Sepher Torath Mosheh

Sepher Torath Mosheh

Studies in the Composition and Interpretation of Deuteronomy

Edited by DANIEL I. BLOCK and RICHARD L. SCHULTZ

HENDRICKSON PUBLISHERS

***Sepher Torath Mosheh*: Studies in the Composition and Interpretation of Deuteronomy**

P. O. Box 3473
Peabody, Massachusetts 01961-3473

ISBN 978-1-68307-066-5

Cover Design: Karol Bailey

Printed in the United States of America

First Printing—December 2017

Library of Congress Cataloging-in-Publication

A catalog record for this title is available from the Library of Congress.
Hendrickson Publishers Marketing, LLC ISBN 978-1-68307-066-5

This volume is dedicated to the memory of
Harry A. Hoffner Jr.
John A. Wilson Professor of Hittitology Emeritus
at the University of Chicago

Contents

EDITORS' PREFACE AND ACKNOWLEDGMENTS

The figure of Moses towers over the history of Israel generally and the history of prophecy particularly. Of this man, his biographer writes,

> No prophet has risen in Israel like Moses, whom the Lord knew face to face, who did all those signs and wonders the Lord sent him to do in Egypt—to Pharaoh and to all his officials and to his whole land. For no one has ever shown the mighty power or performed the awesome deeds that Moses did in the sight of all Israel. (Deut 34:10–12 NIV)

And the reach of the book that consists largely of Moses' valedictory addresses to his congregation on the plains of Moab extends over the entire canon, both the Hebrew Bible and the New Testament. Of the five books that make up the Pentateuch (known in Judaism as the Torah), Deuteronomy is without rival in its influence. This "book of the Torah of Moses" (סֵפֶר תּוֹרַת מֹשֶׁה) was the heart of the Pentateuch, which priests were to teach and model,[1] which psalmists praised,[2] to which the prophets appealed,[3] by which faithful kings ruled[4] and righteous citizens lived, and by which prophetic authors assessed Israel's spiritual condition. Christians, who have been nourished on the New Testament, will find in Deuteronomy the Hebrew Bible's analogue to the Gospel of John (it offers a profoundly theological narration of Israel's experience of salvation from Egypt) and to St. Paul's Epistle to the Romans (it offers the most systematic presentation of the theology arising out of the nation's experience of redemption).

The present volume reflects the ongoing general interest of biblical scholars in Deuteronomy in general and in the critical issues that serious study of this book raises in particular. All the essays included here were first presented at "Debating Deuteronomy: A Colloquium on the Torah of Moses," held at Wheaton College, September 24–26, 2015. Our expressions of gratitude must begin with those who made this colloquium possible. We are grateful to the administrators of Wheaton College for

---

[1] Deut 33:10; 2 Chr 15:3; 19:8; Mal 2:6, 9; cf. Jer 18:18; Ezek 7:26; Ezra 7:10.

[2] Pss 19:7–14; 119; etc.

[3] 2 Kgs 22:16; Isa 8:20; 30:9; 51:7; Hos 4:6; Amos 2:4; Zech 7:12; cf. Dan 9:11, 13.

[4] 1 Kgs 2:2–4; 2 Kgs 14:6; 22:11; 23:25.

creating a climate in which conversations like this may be held freely and openly, and for providing the facilities for the colloquium. Harbor House and its Board Room provided a delightful venue for formal and informal conversation among the participants, and Kristin Siewert hosted us graciously. To the scholars who participated in the program we express our appreciation for their hard work and the cordiality with which they engaged in discussion. Special thanks are due to Jeffrey Tigay, the foremost Jewish authority on Deuteronomy in our time, who presented a stimulating lecture on Thursday evening, and who then listened and watched patiently and graciously as evangelical Christian scholars wrestled with his favorite part of the Hebrew Bible, offering wise words of counsel at critical moments.

We owe special thanks to Michelle Knight, who took care of the bookwork involved in a project like this, and for Ellen Block and Carol Schultz, who assisted in the administration of the social aspects of the event. This colloquium could not have been held without the generous support of interested persons. We are deeply grateful for the major portion of the funding for the event that was provided by the Daniel and Ellen Block Fund for Old Testament Studies, established by their son and daughter-in-law, Jason and Carolyn Block. This was supplemented by monies from the Blanchard and Gunther H. Knoedler Chairs of Old Testament.

Converting presented papers into forms suitable for publication involved another set of persons, without whose assistance this published product would never have seen the light of day. We are deeply grateful to Hendrickson Publishers for making these essays available to the public in printed form. From the beginning, their enthusiasm and support have sustained all of those involved. We are especially grateful to Jonathan Kline, the Hendrickson editor charged with making what scholars do look acceptable to the public. Not only has he worked tirelessly on editing the manuscripts, but he also has consistently dealt with the idiosyncrasies and infelicities of the contributors' submissions with grace and respect. This volume is a monument to his disciplinary expertise, close attention to detail, energy, industry, and sensitivity. We would also like to express our appreciation to all the other staff at Hendrickson who have contributed to the production and marketing of this book, for their obvious commitment to both excellence and Christian ministry in their publications.

It has been a privilege to work with the scholars whose essays are included here. We are grateful for the seriousness and grace with which they presented their research at the colloquium and responded to our edits. I (Dan) am also very grateful to my colleague Richard Schultz, who served as cochair of the colloquium and coeditor of this volume. This volume could not have been produced without the assistance of our graduate students. While they have not signed their names, the work of Holly

Brackin, James Cuénod, Michelle Knight, Daniel Lanz, Meredith Morris, Cooper Smith, and Franklin Wang underlies many aspects of the book: proofreading essays, creating bibliographies and lists of abbreviations, checking footnotes for stylistic consistency, and indexing. We are deeply grateful to them. We are also grateful to our wives, Carol Schultz and Ellen Block, for standing by us and giving us space to work on projects like this.

With great respect, we dedicate this volume to the memory of Harry Hoffner, John A. Wilson Professor of Hittitology Emeritus at the University of Chicago. Harry was a scholar of first rank on all things Hittite. However, he was also an evangelical scholar of first rank, who, in response to a student's question at a conference on the Bible and archaeology, wisely encouraged young scholars "to be good at what they do and to be good." The former comment related to their professional work, the latter to their lives and their disposition toward their conversation partners in the academy. Harry modeled both qualities with uncommon grace and modesty. We were delighted when he agreed to contribute a paper to this collection entitled "Deuteronomic Law and Ancient Near East Law Codes." Sadly, his untimely, accidental death precluded his participation in the colloquium and hence his contribution to this collection of essays. We extend our deep condolences to his widow, Wini Hoffner.

While many associates have contributed to this project, ultimate praise must go to "YHWH the God of Israel," who rescued his people from the slavery of Egypt, and who in his incarnation was called Jesus, for he would rescue his people from their sins (Matt 1:21). May this volume bring great glory to God our Savior, and may it enhance our understanding of the Torah of Moses, which guides all who read it in the way of righteousness (Deut 16:20)!

Contributors

Bill T. Arnold Asbury Theological Seminary (Wilmore, Kentucky)

Richard E. Averbeck Trinity Evangelical Divinity School (Deerfield, Illinois)

Daniel I. Block Wheaton College (Wheaton, Illinois)

Michael A. Grisanti The Master's Seminary (Los Angeles, California)

Neal A. Huddleston Trinity Evangelical Divinity School (Deerfield, Illinois)

J. Gordon McConville University of Gloucestershire (Cheltenham, United Kingdom)

Sandra L. Richter Westmont College (Santa Barbara, California)

Richard L. Schultz Wheaton College (Wheaton, Illinois)

Brent A. Strawn Emory University (Atlanta, Georgia)

Carsten Vang Lutheran School of Theology (Aarhus, Denmark); University of South Africa (Pretoria, South Africa)

Peter T. Vogt LifePoint Church (Maplewood, Minnesota)

K. Lawson Younger Jr. Trinity Evangelical Divinity School (Deerfield, Illinois)

Markus Zehnder Biola University (La Mirada, California); Ansgar University College and Theological Seminary (Kristiansand, Norway); Evangelische Theologische Faculteit (Leuven, Belgium)

ABBREVIATIONS

General Abbreviations

Akk.	Akkadian
ANE	Ancient Near East
AT	Altes Testament
BCE	Before the Common Era
be.	bottom edge
BHQ	*Biblia Hebraica Quinta*
BHS	*Biblia Hebraica Stuttgartensia*
BrTf	Hittite Bronze Tablet (subordination treaty of Tudḫaliya IV of Ḫatti with Kurunta of Tarḫuntašša)
ca.	circa
Cairo	Cairo Geniza
CC	Covenant Collection
CE	Common Era
CEB	Common English Bible
cf.	compare
ch(s).	chapter(s)
col.	column
D	the extant canonical form of Deuteronomy; the Deuteronomist document or source
DC	Deuteronomic Collection
DH	Deuteronomistic History
DSS	Dead Sea Scrolls
Dtr	Deuteronomist
Dtr^1	first version of DH according to Cross
Dtr^2	second version of DH according to Cross
DtrH	exilic redactor according to Smend; or, Deuteronomic History
DtrN	postexilic redactor according to Smend
E	Lines based on Edel's reconstruction from: Elmar Edel, *Der Vertrag zwischen Ramses II. von Ägypten und Ḫattušili III. von Ḫatti.* Wissenschaftliche Veröffentlichung der Deutschen Orient-Gesellschaft 95. Berlin: Gebr. Mann, 1997
EA	El-Amarna tablets
ed(s).	editor(s), edited by; edition
e.g.	*exempli gratia*, for example

esp.	especially
EST	Esarhaddon's Succession Treaty
ESV	English Standard Version
ET	English Translation
et al.	*et alii*, and others
f(f).	and the following one(s)
fasc.	fascicle
ft.	feet
G	the base stem (*Grundstamm*) of a verb
Gt	the base stem (*Grundstamm*) of a verb with an infixed *t*
H	Holiness Code
HC	Holiness Collection
HDT^{2}	Hittite Diplomatic Text
ibid.	*ibidem*, in the same place
idem.	the same
i.e.	*id est*, that is
Impv	imperative
J	Jahwist document or source
JE	editorial combination of the Jahwist and Elohist sources
JEDP	Documentary Hypothesis positing the distinct identity and editorial combination of four original literary sources
Jr. v. Chr.	= BCE
LB	Late Bronze Era
LH	Laws of Hammurapi
LXX	Septuagint (the Greek Old Testament)
LXX^{Lmin}	Septuagint Lucianic miniscules
m.	meters
MA	Middle Assyrian
MB	Middle Babylonian
Mss	Manuscripts
Ms T	Tayinat Manuscript
MT	Masoretic Text
MT^{L}	Masoretic Text Codex Leningradensis
NA	Neo-Assyrian
NASB	New American Standard Bible
NB	Neo-Babylonian
NCB	New Century Bible
NIV	New International Version
NJPS	Tanakh: The Holy Scriptures: The New JPS Translation according to the Traditional Hebrew Text
NRSV	New Revised Standard Version
NT	New Testament
OA	Old Assyrian
OAram.	Old Aramaic

OB	Old Babylonian
obv.	obverse
OG	Old Greek Version of the Old Testament
OL	Old Latin
orig.	original
OT	Old Testament
P	Priestly document or source; Parity
p(p).	page(s)
pl.	plural
Pls.	Plates
PN	personal name/place name
r.	*recto* (tablet front)
repr.	reprint
rev.	revised; reverse
RS	Ras Shamra
RSV	Revised Standard Version
S	Subordination
σ′	Symmachus
Sam(Pent)	Samaritan Pentateuch
s.v.	*sub verbo* ("under the word")
Syr	Syriac
T.	Tell
Targ	Targum
θ′	Theodotion
trans.	translator, translated by
TSA	Tell Sabi Abyad
Urdt	Urdeuteronomium, the earliest form of Deuteronomy
v(v).	verse(s); *verso* (tablet back)
VTE	Vassal-Treaties of Esarhaddon
Vulg	Vulgate
x	times
YHWH	the consonants of the divine name in the Hebrew Bible, conventionally rendered LORD in English translations

Symbols

( )	encloses words added to a gloss for sense in non-Hebrew texts (and occasional parenthetical additions), except for SAA 2.6-T
[ ]	encloses reconstructed text
< >	encloses scribal omissions; or, in biblical text, marks an emendation
⌜ ⌝	encloses partially damaged signs/letters
!	(superscript) indicates a scribal error in transcription

?	(superscript) indicates an uncertain reading and/or gloss in transcription
×	(subscript) multiplication symbol appears immediately before a sign written within the previous sign (e.g., $KA_{\times}U$ = KA, Akk. *pû* "mouth")
:	a colon in transcription indicates the orthographic transposition of the signs between which it appears (e.g., Eblaite nita:udu for udu-nita, "ram")
. . .	a break of unspecified length
⸗	the fraktur-hyphen marks clitic boundaries (Hittite)
∡	*Glossenkeil*, a scribal convention in Hittite that marks stylistically inappropriate terms and collocations (especially Luwian intrusions)
italics	indicates a foreign term in glosses of all non-Hebrew texts; indicates words added to a gloss for sense in all Hebrew texts and in SAA 2.6-T

Ancient Sources

Dead Sea Scrolls

$4QDeut^{n}$	$Deuteronomy^{n}$
$4QJosh^{a}$	$Joshua^{a}$
$4QPhyl^{n}$	$Phylacteries^{n}$

Josephus

Ant.	*Jewish Antiquities*
J.W.	*Jewish War*

Philo

Dreams	*On Dreams*

Babylonian Talmud

ʿAbod. Zar.	*ʿAbodah Zarah*
Ḥul.	*Ḥullin*

Targumic Texts

T^{JNF}	Targum Pseudo-Jonathan and Neofiti

T^O	Targum Onqelos
Tg. Neb.	Targum of the Prophets

Other Rabbinic Works

Sipre Deb.	Sipre Deuteronomy

Journals, Series, and Reference Works

AB	Anchor Bible
ABD	*Anchor Bible Dictionary*. Edited by D. N. Freedman. 6 vols. New York: Doubleday, 1992
ABRL	Anchor Bible Reference Library
ABS	Archaeology and Biblical Studies
AfO	*Archiv für Orientforschung*
AION	*Annali dell'Istituto Orientale di Napoli*
AnBib	Analecta Biblica
ANEM	Ancient Near Eastern Monographs
ANETS	Ancient Near Eastern Texts and Studies
AnOr	*Analecta Orientalia*
AnSt	*Anatolian Studies*
AOAT	Alter Orient und Altes Testament
AoF	Altorientalische Forschungen
AOTC	Abingdon Old Testament Commentary
ApOTC	Apollos Old Testament Commentary
Aramazd	*Aramazd: Armenian Journal of Near Eastern Studies*
ARES	Archivi reali di Ebla, Studi
ARET	Archivi reali di Ebla, Testi
ASJ	Acta Sumerologica (Japan)
ASORAR	American Schools of Oriental Research Archaeological Reports
AT	Wiseman, Donald J. *The Alalakh Tablets*. Occasional Publications of the British Institute of Archaeology at Ankara, no. 2. London: The British Institute of Archaeology at Ankara, 1953
ATD	Das Alte Testament Deutsch
AuOr	*Aula Orientalis*
BA	*Biblical Archaeologist*
BAR	*Biblical Archaeology Review*
BASOR	*Bulletin of the American Schools of Oriental Research*
BBB	Bonner biblische Beiträge
BBR	*Bulletin for Biblical Research*
BBRSup	Bulletin for Biblical Research: Supplement Series

BDAG	Danker, F. W., W. Bauer, W. F. Arndt, and F. W. Gingrich. *Greek-English Lexicon of the New Testament and Other Early Christian Literature*. 3rd ed. Chicago: University of Chicago Press, 2000
BEATAJ	Beiträge zur Erforschung des Alten Testaments und des antiken Judentum
BECNT	Baker Exegetical Commentary on the New Testament
BETL	Bibliotheca Ephemeridum Theologicarum Lovaniensium
Bib	*Biblica*
BIBAL	Berkeley Institute of Biblical Archaeology and Literature
BibInt	Biblical Interpretation Series
BibOr	Biblica et Orientalia
BJS	Brown Judaic Studies
BKAT	Biblischer Kommentar, Altes Testament. Edited by M. Noth and H. W. Wolff
BN	*Biblische Notizen*
BoSt	Boghazköy Studien
BR	*Biblical Research*
BRev	*Bible Review*
BrTf	Otten, Heinrich. *Die Bronzetafel aus Boğazköy: Ein Staatsvertrag Tutḫalijas IV*. Studien zu den Boğazköy-Texten, Beiheft 1. Wiesbaden: Harrassowitz, 1988
BWANT	Beiträge zur Wissenschaft vom Alten und Neuen Testament
BZABR	Beihefte zur Zeitschrift für altorientalische und biblische Rechtsgeschichte
BZAW	Beihefte zur Zeitschrift für die alttestamentliche Wissenschaft
CAD	*The Assyrian Dictionary of the Oriental Institute of the University of Chicago*. Chicago: The Oriental Institute of the University of Chicago, 1956–2006
CBET	Contributions to Biblical Exegesis and Theology
CBQ	*Catholic Biblical Quarterly*
CHANE	Culture and History of the Ancient Near East
CHD	*The Hittite Dictionary of the Oriental Institute of the University of Chicago*. Chicago: The Oriental Institute of the University of Chicago, 1980–. For an online version of the ongoing project see http://ochre.lib.uchicago.edu/eCHD/
ColAnt	Colloquia Antiqua
ConBOT	Coniectanea Biblica: Old Testament Series
COS	*The Context of Scripture*. Edited by William W. Hallo. 3 vols. Leiden: Brill, 1997–2002
CSMSJ	*The Canadian Society for Mesopotamian Studies Journal*
CTH	Laroche, Emmanuel. *Catalogue des textes hittites*. Études et commentaires 75. Paris: Klincksieck, 1971

CTR	*Criswell Theological Review*
CurBS	*Currents in Research: Biblical Studies*
DBH	Dresdner Beiträge zur Hethitologie
DCH	*Dictionary of Classical Hebrew*. Edited by D. J. A. Clines. 9 vols. Sheffield: Sheffield Phoenix Press, 1993–2014
DJD	Discoveries in the Judean Desert
DNWSI	*Dictionary of the North-West Semitic Inscriptions*. J. Hoftijzer and K. Jongeling. 2 vols. Leiden: Brill, 1995
DPL	*Dictionary of Paul and His Letters*. Edited by G. F. Hawthorne and R. P. Martin. Downers Grove, IL: InterVarsity Press, 1993
EDNT	*Exegetical Dictionary of the New Testament*. Edited by H. Balz and G. Schneider. ET. 3 vols. Grand Rapids: Eerdmans, 1990–1993
ErIsr	*Eretz-Israel*
FAT	Forschungen zum Alten Testament
FCI	Foundations of Contemporary Interpretation
FRLANT	Forschungen zur Religion und Literatur des Alten und Neuen Testaments
FZPhTh	*Freiburger Zeitschrift für Philosophie und Theologie*
HALAT	*Hebräisches und aramäisches Lexikon zum Alten Testament*. Ludwig Koehler, Walter Baumgartner, and Johann J. Stamm. 2 vols. Leiden: Brill, 2004
HALOT	*The Hebrew and Aramaic Lexicon of the Old Testament*. Ludwig Koehler, Walter Baumgartner, and Johann J. Stamm. Translated and edited under the supervision of Mervyn E. J. Richardson. 4 vols. Leiden: Brill, 1994–2000
HAT	Handbuch zum Alten Testament
HBM	Hebrew Bible Monographs
HBS	Herders Biblische Studien
HdO	Handbuch der Orientalistik
HDT^2	Beckman, Gary M., and Harry A. Hoffner. *Hittite Diplomatic Texts*. 2nd ed. Writings from the Ancient World 7. Atlanta: Scholars Press, 1999
HOTTP	Hebrew Old Testament Text Project
HSM	Harvard Semitic Monographs
HSS	Harvard Semitic Studies
HThKAT	Herders Theologischer Kommentar zum Alten Testament
HTR	*Harvard Theological Review*
HUCA	*Hebrew Union College Annual*
HUCM	Monographs of the Hebrew Union College
ICC	International Critical Commentary
IEJ	*Israel Exploration Journal*
Int	*Interpretation*
ISBL	Indiana Studies in Biblical Literature

JAC	*Jahrbuch für Antike und Christentum*
JAJ	*Journal of Ancient Judaism*
JANER	*Journal of Ancient Near Eastern Religions*
JBL	*Journal of Biblical Literature*
JCS	*Journal of Cuneiform Studies*
JESOT	*Journal for the Evangelical Study of the Old Testament*
JETS	*Journal of the Evangelical Theological Society*
JNES	*Journal of Near Eastern Studies*
JSJ	*Journal for the Study of Judaism in the Persian, Hellenistic, and Roman Periods*
JSJSup	Journal for the Study of Judaism: Supplement Series
JSNT	*Journal for the Study of the New Testament*
JSOR	*Journal of the Society of Oriental Research*
JSOT	*Journal for the Study of the Old Testament*
JSOTSup	Journal for the Study of the Old Testament: Supplement Series
JTI	*Journal for Theological Interpretation*
JTS	*Journal of Theological Studies*
KAI	*Kanaanäische und aramäische Inschriften*. Herbert Donner and Wolfgang Röllig. 2nd ed. Wiesbaden: Harrassowitz, 1966–1969
KTU	*Die keilalphabetischen Texte aus Ugarit*. Edited by M. Dietrich, O. Loretz, and J. Sanmartín. Münster: Ugarit-Verlag, 2013. 3rd. enl. ed. of *KTU: The Cuneiform Alphabetic Texts from Ugarit, Ras Ibn Hani, and Other Places*. Edited by M. Dietrich, O. Loretz, and J. Sanmartín. Münster: Ugarit-Verlag, 1995
KUB	*Keilschrifturkunden aus Boghazköi*. Berlin: Akademie, 1921–
LACUS	Linguistic Association of Canada and the United States
LAI	Library of Ancient Israel
LAPO	Littératures anciennes du Proche-Orient
LCL	Loeb Classical Library
LHBOTS	The Library of Hebrew Bible/Old Testament Studies
LNTS	Library of New Testament Studies
LS	*Louvain Studies*
LSAWS	Linguistic Studies in Ancient West Semitic
LSJ	Liddell, H. G., R. Scott, H. S. Jones. *A Greek-English Lexicon*. 9th ed. with revised supplement. Oxford: Clarendon, 1996
L.T.	Eidem, Jesper. *The Royal Archives from Tell Leilan: Old Babylonian Letters and Treaties from the Lower Town Palace East*. Archaeological introduction by Lauren Ristvet and Harvey Weiss. PIHANS 117. Leiden: Nederlands Instituut voor het Nabije Oosten; Yale University Press, 2011

MDOG	*Mitteilungen der Deutschen Orient-Gesellschaft*
MIOF	*Mitteilungen des Instituts für Orientforschung*
MRS	Mission de Ras Shamra
ms T	Lauinger, Jacob. "Esarhaddon's Succession Treaty at Tell Tayinat: Text and Commentary." *Journal of Cuneiform Studies* 64 (2012): 87–123
MVAG	Mitteilungen der Vorderasiatisch-ägyptischen Gesellschaft. Vols. 1–44. 1896–1939
NAC	New American Commentary
NEAEHL	*The New Encyclopedia of Archaeological Excavations in the Holy Land*. Edited by E. Stern. 4 vols. Jerusalem: Israel Exploration Society & Carta, 1993
NIB	*The New Interpreter's Bible*. Edited by L. E. Keck. 12 vols. Nashville: Abingdon, 1994–2004
NIBCOT	New International Biblical Commentary on the Old Testament
NICOT	New International Commentary on the Old Testament
NIDB	*New International Dictionary of the Bible*. Edited by J. D. Douglas and M. C. Tenney. Grand Rapids: Zondervan, 1987
NIDNTT	*New International Dictionary of New Testament Theology*. Edited by C. Brown. 4 vols. Grand Rapids: Zondervan, 1975–1985
NIDNTTE	*New International Dictionary of New Testament Theology and Exegesis*. Edited by Moisés Silva. 5 vols. Grand Rapids: Zondervan, 2014
NIDOTTE	*New International Dictionary of Old Testament Theology and Exegesis*. Edited by W. A. VanGemeren. 5 vols. Grand Rapids: Zondervan, 1997
NIVAC	New International Version Application Commentary
NovTSup	Novum Testamentum: Supplement Series
NSBT	New Studies in Biblical Theology
NTL	New Testament Library
NTS	*New Testament Studies*
OAC	Orientis Antiqui Collectio
OBO	Orbis biblicus et Orientalis
ÖBS	Österreichische biblische Studien
OBT	Overtures to Biblical Theology
OED	*Oxford English Dictionary*
OPSNKF	Occasional Publications of the Samuel Noah Kramer Fund
OrAnt	*Oriens Antiquus*
OTE	*Old Testament Essays*
OTG	Old Testament Guides
OTL	Old Testament Library
OTS	Old Testament Studies

OtSt	*Oudtestamentische Studiën*
PBM	Paternoster Biblical Monographs
PEQ	*Palestine Exploration Quarterly*
PIHANS	Publications de l'Institut historique-archéologique néerlandais de Stamboul
R2-H3	Edel, Elmar. *Der Vertrag zwischen Ramses II. von Ägypten und Ḫattušili III. von Ḫatti*. Wissenschaftliche Veröffentlichung der Deutschen Orient-Gesellschaft 95. Berlin: Gebr. Mann, 1997
RA	*Revue d'assyriologie et d'archéologie orientale*
RB	*Revue biblique*
RBS	Resources for Biblical Study
RIMA	The Royal Inscriptions of Mesopotamia, Assyrian Periods
RIME	The Royal Inscriptions of Mesopotamia, Early Periods
RINAP	Royal Inscriptions of the Neo-Assyrian Period
RSR	*Recherches de science religieuse*
SAA	State Archives of Assyria
SAA 2	Parpola, Simo, and Kazuko Watanabe. *Neo-Assyrian Treaties and Loyalty Oaths*. SAA 2. Helsinki: Helsinki University Press, 1988
SAA 2.6-T	A composite text that consists of SAA2.6 and ms T.: Text no. 6 in Parpola, Simo, and Kazuko Watanabe. *Neo-Assyrian Treaties and Loyalty Oaths*. SAA 2. Helsinki: Helsinki University Press, 1988; Lauinger, Jacob. "Esarhaddon's Succession Treaty at Tell Tayinat: Text and Commentary." *Journal of Cuneiform Studies* 64 (2012): 87–123.
SAAS	State Archives of Assyria Studies
SAK	*Studien zur Altägyptischen Kultur*
SBAB	Stuttgarter biblische Aufsatzbände
SBLABS	Society of Biblical Literature Archaeology and Biblical Studies
SBLAIL	Society of Biblical Literature Ancient Israel and Its Literature
SBLDS	Society of Biblical Literature Dissertation Series
SBLEJL	Society of Biblical Literature Early Judaism and Its Literature
SBLMS	Society of Biblical Literature Monograph Series
SBLWAW	Society of Biblical Literature Writings from the Ancient World
SBT	Studies in Biblical Theology
SBTS	Sources for Biblical and Theological Study
ScrB	*Scripture Bulletin*
ScrHier	Scripta Hierosolymitana

SEE-J	Scandinavian Evangelical E-Journal
Sem	*Semitica*
Sf	Fitzmyer, Joseph A. *The Aramaic Inscriptions of Sefire.* 2nd, rev. ed. Biblica et Orientalia 19/A. Rome: Pontificial Biblical Institute, 1995
SHBC	Smyth & Helwys Bible Commentary
SIL	Summer Institute of Linguistics
SOTBT	Studies in Old Testament Biblical Theology
SR	*Studies in Religion*
SSN	Studia Semitica Neerlandica
SSS	Semitic Study Series
StBoT	Studien zu den Boğazköy-Texten (Wiesbaden 1965 ff.)
StBoTB	Studien zu den Boğazköy-Texten: Beihefte (Wiesbaden 1988 ff.)
StIr	*Studia Iranica*
StPohl	Studia Pohl
TA	*Tel Aviv*
TCS	Texts from Cuneiform Sources
TDNT	*Theological Dictionary of the New Testament.* Edited by G. Kittel and G. Friedrich. Translated by G. W. Bromiley. 10 vols. Grand Rapids: Eerdmans, 1964–1976
Them	*Themelios*
THeth	Texte der Hethiter
ThWAT	*Theologisches Wörterbuch zum Alten Testament.* Edited by G. J. Botterweck and H. Ringgren. Stuttgart: Kohlhammer, 1970–
TLCANE	Kitchen, Kenneth A., and Paul J. N. Lawrence. *Treaty, Law and Covenant in the Ancient Near East.* Wiesbaden: Harrassowitz, 2012. Issued in three volumes—Part 1: The Texts; Part 2: Text, Notes and Chromograms; Part 3: Overall Historical Survey.
TLNT	*Theological Lexicon of the New Testament.* Edited by C. Spicq. Translated and edited by J. D. Ernest. 3 vols. Peabody, MA: Hendrickson, 1994
TLOT	*Theological Lexicon of the Old Testament.* Edited by E. Jenni, with assistance from Claus Westermann. Translated and edited by Mark E. Biddle. 3 vols. Peabody, MA: Hendrickson, 1997
TLZ	*Theologische Literaturzeitung*
TOTC	Tyndale Old Testament Commentaries
TRE	*Theologische Realenzyklopädie.* Edited by G. Krause and G. Müller. Berlin: de Gruyter, 1977–
TUAT	*Texte aus der Umwelt des Alten Testaments*
TynBul	*Tyndale Bulletin*
UCOP	University of Cambridge Oriental Publications

UISK	Untersuchungen zur indogermanischen Sprach- und Kulturwissenschaft
VT	*Vetus Testamentum*
VTSup	Supplements to Vetus Testamentum
VWGT	Veröffentlichungen der Wissenschaftlichen Gesellschaft für Theologie
WBC	Word Biblical Commentary
WO	*Die Welt des Orients*
WTJ	*Westminster Theological Journal*
WUNT	Wissenschaftliche Untersuchungen zum Neuen Testament
WVDOG	Wissenschaftliche Veröffentlichungen der deutschen Orientgesellschaft
ZABR	*Zeitschrift für altorientalische und biblische Rechtgeschichte*
ZAW	*Zeitschrift für die alttestamentliche Wissenschaft*

Introduction

Daniel I. Block

Having participated in the Ezekiel Consultation of SBL for several decades I have personally been encouraged by the shrinking of the divide between mainstream and evangelical scholarship in many areas of Hebrew Bible research. However, when I moved into pentateuchal studies, focused particularly on Deuteronomy, I encountered a very different world. In few areas of critical biblical research is the chasm between the two approaches as broad as in discussions of the book of Deuteronomy. The issues relate not only to the provenance of the book, but also to its origin and composition, its ideology, its ethic, and its relationship to other biblical books. Evangelicals differ in their responses to historical-critical scholarship. Some avoid it as much as possible; others consider neither critical methodologies nor the results of critical scholarship to be threatening to their evangelical convictions.

The essays in this volume consist of invited papers by recognized Old Testament scholars with a particular interest in Deuteronomy. These were presented at a special colloquium on the book at Wheaton College, held September 24–26, 2015. The purpose of this colloquium was to explore together historical, literary, theological, and ethical issues at the heart of the tensions evangelicals feel when they interact with mainstream scholarship. In addition to the contributors to the colloquium proper, we had the distinct privilege of having the foremost Jewish authority on the book of Deuteronomy, Jeffrey Tigay, in our midst. We treasured his responses to the papers and were stimulated by a special guest lecture from this esteemed scholar on the history of Jewish interpretation of the *ḥērem* ordinance.

Before I introduce the individual essays, a further word on nomenclature is required. It is difficult to find an appropriate label for the interpretive stance the contributors to this volume represent. They reflect a broad spectrum of theological and hermeneutical perspectives within evangelicalism, and all subscribe to the statement on Scripture that unites the fellows of the Institute for Biblical Research: belief in "the unique divine inspiration, integrity, and authority of the Bible." But this statement is very general, neither declaring this to be a distinctly evangelical stance, nor prescribing or delimiting what sorts of hermeneutical approaches are deemed to fall within the label.

Whereas the contributors to this volume have little difficulty identifying themselves as evangelicals, as historically and traditionally conceived, the search for a new label is difficult. Perhaps here in the introduction to this book we should be content with describing our hermeneutic, rather than labeling it. Identifying the marks of a distinctly evangelical hermeneutic is precarious business, because few represent the paradigm described completely. However, we must begin somewhere.

First, evangelical biblical scholars treat the object of their study as Scripture, not merely as a literary artifact in a museum that may be dispassionately analyzed. Among other entailments, this means that we stand before the text with reverence and awe, and seek to draw from it spiritual nurture and instruction, even as we pursue our textual analysis.

Second, the goal of evangelical biblical exegesis is grasping the life-giving and life-transforming message of the Scriptures. Our primary objective is not historicist determination of the manner or even the contexts in which biblical writings were produced (given the lack of data on these matters our efforts are admittedly speculative), but establishing the authoritative meaning intended by the text.

Third, an evangelical stance toward the Scriptures is typically positivist, rather than suspicious. If the essence of critical scholarship is "The willingness *not* to take a text at face value,"[1] the essence of evangelical scholarship is first to accept the face value of the text. The Scriptures were not written primarily as riddles, whose true significance is realized by reading *against* the grain. While the latter has its place and often yields interesting results, establishing the meaning of biblical texts requires reading *with* the grain.

Fourth, an evangelical hermeneutic is holistic. However the texts were produced, they have been preserved in the canon by the communities of faith as whole documents. This means that, while dividing the text into its constituent sources or redactions may be fruitful, in the end tensions within the text that are often used to identify editorial hands should be treated as essential features of the text, contributing to its final-form message.[2]

---

[1] Michael V. Fox, *Character and Ideology in the Book of Esther* (Columbia: University of South Carolina Press, 1991), 148.

[2] Moshe Greenberg has helpfully identified three criteria by which we may identify secondary alterations to the text: (1) historical anachronisms; (2) syntactical incoherence that cannot be explained on the basis of ancient literary habits or textual corruption; (3) contradictions that cannot be accounted for on rhetorical grounds. See Moshe Greenberg, "What Are Valid Criteria for Determining

Fifth, while not becoming a slave to any single method, evangelical scholars utilize responsibly whatever hermeneutical strategy may clarify biblical texts: source, redaction, form, tradition, lexical, literary, rhetorical, historical, and cultural analyses, as well as speech act theory. These are not methods to be feared, but rather to be harnessed in the pursuit of meaning in biblical texts.

Sixth, evangelical scholars base their conclusions on evidence, which means they treat alternative interpretations with respect (rather than disdain), and they repudiate *ad hominem* arguments.

Seventh, evangelical scholars view biblical writings (1) within the context of the entire canon, and seek to locate texts they are analyzing within the history of divine revelation, which climaxes in the incarnation, life, death, and exaltation of Jesus Christ as Lord, and (2) within the context of the process whereby the canon was produced.

Given these features, it is not surprising that evangelical scholars often feel a greater kinship with conservative Jewish and Roman Catholic scholars than with mainstream Protestant scholars. For many of us, our faith commitments are primary, and we approach the Scriptures with believing reverence and awe. In the Scriptures, we hear the voice of God, not merely the reflections of human authors.

Our colloquium on Deuteronomy afforded the evangelical scholars involved an opportunity to give expression to specific topics related to this book that they have recently engaged or that have been an ongoing concern of theirs. As was the case with the earlier colloquium on Isaiah and the volume that was produced therefrom,[3] the diversity of the participants' styles, interpretive frameworks, and specializations enlivened the conversation when we met at Wheaton College and contributed to a volume that introduces readers to the critical issues that Deuteronomy presents and to the variety of approaches with which evangelical scholars address them. The participants did not agree on all points, but the conversations were cordial and the fellowship was warm. However, we must acknowledge at the outset that, although the versions of the papers here have been significantly modified in view of the discussions around the table, the individual scholars are all responsible for their own papers. That they are gathered in this volume does not mean they accept either the methods or the conclusions of their colleagues; nor does it mean that the coeditors agree with all positions presented in the papers that follow.

Inauthentic Matter in Ezekiel?" in *Ezekiel and His Book*, ed. Johann Lust, BETL 74 (Leuven: Leuven University Press, 1986), 123–35.

[3] *Bind Up the Testimony: Explorations in the Genesis of the Book of Isaiah,* ed. Daniel I. Block and Richard L. Schultz (Peabody, MA: Hendrickson, 2015).

Peter Vogt begins this collection by tracing the history of the critical interpretation of the book of Deuteronomy. The scholarly issues he discusses relate primarily to matters of the date, purpose, ideology, and composition/structure of Deuteronomy. The figure of Moses has receded increasingly into the background, and the date for the composition of the present book gets pushed later and later. Although the designation "evangelical" was not used to identify a theological or hermeneutical movement until well into the twentieth century, Vogt observes that until recently a conservative Christian response to critical scholarship on Deuteronomy has been largely reactive, rather than proactive. This has changed significantly in the past few decades, as a more confident and assertive evangelical cadre of scholars has entered into the conversations on the book at the highest technical levels.

Neal Huddleston's and K. Lawson Younger Jr.'s papers are two parts of a single larger, exhaustive project analyzing ancient Near Eastern treaty traditions and their relationship to biblical texts. Huddleston identifies seven unique ancient Near Eastern treaty traditions that appeared between 2300 and 600 BCE. Selecting several texts from each group, he compares the respective traditions and then concludes by briefly relating their functions and forms to the book of Deuteronomy. Lawson Younger joins the conversation in the next paper, as he and Huddleston jointly offer a more sustained consideration of the relationship between ancient Near Eastern treaty traditions and Deuteronomy. After examining the links between the maledictions in Deuteronomy and in the Esarhaddon Succession treaties and finding them tenuous, Huddleston and Younger reflect on how ancient Israel could have been influenced by Late Bronze Age and Early Iron Age Hittite cultural traditions.

Since the eighteenth century, critical scholars have linked the composition of Deuteronomy with the discovery of the Torah scroll that Josiah's men found while they were refurbishing the temple in Jerusalem (2 Kgs 22), which pushed the date of composition into the late seventh century BCE. After offering a helpful survey of the history of this interpretation, Michael Grisanti assesses its validity, presenting innerbiblical evidence for an earlier date for the book, and concluding by summarizing recent evangelical responses to this evidence.

Bill Arnold's paper addresses the issue of whether and in what sense Deuteronomy might be considered a pseudepigraph, a document purported to derive from Moses but which actually was produced much later. Most evangelical scholars have understood the book to represent in some fashion the very speeches of Moses on the plains of Moab (an approach Arnold labels *ipsissima verba*). However, Arnold suggests that, although Deuteronomy is grounded in the authoritative revelation (*traditum*) given to and through Moses, it is the product of centuries of expansion, reworking, and rewriting by Mosaic scribes. While not necessarily preserving the very words of Moses, these scribes have preserved his voice, and the authority of his teaching remains undiminished.

Taking his cue from Deut 6:21 and 9:7, in which Moses the speaker describes his audience as having been slaves in Egypt and rebellious against YHWH since they left Egypt, Brent Strawn explores the extraordinary rhetoric of Deuteronomy. Most of the people standing before Moses on the plains of Moab had not even been born when the Israelites were rescued from their slavery. However, by transporting the audience back in time and space, the book incorporates a rhetoric that is both trans- and suprahistorical, calling on hearers in every generation to celebrate their rescue from slavery and to warn them of the constant danger of rebellion against YHWH. While Deuteronomy is about both *then* and *now* along with *what yet will be*, the clear accent in terms of literary effect is on *now*.

Treating the command to love the גֵּר (alien) in Deut 10:19 and Lev 19:34 and related texts as a test case, Markus Zehnder explores the relationships among the so-called "Book of the Covenant," the "Holiness Code," and the Deuteronomic law collection. Critical scholarship has tended to highlight perceived contradictions in these documents and to use internal evidence to ascribe relative dates to the documents—dates that typically run counter to the sequence in which they appear in the pentateuchal narratives. In fact, some have argued that later versions of the laws have intentionally supplanted earlier versions. Zehnder establishes that, while exhibiting significant differences, these documents are not contradictory, let alone intended to displace earlier versions of the laws. Rather, they are to be read together as complementary, alongside each other, and the differences reflect new circumstances in which the laws are to be applied.

Richard Averbeck deals with a similar issue, but uses the regulations concerning Israel's cult in the respective documents as his test case. He observes many parallels across the respective legal documents in the prescriptions for specific cultic practices, and notes that all three (the Book of the Covenant, the Holiness Code, and the Deuteronomic law collection) are framed by cultic regulations. In so doing, he shows that the three documents agree in highlighting that, in Israel, faithfulness to YHWH and obedience to the law begins and ends with the people's relationship to YHWH, which is the essential purpose of the cult. Apart from this cultic context, the remainder of the laws make no sense.

Gordon McConville's essay on "Wisdom and Torah in Deuteronomy" is the shortest in this volume. His aim is to examine the profile of "wisdom" in the book and then to explore the relationship between wisdom and torah. He argues that Deuteronomy and the wisdom literature have their own irreducible individuality, which derives from their distinctive engagements with ancient Near Eastern traditions: Deuteronomy is oriented toward the ancient heritage of treaty and law, while Israelite wisdom is oriented to ancient Near Eastern wisdom. Nevertheless, both are characterized as fully in the service of YHWH.

In keeping with their dating of Deuteronomy to the period of Josiah or later, critical scholars almost universally assume that the eighth-century prophet Hosea antedates this book. The links between Hosea and Deuteronomy are most obvious in Deut 8:12–14 and Hos 13:4–6, Hos 2:10[ET 8] and Deut 8:13/17:16–17, and Hos 4:13 and Deut 12:2. Upon closer examination of these texts, Carsten Vang concludes that Deuteronomy reflects a fixed covenantal tradition that is older than the eighth century BCE.

In her paper on Deut 27, Sandra Richter searches for the historical context in which the ritual at Shechem (between Mounts Gerizim and Ebal) might have been significant for the Israelites, and in so doing offers evidence for the provenance of the book of Deuteronomy. After declaring that there are only two options—Late Bronze/Iron I and the Persian/Hellenistic period of Samarian worship on Mount Gerizim, prior to the Hasmonean destruction in 114 BCE—Richter examines the archaeological and textual evidence. She concludes that the former argues unambiguously for the earlier date, while the latter, though slightly less firm, points in the same direction.

The final essay, written by me, is the only one in this volume that addresses the influence of the book of Deuteronomy in the New Testament. Against the grain of prevailing New Testament scholarship, I argue that in Gal 1 the apostle Paul identifies himself as a prophet in the tradition of Moses (cf. Deut 18:9–22), which means that he cannot disagree fundamentally with Moses. Acknowledging this to be a limited foray into the discussion of the relationship between Paul and Moses, I use circumcision as a test case. I argue that Paul's and Moses' dispositions toward physical circumcision were remarkably similar; both "servants of God" placed greater weight on spiritual than on external physical markers of faith, specifically on the circumcision of the heart.

Although all the essays in this volume relate to the critical study of the book of Deuteronomy, they are quite diverse in their goals, style, and content. However, taken together they offer a window into the state of evangelical Deuteronomy scholarship in the second decade of the twenty-first century.

CHAPTER 1

Deuteronomy: A History of Interpretation and Evangelical Responses

Peter T. Vogt

The book of Deuteronomy has long been the subject of intense scholarly scrutiny and analysis. There are few other areas of scholarly inquiry in which the divide between "mainstream" and conservative evangelical biblical scholarship is as great.[1] This paper will examine the history of interpretation of Deuteronomy in terms of how mainstream scholarship has approached the book, as well as surveying conservative responses and alternative evangelical approaches.

Early Modern Approaches to Deuteronomy

An exhaustive study of the history of interpretation of Deuteronomy is well beyond the scope of this paper; the number of works on Deuteronomy is, quite simply, staggering. I will highlight some representative approaches and issues and illustrate how those issues have been handled.[2] I will then examine evangelical responses to those approaches and their impact.

---

[1] Adequately defining *mainstream* and *evangelical* is a challenging task. For a helpful discussion of the theological parameters of "evangelicalism," see Timothy Larsen, "Defining and Locating Evangelicalism," in *The Cambridge Companion to Evangelical Theology*, ed. Timothy Larsen and Daniel J. Treier (Cambridge: Cambridge University Press, 2007), 1–14. Although the scholars discussed in the "Evangelical Approaches" section below would self-identify as "evangelicals," for our purposes it is less important to highlight *theological* distinctives of evangelicalism than to distinguish between evangelical approaches to *biblical hermeneutics* and the approaches of other, "mainstream" scholars. For a helpful description of evangelical hermeneutics, see the introduction to this volume by Daniel I. Block.

[2] The description and analysis of various views presented here constitute a revised version of those presented in Peter T. Vogt, *Deuteronomic Theology and the Significance of Torah: A Reappraisal* (Winona Lake, IN: Eisenbrauns, 2006). Material from that book is reproduced here with kind permission of the publisher.

The three main issues that have absorbed the attention of scholars and that divide evangelical and mainstream scholarship are the date, purpose and ideology, and composition and structure of Deuteronomy. Though they are interrelated, we will examine them separately to better identify trends.

Date

Modern critical study of Deuteronomy began with the 1805 dissertation of Wilhelm M. L. de Wette, in which he maintained that Deuteronomy reflected the reforms of Josiah.[3] Jerome had previously posited that the book Josiah's men found in the temple (2 Kgs 22:3–13) was Deuteronomy,[4] but de Wette is credited with the idea that the book itself was intimately associated with Josiah's reforms. De Wette held that the centralization law in Deut 12 could only have come from a period later than the rest of the Pentateuch because centralization is neither assumed nor valued in the latter. Moreover, he maintained on the basis of literary style that Deuteronomy is the work of a different author than Genesis–Numbers (which, like Deuteronomy, he saw as a unity), though he believed that neither work was written by Moses. De Wette maintained that the time of the Josianic reforms was the period most suited to the law of centralization as found in Deuteronomy.[5]

Consideration of the date of Deuteronomy saw significant advancement through the work of Julius Wellhausen, who argued for the existence of three sources in the Pentateuch: JE, D, and P.[6] While Wellhausen acknowledged that this idea was not unique to him,[7] we credit him with popularizing the now famous "Documentary Hypothesis" and articulating the significance of this view for understanding the history of Israel and the development of the literature of the Pentateuch. For our purposes, Wellhausen's contributions were most significant, because he posited that

---

[3] For a concise treatment of premodern interpretation of Deuteronomy, see Daniel I. Block, *Deuteronomy*, NIVAC (Grand Rapids: Zondervan, 2012), 26–28.

[4] Moshe Weinfeld, "Deuteronomy: The Present State of Inquiry," *JBL* 86 (1967): 249.

[5] See the helpful presentation of de Wette and his contribution to Deuteronomic studies in Gordon J. Wenham, "The Structure and Date of Deuteronomy" (PhD diss., University of London, 1970), 16–43.

[6] Julius Wellhausen, *Prolegomena to the History of Israel* (Edinburgh: A & C Black, 1885; repr. Atlanta: Scholars, 1994). While Wellhausen acknowledged that E once existed as an independent source, he noted that we know of it only as "extracts embodied in the Jehovist narrative" (ibid., 8).

[7] Ibid., 4. Some of Wellhausen's conclusions were anticipated by Eduard Reuss and his student Karl H. Graf.

centralization in Deuteronomy is key to understanding the nature of the reforms in support of which the book was composed.

Wellhausen's work helped establish Deuteronomy as an important starting point for the study of the Old Testament. Wellhausen saw Deuteronomy as representing a midpoint between JE and P. That is, JE was earlier than Deuteronomy, originating in the period of the monarchy but prior to the destruction of the Northern Kingdom by Assyria in the eighth century BCE.[8] Deuteronomy was "composed in the same age as that in which it was discovered," namely, during the reign of Josiah.[9] P was written at a later time and assumes many of the innovations presented in Deuteronomy.

Wellhausen further maintained that the development of Israelite religion can be traced through the source documents of the Pentateuch. He saw in the sources an evolution from a free, spontaneous, and natural religion to a more formalized, artificial expression of faith. The different sources, which represent different stages in the history of religion in Israel, each present a different view of the religion. In this way, he determined the date of the sources. Deuteronomy, most closely associated with the D source, is chronologically the midpoint between JE and P, and is seen as deriving from the monarchic period.

The Documentary Hypothesis emerged as the dominant method in pentateuchal criticism and remained so until about 1970. To be sure, some modified the theory as posited by Wellhausen. But the development of the traditio-historical approach by Albrecht Alt, who saw continuity between events and their description in the pentateuchal sources, as well as archaeological discoveries by William Albright, firmly established the Documentary Hypothesis in modern pentateuchal interpretation.[10] Most notably, adherents of these newer approaches (exemplified by the Alt and Albright "schools") sought to harmonize their findings with the traditional sources and dates postulated in the nineteenth century. In this way, source criticism served to establish Deuteronomy as a product of the monarchic period.

The date of Deuteronomy was further advanced in modern scholarship through the discovery of ancient Near Eastern treaties and the patterns associated with them. Since George Mendenhall identified covenant treaty structures from Hittite documents and proposed that covenant texts

---

[8] Ibid., 9.

[9] Ibid.

[10] For a discussion of the modern development of the Documentary Hypothesis, see Gordon J. Wenham, "Pondering the Pentateuch: The Search for a New Paradigm," in *The Face of Old Testament Studies: A Survey of Contemporary Approaches*, ed. David W. Baker and Bill T. Arnold (Leicester: Apollos, 1999), 116–44.

in the Old Testament correspond to ancient Hittite treaty forms,[11] much scholarly attention has been directed toward refining and revising this theory. It is almost universally agreed that the present text of Deuteronomy resembles the form of ancient Near Eastern suzerain-vassal treaties. However, some far less settled questions remain.

There is no solid consensus as to *which* ancient Near Eastern treaties served as the model for the present form of Deuteronomy. Mendenhall argued that the covenant texts of the Old Testament resemble most closely exemplars of the Hittite Empire of the second millennium BCE.[12] This would suggest a second-millennium BCE date for Deuteronomy.

Moshe Weinfeld and others responded by noting the similarities between Deuteronomy and the Vassal Treaties of Esarhaddon (VTE). They posited that these first-millennium BCE treaties served as the model for Deuteronomy, and accordingly support the contention that Deuteronomy is the product of the monarchic period and, more specifically, the seventh century BCE.[13]

Andrew Mayes claimed that to appeal to the alleged treaty form of Deuteronomy is to miss the significance of the treaty "tradition." Since Deuteronomy in its present form is not presented as a treaty document, but rather has adopted some of the language and form of a broad treaty tradition, attempts to identify which period of the tradition is represented in Deuteronomy are not helpful. In his view, arguments for the date of Deuteronomy based on adherence to a supposed treaty form are "inadmissible."[14]

Beginning in the 1970s, serious concerns began to be raised about the Documentary Hypothesis. Some questioned the basic methodology of source analysis, particularly in light of ancient Near Eastern texts held to be unitary on other grounds but which nevertheless exhibit some of the same characteristics as the biblical texts. Others questioned the archaeological parallels used to support the analysis of source critics. In the 1980s, the consensus began to break down further as some maintained that the J source was the latest source, and that it was actually postexilic and post-Deuteronomic. One of the most significant critiques of the Docu-

---

[11] George E. Mendenhall, "Covenant Forms in Israelite Tradition," *BA* 17 (1954): 50–76.

[12] Ibid., 56–67.

[13] Moshe Weinfeld, *Deuteronomy and the Deuteronomic School* (Oxford: Clarendon, 1972; repr. Winona Lake, IN: Eisenbrauns, 1992), 59–81, esp. 60, and Weinfeld, *Deuteronomy 1–11: A New Translation with Introduction and Commentary*, AB 5 (New York: Doubleday, 1991), 6–9. In the latter (p. 9) Weinfeld argued that Deuteronomy is based on both the old Hittite model (via the "old biblical tradition") and the Assyrian model.

[14] A. D. H. Mayes, *Deuteronomy*, NCB (Grand Rapids: Eerdmans, 1979), 33–34.

mentary Hypothesis emerged in this time. In a landmark work, Norman Whybray presented a powerful argument against the Documentary Hypothesis.[15] Whybray saw the entire Pentateuch as a comprehensive work composed by a single author[16] that should most probably be dated to the postexilic period.[17] According to his theory, since the Pentateuch was the work of a single author, Deuteronomy dates to the postexilic period.

The view that Deuteronomy is later than the monarchic period has gained more widespread support following Whybray's work. For example, Norbert Lohfink maintains that Deuteronomy's vision is largely utopian and could never be realized. In particular, the utopian nature of Deuteronomy may be seen in its treatment of the king and its vision for inclusion of the marginalized. He concludes that the final form of Deuteronomy likely dates to the postexilic period.[18]

Eckart Otto maintains that Deuteronomy developed separately from the rest of the Pentateuch and was later combined with Joshua. In the postexilic period, a "Hexateuch redaction" and later a "Pentateuch redaction" took place. Though based on earlier sources and redactions, the final form of Deuteronomy dates, in Otto's view, to the postexilic era.[19]

Mainstream scholarship now generally agrees that, although Deuteronomy is based on earlier sources and redactions, its final form is late. Possible dates range from the monarchic period (seventh century BCE) to the postexilic era. As Gordon Wenham notes, "the academic community is looking for a fresh and convincing paradigm for the study of the Pentateuch, but so far none of the new proposals seems to have captured the scholarly imagination."[20] The same may be said of dating Deuteronomy.

Purpose and Ideology

Closely related to considerations of the date of Deuteronomy is the book's ideology, which has also been the object of considerable scholarly

---

[15] R. Norman Whybray, *The Making of the Pentateuch: A Methodological Study*, JSOTSup 53 (Sheffield: JSOT Press, 1987).

[16] Ibid., 232–33.

[17] Ibid., 229–30.

[18] Norbert Lohfink, "Distribution of the Functions of Power: The Laws Concerning Public Offices in Deuteronomy 16:18–18:22," in *A Song of Power and the Power of Song: Essays on the Book of Deuteronomy*, ed. Duane L. Christensen, SBTS 3 (Winona Lake, IN: Eisenbrauns, 1993), 346; Lohfink, "The Laws of Deuteronomy: A Utopian Project for a World Without Any Poor?" (Lattey Lecture, St. Edmund's College, Cambridge, 1995), 18.

[19] Eckart Otto, *Deuteronomium 1–11*, vol. 1, *1,1–4,43*, HThKAT (Freiburg im Breisgau: Herder, 2012), 248–56.

[20] Wenham, "Pondering the Pentateuch," 119.

attention.[21] The association of Deuteronomy with the monarchic period in the earliest part of the modern era has led to several significant conclusions about its ideology. As noted above, Wellhausen's source analysis of the Pentateuch located Deuteronomy chronologically between JE and P. But he also recognized ideological differences in the sources. These differences became a criterion for dating the sources, and were important in tracing the development of Israelite religion.

The evolution of Israelite religion may be most readily seen through a comparison of worship as presented in the sources. For example, Wellhausen argued, based on Exod 20:24–25, that JE assumes that many altars will be built for the worship of YHWH.[22] However, Deut 12 changes this law, insisting on one central sanctuary and delegitimizing all others. This firmly fixes the date of Deuteronomy in the seventh century BCE and associates it with the reforms of Josiah.[23] However, P assumes and never argues for the centralization of worship at the one "chosen place."[24] Wellhausen concluded that this can only mean that the transformation of religion envisioned by Deuteronomy had become a reality by the time P was composed. In his view, this ideological change is inextricably linked with the date of the book.

Gerhard von Rad took a different approach. Utilizing the method of form criticism, he sought to identify the *Sitz im Leben* (setting in life) of Deuteronomy. He held that the form of Deuteronomy (which he limited to chapters 4–30)[25] reflects a traditional cultic setting, perhaps a covenant renewal ceremony. However, in Deuteronomy's present form the cultic setting has been largely abandoned, and the older material has been reworked as an instructional address to the people as a whole.[26]

Central to understanding von Rad's view of the ideology of Deuteronomy is his view of authorship (which, in turn, is connected to questions of date). Von Rad maintained that the Levites were responsible for the composition of Deuteronomy, on the grounds that they would have

[21] I understand ideology as representing the system of beliefs (including religious ones), attitudes, values, and assumptions of a community or a part of a community. For a fuller treatment of ideology in Deuteronomy, see Vogt, *Deuteronomic Theology*, 15–20.

[22] Wellhausen, *Prolegomena*, 29.

[23] Ibid., 33.

[24] Ibid., 34–35.

[25] Von Rad followed Noth in treating the first three chapters of the present book of Deuteronomy (as well as chs. 31–34) as an introduction to the Deuteronomistic History (DH). However, he saw significant growth in Deuteronomy during the period of its independent existence prior to its incorporation into DH in the sixth century BCE. See Gerhard von Rad, *Deuteronomy: A Commentary*, OTL (Philadelphia: Westminster, 1966), 12.

[26] Ibid., 15–23.

had access to the religious literature as well as the authority to interpret ancient traditions in light of contemporary concerns. Moreover, given the close association between the theology of the holy war and the ark, and the fact that it was the Levites who maintained the ark, the emphasis on holy war in Deuteronomy suggested that the authors of Deuteronomy were Levites.[27]

More specifically, von Rad believed that the authors of Deuteronomy were "country Levites," who sought, with the support of the "people of the land," to revive the "old patriarchal traditions" of Yahwism, which date back to the amphictyonic period.[28] He based this argument on the relative insignificance of the king in Deuteronomy and the absence of any apparent reference to the Davidic covenant and associated messianic implications. He further maintained that only the country Levites could have possessed the resources and authority to reinterpret and reintroduce older traditions in light of a new context.[29]

Cult centralization holds an unusual place in von Rad's interpretation of Deuteronomy. On the one hand, it was supposedly "the most important special feature of Deuteronomy"[30] and was a necessary result of Deuteronomy's uncompromising insistence that "YHWH is One" (Deut 6:4).[31] Centralization had far-reaching consequences for the religious life of Israel. We should understand the centralizing laws as "a fresh interpretation . . . of the old cultic system, an interpretation which had become necessary owing on the one hand to abuses introduced . . . and on the other to quite new perceptions of Yahweh and his relationship to Israel."[32] These "abuses" and "new perceptions" presumably involve the anthropomorphic conception of YHWH's presence and the rejection of that view by the authors of Deuteronomy.

On the other hand, von Rad cautioned against seeing centralization as the theological center of the book. He saw Deuteronomy's demand for centralization as a relatively late development in the evolution of the book and maintained that centralization was "comparatively easy to remove as a late and final adaptation of many layers of material."[33]

---

[27] Ibid., 24–25. See also Gerhard von Rad, *Studies in Deuteronomy*, trans. D. M. G. Stalker, SBT (London: SCM, 1953), 66–67.

[28] Von Rad, *Studies*, 66–67.

[29] Ibid., 62–67. This view has been challenged. See, e.g., the critique of Weinfeld, *Deuteronomic School*, 53–58.

[30] Von Rad, *Deuteronomy*, 16, 88–89.

[31] Gerhard von Rad, *Old Testament Theology*, vol. 1, *The Theology of Israel's Historical Traditions*, trans. D. M. G. Stalker (New York: Harper & Row, 1962), 226–27; von Rad, *Deuteronomy*, 91.

[32] Von Rad, *Deuteronomy*, 91.

[33] Von Rad, *Studies*, 67.

Far from pervading the entire legal corpus in Deuteronomy, the demand for centralization is emphasized in only seven areas: the altar law (ch. 12), tithes (14:22–29), firstlings (15:19–23), feasts (16:1–17), the central judicial tribunal (17:8–13), provisions for priests (18:1–8), and cities of refuge (19:1–13). This demand is either unknown or contradicted in other laws.[34]

Von Rad also raised the question of whether or not centralization per se was a new concept in Deuteronomy. After all, prior to the establishment of the temple under Solomon, in its various locations the ark may have served as the cultic center to which the tribes journeyed for pilgrimage festivals.[35] Also, the Book of the Covenant begins with its own altar law (Exod 20:24). While von Rad allowed that the altar law in Deuteronomy is different, he maintained that:

> It is not right to regard as its primary aspect . . . an abrupt discontinuance of old usages. There is probably, after all, much that is traditional in this Deuteronomic rule which appears to be so revolutionary. This is evident in the resemblance of the form of the basic Deuteronomic law to the law of the altar in the Book of the Covenant. When compared with the latter, the formulation in Deuteronomy appears to be only a fresh wording.[36]

Thus von Rad seemed cautious about the nature of centralization in Deuteronomy and its significance. For him, the idea of covenant and the need for loyalty to YHWH were more significant than the idea of centralization.

Similar ambiguity surrounds the nature of Deuteronomy. On the whole, von Rad saw Deuteronomy as setting forth a utopian agenda. In its present form the book is a record of preaching, couched in the liturgical form of a covenant renewal ceremony. The aim of this preaching is to inculcate in the people obedience and loyalty to the commands of YHWH.[37] In that respect, Deuteronomy is highly realistic, since the purpose and tenor of the exhortation is to bring people to real obedience to YHWH. However, von Rad also saw in Deuteronomy an attempt "by a 'utopian' anachronism" to revert back to the old amphictyonic order.[38] Deuteronomy represents an effort by reformers of the seventh century

---

[34] Von Rad, *Deuteronomy*, 16, 89. See, e.g., p. 115 (on Deut 16:21–22).

[35] Ibid., 16–17.

[36] Ibid., 90–91. According to von Rad, of the three "centralizing ordinances" in Deut 12 (vv. 1–7; 8–12; 13–19), the third is the earliest because it is worded in the singular. See ibid., 16.

[37] Von Rad, *Theology*, 225.

[38] Von Rad, *Studies*, 64n2. The idea of the amphictyony as promulgated by Noth and understood by von Rad has been largely rejected. This idea was first introduced in Martin Noth, *Das System der zwölf Stämme Israels*, BWANT (Stuttgart: Kohlhammer, 1930).

BCE to recover the lost glory of an earlier, better age in which Israel was ostensibly devoted to YHWH and in which it could rely on the security of his protection. Of course, it would be practically impossible for a monarchic state to revert to the institutions and practices of the premonarchic period. Thus, the vision of Deuteronomy is ultimately utopian.

However, at the same time von Rad saw the book as fiercely realistic in its opposition to syncretism and the influence of Canaanite religion. He noted that "Deuteronomy is in no sense a theoretical compendium of the will of Jahweh: rather it develops its demands" against Canaanite religion, which represented a threat to Yahwism.[39] Therefore, on the one hand, Deuteronomy may be seen as utopian in terms of the era to which it seems to want to return and the way it envisions Israel in every generation as being on the verge of the fulfillment of divine promises. On the other hand, it is fiercely realistic in its expectation that the people of YHWH are to be uncompromisingly loyal to YHWH.

In contrast to von Rad, Weinfeld maintained that Deuteronomy presents not a utopian ideal that could never be implemented but a realistic and revolutionary program of reform. The goal of that reform was the consolidation of power in Jerusalem, both of the king and the temple, and a correction—even repudiation—of earlier thinking and theology. In Weinfeld's view, at the heart of Deuteronomy is a program of centralization that intentionally resulted in "demythologization and secularization." He notes:

> The centralization of the cult was in itself, of course, a sweeping innovation in the history of the Israelite cultus, but its consequences were . . . decisively more revolutionary in nature, in that they involved the collapse of an entire system of concepts which for centuries had been regarded as sacrosanct. . . . [Israelite religious life] was freed from its ties to the cult and was transformed into an abstract religion which did not necessarily require any external expression. Indeed the very purpose of the book of Deuteronomy . . . was to curtail and circumscribe the cultus and not to extend or enhance it.[40]

As a realistic program of reform, Deuteronomy in some form served as the basis for the reforms of Josiah.[41] Indeed, the connection between

---

[39] Von Rad, *Theology*, 227–28.

[40] Weinfeld, *Deuteronomic School*, 190. See also Weinfeld, *Deuteronomy 1–11*, 37.

[41] Weinfeld stated that the form of Deuteronomy that served as the basis for the reforms included "an introduction, a law code (certainly chapters 12–19, which embody the principles of the reform) and the admonition in chapter 28 regarding the rewards for obedience and punishments for violation of the 'terms of the covenant which the Lord commanded Moses to conclude with the Israelites' (Deuteronomy 28:69)" (Moshe Weinfeld, "Deuteronomy's Theological Revolution," *BRev* 12.1 [1996]: 38). See also Weinfeld, *Deuteronomy 1–11*, 9–13.

Deuteronomy and Josiah's reform is so strong that Josiah's reform "might well be called the Deuteronomic Reform."[42] Weinfeld argues further that

> the book of Deuteronomy appears indeed to have the character of an ideal national constitution representing all the official institutions of the state: the monarchy, the judiciary, the priesthood, and prophecy. These institutions are successively referred to in Deut 16:18–18:22 and are depicted not only in realistic terms but also in terms of the ideal at which this neutral circle of scribes was clearly aiming—a national regime which incorporated all the normative, spiritual, and religious circles of the period.[43]

It is clear that in Weinfeld's view Josiah's revolutionary reforms sought to some extent to apply the requirements of the form of Deuteronomy that existed at that time and that they accorded with the theological understanding and ideology of the book.[44]

For Weinfeld, centralization of the cult was at the heart of Deuteronomy's program, and thus Josiah's reforms. What started with the call to eliminate the worship sites of the Canaanites went on to centralize the cult through the elimination even of the YHWH-centered high places. This centralization had far-reaching implications. Before, priests could be consulted in difficult judicial matters at local altars, but the elimination of such altars necessitated changes. This accounts for Deuteronomy's call to appoint judges in the towns.[45] Because centralization resulted in the reduction of the significance of the cult in the day-to-day lives of the Israelites, Weinfeld understood this as "secularization."[46]

---

[42] Weinfeld, "Theological Revolution," 38. However, he noted that at least one aspect of the reforms, the eradication of alien cults, was undertaken *prior* to the discovery of the Book of the Torah. See also Weinfeld, *Deuteronomy 1–11*, 73–74.

[43] Weinfeld, *Deuteronomic School*, 168.

[44] However, it would be simplistic to argue that Weinfeld saw in Josiah's reform simply the application of Deuteronomic principles. Rather, he recognized a more dynamic relationship between the reform and the book of Deuteronomy in which the reform itself (which was based in large part on some form of the book) reshaped the book and contributed to its development.

[45] Weinfeld, *Deuteronomic School*, 233–35.

[46] Weinfeld described Deuteronomy as having a "distinctly secular foundation. Not only do we encounter institutions of a manifestly secular character such as the judiciary . . . the monarchy . . . the military . . . and civil and criminal laws which treat of the family and inheritance . . . loans and debts . . . litigations and quarrels . . . trespassing . . . and false testimony . . . and the like; but . . . even institutions and practices which were originally sacral in character have here been recast in secularized forms. . . . The very book which is so centrally concerned with 'the chosen place' has almost completely ignored the sacral institutions which the chosen place must necessarily imply and without which the conduct of sacral worship is unimaginable" (ibid., 188).

According to Weinfeld, Deuteronomy's program also involved demythologization. Demythologization refers to the tendency to reinterpret earlier theology (which most understand to have been less abstract in its theological constructs) in favor of a more spiritual, abstract understanding. The tendency toward secularization and demythologization may be seen in the following features of Deuteronomy: profane slaughter, an altered understanding of firstlings, reinterpretation of tithes, a changed view of the cultic calendar, a humanitarian motivation for laws, cities of refuge, the elimination of priestly involvement in local judicial matters, the status of Levites, a more abstract conception of God, and a shift in the understanding of the presence of God.[47]

As we have seen, for Weinfeld, Deuteronomy's program is eminently realistic, though he also conceded that it contained some utopian elements. On the one hand, Deuteronomy is realistic in its political agenda to support the reforms of Josiah in the seventh century BCE. On the other hand, Deuteronomy seeks to advance a more abstract, spiritual religion.

Bernard Levinson introduced another approach that has had considerable influence. Like Weinfeld, Levinson saw Deuteronomy (understood as a form of the book that included a law of centralization) as supporting the reforms of Josiah.[48] For him, the authors of this work were scribes who drew on other texts—particularly the Covenant Code—intentionally to support radical transformation of Israelite law, religion, and social structure. Such transformation was unprecedented in the history of Israel.[49]

Levinson agreed with Weinfeld that the authors of Deuteronomy envisioned a radical program of reform. He suggested that this was carried out through a radical transformation of existing law and practice through the use of the very lemmas of the earlier laws.[50] With this reinterpretation, the authors deliberately redefined the nature and role of the judicial system at the local level. Deuteronomy is obviously radical in that it transfers to the central tribunal the authority to adjudicate ambiguous cases and supplants the clan-elder role in the judiciary with the appointment of judges and officers in each town (Deut 16:18).[51] Levinson noted that Deuteronomy is completely silent on the role of clan elders, and that the authors "impose their professionalized judicial system upon the city gate

[47] Moshe Weinfeld, "On 'Demythologization and Secularization' in Deuteronomy," *IEJ* 23 (1973): 230–31. See also Weinfeld, *Deuteronomy 1–11*, 37–44. For a more detailed discussion and evaluation of Weinfeld's view, see Vogt, *Deuteronomic Theology*, 71–93.

[48] Bernard M. Levinson, *Deuteronomy and the Hermeneutics of Legal Innovation* (Oxford: Oxford University Press, 1997), 9.

[49] Ibid., 3–22.

[50] Ibid., 21.

[51] Ibid., 124–27.

as if it were a tabula rasa without traditional legal-historical occupants."[52] According to Levinson, this silence about the elders can "only constitute a deliberate polemic."[53] The purpose of the authors of Deuteronomy was to create an independent judiciary, free of control by the institution of the monarchy. The result is a political system in which the judge does not serve the king; instead, both offices, king and judge, are subject to the authority of the Torah.[54]

For Levinson, Deuteronomy's vision of the program of centralization of justice is both realistic and utopian. On the one hand, it is utopian in its subjugation of all offices to the Torah. On the other hand, it is realistic in its systematic and deliberate reinterpretation of the Covenant Code and the judicial system and procedures described there. Levinson recognized in Deuteronomy both a "draft constitution" and a description of the office bearers of theocracy. He noted that "the Deuteronomic agenda is thus both cultic and judicial, both utopian and practical; it is concerned both with the rewriting of texts and with the transformation of public life."[55]

I conclude by briefly considering the view of Lohfink, who saw Deuteronomy as a utopian text that could not be implemented. The purpose and ideology of the book was to articulate a normative worldview that centered on God's concern for the marginalized. It postulated a "world that is in contrast to all other worlds."[56] According to Lohfink, Deuteronomy envisions a society in which poverty and marginalization are "beyond the borders." In so doing, Deuteronomy contrasts sharply with both the ideologies of the ancient Near East and earlier legal material.[57]

Composition and Structure

My final area of review is the composition and structure of Deuteronomy. As with the previous issues, mainstream scholarship has posited several different possibilities for the composition of the book.

Scholars have described the structure of Deuteronomy in several different ways. The variety in approaches stems from the book itself, which Christopher Wright aptly notes is "so rich in content and texture that, like a rich fruitcake, it can be sliced in various ways."[58] At the same time,

---

[52] Ibid., 125.

[53] Ibid., 126.

[54] Ibid., 126–27.

[55] Ibid., 137.

[56] Lohfink, "Laws of Deuteronomy," 16.

[57] Ibid., 18.

[58] Christopher J. H. Wright, *Deuteronomy*, NIBCOT 4 (Peabody, MA: Hendrickson, 1996), 1.

scholars are divided on whether to understand the book as a unified composition or as a composite representing different strata and layers.

Following Wellhausen's proposal that the Pentateuch represents different sources dating to different time periods, questions arose as to the composition and unity of Deuteronomy. Some have understood its growth in terms of sources, reminiscent of the understanding of the development of the Pentateuch as a whole. They used the change in form of address between second-person singular and plural (*Numeruswechsel*) to identify sources in Deuteronomy.[59] In this approach, the oldest version of Deuteronomy used a singular pronoun, while a later version used plural forms.

Not all accepted this understanding. Lohfink saw the *Numeruswechsel* as a stylistic device intended to capture the attention of the listener.[60] Parts of Deuteronomy considered on other grounds to be a unity (such as Deut 4:1–40) alternate between singular and plural forms of address. This calls into question the reliability of the *Numeruswechsel* as an indicator of disparate sources.[61]

More recently, some have explained the phenomenon of *Numeruswechsel* on rhetorical grounds as well. Timothy Lenchak argued that the change in number represents a deliberate attempt by the author to persuade his audience. Rather than being a merely stylistic issue, the change in address reflects the author's determination to convince his audience that all Israel—as individuals and as a collective—must be radically devoted to YHWH.[62]

After Wellhausen, Martin Noth had the greatest influence on mainstream understanding of the composition and structure of Deuteronomy. In his landmark work *Überlieferungsgeschichtliche Studien*,[63] Noth claimed that Deuteronomy is best seen not as a part of the so-called Hexateuch, but rather as the first part of a Deuteronomistic History (DH), which consists of the books Deuteronomy through Kings. He saw this work as the product

---

[59] See the description and analysis of this approach in Mayes, *Deuteronomy*, 34–38. See also Duane L. Christensen, "Deuteronomy in Modern Research: Approaches and Issues," in *Song of Power*, 3–5.

[60] Norbert Lohfink, *Das Hauptgebot: Eine Untersuchung literarischer Einleitungsfragen zu Dtn 5–11*, AnBib 20 (Rome: Biblical Institute Press, 1963).

[61] Mayes, *Deuteronomy*, 36. The use of *Numeruswechsel* as a criterion for source identification continues, however. Modern versions of the theory are influenced by the work of Martin Noth; see below.

[62] Timothy A. Lenchak, *"Choose Life!": A Rhetorical-Critical Investigation of Deuteronomy 28,69–30,20*, AnBib 129 (Rome: Pontifical Biblical Institute, 1993), 13–16.

[63] Martin Noth, *Überlieferungsgeschichtliche Studien*, 2nd ed. (Tübingen: Niemeyer, 1957). References here are to the English translation of the first 110 pages, which appears in Noth, *The Deuteronomistic History*, JSOTSup 15 (Sheffield: JSOT Press, 1981). The remainder of the work appears in English translation in Noth, *The Chronicler's History*, JSOTSup 50 (Sheffield: JSOT Press, 1987).

of an author, not an editor, who "brought together material from highly varied traditions and arranged it according to a carefully conceived plan."[64] According to Noth, the book of Deuteronomy was composed to serve as the introduction to the larger work. Thus, chapters 1–3 of Deuteronomy are not simply an introduction to the book of Deuteronomy, but function primarily as an introduction to DH.[65] This introduction was placed before an older version of the Deuteronomic law that is essentially the same as that found in Deut 4:44–30:20.[66] Noth also postulated a purpose for this entire composition—to demonstrate that the fall of Jerusalem in 586 BCE was a result of Israel's failure to keep the covenant. As the introduction to DH, Deuteronomy helps explain the nature and terms of that covenant.

Noth's approach signaled a significant departure from that of his predecessors. Since Wellhausen, the study of Deuteronomy was focused largely on identifying the various sources lying behind the final form of the text. In particular, scholars tried to identify the earliest form of Deuteronomy (sometimes called Urdeuteronomium = Urdt) and other sources that were combined with it to form the present book. However, Noth argued for a basic Urdt that was modified by a single author, whose purpose was to explain the fall of Jerusalem and the catastrophe of the exile. To a great degree his analysis consisted of distinguishing between Deuteronomistic and earlier materials.

Mainstream critics adopted Noth's approach in many respects. Some suggested that there were two (or more) versions of DH that have been woven together in the final form of the text. For example, Frank Cross distinguished two versions of DH. The first, Dtr^1, which was composed in the time of Josiah and in support of the Josianic reforms, characteristically emphasized themes of judgment and hope. The second version, Dtr^2, which was composed during the exile (about 550 BCE), was far less hopeful in its outlook. However, Cross noted that he followed Noth in seeing the author of Dtr^1 as truly creative, and did not challenge the general implications of Noth's theory for the book of Deuteronomy.[67]

Noth's approach was significant for the study of Deuteronomy because he made the idea that different voices could be heard in Deuteronomy generally acceptable.[68] Noth's additional proposal that the purpose of the

---

[64] Noth, *Deuteronomistic History*, 10.

[65] Ibid., 12–17.

[66] Ibid., 16.

[67] Frank M. Cross, *Canaanite Myth and Hebrew Epic: Essays in the History of the Religion of Israel* (Cambridge: Harvard University Press, 1973), 274–89. For discussion of how Noth's and Cross' proposals have been modified more recently, see Vogt, *Deuteronomic Theology*, 10–13.

[68] J. Gordon McConville, *Grace in the End: A Study in Deuteronomic Theology*, Studies in Old Testament Biblical Theology (Grand Rapids: Zondervan, 1993), 34.

exilic redactor of Deuteronomy and DH was to explain the exile in terms of failure to keep the terms of the covenant became a criterion for subsequent scholars for identifying redactional layers. Perceived changes in perspective or purpose were used to separate out layers of the text, and each layer was consequently seen to represent a particular ideology. Mark O'Brien rightly notes that "since Noth, the trend has been to concentrate on separating the Deuteronomistic (Dtr) redaction from the earlier material."[69]

While Noth thought primarily in terms of two sources in the present form of Deuteronomy (Urdt and Dtr), later scholars discovered many more layers. Although in principle the number of layers could be unlimited, efforts among mainstream scholars to identify pre-Deuteronomic, Deuteronomic, and Deuteronomistic layers in Deuteronomy (and DH) have reached an impasse. Despite broad acceptance of the fact of later redaction of an Urdt, conclusions about the identification and number of literary strata are diverse and, at times, contradictory.[70] This has led some to pursue new avenues of inquiry.[71]

Beginning with the important work of Robert Polzin, synchronic readings of Deuteronomy became common.[72] Polzin demonstrated that Deuteronomy exhibits a careful and deliberate interplay between the voices of Moses and the narrator of the book, and that the "separate voices of Moses and the narrator gradually fuse as the book progresses toward its conclusion."[73] Apparent contradictions, so often used to identify disparate sources or layers in the book, are the result of a deliberate effort to preserve a "plurality of viewpoints, all working together to achieve a truly multidimensional effect."[74] Polzin's work was significant because it presented a plausible synchronic reading of the text.[75]

---

[69] Mark A. O'Brien, "The Book of Deuteronomy," *CurBS* 3 (1995): 97.

[70] The theory of a later redaction of DH has also been called into question recently. A. Graeme Auld, "The Deuteronomists and the Former Prophets, or What Makes the Former Prophets Deuteronomistic," in *Those Elusive Deuteronomists: The Phenomenon of Pan-Deuteronomism*, ed. Linda S. Schearing and Steven L. McKenzie, JSOTSup 268 (Sheffield: Sheffield Academic, 1999), 116–26, claimed that the influence goes in the opposite direction, i.e., that Kings has influenced Deuteronomy.

[71] According to O'Brien ("Deuteronomy," 101), "interest in tracing the contours of dtr and pre-dtr layers throughout Deuteronomy seems to be waning."

[72] Robert Polzin, *Moses and the Deuteronomist: A Literary Study of the Deuteronomic History*, part 1, *Deuteronomy, Joshua, Judges* (New York: Seabury, 1980); and Polzin, "Deuteronomy," in *The Literary Guide to the Bible*, ed. R. Alter and F. Kermode (Cambridge: Belknap, 1987), 92–101.

[73] Polzin, "Deuteronomy," 92.

[74] Ibid., 93.

[75] Polzin noted that a synchronic reading cannot ignore diachronic considerations, and he maintained that the two approaches are complementary to one another. See Polzin, *Moses*, 2–5.

Since Polzin, there has been an increasing tendency to read Deuteronomy as an organized whole, even among mainstream scholars. The subtleties of argument and the skill of the author(s) or editor(s) of the book are increasingly recognized. Lohfink posited that the book can, in fact, be read as a whole, in which the various parts are interconnected and support a coherent argument.[76] Dennis Olson has also offered a theological reading of the book that seeks to take seriously the development of thought from beginning to end.[77]

Evangelical Responses

From the beginning of the modern era, some have rejected the tenets and conclusions of mainstream scholarship on Deuteronomy. In general, past evangelical responses to Deuteronomy scholarship (and, in many ways, Old Testament scholarship in general) may be fairly described as reactive rather than proactive.

In assessing evangelical responses, it is important to note that, strictly speaking, "evangelicalism" as a movement did not emerge until the late 1920s in the United States (arguably marked by the founding of Westminster Seminary in 1929) and the mid-1940s in Great Britain (with the founding of Tyndale Fellowship). Earlier conservative perspectives were simply part of the overall scholarly conversation and did not constitute a readily identifiable movement.[78]

For the sake of convenience, I shall divide evangelical responses to mainstream scholarship in terms of the three primary issues addressed above.

Date

As noted above, Wellhausen's proposal for the composition and date of the Pentateuch and its implications for understanding Deuteronomy gained widespread acceptance in the scholarly community. Samuel Driver, who largely fit the mold of what would later be called evangelicalism, embraced the Documentary Hypothesis and helped advance and popularize it

[76] Norbert Lohfink, "Zur Fabel des Deuteronomiums," in *Bundesdokument und Gesetz: Studien zum Deuteronomium*, ed. G. Braulik, HBS 4 (Freiburg im Breisgau: Herder, 1995), 65–78.

[77] Dennis T. Olson, *Deuteronomy and the Death of Moses: A Theological Reading*, OBT (Minneapolis: Fortress, 1994).

[78] Gerald Bray, *Biblical Interpretation Past and Present* (Downers Grove, IL: InterVarsity Press, 1996), 539–43.

in the English-speaking world. His commentary on Deuteronomy reflects both the assumptions and conclusions of the Documentary Hypothesis.[79]

However, others rejected the Documentary Hypothesis and "fought against the rise of liberalism."[80] While not specifically focusing on Deuteronomy, James Orr and Oswald Allis represented this resistance camp.[81] As was the case with many others for much of the twentieth century, their work was largely reactive, responding to prevailing views of the composition of the Pentateuch (and, therefore, Deuteronomy).

The tension between evangelicals and mainstream scholarship on Deuteronomy (and the dominance of the Documentary Hypothesis as an explanation for the composition of the Pentateuch) is exemplified by George Manley's work.[82] While engaging with evidence against the scholarly consensus dating Deuteronomy to the reign of Josiah, he articulated a case for a Mosaic date and origin for the book. Despite his careful presentation of evidence, his work was largely ignored. Von Rad's 1964 commentary on Deuteronomy (translated into English two years later) appears to be unaware of Manley's work or the arguments he proposed.[83] This is not uncommon. As Wenham notes,

> conservatives have persistently tried to argue for a much earlier date for Deuteronomy, indeed often for a Mosaic origin of the book. Yet their arguments, even when cogently presented, have fallen on deaf ears; critical scholars may list conservative works in their bibliographies, but they rarely take the trouble to interact with them.[84]

Meredith Kline's work represents another significant evangelical contribution to the discussion of the date of Deuteronomy. Responding to

---

[79] Samuel R. Driver, *A Critical and Exegetical Commentary on Deuteronomy*, ICC (Edinburgh: T&T Clark, 1895), xxxiv–lxxvii.

[80] Bray, *Biblical Interpretation*, 543.

[81] See, e.g., James Orr, *The Problem of the Old Testament Considered with Reference to Recent Criticism* (New York: Scribner's, 1906); and Oswald T. Allis, *The Five Books of Moses: A Reexamination of the Modern Theory That the Pentateuch Is a Late Compilation from Diverse and Conflicting Sources by Authors and Editors Whose Identity Is Completely Unknown*, 3rd ed. (New York: Presbyterian and Reformed, 1969).

[82] George T. Manley, *The Book of the Law: Studies in the Date of Deuteronomy* (London: Tyndale, 1957).

[83] Von Rad, *Deuteronomy*. Manley's work was cited, however, by other evangelicals.

[84] Gordon J. Wenham, "The Date of Deuteronomy: Linch-Pin of Old Testament Criticism, Part One," *Themelios* 10 (1985): 15. Not all evangelicals argue for an early date for the book. James Robson, "The Literary Composition of Deuteronomy," in *Interpreting Deuteronomy: Issues and Approaches*, ed. David G. Firth and Philip S. Johnston (Downers Grove, IL: InterVarsity Press, 2012), 19–59, argued that the rhetorical situation of the book is the exilic period, though its origins are understood as Mosaic.

the discovery of ancient Near Eastern treaty documents, Kline held that the structure of Deuteronomy resembled the treaty pattern of the second millennium BCE. Because treaties from that period included historical prologues (like Deut 1:5–4:49), the book should be dated to the second millennium BCE, since first-millennium BCE treaties lacked this element.[85]

Mainstream scholars reacted to this conclusion by arguing that the absence of historical prologues in extant first-millennium BCE treaties does not conclusively prove their absence from all such treaties. The textual evidence may have been lost, or the prologues may have been presented orally or simply assumed.[86] Consequently, awareness of treaty parallels has not resulted in a consensus concerning the date of Deuteronomy.

Based largely on contextual considerations, evangelicals continued to press for an early date for Deuteronomy. For example, in his 1970 doctoral dissertation, Gordon Wenham presented a case for an early date for Deuteronomy based not only on treaty patterns but also on other factors, while Peter Craigie's argument for an early date for Deuteronomy was still based largely on treaty patterns.[87]

Around 1980, evangelical scholarship shifted from its reactive stance to a more constructive approach. This is evident in discussions of the date of Deuteronomy. Gordon McConville argued for a premonarchic date for Deuteronomy, not on the basis of treaty parallels, but on the basis of the ideological and theological emphases in the book. He noted that the rhetoric of Deuteronomy circumscribes, rather than advances, the powers of the king. This suggests that Deuteronomy opposes the "ANE royal-cultic ideology, in which the king is chief executive in cult and political administration."[88] Deuteronomy's opposition to the "royal-cultic synthesis,"[89] which was expressed further in accounts of the establishment of the monarchy, embedded this ideology into the fabric of Israel's worldview, which enabled Israelite religion and ideologies to survive the exile. McConville claimed that since it is unlikely this theology could

[85] Meredith G. Kline, *Treaty of the Great King* (Grand Rapids: Eerdmans, 1963). Kline took up Mendenhall's approach and applied it to Deuteronomy, arguing that as a whole it has the form of the second-millennium BCE treaties. A similar approach, though not focused exclusively on Deuteronomy, was taken by Kenneth A. Kitchen, *Ancient Orient and Old Testament* (London: Tyndale, 1966).

[86] See John A. Thompson, *The Ancient Near Eastern Treaties and the Old Testament* (London: Tyndale, 1964), 14–15; Thompson, *Deuteronomy: An Introduction and Commentary*, TOTC (London: Inter-Varsity Press, 1974), 51.

[87] Peter C. Craigie, *The Book of Deuteronomy*, NICOT (Grand Rapids: Eerdmans, 1976), 24–28.

[88] J. Gordon McConville, *Deuteronomy*, ApOTC 5 (Downers Grove, IL: Inter-Varsity Press, 2002), 34.

[89] Ibid., 36.

have arisen in the disruptive context of the exile, the book must be dated much earlier.

Elsewhere I have presented a case for a premonarchic date for Deuteronomy based on the implied audience, another internal consideration.[90] Deuteronomy's remarkably positive treatment of Moab, Edom, and Ammon as Israel's "brothers" (Deut 2:4, 8) and recipients of land granted by YHWH does not fit international political realities in either the monarchic or postexilic periods.[91] Similarly, the place of sacrifice and the implied audience argue for a premonarchic date. It is hard to conceive that Deuteronomy could have been written in either the monarchic or postexilic periods without mentioning Jerusalem as "the place" of sacrifice. It seems even less likely that an alternative site, Mount Ebal (Deut 27), would have been named in either of those periods.[92]

Purpose and Ideology

As is the case with the date of Deuteronomy, evangelicals have resisted most mainstream understandings of the purpose and ideology of the book. As I noted above, since Deuteronomy is usually associated with the monarchic period, its purpose and ideology may be seen as advancing relevant political interests. On this issue, evangelicals have tended again to be reactive in their criticism of mainstream scholarship. Given the general evangelical preference for dating the book to the premonarchic period, presentations of its purpose and ideology have largely focused on Moses' audience and Deuteronomy's communication to it. In particular, scholars have emphasized the book's historical significance rather than its rhetorical strategy or its literary devices.[93]

In recent years, evangelicals have focused on the purpose and ideology in differing ways. Rather than simply seeing the final form of the book as coming from Moses' hand, most allow for subsequent editing of the book.[94] This affects the understanding of the purpose and ideology of

---

[90] Peter T. Vogt, " 'These Are the Words Moses Spoke': Implied Audience and a Case for a Pre-Monarchic Dating of Deuteronomy," in *For Our Good Always: Studies on the Message and Influence of Deuteronomy in Honor of Daniel I. Block*, ed. Jason S. DeRouchie, Jason Gile, and Kenneth J. Turner (Winona Lake, IN: Eisenbrauns, 2013), 61–80.

[91] Ibid., 65–72.

[92] Ibid., 72–79. For another attempt to date Deuteronomy based on internal considerations, see Block, *Deuteronomy*, 27–33.

[93] As a representative example, see Craigie, *Deuteronomy*, esp. 30–32.

[94] See Duane L. Christensen and Marcel Narucki, "The Mosaic Authorship of the Pentateuch," *JETS* 32 (1989): 465–71.

the book. Since a complete survey is impossible, I will focus on a couple of representative works.[95]

Wright argues that Deuteronomy should be interpreted based on the standpoint assumed in the book itself. (He maintains that the book is substantially Mosaic in terms of its origin, though he allows for subsequent editing.)[96] This leads him to identify a missiological purpose for the book; Deuteronomy seeks to foster an awareness in the audience that God is actively working in the world through Israel to advance his purposes and plans. In the context of a polytheistic culture, Deuteronomy "bends every rhetorical, literary, emotional, and moral skill to the task of equipping and motivating God's people to live for God's purposes in each generation."[97] This contrasts sharply with Weinfeld and others who see in Deuteronomy a revolutionary, centralizing program of reform in support of the monarchy.

Similarly, Daniel Block sees in Deuteronomy not a political manifesto or program of reform, but a call to the people of God to faithful covenant living in response to God's election of Israel and revelation of himself, and to advance their missional calling.[98] In addition to providing guidance for the administration of the covenant community, the book seeks to inspire the people to live out their relationship with God and thereby serve as a witness of YHWH's grace to the nations. This is essential since Deuteronomy conceives of Israel as a theocracy with "Yahweh as her divine suzerain."[99] This, too, represents a break from the more traditional (mainstream) understanding of Deuteronomy as a support for the claims of the monarchy.

Finally, my own work presents an alternative to the prevailing view that Deuteronomy advances a program of centralization, secularization, and demythologization.[100] Rather than advancing a radical program of centralization in support of the monarchy, Deuteronomy is radical in its insistence on the supremacy of YHWH and the way his people are to respond to this ideology in every aspect of life. Contra Weinfeld and others, I argue further that Deuteronomy centralizes sacrifice but perceives worship as extending into every aspect of life.[101]

---

[95] For a survey of approaches to Deuteronomy with different understandings of its theological purpose and ideology, see Paul A. Barker, "Contemporary Theological Interpretation of Deuteronomy," in *Interpreting Deuteronomy*, 60–90.

[96] Wright, *Deuteronomy*, 7–8.

[97] Ibid., 8.

[98] Block, *Deuteronomy*, 38.

[99] Ibid., 41.

[100] Vogt, *Deuteronomic Theology*.

[101] Ibid., 160–203. See also the shorter treatment of the subject in Peter T. Vogt, "Centralization and Decentralization in Deuteronomy," in *Interpreting Deu-*

As is the case concerning the date of Deuteronomy, recent evangelical study of the purpose and ideology of Deuteronomy has been less reactive and more proactive. This has served to advance the scholarly conversation and debate in constructive ways.

Composition and Structure

The final area I will examine is recent evangelical contributions to discussion of the composition and structure of the book. Once again, with their generally holistic hermeneutic, evangelical scholars break from mainstream approaches. As noted above, many mainstream scholars are rethinking long-standing forms of source-critical analysis. Whybray's work was an important catalyst in this movement, but the seeds for such a trend were planted even earlier.

The canonical approach of Brevard Childs served as a precursor to this change in direction.[102] Childs' emphasis on the final form of the text helped to undermine the notion that issues related to sources and the evolution of the text are primary. Rather, analysis should focus on the final form of the text. Meanwhile, Robert Alter's literary-critical work reinforced efforts to examine the final form, regardless of the underlying compositional process.[103] In particular, Alter's interpretation of literary doublets, type scenes, and the like provided an alternative to the historical-critical approach that saw those features as markers of disparate sources. This corresponds well with Polzin's approach, as described above.

In this area the correspondence between mainstream and evangelical approaches is obvious. Although Childs, Alter, and Polzin are not evangelicals, focus on the final form has gained acceptance in mainstream scholarly debate because of their work. Many evangelicals, who emphasize the final form of the text, are contributing to the broader conversation, despite persistent differences in understandings of the origin and nature of the biblical texts. This is particularly evident in mainstream scholars, such as John Van Seters and Rolf Rendtorff, who argue that the Pentateuch is essentially a single work,[104] sometimes for the same reasons

---

teronomy, 118–38.

[102] The literature on canonical criticism or a canonical approach is extensive. Childs' most significant contributions are *Introduction to the Old Testament as Scripture* (London: SCM, 1979); and *Biblical Theology of the Old and New Testaments: Theological Reflection on the Christian Bible* (Minneapolis: Augsburg Fortress, 1993).

[103] Robert Alter, *The Art of Biblical Narrative*, 2nd ed. (New York: Basic Books, 2011). See also Meir Sternberg, *The Poetics of Biblical Narrative: Ideological Literature and the Drama of Reading*, ISBL (Bloomington: Indiana University Press, 1985).

[104] See Wenham, "Pondering the Pentateuch," 123–32.

that evangelicals do, though there is virtually no agreement as to when or for what purpose(s) the text was written.[105]

With reference to Deuteronomy in particular, James Robson has articulated an understanding that represents current evangelical scholarship in several ways. Robson maintains that "the question of the composition of Deuteronomy is very complex. . . . The difficulty is that the evidence points in different directions. Some evidence points toward an earlier date. . . . However, other evidence points to a final date of production significantly later."[106] While seeking to avoid prejudging the evidence in either direction, after careful analysis of the data he concludes that the relationship between explicit and implicit evidence for understanding the composition of Deuteronomy "needs careful reflection. To regard some statements as self-evident and determinative for the interpretation of all other data is ultimately inconsistent."[107]

Discourse analysis has provided another profitable approach to Deuteronomy's composition. Studies like Jason DeRouchie's advance the understanding of the composition of the book through a careful analysis of participant reference, connection, *inclusio*, and repetition.[108] These studies are significant because they provide additional data for analysis and help ground conclusions on more objective textual data.

As is the case with reference to the date and ideology of Deuteronomy, recent evangelical scholarship on the composition of the book has engaged with mainstream scholarship in important and helpful ways.

Conclusion

This brief overview of the history of interpretation of Deuteronomy and the response from evangelical scholars has highlighted two key developments. First, in the three areas surveyed recent mainstream scholarship has become increasingly fragmented and pluralistic. For example, the lack of consensus on the date of Deuteronomy is a marked change from the early modern era, when the Documentary Hypothesis was widely ac-

---

[105] For similar emphases on the ideological unity of Deuteronomy, see J. Gary Millar, *Now Choose Life: Theology and Ethics in Deuteronomy*, NSBT 6 (Leicester: Apollos, 1998); and Paul Barker, *Deuteronomy: The God Who Keeps Promises* (Melbourne: Acorn, 1998).

[106] Robson, "Literary Composition," 57.

[107] Ibid.

[108] Jason S. DeRouchie, *A Call to Covenant Love: Text-Grammar and Literary Structure in Deuteronomy 5–11* (Piscataway, NJ: Gorgias Press, 2007). See also DeRouchie, "Counting the Ten: An Investigation into the Numbering of the Decalogue," in *For Our Good Always*, 93–125.

cepted and the dates of the various sources were largely agreed upon. Similar lack of agreement characterizes perspectives on the composition of the book and its purpose and ideology.

Second, whereas in the past evangelical scholarship was largely reactive (which is understandable, given the overall academic environment), in recent decades scholars belonging to this group have made many proactive contributions to the study of Deuteronomy. The absence of the same level of scholarly homogeneity among mainstream scholarship coupled with a more confident and assertive evangelical cadre of scholars has resulted in a more collaborative and stimulating environment than at any time in the history of the study of Deuteronomy. Even if evangelicals' work has not been widely accepted, their increasing significance in scholarly conversations is a welcome development.

CHAPTER 2

Ancient Near Eastern Treaty Traditions and Their Implications for Interpreting Deuteronomy

Neal A. Huddleston

A Question of Method: Why Analyze All These Treaties?

In Old Testament studies, two of the more popular comparative models present Deuteronomy as reflecting either a Hittite or a Neo-Assyrian treaty document, the latter type being exemplified in Esarhaddon's Succession Treaties (EST).[1] Interestingly, both models and their permutations are often presented as data to unsuspecting readers.[2] As suggested elsewhere in this volume, genealogical models do not easily account for the textual form or function displayed among ancient Near Eastern treaty materials or in Deuteronomy.[3] A significant by-product of this type of approach is a tacit acceptance of particular models in place of the texts themselves. As they stand, these models remain speculative and theoretical and yield unconvincing results. When imposed, they reduce the complexity of the treaty documents and Deuteronomy to simplified slices ripe for one-to-one correspondences. Indeed, one of the greatest challenges in

---

[1] Special appreciation is due to K. Lawson Younger, who encouraged the publication of this material, carefully read the draft, and offered numerous invaluable insights. The bulk of this essay is a condensed selection from chapter five of my dissertation, "Deuteronomy as *Mischgattung:* A Comparative and Contrastive Discourse Analysis of Deuteronomy and Ancient Near Eastern Treaty Traditions" (PhD diss., Trinity International University, 2015).

[2] The same is true for comparisons made between Deuteronomy and ancient Near Eastern law collections. However, rather than analyzing this genre, this essay is limited to the treaty materials.

[3] See the essay in the present volume by Younger and myself. In no way do I intend hereby to disparage the work of those who have taken these materials seriously, especially as represented by Kenneth Kitchen's and Paul Lawrence's significant achievement in *Treaty, Law and Covenant in the Ancient Near East* (Wiesbaden: Harrassowitz, 2012) (hereafter *TLCANE*).

Deuteronomy studies is to do justice to complex textual traditions without falling prey to oversimplification and reductionism.

It is tempting to analyze only those documents immediately relevant to one's preferred model and to the scholarly opposition. After all, one might argue, there are enough similarities between Deuteronomy and certain documents to warrant such an approach. However, this level of selectivity is problematic. First, it remains dependent on the models and the secondary literature that produced them. Second, it cannot cope with the significant differences between the models and the proposed texts from which they are derived. Third, it does not adequately explain the interrelationships among the ancient Near Eastern treaty documents themselves. All these deficiencies inevitably influence conclusions drawn from comparisons between the model and the biblical text.

Another relevant, but often overlooked, issue concerns the larger question of ancient Near Eastern treaty traditions. What can we actually say without resorting to select preconceived models?[4] Once one is willing to engage the significant pool of treaty material from which distinct traditions can be derived, the question becomes one of method. We may address other significant questions, especially concerning the notable parallels and divergences between these observable traditions, and the implications of these data for the comparative enterprise in Deuteronomy. Therefore, if one desires conclusions that are rooted in data, it is necessary to engage *all* the observable ancient Near Eastern treaty traditions, at least at a descriptive level, *before* comparing them with Deuteronomy.

Similarities between select discourse elements within Deuteronomy and the two popular treaty paradigms are obvious. The most notable similarities expressed in the secondary literature are the historiographic and maledictory material reflected in the Hittite and Neo-Assyrian treaty traditions, respectively. Nevertheless, Deuteronomy also exhibits significant differences. The voice of a narrator, for instance, never appears in the ancient Near Eastern treaty materials. Yet in Deuteronomy the voice of the narrator is a primary voice, and more importantly, the primary framer of the document. Indeed, collapsing this distinct voice with the many other voices of Deuteronomy is sufficient in itself to call into question the traditional comparative models. That is, as a matter of method one should keep the narrator's time and the narrated time distinct in any comparison, if one wishes to preserve the text's own voice. How one interacts with the narratorial voice directly influences how one interprets the opening lines

[4] See the helpful summary provided in Amnon Altman, "How Many Treaty Traditions Existed in the Ancient Near East?" in *Pax Hethitica: Studies on the Hittites and Their Neighbours in Honour of Itamar Singer*, ed. Yoram Cohen, Amir Gilan, and Jared L. Miller, StBoT 51 (Wiesbaden: Harrassowitz, 2010), 17–36.

of the book, its overall structure, and everywhere else the narrator speaks (or is absent).

Similarly, the exhortation plays a significant role in the content and discourse structure of Deuteronomy. However, in the ancient Near Eastern material the exhortation is essentially limited to projected speech and is not a significant discourse type either statistically or functionally. While Deuteronomy contains treaty elements, it is not itself a treaty document. Rather, in overall form and function Deuteronomy represents a paraenesis cast in the historiographic tradition of ancient Israel.

In light of these challenges, the way forward requires examining the relevant documents as texts in their own right and then deriving an observable textual tradition where reasonable. This essay therefore offers a succinct description at the discourse level of the most complete ancient Near Eastern treaty texts. The discourse analysis then provides the foundation for determining the forms of their respective treaty traditions. In turn, we will observe seven unique ancient Near Eastern treaty traditions that appeared from 2300 to 600 BCE. While this is not the place to include the full analysis of each treaty text, or even to refer to every document analyzed for this study, the essay will engage these texts on their own merits through illustrative citations.[5] Several texts are chosen as exemplars for their respective treaty group, based on complexity, length, and historical situation.[6] Each tradition is then briefly compared and contrasted with

[5] As background for this discussion, all published treaty documents dating from 2300 to 600 BCE were examined using a discourse method focusing primarily on the clause and upward. It is impractical to incorporate lengthy textual extracts into an essay, though numerous citations do appear. It is also essential to take note of the most recent finds as well as some of the treaty material overlooked in the massive work of Kitchen and Lawrence (*TLCANE*), as this additional material contributes significantly to the discussion. See the noted lacunae in the table of treaties that concludes this essay. An interested reader can easily compare the discussion here with the full texts conveniently provided in *TLCANE* (see the key in the table). Nevertheless, for detailed analysis I recommend original editions, as well as their updates and new joins, where relevant. For recently published treaties not present in *TLCANE*, see Jesper Eidem, *The Royal Archives from Tell Leilan: Old Babylonian Letters and Treaties from the Lower Town Palace East*, PIHANS 117 (Leiden: Nederlands Instituut voor het Nabije Oosten, 2011); Jacob Lauinger, "Esarhaddon's Succession Treaty at Tell Tayinat: Text and Commentary," *JCS* 64 (2012): 87–123; Michaël Guichard, "Un traité d'alliance entre Larsa, Uruk et Ešnunna contre Sabium de Babylone," *Sem* 56 (2014): 9–34; Ahmet Ünal, "A Hittite Treaty Tablet from Oylum Höyük in Southeastern Turkey and the Location of Ḫaššu(wa)," *AnSt* 65 (2015): 19–34.

[6] All translations are mine unless otherwise noted. They are intended only as illustrative of text-linguistic features pertinent to the discussion. All textual analysis is dependent on the respective *editio princeps* unless otherwise noted. Where expedient I preserve line numbers in the English gloss; otherwise they are omitted.

the others at the descriptive level in order to determine features unique to each. In the concluding section I explore a selection from the formal and functional relationships exhibited by these traditions to Deuteronomy. A complete list of the documents examined for this study, given in general chronological order,[7] appears in a table closing this essay.[8]

Before attending to specific traditions, a few comments regarding method are in order. First, I define "treaty tradition" in terms of linguistic typological features reflecting shared *formal* and *functional* elements evident in surface level, content, usage, and where it can be known, physical characteristics and find context. Similarly, while it is reasonable to suppose that a lone extant exemplar represents an entire tradition, this study applies the category "tradition" only to groups of documents that fulfill the following criteria: at minimum two texts from similar chronological and geo-linguistic circumstances, where one is not a copy of the other, and where both share similar discourse patterning. I therefore distinguish between unique treaties that *may* represent an underlying tradition (e.g., the Old Elamite treaty) and treaties that belong to an extant larger

[7] Middle Babylonian and Hittite materials represent exceptions to this organization. Rather than listing the Middle Babylonian and Hittite treaties together, I group them as discrete units to facilitate the discussion. As will be seen, the Middle Babylonian material is a simplified form of its Hittite counterpart. Similarly, the discussion generally follows the table except when it is clearer to group key texts according to their formal linguistic characteristics.

[8] I have not included highly fragmentary and unpublished texts in the discussion or in the closing table. Beckman lists a number of treaties too broken or fragmentary for including in *HDT*²; see his *Hittite Diplomatic Texts*, ed. Harry A. Hoffner, 2nd ed., SBLWAW 7 (Atlanta: Scholars Press, 1999), 6–7. A number of these are likewise not surveyed here, but are listed for the sake of completeness. The Middle Babylonian text group constitutes the following: Telipinu of Ḫatti and Išputaḫšu of Kizzuwatna (*CTH* 21.I/II; also in Hittite), Taḫurwaili of Ḫatti and Eḫeya of Kizzuwatna (no *CTH* number). The Hittite text group constitutes the following: a king of Ḫatti and the *ḫapiru* (*CTH* 27), a king of Ḫatti and Ḫuḫazalma of an unknown polity (*CTH* 28), Šuppiluliuma I of Ḫatti and *Šarri-kušuḫ of Carchemish (CTH* 50), Šuppiluliuma II of Ḫatti and Talmi-Teššub of Carchemish (*CTH* 122). Kitchen adds the following: an unknown king of Ḫatti and an unknown ruler of Kizzuwatna (*CTH* 132; see *TLCANE* 1:1086 no. 43), Šuppiluliuma II (?) of Ḫatti and an Eḫli-šarruma (?) of an unknown polity (*CTH* 123; see *TLCANE* 1:1086 no. 78), and an unknown ruler of Ḫatti and an unknown ruler of Mukiš (*CTH* 136; see *TLCANE* 1:1086 no. 79). The Hellenistic treaties between Hannibal of Carthage and Philip V of Macedon, between Rome and Lycia, etc. are deemed chronologically too late to be relevant and are therefore not included (see *TLCANE* no. 102 and no. 103). Finally, the Middle Assyrian treaty between Ili-ipadda (Assyrian *sukkallu rabi'u* and *šar* (*māt*) *Ḫanigalbat,* "the Grand Vizier" and "king of Ḫanigalbat") and the local Sutû (the Niḫsānu tribe) (TSA T04–37), about which some of the content has been made known, remains unpublished (Wiggermann, forthcoming). It likely dates between 1200 and 1180 BCE.

group and *do* represent an underlying tradition (e.g., the Old Babylonian treaties). The former are referred to as representing "potential treaty traditions." Only the latter bear the "treaty tradition" designation. While potential traditions are noted, attested treaty traditions occupy the lion's share of this study.

Second, discourse analysis provides a method that enables an exploration of treaty materials that traditional form-critical methods cannot. This study therefore adopts a discourse methodology that emphasizes a hierarchical model of language.[9] Categories are intentionally descriptive to reflect the discourse type and function of the text under examination, regardless of its language. Structural analysis primarily focuses at the clausal level and upward, while paying close attention to speaker, discourse mainline, and the clustering of discourse level features such as predication patterns. These elements collectively demonstrate the presence of seven unique discourse types among ancient Near Eastern treaty documents: adjuratory, explanatory, historiographic, hortatory, indictment, juridical, and present-procedural. Most of these categories are self-explanatory. Adjuratory discourse involves oath-based texts that are declaratory or promissory and includes the benediction and the malediction. The indictment represents a set of formal charges for violation of conduct, and incorporates features such as the indictment itself, supporting argumentation, and resulting penalties. Finally, juridical discourse incorporates absolute (so-called apodictic) and casuistic (case-law) forms. Where relevant these varieties will receive further explanation. We now turn to the application of these principles for discerning the treaty traditions.

Third Millennium

In the third millennium we find a single observable treaty tradition, which is reflected in a handful of Eblaite treaty documents discovered at Tell Mardiḫ (Ebla). An Old Elamite treaty also appears during this time frame, but as a single exemplar it represents either an ad hoc document or a potential Elamite treaty tradition.[10]

---

[9] The method is Hallidayan in its approach and is based on the work of Robert Longacre; see, e.g., Robert E. Longacre and Shin Ja J. Hwang, *Holistic Discourse Analysis* (Dallas: SIL International, 2012); Robert E. Longacre, "Complementarity: Verb Types and Discourse Types in Biblical Hebrew," in *LACUS Forum XXIX: Linguistics and the Real World*, ed. Douglas W. Coleman, William J. Sullivan, and Arle Lommel (Houston: LACUS, 2003): 123–33; *The Grammar of Discourse*, Topics in Language and Linguistics (New York: Plenum, 1996).

[10] The tablet is from Susa and dates to ca. 2300 BCE, perhaps after the Eblaite treaty material (Sb 8833; see *TLCANE* no. 8). It was made between Narām-Sîn

Tradition 1: Eblaite

The earliest treaty tradition on record hails from the twenty-third century BCE and is constituted by four Eblaite treaties made between an unknown ruler of Ebla and the following subordinates: rulers from Abarsal, Martu, and Dulu, and Yinḫar-Ḫalab of Burman.[11] Of these, Ebla's treaty with Abarsal (ARET 13:5) is the most extensive and representative, making it a fitting exemplar for the group. It boasts Ebla as its only speaker and divides into three sections. Section one (ARET 13:5 r.1.1–6.5) contains a geographic introduction explaining the holdings of the two powers, cast as a series of noun clauses: e.g., "$^{\text{r.1.6}}$Kablul $^{\text{1.7}}$and (its) fortifications (are) $^{\text{1.8}}$in the hand $^{\text{1.9}}$of the king $^{\text{1.10}}$of Ebla" ($^{\text{r.1.6}}$*Kab-lu*$_5$*-ul*^{ki} $^{\text{1.7}}$*ù* bàd-bàd^{ki} $^{\text{1.8}}$*in* šu $^{\text{1.9}}$en $^{\text{1.10}}$*Ib-la*^{ki}).

Section two (r.6.6–be.2.2) is signaled by a transition to juridical discourse (i.e., stipulations) that includes casuistic discourse (i.e., case law) marked by *su-ma* and *ʾà-na-sa* ("if" clauses): e.g., "$^{\text{r.6.6}}$Whoever $^{\text{6.8}}$insults (his) $^{\text{6.7}}$king . . . $^{\text{r.6.11}}$he shall die. $^{\text{r.6.12}}$If (he is) $^{\text{6.13}}$a leader (in) Abarsal . . . (etc.)" ($^{\text{r.6.6}}$*ma-nu-ma* $^{\text{6.7}}$en $^{\text{6.8}}$áš . . . $^{\text{r.6.11}}$ug$_7$ $^{\text{r.6.12}}$*su-ma* $^{\text{6.13}}$lú-igi *A-bar*-SAL$_4^{\text{ki}}$ . . .). Contingency is also asyndetic or contextually derived. The apodosis (the "then" clause) in the following provision is of special interest: "(But) $^{\text{r.10.6}}$if $^{\text{10.7}}$you do not request (an exception . . .), $^{\text{r.10.8}}$you have failed

---

of Akkad and an unknown Elamite ruler of Awan. This is the earliest known Elamite inscription and possesses a number of lacunae, two factors that create significant challenges for its interpretation. See Heidemarie Koch, "Elams Vertrag mit dem akkadischen König Narām-Sîn," in *TUAT*, Neue Folge, Band 2, *Staatsverträge, Herrscherinschriften und andere Dokumente zur politischen Geschichte*, ed. Bernd Janowski and Gernot Wilhelm (Gütersloh: Gütersloher Verlagshaus, 2005), 283–84. The document is probably a parity treaty, and the earliest of such texts found in a temple, suggesting divine assurance for the compliance of both parties to its contents. See Altman, "How Many Treaty Traditions," 19. Two speakers appear: a combined voice consisting of Narām-Sîn and the Elamite ruler, and the Elamite ruler alone as the primary voice. The combined voice is marked by the first-person plural in the first and second-to-last sections, bracketing the body of the treaty with an introductory adjuratory-promissory list of divine witnesses and what appears to be a final consequential affirmation. The entire text consists of adjuratory-promissory discourse, that is, promissory oath clauses. A formulaic divine invocation is followed by promissory oaths in each of the six sections of the body. The fifth occurrence of the pattern also includes two benedictions over Narām-Sîn's wife. The Elamite king utters a final benediction over Narām-Sîn as treaty closure. Given the prevalence of maledictory content in later treaty traditions, it is noteworthy that this text appears without this feature. In general, the document's purely adjuratory nature reflects an early witness to the general paradigm of the Old Babylonian treaty tradition (see below).

[11] For texts and translations, see Pelio Fronzaroli, *Testi di cancelleria: i rapporti con le città (Archivio L. 2769)*, with collaboration by Amalia Catagnoti, ARES 13 (Rome: Missione Archeologica Italiana in Siria, 2003).

the oil-oath" ([r.10.6]*su-ma* [10.7]nu du$_{11}$-ga [r.10.8]ì a-è).[12] Variations of the formula "(contingency X), you have failed the oil-oath (ì a-è)" appear several times in the treaty and always function as a concluding consequence for their respective paragraphs.[13] Procedures also appear that provide qualified individuals, the repetition of a goal, tangibles, and general regulations regarding tribute (r.12.13–v.1.6, v.1.7–2.6) and riverine commerce (v.5.9–6.13).

Section three (be.2.3–18) involves a brief series of maledictions. The invocation of the solar deity, Hadad, and Kakab (^{d}Utu ^{d}*ʾÀ-da* $^{(d)}$Mul[AN.AN:AN.AN]) as witnesses (be.2.6) is followed by threatened divine destruction (be.2.7–14): "[be.2.7]May their utterance [2.8]by (its very) expression make (the evildoer) perish! (And) [2.12]may they not supply [be.2.11b]drinking water [be.2.9]for (their) caravans . . . (while) [be.2.13]refusing (them) [2.14]lodging!" ([be.2.7]du$_{11}$-ga-*sù* [2.8]*in* ⌜*zé*⌝ zàḫ [be.2.9]*ʾa*$_{5}$*-na* kas$_{4}$-kas$_{4}$ . . . [be.2.11b]a-nag [2.12]nu túm [be.2.13]*ma-in* [2.14]tuš). A final juridical oil-oath formula provides a fitting conclusion to the treaty: "[be.2.15]And (if) you [2.17]go (down) [2.16]an evil road, [be.2.18]you have failed the oil-oath" ([be.2.15]*an-da-ma* [2.16]kaskal ḫul [2.17]du [be.2.18]ì a-è).

The three remaining Eblaite treaties reflect similar, if not identical, discourse patterning. First, ARET 13:6 is an incomplete tablet probably excerpted from a larger treaty.[14] It asserts Ebla's support of Yinḫar-Ḫalab's right to rule Burman in the face of internal strife and demands the protection of Yinḫar-Ḫalab's Eblaite wife. The regular presence of *šumma*, including positions of aperture and closure (r.1.1, r.3.3, r.5.4, v.3.1′, v.6.8), marks it as entirely juridical. Second, in ARET 13:20 Ebla regulates Martu's annual treaty-renewal offerings and military conscription in the event of aggression from Mari.[15] It opens with an explanatory title marking the text as a treaty: "[r.1.1]The tablet [1.2]of the oil offering (between) [1.3]Mart[u] [1.4]an[d] [1.5]Ebla" ([r.1.1]dub [1.2]nídba ì-⌜giš⌝ [1.3]*Mar-t*[*u*^{ki}] [1.4]*w*[*a*] [1.5]*Ib-la*^{ki}). Juridical discourse follows, appearing with understood contingency and divided by four occurrences of an oil-oath formula (r.3.13, r.5.4, r.6.6′, v.1.4′), similar to those in the Abarsal text: ". . . you have failed the oil-oath" (a-è ì-giš || ì a-è). The treaty concludes with a list of personal names, likely indicating human witnesses.[16] Third, in ARET 13:21 Ebla regulates Dulu's required cultic offerings, tribute, and military conscription. The presence of the collocation "once in the year" ([v.1.4′]*i*[*n*] [v.2.1]1 mu) regarding sacrificial animals indicates an annual tribute context for the

---

[12] For an explanation of the idiom "to divert the oil" (ì a-è), see Fronzaroli, *Testi di cancelleria*, 62, 197–98.

[13] See r.10.6–8, r.10.17–19, r.11.16–20, r.12.9–12, v.1.2–6, v.2.17–3.1, v.4.2–4, v.5.1–8, v.7.5–7, v.11.20–12.1, and v.13.6–8.

[14] Fronzaroli, *Testi di cancelleria*, 79.

[15] Ibid., 204.

[16] Ibid., 204, 208.

document.[17] Its juridical section also appears with the oil-oath formula (a-è ì-giš v.1.2, v.4.6) and implied contingency. A concluding explanatory statement similar to the explanatory title in ARET 13:20 appears as its colophon: "$^{\text{v.4.7}}$The tablet of $^{\text{4.8}}$the [oil] offering (between) $^{\text{4.9}}$[Dul]u (and) $^{\text{4.10}}$Eb[la] $^{\text{4.11}}$[(in reference to their) alliance]" ($^{\text{v.4.7}}$dub $^{\text{4.8}}$⸢nídba⸣ [ì]-giš $^{\text{4.9}}$[*Du-l*]*u*^{ki} $^{\text{4.10}}$*Ib*-[*la*]^{ki} $^{\text{4.11}}$[GIŠ-sur$_{\times}$]).

In sum, several features appear in two or more of these texts, collectively suggesting an Eblaite treaty tradition. First, all four treaties employ juridical discourse as their primary discourse type, where case law is marked explicitly by *šumma* (Abarsal, Yinḫar-Ḫalab) and asyndeton (Abarsal) or asyndeton alone (Martu, Dulu). Second, two treaties possess an explanatory line naming all contracting partners with either a title (Martu) or a colophon (Dulu): "the tablet of the oil offering (between) PN1 (and) PN2" (dub nídba ì-giš PN1 (*wa*) PN2). Third, three treaties (Abarsal, Martu, Dulu) employ an oil-oath formula as paragraph closure in the juridical section, and in one case as treaty closure (Abarsal): " . . . you have failed the oil-oath" (a-è ì-giš or ì a-è). Fourth, the juridical sections in the treaties with Abarsal and Dulu boast annual tribute clauses dedicated to the local cult. Fifth, though malediction occurs only in ARET 13:5, it is probably a traditional element, based on the nature of treaties as oath documents (cf. the remaining six treaty traditions). Sixth, three texts involve treaties between Ebla and other people groups rather than explicitly named individuals, implying an intended generic imposition on whoever is ruling at the time. Finally, two features appear once in the Abarsal text and *may* reflect a larger Eblaite tradition: a formulaic geographic explanation of territorial control, and procedures placed in conjunction with its juridical material.

Second Millennium

After a gap between the twenty-third and nineteenth centuries BCE, two additional treaty traditions appear. They are represented by several treaty documents composed in Old Assyrian and Old Babylonian, the former having been discovered at Kültepe and the latter at Tell Leilan and Mari. After another gap between the eighteenth and fifteenth centuries BCE, two more treaty traditions appear. These traditions are represented by our largest group of treaty documents, collectively composed in Middle Babylonian[18] and Hittite. The former were discovered at Alalaḫ,

[17] See ibid., 214.

[18] I employ "Middle Babylonian" as a convenient reference to the general time period of the Akkadian texts dealt with here. It includes their various translational

Ras Shamra (Ugarit), and Boğazköy, while the Hittite documents were found primarily at Boğazköy.[19] Three additional Old Babylonian treaties also date from the eighteenth century BCE, but were found in unique locations and exhibit unique discourse features.[20] They represent either ad hoc

---

forms in a dialect more specifically known as peripheral Akkadian, representing a non-native speaker's use of the *lingua franca*.

[19] But now see the new Hittite-language treaty discovered at Oylum Höyük (Oy. 12–401).

[20] The first was found at Ishchali in the Diyala region and was made between the city-states of Šadlaš and Nērebtum (Diyala No. 326). See Samuel Greengus, *Old Babylonian Tablets from Ishchali and Vicinity*, PIHANS 44 (Istanbul: Nederlands Historisch-Archaeologisch Instituut, 1979); Wu Yuhong, "The Treaty between Shadlash (Sumu-Numhim) and Neribtum (Hammi-dushur)," *JAC* 9 (1994): 124–36. Its stipulations are couched in juridical garb and apply to both parties, rather than employing unilateral language; it lacks oath-taking language; and the speaker is unclear. The second is a fragment from a treaty between Ilumgāmil of Uruk and an unknown ruler. It bears an injunction marked by asseverative *lū* with the durative, indicating adjuratory discourse ("I will indeed keep peace," *lu-ú a-sa-li-im*; i 4) and possibly reflecting the paradigm evident at Tell Leilan and Mari. The third was found at Alalaḫ and involves an agreement between Abba-AN of Yamḫad (Aleppo) and Yarīm-Lîm of Alalaḫ (AT *456). See Donald J. Wiseman, "Abban and Alalaḫ," *JCS* 12 (1958): 124–29; Anne E. Draffkorn, "Was King Abba-AN of Yamḫad a Vizier for the King of Ḫattuša?" *JCS* 13 (1959): 94–97; W. G. Lambert, "A Vizier of Ḫattuša? A Further Comment," *JCS* 13 (1959): 132; see also the combined gloss in Dennis J. McCarthy, *Treaty and Covenant: A Study in Form in the Ancient Oriental Documents and in the Old Testament*, AnBib 21 (Rome: Pontifical Biblical Institute, 1981), 307–8; see also the updated version in *TLCANE* 1:231–34. Amnon Altman suggests that the document lies somewhere between a private contract and an international treaty. See his "Reflections on the Alalaḫ Text AT 456," in *Looking at the Ancient Near East and the Bible through the Same Eyes: A Tribute to Aaron Skaist*, ed. Kathleen Abraham and Joseph Fleishman (Bethesda, MD: CDL, 2012), 1–12. Its primary topic is the grant of Alalaḫ to Yarīm-Lîm in place of Irrite, which was destroyed when Abba-AN seized it. A broken list of towns (lines 1–18) is followed by historiographic discourse detailing why Abba-AN gave Alalaḫ to Yarīm-Lîm, and is marked primarily by the preterite: e.g., "he (a rebel subordinate) made all the [la]nd become enemies with Abba-[A]N the kin[g]" ([23][*ma-*]*a*?*-tam ka-la-ša it-ti ab-ba-*[A]N *šarr*[*im*] [24]*ú-ša-ak-ki-ir-ma*). Importantly, it represents the earliest example to date of the historical prologue, demonstrating that the section existed before the later Hittite form. See Amnon Altman, *The Historical Prologue of the Hittite Vassal Treaties: An Inquiry into the Concepts of Hittite Interstate Law*, Bar-Ilan Studies in Near Eastern Languages and Culture (Ramat-Gan: Bar-Ilan University Press, 2004), 479–80; so "Reflections," 12. Abba-AN concludes the historiographic section with a succinct version of his oath to Yarīm-Lîm: "What I gave you I will never take away!" (*šum-ma ša ad-di-nu-ku-um-mi e-le-eq-qú-*[*ú*]; line 42). The promise is marked by an inverse *šumma* clause with the durative, indicating an inherent self-imprecation should Abba-AN fail to keep his oath (for inverse *šumma*, see the note regarding AT 2 21–22). Case-law comprises the next section (lines 43–67): e.g., "If a descend[ant] of Yarīm-Lîm [se]lls (one of) his cities fo[r silve]r . . . , he may also give it to a descendant of

arrangements or perhaps potential traditions. Finally, a single Ugaritic treaty tablet found at Ras Shamra dates from the late thirteenth century BCE, constituting an ad hoc document or perhaps marking a potential Ugaritian treaty tradition.[21]

Tradition 2: Old Assyrian

The second treaty tradition is based first on two broken Old Assyrian treaties from the nineteenth century BCE. Both were discovered at Kültepe, which connected the city of Assur with its "trade colonies" (sing. *kārum*), and involve parity treaties that Assyrian merchants concluded with rulers from Kaneš and Ḫaḫḫum.[22] The voice of the merchants governs both, employing the second person for their respective ruler. A broken list of oath-deities likely marks an initiatory set of oaths (Kt.00/k 6:1–4; lost in Kt.00/k 10), followed by an imposed adjuratory matrix for the bulk of both texts. Interestingly, this last section generally reflects the

---

Abba-AN, (but) he must not give (it) to another" (^{57b}*šum-ma wa-ar-ki*[*-it* ^{58} ^{I}*i*]*a-ri-im-li-im i-na āli*^{ki}*-šu a-n*[*a* KUG.BABBAR-*i*]*m* ^{59}[*i-na-*]*ad-di-nu* . . . ^{60b}*a-na wa-ar-ki-it* ^{61} ^{I}*ab-ba-*AN*-ma i-na-ad-di-in* ^{62}*a-na ša-ni-im ú-ul i-na-ad-di-in*). A declaration of the vassal's compliance marked by the preterite closes the treaty (lines 68–76; cf. L.T.-2), where a series of personal names collectively function as human witnesses (cf. ARET 13:20).

[21] I follow Pardee in referring to it as a "suzerainty treaty" («le traité d'alliance»), made between Šuppiluliuma II of Ḫatti and Niqmadu III of Ugarit (KTU 3.1). The discourse structure of the tablet is simple, consisting of historiographic discourse with embedded explanation, followed by juridical-absolute discourse with an exclusive topical focus on tribute: e.g., "^{18}And so, (this is) the tribute that [Ni]qmadu [shall bring] ^{19}to the Sun goddess of Arinna: (*tribute list*). ^{24}(This is) the tribute of Niqmadu, king of ^{25}Ugarit, which he shall bring to the Sun, ^{26}Great King, his lord: (*tribute list*)" (^{18}*h*⌜*l*⌝*ny* . *ảrgmn* . *d*[*ybl n*]*qmd* ^{19}*l špš* . *ảrn* . . . ^{24}*ảrgmn* . *nqmd* . *mlk* ^{25}*ủgr*⌜*t* .⌝ *d ybl* . *l špš* ^{26} ⌜*m*⌝*lk* . *rb* . *bʿlh* . . . ; 3.1:18–26). It reflects the Syrian I group (see below) in its inclusion of the tribute stipulation, but is markedly simpler in all other respects due to its incompleteness. For editions and discussion, see Jean Nougayrol, *Le palais royal d'Ugarit IV: Textes accadiens des archives sud*, ed. Claude F. A. Schaeffer, 2 vols., MRS IX (Paris: Imprimerie nationale and Librairie C. Klincksieck, 1956), 44–46; Gary N. Knoppers, "Treaty, Tribute List, or Diplomatic Letter: KTU 3.1 Reexamined," *BASOR* 289 (1993): 81–94; and especially Dennis Pardee, "Le traité d'alliance RS 11.772+," *Sem* 51 (2003): 5–31; Pierre Bordreuil and Dennis Pardee, *A Manual of Ugaritic*, LSAWS 3 (Winona Lake, IN: Eisenbrauns, 2009), Text 36.

[22] Kt.00/k 6 and Kt.00/k 10, respectively. See Veysel Donbaz, "An Old Assyrian Treaty from Kültepe," *JCS* 57 (2005): 63–68; Cahit Günbatti, "Two Treaty Texts Found at Kültepe," in *Assyria and Beyond: Studies Presented to Mogens Trolle Larsen*, ed. Mogens Trolle Larsen and Jan Gerrit Dercksen (Leiden: Nederlands Instituut voor het Nabije Oosten, 2004): 249–64.

juridical matrix in an Old Babylonian treaty between Assyrian merchants and Till-Abnû of Apum (L.T.-5), where contingency prevails.

Either *inūmī* ("when") or *šumma* marks the protasis, and the apodosis expresses negative impositions marked by *lā* and the durative with subjunctive *-ni* (equivalent to oath-bearing *-u* in Old Babylonian and *-ūni* in Neo-Assyrian):[23] e.g., "If a citizen of Aššur is indebted to a citizen of Kaneš and [go]es to another country, they must not seize another merchant, a stranger, or his brother in his place; they will certainly seek the debtor (for) the fixed (amount)!" (^{72b}*šu-ma* DUMU *A-šùr a-na* DUMU *Kà-ni-iš* ^{73}*i-ta-aḫ-ba-al-ma a-na ma-tim* ^{74}*ša-ni-tim i-ta-*[*lá-a*]*k a-pu-ḫi-šu* ^{75}*tám-kà-ra-am ša-ni-a-am a-ḫi-a-am* ^{76}*ú a-ḫu-šu lá i-ṣa-bu-tù-ni ḫa-bu-lá-nam* ^{77}*ší-im-tám lu i-šé-e-ú-ni*; Kt.00/k 6:72b–77). That is, the *-ni* particle marks the stipulatory section as oath-based rather than juridical. Positive impositions are marked by the durative alone, with subjunctive *-ni*, with *lū*, or with both (e.g., Kt.00/k 10 iv 15b–22). The Ḫaḫḫum text also shares similar non-abrogation language with the materials from Tell Leilan, assuring the integrity of the oath for the life span of the one adjured: "From this day, while you live . . ." (*iš-t*[*ù* *u*$_4$]*-mì-im a-nim a-dí-i ba-al-ṭá-tù-nu-ni*; Kt.00/k 10 iv 23′).

Two clauses conclude the Kaneš treaty (Kt.00/k 6; perhaps lost on the missing left edge of Kt.00/k 10). The first invokes the collective oath-deities and suggests an understood malediction: "These gods, lor[ds of] your [o]ath, will look upon you!" (DINGIR$^{lu\text{-}ú}$ *a-ni-ú-tum be-e*[*l m*]*a-mì-tí-kà i-dá-gu*$_5$*-lu-kà*; Kt.00/k 6:89b). The second is a colophon: "The oath [of . . .], Great [King] of Kaneš" (⌜*ma*⌝*-mì-tum*! [*ša* . . . LUGAL] GAL *Kà-ni-šé-e-im*; Kt.00/k 6:89c–90).

When compared with the more extensive Tell Leilan (L.T.) and Mari material (see below), the Kültepe documents form a simplified treaty tradition that incorporates the following features (also reflected in L.T.-5). The tradition opens with an invocation of the oath-deities, followed by an imposed adjuratory matrix outlining specific stipulations (juridical in L.T.-5). This section appears with non-abrogation language and concludes with an implicit malediction and explanatory postscript. Finally, both the Kültepe documents and L.T.-5 are designed to protect the commercial interests of both the city-states and their transient merchants (cf. the Ebla material). I therefore refer to this paradigm as the Assyrian merchant treaty tradition.

Tradition 3: Old Babylonian

Our investigation into the third treaty tradition begins with an Old Babylonian treaty made between Sîn-iddinam of Larsa and Sîn-kāšid of Uruk

[23] See Karl Hecker, *Grammatik der Kültepe-Texte*, AnOr 44 (Rome: Pontifical Biblical Institute, 1968), §106e.

with Ibâl-pī-El I of Ešnunna (*CUNES* 49–04–176),[24] likely from ca. 1844 or 1843 BCE.[25] The combined voice of Sîn-iddinam and Sîn-kāšid opens the document with a brief oath-deity list and an adjuratory declaration, in the third person, of Ibâl-pī-El's compliance: "^{3}Ibîl-pi-El swore ^{1}before Sîn of [the Heaven]s, Išḫar[a] of Išur, ^{2}Tišpak, (and) Iškur (Adad)" (^{1}*a-na* ^{d}EN.ZU *ša* [*ša-me*]-⸢*e*⸣ ^{d}*iš-ḫa-r*[*a*] / ⸢*ša*⸣ *i-šur*^{ki} ^{2} ^{d}*Tišpak* ^{d}*Iškur* ^{3}*i-bi-il-pi-el it-ma*; obv. 1–3). The voice of Ibâl-pī-El governs the remainder of the tablet, presenting a series of self-imposed oaths marked by oath-bearing *-u*, which indicates implicit stipulations: e.g., "^{6}I will not abandon ^{4}Sîn-iddinam king of Larsa ^{5}or Sîn-kāšid king of Uruk" (^{4} ^{d}EN.ZU-*i-dí-nam* LUGAL *larsa*^{ki} ^{5}*ù* ^{d}EN.ZU-*ka-ši-id* LUGAL *unu*^{ki} ^{6}*la e-ze-bu-ma*; obv. 4–6). Though it provides a remarkable reflection of the Leilan and Mari treaties, it lacks their customary oath imperative *tama* and non-abrogation language (see below).

Five Old Babylonian treaties were discovered at Tell Leilan (ancient Šeḫnā/Šubat-Enlil) and date from the first half of the eighteenth century BCE. The treaty of Qarni-Lim of Andarig and Ḫāya-abum of Apum with an unknown ruler of Sûmum (L.T.-1) is the longest and most complex, making it a fitting exemplar.[26] Like the other Leilan materials, L.T.-1 may represent one of two related unilateral documents sworn by each party to the other.[27] However, I interpret it as a subordination treaty, because of the adjured partner's position over the relatively unimportant principality of Sûmum. What is preserved breaks into two primary sections; the ending is lost.

Section one opens with an oath-deity list to which the vassal is adjured to swear with the formula "Before X deity swear!" (^{d}X *tama*; L.T.-1 i 1–14): e.g., "^{4}Before Adad of Heaven swear!" (^{4} ⸢^{d}IM⸣ *ša ša-me-*⸢*e*⸣ *ta-ma*; i 4). The list follows a standardized format also evident in three other Leilan treaties: international deities, great gods of important cultic centers, local deities specific to the treaty participants, and a concluding general overview of deities belonging to "heaven, earth, water."[28] Tablet scoring shifts to an official statement that the subordinate carried out the

---

[24] Guichard, "Un traité d'alliance."

[25] Ibid., 19–24.

[26] See plates 107–115 and 142–144 in Eidem, *Royal Archives from Tell Leilan*, 577–85, 613–15.

[27] Ibid., 311; Jesper Eidem, "An Old Assyrian Treaty from Tell Leilan," in *Marchands, diplomates et empereurs: Études sur la civilisation mésopotamienne offertes à Paul Garelli*, ed. Dominique Charpin, Francis Joannès, and Paul Garelli (Paris: Editions recherche sur les civilisations, 1991), 191. See the "small tablet" and "large tablet" discussion in Eidem, *Royal Archives from Tell Leilan*, 319–21; Jesper Eidem, "Apum: A Kingdom on the Old Assyrian Route," in *Mesopotamia: the Old Assyrian Period*, ed. K. R. Veenhof, Jesper Eidem, and Markus Wäfler, OBO 160 (Göttingen: Vandenhoeck & Ruprecht, 2008), 311–15.

[28] L.T.-2, 3, 5; see Eidem, *Royal Archives from Tell Leilan*, 329–30; Eidem, "Apum," 325–26.

proper oath procedures: "^{19}[To Qa]rni-Lim son of Muti-Addu, the king of [An]darig, ^{20}[and (to) the kin]g of Apum . . . [X of] Sûm[u]m ^{25}[swo]re" (^{19}[*a-na qa*]*r-ni-li-im* DUMU *mu-ti-*⸢^{d}IM⸣ LUGAL-[*an*]-*da-ri-*[*i*]*g* ^{20}[*ù* LUGA]L *a-pí-im*^{ki} . . . *sú-*⸢*ú*⸣*-m*[*i-i*]*m*^{ki} [*it*]-*mu*; i 24–25). The section is written from the perspective of the two sovereigns (or their representatives), with the vassal adjured first and his actions then put on record.

Section two opens with the voice of the subordinate, who employs adjuratory language to confirm that he has fulfilled the oaths required in the first section: "[By the life of the god]s [have I sw]orn" (^{1}[*ni-iš* DINGIR^{me}]^{š} *za-a*[*k-ra-ku*]; i 1′). Similar to the Kültepe material, specific stipulations are couched in adjuratory language marked by oath-bearing *-u*, albeit self-imposed by the adjured party: e.g., "^{2}To a kin[g], a noble, or [any] free per[son] . . . ^{4}I did [n]ot say thu[s], I will not say, ^{5}I did not send, I will not send, ^{6}I will not command, saying . . ." (^{2}*a-na* LUG[AL] *ra-bi-im ù* DUMU *a-wi-l*[*u-tim šum-šu*] . . . ^{4}*ki-a-*[*am l*]*a aq-bu-ú la a-qa-ab-b*[*u-ú*] ^{5}*la aš-pu-ru la-a a-ša-pa-r*[*u*] ^{6}*la ú-wa-a-r*[*u*] *um-ma a-na-ku-ma*; i 2′–6′). Non-abrogation language also appears throughout: e.g., "While I live . . ." (⸢*a-di ba*⸣*-al-ṭà-ku*; vi 13.1).

The remaining Leilan treaties open with a deity list similar to the one in our exemplar, via the sovereign's voice in L.T.-2, L.T.-3, and L.T.-4, and the merchant's voice in L.T.-5: e.g., "Before Sîn of Heaven swear!" (^{d}EN.ZU *ša ša-me-e ta-ma* in L.T.-1 i 2, L.T.-2 i 2, and L.T.-3 i 3; ^{d}EN.ZU *ša* IB *ta-ma* in L.T.-5 i 6). Similarly, a declaratory summary regarding the subordinate's compliance with the oath procedure immediately follows in L.T.-3 (though in L.T.-2 as a colophon): "[By t]hese [gods] Till-Abnû . . . [swo]re" ([DINGIR^{meš} *a*]*n-nu-ti-in* ^{I}*ti-la-ab-nu-u* . . . [*it-m*]*u-ú*; L.T.-3 i 20–24). All then switch to the voice of the adjured, employing linguistic patterning similar to that of L.T.-1 to pragmatically mark stipulations sworn by the adjured. Although the first column is very broken, L.T.-4 boasts a clear preterite with oath-bearing *-u* "I swore" (*áz-ku-ru*; i 5′), indicating compliance to the preceding adjurations, similar to L.T.-1 (i 26–i 1′; which employs the stative *za-a*[*k-ra-ku*]). L.T.-2 (column vi) and L.T.-3 (iv 8′–v 35′ and perhaps most of column vi) boast a concluding set of self-imposed maledictions absent in our exemplar and the remaining Leilan treaties: e.g., "[May Šamaš above] remove my [s]eed!" ([^{d}UTU *e-le-nu-um z*]*e-ri li*$^{!}$-⸢*il*$^{!}$⸣*-qú-ut*; L.T.-2 vi 2′; see vi 7″ etc.; L.T.-3 iv 14′ etc.). Significantly, L.T.-3 also boasts the "maximum effort—minimum yield" malediction, or futility curse, a variety also present in Deuteronomy (28:30–31, 38–41), and is topically parallel to Lev 26:26:[29]

---

[29] Leviticus 26:26 has also been compared to the Sefire treaty material (Sf 1 A 24). A similar curse is found on the Tell Fakhariyah bilingual (Aramaic line 22 || Akkadian lines 35–36) and Bukān (lines 6–8) inscriptions. For a discussion

Table 1

L.T.-3 v 24b′–28′	***Lev 26:26***
[24b][I]*ti-la-ab-nu-ù* ÌR-*di-šu* [25]*ù ma-a-at ḫa-na ka-*[*l*]*u-šu* [26]*ti-nu-ra-am ù ú-tu-na-am* [27]*li-ip-ḫu-ru-ma i-na pu-uḫ-ri-šu-nu* [28]NINDA *a ú-ma-al-lu-ú*	וְאָפוּ עֶשֶׂר נָשִׁים לַחְמְכֶם בְּתַנּוּר אֶחָד וְהֵשִׁיבוּ לַחְמְכֶם בַּמִּשְׁקָל וַאֲכַלְתֶּם וְלֹא תִשְׂבָּע׃
May Till-Abnû, his servants, and al[l] his country of Ḫana assemble (before) an oven or furnace, but not provide (any) bread among their gathering!	. . . then ten women will bake your bread in one oven and will give your bread back by weight, but you will eat and not be satisfied!

Four additional Old Babylonian treaties from the same time period but found at Mari reflect these discourse features. All are governed by the voice of Zimrī-Lîm. Two are parity treaties, concluded with Ḫammurapi of Babylon (M.6435 + M.8987)[30] and with Ibâl-pī-El II of Ešnunna (A.361);[31] the third is a subordination treaty[32] concluded with Atamrum of Andarig (A.96); and the fourth is a fragment of a treaty concluded with a ruler of Kurda (M.7750).[33] Three appear with adjuratory *tama* (imperative, "swear!") directed toward the adjured in the context of a deity list. A preterite declaration regarding the adjured partner's compliance to the oath follows in the Babylon text (M.6435 + M.8987 3–4; likely lost in A.361 and M.7750). The Andarig text is exceptional, opening with the declaration rather than the expected list (so the Larsa/Ešnunna treaty, see below): "[1]By Šamaš o[f Heaven] [2]Atamrum . . . [3]swore" ([1] [d]UTU *š*[*a ša-me-e*] [2] [I]*a-tam-rum* . . . [3]*it-ma*; A.96:1–3).[34] Implicit stipulations follow,

of these texts, see K. Lawson Younger Jr., "The 'Contextual Method': Some West Semitic Reflections," in *COS* 3:xxxvii–xxxix.

[30] Jean-Marie Durand, "Fragments rejoints pour une histoire élamite," in *Fragmenta Historiae Elamicae: Mélanges offerts à M.-J. Stève*, ed. M.-J. Stève et al. (Paris: Editions recherche sur les civilisations, 1986): 111–28; revised in Jean-Marie Durand, *Les Documents épistolaires du palais de Mari, I*, LAPO 16 (Paris: Cerf, 1997), 452–53.

[31] Dominique Charpin, "Un traité entre Zimrî-Lim de Mari et Ibâl-pî-El II d'Ešnunna," in *Marchands, diplomates et empereurs: Études sur la civilisation mésopotamienne offertes à Paul Garelli*, ed. Dominique Charpin, Francis Joannès, and Paul Garelli (Paris: Editions recherche sur les civilisations, 1991), 139–66.

[32] See Francis Joannès, "La traité de vassalité d'Atamrum d'Andarig envers Zimri-Lim de Mari," in *Marchands*, 170.

[33] Ibid.

[34] Altman interprets the document as a loyalty oath and as a "small tablet," presumably based on its diminutive size and brevity; see his "How Many Treaty Traditions," 23n29.

cast in adjuratory discourse marked by oath-bearing *-u* and sworn in the first person by the adjured (lost in M.7750). Non-abrogation language likewise appears, reflecting the fuller Kültepe form: e.g., "[4]From this day, [5]while I live . . ." ([4]*iš-tu* u_4*-mi-im an-ni-i-im* [5]*a-di ba-al-ṭà-ku*; A.96:4–5, so also M.6435 + M.8987 line 5). The voice of Zimrī-Lîm concludes the Ešnunna treaty with maledictions marked by the precative. The Mari treaties represent a local paradigm very similar to the Leilan material.

In sum, the Larsa/Ešnunna treaty, the first four Leilan treaties, and the Mari treaties collectively form a general Old Babylonian treaty tradition that incorporates the following features. The adjuring party first invokes the oath-deities with the imperative *tama* aimed at the adjured party, followed by a declaration regarding that party's compliance to the oath. The adjured party then confirms this compliance and utters a series of oaths that implicitly reflect specific stipulations supported by non-abrogation language. Self-imposed maledictions close the tradition. Finally, it is important to note that both parity and subordination treaties in the general Old Babylonian treaty tradition used unilateral language.

Traditions 4–5: Middle Babylonian

Our investigation into the fourth and fifth treaty traditions begins first with a group of Middle Babylonian parity treaties and then considers the larger group of subordination treaties. The treaty between Ramesses II and Ḫattušili III (*CTH* 91; hereafter R2-H3) is a fitting exemplar for the parity group because of its length and completeness. Significantly, R2-H3 also exhibits features found in *both* Middle Babylonian parity and subordination treaties.

Parity Paradigm

R2-H3 was discovered in the Boğazköy archives and dates from 1259 BCE. It represents the only parity treaty for which we also possess its international counterpart, the Egyptian treaty between Ḫattušili and Ramesses (hence H3-R2). Our discourse analysis concerns the Babylonian version and employs the edition of Edel, who reconstructs its lacunae based in part on the Egyptian counterpart.[35] R2-H3 divides into three sections.

[35] My citations are based on the eclectic edition of Elmar Edel, *Der Vertrag zwischen Ramses II. von Ägypten und Ḫattušili III. von Ḫatti*, WVDOG 95 (Berlin: Gebr. Mann, 1997). R2-H3 is written in "Egyptianized" Akkadian, as an apparent translation of an Egyptian original produced by an Egyptian scribe. The Egyptian version of the treaty presents Ḫattušili as the principal voice (hence the reversed designation H3-R2), and is displayed on an outer wall of the Great Temple of

Section one opens with an explanatory title: “[1][The treaty of R]ia-maš[eša mai]-Amana, Great King, King of [the land of Egypt, (which) he made on a tablet of silver] [2]together with Ḫattušili, G[reat King], King of the land of Ḫatti . . .” ([1]*[ri-ki-il-tu ša* ^{m}*R]i-a-ma-š[e-ša ma-a-i]-*⸢^{d}*a*⸣*-ma-*⸢*na* LUGAL⸣.GAL LUGAL [KUR *Mi-iṣ-ri-i i-pu-šu* UGU *ṭup-pi ša* KÙ.BABBAR] [2]*qà-du* ^{m}*Ḫa-at-tu-ši-li* [LUGAL.GA]L LUGAL KUR *Ḫa-at-ti*; R2-H3 r.1.1–2.1). Ramesses is the sole speaker throughout. A historiographic document content clause follows, emphasizing existing treaty relations rather than past events, and employing the perfective for the mainline: e.g., “Look! Now I have provided [8]go[od] brotherhoo[d] (and) good peace between [u]s forever” (*a-mur a-nu-ma at-ta-din* [8]ŠEŠ*-ut-t[a* SI]G_5 *sa-la-ma* SIG_5 *i-na be-ri-i[n-]ni a-di da-ri-ti*; r.7.2–8.1).

Section two is composed principally of juridical discourse in the form of case-law: e.g., “Now if an outside enemy [28]comes . . . and Ḫattušil[i,

---

Amūn-Reʿ at Karnak, and on the Ramesseum. See Edel’s edition (ibid.). H3-R2 opens with a preface absent in its Akkadian counterpart, providing a date and a historiographic account of the official circumstances of the treaty’s arrival in Egypt: e.g., “Year 21, the first (month) of Winter, day 21, under the majesty of the King of Upper and Lower Egypt, Wasmuʿariʿa satepnariʿa, Son of Re, Riʿamasesa mai-amana” (*rnpt-sp* 21 *tpỉ prt sw* 21 *ḫr ḥm n nỉ·swt-bỉt wsr-mꜣʿt-rʿ stp·n-rʿ sꜣ rʿ rʿ-msỉ-sw mrỉ ỉmn*; H3-R2 1.1.1–1.2.1); also: “A copy of the silver tablet that the Great King of Ḫatti, Ḫattušili, granted to be sent to Pharaoh . . .” (*mỉtt n pꜣ-ʿnw n ḥḏ rdỉ·n wr-ʿꜣ n ḫt ḫtsl ỉnỉ·tw r pr-ʿꜣ*; 3.4.4). The voice of Ramesses governs the preface, while that of Ḫattušili governs the treaty proper. The body of H3-R2 essentially reflects the discourse patterning and content of R2-H3, including a historiographic introduction with a topical focus on treaty relations: e.g., “Look, Ḫattušili the Great King of Ḫatti [allied] himself through a treaty <on a tablet of silver> with Wasmuʿariʿa satepnariʿa . . . !” (*ptr [ỉr]wy sw ḫtsl pꜣ-wr-ʿꜣ n ḫt m nt-ʿ <ḥr ʿn n ḥḏ> ỉrm wsr-mꜣʿt-rʿ stpn-rʿ*; 7.2.9–7.3.9). Note that the Egyptian term for “treaty” (*nt-ʿ*, 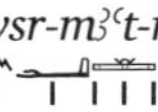) glosses *rikiltu* here. Oddly, the oath-deity list and concluding curses-blessings separate the treaty’s conclusion of the extradition stipulation from its beginning. The error probably resulted from Egyptian translators reading the original’s columns in the order of 1, 2, 4, 3. See Anthony Spalinger, “Considerations on the Hittite Treaty between Egypt and Hatti,” *SAK* 9 (1981): 348–49. For an extant example of the left-right obverse and right-left reverse, see the Hittite bronze tablet (BrTf), especially photos 1–2 in Heinrich Otten, *Die Bronzetafel aus Boğazköy: Ein Staatsvertrag Tutḫalijas IV*, StBoTB 1 (Wiesbaden: Harrassowitz, 1988). A description of the two Hittite state seals closes the treaty. Although R2-H3 and H3-R2 are parallel texts, they exhibit some important differences. First, the Egyptian version is longer and includes additional features, such as its opening and closing descriptions. Second, it contains the deity-list, benedictions, and maledictions lost in the Akkadian version. Third, the Egyptian version includes information not present in R2-H3, including the war between Egypt and Ḫatti, the death of Muwatalli, and reference to two previous treaties (cf. *CTH* 134, a Hittite-language treaty between Tudḫaliya I [?] and Amenophis II [?]). For discussion see Kenneth A. Kitchen, *Ramesside Inscriptions, Translated and Annotated: Notes and Comments*, vol. 2, *Ramesses II, Royal Inscriptions* (Cambridge: Blackwell, 1999), 141–42.

King of the land of Ḫatt]i, sends to me as follows: 'Come to me ^{29}for my assistance against him!,' then Ri[amašeša] . . . ^{30}shall send his armies and his chariots . . ." (⸢*ù*⸣ *šum-ma* ^{lú}KÚR *ša-nu-ú* ^{28}*il-la-ka* . . . ⸢*ù*⸣ ^{m}*Ḫa-at-tu-ši-l*[*i*] . . . *i-šap-pár a-na a-ia-ši* ⸢*um-ma*⸣*-a al-ka a-na a-ia-ši* ^{29}*a-na re-ṣu-ti-ia a-na ša-a-šu ù* ^{m}*Ri*[*-a-ma-še-ša*] . . . ^{30}*i-šap-pár* ÉRIN^{meš}-⸢*šu*⸣ ^{giš}GIGIR⸢^{meš}⸣*-šu*; r.27.4–30.1).

Section three is analyzed according to the reconstruction of Edel,[36] based on formulaic Hittite treaty material and the Egyptian version. It opens with a brief introduction (E1–2), followed by a divine invocation and lengthy deity list (E10–57): e.g., "$^{\text{E3}}$[(As for) the Thousand Gods . . .] $^{\text{E4}}$[I have] sum[moned] them [as witnesses.] $^{\text{E5}}$Now let them continually hear . . ." ($^{\text{E3}}$[*LI-IM* DINGIR^{meš} . . .] $^{\text{E4}}$*n=aš kut*[*ruwaḫḫun*] $^{\text{E5}}$*nu ištamaškandu*; E3–4). Maledictions and benedictions conclude the treaty: e.g., "[And if Riamašeša . . . and the people of the land of Egypt do not keep this treaty, (then) indeed the gods (and)] $^{2'}$goddess[es . . . will destroy the seed] $^{3'}$of Riama[šeša . . . together with the people of the land of Egypt!] ([*ù šum-ma* ^{m}*Ri-a-ma-še-ša* . . . *ù* DUMU^{meš} KUR *Mi-iṣ-ri-i ri-ki-il-ta an-ni-ta la-a i-na-aṣ-ṣa-ru a-di* DINGIR^{meš} LÚ^{meš}] $^{2'}$DINGIR^{meš} MUNUS[^{meš} . . . *ú-ḫal-la-qú* NUMUN] $^{3'}$*ša* ^{m}*Ri-a-ma*[*-še-ša* . . . *qa-du* DUMU^{meš} KUR *Mi-iṣ-ri-i*]; v.0.3′–3.1′); "[But if Riamašeša . . .] $^{4'}$and the people of <the land of> E[gypt do keep this treaty, (then) indeed the gods of the oath will protect them] $^{5'}$and [make] t[heir] faces [glad!]" ([*ù šum-ma* ^{m}*Ri-a-ma-še-ša* . . .] $^{4'}$*ù* ⸢DUMU⸣^{meš} <KUR> *M*[*i-iṣ-ri-i ri-ki-il-ta an-ni-ta i-na-aṣ-ṣa-ru a-di* DINGIR^{meš} *ša ma-mi-ti i-na-aṣ-ṣa-ru-šu-nu-ti*] $^{5'}$*ù pa-ni-š*[*u-nu ú-na-am-ma-ru*]; v.3.2′–5.1′). Two instances of "The seal [of . . .]" ($^{10'\ \text{na4}}$KIŠI[B *ša* . . .] $^{11'\ \text{na4}}$KIŠIB *ša* [. . .]) are all that remain of the seals in the Akkadian version.

Two parity treaties from the fifteenth-century Alalaḫ archives complement this picture. They were concluded between Idrimi of Alalaḫ and Pilliya of Kizzuwatna (AT 3), and between Niqmepa of Alalaḫ and Ir-Adad/Teššub of Tunip (AT 2).[37] AT 3 opens with an explanatory title and a subordinate clause introducing the document's content in the past tense (preterites): "The treaty [tab]let when Pilliya and Idrimi swore the oath of the gods, and bound this treaty [bet]ween them" (^{1}[*ṭup*]*-pi ri-ik-ši* ^{2}*i-nu-ma* ^{m}*pil-li-ia* ^{3}*ù* ^{m}*id-ri-mi ni-iš* DINGIR^{meš} *iz-ku-ru* ^{4}*ù ri-ik-ša-am an-ni-e-im* ^{5}[*i-na b*]*i-ri-šu-nu ir-ku-šu*; AT 3 1–5). Juridical discourse follows, followed in turn by a maledictory conclusion, marked by the precative: "May the Storm deity, Šamaš, Išḫara, (and) all the gods dest[roy] whoever trans-

[36] Edel, *Der Vertrag zwischen Ramses II. von Ägypten und Ḫattušili III. von Ḫatti*, 66, 70.

[37] For both AT 3 and AT 2, see Donald J. Wiseman, *The Alalakh Tablets*, OPSNKF 2 (London: British Institute of Archaeology at Ankara, 1953).

gresses the words of this treaty tablet!" (^{44}*ma-an-nu-e a-wa-ti ša ṭup-pí* ^{45}*an-ni-e-im i-ti-iq* ^{46} ^{d}IM ^{d}UTU ^{d}*iš-ḫa-ra* DINGIR^{meš} *ka-li-šu-nu* ^{47}*li-ḫal-li-*[*qú-šu*]; AT 3 44–47). AT 2 reflects these features with the following differences: its historiographic content clause appears on the mainline, and its stipulatory section is a unilateral juridical and predominantly adjuratory matrix (cf. the Old Babylonian tradition). The latter is marked by inverse *šumma lā* + durative (or the durative alone) for positive impositions: e.g., "^{21}If a fugitive . . . of my country fl[ees] to your country, ^{22}you must seize and return him" (^{21}*šum-ma* ^{lú}*mu-un-na-ab-tù* . . . *ša* KUR-*ia a-na* KUR-*ka in-na*[-*ab-bi-it*] ^{22}*šum-ma la ta-ṣa-bat ù la tu-te-er-šu*; AT 2 21–22).[38]

Five additional parity treaties from the fourteenth- and thirteenth-century Ras Shamra archives complete the picture.[39] The treaty between Niqmadu II of Ugarit and Aziru of Amurru (RS 19.68) opens with a historiographic document content clause marked by the perfective: "On this day Niqmadu king of Ugar[i]t and Aziru king of Amu[rru] made an oath between them" (^{1}*iš-tu* UD-*mi an-ni-im* ^{2} ^{m}*niq-ma-*^{d}IM *šàr* ^{uru}*u-ga-r*[*i-i*]*t*^{ki} ^{3}*ù* ^{m}*a-zi-ru šàr* ^{uru}*amu*[*rru*]^{ki} ^{4}*ma-mi-tam i-na be-ri-šu-nu* ^{5}*i-te-ep-šu-nim*; RS 19.68.1–5a). A unilateral juridical matrix follows (lines 5b–41), and concludes with a malediction. Aside from the lack of a title and its unilateral formulation, the overall interdiscourse patterning of RS 19.68 reflects that of AT 3. A treaty arbitrated by Ini-Tešub[40] between the people of Carchemish and the people of Ugarit (RS 17.146) likewise begins with a historiographic document content clause. Bilateral adjuratory stipulations follow, marked by oath-bearing *-ni*: e.g., "Now, if within Carchemish merchants with endowed capital from the king of Ugarit are killed and their murderers are seized, then the citizens of Carchemish . . . shall make full restitution" (^{6}*ma-a šum-ma-me-e* $^{\text{lú.meš}}$*tamkârî ša ma-an-da-ti* ^{7}*ša šàr* KUR ^{uru}*u-ga-ri-it* ŠÀ-*bi* KUR ^{uru}*kar-ga-mis* ^{8}*i-du-ku-mì ù* $^{\text{lú.meš}}$*da-i-ku-šu-nu iṣ-ṣa-ba-tum-mì* ^{9}*ù* DUMU^{meš} KUR ^{uru}*kar-ga-mis* . . . *ú-šal-la-mu-ni*; RS

---

[38] Inverse *šumma* is a type of implicit imprecation where the negative is semantically equivalent to a positive imposition and the positive (i.e., no negative) is semantically equivalent to a prohibition. Syntactically it consists of an explicit protasis and an assumed malediction in the implied apodosis. These notions may be simplified as "If X occurred/occurs/will occur, (may I be cursed)!" (≈ "X did not/does not/will not occur!"), or as "If X did/does/will not occur, (may I be cursed)!" (≈ "X did/does/will occur!").

[39] RS 19.68, RS 17.230, RS 18.19, RS 17.146, RS 18.115; for all of these see Nougayrol, *Le palais royal d'Ugarit IV*.

[40] At this time Ini-Tešub functioned as the third Hittite viceroy in Carchemish, likely under his cousin Tudḫaliya IV, and was probably first appointed under Ḫattušili III over the Hittite-controlled north Syrian territories. See the discussion in Trevor R. Bryce, *The Kingdom of the Hittites* (Oxford: Oxford University Press, 2005), 313.

17.146.6–11).[41] An implicit malediction closes the treaty with a brief list of oath-deities. The three remaining Ras Shamra treaties are likewise arbitrated and reflect these discourse elements, though two (RS 17.230, RS 18.19) lack a maledictory conclusion.

In sum, the Alalaḫ treaties are sealed; appear with an explanatory title, an introductory document content clause, and juridical discourse; deal solely with extradition; and close with a malediction. Neither possesses benedictions. Differences appear in their seals, the subordination or lack thereof for the document content clause, the bilateral vis-à-vis unilateral formulation of AT 3 and AT 2, respectively, the significant presence of adjuratory stipulations in AT 2, and its closing colophon. All five Ras Shamra texts are sealed, open with a historiographic document content clause, employ either juridical or adjuratory discourse for stipulatory framing, and may close with malediction, but possess no benediction. R2-H3 fully reflects these elements, with the addition of explicit oath-deities and a benediction. Collectively, R2-H3 and the Alalaḫ and Ras Shamra treaties reflect similar interdiscourse structures, indicating a Middle Babylonian parity treaty tradition.

General Paradigm

The bulk of the remaining Middle Babylonian texts involve subordination treaties. For convenience I present them in three groups based on the significant number of documents pertaining to Syrian rulers ("Syrian" is used only as a convenient geographic referent), as well as similarities and differences in their collective discourse features. While we could refer to these patterns as a subordination paradigm, a few parity treaties also exhibit features unique to this tradition (i.e., R2-H3/H3-R2, *CTH* 41.I). It is therefore simply referred to as the general paradigm.

Syrian I Group

We begin the investigation of Middle Babylonian subordination treaties with four agreements made with Syrian rulers and sharing similar interdiscourse features. They are collectively referred to as the Syrian I treaty group:[42] Šuppiluliuma I of Ḫatti and Aziru of Amurru (*CTH* 49.I), Tette of Nuḫašše (*CTH* 53), Muršili II of Ḫatti and Niqmepa of Ugarit (*CTH* 66), Ḫattušili III of Ḫatti and Bentešina of Amurru (*CTH* 92).

The texts in the Syrian I group share the following features. The voice of the respective Great King opens three treaties with performa-

[41] For *maddattu* as "endowment capital" see *CAD* (M 1:15).

[42] The terminology is borrowed from Beckman *HDT*², 36. The edition of del Monte is employed throughout for all citations: *Il trattato fra Muršili II di Ḫattuša e Niqmepaʿ di Ugarit*, OAC 18 (Rome: Istituto per l'Oriente C. A. Nallino, 1986).

tive *umma* and accompanying epithets: e.g., "^{1}Thus (declares) My Majesty, Šuppiluliuma, Great King, ^{2}King of the land of Ḫatti, Hero:" (^{1}*um-ma* ^{d}UTU-*ši* ^{m}*šu-up-pí-lu-li-u-ma* LUGAL.GAL ^{2}LUGAL KUR ^{uru}*ḫa-at-ti* UR.SAG; *CTH* 53 i 1–2). A historiographic introduction outlining past relations follows, marked by the preterite and perfective: e.g., "^{9}Then I, My Majesty, sent troops and horses for his assistance, ^{10}and they led away the king of the land of Mitanni" (^{9}*ù* ^{d}UTU-*ši* ERÉN^{meš} ANŠE.KUR.RA$^{ḫi.a}$ *a-na ti-il*$_{5}$*-lu-ti-šu aš-pur* . . . ^{10}*ù* LUGAL KUR ^{uru}*mi-it-ta-an-ni* . . . *e-tab-ku*; *CTH* 53 i 9–11).

Two treaties appear with procedural discourse outlining annual tribute requirements, possibly as stipulatory aperture (following a break in each tablet): e.g., "once a year [. . . X shekels of gold] (shall be) his tribute, and may they weigh (it) with the weights of the merchants of Ḫatti, and may Tette come to My Majesty" ([. . .] ^{1}*i-na* MU.1.KAM *lu-ú ar-kam-ma-an-na-šu* ^{2}*ù i-na* NA$_{4}$$^{ḫi.a}$ $^{lú.meš}$DAM.GÀR *ša* KUR *ḫa-at-ti* ^{3}*li-ša-aq-qí-lu ù* ^{m}*te-it-te a-na* UGU ^{d}UTU-*ši* . . . ^{5}*li-il*$_{5}$*-li-ik*; *CTH* 53 ii 1–5). Juridical discourse follows in each, with a formulaic consequential clause appearing several times: e.g., "if Tette with all his heart does not campaign with his troops and chariots, and does not fight with the enemy . . . then he has broken the oath!" (^{23}*šum-ma* ^{m}*te-it-te i-na kúl* ŠA-*šu iš-tu* ÉRIN^{meš}-[*šu*] ^{24} ^{giš}GIGIR^{meš}-*šu ú-ul i-na-muš ù it-ti* ^{lú}KÚR ^{25}*la-a in-tù-uḫ-ḫa-ṣa* . . . *ù iš-tu ma-mi-ti i-te-te-eq*; *CTH* 53 ii 7–32).[43] Similarly, a significant number of standardized stipulations appear throughout the group.

An adjuratory oath-deity list follows in at least two of the treaties, bracketed by a catchphrase employing *lū* with the stative: "[Now, within this treaty] ^{86}may [the thousand god]s assemble, may [they listen, and be witnesses!] . . . $^{87–110}$*deity list* . . . ^{111}[For] this treaty and [for the oath may they be witnesses!]" ([*ù i-na lìb-bi ri-ik-sí an-ni-i* ^{86}*li-im* DINGIR]^{meš} *li-ip-ḫu-ru l*[*il-te-mu-ú ù lu-ú ši-bu-tù*] $^{87–110}$*deity list* ^{111}[*a-na*] *an-ni-i ri-ik-sí ù* [*a-na ma-mi-ti lu-ú ši-bu-tu*$_{4}$]; *CTH* 66 85–111).[44] The group concludes with a standardized malediction-benediction: e.g., "Whatever words of the treaty and oath are written within this tablet—if Tette does not keep these words of the treaty and oath, then [he] has broken the oath, even the oath of these gods! May (the gods) dest[roy] Tette, [with his head,] his [w]ives . . . !" (*mi-i-nu-me-e a-wa-te*^{meš} *ša ri-ik-si* ^{47}*ù ša ma-mi-ti i-na lìb-bi ṭup-pí an-ni-i-ti šaṭ-rat-at* ^{48}*šum-ma* ^{m}*te-it-te a-wa-te*^{meš} *an-na-ti ša ri-ik-si* ^{49}*ù ma-mi-ti la-a i-na-ṣar ù iš-tu ma-mi-ti* ^{50}[*i*]*-te-te-eq ù né-eš* DINGIR^{meš} *an-nu-tì*

[43] The writing *intuḫḫaṣ* is a variation of *imtaḫḫaṣ*, the Gt durative of *maḫāṣu* (see *CAD* M 1:72).

[44] The beginning of the list is broken in *CTH* 53 and *CTH* 49.I, where the *lū* + stative catchphrase appears (*CTH* 53 iv 45–46) or is partially reconstructed (*CTH* 49.I A rev. 10–11) at their conclusions.

^{m}*te-it-te* [*qa-du* SAG.DU-*šu* ^{51}D]AM^{meš}-*šu* . . . *lu-ḫal-l*[*i-qú-šu-nu*]; *CTH* 53 iv 46–52).

Syrian II Group

Two documents resembling the Syrian I group boast a few unique features. They are therefore referred to as the Syrian II group: the treaties between Šuppiluliuma I of Ḫatti and Niqmadu II of Ugarit (*CTH* 46, et al.),[45] and between Muwatalli II of Ḫatti and Talmi-Šarrumma of Aleppo (*CTH* 75).[46]

CTH 75 is exceptional in that it represents a copy of a treaty made between Muršili II and Talmi-Šarrumma that was lost but then reformulated under Muwatalli II. In the opening section Muwatalli explains this unusual circumstance. The document thus appears with two initiating declaratory *umma* clauses, followed by their respective historiographic and stipulatory sections, where the treaty proper employs adjuratory rather than juridical discourse.

Interestingly, *CTH* 46 possesses two stipulatory sections introduced as quotations and framed by historiographic discourse: "Now, Šuppiluliuma . . . has thus made a treaty for Niqmadu . . . as follows: 'If in the future . . . *stipulation* . . . ' My Majesty . . . accordingly made a treaty forever" (^{3}*anumma-ma* ^{m}*šu-up-pí-lu-lim-ma* . . . *ri-kí-il-ta* ^{5}*a-na* ^{m}*níq-iq-ma-an-da* . . . ^{6}*a-kán-an-na ir-ku-us* ^{7}*um-ma-a šum-ma-mi i-na* EGIR-*ki* UD-*mi* . . . ^{19}*a-di ṣa-a-ti* ^{d}UTU-*ši* . . . *ri-kí-il-ta* ^{20}*kán-na-a ir-ku-us*; *CTH* 46 B obv. 3–20). Neither treaty employs the standardized language of the Syrian I group.

Finally, *CTH* 46 formulates its witness list with an implicit malediction: "Now, (as for) the one who alters the words of this tablet, the thousand gods shall know: $^{17b-21}$*oath-deities*" (^{16}*ù ša a-ba-te*^{meš} *tup-pí ša ri-kí-il-ti an-na-a-ti* ^{17}*ú-ša-aš-na-a* 1 *li-im* DINGIR^{meš} *lu-ú i-di* . . . ; *CTH* 46 A rev. 16–21). *CTH* 75 includes only human witnesses couched in historiographic discourse: "In Ḫatti [. . . the s]cribe wrot[e] this tablet in the pre[sence of] $^{17-22}$*human witnesses*" (^{17}*ṭup-pa an-na-a i-na* ^{URU}*ḫa-at-ti a-na* [*pa-ni*] $^{17-22}$*human witnesses* [. . . *ṭu*]*p-šar iš-ṭu*[*r*]; *CTH* 75 rev. 17–22).

Non-Syrian Treaties

Six texts constitute non-Syrian treaties. Two of these pertain to Šuppiluliuma I of Ḫatti and Šattiwazza of Mitanni (*CTH* 51.I, *CTH* 52.I). Together they comprise a single document, where *CTH* 52.I functions as a

[45] *CTH* 46: RS 17.340, RS 17.369A; see Nougayrol, *Le palais royal d'Ugarit IV*, 48–52.

[46] Ernst Friedrich Weidner, *Politische Dokumente aus Kleinasien: Die Staatsverträge in akkadischer Sprache aus dem Archiv von Boghazköi*, BoStu 8 and 9 (Leipzig: Hinrichs, 1923), 80–88.

type of supplement to *CTH* 51.I.[47] *CTH* 52.I opens with declaratory *umma* (without accompanying royal epithets; obv. 1a), followed immediately by a historiographic introduction (obv. 1b–rev. 6), while *CTH* 51.I lacks opening *umma*. A juridical matrix follows in *CTH* 51.I (obv. 59–rev. 34), where embedded explanatory discourse continues both treaties, providing a deposit clause marked by the stative: e.g., "[35]A copy of this tablet is deposited before the Sun-goddess of Ari[nn]a . . . [36]and (a copy) is deposited in the land of Mitanni before the Storm deity, lord of the *kur*[*i*]*nnu* of Kaḫat" ([35]*me-ḫi-ir ṭub-bi an-ni-ti a-na pa-ni* ᵈUTU ᵘʳᵘ*a-ri-i*[*n-n*]*a ša-kin-in* . . . [36]*ù i-na* KUR ᵘʳᵘ*mi-it-ta-an-ni a-na pa-ni* ᵈU EN *ku-r*[*i-i*]*n-ni šá* ᵘʳᵘ*ka-ḫat* GAR-*in*; *CTH* 51.I rev. 35–36). An injunction for regular review of the treaty concludes the stipulatory section: e.g., "It must be read repeatedly and always in the presence of the king of Mitanni and in the presence of the people of Ḫurri" (*e-im-mu-ti e-im-mu-ti-ma a-na pa-ni* LUGAL KUR ᵘʳᵘ*mi-it-ta-an-ni* [37]*ù pa-ni* DUMUᵐᵉš KUR ᵘʳᵘ*ḫar-ri li-el-ta-az-zu-u*; *CTH* 51.I rev. 36–37). An invocation of bracketed oath-deities is followed by a concluding malediction and benediction; the supplement appears with a second set of maledictions and benedictions sworn in the first person by the subordinate. Both documents reflect the Syrian I group, but add an explanatory deposit clause and a juridical reading clause as stipulatory closure.

Four broken treaties from Boğazköy support the observations from both parity and Syrian I/II groups: Tudḫaliya II or Šuppiluliuma I of Ḫatti and Šunaššura II (?) of Kizzuwatna,[48] a king of Ḫatti and Paddatiššu of Kizzuwatna,[49] Tudḫaliya II or Šuppiluliuma I with Labʾu and Tunip,[50] Muršili II of Ḫatti and Tuppi-Teššub of Amurru.[51] Of these, *CTH* 41.I boasts the most complete interdiscourse relationships. Here a seal superscription provides aperture, followed by an *umma* declaration with epithets (i 1), a historiographic introduction (i 2–33), and adjuratory discourse (i 34–44) that initiates a juridical stipulatory section. These features collectively reflect interdiscourse elements from both parity and subordination groups, indicating that their patterning is not mutually exclusive.

The Syrian I documents reflect similar interdiscourse patterns and standardized stipulations. The Syrian II group reflects the Syrian I group in simplified and exceptional form: its stipulations are uniquely formulated, its witness list is uniquely framed, and it lacks a maledictory-benedictory conclusion. The *CTH* 51.I and *CTH* 52.I pair further support the features

---

[47] Beckman, *HDT*², 41–42; so Altman, *Historical Prologue*, 264.

[48] *CTH* 41.I; Weidner, *Politische Dokumente aus Kleinasien*, 88–111.

[49] *CTH* 26; Gerhard R. Meyer, "Zwei neue Kizzuwatna-Verträge," *MIOF* 1 (1953): 108–23.

[50] *CTH* 135; Weidner, *Politische Dokumente aus Kleinasien*, 137–46.

[51] *CTH* 62.I; ibid., 76–79; del Monte, *Il trattato fra Muršili II di Ḫattuša e Niqmepaʿ di Ugarit*, 156–59.

discerned in the Syrian I group, and contribute an embedded explanatory deposit clause and a concluding juridical reading clause as possible stipulatory closure. Several non-Syrian Hittite-language treaties likewise exhibit structural features unique to both the Middle Babylonian Syrian I and II patterns (e.g., *CTH* 67–69, 76, 89). The larger paradigm is therefore best interpreted as a general Middle Babylonian treaty tradition, a pattern expressed in comprehensive and limited forms. In sum, these collectively boast the following features: an *umma* declaration with royal epithets as treaty aperture, historiographic account of past relations, juridical matrix with a procedural tribute stipulation as possible aperture, possible embedded explanatory deposit clause and concluding juridical reading clause as stipulatory closure, standardized juridical language with the consequential formula "you have broken the oath!" (*ištu māmīti ītetiq*), invocation of the oath-deities with potential bracketing, a maledictory and benedictory conclusion, and an explanatory colophon as treaty closure.

Traditions 4–5 Continued: Hittite

While the Hittite-language treaty traditions reflect their Middle Babylonian counterparts, differences appear that warrant treating them separately. These unique differences will be summarized after first discussing the parity and general treaty paradigms.

Parity Paradigm

Hittite-language parity treaty documents are few and fragmentary.[52] The treaty between Zidanta II of Ḫatti and Pilliya of Kizzuwatna (*CTH* 25) lacks the explanatory title of the Middle Babylonian parity treaties, opening instead with a historiographic document content clause. Juridical discourse follows, where contingency is marked with *mān . . . nu* or an asyndetic apodosis (so BrTf; see below). In the treaty between Tudḫaliya II (?) of Ḫatti and Šunaššura I (?) of Kizzuwatna (*CTH* 41.II + 131), *natta* with the present marks prohibition rather than the *lē* typical elsewhere:[53] e.g., "[7][If the king of the land of Mitt]anni also takes up hostility against the king of Ḫatti, [Šun]aššura [8][. . .] shall [n]ot give . . . , he shall not allow him right through his country, but he shall defend his own country"

[52] *CTH* 25 (Heinrich Otten, "Ein althethitischer Vertrag mit Kizzuvatna," *JCS* 5 [1951]: 129–32); *CTH* 41.II + 131 (Giuseppe F. del Monte, "Note sui tratti fra Ḫattuša e Kizuwatna," *OrAnt* 20 [1981]: 203–21); *CTH* 134 (Itamar Singer, "The Kuruštama Treaty Revisited," in *Šarnikzel: Hethitologische Studien zum Gedenken an Emil Orgetorix Forrer (19.02.1894–10.01.1986)*, ed. Detlev Groddek and Sylvester Rößle, DBH 10 [Dresden: Technische Universität, 2004], 597–602).

[53] See *CHD* (1:419).

(^{7}[*ma-a-an-kán* LUGAL KUR ^{URU}*mi-it-t*]*a-an-ni-ma IT-TI* LUGAL ⌜^{URU}⌝*ḫa-at-ti ku-u-ru-ur e-ip-zi* [^{I}*šu-n*]*a-aš-šu-ra-aš-ši* ^{8}[. . . *Ú*]*-UL pa-a-i A-NA* KUR-*SU-wa*$^{!}$*-an*$^{?}$*-kán iš-tar-na ar-ḫa Ú-UL tar-na-i nu-za* KUR-*SÚ pa-aḫ-ša*; *CTH* 131 rev. 7′–8′). Interestingly, a nominal formula marks reciprocal stipulations in *CTH* 41.II: e.g., "[Now that wh]ich (pertains to) Šunaššura (shall be) the s[am]e" ([*Ù Š*]*A* ^{I}*šu-na-aš-šu-ra a-p*[*i-ni-iš-š*]*a-an*; iii 8, see also ii 5′, iii 13, 18). Closing sections are lost in both treaties. What is legible in a third treaty, made between Tudḫaliya I (?) of Ḫatti and Amenophis II (?) of Egypt (*CTH* 134), consists of bilateral stipulations. In sum, these treaties exhibit the following characteristics: a historiographic document content clause as aperture, no historiographic statement of past relations, and bilaterally framed stipulations.

General Paradigm

In the Hittite-language corpus the subordination treaty of Tudḫaliya IV of Ḫatti with Kurunta of Tarḫuntašša (BrTf), inscribed on a bronze tablet discovered at Boğazköy, represents the tradition because of its completeness, length, and complexity.[54] While it reflects the more comprehensive general treaty paradigm observed in the Middle Babylonian material, it also possesses the most sophisticated interdiscourse relationships and the largest number of sections among the ancient Near Eastern treaty materials. The voice of Tudḫaliya governs or is supported by several other voices throughout. Based on discourse patterning, BrTf divides into four primary sections.

Section one opens with elliptical *UMMA* and royal epithets: e.g., "^{1}Thus (says) the *tabarna*, Tudḫaliya (IV), Great King, King of the land of Ḫatti, Hero, ^{2}son of Ḫattušili (III)" (^{1}*UM-MA ta-ba-ar-na* ^{m}*Tu-ut-ḫa-li-ya* LUGAL.GAL LUGAL KUR ^{URU}*ḪA-AT-TI* UR.SAG ^{2}DUMU ^{m}*Ḫa-at-tu-ši-li*; BrTf i 1–2).[55] A historiographic account of past relations follows, where the storyline is primarily marked by the preterite: e.g., "^{6}When my father Ḫattušili became hostile against Urḫi-Teššub . . . ^{8}and removed him from kingship, ^{9}then in Kurunta no offense of any sort remained" (^{6}*A-BU-YA ku-wa-pí* ^{m}*Ḫa-at-tu-ši-li-iš A-NA* ^{m}*Úr-ḫi-te-eš-šu-up-aš*⌉ . . . *me-na-aḫ-ḫa-an-da ku-ru-ri-aḫ-ta* ^{8}*na-an* LUGAL-*iz-na-an-ni ar-ḫa ti-it-ta-nu-ut* ^{9}*A-NA*^{m} ^{D}LAMMA-

[54] See the edition of Otten, *Die Bronzetafel aus Boğazköy*.

[55] The performative introduction appears in eighteen Hittite treaties. Half are separated from the historiographic introduction by tablet scoring (Hittite: BrTf, *CTH* 62.II, *CTH* 68, *CTH* 76, *CTH* 105, *CTH* 89; Middle Babylonian: *CTH* 62.I, *CTH* 75 2x, *CTH* 92) and half are not (Hittite: *CTH* 133, *CTH* 49.II, *CTH* 42, *CTH* 69; Middle Babylonian: *CTH* 41.I, *CTH* 52.I, *CTH* 53, *CTH* 46, *CTH* 66). The frequency of the performative introduction suggests an emic division that, in combination with its performative focus, indicates a distinct treaty-tradition element.

ma-kán wa-aš-túl Ú-UL ku-it-ki a-aš-ta; i 6–9). An explanation of the boundaries and holdings of Tarḫuntašša is embedded, frequently marked with a nominal clause: e.g., "[18]So his boundaries are set as follows: from the land of Pitašša, [19]your boundaries (are) Mount Ḫauwā, the ⸗*kantanna* of the town Zarniya, (and) the town Šanantarwa" ([18]ZAG^MEŠ^-*ma-aš-ši ki-iš-ša-an ti-ya-an-te-eš IŠ-TU* KUR ^URU^*Pí-ta-aš-ša-at-ta* [19] ^ḪUR.SAG^*Ḫa-u-wa-a-aš* ⸗*kán-ta-an-na* ^URU^*Za-ar-ni-ya-aš* ^URU^*Ša-na-an-tar-wa-aš* ZAG-*aš*; i 18–19).[56] Juridical discourse related to the listed holdings is also embedded in the historiographic account.

Its remaining three sections are summarized as follows. Section two consists primarily of juridical discourse with embedded historiographic and maledictory discourse as support material. Section three constitutes the oath-deity list followed by malediction and then benediction. The final section provides an explanatory human witness list, and an explanation of the tablet's copies and seals: e.g., "[46]Now one tablet in the presence of the Sun-goddess of Arinna (etc.) . . . is in place, [51]and Kurunta King of the land of Tarḫuntašša possesses one tablet in his palace" ([46]*nu* DUB I^KAM^ *A-NA PA-NI* ^D^UTU ^URU^*A-ri-in-na* (etc.) . . . GAR-*ri* [51]DUB I^KAM^-*ma* ^m^ ^D^LAMMA-*aš* LUGAL KUR ^URU^ ^D^U-*ta-aš-ša I-NA* É-*ŠU ḫar-zi*; iv 46–51).

Eleven Hittite-language treaties[57] share similar interdiscourse features with BrTf. First, the voice of the Great King opens several with a verbless *UMMA* declaratory frame and accompanying royal epithets. A historio-

---

[56] The ⸗*kantanna* was apparently a topographical feature; see Otten, *Die Bronzetafel aus Boğazköy*, 32; H. Craig Melchert, *Cuneiform Luvian Lexicon*, Lexica Anatolica 2 (Chapel Hill, NC: n.p., 1993), 100.

[57] Arnuwanda I of Ḫatti and the men of Išmerika, *CTH* 133 (Aharon Kempinski and Silvin Košak, "Der Išmeriga-Vertrag," *WO* 5 [1970]: 191–217); Arnuwanda I (?) of Ḫatti and the Kaška people, *CTH* 137 (for text see Einar von Schuler, *Die Kaškäer: Ein Beitrag zur Ethnographie des alten Kleinasien* [Berlin: de Gruyter, 1965], 134–39; translation in *TLCANE*, 1:355–64); Šuppiluliuma of Ḫatti and Aziru of Amurru, *CTH* 49.II (del Monte, *Il trattato fra Muršili II di Ḫattuša e Niqmepa*ᶜ *di Ugarit*, 128–41); Muršili II of Ḫatti and Tuppi-Teššub of Amurru, *CTH* 62.II (ibid., 160–77); Muršili II of Ḫatti and Targasnalli of Ḫapalla, *CTH* 67 (Johannes Friedrich, *Staatsverträge des Ḫatti-Reiches in hethitischer Sprache I*, MVAG 31/1 [Leipzig: Hinrichs, 1926], 51–94, 180); Muršili II of Ḫatti and Manapa-Kurunta of Mira-Kuwaliya, *CTH* 68 (ibid., 95–179, 180–81); Muršili II of Ḫatti and Manapa-Tarḫunta of the Šeḫa River land, *CTH* 69 (Johannes Friedrich, *Staatsverträge des Hatti-Reiches in hethitischer Sprache II*, MVAG 34/1 [Leipzig: Hinrichs, 1930], 1–41); Muwatalli II of Ḫatti and Alakšandu of Wiluša, *CTH* 76 (ibid., 42–102); Tudḫaliya IV (?) of Ḫatti and Ulmi-Teššub of Tarḫuntašša, *CTH* 106 (Theo P. J. van den Hout, *Der Ulmitesub-Vertrag: Eine prosopographische Untersuchung*, StBoT 38 [Wiesbaden: Harrassowitz, 1995]); Šuppiluliuma I of Ḫatti and Ḫuqqana of Ḫayasa, *CTH* 42 (Friedrich, *Staatsverträge des Hatti-Reiches in hethitischer Sprache II*, 103–63); Šuppiluliuma I (?) of Ḫatti and an unknown ruler of Oylum Höyük, Oy. 12–401 (Ünal, "Hittite Treaty Tablet from Oylum Höyük").

graphic introduction follows (lost in *CTH* 67 and *CTH* 106) with the preterite marking the mainline. Juridical discourse and a procedural tribute stipulation may be embedded in this section (i.e., *CTH* 49.II i 3–9, 10–13, respectively, the sole Hittite-language treaty with this clause).

Juridical discourse follows, where contingency appears in a variety of ways, with *mān* . . . *nu* or *mān* and an asyndetic apodosis being the most common. Formulaic stipulations also appear (especially in *CTH* 67–69 and *CTH* 76). A reading clause marked by the imperative concludes the juridical section in two texts: e.g., "Now, let th[em read] this tablet before you three times annually, which for you, Ala[kšandu], I had [made]; and you, Alakšandu, must know it" ([73]*nam-ma* ⸢*ki*⸣*-i ku-it ṬUP-PU tu-uk* [I]*a-la*[*-ak-ša-an-du-uš i-ya-*]*u-*⸢*un*⸣ [74]*ne-it-ták-kán* MU.KAM-*ti* MU.KAM-*ti pí-ra-an* 3-*Š*[*Ú ḫal-zi-eš-ša-an-*]*du* [75]*na-at-za-kán zi-ik* [I]*a-la-ak-ša-an-du-uš ša-*⸢*ki*⸣ . . . ; *CTH* 76 iii 73–75). Tablet scoring often appears in conjunction with formulaic utterances marking closure for a given stipulation: e.g., (*mān*) . . . *nu*⸗*kan* (*kāšma*) *MĀMĒTUM šarratti*, "(If) . . . then you have (hereby) transgressed the oath!" (e.g., *CTH* 49.II ii 39, 46, iii 16, 34; *CTH* 62.II iii 11; cf. the Eblaite oil-oath formula); (*mān*) . . . *nu kāšma zik* PN *ANA PĀNI* DINGIR[MEŠ] *waštaši*, "(If) . . . then you, PN, have hereby sinned against the gods!" (e.g., *CTH* 68 C ii 46–47, B iii 28–29; *CTH* 76 ii 55–56).[58]

An oath-deity list typically follows the juridical section and may appear in optional bracketing. Most of these treaties also appear with maledictory and/or benedictory discourse in various states of preservation (lost in *CTH* 49.II and *CTH* 68). While this adjuratory section is fairly standardized, it possesses more variation than its Middle Babylonian counterpart. Four of these texts bear a colophon providing the tablet copy number:[59] e.g., "The [first] tablet o[f Alak]šandu" (DUB [1[KAM]] *Š*[*A* [I]*a-la-ak*]*-ša-an-du*; *CTH* 76 A 47).

A number of pattern variations are worth noting among these documents: witness lists may be fronted (*CTH* 133, *CTH* 137) or embedded (*CTH* 42); explicit tablet deposition is infrequent, irregularly placed, and incorporated within multiple discourse types; human witnesses appear

[58] Ünal suggests a similar formula in the lacuna immediately before the line score in Oy. 12–401 (obv. 10); see Ünal, "Hittite Treaty Tablet from Oylum Höyük," 25. Since only the top of the obverse (and thus the bottom of the reverse) is preserved in this broken treaty, it is impossible to know how long it was. Its first predicate is a preterite, likely marking a historiographic introduction. What is left of the body indicates the injunctive use of the present (perhaps prohibition with *ŪL* + present; see Ünal's reconstruction) and *mān* ("if") for marking casuistic discourse. It concludes with an oath-deity list. Aside from its apparently single-column nature, Oy. 12–401 reflects the other Hittite treaties at the discourse level.

[59] See *CTH* 62.II, *CTH* 69, *CTH* 76, and *CTH* 42. See also BrTf, *CTH* 146 and *CTH* 89.

irregularly (*CTH* 106; cf. BrTf); adjuration infrequently formulates the stipulatory section (*CTH* 42; cf. AT 2, RS 17.146, RS 18.115). Embedded historiographic and explanatory discourse types also provide numerous support roles among the stipulatory sections. Interestingly, indictment discourse appears in two treaties: as stipulatory support in one (*CTH* 42 iii 53–58), and as a motivating introduction for another (*CTH* 146 obv. 1–40).

Two additional treaties reflect the general paradigm but with fewer nuances: Tudḫaliya IV of Ḫatti and Šaušgamuwa of Amurru,[60] and Ḫattušili III of Ḫatti and the town Tiliura.[61] The latter (*CTH* 89) exhibits the most striking differences, lacking a witness list, benedictions, and maledictions. Similarly, several broken texts provide additional examples of the inter-discourse patterns found in the general Hittite-language treaty tradition,[62] as well as exhibiting some differences in their ordering of discourse elements: e.g., a witness list appears after the benediction in *CTH* 141 but before the juridical section in *CTH* 138.1 (cf. *CTH* 137).

In sum, the general comprehensive paradigm observed for the Middle-Babylonian material applies to the bulk of the Hittite-language material, though limited forms appear in two cases (*CTH* 105, *CTH* 89).

Differences from the Middle Babylonian Traditions

The differences between the Hittite and Middle Babylonian treaties are somewhat surprising. Texts in the Hittite-language parity group lack

[60] *CTH* 105; Cord Kühne and Heinrich Otten, *Der Šaušgamuwa-Vertrag: Eine Untersuchung zu Sprache und Graphik*, StBoT 16 (Wiesbaden: Harrassowitz, 1971).

[61] *CTH* 89; J. M. Gonzáles Salazar, "Tiliura, un ejemplo de la politica fronteriza durante el imperio hitita (*CTH* 89)," *AuOr* 12 (1994): 159–76.

[62] Šuppiluliuma I of Ḫatti and Šattiwazza of Mitanni, *CTH* 51.II (Emmanuel Laroche, "Fragments hittites du traité mitannien de Šuppiluliuma Ier," *Ugaritica* 6 [1969]: 369–73); Šattiwazza of Mitanni and Šuppiluliuma I of Ḫatti, *CTH* 52.II (Johannes Friedrich, "Ein Bruchstück des Vertrages Mattiwaza-Suppiluliuma in hethitischer Sprache?" *AfO* 2 [1924]: 119–24); Tudḫaliya I (?) of Ḫatti and Amenophis II (?) of Egypt, *CTH* 134 (Singer, "Kuruštama Treaty Revisited," 597–602); Tudḫaliya IV or Šuppiluliuma II of Ḫatti and the rulers of Alašiya (Cyprus), *CTH* 141 (Heinrich Otten, "Neue Quellen zum Ausklang des Hethitischen Reiches," *MDOG* 94 [1963]: 10–13; Gerd Steiner, "Neue Alašija-Texte," *Kadmos* 1 [1962]: 130–38); the indictment of Mita of Paḫḫuwa and a treaty with the elders of several Anatolian communities, *CTH* 146 (for text see Silvio Reichmuth, "Mita von Pahhuwa (*CTH* 146)," in *Hethitologie in Dresden: Textbearbeitungen, Arbeiten zur Forschungs- und Schriftgeschichte*, ed. Robert Fischer, Detlev Groddek, and Henning Marquardt, DBH 35 [Wiesbaden: Harrassowitz, 2011]: 109–44; Aram Kosyan, "Arnuwandas I in the East," *Aramazd* 1 [2006]: 72–97; Giulia Torri, "Militärische Feldzüge nach Ostanatolien in der mittelhethitischen Zeit," *AoF* 32 [2005]: 386–400; for translation see *HDT*^{2}, no. 27A); four treaties related to an unknown ruler of Ḫatti and the Kaška people, *CTH* 138.1, *CTH* 138.2, *CTH* 139, *CTH* 138.3 (in German/English translation only; see *TLCANE* and von Schuler, *Die Kaškäer*).

an explanatory prescript and title (perhaps due to breaks), but appear with a reciprocal stipulatory formula not apparent in the Middle Babylonian group.

As for the general paradigms, the placement of the procedural tribute stipulation and the maledictions/benedictions differ. The ordering of the latter is consistent in the Middle Babylonian material but is occasionally switched in the Hittite-language material. Furthermore, the Middle Babylonian group not only lacks any additional malediction directed toward an impersonal third party, but also lacks the possible addition of a human witness list. The Hittite-language material boasts a significantly larger range of formulaic yet flexible utterances for closing its stipulatory paragraphs. The corresponding Middle Babylonian formula, however, is limited to a single, non-variable utterance. Similarly, the Hittite-language treaty texts may appear with indictment discourse as treaty support. In conclusion, the general Hittite-language treaty tradition is collectively more comprehensive, complex, and fluid than its Middle Babylonian counterpart. These differences are probably due in part to the peripheral and translational nature of the Middle Babylonian documents.

First Millennium

Following a gap between 1210 and 824 BCE, our last two treaty traditions appear. Three Old Aramaic stelae probably from Sefire comprise the sixth tradition, and a set of Neo-Assyrian tablets comprises the seventh tradition. The latter were found at Aššur, Nimrud, Nineveh, and Tell Tayinat. Two Neo-Babylonian treaties also belong to this period, but their provenience, physical material, and discourse structure mark them as either ad hoc arrangements or perhaps potential treaty traditions.[63]

[63] For text and analysis, see Simo Parpola and Kazuko Watanabe, *Neo-Assyrian Treaties and Loyalty Oaths*, SAA 2 (Helsinki: Helsinki University Press, 1988). The first is a parity treaty between Šamši-Adad V of Assyria and Marduk-zakir-šumi I of Babylon; it dates roughly from 824 BCE, is inscribed on a polished black stone fragment, and was found in the secondary context of Assurbanipal's library. See John A. Brinkman, "Political Covenants, Treaties, and Loyalty Oaths in Babylonia and between Assyria and Babylonia," in *I trattati nel mondo antico: forma, ideologia, funzione*, ed. Luciano Canfora, Mario Liverani, and Carlo Zaccagnini (Rome: L'Erma di Bretschneider, 1990), 96. It consists of a few stipulations couched in adjuratory discourse that appears with and without inverse *šumma, lā* with the perfective and oath-bearing *-u* for the positive, and the perfective and oath-bearing *-u* for the negative: e.g., "[. . . in the loyal]ty of their heart he shall trust" ([*ina ku-u*]*n* ŠÀ-*bi-šú-nu la it-ták-lu*; obv. 5′). A series of maledictions also appears, and in substance these reflect those in the epilogue of Hammurapi's Laws (ca. eighteenth/seventeenth century), to the extent that they provided the means for the editor's

Tradition 6: Old Aramaic

Our investigation of the sixth treaty tradition is grounded on the three eighth-century Old Aramaic treaty texts from Sefire, made between Bar-Gaʾyah of KTK and Matīʿʾēl of Arpad.[64] The revised edition of Fitzmyer serves as the primary basis for the analysis.[65] Collectively, the voice of the sovereign governs all three, including the united voice of the sovereign and vassal, and the vassal alone. Sf 1 functions as the basis for the discussion, and divides into three sections.

Section one opens with a lengthy explanatory title: "The treaty of Bar-Gaʾyah king of KTK with Matīʿʾēl Bar-ʿAttarsamak king of [Arpad] . . ." (*⸢ʿ⸣dy br gʾy⸢h m⸣lk ktk ʿm mtʿʾl br ʿtrsmk ml⸢k⸣* [*ʾrpd*]; Sf 1A 1). A subordinate document content clause then introduces the deity list: "So this (is) the treaty that Bar-Gaʾ[yah] cut [before Aššur] . . . [8–12]*deity list* . . ." (*wʿdyʾ ʾl⸢n⸣ zy gzr br g⸢ʾ⸣*[*yh qdm ʾšr*] . . . [8–12]*deity list* . . . ; Sf 1A 7–12). A lengthy maledictory series follows, containing several futility curses recognizable through the "maximum effort—minimum yield" motif and heightened by the stylized number "seven": e.g., "and may seven mares nurse a colt but it not be sat[ed]" (*wšbʿ ssyh yhynqn ʿl wʾl yš*[*bʿ*]; Sf 1A 22).[66] Ritual curses

reconstruction of the broken clauses; see Parpola and Watanabe, *Neo-Assyrian Treaties*, 4n1. The second Neo-Babylonian text hails roughly from 652 BCE, was drawn up between Assurbanipal of Assyria and a series of Babylonian allies, and appears on a broken single-column tablet from Nineveh. Its extant surface-level features reflect those of the first Neo-Babylonian parity treaty but exhibit a number of unique discourse elements: the voice of the subordinate allies dominates, its adjuratory stipulations are formulated differently, and formulaic non-abrogation language appears: "From this day for as many days as we live . . ." (*ul-tu* UD-*mu an-ni-i a-di* UD-*mu ma-la bal-ṭa-a-ni*; obv. 3, 17a, 32b; cf. the Old Babylonian treaties). See A. Kirk Grayson, "Akkadian Treaties of the Seventh Century B.C.," *JCS* 39 (1987): 140.

[64] These treaty partners are explicit in Sf 1 and Sf 2. Though debated, the PN "[Bar-Gaʾya]h" perhaps appears in Sf 3 (line 25), for there is room for only five letters and no other proposal has gained acceptance; see Joseph A. Fitzmyer, *The Aramaic Inscriptions of Sefire*, BibOr 19/A (Rome: Pontificial Biblical Institute, 1995), 161. Like Sf 1–2, Sf 3 is engraved on basalt, mentions the kings of Arpad as subordinates, is written without word dividers, and exhibits similar orthography and syntax to those of Sf 1–2.

[65] Fitzmyer, *Aramaic Inscriptions of Sefire*.

[66] The bilingual (Old Aramaic and Akkadian) Hadad-yiṯʿi inscription from Tell Fakhariyah reflects a similar ninth-century situation in a different context. Here a series of futility curses are parallel in topic to those in Sf 1–2 and the later Bukān inscription (ca. 700 BCE). Their presence in these Aramaic contexts, as well as biblical texts, may suggest a West Semitic formulation, though this possibility is uncertain. See the bibliography in Alan R. Millard, "Hadad-Yithʿi," *COS* 2.34:154n115. Note also the caveats with Sumerian examples in Alan R. Millard, "The Tell Fekheriyeh Inscriptions," in *Biblical Archaeology Today, 1990:*

also appear: e.g., “[And just as] this calf is cut in two, thus may Matīʿʾēl be cut in two, and his nobles be cut in two!” ([*wʾyk z*[40]*y*] ⸢*y*⸣*gzr ʿglʾ znh kn ygzr mtʿʾl wygzrn rbwh*; Sf 1A 39–40). Among the three stelae, ritual curses are unique to Sf 1, though they appear in the earlier Šattiwazza and Šuppiluliuma treaty (e.g., *CTH* 52.I rev. 46–47) and in the roughly contemporaneous Neo-Assyrian Aššur-nirari and Matiʾ-ilu treaty, and they are not uncommon in other ancient Near Eastern genres.[67]

Section two comprises predominantly casuistic discourse, where *whn* marks the protasis and the injunctional prefix the apodosis: e.g., “Now if one of the kings comes and surrounds <me>, [(then) your] ar[my] must come [29][to me] . . .” (*wh*⸢*n*⸣ *y*⸢ʾ⸣*th ḥ*⸣*d mlkn wys*⸢*b*⸣*n*<*y*> *yʾth* ⸢*ḥ*⸣[*ylk* [29]*ʾly*] . . . ; Sf 1B 28–29). Standardized stipulations seem to appear in Sf 1 and Sf 2, but not as fully as in the Middle Babylonian materials. A fluid formulaic apodosis provides closure several times in all three stelae (cf. the Eblaite, Akkadian, and Hittite materials): e.g., “ . . . (then) you have betrayed all the gods of the treaty wh[o (are) in this inscription!]” (. . . *šqrtm lkl* ʾ⸢*l*⸣*hy ʿdyʾ* ⸢*z*⸣[*y bsprʾ znh*]; Sf 1B 23). Intriguingly, historiographic discourse provides juridical support in Sf 3, similar to several instances found in the Hittite general-comprehensive treaty tradition: e.g., “But now the gods have restored the fortunes of [25]the hou[se of my father, and the house of] my father [has become great], and Talʾayim has returned to [Bar-Gaʾya] h . . .” (*wkʿm hšbw ʾlhn šybt by*[25][*t ʾby wrbh byt*] ⸢ʾ⸣*by wšbt tlʾym l*[*br gʾy*]⸢*h*⸣ . . . ; 24–25). Section three constitutes an adjuratory conclusion for Sf 1 that includes oaths by both treaty partners, benediction, and malediction. Sf 2 also concludes with malediction.

In sum, the Old Aramaic treaty tradition incorporates a maledictory introduction, a juridical matrix with standardized stipulatory language and paragraph closure, and a maledictory conclusion. Items appearing in only one of the Sefire documents that also appear in earlier treaty materials include the following: an explanatory title and document content clause (Middle Babylonian parity tradition); a fronted deity list (Hittite treaties, see *CTH* 133 and *CTH* 137); a possible fronted benediction (a Hittite treaty, *CTH* 137, text 2 ii 16–17); an explanatory summary regarding treaty relations (R2-H3/H3-R2); embedded historiographic support for

---

Proceedings of the Second International Congress on Biblical Archaeology (Jerusalem: Israel Exploration Society, 1993), 521–22. The presence of the futility curse in Old Babylonian treaty material at Tell Leilan (see especially L.T.-3 24b′–28′) further justifies Millard’s suggestion: “Rather than making a firm distinction between West Semitic and Babylonian curses, it may be preferable to envisage a reservoir of tradition common to both” (ibid., 522).

[67] See the summary in Anne Marie Kitz, *Cursed Are You! The Phenomenology of Cursing in Cuneiform and Hebrew Texts* (Winona Lake, IN: Eisenbrauns, 2014), 82–95.

related stipulations (Hittite general-comprehensive tradition); concluding adjuratory elements (Hittite general-comprehensive tradition).

Tradition 7: Neo-Assyrian

The seventh and last treaty tradition is represented by Neo-Assyrian documents.[68] The succession treaty of Esarhaddon is the chosen collective exemplar for this corpus because of its completeness, length, and relative complexity (SAA 2.6-T).[69] The voice of the sovereign governs the whole, and the voice of the subordinate also appears. It divides into three sections.

Section one opens with an explanatory title (1–12) introducing all contracting partners with epithets and their further associates: e.g., "[1]The treaty of Esarhaddon, (king of the world), king of the land of Assyria, [2]the son of Sennacherib . . . [3]with Ḫumbarēš the ruler of the city of Naḫšimarti, [4](with) his sons . . ." ([1]*a-de-e ša* ^{m}*aš-šur*-PAB-AŠ (MAN ŠÚ) MAN KUR *aš-šur*$^{\mathrm{(ki)}}$ [2]DUMU ^{m} ^{d}30-PAB.MEŠ-SU . . . [3]TA ^{m}*ḫum-ba-re-eš* ^{lú}EN-URU ^{uru}*na-aḫ-ši-mar-ti* [4](TA) DUMU^{meš}-*šú* . . . ; 1–4). A subordinate document content clause marked by the preterite and a deity list follows: "*the treaty that,* [13]in the presence of . . . *deity list* . . . [23]the gods of the lands, all of them, he strengthened, [24]*which* he drew up, *and which* he established" ([13]*ina* IGI . . . *deity list* . . . [23]DINGIR^{meš} KUR.KUR DÙ-*šú-nu ú-dan-nin-*[*u-ni*] [24]*iṣ-ba-tu iš-ku-nu-n*[*i*]; 13–24). These oath-deities are then invoked, marked by an initial imperative and a series of ditto signs: e.g., "[25]*Before* Aššūr, father of the gods, ruler of the lands, must each of you s[wear]! [26]*Before* Anu, Illil, *and* Ea, ditto! . . ." ([25] ^{d}*aš-šur* AD DINGIR^{meš} EN KUR.KUR *ti-t*[*am-ma-a*] [26] ^{d}*a-num* ^{d}EN.LÍL ^{d}É.A MIN . . . ; 25–26). An explanatory summary reflecting the opening concludes the section, thereby forming an *inclusio*.

Section two is stipulatory but is written in essentially adjuratory garb, where positive injunctions are marked by *lā* with the durative and oath-bearing *-ūni*, as well as implicit and explicit inverse *šumma* clauses, etc.: e.g., "Assurbanipal . . . this very *prince*, shall you obey!" (*šum-ma*

---

[68] For the majority of these, see Parpola and Watanabe, *Neo-Assyrian Treaties*.

[69] I employ a composite text that incorporates SAA 2.6 and the preliminary critical edition of ms T by Jacob Lauinger, "Esarhaddon's Succession Treaty at Tell Tayinat." Hundreds of fragments comprising eight manuscripts constitute SAA 2.6, all associated with the Nabû temple of Calaḫ, and made with several different "city rulers" on the eastern extremity of Assyria. Ms T comprises a single manuscript found in a Neo-Assyrian temple at Tayinat, on the western extremity of the Assyrian empire, and reflects a treaty made with an unnamed governor of Kunalia, sixteen of his officials, and "all the men of his hands" (ms T i 3–11). All manuscripts involve essentially the same text.

^{m}*aš-šur*-DÙ-A . . . *ḫa-an-nu-um-ma la ta-da-gal-a-ni*; 58.3–60.2).[70] The collocation *šumma attunu* regularly provides paragraph aperture in both this section and the next. Juridical discourse briefly appears (83–91, 198–211).

Section three constitutes the bulk of the document and its conclusion. Here maledictory discourse predominates and is frequently marked by the precative and vetitive: e.g., "May Mullissu, his [i.e., Aššūr's] beloved spouse, make the utterance of his mouth evil, and may she not intercede for you!" ([417] ^{d}NIN.LÍL *ḫi-ir-tu na-ram-ta-šú a-mat* KA-*šú* [418]*li-lam-mìn-ma a-a iṣ-bat ab-bu-ut-ku-un*; 417.1–418.2). The voice of the subordinate also appears, providing a series of promissory oaths (494–512) and breaking the section roughly into two parts, where the first emphasizes divine agency (so-called "Standard Curse" section) and the second emphasizes ritual malediction (so-called "Ceremonial Curse" section). A series of simile curses follows, employing the formula *kī ša* X *kī ḫannî* [+ volitional form] ("Just as X, like this [may . . .]") and appearing with interspersed curses of deprivation-for-blessing (545–546, 573–575, 649–651, etc.). Several instances of the simile curse exhibit performative action with actual objects, indicated by a demonstrative: e.g., "(Ditto, ditto:) Just as (this) ewe is cut open *and* the flesh of (her) young is placed in her mouth, like this may you be made to consume the flesh of your brothers, your sons, *and* your daughters in your hunger!" ([547](KI.MIN KI.MIN) *ki-i šá* U_8 *(an-[n]i)-tú šal-qa-(tu)-u-ni* UZU *šá* DUMU-(*šá*) [548]*ina pi-i-šá šá-kín-u-ni ki-i ḫa-an-ni-e* [549]UZU$^{(meš)}$ *šá* ŠEŠ^{meš}-*ku-nu* DUMU^{meš}-*ku-nu* DUMU.MÍ^{meš}-*ku-nu* [550]*a-na bu-ri-ku-nu lu-šá-kil-u-ku-nu*; 547–550). The ritual curse also appears in the Sefire material (see Sf 1A 35–42).

Several essentially complete Neo-Assyrian documents fill out the structural picture, where the voice of the monarch or his representative governs each. The first is a subordination treaty made ca. 754 BCE between Aššur-nirari V and Matiʾ-ilu of Arpad (SAA 2.2). While the title is lost, interdiscourse relationships appear in the document's remnants, which include a series of ritual maledictions. Adjuratory stipulations follow, marked by inverse *šumma* and oath-bearing *-ūni*, etc.: e.g., "You must not hide (or) protect (him)" (*šúm-mu tu-pa-za-ru-ni ta-ḫa-ṣi-nu-*[*u*]*-ni*; iii 22′). More maledictory content follows, and the treaty closes with a deity list.

The second document is a subordination treaty made ca. 676 BCE between Esarhaddon and Baal of Tyre (SAA 2.5). It opens with an explanatory title presenting the contracting partners of the treaty. Juridical discourse resumes the text after a break (i 5′–iii 17′, iii 22b′–30′), which contains an explanatory geographic summary (iii 18′–22a′) outlining

[70] Lit., "If you do not obey Assurbanipal, this very *prince, may you be cursed!*" For inverse *šumma* in adjuratory discourse, see the note regarding AT 2 21–22.

Baal's jurisdiction. A maledictory conclusion follows (iv 1′–19′), and an explanatory colophon providing a document content clause provides closure: "The trea[t]y tablet established with Baal of Ty[re]" (*ṭup-pi a-d*[*e*]*-e kun-nu šá* ^{I}*ba-a-lu* ^{kur}*ṣu*[*r-ra-a-a*]; iv 20′).

The third document is a subordination treaty made ca. 652 BCE between Assurbanipal and the Arab tribe of Qedar (SAA 2.10). It too opens with an explanatory title naming the treaty partners, but an implicit divine invocation appears next, where the imperative should probably be understood: "[(Swear by) Aššur], Mullissu, (and) Š[erua]!" ([*aš-šur*] ^{d}NI[N].LÍL $^{d!}$*š*[*e*$^{!}$*-ru-u-a*]; obv. 3′). Adjuratory stipulations follow, and the broken ending constitutes a deity list.

The fourth document is an accession treaty made ca. 669 BCE by the dowager queen Zakutu on behalf of Assurbanipal (SAA 2.8), shortly after his father's death, and is probably an excerpt from a larger document. It opens with an explanatory title identifying the contracting parties, while a deity list in a broken apodosis marks an opening malediction. An adjuratory stipulatory sequence makes up the final section (rev. 2–27), appearing with *lā* and oath-bearing *-ūni* for positive injunctions and conditional *šumma attunu* as paragraph aperture: e.g., "[I]f [yo]u hear about the killing or destroying of Assurbanipal . . . , [you must] come (and) [in]form[71] Zakutu [his mother] and Assurbanipal . . ." ([*š*]*um-ma* ^{8}[*at-tu*]*-nu šá da-a-ki ù ḫul-lu-qí* ^{9}[*šá* ^{I}*aš-šur*]-DÙ-A . . . *ta-šam-ma-a-ni* ^{10}[*la ta*]*l-la-ka-nin-ni uz-ni šá* ^{mí}*za-ku-te* ^{11}[AMA-*šú*] ⌜*ù*⌝ *šá* ^{I}*aš-šur*-DÙ-A . . . ^{12}[*la tu-pa*]*t-ta-a-ni*; rev. 9b–12a). The typical invocation of oath-deities and maledictory conclusion are omitted.

Three additional subordination treaties (SAA 2.11, SAA 2.12, SAA 2.13), a succession treaty (SAA 2.3), and an accession treaty (SAA 2.4) extend our analysis. With the exception of SAA 2.12, which is a brief treaty extract, all are fragmentary and reflect the following discourse components (among others). Where discernible, the voice of the sovereign governs the whole. The explanatory title naming contracting partners is preserved in the treaty between Sîn-šarru-iškun and Babylonian allies (SAA 2.11 obv. 1–5). A broken oath-deity list follows in the same treaty, suggesting an opening declaratory invocation (the predicate is lost; SAA 2.11 obv. 6). Stipulations are formulated with juridical discourse in SAA 2.13, but with adjuratory discourse everywhere else. A maledictory conclusion also appears.

In sum, the Neo-Assyrian corpus is primarily adjuratory, exhibiting fairly consistent discourse features. Where extant, an explanatory title provides treaty aperture and identifies all contracting partners. Divine invocation may follow, with the exception of the Aššur-nirari and Matiʾ-ilu

[71] Lit., "open the ear of."

text, where it seems to close the document. In two cases (SAA 2.2, SAA 2.8) maledictory discourse appears next; otherwise the stipulatory section commonly follows and is primarily adjuratory—though in two texts it is juridical (SAA 2.5 and SAA 2.13). The exemplar (SAA 2.6-T) includes both adjuratory and juridical discourse in its stipulatory material. With the exception of the Zakutu treaty, all documents with a complete ending conclude with maledictory discourse. A colophon provides closure in a few texts, which also functions as a subordinate document content clause in the exemplar and as a mainline document content clause in SAA 2.5. Finally, it is significant that *none* of the documents in the Neo-Babylonian or Neo-Assyrian corpora appears with historiographic discourse as a mainline feature. The closest possibilities appear in the form of projected speech in the exemplar (SAA 2.6-T 351–352, 358–359) and a few subordinate clauses (SAA 2.10 obv. 4′–11′) that provide setting for their governing adjuration.

Comparison and Contrast: Seven Ancient Near Eastern Treaty Traditions

The seven treaty traditions I have examined all share clusters of interdiscourse features, while displaying their own unique characteristics. Our concern here is not to offer a historical reconstruction positing putative connections between overlapping clusters, but simply to note significant similarities and differences.

First, all primary constituents in the Eblaite tradition appear in later treaty traditions and are outlined according to their order of appearance. Its (apparently elliptical) explanatory title introduces the tradition and identifies all contracting partners with the idiom "the tablet of the oil offering between PN1 (and) PN2" (dub nídba ì-giš PN1 (*wa*) PN2). This feature is reflected in similar titular explanatory elliptical clauses in the Middle Babylonian parity tradition, as well as in the Sefire and Neo-Assyrian traditions. An analogue of the Eblaite explanatory geographic summary of holdings appears in the Hittite general-comprehensive paradigm, where it is embedded in a juridical matrix rather than occupying the Eblaite introductory position. On the one hand, the Eblaite performative declaration "Thus (says) the king of PN1 to PN2" (*en-ma* en PN1 *ʾa$_5$-na* PN2), which functions as paragraph aperture in its juridical section, reflects the *umma* declarations providing treaty aperture in the Middle Babylonian and Hittite-language general-comprehensive traditions. On the other hand, its motive-consequence formula " . . . you have failed the oil-oath" (a-è ì-giš or ì a-è) as paragraph closure more closely approximates the function and semantics of the corresponding feature in the Middle

Babylonian and Hittite general-comprehensive traditions and the Sefire tradition: "you have broken the oath" (*ištu māmīti ītetiq*) or " . . . then you have (hereby) transgressed the oath" (*nu⸗kan* (*kāšma*) *MĀMĒTUM šarratti*, et al.), and " . . . you have betrayed all the gods of the treaty who (are) in this inscription" (*šqrtm lkl ʾlhy ʿdyʾ zy bsprʾ znh*), respectively. The Eblaite juridical matrix also contains procedural discourse reflecting a number of underlying economic concerns, which are intriguingly reflected in the uncommon procedural tribute stipulations of the Middle Babylonian and Hittite general-comprehensive traditions. The Eblaite adjuratory conclusion incorporates a list of human rather than divine names, probably representing oath-takers/witnesses instead of the ubiquitous oath-deity lists of the later traditions. However, a human witness list appears in the Hittite-language general-comprehensive tradition, albeit in explanatory form. The closing explanatory colophon appears in some form throughout the ancient Near Eastern treaty traditions (the Sefire material being the exception). Finally, the Eblaite tradition lacks a closing malediction, an explicit invocation of oath-deities, and any historiographic discourse.

Second, many of the primary constituents of the general Old Babylonian and the Assyrian merchant treaty traditions appear in later paradigms. Both open with an invocation of their respective oath-deities, a feature shared with the Sefire and Neo-Assyrian traditions (immediately after their respective titles). The invocation regularly appears after the juridical matrices of the Middle Babylonian and Hittite-language general-comprehensive traditions (though fronted in *CTH* 133 and *CTH* 137). The stipulatory section of both the Old Babylonian and Old Assyrian traditions is primarily couched in adjuratory discourse (though juridical discourse appears in L.T.-5). In the general paradigm, stipulations are sworn by the adjured in the first person, and in the merchant paradigm they are imposed. Both juridical and adjuratory discourse make up the specific stipulations of the Middle Babylonian parity tradition, while adjuratory discourse comprises the bulk of the corresponding section of the Neo-Assyrian tradition (which also contains some juridical material). All remaining traditions employ a juridical matrix. Both the Old Babylonian and Old Assyrian traditions close with an explicit self-imposed set of maledictions. This type of closure is common throughout the traditions that follow, albeit not in the first person. Two items are unique to the Old Babylonian and Old Assyrian traditions: a declaratory summary of the contracting partner's compliance to the oath-taking procedure and/or stipulatory adjurations, and non-abrogation language functioning as paragraph aperture: i.e., "(from this day) while X live(s)" ([*ištu ūmim annîm*] *adi balṭā* + suffix). The former's placement is flexible, where it appears most often in the introduction but sometimes as treaty closure. A closing date notice is also unique.

Third, many of the primary constituents of the Middle Babylonian and Hittite-language treaty traditions appear in other paradigms. In addition to the features already noted, the general-comprehensive paradigms employ standardized stipulatory language, a feature likely reflected in the Sefire materials (if they are not versions of the same parent document). Similarly, benedictions appear in the conclusion of the general-comprehensive traditions, also reflected by the Sefire tradition, though the feature appears in an earlier position within the latter (and in a single Hittite document: *CTH* 137, text 2). Benediction is essentially confined to these treaty traditions (excluding single witnesses such as the Narām-Sîn treaty). The Hittite-language general-comprehensive paradigm embeds historiographic discourse as support material in its stipulatory section, a device also employed in the Sefire material. Likewise, an oath clause appears before the concluding maledictions and benedictions of both traditions. Features unique to the Middle Babylonian and Hittite-language general-comprehensive traditions include the following: a historiographic introduction presenting the contracting partner's past relationship, explicit procedural treaty stipulation (though the Ebla tradition and some single texts employ procedural discourse for economic and gift purposes), an embedded explanatory document deposit clause, a juridical reading clause providing closure for the stipulatory section, and bracketing of the oath-deities. The Hittite-language general-comprehensive tradition also employs indictment and explanatory discourse as stipulatory support, and additional malediction aimed at an impersonal third party in its conclusion (aimed toward protecting the rights of all treaty partners). A feature unique to the Middle Babylonian parity tradition is a historiographic document content clause as an element of the title, whereas its Hittite-language counterpart employs the same as treaty aperture. The former also appears with a subordinate document content clause that is reflected in the Sefire material and the SAA 2.6-T exemplar.

Fourth, virtually all the primary constituents of the Sefire treaty tradition appear in earlier paradigms. In addition to the items already noted, this tradition appears with a ritual maledictory form employing "Just as (this) X, [may . . .]" (*ʾyk zy* X (*znh*) [+ volitional form]), a formula also appearing in the Neo-Assyrian tradition: "Just as (this) X, [may . . .]" (*kī ša* X (*anniu*) [+ volitional form]). The ritual curse also appears in an earlier Middle Babylonian text (*CTH* 52.I) and in much earlier antecedents. Likewise, the Sefire tradition possesses a futility curse form that also appears in an Old Babylonian treaty (L.T.-3) and in non-treaty Sumerian and Old Aramaic texts. A feature unique to the Sefire tradition is the explanatory summary regarding treaty relations, although the element appears in the R2-H3/H3-R2 pair and the SAA 2.6-T exemplar.

Fifth, all of the primary constituents of the Neo-Assyrian treaty tradition appear in the summarized paradigms. A few specific elements are unique to the tradition, the most important of which is the "You/If you . . ." (*šumma attunu*) as paragraph aperture in stipulatory and maledictory sections. Lastly, as in the Eblaite tradition, historiographic discourse does not appear in the Neo-Assyrian tradition, though it appears as projected speech in SAA 2.6-T. Because historiographic discourse appears in some significant capacity within the other five ancient Near Eastern treaty traditions, and in light of the Eblaite tradition as the earliest potential antecedent, its absence is conspicuous in the Neo-Assyrian material as the chronologically final tradition (assuming that this tradition had some awareness of other traditions).

These points demonstrate, at least in part, the complexity of the various ancient Near Eastern treaty traditions that can be identified through the extant data. They also reveal the depth and breadth of the conceptualization and utilization of "treaty" throughout the ancient Near Eastern world. In contrast, the data also establish a surprising simplicity and lack of originality in the Neo-Assyrian treaty tradition when compared with its predecessors, including the contemporaneous though more sophisticated Old Aramaic treaty tradition.

How Do These Traditions Relate to Deuteronomy?

The goal of our investigation has been a discourse analysis of ancient Near Eastern treaty texts and their respective traditions. When one compares these traditions to the discourse constellations of Deuteronomy,[72] a complex picture emerges. Deuteronomy does indeed share discourse features that characterize the observed treaty traditions. Nevertheless, a significant number of discourse elements are unique to Deuteronomy, such as the narratorial voice and predictive, instructional, and epitaphic discourse, among other discourse features. The following observations summarize how these ancient Near Eastern treaty traditions compare and contrast with Deuteronomy on both formal and functional grounds.

First, for the sake of argument, let us set aside the more salient narratorial elements. Distinguishing the voice of the narrator from the remaining voices in Deuteronomy is vital in the comparative enterprise,

---

[72] A discourse analysis of Deuteronomy lies beyond the purview of this brief essay, and is indeed worthy of a book-length project. For an inaugural investigation that reflects the method employed for observing these ancient Near Eastern treaty traditions as applied to Deuteronomy, see chapter four of my dissertation, "Deuteronomy as *Mischgattung*."

because this voice stands apart in its narratorial time from its narrated time. That is, the voices of Moses and YHWH are the primary vehicles for carrying the treaty analogue forward, rather than the voice of the narrator. For example, this distinction is significant in the opening lines of Deuteronomy (1:1–5). While they are traditionally viewed as analogous to a treaty title and preamble (e.g., *TLCANE*), they are in fact the words of the narrator, and are therefore beyond the narrated time of Moses: "These are the words that Moses spoke to all Israel beyond the Jordan. . . . Moses began to explain this *Tôrâ*, saying . . ." (אֵלֶּה הַדְּבָרִים אֲשֶׁר דִּבֶּר מֹשֶׁה אֶל־כָּל־יִשְׂרָאֵל בְּעֵבֶר הַיַּרְדֵּן . . . הוֹאִיל מֹשֶׁה בֵּאֵר אֶת־הַתּוֹרָה הַזֹּאת לֵאמֹר; 1:1–5). When one sets aside the voice of the narrator, then Deuteronomy lacks features common to treaty introductions, such as the explanatory title (cf. the Eblaite, Middle Babylonian, Old Aramaic, and Neo-Assyrian traditions) or the document content clause (cf. the Middle Babylonian, Hittite, Old Aramaic, and Neo-Assyrian traditions). It should therefore be viewed as remarkable that generically the narrator appears to apply a semblance of these features in the opening lines of Deuteronomy, at least from the perspective of interpreters who apply the treaty analogue here.

Second, several interdiscourse elements reflected throughout the treaty corpora appear among the remaining voices of Deuteronomy. Similarities to the Eblaite tradition are limited to a juridical tribute clause and procedural texts that focus solely on economics (see Deut 14:22–29). Similarities to the Neo-Assyrian tradition are also limited, pertaining only to the maledictory content and the non-human witnesses common to most traditions (but without a deified heavens and earth; personified in Deuteronomy—see 4:26; 30:19; 31:28). The Old Babylonian and Old Assyrian traditions share both features in addition to non-abrogation language, and L.T.-3 employs futility curses topically similar to those in Deuteronomy (28:30–31, 38–41). The Sefire material shares more features with Deuteronomy, including the use of historiographic discourse as stipulatory support material (e.g., Deut 23:6; cf. 26:5–9), the invocation of a deified heaven and earth, the use of parallel benediction and malediction (see Deut 28:3–6 || 16–19), and the presence of the futility curse. The Middle Babylonian general tradition shares even more features, including the historiographic introduction (e.g., Deut 1:6–3:29; cf. 5:1–33; 9:1–11:32; etc.), the present-procedural tribute clause, the reading and deposition clauses (see Deut 31:10–13, 26), the invocation of a deified heaven and earth, and parallel benedictory and maledictory discourse. The Hittite general treaty tradition is closer still, incorporating all the aforementioned Middle Babylonian features in addition to the use of historiographic and indictment discourse for stipulatory support (cf. Deut 32:1–38). Similarly, Deuteronomy's use of promissory discourse to reflect benefit and detriment is reflected in BrTf (cf. the Hittite tradition). Hence, at a discourse level the bulk of Deuteronomy most closely resembles the interdiscourse modeling of the Middle Babylonian and Hittite treaty traditions, and it least resembles those of the Eblaite and Neo-Assyrian traditions. Nevertheless, Deuteronomy transforms these interdiscourse relationships in significant ways, including their literary form, relative positioning and order, and internal functions (see below). If one interprets Deuteronomy as a subversive document aimed at the Assyrian state, it is truly remarkable that it reflects so little of the Neo-Assyrian treaty tradition, and those features that it does reflect represent common fare among significantly older traditions.

Third, absent from Deuteronomy are the following treaty elements: an introductory performative declaration (such as כֹּה־אָמַר יְהוָה, "thus says YHWH," a collocation not present in Deuteronomy), a declaratory summary of Israel's compliance to an oath procedure (but cf. Josh 8:30–35), a declaratory oath clause placing the document contents officially on record (but see Exod 34:27),[73] a geographic summary explicitly outlining Israel's (potential) holdings (but cf. Num 34:2–12), ritual curses (but cf. Gen 15:10, 17, with Jer 34:18–19), and official human oath-witnesses (but see Josh 24:22). According to Dennis McCarthy, Deuteronomy represents the most exemplary Old Testament book for observing the treaty analogue.[74] The absence of these interdiscourse elements in Deuteronomy is therefore surprising, for they do appear in other treaty-related contexts within the Hebrew Bible.

Fourth, while the treaty elements contained within Deuteronomy reflect some of the functions of their ancient Near Eastern counterparts, they are executed in an entirely unique way. For example, securing some level of economic control is a dominant feature throughout the ancient Near Eastern treaty corpora. While Deuteronomy contains tribute clauses, its focus is communal. The procedures and injunctions for gifting cult and

---

[73] It is tempting to interpret the reading clause (Deut 31:10–13) or the deposit clause (Deut 31:26) of Deuteronomy as presenting it as an official document in a way similar to how the declaratory oath clauses function in the Old Babylonian and Sefire traditions (e.g., L.T.-1 i 19–25; Sf 1 A 7–13). However, neither of these sections appears with oath-based language in Deuteronomy. That is, they do not appear with adjuratory discourse. The reading clause is descriptively introduced by the narrator, using historiographic discourse (31:9–10a), and the clause itself is an exhortation (hortatory discourse). The deposit clause is similarly introduced by the narrator (31:24–25), and the clause itself is an instructional text (a discourse type entirely absent from our ancient Near Eastern treaty corpora). The closest Deuteronomic approximation to the declaratory oath clause is the attributive relative materials that reflect the ubiquitous formula "which X swore to your ancestors" (Deut 1:8, 35; 4:31; 7:8; etc.). However, these are all offline clauses, and each refers to a prior oath rather than the current document.

[74] McCarthy, *Treaty and Covenant*, 157–59.

community are motivated first by thanksgiving for YHWH's provision, and second by a concern for those with genuine needs. Additionally, the analogous gifting sections in Deuteronomy are aimed directly at the community rather than a body politic, and trade is of no concern whatsoever. The economic growth of the state is not a concern of the deuteronomic paradigm. It is quite the opposite. YHWH ironically promises to provide for his people, rather than demanding that they provide for him. What is more, the promised provision is conditioned on covenant faithfulness, which in part requires the community to look to the material necessities of its needy members. Indeed, Israel's future kings are prohibited from amassing wealth (Deut 17:17), a stipulation consistent with the communal concerns of the book. Similar contrasts apply to all other functional purposes shared between Deuteronomy and the treaty traditions. Neither the apotropaic nor quasi-deified characteristics evident in certain treaty documents (e.g., the Old Babylonian treaty tradition, SAA 2.6-T, etc.) have any direct bearing in Deuteronomy, nor do the functions of procuring and fortifying political hegemony[75] or of securing dynastic succession.

In sum, Deuteronomy transforms all formal and functional discourse elements that are also reflected among the seven observed treaty traditions. Indeed, the level of this transformation places Deuteronomy firmly beyond simple one-to-one associations with a specific treaty tradition or a specific treaty document. Similarly, Deuteronomy evinces a significant number of unique formal discourse features and functional purposes not present among the analogues. Notable among these are its overarching prophetic function, marked by hortatory and predictive discourse and presented by the all-pervasive voice of Moses, and its program of generational cultural transformation through the ever-present illocutionary "today."

* * * * *

[75] All ancient Near Eastern treaties were explicitly designed to exert political control over one or both of the respective treaty partners, whether they were subordinates or putative equals. Political machination was (and still is) part and parcel of the treaty-making process. Deuteronomy, however, legislates the opposite. Its *ḥērem* laws, cultic and dietary regulations, and prohibitions for future kings all spring from an ideology that ideally leaves little room for brokering treaties with other nations, and none at all for those considered "Canaanite." That is, rather than functioning as a mechanism of political control over another body politic, Deuteronomy provides the foundation for an entirely unique relationship between YHWH and his people. Many benefits are promised to a faithful Israel, including the blessing that "YHWH will make you the head and not the tail, and you will only go up and not down" (וּנְתָנְךָ יְהוָה לְרֹאשׁ וְלֹא לְזָנָב וְהָיִיתָ רַק לְמַעְלָה וְלֹא תִהְיֶה לְמָטָּה; Deut 28:13a). The political implications of this benediction are clear. Nevertheless, it is a promised result of covenant faithfulness to YHWH, rather than the driving function or purpose of Deuteronomy as a document.

The following table represents all treaty-related documents underlying the study above. It is arranged essentially in chronological order (by date or century BCE), but also by language and document type (genre). "K" (Kitchen and Lawrence) represents *TLCANE* numbers for each treaty; italicized *TLCANE* numbers indicate that the corresponding treaty appears there in English translation only. Select texts that are not actual treaties are marked by an initial asterisk (e.g., *Stela of Vultures, K *1) and are only included here because of the attention *TLCANE* devotes to them. An em-dash ("—") marks treaties that do not appear in *TLCANE*. The first column numbers each document, where parenthetic numbering marks non-treaty texts. Known parity and subordination treaties are labeled (P) and (S) respectively in the genre column. Select languages are abbreviated as follows: Old Aramaic (OAram.), Old Assyrian (OA), Old Babylonian (OB), Middle Assyrian (MA), Middle Babylonian (MB), Neo-Assyrian (NA), and Neo-Babylonian (NB).

Table 2. Ancient Near Eastern Treaty-Related Documents

	Text	*Description*	*Genre*	*Find Spot*	*Language*	*BCE*	*K*
		Third Millennium					
(1)	*Stela of Vultures	Stela referencing a treaty between Eanatum of Lagash and an unnamed ruler of Umma	Victory Stela	Girsu	Sumerian	25th	*1
1.	ARET 13:5	A ruler of Ebla and a ruler of Abarsal	Treaty (S)	T. Mardiḫ	Eblaite	23rd	2
2.	ARET 13:6	A treaty excerpt between a ruler of Ebla and Yinḫar-Ḫalab of Burman	Treaty (S)	T. Mardiḫ	Eblaite	23rd	5
3.	ARET 13:20	A ruler of Ebla and a ruler of Martu	Treaty (S)	T. Mardiḫ	Eblaite	23rd	6
4.	ARET 13:21	A ruler of Ebla and a ruler of Dulu	Treaty (S)	T. Mardiḫ	Eblaite	23rd	4
(2)	*ARET 13:10	Letter referencing a treaty between a ruler of Mari and Ḥenna-Damu of Manuwat	Letter	T. Mardiḫ	Eblaite	23rd	*3
(3)	*ARET 13:18	School exercise with clauses from a treaty between a ruler of Ebla and a ruler of Armi	School Exercise	T. Mardiḫ	Eblaite	23rd	*7
5.	Sb 8833	Narām-Sîn of Akkad and an Elamite ruler of Awan	Treaty (P)	Susa	Elamite	23rd	8
		Second Millennium					
6.	Kt.00/k 6	Assyrian merchants and a ruler of Kaneš	Treaty (P)	Kültepe	OA	19th	16
7.	Kt.00/k 10	Assyrian merchants and a ruler of Ḫaḫḫum	Treaty (P)	Kültepe	OA	19th	17
(4)	*Kt. n/k 794	Letter referencing a treaty between Assyrian merchants and an unnamed ruler of an unnamed city	Letter	Kültepe	OA	19th	*15

	Text	Description	Genre	Find Spot	Language	BCE	K
8.	*CUNES* 49-04-176	Sîn-iddinam of Larsa and Sîn-kāšid of Uruk with Ibâl-pī-El I of Ešnunna (Guichard 2014:26–27)	Treaty	Larsa? Ešnunna?	OB	1844/1843	—
9.	L.T.-1	Treaty between Qarni-Lim of Andarig and Ḫāya-abum of Apum with an unknown ruler of Sûmum	Treaty (S)	T. Leilan (Šeḫnā/Šubat-Enlil)	OB	mid-18th	—
10.	L.T.-2	Mutiya of Apum and Ḫazip-Teššub of Razamā	Treaty	T. Leilan	OB	mid-18th	—
11.	L.T.-3	Till-Abnû of Apum and Yamṣi-Ḫatnû of Kaḫat	Treaty	T. Leilan	OB	mid-18th	—
12.	L.T.-4	Till-Abnû of Apum and Yamṣi-Ḫatnû of Kaḫat (?)	Treaty	T. Leilan	OB	mid-18th	—
13.	L.T.-5	Till-Abnû of Apum and Assyrian merchants	Treaty (P)	T. Leilan	OB	mid-18th	24
14.	M.6435 + M.8987	Zimrī-Lîm of Mari and Ḫammurapi of Babylon	Treaty (P)	Mari	OB	mid-18th	21
15.	A.361	Zimrī-Lîm of Mari and Ibâl-pī-El II of Ešnunna	Treaty (P)	Mari	OB	mid-18th	20
16.	A.96	Zimrī-Lîm of Mari and Atamrum of Andarig	Treaty (S)	Mari	OB	mid-18th	22
17.	M.7750	Fragment of a treaty between Zimrī-Lîm of Mari and an unknown ruler of Kurda	Treaty	Mari	OB	mid-18th	23
18.	Diyala no. 326	The city-states of Šadlaš and Nērebtum	Treaty	Ishchali	OB	mid-18th	18
19.	W 19900,147	Fragment of treaty between Ilumgāmil of Uruk and an unknown ruler	Treaty	Uruk	OB	mid-18th	19
20.	AT *456	Abba-AN of Yamḫad (Aleppo) and Yarīm-Lîm of Alalaḫ	Treaty (S)	Alalaḫ	OB	mid-18th	29
21.	AT 2	Niqmepa of Alalaḫ and Ir-Adad/Teššub of Tunip	Treaty (P)	Alalaḫ	MB	15th	42

	Text	Description	Genre	Find Spot	Language	BCE	K
22.	AT 3	Idrimi of Alalaḫ and Pilliya of Kizzuwatna	Treaty (P)	Alalaḫ	MB	15th	41
23.	*CTH* 26	Fragmentary treaty between a king of Ḫatti and Paddatiššu of Kizzuwatna	Treaty (P)	Boğazköy	MB	15th	39
24.	*CTH* 41.I	Fragmentary treaty between Tudḫaliya II or Šuppiluliuma I of Ḫatti and Šunaššura II (?) of Kizzuwatna	Treaty (P)	Boğazköy	MB	early 14th	51
25.	*CTH* 135	Fragmentary treaty between Tudḫaliya II/Šuppiluliuma I with Labʾu and Tunip	Treaty	Boğazköy	MB	early 14th	52
26.	RS 19.68	Niqmadu II of Ugarit and Aziru of Amurru	Treaty (P)	Ras Shamra	MB	14th	—
27.	*CTH* 46	Šuppiluliuma I of Ḫatti and Niqmadu II of Ugarit	Treaty (S)	Ras Shamra	MB	14th	61
28.	*CTH* 49.I	Šuppiluliuma I of Ḫatti and Aziru of Amurru (cf. *CTH* 49.II)	Treaty (S)	Boğazköy	MB	14th	58A
29.	*CTH* 51.I	Šuppiluliuma I of Ḫatti and Šattiwazza of Mitanni (cf. *CTH* 51.II)	Treaty (S)	Boğazköy	MB	14th	55A
30.	*CTH* 52.I	Šattiwazza of Mitanni and Šuppiluliuma I of Ḫatti (cf. *CTH* 52.II)	Treaty (S)	Boğazköy	MB	14th	56A
31.	*CTH* 53	Šuppiluliuma I of Ḫatti and Tette of Nuḫašše	Treaty (S)	Boğazköy	MB	14th	57
32.	*CTH* 62.I	Fragmentary treaty between Muršili II of Ḫatti and Tuppi-Teššub of Amurru (cf. *CTH* 62.II)	Treaty (S)	Boğazköy	MB	14th	62A
33.	*CTH* 66	Muršili II of Ḫatti and Niqmepa of Ugarit	Treaty (S)	Ras Shamra	MB	14th	63
34.	*CTH* 75	Muwatalli II of Ḫatti and Talmi-Šarrumma of Aleppo (a copy of an earlier treaty between Muršili II and Talmi-Šarrumma, lost and then reformulated by Muwatalli II)	Treaty (S)	Boğazköy	MB	$14^{th}/13^{th}$	67
35.	RS 17.146	The people of Karkamiš (Ini-Tešub) and the people of Ugarit	Treaty (P)	Ras Shamra	MB	13th	—
36.	RS 17.230	The people of Karkamiš (Ini-Tešub) and the people of Ugarit	Treaty (P)	Ras Shamra	MB	13th	—

	Text	*Description*	*Genre*	*Find Spot*	*Language*	*BCE*	*K*
37.	RS 18.115	The people of Karkamiš (Ini-Tešub) and the people of Ugarit	Treaty (P)	Ras Shamra	MB	13th	—
38.	RS 18.19	A citizen of Ugarit (Ini-Tešub) and a citizen of Karkamiš	Treaty (P)	Ras Shamra	MB	13th	—
39.	*CTH* 92	Ḫattušili III of Ḫatti and Bentešina of Amurru	Treaty (S)	Boğazköy	MB	13th	69
40.	*CTH* 91 (R2-H3)	Ramesses II of Egypt and Ḫattušili III of Ḫatti (primary voice: Ramesses)	Treaty (P)	Boğazköy	MB	1259	71A
41.	Edel 1997 (H3-R2)	Ḫattušili III of Ḫatti and Ramesses II of Egypt (primary voice: Ḫattušili)	Treaty (P)	Ramesseum, Karnak	Egyptian	1259	71B
42.	*KTU* 3.1	Šuppiluliuma II of Ḫatti and Niqmadu III of Ugarit	Treaty (S)	Ras Shamra	Ugaritic	late 13th	77
(5)	*BM 121033 (Machinist 1978)	Epic of Tukulti-Ninurta I—part of a “treaty indictment ceremony” referencing a treaty between Tukulti-Ninurta I of Assyria and Kaštiliaš IV of Babylonia	Indictment Prayer	Nineveh	MA	late 13th	*75
43.	*CTH* 25	Zidanta II of Ḫatti and Pilliya of Kizzuwatna	Treaty (P)	Boğazköy	Hittite	15th	40
44.	*CTH* 134	Tudḫaliya I (?) of Ḫatti and Amenophis II (?) of Egypt	Treaty (P)	Boğazköy	Hittite	late 15th	—
45.	*CTH* 138.1	An unknown ruler of Ḫatti and the Kaška people	Treaty (S)	Boğazköy	Hittite	late 15th	*46.1*
46.	*CTH* 138.2	An unknown ruler of Ḫatti and the Kaška people	Treaty (S)	Boğazköy	Hittite	late 15th	*46.2*
47.	*CTH* 138.3	An unknown ruler of Ḫatti and the Kaška people	Treaty (S)	Boğazköy	Hittite	late 15th	*48*
48.	*CTH* 139	An unknown ruler of Ḫatti and the Kaška people	Treaty (S)	Boğazköy	Hittite	late 15th	*47*
49.	*CTH* 41.II+131	Tudḫaliya II (?) of Ḫatti and Šunaššura I (?) of Kizzuwatna (cf. *CTH* 41.I)	Treaty (P)	Boğazköy	Hittite	early 14th	50
50.	*CTH* 42	Šuppiluliuma I of Ḫatti and Ḫuqqana of Ḫayasa	Treaty (S)	Boğazköy	Hittite	14th	60

	Text	Description	Genre	Find Spot	Language	BCE	K
51.	*CTH* 49.II	Šuppiluliuma I of Ḫatti and Aziru of Amurru (cf. *CTH* 49.I)	Treaty (S)	Boğazköy	Hittite	14th	58B
52.	*CTH* 51.II	Šuppiluliuma I of Ḫatti and Šattiwazza of Mitanni (cf. *CTH* 51.I)	Treaty (S)	Boğazköy	Hittite	14th	55B
53.	Oy. 12-401	Šuppiluliuma I (?) of Ḫatti and an unknown ruler of Oylum Höyük	Treaty (S)	Oylum Höyük	Hittite	14th	—
54.	*CTH* 52.II	Šattiwazza of Mitanni and Šuppiluliuma I of Ḫatti (cf. *CTH* 52.I)	Treaty (S)	Boğazköy	Hittite	14th	56B
55.	*CTH* 62.II	Muršili II of Ḫatti and Tuppi-Teššub of Amurru (cf. *CTH* 62.I)	Treaty (S)	Boğazköy	Hittite	14th	62B
56.	*CTH* 67	Muršili II of Ḫatti and Targasnalli of Ḫapalla	Treaty (S)	Boğazköy	Hittite	14th	64
57.	*CTH* 68	Muršili II of Ḫatti and Manapa-Kurunta of Mira-Kuwaliya	Treaty (S)	Boğazköy	Hittite	14th	65
58.	*CTH* 69	Muršili II of Ḫatti and Manapa-Tarḫunta of the Šeḫa River land	Treaty (S)	Boğazköy	Hittite	14th	66
59.	*CTH* 133	Arnuwanda I of Ḫatti and the Men of Išmerika	Treaty	Boğazköy	Hittite	14th	53
60.	*CTH* 137	Arnuwanda I (?) of Ḫatti and the Kaška People	Treaty	Boğazköy	Hittite	14th	54
61.	*CTH* 146	The indictment of Mita of Paḫḫuwa and a treaty of Arnuwanda I/ Tudḫaliya III with the elders of several Anatolian communities	Treaty	Boğazköy	Hittite	14th	—
62.	*CTH* 76	Muwatalli II of Ḫatti and Alakšandu of Wiluša	Treaty (S)	Boğazköy	Hittite	13th	68
63.	*CTH* 89	Ḫattušili III of Ḫatti and the town Tiliura	Treaty	Boğazköy	Hittite	mid-13th	*70*
64.	*CTH* 105	Tudḫaliya IV of Ḫatti and Šaušgamuwa of Amurru	Treaty (S)	Boğazköy	Hittite	late 13th	72
65.	*CTH* 141	Tudḫaliya IV or Šuppiluliuma II of Ḫatti and the rulers of Alašiya	Treaty	Boğazköy	Hittite	late 13th	80
66.	BrTf (Otten 1988)	Tudḫaliya IV of Ḫatti and Kurunta of Tarḫuntašša	Treaty (S)	Boğazköy	Hittite	1230	73
67.	*CTH* 106	Tudḫaliya IV (?) of Ḫatti and Ulmi-Teššub of Tarḫuntašša	Treaty (S)	Boğazköy	Hittite	1210	74

	Text	*Description*	*Genre*	*Find Spot*	*Language*	*BCE*	*K*
		First Millennium					
68.	SAA 2.1	Šamšī-Adad V of Assyria and Marduk-zākir-šumi I of Babylon	Treaty (P)	Nineveh	NB	824	89
69.	SAA 2.2	Aššur-nērārī V of Assyria and Matīᵓēl of Arpad	Treaty (S)	Nineveh	NA	754	90
70.	Sf 1	Bar-Gȧyah of KTK and Matīᵓēl of Arpad (1)	Treaty	Sefire?	OAram.	ca. 750	87
71.	Sf 2	Bar-Gȧyah of KTK and Matīᵓēl of Arpad (2)	Treaty	Sefire?	OAram.	ca. 750	88
72.	Sf 3	Bar-Gȧyah of KTK and Matīᵓēl (?) of Arpad (3)	Treaty	Sefire?	OAram.	ca. 750	86
73.	SAA 2.3	Fragmentary treaty between Sennacherib of Assyria and an unknown ruler of an unknown polity	Succession Treaty	Assur	NA	683	91
74.	SAA 2.4	Fragmentary treaty between Esarhaddon of Assyria—accession oaths	Accession Treaty	Nineveh	NA	681	92
75.	SAA 2.5	Esarhaddon of Assyria and Baal of Tyre	Treaty (S)	Nineveh	NA	676	93
76.	SAA 2.6-T	Esarhaddon of Assyria and various officials	Succession Treaty	Nimrud; Assur; Tayinat	NA	672	94
(6)	*SAA 2.7	Fragmentary oath by Esarhaddon of Assyria—a loyalty oath reflecting NA treaty elements	Loyalty Oath	Nineveh	NA	670	*95
77.	SAA 2.8	Queen Zakutu of Assyria and Šamaš-šumu-ukin and all Assyria—accession treaty for Assurbanipal	Accession Treaty	Nineveh	NA	669	96
78.	SAA 2.9	Assurbanipal of Assyria and Babylonian allies	Loyalty Oath; Treaty? (S)	Nineveh	NB	652	98
79.	SAA 2.10	Assurbanipal of Assyria and the Arab Qedar tribe	Treaty (S)	Nineveh	NA	652	97

	Text	Description	Genre	Find Spot	Language	BCE	K
80.	SAA 2.13	Fragmentary treaty between an unknown ruler of Assyria and an unknown Arab (?) treaty partner	Treaty (S)	Nineveh	NA	ca. 650	101
81.	SAA 2.11	Fragmentary treaty between Sîn-šarru-iškun of Assyria and Babylonian allies (?)	Treaty (S)	Nineveh?	NA	627–612	99
82.	SAA 2.12	Extract of a treaty between Sîn-šarru-iškun of Assyria and an unknown treaty partner	Treaty (S)	Assur	NA	627–613	100

CHAPTER 3

Challenges to the Use of Ancient Near Eastern Treaty Forms for Dating and Interpreting Deuteronomy

K. Lawson Younger Jr. and Neal A. Huddleston

Introduction

It is abundantly clear to everyone who reads ancient Near Eastern treaties that this genre was utilized in the composition of the book of Deuteronomy. It is also clear from a perusal of the secondary literature in Biblical Studies that most efforts in studying the ancient Near Eastern treaties have focused on their value in dating the composition of Deuteronomy (usually following either Hittite or Neo-Assyrian analogues). Yet an objective study of all the data involves examination of a tremendous amount of material from the ancient Near East. The massive achievement of the 2012 work of Kenneth A. Kitchen and Paul Lawrence, *Treaty, Law and Covenant in the Ancient Near East* (hereafter *TLCANE*), illustrates the huge scope of such a task.[1] This task is further compounded by the fact that the corpus of materials is continuing to expand; Kitchen and Lawrence have not included recently discovered and published treaties that must be added to the discussion.[2]

---

[1] Kenneth A. Kitchen and Paul J. N. Lawrence, *Treaty, Law and Covenant in the Ancient Near East* (Wiesbaden: Harrassowitz, 2012). For an outstanding general survey of treaty and covenant in the Hebrew Bible, see Samuel Greengus, "Covenant and Treaty in the Hebrew Bible and in the Ancient Near East," in *Ancient Israel's History: An Introduction to Issues and Sources*, ed. Bill T. Arnold and Richard S. Hess (Grand Rapids: Baker Academic, 2014), 91–126.

[2] Examples include several Old Babylonian treaties from Tell Leilan, on which see Jesper Eidem, *The Royal Archives from Tell Leilan: Old Babylonian Letters and Treaties from the Lower Town Palace East*, PIHANS 117 (Leiden: Nederlands Instituut voor het Nabije Oosten, 2011). See also the important new Neo-Assyrian manuscript in Jacob Lauinger, "Esarhaddon's Succession Treaty at Tell Tayinat: Text and Commentary," *JCS* 64 (2012): 87–123.

Even though treaties were utilized throughout ancient Near Eastern history for over three millennia, we have only around one hundred treaties to study (not counting the biblical data).[3] Yet the amount of literature devoted to this topic—whether oriented to the ancient Near Eastern or the biblical data—can be daunting.

The purpose of this essay is straightforward: to point out and discuss three fundamental challenges facing scholars as they engage this material, in each case with accompanying methodological concerns. The essay will highlight difficulties with some works that have been dependent on particular assumptions. In a separate essay included in this volume, Neal Huddleston offers a fresh perspective regarding ancient Near Eastern treaty traditions and their relationship to Deuteronomy, as demonstrated from a discourse analysis of these materials.[4] In a sense, both articles serve as an up-to-date status report. We believe this is important in and of itself, regardless of what one does with Deuteronomy (a composition that is more than just an ancient Near Eastern treaty, in any case). Such an analysis yields positive results in the comparative enterprise, for the thorough study of the larger treaty corpus provides more cautious and sustainable conclusions, which reflect these texts in their own right.

Challenge 1: Kitchen Issues—Can the Generic Connections Be Traced?

How do we explain similarities between treaties from different languages and cultures? Is there a type of "genealogical tree" for treaties in the ancient Near East? Kitchen and Lawrence seem to have such an understanding, seeing developments and interconnections throughout the three millennia of extant treaties included in their work. This leads them to posit interconnections that are highly speculative.[5]

In their discussion of the Hittite treaty network (1380–1180 BCE), Kitchen and Lawrence (*TLCANE* 3:250) argue that during this period:

---

[3] For a full list, see the table "Ancient Near Eastern Treaty–Related Documents" in the Huddleston essay in this volume.

[4] For fuller discussion regarding many of the points raised in both essays, see Neal A. Huddleston, "Deuteronomy as *Mischgattung:* A Comparative and Contrastive Discourse Analysis of Deuteronomy and Ancient Near Eastern Treaty Traditions" (PhD diss., Trinity International University, 2015).

[5] This criticism is not meant to detract from their very substantial work, but to highlight a basic assumption that can be found among many studies on ancient Near Eastern treaties and Deuteronomy.

> . . . untidily at first, historical prologues, witness-deities, blessings alongside curses and explicit oath and ceremony reappear. It is likely that renewed contacts with Babylon (in opposition to Mitanni) and its long cuneiform heritage of law and treaty brought the knowledge of Kassite treaty-usage (revised by incorporation of features from law-collections' usage as exemplified by Hammurabi) to the Hittite court, along with so much other Babylonian cuneiform lore; cf. pp. 101–102, in Chapter 5 above.

Kitchen and Lawrence (*TLCANE* 3:101–2) state that *one document* single-handedly attests to this: "the Epic of Tukulti-Ninurta I of Assyria (c. 1244–1207 BC)." Table 1 presents the organizational headings for the relevant excerpt exactly as it appears in Kitchen and Lawrence (*TLCANE* 1:645), as well as its accompanying "chromogram" labels (*TLCANE* 2:253, 262).[6] The translation of the excerpt is ours, and incorporates *TLCANE*'s headings for explanatory purposes.

1 Initial Address

Col. ii. (13) O Šamaš, lord of [judg]ment, I have observed your oath,
I feared your greatness.
(14) The one who does not [. . .] transgressed before your [divinity(?)],
(but) I observed your verdict.

2 Prologue

(15) When our fathers made a treaty before your divinity,
(16) (and) confirmed an oath between them,
they invoked your greatness.

5 Witness

(17) The one who from former times was the irreversible judge of our fathers,
You are the hero;
(18) and the one who sees now our loyalty,
You are the god who makes (things) right.

6c Curse

(19) Why has the king of the Kassites cancelled your plan and verdict from former times?
(20) He did not fear your oath;
he transgressed your regulations;

[6] For the primary edition, with commentary, on the section concerned, see Peter Machinist, "The Epic of Tukulti-Ninurta I: A Study in Middle Assyrian Literature" (PhD diss., Yale University, 1978). See also Benjamin R. Foster, *Before the Muses: An Anthology of Akkadian Literature*, 3rd ed. (Bethesda, MD: CDL, 2005), 298–317.

he plotted malice;
(21) he has made his sacrilege great before you,
Judge me, O Šamaš!

6b Blessing on Obedient Party

(22) (But) [as for] the one who did not commit sacrilege [against] the king of the Kassites,
[act favorably toward him].

11 Sanctions

(23) By your great [. . .] bestow the total victory on the observer of oaths,
(24) [The one who does not do] your regulations destroy his people in the decisive defeat of battle!

Table 1. TLCANE no. 75 Indictment Prayer Organization from the Epic of Tukulti-Ninurta

Lines	*Numerical Key*	*Text Headings*	*Chromogram Labels*
13′–14′	1	Initial Address	Title and/or Preamble
15′–16′	2	Prologue	Prologue
	3		Laws or Stipulations
17′–18′	5	Witness	Witnesses
19′–21′	6c	Curse	Curses
22′	6b	Blessing on Obedient Party	Blessings
23′–24′	11	Sanctions	Sanctions

A few comments on the text and *TLCANE*'s accompanying labels are in order. The text itself represents an "indictment prayer" functioning as one element within a "treaty indictment ceremony,"[7] the whole of which is embedded in a larger epic poem. In Table 1, Kitchen and Lawrence have treated this prayer as though it were a treaty, dividing it up into treaty components. Their number 2 is only a record that a treaty was made for the purposes of the indictment itself; it in no way alludes to a historical prologue within the treaty referred to. Nevertheless, they have inferred from this that the original treaty contained a historical prologue. But this is not evident. Kitchen and Lawrence (*TLCANE* 3:101) argue that

[7] Ibid., 217.

> from the passage concerned, it is directly possible to deduce the basic format of the document there alluded-to, in particular the antecedent history (as in a prologue, 2), the existence of stipulations (3) as these had been transgressed; possible deposition (4a) of the treaty with the deity before whom it had been sworn, and as witness (5); plus attendant curses (6c) invoked on Kashtiliash because of his transgression; and by contrast the claim for blessing (6b) because of his innocence by the Assyrian king. Sanctions (11) could then be called down upon the offender.

Furthermore, though they assert that "lines 13′–14′ serve as a preamble" (their 1; *TLCANE* 2:65), these lines are an explicit invocation of the deity Šamaš as divine judge. Lines 17′–18′ remind Šamaš of his duty to exercise justice and vindicate the wronged: "You are the hero, who since times past were the judge of our fathers, not changing (verdicts), And you are the god who now watches over our loyalty, setting (things) right" (Machinist's gloss).[8] The lines neither invoke the deity as a witness (Kitchen and Lawrence's 5), nor allude to such an invocation in the now-lost treaty, though Šamaš was likely present in such a list—this deity is well known for his role as divine judge, especially pertaining to the expectations incumbent on Mesopotamian royalty. That is, the Šamaš reference is too generic to suggest a witness list, not to mention the other deities that would be on such a list or its supposed position in the treaty.

Lines 19′–21′ contain the heart of the prayer, providing a series of specific indictments against the oath-breaker. While Kitchen and Lawrence label the section as a curse (their 6c), it contains no form of malediction or any allusion to such. However, malediction does explicitly conclude the prayer in lines 23′–24′ (their proposed 11). The indictment prayer refers to a broken treaty in only general terms and in no way specifically reflects the constituent parts of the violated agreement. Its purpose resides in delivering formal charges against Kaštiliaš with supporting argumentation that Šamaš might prosecute justice. Regarding the general treaty references in the prayer, Machinist states that "no real history of the relations between Assyria and Babylonia is offered, nor are the treaty stipulations which Kaštiliaš is accused of violating actually spelled out."[9] Indeed, more specific details for the violated treaty occur elsewhere in the epic.[10] The elements within the prayer most closely approximating a treaty analogue are its two closing exhortations, perhaps reflecting an original blessing (line 22′) and curse (lines 23′–24′).

---

[8] Ibid., 77.

[9] Ibid., 217.

[10] Stipulations apparently included the keeping of state secrets (Aii 3), border arrangements (Aii 4; Aiii 2), and mutual non-aggression (Aiii 3–12). Malediction also closes the epic (Bvi 38–40).

In sum, the prayer is an indictment concluding with a brief exhortation. It reflects general themes from the now-lost treaty original but expresses no details beyond the closing exhortation. It is a plea for justice that provides a principal argument in support of the epic's larger purpose in justifying Assyria's war against Babylon.[11] The deities of both Assyria and Babylon are proponents in Assyria's hostile takeover, and their primary agent against Kaštiliaš is Tukulti-Ninurta himself. The bottom line is that the prayer refers only generally to a broken oath and does not reflect any sort of treaty tradition. Most importantly, there is no actual Kassite treaty! Kitchen and Lawrence's model imposes on this indictment prayer a hypothetical treaty tradition that is based on inference.

Their approach seems to be based on a conviction that there must be genealogical connections and that these must be explicated. From this, Kitchen and Lawrence speculate that, even though early-to-mid-second-millennium treaties do not use this overall formulation, "the hint of the ultimate origin" comes from Babylonia itself, specifically the law collections of Lipit-Ishtar and Hammurabi, which follow precisely this format with the exception of 5 divine witnesses, "which are never invoked in law texts" (*TLCANE* 3:101). Thus, Kitchen and Lawrence assume that these serve as precedents for a change to the format of treaties, which chronologically follow that of the major law collections (*TLCANE* 3:102). They further speculate:

> The Kassite regime that took over Babylon may thus be credited with this new departure; and so the reported treaties of Burnaburiash (I) with Puzur-Assur III of Assyria, and of Karaindash of Babylon with Assur-bel-nisheshu *could* possibly have taken the new Kassite usage in Mesopotamia that far back, during most of the 15th century BC,—to be used in Mesopotamia for the rest of the Kassite period (i.e., down to c. 1160 BC) (emphasis added).

Yet Kitchen and Lawrence must posit a genealogical connection with the Hittites. So they speculate that:

> It is possible that, at this time [the mid-fifteenth century, during the reign of Thutmose III], the Babylonians (and even the Assyrians) sent such embassies of alliance to Hatti as well as to Egypt, so as to encircle the Mitannian military menace politically;—and that the Mesopotamian model was then adopted in these cases. Thus, its basic features were built into Hittite treaty-making definitively not later than Suppiluliuma I after some initial experimentation under his immediate predecessors.

Their entire discussion is based on a questionable analysis of a prayer as if it contained a treaty format, which is followed by a series of speculations, all seemingly driven by an underlying assumption that there is some

[11] Machinist, "Epic of Tukulti-Ninurta," 43.

type of interconnection between all ancient Near Eastern treaties—one that results in a genealogical tree. Similar argumentation underlies their analysis of the Stela of Vultures (*TLCANE* no. 1) (which is clearly a victory memorial); a piece of Eblaite correspondence (ARET 13:10; *TLCANE* no. 3); an Eblaite exercise tablet (ARET 13:18; *TLCANE* no. 7); and an Old Assyrian letter (Kt. n/k 794; *TLCANE* no. 15).

Perhaps in the future, Kassite treaties will be discovered. If we had some exemplars, we might be able to argue for their influence on the Hittite treaty tradition. But at the present time, we do not possess such evidence, and we must refrain from speculation. At the end of the day, the assumption that there was some type of genealogical tree of ancient Near Eastern treaty interconnections must be rejected. We must resist the compulsion to explain the existence of similarities as *always* being the result of borrowing and/or influence. There were unquestionably interconnections throughout the ancient Near East, and, due to the conservative nature of ancient Near Eastern societies, some of these interconnections might have been long lived. However, we must be cautious where data are insufficient, and we must be willing to permit indigenous developments.[12]

Challenge 2: Dating Curses

Soon after the discovery and publication of the vassal treaties of Esarhaddon (VTE)—or better, Esarhaddon's Succession Treaties (EST)[13]—

[12] See Noel Weeks, *Admonition and Curse: The Ancient Near Eastern Treaty/Covenant Form as a Problem in Inter-Cultural Relationships* (London: T&T Clark, 2004). Weeks argues that treaty form is largely an inner-cultural development rising from primarily independent and internal development. Apparent similarities between treaty forms are explainable in psychological terms where humans find similar ways to deal with similar situations.

[13] For this terminology see Lauinger, "Esarhaddon's Succession Treaty." Since these functioned as loyalty oaths to the future king instead of the current monarch, Altman excludes the EST from his discussion of the Neo-Assyrian treaty tradition; see Amnon Altman, "How Many Treaty Traditions Existed in the Ancient Near East?" in *Pax Hethitica: Studies on the Hittites and Their Neighbours in Honour of Itamar Singer*, ed. Yoram Cohen, Amir Gilan, and Jared L. Miller, StBoT 51 (Wiesbaden: Harrassowitz, 2010), 29–30n71; Altman, *Tracing the Earliest Recorded Concepts of International Law: The Ancient Near East (2500–330 BCE)*, ed. Randall Lesaffer, Legal History Library 8/Studies in the History of International Law (Leiden: Martinus Nijhoff, 2012), 190. However, Parpola concludes that "alliance pact[s]" were a type of vassal treaty, and that they "did not differ formally from other treaty types and are therefore to be taken as political agreements" (Simo Parpola, "International Law in the First Millennium," in *A History of Ancient Near Eastern Law*, ed. Raymond Westbrook, HdO 1/72 [Leiden: Brill, 2003], 1054–59). He posits the EST was a fluid example that applies equally to both of these catego-

scholars such as Rintje Frankena[14] and Moshe Weinfeld[15] argued that the curses of Deut 28:26–33 were dependent on curses in the EST. That is, in their view the EST's curses were the Assyrian *Vorlage* for Deuteronomy. More recently, scholars have argued that not only are the curses modeled on the EST but that they also constitute a conscious polemic replacement of these oaths in an attempt to subvert the Neo-Assyrian empire. Some have argued that Deuteronomy copies directly from the EST's curses. In their view, this "*Ur-Deuteronomium*" is composed of Deut 6:4–5; 13; and 28. Currently, this is a very popular view.[16]

The foundational argument rests on the suggestion that the curses of Deut 28 are "borrowed" from the EST, and this, in turn, rests on the work of Moshe Weinfeld. In fact, scholars holding this view depend directly on the presumed validity of Weinfeld's ordering of the two maledictory sections in Deuteronomy and the EST.[17] Additionally, he presents the

---

ries, suggesting that the Assyrian emic perspective regarding such documents was not categorically stringent. All varieties are termed *adê* without distinction. Fales is undoubtedly correct in defining the EST "as a covenant of loyalty to the Assyrian Crown in view of the planned succession of Assurbanipal" applicable to both "Assyrian-ruled provinces and polities subjected to vassalage" (Frederick Mario Fales, "After Taʿyinat: The New Status of Esarhaddon's *adê* for Assyrian Political History," *RA* 106 [2012]: 147). Consequently, the EST are best treated as a collection of succession treaties for Esarhaddon's heir.

14 Rintje Frankena, "The Vassal-Treaties of Esarhaddon and the Dating of Deuteronomy," *OtSt* 14 (1965): 122–54.

15 Moshe Weinfeld, "Traces of Assyrian Treaty Formulae in Deuteronomy," *Bib* 46 (1965): 418–19; Weinfeld, *Deuteronomy and the Deuteronomic School* (Oxford: Clarendon, 1972; repr., Winona Lake, IN: Eisenbrauns, 1992), 117–22.

16 Space does not allow for a discussion of Deut 6 and 13. For evaluation of these passages, see Markus Zehnder, "Building on Stone? Deuteronomy and Esarhaddon's Loyalty Oaths (Part 1): Some Preliminary Observations," *BBR* 19 (2009): 341–74; Zehnder, "Building on Stone? Deuteronomy and Esarhaddon's Loyalty Oaths (Part 2): Some Preliminary Observations," *BBR* 19 (2009): 511–35; Carly L. Crouch, *Israel and the Assyrians: Deuteronomy, the Succession Treaty of Esarhaddon, and the Nature of Subversion*, ANEM 8 (Atlanta: SBL Press, 2014). Since the real substance of the argument depends on Deut 28, it is sufficient to deal only with this text. Our study complements Zehnder's and Crouch's studies, which also address Deut 28, and portions of our discussion below draw heavily from Crouch's work in particular.

17 Given the dependence of many contemporary scholars on Weinfeld's parallels, it is important to note that Weinfeld's argument is not polarized. That is, he argues for "both-and," in that he interprets Deuteronomy as containing a covenantal core that both reflects Hittite subordination treaty patterning and incorporates the Assyrian loyalty oath as expressed by Esarhaddon's text: "Deuteronomy is actually dependent on two models of covenant: the Hittite one and the Assyrian one. The Hittite model is old and seems to underlie the old biblical covenantal tradition. Deuteronomy shows connections with both sets of loyalty oaths: one of the second millennium and the other of the first millennium. The Hittite model pervaded

comparison in absolute categories: "In VTE [EST] 419–30 we encounter a series of imprecations identical with those of 28:26–35."[18] By "identical" he refers to topic and order,[19] for the wording is significantly different in each case. Therefore, it is imperative to perform a thorough contextual analysis to see how valid this assumption is.

To facilitate the analysis, the texts are placed in fuller parallel than they are in Weinfeld's selective presentation,[20] which is cast in bold here to highlight his argument. The division into "Sets" is based on Weinfeld's presentation. Although he does not number these, the order presented here is his, and their numbering facilitates analysis and discussion.

Since the argument is for dependence of Deuteronomy on EST, the text of EST is presented in the first column.[21] The various manuscripts of EST are found on ruled tablets that divide the curses into individual sections (see Figure 1 [below]). This is reflected in the numbered paragraph divisions (the superscripted numbers are the lines). Thus, the ruled sections of the EST match the first three Sets: §39 (lines 419–421) = Set 1; §40 (lines 422–424) = Set 2; and §41 (lines 425–427) = Set 3. However, the ruled section §42 comprises Set 4 (lines 428–429a); Set 5 (line 429b–430a); and Set 6 (line 430b). Finally, §§63–64 (lines 526–533) make up Set 7. In Table 2, the hard, horizontal lines of the rows in the table represent the rulings that divide these paragraph sections (Sets 1–3, Set 7 [columns 1–2]). The dotted, horizontal lines between Sets 4–6 represent the division that Weinfeld made in his comparative analysis.

The Assyrian text is presented as individual sentences with the sentences or clauses of the Deut 28 passage in parallel to the right for easy comparison. The translations of the Akkadian and the Hebrew are ours. When there is no text parallel to the other text, this is reflected by empty space in the table.

the old biblical tradition, which Deuteronomy used and reworked in accordance with the prevalent covenantal pattern reflected in the EST" (Moshe Weinfeld, *Deuteronomy 1–11: A New Translation with Introduction and Commentary*, AB 5 [New York: Doubleday, 1991], 9).

[18] Weinfeld, *Deuteronomic School*, 117.

[19] Ibid., 121.

[20] Ibid., 117–18.

[21] There are a number of manuscripts of the EST. The text here is based on the critical edition of Simo Parpola and Kazuko Watanabe, *Neo-Assyrian Treaties and Loyalty Oaths*, SAA 2 (Helsinki: Helsinki University Press, 1988), 45–46, 51; §§39–42, 63–64. Manuscript T (see below) has also been fully consulted.

Table 2. Comparison of Esarhaddon's Succession Treaty and the Curses of Deut 28:22–33

Set	*EST Text*	*EST Gloss*	*Deut 28 Gloss*	*Deut 28 Text*
1	§39 [419] d30 *na-an-nar* AN-*e u* KI.TIM *ina* SAḪAR.ŠUB-*pu* [420]*li-ḫal-lip-ku-nu*	**May Sîn, moonlight of heaven and earth, clothe you with "leprosy"!**	[27] **YHWH will attack you with the inflammation of Egypt**, with boils [with hemorrhoids], **with festering rash** and with itch, **from which you cannot be cured.**	27 יַכְּכָה יְהוָה בִּשְׁחִין מִצְרַיִם וּבָעֳפָלִים [וּבַטְּחֹרִים] וּבַגָּרָב וּבֶחָרֶס אֲשֶׁר לֹא־תוּכַל לְהֵרָפֵא
	ina IGI DINGIR.MEŠ *u* LUGAL *e-rab-ku-nu a-a iq-bi*	**May he not permit your entrance before the gods and the king!**		
	[421]*ki-i sér-ri-me* MAŠ.DÀ (*ina*) EDIN *ru-up-da*	Wander the steppe like an onager (or) a gazelle!		
2	§40 [422] dUTU *nu-úr šá-ma-mi u kaq-qar di-in ket-ti* (*me-šá-ri*) [423]*a-a i-di-in-ku-nu*	**May Šamaš**, sunlight of heavens and ground, **not give you a just judgment** *and* (justice)!	[28] **YHWH will attack you with madness, blindness, and confusion of mind;**	28 יַכְּכָה יְהוָה בְּשִׁגָּעוֹן וּבְעִוָּרוֹן וּבְתִמְהוֹן לֵבָב
	ni-ṭil IGI.2.MEŠ-*ku-nu liš-ši-ma*	**May he remove both of your eyes!**	[29] **at midday you will grope about in the dark like a blind man;**	29 וְהָיִיתָ מְמַשֵּׁשׁ בַּצָּהֳרַיִם כַּאֲשֶׁר יְמַשֵּׁשׁ הָעִוֵּר בָּאֲפֵלָה
	[424]*ina ek-le-ti i-tal-la-ka*	**Roam around continuously in darkness!**	**and you will truly not be prosperous in your ways;**	וְלֹא תַצְלִיחַ אֶת־דְּרָכֶיךָ
			and you will surely be oppressed and robbed constantly,	וְהָיִיתָ אַךְ עָשׁוּק וְגָזוּל כָּל־הַיָּמִים
			and there will be no deliverer.	וְאֵין מוֹשִׁיעַ

3	§41 [425] ᵈMAŠ *a-šá-rid* DINGER.MEŠ *ina šil-ta-ḫi-šu šam-ri li-šam-qit-ku-nu*	**May Ninurta,** foremost of the gods, **fell you with his ferocious arrow!**	[25] YHWH will allow you to be defeated before your enemies;	[25] יִתֶּנְךָ יְהוָה נִגָּף לִפְנֵי אֹיְבֶיךָ
	[426]MÚD.MEŠ-*ku-nu li-mal-[li]* EDIN	**May he fill the steppe with your blood!**		
			you will go out against them one way but flee before them seven ways; and you will become a horror object to all the kingdoms of the earth;	בְּדֶרֶךְ אֶחָד תֵּצֵא אֵלָיו וּבְשִׁבְעָה דְרָכִים תָּנוּס לְפָנָיו וְהָיִיתָ לְזַעֲוָה לְכֹל מַמְלְכוֹת הָאָרֶץ
	UZU-[*k*]*u-nu* Á.MUŠEN *zi-i-bu* [427]*li-šá-kil*	**May he feed your flesh to the eagle (and) the vulture!**	[26] and **your corpses will be food for all the birds of the air and the beasts of the earth;**	[26] וְהָיְתָה נִבְלָתְךָ לְמַאֲכָל לְכָל-עוֹף הַשָּׁמַיִם וּלְבֶהֱמַת הָאָרֶץ
			and there will be no one to frighten (them) away.	וְאֵין מַחֲרִיד
4	§42 [428] ᵈ*dil-bat na-bat* MUL.MEŠ *ina ni-ṭil* IGI.2-*ku-nu ḫi-ra-a-te-ku-nu* [429]*ina* ÚR LÚ.KÚR-*ku-nu li-šá-ni-il*	**May Venus, the brightest of the stars, cause your wives to lie down in the sight of both your eyes in the lap of your enemy!**	[30] **You shall be engaged to a woman; but another man shall rape [lie with] her.**	[30] אִשָּׁה תְאָרֵשׂ וְאִישׁ אַחֵר יִשְׁגָּלֶנָּה [יִשְׁכָּבֶנָּה]
5	DUMU.MEŠ-*ku-nu* [430]a-a *i-bé-lu* É-*ku-un*	**May your sons not reign over your house!**	**You shall build a house; but not live in it.**	בַּיִת תִּבְנֶה וְלֹא-תֵשֵׁב בּוֹ
			You shall plant a vineyard; but not enjoy it. [31] Your ox shall be butchered before your eyes; but you shall not eat of it. Your donkey shall be stolen in front of you; but shall not be restored to you. Your sheep shall be given to your enemies, and you will have no deliverer. [32] Your sons and daughters shall be given to another people; while you look on, you will strain your eyes looking for them all day and your hand will be powerless.	כֶּרֶם תִּטַּע וְלֹא תְחַלְּלֶנּוּ [31] שׁוֹרְךָ טָבוּחַ לְעֵינֶיךָ וְלֹא תֹאכַל מִמֶּנּוּ חֲמֹרְךָ גָּזוּל מִלְּפָנֶיךָ וְלֹא יָשׁוּב לָךְ צֹאנְךָ נְתֻנוֹת לְאֹיְבֶיךָ וְאֵין לְךָ מוֹשִׁיעַ [32] בָּנֶיךָ וּבְנֹתֶיךָ נְתֻנִים לְעַם אַחֵר וְעֵינֶיךָ רֹאוֹת וְכָלוֹת אֲלֵיהֶם כָּל-הַיּוֹם וְאֵין לְאֵל יָדֶךָ

6	LÚ.KÚR *a-ḫu-u li-za-i-za mim-mu-ku-un*	**May a foreign enemy divide up your possessions!**	[33] **A people whom you do not know shall consume the fruit of your ground and of all your labors;**	33 פְּרִי אַדְמָתְךָ וְכָל־יְגִיעֲךָ יֹאכַל עַם אֲשֶׁר לֹא־יָדָעְתָּ
			and you will be indeed oppressed; and you will be crushed continually.	וְהָיִיתָ רַק עָשׁוּק וְרָצוּץ כָּל־הַיָּמִים
7			[22] YHWH will attack you with consumption, with fever, with inflammation, with feverish heat, with drought, with blight and mildew; and they will pursue you until you perish.	22 יַכְּכָה יְהוָה בַּשַּׁחֶפֶת וּבַקַּדַּחַת וּבַדַּלֶּקֶת וּבַחַרְחֻר וּבַחֶרֶב וּבַשִּׁדָּפוֹן וּבַיֵּרָקוֹן וּרְדָפוּךָ עַד אָבְדֶךָ
	§63 [526]KI.MIN KI.MIN DINGIR.MEŠ *ma-la ina ṭup-pi a-d[e]-e an-[ni-e* MU-*šú-nu zak-ru]* [527]*am-mar* SIG_4 *kaq-qu-ru lu-si-qu-ni-ku-nu*	Ditto, ditto: **may all the gods** —as many as [are invoked by their names] in this treaty tablet—make the ground as narrow as a brick for you.		
	[528]*kaq-qar-ku-nu ki-i* AN.BAR *le-pu-šú*	**May they make your ground like iron;**	[23] **and the heavens over your head shall be bronze; and the earth under you iron.**	23 וְהָיוּ שָׁמֶיךָ אֲשֶׁר עַל־רֹאשְׁךָ נְחֹשֶׁת וְהָאָרֶץ אֲשֶׁר־תַּחְתֶּיךָ בַּרְזֶל
	me-me-ni [529]*ina* ŠÀ-*bi lu la i-par-ru-ʾa*	**and may nothing sprout within it.**		
	§64 [530]*ki-i šá* TA ŠÀ AN-*e šá* UD.KA.BAR A.AN *la i-za-nun-a-ni* [531]*ki-i ḫa-an-ni-e zu-un-nu na-al-šú ina* ŠÀ A.ŠÀ.MEŠ-*ku-nu* [532]*ta-me-ra-ti-ku-nu lu la [i]l-lak*	**Just as rain does not shower from a brazen heaven so may rain and dew not come upon your fields and your meadows;**	[24] YHWH will change the rain of your land into powder;	24 יִתֵּן יְהוָה אֶת־מְטַר אַרְצְךָ אָבָק
	ku-um zu-un-nu [533]*pe-eʾ-na-a-ti ina* KUR-*ku-nu li-iz-nu-na*	instead of rain may burning coals shower on your land.	and dust shall come down upon you from the heavens until you are destroyed.	וְעָפָר מִן־הַשָּׁמַיִם יֵרֵד עָלֶיךָ עַד הִשָּׁמְדָךְ

It is clear from the bold text in Table 2, especially in the biblical material, that Weinfeld has presented the evidence selectively, choosing to leave out material that might bring his thesis into question. This affects the internal integrity of each text (see further below). When one looks more closely at the individual sets of curses, additional problems quickly surface.

In Set 1, Weinfeld argues that the maledictions are based on the topic "leprosy," a condition regularly associated with the deity Sîn, and that this suggests a Mesopotamian connection in Deut 28:27. Sîn was indeed the god usually held responsible for the condition of *saḫaršubbû*,[22] generally rendered "leprosy." It is likely that *saḫaršubbû* refers to generalized skin lesions of characteristic types organized around that of Hansen's disease (leprosy), perhaps similar to how chicken pox was probably the major cause of *ašû*, another ancient syndrome involving generalized skin lesions of characteristic types.[23] *Saḫaršubbû* is lexically equated with *garābu*, "granular, white skin lesions."[24] Hebrew גָּרָב is cognate with *garābu* (*HALOT*, 201). However, *garābu* does not occur in Neo-Assyrian treaty curses.[25] Therefore, the usage of גָּרָב in Deut 28:27 is not evidence of borrowing, particularly since it is doubtful that a Hebrew author would know the lexical equation, and since it is even more doubtful that any Hebrew reader would have been able to make this connection. In the biblical texts, גָּרָב refers to a "festering rash" or "boil-scar" that, like any other defect, disqualifies high priests from service (Lev 21:20), or, in parallel, that disqualifies animals from sacrifice (Lev 22:22). Interestingly, *garābu*-lesions were observed in sheep,[26] even though sheep, cattle, and horses are not subject to Hansen's disease. Along with Deut 28:27, the Levitical passages mentioned above contain the only occurrences of גָּרָב in the Hebrew Bible. The parallel certainly would have been more compelling if the Esarhaddon text had used the word *garābu* rather than *saḫaršubbû*, or if the biblical text had used צָרַעַת, which would have aligned better with *saḫaršubbû*.

---

[22] The curse is known in much earlier times in *kudurrû*. For example, the *kudurru* of the Kassite king Meli-Šipak (1186–1172) reads: [41] ^{d}*Zuen* . . . [48]SAḪAR. ŠUB.BA-*a* [49]*ki-ma ṣu-ba-ti* [50]*pa-ga-ar-šu* [51]*li-la-bi-iš-ma* [52]*a-di* u_4*-um bal-ṭu* [53]É-*su li-za-mi-ma* [1]*ki-ma ú-ma-am* [2]*ṣe-ri ṣe-ra li-ir-pu-ud* [3]*re-bi-it* URU-*šu* [4]*a-a ik-bu-us*, "May Sîn . . . clothe his body with leprosy (*saḫaršubbû*) like a garment and while he is alive, may he be deprived of his house and may he roam the wilderness like a wild animal but not walk over the streets of his city" (William John Hinke, *Selected Babylonian* kudurru *Inscriptions*, SSS 14 [Leiden: Brill, 1911], 48–53). The same curse also occurs in the treaty of Aššur-nērārī V with Matīʾēl (SAA 2.2, iv.4–7).

[23] JoAnn Scurlock and Burton R. Andersen, *Diagnoses in Assyrian and Babylonian Medicine: Ancient Sources, Translations, and Modern Medical Analyses* (Urbana: University of Illinois Press, 2005), 723–24nn139–40.

[24] Ibid., 231.

[25] Weinfeld notes *garābu* as a cognate of Hebrew גָּרָב but, importantly, does not note its absence in Neo-Assyrian treaty curses.

[26] Scurlock and Andersen, *Diagnoses in Assyrian and Babylonian Medicine*, 232.

Three additional skin maladies are mentioned in the curse of Deut 28:26. The first, שְׁחִין, is specified as "of Egypt," in a reference to the "inflammation of Egypt," namely, a plague of YHWH in the Exodus tradition (Exod 9:8–11). Furthermore, it occurs as a prominent cause of uncleanness detailed in Leviticus (13:18–23). The second malady, עֳפָלִים, "boils" (Qere: טְחֹרִים, "hemorrhoids"), appears as a plague of YHWH against the Philistines (1 Sam 5–6). Neither of these words (עֳפָלִים or טְחֹרִים) has an Akkadian cognate or semantic equivalent that occurs in Neo-Assyrian treaty curses.[27] The third malady, חֶרֶס, "scratch" or "itch," is a hapax legomenon.[28] None of the Hebrew terms is cognate with Akkadian terms occurring in the Neo-Assyrian treaty curses, including the EST. These terms collectively tie the Deuteronomic malediction to the Exodus plague tradition and/or to the laws concerning separation resulting from uncleanness, an observation solidified by the explicit mention of Egypt. Moreover, the biblical text fails to reflect the verbal notion "clothe with leprosy (*saḫaršubbû*)" (see Set 1). Therefore, the proposed direct Mesopotamian connection to Sîn must be rejected, for there is nothing in the text of Deuteronomy that signals a clear connection. In addition, the Akkadian section (§39) is composed of three component clauses (utilizing, in order, precative, vetitive, and imperative verbal forms). The biblical text lacks the important second and third parts to this "Sîn-curse" section: no mention of denial of access to gods and king, and no mention of the notion "wandering the steppe"—a component that is fundamental to the Akkadian curse (see the citation above from the *kudurru* of the Kassite king Meli-Šipak). In form, "the Deuteronomy text bears no more than a passing resemblance to the EST passage, eliminating symmetry between target and source texts as an indicator of the texts' relationship."[29] Carly Crouch rightly observes that "the only real similarity between these texts is the use of skin disease as curse material, and that is far from distinctive."[30]

In Set 2, the curses in the EST and Deut 28 are similar in their statements about the removal of eyesight and roaming around continuously in the dark (EST) and being struck with blindness and groping in the dark (Deut 28). However, Crouch rightly declares that "the symmetry of these two passages is so poor as to defy visual representation. . . . What little

---

[27] There are three possible Akkadian terms for hemorrhoids, *umṣātu*, *uršu*, and *baṣkiltu*; ibid., 149–50. None of these occurs in the Neo-Assyrian treaty curses.

[28] It may be cognate with Akkadian *ḫarāsu*, which appears to be a malady involving skin lesions and itching (see *CAD* Ḫ, s.v. *ḫarāsu*). Scurlock and Andersen suggest that this might be onchocerciasis, which is caused by a roundworm transmitted by the bite of black flies and whose commonest symptoms are itching of the skin and blindness (ibid., 86). However, this Akkadian term does not appear in any treaty curse from the Neo-Assyrian period.

[29] Crouch, *Israel and the Assyrians*, 54.

[30] Ibid., 57.

overlap there is, in other words, is highly unlikely to have functioned successfully as a signal—especially not one on which the entirety of the allusion, in the absence of additional terminological overlap, was obliged to rely."[31] In Deut 28:28 the "madness, blindness, and confusion of mind" in the context of the prior afflictions (v. 27) most clearly refer to physical and psychological maladies[32] rather than to an underlying "judicial blindness."[33] Although many interpret "the mention of blindness" in Deut 28 "as parallel and alluding to VTE's [EST's] mention of loss of eyesight, Deuteronomy's usage is more obviously understood as an elaboration of the theme of madness, culminating in a description of the addressee's consequent social vulnerability."[34] The simile in verse 29, "like a blind man in the dark," functions as a comparative figure of speech—that is, the madness makes a person function like a blind man in the dark. This also explains the next clause of the verse, "and you will not be prosperous in your ways" (due to madness and confusion of mind).

In addition, social injustice in the Neo-Assyrian curse is the product of the direct agency of the deity Šamaš, whereas in the proposed Deuteronomy parallel, human beings are the agents. In fact, the biblical text consistently presents YHWH as just (cf. Deut 32:4). While the Hebrew text clearly ties the lack of prosperity and accompanying oppression and thievery grammatically with the initial maladies (madness, blindness, and confusion of mind) by the use of a *weqatal* verbal form (וְהָיִיתָ), both it and the presence of two agents separate the infliction of maladies and the deprivation of justice as categorically unique. Although the texts bear superficial similarities, as in Set 1 their relationship is so generalized as to nullify the contention that Deuteronomy intends to allude to the Esarhaddon text, let alone that it intends to borrow from it directly.[35]

The curses in Set 3 exhibit some similarities, especially in the references to carrion birds and the descriptions of the addressees as food for the animals (Akkadian is plural; Hebrew is singular). Both are based on the well-known fear in the ancient Near East of restless spirits who have not received a proper burial.[36] However, while the "Ninurta-curse" follows immediately after the "Šamaš-curse," in Deut 28 the curse in question precedes Sets 1 and 2. Once again, as Crouch points out, "the ter-

[31] Ibid., 58.

[32] Jeffrey H. Tigay, *Deuteronomy*, דברים, JPS Torah Commentary (Philadelphia: Jewish Publication Society of America, 1996), 264; Daniel I. Block, *Deuteronomy*, NIVAC (Grand Rapids: Zondervan, 2012), 655.

[33] Weinfeld, *Deuteronomic School*, 121.

[34] Crouch, *Israel and the Assyrians*, 59.

[35] Ibid.

[36] Ibid., 60.

minological overlap is limited and the symmetry is weak."[37] The motif of leaving corpses on the field of battle occurs very early and continues throughout all of ancient Near Eastern history. It is found in an earlier Old Babylonian curse series (i.e., LH 51:12–16), and the iconographic rendering of birds feasting on the dead for treaty breach is likewise an early conception (e.g., the Stela of Vultures). It occurs in several other ancient Near Eastern inscriptions and is also common in the biblical texts.[38] This removes all grounds for seeing this curse in Deut 28 as unique or directly dependent on the EST. The curse appears to come from a common pool of ancient Near Eastern maledictions, rather than from a specific document. Apparently overlooked by many scholars is the fact that the same curse can also be used with a different deity in a different place in the same treaty. In lines 519–520, one reads:

> 519 dIGI.DU EN *a-šá-(re-du* UZU.MEŠ-*ku-nu)* 520Á.MUŠEN *zi-i-bu* (*li-šá-kil*)
>
> May Pālil, the foremost lord, feed your flesh to the eagle (and) the vulture!

So, did Deut 28:26 "borrow" from this "Pālil-curse" or from the "Ninurta-curse"? Obviously, from neither!

Furthermore, not only does this curse in Deut 28:26 occur before Sets 1 and 2, but Weinfeld also fails to quote the whole curse (once again, grammatically the *weqatal* verbal form at the beginning of verse 26 is a sequential form tying it to the preceding verse). The specific wording of verse 25 demonstrates that this curse sequence is not dependent on a Neo-Assyrian counterpart. The syntagm "you will go out against them one way but flee before them seven ways" clearly reflects a West Semitic curse formula seen in the Sefire and Bukān inscriptions.[39]

In Set 4, the correlation of maledictions is topically similar: sexual abuse of a woman. However, a careful comparison reveals two important differences. First, the stolen "wives" in the Esarhaddon text are already in fruitful relationships with their husbands, as the next line in the Akkadian implies existing children. In Deuteronomy, the relationship has not been consummated, as suggested by the following sequence beginning with building a home, acquiring property, and then having children. This distinction is confirmed by the specific betrothal term, ארשׂ. Second, the two maledictions in the proposed comparison involve different kinds of curses. In Deuteronomy, this is a futility curse—in fact, the beginning of

[37] Ibid., 60.

[38] Gen 40:19; 1 Sam 17:44–46; 1 Kgs 14:11; 16:4; Isa 18:6; Jer 7:33; 15:3; 16:4; 19:7; 34:20; Ezek 39:17–20; Ps 79:2.

[39] Sf I A 21–24, 27–28; II A 1–3a, 5–6 (*KAI* nos. 222–224; *COS* 2.82:213–17). Bukān 5′–8′. See *COS* 3.89:219; André Lemaire, "Une inscription araméenne du VIIe siècle avant J.-C. trouvée à Bukân," *StIr* 27 (1998): 15–30; *KAI* no. 320.

a series of futility curses. Futility curses are absent in the Neo-Assyrian material. However, they are present in the Sefire documents, as the nearest analogy. More importantly, this and another specific Deuteronomic curse are parallel in both topic and kind to similar maledictions in an Old Babylonian treaty from Tel Leilan, though the notion of "betrothal" is absent there as well:

Table 3

L.T.-3 v 10′–11′	**Deut 28:38**
[10]*šu-bu-ul-ṭam še-ri-iḫ* *ma-a-at a-pí* [11]*a i-ib-ni*	זֶרַע רַב תּוֹצִיא הַשָּׂדֶה וּמְעַט תֶּאֱסֹף
May an (entire) furrow in the country of Apu(m) not produce a (single) sprout of grain!	Much seed will you take out to the field, but little will you gather . . .
L.T.-3 v 31′–32′	**Deut 28:30**
[31]*i-na pí-li-is i-ni-ia* ᵐⁱDAM [32]*ša-nu-um li-ḫu-uz*	אִשָּׁה תְאָרֵשׂ וְאִישׁ אַחֵר יִשְׁגָּלֶנָּה [יִשְׁכָּבֶנָּה]
Let another (man) take (my) wife in (full) view of my eyes!*	You shall be engaged to a woman; but another man shall rape [lie with] her.

*For the rare *pilsu* ("view, vista"), see *CAD* P, 378.

In the case of the EST, Venus is Ištar; and Ištar is a goddess of reversals with the ability to render a person powerless.[40] The epilogue for the Laws of Hammurapi makes clear Ištar's penchant for reversals: "may [Ištar] turn his good fortunes to bad, may she break (*lišbir*) his weapon (*kakkašu*) on the field of battle and strife!" Of Ištar it was frequently said: "to grant potency is hers, to remove potency is hers."[41] Thus Ištar is implored in the "Venus-curses" (Sets 4–6) to reverse the correct and normal outcome for a monarch. The "Venus-curses" are reversals, whereas the Deuteronomy curses are futility curses.

Weinfeld separates the lines of the treaty and the verses of Deut 28 into separate parallels (hence, Sets 4, 5, and 6),[42] even though in the Esar-

---

[40] Ilona Zsolnay, "Ištar, 'Goddess of War, Pacifier of Kings': An Analysis of Ištar's Martial Role in the Maledictory Sections of the Assyrian Royal Inscriptions," in *Proceedings of the 53ᵉ Rencontre Assyriologique Internationale*, vol. 1, *Language in the Ancient Near East*, ed. Leonid Kogan et al., Babel und Bibel 4/Annual of Ancient Near Eastern, Old Testament, and Semitic Studies (Winona Lake, IN: Eisenbrauns, 2010), esp. 396.

[41] Robert D. Biggs, šà.zi.ga*: Ancient Mesopotamian Potency Incantations*, TCS 2 (New York: J. J. Augustin, 1967), 46.

[42] Weinfeld, *Deuteronomic School*, 118.

haddon text the lines are all part of the "Venus-curse" (lines 428–430). However, for the biblical text this means that the first two clauses of verse 30 are separated from the next two clauses. The remainder of verse 30 and all of verse 31 are left out. Then the first clause of verse 32 is included, but not the rest of the verse. Finally, the initial clause of verse 33 is included, but not the remainder. While Weinfeld's presentation makes the parallels look more convincing, it skews the boundaries of the curses in both the Neo-Assyrian treaty and in Deuteronomy. The violation of the integrity of both documents is evident even from a casual glance. One cannot simply manufacture "matches" by manipulating the texts.

Thus, in Set 5 Weinfeld's parallel of maledictions relies on his correlation of the Deuteronomic elements "house" and "sons," which are located in different verses. He elides too much to get these two elements to appear close enough to one another to merit comparison with the second component of the Venus-curse section (i.e., "May your sons not reign over your house!"). When we account for the elements that Weinfeld has elided, they include vineyard, ox, donkey, and sheep (28:30–32).[43] But he compounds his violation of the biblical text. Verses 30–31 comprise a litany of six futility curses[44] that conclude with the clause "and you will have no deliverer" (both here and at the end of v. 32 the use of . . . וְאֵין is a clear closure marker). Syntactically, verse 32 begins a new curse about "your" sons *and daughters* (not just "sons," as in the Assyrian text) being given to another people while the addressee watches and has no power to intervene (i.e., "deliver" them). In short, Weinfeld has manufactured another parallel in the case of his Set 5.

In Set 6, the third component of the Venus-curse section and the curse of Deut 28:33 speak to the loss of goods to an enemy force. Even so, the texts' dissimilarities work against identifying the common features as a convincing case of allusion. Furthermore, the biblical text contains two final clauses that emphasize the continuity, even permanence, of this oppressive situation, an emphasis lacking in the Assyrian text.

Before analyzing Set 7, we must return to an issue mentioned above. In the paragraph immediately following Table 1, we noted that Weinfeld's selectivity influences the internal integrity of each text being compared.

---

[43] Ironically, the following items also appear in the maledictory sections of several Hittite treaties: the loss of land, home, children, vineyard, cattle, and flocks (see *CTH* 62.II; 76; 106; etc.).

[44] Hans Steymans argues that much of this text is secondary ("Eine assyrische Vorlage für Deuteronomium 28,20–44," in *Bundesdokument und Gesetz: Studien zum Deuteronomium*, ed. Georg Braulik, HBS 4 [Freiburg: Herder, 1995], 125). This is a pretext for removing evidence that is contrary to one's theory. See Joshua Berman, "Historicism and Its Limits: A Response to Bernard M. Levinson and Jeffrey Stackert," *JAJ* 4 (2013): 297–309.

Our analysis above has identified some instances of this, but this requires further comment. In the case of the EST, Weinfeld violates the internal curse structure. The structure of the "Standard Curse Section"[45] (§§37–56 = lines 414–493) is composed of six subsections:

The Assyrian Divine Couple: Aššur and Mullissu[46] (lines 414–418)

Six Astral Deities: Anu; Sîn; Šamaš; Ninurta; Venus; and Jupiter (lines 418a–432)

Six Babylonian Deities: Marduk; Ṣarpānitu; Bēlet-ilī; Adad; Ištar; and Nergal (lines 433–456)

Three Specific Female Deities: Mullissu, who dwells in Nineveh; Ištar, who dwells in Arbela;[47] and Gula, the great physician goddess (lines 457–463)

Nine[48] *Peripheral Regional Deities*: Sebettu (Pleiades);[49] Aramiš (or Aramis) of Qarnê and Azaʾi; Adad and Šāla of Kurbaʾil;[50] Šarrat-Ekron (the Queen of Ekron); Bethel and Anat-Bethel; Kubaba and Karḫuḫa of Karkamiš (lines 464–471)

---

[45] This is the designation given in Parpola and Kazuko, *Neo-Assyrian Treaties*, 45.

[46] This Assyrian divine couple established the fate and long life and reign of the Assyrian monarch from the Middle Assyrian period onward. See the words spoken by the high priest to the king during the Middle Assyrian coronation ritual cited in Karl Friedrich Müller, *Das Assyrische Ritual*, MVAG 41.3 (Leipzig: J. C. Hinrichs, 1937), 12–13: col. ii.30–37. This divine couple makes a perfect beginning to the entire standard curse section from an Assyrian point of view.

[47] Ilona Zsolnay, "The Function of Ištar in the Assyrian Royal Inscriptions: A Contextual Analysis of the Actions Attributed to Ištar in the Inscriptions of Ititi through Šalmaneser III" (PhD diss., Brandeis University, 2009).

[48] We base this number on the composite text of Lauinger's "Esarhaddon's Succession Treaty at Tell Tayinat." The Sebettu are lacking in the Tayinat text. After the Aramiš-curse, none of the manuscripts from Nimrud preserves an unbroken transition to the Bethel and Anat-Bethel curse. Thus, until the discovery of the Tayinat tablet, we did not know that two additional curses invoking the pair Adad and Šāla of Kurbaʾil and Šarrat-Ekron ("the Queen of Ekron") follow immediately after the curse invoking Aramiš. For this reason, these curses are now designated §54A and §54B, and the curse invoking Bethel and Anath-Bethel (formerly §54A) is now §54C. The Šarrat-Ekron is undoubtedly PTGYH, the Lady of Ekron of the Ekron Inscription (see *COS* 2.42:164).

[49] Graziani argues that the cult of the Sebettu that spread to Mesopotamia is of West Semitic origin, being unattested in Sumerian religious tradition (Simonetta Graziani, "Note sui Sibitti," *AION* 39 [1979]: 674–85, esp. 681). See also Michael P. Streck, "Die Flüche im Sukzessionsvertrag Asarhaddons," *ZABR* 4 (1998): 183. The curse at the end of Aššur-bēl-kala's inscription (RIMA 2:108, A.0.89.10, lines 6–7) states: "As for the one who removes my inscriptions and my name: the divine Sibitti, the gods of the West (ᵈIM[IN.BI] DINGIR.MEŠ KUR.MAR.TU), will afflict him with a snake-bite." The Sebettu also occur in the Aramaic Sefire Stela (*KAI* 222 I A 10–11: *sbt*).

[50] The Adad temple in Kurbaʾil at the northernmost point of the country was the main cult center for this deity and his consort. See Daniel Schwemer, "The

Conclusion: all the deities: "The great gods of heaven and earth, who dwell in the four quarters of the world, as many as are invoked by their names in this tablet" (lines 472–493).

The subsection from which the writer of Deuteronomy supposedly borrowed is the *Six Astral Deities* subsection[51] (lines 418a–432), which lists Anu, Sîn, Šamaš, Ninurta (Sirius/Mercury), Venus, and Jupiter. Anu opens the subsection because he is "king of the gods," and because he represents one of the three paths in the heavens. He is also the father of Marduk, who opens the next subsection. The important pair Sîn and Šamaš follow Anu, with Sîn, "the moonlight of heaven and earth," preceding Šamaš in the list for two reasons: because (1) Sîn is Šamaš' father and (2) the appearance of Sîn and Šamaš "together" is normally a good omen. Although here in the EST they come back to back, due to the rulings on the tablet, they invoke separate curses. In his discussion of Ninurta as Star and Arrow, Amar Annus notes:

> "Ninurta is the Arrow (Sirius),[52] the great warrior, who slit the throats of the enemies of Assurbanipal with his pointed arrowhead." Ninurta protects Esarhaddon's succession treaty with his arrow: "May Ninurta the foremost among the gods, fell the violator with his fierce arrow . . ."[53]

He also notes that in the astrological materials "there was a kind of duality of Šamaš and Ninurta in the sky because, in an astronomical commentary, Venus is identified as Šamaš at sunrise and as Ninurta at sunset."[54] Since Ninurta is also associated with Mercury,[55] the placement of Ninurta after Šamaš and before Venus in the curses in the EST is purposeful, probably signaling the order Sun, Mercury, Venus. So, then, the placement of Venus (Ištar), "the brightest of the stars," makes sense. Jupiter, "the exalted lord of the gods," works perfectly as the concluding astral deity in this subsection. It also provides a perfect transition to the next subsection.

Storm-Gods of the Ancient Near East: Summary, Synthesis, Recent Studies (Part 1)," *JANER* 7 (2007): 143.

[51] Streck notes the astral aspect in this subsection in "Die Flüche im Sukzessionsvertrag Asarhaddons," 182.

[52] Significantly, the Hymn to Ninurta refers to this deity as Sirius; see Amar Annus, *The God Ninurta in the Mythology and Royal Ideology of Ancient Mesopotamia*, SAAS 14 (Helsinki: Neo-Assyrian Text Corpus Project, 2002), 207–8.

[53] Ibid., 133.

[54] Ibid., 134.

[55] Similarly, at Ugarit Aṯtartu is variously the planet Venus (*Aṯtartu* = Ištar of Nineveh) and the Bow Star (*Aṯtartu ša šadî* = Ištar of Arbela), whereas *Aṯtaru* (*ša šadî*) is the planet Mercury. At Emar, he is equated lexically with Ninurta, Nabû's avatar and a god of warfare. See Mark S. Smith, ed., *The Ugaritic Baal Cycle*, vol. 1, *Introduction with Text, Translation and Commentary of KTU 1.1–1.2*, VTSup 55 (Leiden: Brill, 1994), 24.

This is seen in the wording of the curse ("May Jupiter . . . not show you the entrance of Bēl into Esagil . . ."), as well as in the fact that Jupiter is identified with Marduk, the first deity in the Babylonian subsection. In addition, interestingly, Jupiter heads the list of deities mentioned as witnesses in the treaty document proper (line 13);[56] and Esarhaddon's royal inscriptions note Jupiter for its good omens for Esarhaddon's reign.[57] Clearly, the writer of Deuteronomy 28 has failed to signal—in any kind of adequate way—this astral structuring within the biblical curses. If one wanted to subvert this subsection, one could have accomplished this in many ways. Deuteronomy 28 obviously fails in this regard, if one assumes the text intended to subvert Assyrian imperialism.[58]

Koch has argued that in the EST there is a palindrome (i.e., a chiastic pattern) of deity-curses (Ninurta–Sîn–Šamaš–Ištar–Šamaš–Sîn–Ninurta) and that this pattern is followed closely in Deut 28:25–36.[59] His table shows this structure with the supposed links to Deut 28, reproduced on the next page.[60] However, this is problematic from the start. Koch recognizes that the links between Deut 28:36 and Ninurta are weak.[61] Since there is no palindrome (chiastic pattern) in the Esarhaddon treaty, it is highly unlikely that an ancient Hebrew reader could have discerned one here. This is especially true in light of the foregoing discussion. Since the

---

[56] Of course, the seals of Aššur are present, but the first deity after the ruling is MUL.SAG.ME.GAR, "Jupiter."

[57] See RINAP 4:106, Text 48, lines 55–57a; RINAP 4:197, Text 104, ii.34–41a; RINAP 4:204, Text 105, iii.10–18; RINAP 4:100, Text 1015, ii.9′; but especially see RINAP 4:245, Text 116, r.2–6: "[Bright Jupiter, the giver of decisions on Akkad, came] near [in Simānu (III)] and stood in the place where the sun (^{d}UTU) shines. It was shining brightly (and) its appearance was [red. Its rising was as complete as the rising of the sun. The angry gods were reconciled with Akkad] (and) there were copious [rains] (and) regular floods [in Akkad]. It (Jupiter) reached (its) [hyp]soma [for a second time in the month 'Opening the Door'] and [stayed in its place]. [In order to triumph (and) to show overpowering strength], he (the god Marduk) reveal[ed to me] good omen(s) [concerning the (re)-entering of Esagil {note the curse connected to Jupiter above}. Every month, the gods Sîn (and) Šamaš together, at their appearance, answered me with a firm] 'yes' [concerning the renewing of the gods, the completion of the shrines (and) the cult centers, the stability] of my reign (and) the securing of the throne of my priestly office."

[58] For an introduction to those holding this position, see Crouch, *Israel and the Assyrians*, 5–12.

[59] Christoph Koch, *Vertrag, Treueid, und Bund: Studien zur Rezeption des altorientalischen Vertragsrechts im Deuteronomium und zur Ausbildung der Bundestheologie im Alten Testament*, BZAW 383 (Berlin: de Gruyter, 2008), 241–44. Cf. Crouch, *Israel and the Assyrians*, 70–71.

[60] Ibid., 242.

[61] Ibid., 247. The entire Deuteronomy curse is 28:36–37 (the *weqatal* form links verses 36 and 37), a fact ignored by Koch.

association of any of these deities with the proposed biblical counterpart is very doubtful, there is no real evidence of this supposed palindrome. Koch has simply forced it onto the passage.

Table 4

A	Ninurta-Fluch	25f*
B	Sîn-Fluch	27
C	Šamaš-Fluch	28–29a
D	*ʿšwq*	29b
E	Venus/Ištar-Fluch	30–33a
D′	*ʿšwq*	33b
C′	Šamaš-Fluch	34
B′	Sîn-Fluch	35*
A′	Ninurta-Fluch?	36f*

The curses of Set 7 offer the strongest parallel of all the sets of curses. Three obvious similarities are: (1) the ground or earth (KI/*qaqqaru*, אֶרֶץ) becomes like iron (*parzillu* [AN.BAR], בַּרְזֶל); (2) heaven (*šamû* [AN], שָׁמַיִם) becomes as bronze (*sipparu* [UD.KA.BAR], נְחֹשֶׁת); and (3) there are substitutes for the rain (*zunnu* [noun], *zanānu* [verb], מָטָר). Even so, the differences are significant.[62]

First, as Crouch states, "the VTE [EST] material can hardly be said to have been precisely rendered into Deuteronomy, either with regard to syntax or with regard to meaning."[63] On the contrary, "the superficial similarity of these texts is betrayed by their substantial divergences" and their limited correspondence.[64] A substantial part of each text is without counterpart in the other: lines 526–527 and 532a–533 are lacking in Deut 28; and Deut 28:22 and the last clause of verse 23 are lacking in the Esarhaddon treaty.

Second, as emphasized above, any comparison must maintain the integrity of each text. In the case of Esarhaddon's text, a ruling on the tablet after line 529 (represented as a horizontal line in Table 2 above) separates the curses in lines 530–533 (§64) from lines 526–529 (§63). Subsection

[62] See Crouch, *Israel and the Assyrians*, 65.
[63] Ibid., 66.
[64] Ibid.

64 is the first in a series of four simile curse subsections,[65] each of which utilizes the construction *kī ša*, "Just as . . . ," in the curse: (1) "Just as rain . . ."; (2) "Just as lead . . ."; (3) "Just as a mule . . ."; and (4) "Just as a germinal shoot of malt . . ." Weinfeld's comparison has noted some superficial similarities in vocabulary but none of the contrasts. He has therefore skewed the curse boundaries and violated the integrity of the Esarhaddon text. Lines 526–529 (§63) contain three curses related *only* to the "ground": (1) may it be made as narrow as a brick; (2) may it be made (*as hard as*) iron; and (3) may it sprout nothing within it. Here all the deities of the treaty are invoked to narrow and harden the earth to prevent crops. As noted, since the next curse subsection (lines 530–533, §64) is the first in a series of simile curse sections, it opens with a simile, "Just as rain does not shower from a brazen heaven," which serves as the basis for two curse components: (1) there will be no hydration of any kind and, instead, (2) there will be the raining of burning coals.

Crouch observes that "the elements of the two VTE [EST] curses that do appear in Deuteronomy"—if they have in fact come from the EST—"are garbled: the bronze sky and iron earth are joined together in Deut 28:23."[66] Significantly, verse 23 is grammatically tied to verse 22 (*weqatal* verbal form).[67] Deuteronomy 28:22 is a catalogue of seven afflictions with which YHWH will attack his people. The first four speak of personal bodily afflictions: consumption (perhaps tuberculosis), fever,[68] inflammation (perhaps another word for fever), and feverish heat. The next three—drought,[69] blight, and mildew—evoke plagues of ruin[70] and hence foreshadow the climactic bronze heavens and iron earth of verse 23.

Importantly, Deut 28:24 is syntactically a separate curse. It describes storms of dust (אָבָק, עָפָר) that bring about Israel's destruction. Thus, the curse may be an allusion to the phenomenon of *ḥamsîn* as a constant weather pattern. This is not the same as the Akkadian term *peʾināti* "charcoal, embers," which envisions hot burning coals. Crouch observes that

[65] For a discussion of this type of curse, see Anne Marie Kitz, *Cursed Are You! The Phenomenology of Cursing in Cuneiform and Hebrew Texts* (Winona Lake, IN: Eisenbrauns, 2014), 82–84.

[66] Crouch, *Israel and the Assyrians*, 67.

[67] Scholars who argue for the dependence of Deuteronomy on the EST curses often overlook the grammatical constructions in Deut 28.

[68] The first two terms occur in Lev 26:16.

[69] Understanding חֶרֶב as חֹרֶב, "drought" (see *HALOT*, 350).

[70] Block comments: " 'Blight' apparently refers to premature drying of grain growing in the fields, perhaps because of the desiccating effect of scorching east wind. 'Mildew' seems to involve pathological yellowing of grain, attributable to plant disease, inadequate nutrients in the soil, or drought" (*Deuteronomy*, 654).

had the biblical writer intended to make a clear allusion to the EST, he could have used a phrase like גַּחֲלֵי־אֵשׁ, "burning charcoals," an exact semantic equivalent for *peʾināti*.[71] Crouch concludes:

> The omission of the initial curse that the earth be like brick, the alteration of the purpose of the curse(s), the change in what will now fall from the heavens, and the abandonment of the bronze sky's rhetorical function all distance the Deuteronomy text from the VTE [EST] text. Perhaps some of these divergences might be attributed to acceptability in the target language, but when combined with the overall asymmetry of the two texts they do nothing but weaken the new text's ability to evoke VTE [EST] as its source.[72]

In addition, Lev 26:19 knows this same curse, portraying the heavens as a sheet of metal preventing moisture above the firmament from watering the earth, and the ground hardened as metal resisting cultivation (although it reverses the metals). Weinfeld acknowledges that the fact that "the same malediction is found in Lev 26:19, which appears to be free from Assyrian influence and which has no sign of dependence on Deuteronomy, may perhaps indicate that this metaphor could not be considered characteristically Assyrian."[73]

As Crouch concludes: "Only with significant difficulty, therefore, may Deut 28:23–24 be understood as alluding to VTE [EST] §63 and VTE [EST] §64 for the purpose of signaling Deuteronomy's subversive relationship with VTE [EST]."[74] It seems preferable to posit that the biblical and Neo-Assyrian writers have drawn on common curse similes to formulate different maledictions.

These two curse subsections (lines 526–529 and 530–533; §§63–64) appear 96 lines later in the EST than the primary curse subsection (Sets 1–6, §§39–42, discussed above). However, instead of continuing with material from the Esarhaddon text (i.e., lines 534–536, subsection EST §65), "Deut 28:25 uses nothing recognizable"[75] whatsoever from the Assyrian text (though Deut 28:26 is grammatically tied to 28:25 with the *weqatal* וְהָיְתָה). The proponents of the dependence view apparently would see the biblical writer in Deut 28:26 moving back 110 lines in the Esarhaddon material (i.e., to subsection §41) in continuing his subversive borrowing, while rearranging the claimed parallels to these astral deity curses and failing to make even an implicit polemic.

To sum up, only 20 lines (lines 419–430; 526–533) out of a 670-line inscription make up the core of Weinfeld's thesis. We may hardly deem

[71] Crouch, *Israel and the Assyrians*, 67.
[72] Ibid.
[73] Weinfeld, *Deuteronomic School*, 117n113.
[74] Crouch, *Israel and the Assyrians*, 69.
[75] Ibid.

this "borrowing." Table 5 and Figure 1 (below) show the tablet from Tell Tayinat (ms T; obverse, columns i–iv; reverse, columns v–viii) with the five curse sections outlined in white blocks according to their proposed order in Deuteronomy (A–E). Each block corresponds to the malediction set numbers provided in the textual comparison above (see Table 2). It is important to note that the treaty curses are on the reverse (the back) of the tablet, meaning that the reader had to walk around to the back of the tablet if it were hung, or had authority to turn the tablet, if it were positioned for rotating on its vertical axis.[76] If there were a treaty copy in Jerusalem, it would probably have had the same basic shape and design.[77] The beginning of the supposed sequence comes 526 lines into the text (marked as block A; lines 526–533, §63; ms T vii 17–25),[78] and then backtracks 110 lines to block B (lines 425–427, §41; ms T v, not preserved), and then backtracks 6 lines more to blocks C–D (lines 419–424, §39; ms T v 86–89), and finally jumps ahead to block E (lines 428–430, §42; ms T v, not preserved)!

Table 5. Location of the Putative Parallels between the EST and Deut 28:22–33 on Ms T

Block	*Curse Set(s)*	*Ms T (lines)*	*Deuteronomy*
A	7	vii 17–25 (526–533)	28:22–24
B	3	v—*broken* (425–427)	28:25–26
C	1	v 86–89 (419–421)	28:27
D	2	v—*broken* (422–424)	28:28–29
E	4–6	v—*broken* (428–430)	28:30–33

[76] The ms T tablet was apparently on display in the temple at Tayinat. See the discussion in Jacob Lauinger, "Some Preliminary Thoughts on the Tablet Collection in Building XVI from Tell Tayinat," *CSMSJ* 6 (2011): 11; Timothy P. Harrison and James F. Osborne, "Building XVI and the Neo-Assyrian Sacred Precinct at Tell Tayinat," *JCS* 64 (2012): 137–38.

[77] For a similarly constructed and formatted tablet of this treaty from Nimrud (Kalḫu), see Plates 1 and 9 in Donald J. Wiseman, "The Vassal-Treaties of Esarhaddon," *Iraq* 20 (1958): 1–99; Plates 1–53.

[78] Or 112 lines into the curse sections. Thus the writer of the curses in Deut 28 would have skipped all these lines in order to start his work, assuming that his readers would know this and that Deuteronomy is an intentionally subversive political document.

Obverse (Front) Reverse (Back)

Figure 1. Location of the Putative Parallels between the EST and Deut 28:22–33 on Ms T. (Photos courtesy of Jennifer Jackson.)

Add to this the fact that there is no convincing evidence of borrowing, as discussed above, and what remains is some generic similarity shared by maledictions in a number of different inscriptions.[79] In short, no two maledictions in the Deuteronomy list actually appear in the sequence reflected in the Esarhaddon list. Weinfeld's proposed connection between these two documents at both the topical and sequential levels is remote at best and hardly "identical" (according to his definition of the term).

We have little doubt that at least some learned Judahites knew Akkadian.[80] Based on the discovery of the Tell Tayinat EST, it is certainly

[79] Weeks puts it this way: "Thus we can say there are similarities of themes, perhaps partly in a common order. Given the long history of similar curses and the other overlaps between biblical and treaty curses, this is less than what is needed to prove definite borrowing" (Weeks, *Admonition and Curse*, 168).

[80] Contra Morrow, who states: "the idea that an educated elite of Judah would have been able to read cuneiform during the time period under discussion is implausible" (William S. Morrow, "Tribute from Judah and the Transmission of Assyrian Propaganda," in *"My Spirit at Rest in the North Country" (Zechariah 6.8): Collected Communications to the XXth Congress of the International Organization for the Study of the Old Testament, Helsinki 2010*, ed. Hermann Michael Niemann and Matthias Augustin, BEATAJ 57 [New York: Lang, 2011], 183). This is far too

possible that a copy of this document was located in Jerusalem, perhaps in the palace of the *qēpu* at Ramat Rachel.[81] However, since Judah was a vassal and not a province with a governor (as in the case of Tell Tayinat), there may not have been a copy in Judah, but only in Nineveh. If a copy were in Jerusalem, it would have been there in the days of Manasseh. With the Assyrian withdrawal from the region, it is doubtful it would have survived into the period of Josiah. In any case, it is extremely unlikely that any of these "literate-in-Akkadian" Judahites would have known the treaty so well that they could have discerned from this tiny bit (20 lines) a literary allusion to the Esarhaddon treaty, much less that Deuteronomy was directly subverting it!

Challenge 3: The Problem with Hittites

When one compares the overall structure of Deuteronomy with all the ancient Near Eastern treaty materials, it is evident that Deuteronomy bears a closer resemblance to the late second-millennium Hittite treaty form than any other treaty traditions (see Huddleston's essay in this volume). But this observation carries with it an obvious challenge—there are no clear material links between the Hittites of the empire period and the Israelites.

Although the Hebrew Bible employs the term *ḥittî* in its various permutations, it uses it as a geographic-cultural identifier for individuals and families originating from, or peoples located in, the northern region of the Levant. The application of *ḥittî* to the "children of Heth" (בְּנֵי חֵת) as if they are "Hittites," or the application of the "children of Heth" to *ḥittî*, as if *ḥittî*

---

pessimistic. Even in the mid-ninth century a ruler of Sūḫu could write to the king of Hamat in Akkadian. See Simo Parpola, "A Letter from Marduk-apla-uṣur of Anah to Rudamu/Urtamis, King of Hamath," in *HAMA: Fouilles et recherches de la Fondation Carlsberg, II 2: Les objets de la période dite Syro-Hittite*, ed. P. J. Riis and Marie-Louise Buhl (Copenhagen: Nationalmuseet, 1990), 257–65. If Yariri of Karkamiš around 800 BCE could boast knowledge of four scripts and twelve languages (one of which was Akkadian), it is not implausible to think that a limited number of scribes in Judah during the Assyrian empire's domination of the region could have known Akkadian. See now K. Lawson Younger Jr., "The Scripts of North Syria in the Early First Millennium: The Inscription of Yariri (KARKAMIŠ A15b) Once Again," *Transeuphratène* 46 (2014): 169–83. Finally, the growing number of bilinguals in which Akkadian is one of the languages argues for the ability of some Judahite scribes to have worked in the language.

[81] See also Karen Radner, "Assyrische *ṭuppi adê* als Vorbild für Deuteronomium 28,20–44?" in *Die deuteronomistischen Geschichtswerke: Redaktions- und religionsgeschichtliche Perspektiven zur "Deuteronomismus"-Diskussion in Tora und Vorderen Propheten*, ed. Markus Witte et al., BZAW 365 (Berlin: de Gruyter, 2006), 374–75.

are "Hethites," introduces category confusion on contextual, geographic, linguistic, and historical grounds.[82] In short, the terminology *haḫittî* in the patriarchal narratives describes individuals and their families who exhibited some level of cultural homogeneity with northern peoples regardless of specific political and historical details surrounding Anatolia and Syria-Palestine. Assyrian inscriptions from the time of Tiglath-pileser I (ca. 1091 BCE)[83] onward illustrate that the areas controlled by the Neo-Hittite successor states were referred to as "Ḫatti" due to their connection to the fallen Hittite empire.[84] While this appellation is no doubt geographic, it is also vested with Hittite culture, as the Assyrian interchange of "Ḫatti" with "Karkamiš" demonstrates.[85] The Assyrian conception of "Ḫatti" as the area that encompasses "northern Syria and parts of south-eastern Anatolia, from the Euphrates to the Mediterranean coast and anti-Taurus range, probably comes closest to reflecting what most Iron Age peoples understood by the term."[86] Those "Hittites" mentioned in the lists and in the periods during the Iron Age refer to various people groups associated with the collapse of the Hittite empire and the Neo-Hittite successor states. The application of *ḥittî* to the northern Levant and to individuals with roots in that area avoids category confusion, reflects geographic and onomastic delimiters supplied in the biblical text, and is consistent with the presence of Syro-Hittite realia from that area.

In addition, according to present knowledge, empire-period Hittites only penetrated as far south as Damascus. Around 1340 BCE, the Hittites captured Damascus during Šuppiluliuma I's one-year Syrian campaign against Mitanni and its Syro-Palestinian vassals. However, not long after the campaign, Šuppiluliuma relinquished control of the town in an attempt to achieve peace with the pharaoh.

Following the Egyptian retreat from Qadesh, in 1274 BCE the Hittite army marched as far as the Damascus area and devastated the land. Thus Ḫattušili III related:

---

[82] For a detailed argument see the second chapter in Huddleston, "Deuteronomy as *Mischgattung*."

[83] RIMA 2, 37–43, A.0.87.3, lines 26, 28, 37; A.0.87.4, lines 28, 30, 31. KUR *ḫa-at-te* equates with Karkamiš, but also is used for the region as a whole.

[84] See also Billie Jean Collins, *The Hittites and Their World*, ABLHS 7 (Atlanta: SBL Press, 2007), 198.

[85] John David Hawkins, "Karkamiš," in *Corpus of Hieroglyphic Luwian Inscriptions*, vol. 1, *Inscriptions from the Iron Age, Part 1: Text: Introduction, Karatepe, Karkamiš, Tell Ahmar, Maraş, Malatya, Commagene*, ed. Roberto Gusmani et al., UISK 8.1 (Berlin: de Gruyter, 2000), 73.

[86] Trevor R. Bryce, *The World of the Neo-Hittite Kingdoms: A Political and Military History* (Oxford: Oxford University Press, 2012), 50.

> Because my brother Muwattalli campaigned against the king of Egypt and the king of Amurru, when he defeated the kings of Egypt and Amurru, he went back to Aba. When Muwattalli, my brother defeated Aba/Apa, he . . . went back to Hatti, but he left me in Aba/Apa.[87]

At this time the region around Damascus was called Aba/Apa. Thus, Ḫattušili was in charge of Damascus for a time. However, once again the Hittites did not stay in Apa. After they withdrew, Damascus and its surrounding region marked part of Egypt's northern frontier with the Hittites.[88]

An important handful of distinctly Hittite artifacts have been discovered in the southern Levant. Although this is not the place to rehearse all this evidence,[89] it is important to point out that, relative to other regions, "the Hittite objects from the southern Levant are surprisingly numerous."[90] Significantly, in appearance they seem to reflect "diplomatic gifts" and "Hittite emissaries or functionaries."[91] This comports well with Billie Jean Collins' succinct summary regarding two of these objects—the Megiddo ivory and Aphek bulla—which were products of Hittite-Egyptian diplomacy. Regarding the Late Bronze Age material she states:

> No migration is necessary to explain the Hittites in the Bible . . . the Hittites who came to northern Palestine during the *pax Hethitica-Egyptiaca*, whether their stay was long or short, were sufficient in quantity and, more importantly, in quality to explain the level of cultural transmission that is evident. . . . But at no time were conditions more perfect or [*sic:* for] Palestine, which was perched on the cusp of a new era, more poised to absorb new influences than in the latter half of the thirteenth century.[92]

Collins also argues that occasionally in the Hebrew Bible the term "Hittite" is rooted in a secondary use taken from northern Israel. In this

[87] *KUB* XXI 17 (*CTH* 86) I 14–21, with duplicate *KUB* XXXI 27 2–7, 51. Translation: Richard Henry Beal, *The Organisation of the Hittite Military*, THeth 20 (Heidelberg: C. Winter, 1992), 307. For discussion, see Collins, *Hittites and Their World*, 55; Trevor R. Bryce, *The Kingdom of the Hittites* (Oxford: Oxford University Press, 2005), 240. *KUB* XXI, 17 I 14–21; *KUB* XXXI, 27:208.

[88] Bryce, *World of the Neo-Hittite Kingdoms*, 175.

[89] Itamar Singer, "The Hittites and the Bible Revisited," in *"I Will Speak the Riddles of Ancient Times": Archaeological and Historical Studies in Honor of Amihai Mazar on the Occasion of His Sixtieth Birthday*, ed. Aren M. Maeir and Pierre de Miroschedji (Winona Lake, IN: Eisenbrauns, 2006): 723–56; Amir Gilan, "Hittites in Canaan? The Archaeological Evidence," *BN* 156 (2013): 39–52; Huddleston, "Deuteronomy as *Mischgattung*."

[90] Hermann Genz, "Foreign Contacts of the Hittites," in *Insights into Hittite History and Archaeology*, ed. Hermann Genz and Dirk Paul Mielke, ColAnt 2 (Leuven: Peeters, 2011), 316.

[91] Ibid., 323; so also Gilan, "Hittites in Canaan?" 48.

[92] Collins, *Hittites and Their World*, 218.

view, "Hittite" reflects an embedded cultural memory manifested in a literary convention. The term represents indirect historical precursors when applied to assumed populations in the southern Levant, rather than assuming population displacement for which there is no archaeological evidence.[93] The Hittite artifacts found in Canaan, as well as later cultural influences via a Hittite elite, are best explained as the product of the *pax Hethitica-Egyptiaca*,[94] especially during the thirteenth century.[95]

We must emphasize that there is no archaeological or textual evidence for direct contact between the Anatolian Hittite civilization and the people of Israel. Therefore, apparent Hittite influences in Israel were indirect, most likely filtered and transmitted through the Hittite successor states.[96] These influences may have been brought south prior to the Israelite monarchy, though "elements of Hittite culture in their 'Neo-Hittite' after-life may certainly have been brought into David's court by North Syrian immigrants."[97]

While the kingdom of Hamath may have been a conduit, particularly in the time of David, Elena Devecchi[98] has suggested that Carchemish was likely the principle disseminator of Hittite treaty forms and culture to its north Syrian vassals prior to the empire's collapse. After the demise

---

[93] Ibid., 197–213.

[94] An important phrase borrowed from Singer. See his "Hittites and the Bible Revisited." See also Yoram Cohen, Amir Gilan, and Jared L. Miller, *Pax Hethitica: Studies on the Hittites and Their Neighbours in Honour of Itamar Singer*, StBoT 51 (Wiesbaden: Harrassowitz, 2010), 2.

[95] Collins, *Hittites and Their World*, 213–18.

[96] Although Egypt could potentially have been an intermediary of sorts, particularly in the period of the *pax Hethitica-Egyptiaca*, this is extremely difficult to trace, given the present status of the Egyptian evidence and the challenges of tracing this type of influence.

[97] Harry A. Hoffner, "The Hittites and Hurrians," in *Peoples of Old Testament Times*, ed. D. J. Wiseman (London: Oxford University Press, 1973), 221; so also Hoffner, "Hittite-Israelite Cultural Parallels," in *COS* 3:xxxvi; Hoffner, "Ancient Israel's Literary Heritage Compared with Hittite Textual Data," in *The Future of Biblical Archaeology: Reassessing Methodologies and Assumptions: The Proceedings of a Symposium, August 12–14, 2001 at Trinity International University*, ed. Alan R. Millard and James K. Hoffmeier (Grand Rapids: Eerdmans, 2004), 191–92.

[98] Elena Devecchi, "Treaties and Edicts in the Hittite World," in *Organization, Representation, and Symbols of Power in the Ancient Near East: Proceedings of the 54th Rencontre Assyriologique Internationale at Würzburg, 20–25 July 2008*, ed. Gernot Wilhelm (Winona Lake, IN: Eisenbrauns, 2012), 643–44. Alfonso also posits Aleppo in this role, while noting the likely continuation and transformation of Hittite legal traditions at Carchemish (see Lorenzo d'Alfonso, "Die hethitische Vertragstradition in Syrien [14. – 12. Jh. v. Chr.]," in *Die deuteronomistischen Geschichtswerke: Redaktions- und religionsgeschichtliche Perspektiven zur "Deuteronomismus"-Diskussion in Tora und Vorderen Propheten*, ed. Markus Witte et al., BZAW 365 [Berlin: de Gruyter, 2006], 329).

of the Hittite empire, the king of Carchemish claimed the title "Great King," suggesting that this polity envisioned itself as the continuator of Hittite tradition. If Devecchi is correct, this implies that such influence would have continued up to the destruction of Carchemish by Sargon II in 717 BCE, providing a firm *terminus ad quem* for these influences in the Iron Age. Thus the Late Bronze Age *pax Hethitica-Egyptiaca* and early Iron Age evidence form a potentially contiguous stream of Hittite and then Neo-Hittite cultural awareness and expression for the southern Levant, particularly in Israel. The relatively frequent presence of Late Bronze Age Hittite material in the southern Levant evidences robust international relations with Egypt and provides an ample basis for an early Israelite awareness of Hittite diplomacy. Thus, the data leave open the possibility of an early awareness of Hittite diplomacy in ancient Israel and demonstrate later cultural and trade interactions with the Syro-Hittite successor states. However, we must emphasize again that there is no material evidence indicating a direct link.

For this reason, we do not attempt a historical reconstruction specifying the means by which biblical Israel came into contact with early Hittite cultural influences. Concerning possible mechanisms of influence, the texts and material artifacts are silent. They do, however, describe a rich cultural milieu where such contact could have occurred at a number of points during the Late Bronze Age and subsequent Neo-Hittite context. In our estimation, when we account for the total picture, it is reasonable to suggest a Late Bronze Age awareness of "Hittite" (Anatolian) cultures in the southern Levant that persisted throughout the monarchic period, both in Israel and in Judah.

Conclusion

We have demonstrated that the use of ancient Near Eastern treaty forms for dating and interpreting Deuteronomy presents significant challenges. Furthermore, there are several significant chronological gaps in the preservation of the ancient Near Eastern treaties. The first gap is between the twenty-third and nineteenth centuries, the second is between the mid-eighteenth and fifteenth centuries, and the third is between 1210 and 824 BCE (a span of almost four hundred years).[99] Recognition of these gaps should warn scholars to be cautious in their discussions and conclusions, since there are narrative texts from these chronological gaps that

[99] For quick reference, see the table at the end of Huddleston's essay in this volume.

allude to various treaties being made, yet we do not have extant copies. Many more treaties were made than the extant exemplars attest to.

Moreover, all three challenges highlighted above operate on the assumption that the treaty form, so evident in a reading of Deuteronomy, is the product of some kind of influence on Israel. However, given the continual discovery of additional treaties from the ancient Near East, there is reason to wonder to what extent the treaty materials found in the Hebrew Bible, including Deuteronomy, are simply part of a broad cultural continuum. In this case, Deuteronomy has drawn on this broader cultural phenomenon, and is therefore not directly dependent on *one* particular treaty document or tradition from the ancient Near East. Clearly, Deuteronomy is a *Mischgattung* that functions as a unique work in its own right. Insofar as it reflects the treaty form, the book of Deuteronomy may better be understood as part of the ancient Near Eastern cultural continuum.

CHAPTER 4

Josiah and the Composition of Deuteronomy

Michael A. Grisanti

Introduction

In scholarly discussions concerning the dating for the composition of Deuteronomy, the connection of this biblical book to the setting of the Judean king Josiah reigns supreme.[1] This connection is often regarded as a beginning point for understanding other sections of the Old Testament. For example, Rainer Albertz wrote that "the most important decision in the history of Israelite religion is made with a dating of an essential part of Deuteronomy to the time of Josiah."[2] Writing about the development of the Deuteronomistic History, Marvin Sweeney observed:

> [The] remarkable narrative about Josiah in the DtrH has proved to be a pivotal text in scholarly discussion and has shaped the entire discipline of Hebrew Bible studies. It provides the fundamental linchpin by which modern critical scholarship reconstructs the development of Israelite/Judean religion and the compositional history of much of biblical literature.[3]

Finally, in 1992 Steven McKenzie wrote that the "acceptance of this viewpoint has continued such that, to the extent that any position in biblical studies can be regarded as the consensus viewpoint, the existence of the DH has achieved almost canonical status."[4]

Undoubtedly, how one handles the role of Josiah and his reforms in the composition of Deuteronomy looms large on the stage of Old Testament scholarship. This essay seeks to provide a brief overview of the development of the connection of Josiah and his reforms to the composition

---

[1] I express my thanks to my teaching assistant, Peter Goeman, for reading this essay in several iterations and for his assistance in matters of formatting and style.

[2] Rainer Albertz, *A History of Israelite Religion in the Old Testament Period*, OTL (Louisville: Westminster John Knox, 1994), 1:199.

[3] Marvin Sweeney, *King Josiah of Judah: The Lost Messiah of Israel* (Oxford: Oxford University Press, 2001), 5.

[4] Steven L. McKenzie, "Deuteronomistic History," *ABD* 2:161.

of Deuteronomy—its origin with Wilhelm M. L. de Wette, the adjustments introduced by Julius Wellhausen, and the continuing "conversation" by proponents of the Deuteronomistic History (DH hereafter—discussed below). After offering some supporting evidence used by those who affirm the connection of Josiah to the composition of Deuteronomy (with some brief responses), the essay concludes with a sketch of some scholarly challenges to this connection.

Josiah's Reforms and the Composition of Deuteronomy: The Roots of the Connection[5]

As part of the development of the JEDP theory, by the late eighteenth century, the alleged documents E and J were assigned to a post-Mosaic era and P was just beginning to receive attention as a distinct source. In that context, de Wette (1780–1849) proposed that Deuteronomy was written not by Moses, but rather by an unknown author in the time of King Josiah.

De Wette's primary goal was to demonstrate that Deuteronomy was written later than the other four books of the Pentateuch.[6] He maintained that "the book of Deuteronomy was not simply a blueprint for the Josianic reforms of the seventh century BCE, but was also the product of the period in which it was used."[7] Although this basic suggestion had originated as far back as Benedict de Spinoza and his Enlightenment peers in the seventeenth century,[8] de Wette's dissertation became famous "because

[5] Limitations of space preclude detailed presentation of the historical development of a Josianic context for the "authorship" of Deuteronomy. More information is available in Peter Vogt's essay in this volume, "Deuteronomy: A History of Interpretation and Evangelical Responses."

[6] John W. Rogerson, *W. M. L. de Wette, Founder of Modern Biblical Criticism: An Intellectual Biography*, JSOTSup 126 (Sheffield: Sheffield Academic, 1992), 40.

[7] Peter T. Vogt, " 'These Are the Words Moses Spoke': Implied Audience and a Case for a Pre-Monarchic Dating of Deuteronomy," in *For Our Good Always: Studies on the Message and Influence of Deuteronomy in Honor of Daniel I. Block*, ed. Jason S. DeRouchie, Jason Gile, and Kenneth J. Turner (Winona Lake, IN: Eisenbrauns, 2013), 61.

[8] Spinoza identified Ezra as the author of Deuteronomy (Benedict de Spinoza, *Theological-Political Treatise*, ed. J. Israel, trans. M. Silverthorne and J. Israel, Cambridge Texts in the History of Philosophy [Cambridge: Cambridge University Press, 2007], 127–29), while Richard Simon pointed to an anonymous priest of the exilic period (2 Kgs 17:28) (see Rudolf Smend, *From Astruc to Zimmerli: Old Testament Scholarship in Three Centuries*, trans. M. Kohl [Tübingen: Mohr Siebeck, 2007], 10). Nestle pointed to some early church fathers (Athanasius, Chrysostom, Jerome, and Theodoret) who made the same identification (Eberhard Nestle, "Das Deuteronomium und 2 Könige 22," *ZAW* 22 [1902]: 312–13). De Wette offers a

it is supposed to have established that Deuteronomy was the law book discovered in the temple in the reign of Josiah in 622 BCE, and that Deuteronomy must have been written in the seventh century."[9]

Although others had seen connections between Josiah's reforms and the book of Deuteronomy, de Wette introduced a more concrete statement of that possibility, laying the groundwork for generations of Old Testament scholars after him. De Wette regarded Deuteronomy (his document D) as significantly different from the other books of the Pentateuch. The thematic similarities of sections of Deuteronomy and 2 Kgs 22–23 offer support for his conclusions.

De Wette contributed significantly to the ongoing scholarly discussion of how best to understand the way the Bible (including the Pentateuch) came into being. In the decades to follow, that understanding became more concrete and better known. Due to space limitations, this essay considers just one individual who helped establish the place of Deuteronomy in the development of the Documentary Hypothesis.

Although Julius Wellhausen (1844–1918) introduced some refinements to the scholarly consensus regarding the origins of the Pentateuch (e.g., the Documentary Hypothesis, or JEDP theory), his main contribution was to present a simplified and coherent set of ideas.[10] The wide reception of his books contributed to the massive spread of the Documentary Hypothesis throughout the world (including the hypothesis concerning Josiah's role in the composition of Deuteronomy).

By Wellhausen's time, "De Wette's thesis was widely accepted, becoming the linchpin in modern critical theory of the Pentateuch . . . Deuteronomy (Source D) had become one of the four pillars of pentateuchal theory."[11] Although scholars regarded de Wette as the foundation for their understanding of Deuteronomy, they generally rejected his idea that Deuteronomy was the latest book of the Pentateuch. According to Rudolf Smend, "later 19th century research brought the proof, finally presented by Wellhausen, that the relationship is largely the reverse, i.e., that Deuteronomy should not

---

lengthy list of scholars who questioned the genuineness of the books of Moses (W. M. L. de Wette, *A Critical and Historical Introduction to the Canonical Scriptures of the Old Testament*, trans. Theodore Parker [Boston: Charles C. Little and James Brown, 1843], 2:161–64). See also Paul B. Harvey Jr. and Baruch Halpern, "W. M. L. de Wette's *'Dissertatio Critica . . .'*: Context and Translation," *ZABR* 14 (2008): 48n4.

[9] Rogerson, *De Wette: Founder of Modern Biblical Criticism*, 39–40.

[10] Julius Wellhausen, *Prolegomena to the History of Ancient Israel* (Edinburgh: A. & C. Black, 1885; repr., Atlanta: Scholars Press, 1994).

[11] Jack Lundbom, *Deuteronomy: A Commentary* (Grand Rapids: Eerdmans, 2013), 6. See also H. H. Rowley, *Men of God: Studies in Old Testament History and Prophecy* (London: Nelson, 1963), 161; Otto Eissfeldt, *The Old Testament: An Introduction,* trans. P. R. Ackroyd (New York: Harper & Row, 1965), 173.

be placed at the end of the Pentateuch but belongs approximately to the middle of its history."[12]

The connection between the book of the law discovered during Josiah's reign and the book of Deuteronomy appears patently obvious to most critical scholars.[13] Although some suggest that de Wette's understanding of the basic features of the composition of Deuteronomy has undergone little alteration,[14] others have rejected several aspects of de Wette's thesis, offering other models in its place.[15] For example, after pointing out ways scholars have rejected and added to de Wette's proposal, Moshe Weinfeld notes that "one can no longer speak of a new book written in the time of Josiah but about compiling old traditions and reworking them in the spirit of a new historical and social reality."[16]

Josiah's Reforms and the Composition of Deuteronomy: Recent Modifications to the Connection[17]

In the wake of discoveries in ancient Near Eastern literature and growing frustrations with various aspects of the Documentary Hypothesis, many critical scholars have moved away from focusing on literary sources, preferring to emphasize the development of traditions. They have begun regarding Deuteronomy less as document D discovered during Josiah's reign, and more as an ideological engine that influenced the Former Prophets, Joshua–Kings.

---

[12] Smend, *From Astruc to Zimmerli*, 48.

[13] Philip R. Davies bluntly stated that "it takes no genius to see that the identification of Deuteronomy with the Josianic law book is precisely what the author of 2 Kings 22 intends" ("Josiah and the Law Book," in *Good Kings and Bad Kings: The Kingdom of Judah in the Seventh Century BCE*, ed. Lester Grabbe, LHBOTS 393 [London: T&T Clark, 2005], 69).

[14] Rudolf Smend, "Ein Theologe zwischen den Fronten," in *Wilhelm Martin Leberecht de Wette: Ein Universaltheologe des 19. Jahrhunderts*, ed. H.-P. Mathys and K. Seybold, Studien zur Geschichte der Wissenschaften in Basel, Neue Folge 1 (Basel: Schwabe, 2001), 25.

[15] Duane L. Christensen, "Deuteronomy in Modern Research: Approaches and Issues," in *A Song of Power and the Power of Song: Essays on the Book of Deuteronomy*, ed. Duane L. Christensen, SBTS 3 (Winona Lake, IN: Eisenbrauns, 1993), 4–8. Cf. Moshe Weinfeld, "Deuteronomy: The Present State of Inquiry," in ibid., 22–35; Norbert Lohfink, "Recent Discussion on 2 Kings 22–23: The State of the Question," in ibid., 37–61.

[16] Weinfeld, "State of Inquiry," 35.

[17] Because of space limitations, this summary of the place of Josiah's reforms in the composition of Deuteronomy (and DH) focuses primarily on the views as they relate to Josiah.

Martin Noth and the Inception of DH

In the years following the placement of Deuteronomy in the context of the Josianic reforms, scholars began investigating whether or not there was an Urdeuteronomium, or "proto-Deuteronomy."[18] Some suggested that chapters 12–26 made up the scroll discovered during Josiah's reign, and that chapters 1–4 and 5–11 were distinct introductions to that scroll.[19] Martin Noth's proposal that the book of Deuteronomy (the work of a single author) represented the introduction to the entire DH (Deuteronomy to 2 Kings) offered a potential resolution to this debate.[20] Deuteronomy 1–4 was considered the introduction not simply to the legal section (chs. 12–26), but to the entirety of DH. According to Noth, DH was completed sometime after 562 BCE (the last event recorded in 2 Kings).[21] Although Noth affirmed that the present form of Deuteronomy dates from the exilic period, according to Dillard and Longman he granted that it "contains many ancient materials."[22]

As was true in de Wette's proposal, DH scholars generally saw Deut 12:5 and subsequent "name" references in that book as veiled allusions to the Jerusalem temple and an essential part of the law of cult centralization.[23] They suggested that DH authors used general terminology rather than concrete language (e.g., Jerusalem, city, the house, David, etc.) to avoid sounding anachronistic.[24] Weinfeld summarizes, stating that the "deuteronomic composition is the creation of scribal circles which began their literary project some time prior to the reign of Josiah and were still at their work after the fall of Judah."[25] These allusions prepared the way for the claim, made by the Deuteronomistic historian (= Deuteronomist or Dtr), that Jerusalem (i.e., the temple) was the place that YHWH chose

---

[18] Lundbom, *Deuteronomy*, 8. Scholars assumed that the scroll found by Hilkiah could not have included all of the current book of Deuteronomy.

[19] Ibid.; cf. de Wette, *Canonical Scriptures* 2:131; Julius Wellhausen, *Die Composition des Hexateuchs und der historischen Bücher des Alten Testaments*, 3rd ed. (Berlin: Reimer, 1889), 191–95; S. R. Driver, *A Critical and Exegetical Commentary on Deuteronomy*, ICC (Edinburgh: T&T Clark, 1895), lxvi–lxxii, 135; etc.

[20] Martin Noth, *The Deuteronomistic History*, JSOTSup 15 (Sheffield: JSOT, 1981), 12–14.

[21] Noth, *Deuteronomistic History*, 12.

[22] Tremper Longman III and Raymond B. Dillard, *An Introduction to the Old Testament*, 2nd ed. (Grand Rapids: Zondervan, 2006), 108–9.

[23] E.g., Moshe Weinfeld, *Deuteronomy and the Deuteronomic School* (Oxford: Clarendon, 1972; repr., Winona Lake, IN: Eisenbrauns, 1992), 4.

[24] Ibid., 6.

[25] Ibid., 9. Weinfeld (ibid., 8–9) suggests that the orations that refer to centralized worship may have eventually been used in cultic worship, but they did not necessarily originate in a cultic setting. In other words, the centralization emphasis did not originate in a cultic setting but helped create that setting in a centralized location.

for his dwelling. Accordingly, all Israelite worship had to be centralized there, and worship or sacrifice elsewhere was regarded as illegitimate. Jeffrey Niehaus summarizes a common view among DH proponents that "the insistence on centralization of worship in Jerusalem was part of the larger Deuteronomic reform movement, which enlisted the support of Josiah and which had as its advocate the prophet Jeremiah."[26]

According to Noth, Josiah and his reformation played a less significant role in the composition of Deuteronomy than that proposed by de Wette and other JEDP theory proponents. Noth argued that the Deuteronomist compiled DH by drawing on a variety of ancient sources to produce his history of Israel. The scroll discovered by Hilkiah may have been a reworked version or exposition of the Decalogue (Deut 4:44–30:20).[27] According to Peterson's summary of Noth, Dtr wrote with a theological perspective to explain "the failure of the monarchy, why the nation of Israel had lost the land, and why it found itself in exile" (primarily a negative perspective).[28]

Further Revisions of DH: "Double Redaction" Views

Frank Cross and the "Harvard School"

In light of numerous passages that introduced a hope for the future, some scholars dismissed the notion that Dtr focused primarily on the downfall of the kingdoms of Israel and Judah.[29] For example, Frank Cross proposed preexilic and postexilic redactions of the DH (a view known as the "Double Redaction" or "Harvard School" view). Dtr^1 produced the

---

[26] Jeffrey Niehaus, "The Central Sanctuary," *TynBul* 43 (1992): 21.

[27] Noth, *Deuteronomistic History*, 6–10, 16, 31–33, 76, 116. For Noth (ibid., 4), "Deuteronomic" referred to something that was drawn from "Urdeuteronomy," while "Deuteronomistic" signified something deriving from an exilic revision, material influenced by Deuteronomy.

[28] Brian N. Peterson, *The Authors of the Deuteronomistic History: Locating a Tradition in Ancient Israel* (Minneapolis: Fortress, 2014), 10–11. Peterson (ibid., 11) observes that Noth affirmed the unity of DH in its final form, "with the author(s) presenting a clearly focused end goal."

[29] This essay can only sketch the development of views concerning DH. For helpful surveys of the origin and development of DH, see Jeremy M. Hutton, *The Transjordanian Palimpsest: The Overwritten Texts of Personal Exile and Transformation in the Deuteronomistic History*, BZAW 396 (New York: de Gruyter, 2009); Mark A. O'Brien, "The Book of Deuteronomy," *CurBS* 3 (1995): 95–128; Sandra L. Richter, "Deuteronomistic History," in *Dictionary of the Old Testament: Historical Books*, ed. Bill T. Arnold and H. G. M. Williamson (Downers Grove, IL: InterVarsity Press, 2005), 219–30; Thomas Römer and A. de Pury, "Deuteronomistic Historiography (DH): History of Research and Debated Issues," in *Israel Constructs Its History: Deuteronomistic Historiography in Recent Research*, ed. A. de Pury, Thomas Römer, and Jean-Daniel Macchi, JSOTSup 306 (Sheffield: Sheffield Academic, 2000), 24–141.

first redaction of this history in the time of Josiah, while Dtr^2 modified and updated the DH in the exilic period.[30] Cross proposed that, throughout this history, Dtr^1 consistently interacted with the consequences of the rebellion of Jeroboam I and the implications of David's faithfulness.[31] By paralleling judgment and hope, Dtr^1 communicated the central concerns of the Josianic reforms.[32] Later proponents of DH gave less attention to Josiah and his reforms in their explanation of the origin and development of DH than had de Wette, Wellhausen, and supporters of the JEDP paradigm. In the context of DH, Josiah's reforms provide an essential part of the historical presentation of Dtr^1. Dtr^2 wrote the conclusion to DH by the time of the exile, bringing the document up to date with the sad news of exile, which seemed to extinguish the hopes of Josiah's time.[33]

Rudolf Smend and the "Göttingen School"

Rudolf Smend and some of his students (the "Göttingen School") offered a different "Double Redaction" view. The initial Dtr completed his work in the exilic period (DtrH), and a postexilic redactor (DtrN) highlighted the role of the law in Israel's history.[34] One of Smend's students later posited a second postexilic redactor, who added various predictive or prophetic passages to DH.[35] In Smend's view, Josiah and his reforms played no significant role in the composition of Deuteronomy as part of DH.[36]

---

[30] Frank M. Cross, "The Themes of the Book of Kings and the Structure of the Deuteronomistic History," in *Canaanite Myth and Hebrew Epic: Essays in the History of the Religion of Israel* (Cambridge: Harvard University Press, 1973), 274–89; cf. Richard D. Nelson, *The Double Redaction of the Deuteronomistic History*, JSOTSup 18 (Sheffield: JSOT Press, 1981), esp. 13–28; Norbert Lohfink, "The Cult Reform of Josiah of Judah: 2 Kings 22–23 as a Source for the History of Israelite Religion," in *Ancient Israelite Religion: Essays in Honor of Frank Moore Cross*, ed. P. Miller, P. Hanson, and S. D. McBride (Philadelphia: Fortress, 1987), 459–75.

[31] Cross, "Themes," 278–85.

[32] Ibid., 284; Richter, "Deuteronomistic History," 223.

[33] Cross, "Themes," 285.

[34] Rudolf Smend, *Die Entstehung des Alten Testaments*, Theologische Wissenschaft 1 (Stuttgart: Kohlhammer, 1978), 111–39; Smend, "The Law and the Nations: A Contribution to Deuteronomistic Tradition History," in *Reconsidering Israel and Judah: Recent Studies on the Deuteronomistic History*, ed. G. Knoppers and J. Gordon McConville (Winona Lake, IN: Eisenbrauns, 2000), 95–110; for the German original, see Smend, "Das Gesetz und die Völker: Ein Beitrag zur deuteronomistischen Redaktionsgeschichte," in *Probleme biblischer Theologie: Gerhard von Rad zum 70. Geburtstag*, ed H. W. Wolff (Munich: Kaiser, 1971), 494–509.

[35] Walter Dietrich, *Prophetie und Geschichte: Eine redaktionsgeschichtliche Untersuchung zum deuteronomischen Geschichtswerk*, FRLANT 108 (Göttingen: Vandenhoeck & Ruprecht, 1972), 107–9, 143–44.

[36] Numerous adjustments to the views of de Wette, Cross, Smend, and others have been offered over the years.

Ongoing Discussion

Although some have observed that Josiah's involvement in the composition of the book of Deuteronomy is a linchpin of Old Testament scholarship, others note that the views on DH are so varied that no consensus can be found. Scholars do not agree on whether some early form of Deuteronomy dates to the time of Hezekiah, Manasseh, or Josiah, or on how much of Deuteronomy existed in Josiah's time.[37]

However, scholars have raised other pressing questions relating to Josiah's role in Deuteronomy's composition. Richard Lowery suggests that the reforms of Josiah's reign stemmed from political or economic considerations rather than from an early form of Deuteronomy or a centralization of the cult agenda.[38] Others dismiss the strength of the connection between Deuteronomy and Josiah's reforms on "literary" grounds, concluding that "the narrational links that appear to exist between the reform and the discovery of the law book or its supposed contents are secondary and tendentious."[39] Finally, some reject the basic historicity of the reform altogether, regarding it as a "secondary literary construct that promotes postexilic theological and didactic aims."[40]

---

[37] Lundbom, *Deuteronomy*, 7–10.

[38] Richard H. Lowery, *The Reforming Kings: Cult and Society in First Temple Judah*, JSOTSup 120 (Sheffield: Sheffield Academic, 1991), 190–95. Cf. Gustav Hölscher, "Komposition und Ursprung des Deuteronomiums," *ZAW* 40 (1923): 161–255. Hölscher believed that Deuteronomy and its centralization agenda were postexilic creations and thus from a period long after Josiah's reforms.

[39] David A. Glatt-Gilad, "Revealed and Concealed: The Status of the Law (Book) of Moses within the Deuteronomistic History," in *Mishneh Todah: Studies in Deuteronomy and Its Cultural Environment in Honor of Jeffrey H. Tigay*, ed. N. S. Fox, D. Glatt-Gilad, M. Williams (Winona Lake, IN: Eisenbrauns, 2009), 186. For proponents of this view, see Christof Hardmeier, "King Josiah in the Climax of the Deuteronomic History (2 Kings 22–23) and the Pre-Deuteronomic Document of a Cult Reform at the Place of Residence (23.4–15): Criticism of Sources, Reconstruction of Literary Pre-Stages and the Theology of History in 2 Kings 22–23," in *Good Kings and Bad Kings*, 123–63, esp. 157–59. W. Boyd Barrick regards the connection between the book of Deuteronomy and the DH (and Josiah's reforms) as "a post-Josianic," probably postexilic, literary invention (Barrick, *The Kings and the Cemeteries: Toward a New Understanding of Josiah's Reform*, VTSup 88 [Boston: Brill, 2002], 114; see 112–14); cf. Ronald E. Clements, "The Deuteronomic Law of Centralisation and the Catastrophe of 587 BCE," in *After the Exile: Essays in Honour of Rex Mason*, ed. J. Barton and D. Reimer (Macon, GA: Mercer University Press, 1996), 8–13; Clements, "Deuteronomy and the Jerusalem Cult Tradition," *VT* 15 (1965): 300–312.

[40] Glatt-Gilad, "Revealed and Concealed," 187. For proponents of this skeptical view, see Davies, "Josiah and the Law Book," 65–77. According to Lowell K. Handy, the Josianic reform narrative was "clearly *not* contemporary with the events described in it and, in all probability, was written by persons unrelated to the reign of Josiah altogether . . . the Josianic reform narratives of Kings would have to be construed as . . . non-contemporary and unreliable" ("Historical

Martin Noth's pioneering suggestion that Deuteronomy provided the introduction to a coherent history of Israel (DH = Joshua–2 Kings) has had a far-reaching impact on Old Testament scholarship. As had been happening since the early 1900s, Noth pulled away from the idea of written documents underlying the Old Testament and began tracking oral traditions that developed over the centuries before they reached book form. He argued that an exilic writer composed a history of Israel with a Deuteronomic flavor. Maintaining that Josiah and his reforms played a significant role in that developing history, later proponents of DH offered divergent explanations of how various authors brought that history together. In the current landscape of Deuteronomy studies, there is no consensus on whether Josiah's reforms provided the setting for the composition of some of the book of Deuteronomy.

Josiah's Reforms and the Composition of Deuteronomy: Intertextual Evidence for the Connection

As noted above, critical scholars cannot agree on the composition of Deuteronomy or the process by which DH came into being. Nevertheless, we still often read that "De Wette's conclusions concerning Deuteronomy retain considerable force today."[41] As late as 2009 Michael Coogan stated that "a majority of scholars, if by no means all, continue to follow some version of the classic formulation of the Documentary Hypothesis [including de Wette's contribution] summarized here."[42]

Institutional Evidence

Reflecting this "consensus," many critical scholars contend that Deuteronomy is "fundamentally a late work whose purpose was not to anticipate Israel's sacred history but to reflect upon it, and to assess and critique that history in terms of Israel's adherence to or disobedience of the covenant principles enshrined within it."[43] Is that a justified conclu-

---

Probability and the Narrative of Josiah's Reform in 2 Kings," in *The Pitcher Is Broken: Memorial Essays for Gösta Ahlström*, ed. S. Holloway and L. K. Handy, JSOTSup 190 (Sheffield: Sheffield Academic, 1995), 275.

[41] Harvey and Halpern, "W. M. L. de Wette's *'Dissertatio Critica . . . ,'* " 61.

[42] Michael D. Coogan, *A Brief Introduction to the Old Testament* (New York: Oxford University Press, 2009), 46.

[43] Eugene H. Merrill, "Deuteronomy and History: Anticipation of Reflection?" *Faith & Mission* 18 (2000): 57.

sion based on the evidence generally cited? The next two subsections will consider two categories of argumentation often offered by proponents of the Josianic setting for the composition of Deuteronomy. Of the various institutions and elements that made up Israelite society (e.g., priesthood, prophetism, military, law, etc.), proponents of a Josianic time frame for the composition of Deuteronomy give special attention to the central sanctuary and "kingship."[44] The final subsection will consider the linguistic evidence that is offered as providing clear evidence that Deuteronomy drew on Josiah's reforms.

The Central Sanctuary

Deuteronomy 12:5–14 requires that God's chosen people worship at a place that YHWH will choose and where he has put his name. Unlike what characterized Israelite worship before the conquest of Canaan (Exod 18:12; Deut 12:8–9), their worship could only take place in designated places (primarily where the tabernacle and, later, the temple were located). In light of this, many scholars have concluded that Deut 12–26 must derive from the time of Josiah's reforms (or later), since he focused on removing places of pagan worship (2 Kgs 23:4–20; 2 Chr 34:3–7) and on rejuvenating worship at the temple (2 Kgs 22:3–7; 23:2, 9; 2 Chr 34:8; 35:2–3).[45] These scholars often point out that Israel's worship of YHWH rarely (if ever) perfectly matched the instructions found in Deut 12, suggesting that those instructions must not have existed until much later in Israel's history (long after Josiah).

Even though the exclusive worship of Israel's God may have predated Deuteronomy and Josiah's reforms, Mark O'Brien argues that centralization of worship was regarded as a distinctive Deuteronomic theme that directly affected Josiah's reforms (cf. 2 Kgs 23:4–20).[46] Norbert Lohfink states that "cult centralization remains the surest reform measure to link with the Deuteronomic legislation of that period."[47] Even so, DH scholars are not agreed on how much of this emphasis on centralization or which

---

[44] Several points in this section are taken from Merrill, "Deuteronomy and de Wette: A Fresh Look at a Fallacious Premise," *JESOT* 1 (2012): 35–36; and Merrill, "Deuteronomy and History," 60–65.

[45] Ernest W. Nicholson, *Deuteronomy and Tradition* (Philadelphia: Fortress, 1967), 5–17. According to de Wette, Deut 12 exemplified "legislation, which indicates later circumstances, namely the temple in Jerusalem" (W. M. L. de Wette, *Lehrbuch der historisch-kritischen Einleitung in die kanonischen und apokryphischen Bücher des Alten Testaments* [Berlin: G. Reimer, 1833], 201, as cited by Niehaus, "Central Sanctuary," 21).

[46] O'Brien, "Book of Deuteronomy," 99.

[47] Lohfink, "Cult Reform of Josiah," 466.

specific phrases derive from the version of Deuteronomy that existed in Josiah's day or from the developments in DH.[48]

The central idea of Deut 12 obviously served as a key part of Josiah's reforms in the seventh century BCE. De Wette had argued that Deuteronomy's emphasis on a central sanctuary must reflect later Josianic-era legislation since worship was permitted at local shrines in spite of Deuteronomy's prohibition against such locations for worship.[49] However, as Eugene Merrill notes, the reason de Wette concluded that Deuteronomy embodied theological ideas "later" than those found in the rest of the Pentateuch was because he already had determined that Deuteronomy must be a later composition than J and E, and that consequently Deuteronomy might be "the book of the law" found at the temple.[50] By itself, the fact that Josiah's reforms may have drawn on Deuteronomic exhortations does not argue that those reforms contributed to the composition of Deuteronomy during his reign.

Furthermore, the critical consensus of the composition of Deuteronomy in a Josianic time frame stands in tension with the following texts. First, according to 2 Chr 34:3–7, Josiah began purging the land of pagan places of worship twelve years before the book of the law was discovered by Hilkiah. In the same way that the Israelites were commanded by Moses to do so as part of their conquest of Canaan (Deut 7:5, 25), every godly king should have conducted this kind of purging. Second, Hezekiah's efforts to purge pagan altars from Israel (2 Kgs 18:4, 33; 2 Chr 31:1) predate Josiah by several decades and give no indication that his actions were occasioned by a monarchic "Mosaic" document. Rather, his conduct clearly presupposes what Deut 7 and 12 demanded of Israel. Third, Hezekiah was clearly aware of what God intended to do to Israel if it were to commit covenant treachery (i.e., the covenant curse—2 Chr 29:9; cf. Deut 28:25; and 2 Chr 30:9; cf. Deut 30:2). Fourth, the expressions "book of the law" (סֵפֶר הַתּוֹרָה, 2 Kgs 22:8); the Lord's "commandments" (מִצְוֹת), "testimonies" (עֵדוֹת), and "statutes" (חֻקִּים, 2 Kgs 23:3; 2 Chr 34:31); and "covenant" (בְּרִית, 2 Kgs 23:2–3, 21; 2 Chr 34:30–32) are also used in descriptions of Manasseh's treachery (2 Chr 33:8) and of the conduct of Jehoshaphat (250 years before Josiah; 2 Chr 19:10), as well as in descriptions of God's expectations of Solomon and Solomon's rebellion against them (1 Kgs 2:3; 3:14; 6:12; 8:58, 61; 9:6; 11:11, 33–34, 38). This repeated vocabulary suggests that these issues predated Josiah and cannot be limited to his reign.

---

[48] See O'Brien, "Book of Deuteronomy," 99–100, for a summary of alternatives.

[49] W. M. L. de Wette, *Opuscula Theologica* (Berlin: G. Reimer, 1830), 163–65.

[50] Merrill, "Deuteronomy and de Wette," 26n3, drawing on Rogerson (*De Wette: Founder of Modern Biblical Criticism*, 40–41).

Finally, the simple fact that the law in Deut 12:5 had not been perfectly practiced by Israel either before or after Solomon built the temple does not mean that the requirements of Deut 12 could not have antedated Israel's rebellion.[51] Neither is it compelling to conclude that Deut 12 "was written as part of a reform effort in Josiah's day, any more than Israel's persistent syncretism, from the wilderness wanderings onward, necessitates a seventh century date for Deuteronomy's polemic against idolatry."[52]

Kingship

According to Deut 17:14–20, YHWH demanded that Israel install a king of his choosing, a fellow Israelite rather than a foreigner, and one who would commission a fresh copy of the book of the law. God required that each Israelite king regularly read that law, which would cause him to fear YHWH and to obey God's covenant requirements. YHWH prohibited each Israelite king from acquiring many horses and wives and silver and gold. As part of their argument for a Josianic (or later) composition of Deuteronomy, DH proponents point out that no king ruled over Israel until the eleventh century, long after an alleged Mosaic setting. They contend that the choice of Saul (1 Sam 8:4–5, 19–20) and the reign of Solomon (1 Kgs 4:26; 10:26–29; 11:3–4) resonate with the requirements laid out in Deut 17.[53] Finally, they argue that the regal instructions of Deut 17 more directly address the historical realities that plagued Israel during the divided monarchy period (compared with the time of Moses or the early period of the Israelite monarchy). They imply that the disobedience of the requirements of the stipulations of Deut 17 during the united and divided monarchy suggests that those laws did not exist before those patterns of disobedience characterized the Israelite monarchy.

In response,[54] the critical view of a Josianic (or later) setting for the composition of the regal requirements in Deut 17 disregards the anticipation of kingship as part of the Abrahamic covenant (Gen 17:1–21),[55] a promise that occurs in several other pentateuchal passages as well. It

---

[51] The fact of a law's existence does not require perfect obedience to that law.

[52] Niehaus, "Central Sanctuary," 17.

[53] Gary N. Knoppers, "The Deuteronomist and the Deuteronomic Law of the King: A Reexamination of a Relationship," *ZAW* 108 (1996): 329–46; Ernest Nicholson, " 'Do Not Dare to Set a Foreigner Over You': The King in Deuteronomy and 'The Great King,' " *ZAW* 118 (2006): 46–61; Marvin A. Sweeney, "The Critique of Solomon in the Josianic Edition of the Deuteronomistic History," *JBL* 114 (1995): 607–22; Gerhard von Rad, *Deuteronomy*, OTL (Philadelphia: Westminster, 1966), 118–20.

[54] For McConville's contention that Deuteronomy's instruction concerning kingship does not match the realities of Josiah's day, see the final section of this essay.

[55] Cf. Gen 35:11; 36:31; 49:10; Num 24:17. Those who date these sections of Genesis to the ninth century BCE do not recognize that tension.

also ignores the fact that the monarchic tendency of self-aggrandizement reflected in multiplying horses, wealth, and women characterized ancient Near Eastern governance long before the time of Moses.[56] Furthermore, the absence of some such covenant regulations for kingship prior to Josiah's time, 350 years after the first king ruled over Israel, seems odd.[57]

Although the Pentateuch and historical books provide numerous examples of Israel failing to comply with parameters laid out in the Mosaic law, by itself this does not constitute evidence that those parameters did not exist until later in the history of the divided monarchy.

Linguistic Evidence

The most significant line of evidence cited by proponents of a Josianic setting for the composition of the book of Deuteronomy draws on the connection between the historiographic descriptions of Josiah's reform and the legal statements found in Deuteronomy. This section will consider this "terminological resonance" as customarily presented and examine whether the sinful practices and beliefs addressed by Josiah's reforms are present in texts (and historical settings) from before the time of Josiah.

Most scholars affirm that the Josianic reform (2 Kgs 22–23) draws heavily on Deuteronomy. The narratives suggest that the purge carried out by the young king in Jerusalem, Judah, and sites in the north took place immediately after the discovery of the scroll at the temple. Whatever "the book of the law" was or said, it seemed to motivate Josiah to expand the reform efforts he had initiated ten years earlier (2 Chr 34:3–7).

Remarkably, the details of Josiah's reforms all seem to match the prohibitions of Deuteronomy in content, vocabulary, and phraseology.[58] Mark Biddle has helpfully noted the following parallels between 2 Kgs 23 and Deuteronomy:[59]

---

[56] Yutaka Ikeda, "Solomon's Trade in Horses and Chariots in Its International Setting," in *Studies in the Period of David and Solomon and Other Essays*, ed. T. Ishida (Winona Lake, IN: Eisenbrauns, 1982), 215–38; Bernard M. Levinson, "The Reconceptualization of Kingship in Deuteronomy and the Deuteronomic History's Transformation of the Torah," *VT* 51 (2001): 511–18; Knoppers, "Deuteronomic Law of the King," 329.

[57] For issues not addressed in this essay (e.g., the presupposition of historical events, purported legal development), see Merrill ("Deuteronomy and History," 65–67), who argues that these issues do not support a Josianic time frame for the composition of Deuteronomy.

[58] Nicholson, *Deuteronomy and Tradition*, 3; Artur Weiser, *Old Testament: Its Formation and Development*, trans. D. M. Barton (New York: Association, 1961), 127–28; Weinfeld, *Deuteronomic School*, 320–59.

[59] The following list is adapted from Mark E. Biddle, *Deuteronomy*, SHBC (Macon, GA: Smyth & Helwys, 2003), 3.

- "to keep his commandments, and his statutes, and his testimonies" (2 Kgs 23:3; Deut 6:17; compare Deut 4:40, 45; 6:2, 20; etc.)
- "with all his heart and all his soul (and all his might)" (2 Kgs 23:3, 25; Deut 4:29; 6:5; 10:12; 11:13; 13:4[ET 3]; 26:16; 30:2, 6, 10)
- burning the vessels of Asherah (2 Kgs 23:4, 6, 15; Deut 7:5; 12:3)
- "the sun, the moon, the stars, and the hosts of heaven" (2 Kgs 23:5; Deut 4:19; 17:3)
- "beat it to dust" (2 Kgs 23:6, 15; Deut 9:21)
- "male cult prostitutes" (2 Kgs 23:7; Deut 23:18[ET 17])
- "to cause his son or his daughter to pass through the fire" (2 Kgs 23:10; Deut 18:10; compare Deut 12:31)
- "broke the מַצֵּבוֹת" (2 Kgs 23:14; Deut 12:3; compare Deut 7:5)
- "provoke YHWH to anger" (2 Kgs 23:19, 26; Deut 4:25; 9:18; 31:29; 32:16, 21)
- "mediums and wizards" (2 Kgs 23:24; Deut 18:11)
- "idols (גִּלֻּלִים) and abominations (שִׁקּוּצִים)" (2 Kgs 23:24; Deut 29:16)
- "[YHWH's] name there" (2 Kgs 23:27; Deut 12:5, 11, 21; 14:23, 24; 16:2, 6, 11; 26:2)

Many have noted the terms and phrases shared by the book of Deuteronomy and 2 Kgs 22–23. Scholars often conclude that this resonance of expressions demonstrates that Deuteronomy draws heavily on Josiah's speech and the "book of the law" discovered during his reign, and they utilize this evidence to support their dating of Deuteronomy to the time of Josiah (or beyond). In addition to these terminological links between Deuteronomy and 2 Kgs 22–23, the fact that many of the cited expressions occur long before Josiah's day demands attention. The examples given below clearly show that arguments for a Josianic dating of Deuteronomy often overlook the fact that those terms also frequently occur in Joshua–2 Kgs 22, in passages narrating events long before Josiah's time. On the one hand, these narratives address the same sinful practices carried out in various earlier historical circumstances. On the other hand, the few Israelite kings who sought to extinguish those practices reflected the long-standing divine repudiation of those practices. These attempts at "reform" took place long before Josiah and were arguably based on the Deuteronomic stipulations (along with similar ones in the rest of the

Pentateuch). This reality suggests that the laws of Deuteronomy do not originate with Josiah's reforms but are the driving force for all of these monarchial reform efforts.[60]

The Authority Base for Proper Covenant Conduct

"The book of the law" (סֵפֶר הַתּוֹרָה, 2 Kgs 22:8, 11). This expression draws on the command that each Israelite king was to copy the book of Deuteronomy at the beginning of his reign: "He shall write (כָּתַב) for himself in a book (סֵפֶר) a copy of this law (תּוֹרָה)" (Deut 17:18). The phrases "written in this book of the law" and "the book of the law of Moses" occur frequently (Deut 28:61; 29:20[ET 21]; 30:10; 31:26; Josh 1:8; 8:31, 34; 23:6; 24:26; 2 Kgs 14:6 [Amaziah]). A slight variant of this expression, "the words of this law" written in a book, also occurs (Deut 28:58; 31:24; 2 Chr 25:4 [Amaziah]; 2 Kgs 23:24 [Josiah]). The five occurrences of "book of the law" in the book of Joshua suggest that some version of this source existed during the time of Joshua, Moses' replacement. Both versions of the expression are also used in a description of the rebellion of Amaziah, who preceded Josiah by more than 150 years.

Descriptions of the Treachery or Consequences of Idolatry

Various verbs and nouns are used with some regularity to describe Israel's penchant for abandoning YHWH and worshipping other gods, provoking him and therefore facing divine punishment. In 2 Kgs 22:15–20, the prophetess Huldah warns of God's imminent punishment of Judah because it had pursued other gods. In this statement, she announces the fulfillment of "all the words of the book that the king of Judah has read" (v. 16). The verb "to abandon, forsake" (עָזַב, v. 17), which occurs more than 30 times in Deuteronomy–2 Chronicles, describes the nation's (as late as during Hezekiah's reign; 2 Chr 29:6) or a ruler's conduct before the time of Josiah.[61] It is included in warnings for or descriptions of Solomon (1 Kgs 9:9; 1 Chr 28:9; 2 Chr 7:19, 22), Rehoboam (2 Chr 12:1, 5), Abijam (2 Chr 13:11), Asa (2 Chr 15:2), Ahab (1 Kgs 18:18), Joash (2 Chr 24:18, 20, 24), Amon (2 Kgs 21:22), and Pekah (2 Chr 28:6). Two preexilic prophets also use this verb to describe Israel's covenant treachery in the eighth century BCE (Hos 4:10; Isa 1:4, 28; cf. also 65:11).

"Other gods" (אֱלֹהִים אֲחֵרִים, 2 Kgs 22:17 = 2 Chr 34:25). This expression occurs 63 times in the Old Testament and is used to describe the pagan gods Israelites were tempted to worship. It occurs 45

---

[60] A chart summarizing the expressions surveyed in the following subsections can be found at the end of the section below.

[61] Deut 28:20; 29:24[ET 25]; 31:16; Josh 24:16; Judg 2:12–13; 10:6, 10, 13; 1 Kgs 11:33; 19:10, 14; 2 Kgs 17:16; etc.

times in Exodus, Deuteronomy, Joshua–2 Kings (missing in 2 Samuel), 2 Chronicles, and Hosea (with the greatest concentration being in Deuteronomy: 18 times).[62] Joshua affirms that worshipping other gods is absolutely unacceptable for God's chosen nation (Josh 23:16; 24:2, 16), while the book of Judges depicts Israel's tendency to do just that (Judg 2:12, 17, 19; 10:13). YHWH warned Solomon not to worship other gods (1 Kgs 9:6, 9), a warning he eventually ignored (1 Kgs 11:4, 10). Kings Jeroboam and Ahaz worshipped other gods themselves and caused the Israelites to do the same (1 Kgs 14:9; 2 Chr 28:25). The biblical historians summarize the Northern Kingdom's devotion to the worship of other gods (2 Kgs 17:7) in clear violation of the standard YHWH had set before them (2 Kgs 17:35, 37). Naaman, the Syrian convert to the worship of YHWH, gladly declared that he would no longer offer sacrifices to any other gods but YHWH (2 Kgs 5:17). The frequent warnings against the worship of "other gods" demonstrate an abhorrence of idolatry long before Josiah's time.

"Idols" (גִּלֻּלִים, 2 Kgs 23:24). This noun often refers pejoratively to forbidden objects of worship. Deuteronomy 29:15[ET 16] speaks of idols worshipped by the Egyptians during Israel's sojourn there. King Asa removed these abhorrent images from Judah (1 Kgs 15:12), while other kings, including Ahab (1 Kgs 21:26), Manasseh (2 Kgs 21:11), and Amon (2 Kgs 21:21), served those objects of divine disdain. The narrator's sweeping indictment of the Northern Kingdom condemns it for worshipping these idols (2 Kgs 17:12). Rather than connecting Josiah's reforms tightly to Deuteronomy, the noun גִּלֻּלִים points to offenses practiced before and after the events recorded in the book of Deuteronomy.

"Provoking (כָּעַס) YHWH to anger" (2 Kgs 23:19, 26). The pagan worship sites in Judah and Jerusalem that Josiah removed had been erected by his royal predecessors, provoking YHWH's anger (2 Kgs 23:19). However, even after Josiah removed them, YHWH did not withdraw his threats to impose the covenant curses on his people (2 Kgs 23:26). Although Deuteronomy emphasizes that idolatry would provoke YHWH's anger (4:25; 9:18; 31:29; 32:16, 21), Israel's historians cite numerous examples of Israelite kings who worshipped false gods: Jeroboam I (1 Kgs 14:9, 15; 15:30), Baasha (1 Kgs 16:2, 7), Elah (1 Kgs 16:13), Omri (1 Kgs 16:26), Ahab (1 Kgs 16:33; 21:22), Ahaziah (1 Kgs 22:54[ET 53]), Ahaz (2 Chr 28:25), and Manasseh (2 Kgs 21:6, 15; 2 Chr 33:6). The prophets Isaiah (65:3) and Hosea (12:15) reinforce YHWH's denunciation of the Northern Kingdom, the conduct of which provoked his anger (2 Kgs 17:11, 17).

[62] It also occurs 18 times in Jeremiah. I did not include those occurrences since Jeremiah's ministry began in Josiah's thirteenth year and extended well beyond his reign.

"Bring disaster" (מֵבִיא רָעָה). In the face of Israel's repeated covenant treachery, YHWH threatened to bring judgment upon his covenant nation. The prophet Huldah's warning that he would "bring disaster" (מֵבִיא רָעָה) on his people matched what was spelled out in the book of the law (2 Kgs 22:16). This warning was also announced against Jeroboam I (1 Kgs 14:10) and Amon (2 Kgs 21:12). A related verbal phrase, "he will harm you" (*hiphil* of רעע, Josh 24:20; Isa 31:2), affirms a similar idea.

Divinely Prescribed Actions to Stamp Out Various Aspects of Idolatry

Burning (שָׂרַף) or tearing down (נָתַץ) pagan utensils and installations (2 Kgs 23:4, 6, 8, 11, 15, 16, 20; 2 Chr 34:5). From the time of Deuteronomy through the Israelite monarchy, godly leaders burned or tore down pagan objects of worship.[63] What Josiah described and practiced is well attested in the centuries before his time.

Pulverizing pagan utensils (2 Kgs 23:6, 15 = 2 Chr 34:4, 7). Besides burning pagan utensils, the Israelites destroyed pagan items by grinding them to dust (Exod 32:20 = Deut 9:21; 2 Chr 15:16 [Asa]). The event referred to in Deut 9:21 occurred almost forty years prior to its mention in that context.

The condemnation of cult prostitutes (2 Kgs 23:7). In spite of the divine prohibition against Israelite men or women serving as cult prostitutes (Deut 23:18[ET 17]), such individuals existed during Rehoboam's reign (1 Kgs 14:24). Long before Josiah's day, Kings Asa and Jehoshaphat removed all male prostitutes from Judah (1 Kgs 15:12; 22:46). The prophet Hosea condemned them as well (Hos 4:14).

The prohibition of mediums and necromancers (2 Kgs 23:24). Josiah's removal of mediums and necromancers conforms to the prohibitions spelled out in Leviticus (19:31; 20:6, 27) and Deuteronomy (18:11). King Saul removed them from Israel (1 Sam 28:3), but he was later condemned for consulting a medium for his own purposes (1 Chr 10:13). In the sweeping indictment of the Northern Kingdom's infidelity that precipitated its end as a nation, the historian condemns that nation for regularly practicing divination and necromancy (2 Kgs 17:17). Manasseh's treachery included consulting mediums and necromancers (2 Kgs 21:6 = 2 Chr 33:6). Josiah's reforms were neither novel nor innovative. The eighth-century prophets Isaiah (2:6) and Micah (5:11) condemned these practices as well. Inasmuch as Israelite involvement with mediums and the practice of necromancy predated Josiah by centuries, his reforms were

[63] Exod 32:20; 34:13; Deut 7:5, 25; 12:3; 13:17[ET 16]; Josh 6:24; 7:15; Judg 2:2; 6:28, 30–32; 1 Kgs 13:2; 15:13; 2 Kgs 10:26–27; 11:18; 1 Chr 14:12; 2 Chr 15:16; 33:3; Mic 1:7.

driven by divinely established pentateuchal standards that also antedated his reign by several centuries.

Designations for Fidelity to YHWH

"To go after" (לָלֶכֶת אַחַר). Although this phrase sometimes refers to following another person (Gen 24:5, 8), usually it is used theologically of following other gods (Deut 11:28; 28:14; 29:17[ET 18]; Judg 2:19; 1 Kgs 21:26), of following God's requirements (Lev 18:4; Deut 8:6; 10:12; 26:17; 30:16; Josh 22:5; Judg 2:22; 1 Kgs 2:3; 3:3; 6:12; 8:25, 58, 61; etc.[64]), or of following after YHWH (2 Kgs 23:3 = 2 Chr 34:31). This concept clearly preceded Josiah.

"To keep" (לִשְׁמֹר). In addition to occurring by itself, this verb occurs with the previous expression ("to walk/follow after") to describe the obedience God expected from his chosen nation (Deut 5:29; 26:17–18; 30:16; Josh 22:5; 1 Kgs 2:3; 8:58, 61; 2 Kgs 23:3 = 2 Chr 34:31; 1 Chr 29:19). As with the expression "to go after," God's requirement that his people keep his commandments is clearly attested long before the time of Josiah.

"With all one's heart" (בְּכָל־לֵב/לֵבָב). This prepositional phrase (often accompanied by בְּכָל־נֶפֶשׁ, "with all one's soul") expresses the wholehearted obedience that God expects of his covenant people.[65] This phrase does not link Deuteronomy tightly with 2 Kgs 23; rather, its widespread use in the historical books reflects its pervasiveness. Although the Old Testament applies this expression to the loyalty God expected from all Israelites, the phrase also occurs with reference to Israelite kings—David, Solomon, Jeroboam I, Asa, Jehoshaphat, Jehu, Hezekiah, and Josiah.

Promises of Divine Presence to Continue despite Covenant Curses

"My name will be there" (יִהְיֶה שְׁמִי שָׁם, 2 Kgs 23:27). Deuteronomy emphasizes that Israel must worship YHWH at the place where he puts his name (12:5, 11, 21; 14:23–24; 16:3, 6, 11; 26:2). During Solomon's reign, YHWH had referred to the recently completed temple in Jerusalem as the place where he had put his name (1 Kgs 8:16, 29 = 2 Chr 6:20; 1 Kgs 9:3 = 2 Chr 7:16). Included with the prophet Ahijah's promise that YHWH would give Jeroboam I ten Israelite tribes, YHWH declared that Jerusalem, where YHWH put his name (1 Kgs 11:36), would remain with

[64] Second Kings 10:31 refers to Jehu, who did not walk according to God's requirements.

[65] It occurs 26 times in Deuteronomy–2 Chronicles (Deut 4:29; 6:5; 10:12; 11:13; 13:4[ET 3]; 26:16; 30:2, 6, 10; Josh 22:5; 23:14; 1 Sam 7:3; 12:20, 24; 1 Kgs 2:4; 8:23, 48; 2 Kgs 14:8; 10:31; 23:3[ET 2]; 2 Chr 6:14, 38; 15:12, 15; 22:9; 31:21).

David. The historian reports that King Rehoboam established his reign in "the city that YHWH had chosen from all the tribes of Israel to put his name" (1 Kgs 14:21; 2 Chr 12:13; cf. Deut 12:5). Because of the depth of Manasseh's wickedness, YHWH declared, in 2 Kgs 23:27, that he would bring the covenant curses on his people in spite of Josiah's reform. In so doing he would be rejecting Jerusalem and the temple, even though he had said, "My name will be there." As with the other expressions, the notion of YHWH putting his name in the chosen place originated long before the reign of Josiah.

Table 1. Key Expressions Shared by Deuteronomy and 2 Kings 22–23

Expression*	Occurrences in Deuteronomy	Occurrences in Josh 1 through 2 Kgs 21, and in the pre-Josianic prophets	Occurrences in 2 Kgs 22–23
The Authority Base for Proper Covenant Conduct			
"the book of the law"	17:18; 28:58; 29:20[ET 21]	Josh 1:8; 8:31, 34; 23:6; 24:26; 2 Kgs 14:6; 2 Chr 25:4; Hos 4:10; Isa 1:4, 28; 65:11	22:8, 11; 23:24
Descriptions of the Treachery or Consequences of Idolatry			
"abandon"	28:20; 31:16	Josh 24:16; Judg 2:12–13; 10:6, 10, 13; 1 Kgs 11:33; 19:10; 2 Kgs 17:16; et al.	22:17 = 2 Chr 34:25
"other gods"	5:7; 6:14; 7:4; 11:28; 28:14; 29:25[ET 26]; 30:17; et al.	Josh 23:16; 24:2, 16; Judg 2:12, 17; 10:13; 1 Kgs 9:6, 9; 11:4, 10; 14:9 = 2 Chr 28:25; 2 Kgs 5:17; 17:7, 35, 37; Hos 3:1; et al.	22:17 = 2 Chr 34:25
"idols"	29:16[ET 17]	1 Kgs 15:12; 21:26; 2 Kgs 17:12; 21:11, 21	23:24
"provoking YHWH to anger"	4:25; 9:18; 31:29; 32:16, 21	1 Kgs 14:9, 15; 15:30; 16:2, 7, 13, 26, 33; 21:22; 22:54 [ET 22:53]; 2 Kgs 17:11, 17; 21:6, 15; 2 Chr 28:25; 33:6	23:19, 26
"bring disaster"	29:20[ET 21]; 31:17, 21, 29; 32:23	Judg 2:15; 2 Sam 12:11; 1 Kgs 9:9; 14:10; 2 Kgs 21:12; cf. Josh 24:20; Isa 31:2	22:16, 20
Divinely Prescribed Actions to Stamp Out Various Aspects of Idolatry			
burning or tearing down pagan sites	7:5, 25; 12:3; 13:17[ET 16]	Josh 6:24; 7:15; Judg 2:2; 6:28, 30–32; 1 Kgs 13:2; 15:13; 2 Kgs 10:26–27; 11:18; 1 Chr 14:12; 2 Chr 15:16; 33:3; Mic 1:7	23:4, 6, 8, 11, 15, 16, 20; 2 Chr 34:5
pulverizing pagan utensils	9:21 = Exod 32:20	2 Chr 15:16 [Asa]	23:6, 15 = 2 Chr 34:4, 7

condemnation of cult prostitutes	23:18[ET 17]	1 Kgs 14:24; 15:12; 22:46; Hos 4:14	23:7
prohibition of mediums and necromancers	18:11; cf. Lev 19:31; 20:6, 27	1 Sam 28:3; 1 Chr 10:13; 2 Kgs 17:17; 21:6 = 2 Chr 33:6; Isa 2:6; Mic 5:11	23:24
Designations for Fidelity to YHWH			
"to go/follow after"	8:6; 10:12; 26:17; 30:16	Josh 22:5; 1 Kgs 2:3; 3:3; 6:12; 8:25, 58, 61; et al.	23:3 = 2 Chr 34:31
"to keep"	5:29; 26:17–18; 30:16	Josh 22:5; 1 Kgs 2:3; 8:58, 61; 1 Chr 29:19	23:3 = 2 Chr 34:31
"with all his heart"	4:29; 6:5; 10:12; 26:16; 30:2, 6; et al.	Josh 22:5; 1 Sam 7:3; 12:20, 24; 1 Kgs 8:48; 14:8; 2 Chr 15:12, 15; 22:9; 31:21; et al.	23:3 = 2 Chr 34:31
YHWH Promises His Presence Will Continue despite Covenant Curses			
"my name will be there"	12:5, 11, 21; 14:23–24; 16:3, 6, 11; 26:2	1 Kgs 8:16, 29 = 2 Chr 6:20; 1 Kgs 9:3 = 2 Chr 7:16; 1 Kgs 11:36; 14:21; 2 Chr 12:13	23:27

*This chart does not distinguish between slight variations of a given expression.

Summary

The preceding discussion demonstrates that the terminological connections between Josiah's reforms and the book of Deuteronomy tell only part of the story. Many phrases cited by scholars as evidence for a Josianic setting for the composition of Deuteronomy (or part of Deuteronomy) may actually serve to demonstrate a much earlier date for the book. Of course, the weight one grants to this evidence depends upon one's view of the reliability of the narratives in describing earlier events. In any case, the historians were obviously convinced that the issues addressed by Josiah's reform efforts had plagued Israel for a long time and that they violated fundamental principles grounded in Mosaic law. This reality[66] speaks against the "consensus of modern scholarship" that Deuteronomy must derive in some primary fashion from the time of King Josiah.

[66] For helpful studies on this general subject, see especially Carsten Vang's essay in this volume ("When a Prophet Quotes Moses: On the Relationship between the Book of Hosea and Deuteronomy"); and Vang, "God's Love According to Hosea and Deuteronomy: A Prophetic Reworking of a Deuteronomic Concept?" *TynBul* 62 (2011): 173–94. See also Mark F. Rooker, "The Use of the Old Testament in the Book of Hosea," *CTR* 7 (1993): 51–66, esp. 60–65; and Justin M. Fuhrmann, "Deuteronomy 6–8 and the History of Interpretation: An Exposition on the First Two Commandments," *JETS* 53 (2010): 37–63.

Josiah's Reforms and the Composition of Deuteronomy: Challenges to the Connection

The connection between Josiah and his reforms and the composition of Deuteronomy is a consensus position in critical biblical scholarship. The final section of this essay surveys alternative approaches to the link between Josiah's reforms and the book of Deuteronomy, beginning with scholars who defend Mosaic authorship and date the book near the time of the conquest of Canaan[67] and proceeding to those who argue that Deuteronomy reached a form approximating what now exists later in the first millennium BCE. What unites these interpreters is the seriousness with which they take the internal evidence of the book, which claims in some sense to preserve the words of Moses. In their view, the book of Deuteronomy provided the theological authority for the life to which YHWH called Israel, as well as the divine authority behind the prophets' denunciation of Israel's repeated acts of covenant treachery.

Peter Vogt: Deuteronomy is predominantly from Moses' time but was completed in a premonarchic setting

Various scholars[68] regard the book of Deuteronomy as predominantly the words Moses wrote as God's instrument for the sake of his generation and the ones to follow. These words are part of inspired Scripture and were passed on carefully by scribal figures, allowing for inspired scribal/prophetic figures to insert certain post-Mosaic elements in the work that left Moses' hand.[69]

Vogt notes correctly that, in the world of Old Testament studies, the "association of Deuteronomy with the monarchic period became the prevailing critical understanding of the book."[70] In various published works, Vogt has presented generally overlooked evidence for a premonarchic

[67] No effort is made in this essay to argue for either an early (ca. 1446 BCE) or a late date (ca. 1266 BCE) of the exodus, since this issue does not significantly affect this presentation.

[68] A selection of these authors includes M. Grisanti, "Deuteronomy," in *The Expositor's Bible Commentary*, ed. T. Longman III and D. Garland, rev. ed. (Grand Rapids: Zondervan, 2012) 2:459–61; R. K. Harrison, *Introduction to the Old Testament, with a Comprehensive Review of Old Testament Studies and a Special Supplement on the Apocrypha* (Grand Rapids: Eerdmans, 1969), 636–40; P. Craigie, *The Book of Deuteronomy*, NICOT (Grand Rapids: Eerdmans, 1976), 20–29; and E. Merrill, *Deuteronomy*, NAC (Nashville: Broadman & Holman, 1994), 22–23.

[69] See the *Post-Mosaica* listed as part of the summary of Daniel Block's view below.

[70] Vogt, "These Are the Words Moses Spoke," 61.

dating for Deuteronomy. In discussions of the date of Deuteronomy's composition, scholars have argued for a second- or first-millennium BCE date based on ancient Near Eastern treaty structures[71] and ancient law codes (e.g., the Code of Hammurabi).[72]

Vogt appeals to three passages to argue that Deuteronomy is best seen as addressed to a premonarchic audience.[73] First, he examines Deut 2:1–23, which compares God's gift of the land of Canaan to Israel to his gifts of different lands to the Edomites, Ammonites, and Moabites (1:8, 21, 25, 35, 39 compared with 2:5, 9, 19). Although YHWH gave land to all these nations, he entered into a unique covenant relationship only with Israel.[74] YHWH demanded that the Israelites neither show hostility toward the Edomites (identified as Israel's "brothers"; 2:4, 8), Moabites, and Ammonites, nor provoke them to engage Israel in battle (2:5, 9, 19), because he gave these three peoples their respective lands (2:5, 9, 19). These nations were also recipients of his sovereign care. While there is tension over the Israelites' request to pass through their territory, there is no hint of an adversarial relationship. As Vogt notes, this contrasts sharply with the hostility of these nations toward Israel from the period of the judges through the divided monarchy (Judg 3:30; 1 Sam 11:8–11; 14:47; 2 Sam 8:2; 2 Kgs 3:24; 8:20, 22; 2 Chr 26:8; 27:5; etc.). The biblical prophets scathingly denounced these three nations and announced divine judgment upon them (Isa 11:14; Jer 9:26; 25:21; Amos 1–2; Zeph 2:8–11; etc.). Instead of treating Israel as a "brother," Edom acted violently against it (Obad 10). Vogt correctly acknowledges the difficulty of

---

[71] For defense of a second-millennium BCE date, see Craigie, *Book of Deuteronomy*, 24–28; Kenneth A. Kitchen, *Ancient Orient and Old Testament* (London: Tyndale, 1966), 90–102; Meredith G. Kline, *Treaty of the Great King* (Grand Rapids: Eerdmans, 1963), 27–44; Merrill, *Deuteronomy*, 32–37; Gordon J. Wenham, "The Structure and Date of Deuteronomy" (PhD diss., University of London, 1970), 182–216. Scholars arguing for a first-millennium BCE date include A. F. Campbell, "An Historical Prologue in a Seventh-Century Treaty," *Bib* 50 (1969): 534–35; Rintje Frankena, "The Vassal-Treaties of Esarhaddon and the Dating of Deuteronomy," *OtSt* 14 (1965): 122–54; Delbert R. Hillers, *Covenant: The History of a Biblical Idea* (Baltimore: Johns Hopkins, 1969), 120–42; Dennis J. McCarthy, *Treaty and Covenant*, AnBib 21 (Rome: Pontifical Biblical Institute, 1963), 27–152; Weinfeld, *Deuteronomic School*, 116–46.

[72] For a defense of a second-millennium date, see G. Wenham, "The Date of Deuteronomy: Linch-pin of Old Testament Criticism," *Them* 10.3 (1985): 19; for a first-millennium BCE date, see Weinfeld, *Deuteronomy 1–11*, 6–9; Weinfeld, *Deuteronomic School*, 146–57.

[73] Vogt ("These Are the Words Moses Spoke," 64) recognizes that while the "implied audience" by itself cannot be the sole means of dating a book, it can support a general time frame for the book's composition.

[74] Christopher J. H. Wright, *Deuteronomy*, NIBCOT (Peabody, MA: Hendrickson, 1996), 36.

locating Deut 2 and its view of Edom as a “brother” to Israel in the monarchic period; it would have made no sense to a seventh-century-BCE audience.[75]

Second, Vogt considers Deut 12 and 27, which address the “place” of the divinely demanded sacrifices. In Deut 12, YHWH demands that Israel worship him in the place in which he has established his name.[76] Remarkably, while Deut 12 fails to name this divinely prescribed place, in chapter 27 Mount Ebal is identified as the place to which YHWH calls his people to pronounce the curses. Beginning with the book of Joshua, later texts generally name the place where Israel worshipped YHWH. Significantly, that place of worship was not constant, but moved to different locations over time: Shiloh, Bethel, Mizpah, Gilgal, Hebron, Gibeon, and Jerusalem.

According to Deut 12, YHWH calls for wholehearted loyalty demonstrated by worshipping him at his chosen place. Although not named specifically, that place contrasted sharply with pagan places of worship. If Deuteronomy was composed in a monarchic (or later) setting, and if a key element of the historian’s agenda was to highlight the centralization of worship in Jerusalem, neither the absence of the name of a particular place in Deut 12 nor the surprising naming of Mount Ebal in chapter 27 as the divinely mandated place for the national covenant assembly makes sense.[77]

Vogt recognizes that, while his argument about the implied audience of Deuteronomy does not settle the debate concerning the date of Deuteronomy’s composition, it points out a major weakness in a conclusion that is part of the scholarly consensus. Most who see Josiah’s reforms as the occasion that generated much of the legislation found in what came to be called Deuteronomy enthusiastically affirm that Deuteronomy was, in fact, a product of the monarchic period, intended in part to solidify the claims of the monarchy and priesthood in Jerusalem.[78] However, the implied audience of Deuteronomy suggests that Josiah and his reform had no substantive role to play in the writing of Deuteronomy.

---

[75] Vogt, “These Are the Words Moses Spoke,” 70.

[76] For discussions of whether this refers to a single central sanctuary or other divinely authorized sanctuaries, see Gordon J. Wenham, “Deuteronomy and the Central Sanctuary,” *TynBul* 22 (1971): 109–16; Merrill, *Deuteronomy*, 223–24; J. Gordon McConville and J. G. Millar, *Time and Place in Deuteronomy*, JSOTSup 179 (Sheffield: Sheffield Academic, 1994), 117–23; J. Gordon McConville, *Deuteronomy*, ApOTC (Downers Grove, IL: InterVarsity Press, 2002), 230–32.

[77] Since Mount Ebal was in Assyrian territory during Hezekiah’s reign, it makes little sense for Deuteronomy to call for a national assembly in enemy territory.

[78] Vogt, “These Are the Words Moses Spoke,” 70.

Daniel Block: Deuteronomy was completed by the time of King David

After citing references within Deuteronomy, the Old Testament, and the New Testament that link Moses to the authorship of Deuteronomy, Block nuances his view to suggest that Moses transcribed a version of his speeches contained in the book before his death.[79] While references to "the voice of YHWH" appear in Deuteronomy (31:14b, 16b–21, 23b; 32:49–52; 34:4b), "the voice of Moses"[80] dominates the book (1:6–4:40; 5:1b–26:19; 27:1, 9, 12–26; 28:1–69[ET 29:1]; 29:1[ET 2]–30:20; 32:1–43, 46b–47; 33:2–29). The voice of the narrator, represented by third-person statements about Moses and historical notes, makes up the rest of the book (64 verses total).[81] Block suggests that Joshua and the Israelites carried across the Jordan River a written copy of all of Deuteronomy except the narrative sections, historical notes, and other post-Mosaic elements.[82] In his view, a form of the current book of Deuteronomy was produced no earlier than the time of Joshua and no later than the ninth century BCE, prior to the ministries of Elijah and Elisha. According to Block, "it is reasonable to suppose that by David's time Deuteronomy more or less as we have it existed as the last scroll of the Pentateuch."[83]

---

[79] Daniel I. Block, "Recovering the Voice of Moses: The Genesis of Deuteronomy," *JETS* 44 (2001): 385; republished in *The Gospel according to Moses: Theological and Ethical Reflections on the Book of Deuteronomy* (Eugene, OR: Wipf & Stock, 2012), 21–67.

[80] Bill Arnold's reference to "the Mosaic voice" is quite different from what Block means here by "the voice of Moses." For Arnold, "the Mosaic voice" refers to the basic message of Deuteronomy, adjusted and supplemented in the light of changing historical circumstances ("Deuteronomy as the *Ipsissima Vox* of Moses," *JTI* 4 [2010]: 68–74). For Block, the "voice of Moses" refers to those sections of Deuteronomy that the book of Deuteronomy attributes to Moses ("Recovering the Voice of Moses," 390–92).

[81] Block, "Recovering the Voice of Moses," 391–92.

[82] Daniel I. Block, *Deuteronomy*, NIVAC (Grand Rapids: Zondervan, 2012), 30–31. The examples cited include the following: "(a) expressions like (lit.) 'across the Jordan in the wilderness in the Arabah opposite Suph' (1:1), and 'to this day' (2:22; 3:14; 10:8); (b) parenthetical historical notes (2:10–12; 2:20–23; 3:9, 11, 13b–14); (c) the use of the past tense in 2:12, 'just as Israel did in the land the LORD gave them as their possession'; (d) the obituary of Moses (32:48–52; 34:1–12); (e) the reference to Dan as a northern extremity (34:1); (f) the use of Israelite tribal names for geographic regions of Canaan (34:1–3); (g) the observation that since the death of Moses no prophet like him has risen in Israel, that is, no one whom YHWH knew face to face (34:10), which makes sense only if the narrator was aware of the historical significance of Moses' own prediction concerning the prophetic institution in 18:15–22 and knew at least a few prophetic figures with whom Moses could be compared."

[83] Ibid., 31–32.

Brian Peterson: Deuteronomy was substantially completed by priestly individuals by the time of David and possibly finalized in Jeremiah's time

In a recent monograph, Brian Peterson goes against the grain of the scholarly consensus by proposing a relatively early date for the composition of Deuteronomy as well as DH.[84] Although a detailed consideration of DH remains outside the focus of this essay, Peterson's understanding of the date of the composition of DH provides an important backdrop to his view of the composition of Deuteronomy. He proposes that "Abiathar, the priest, his sons Jonathan and Ahimelech, their priestly descendants, and finally Jeremiah and Baruch all may have had a key role to play in formulating what has come to be known as the 'Deuteronomistic History.' "[85]

Following the lead of many conservative scholars, Peterson affirms that the bulk of Deuteronomy was composed by Moses by the time of Israel's conquest of the Amorites in the Transjordan region. He points to the similarities between the structure of Deuteronomy and the second-millennium Hittite treaties,[86] as well as to a series of linguistic features[87] that support this view.

Peterson devotes a chapter of his monograph to two expressions, "across the Jordan" and "until this day."[88] He considers where they appear in DH (including Deuteronomy) and their implications for dating the composition. While the first expression occurs primarily in Deut 1–4 and Joshua, the second occurs many times throughout Deuteronomy–2 Kgs 21.[89] With regard to Deuteronomy, in Peterson's view, both expressions point to a time of composition before the ninth century BCE (that is, long before the time of Josiah).[90]

In the second half of his monograph ("An Analysis of the Texts"), Peterson examines the evidence for the editing of the book of Deuteronomy,[91] concluding that the majority of the post-Mosaic shaping occurs in Deut 1–4 and 31–34. This editorial activity could have involved Joshua, Abiathar, and Jeremiah.[92] He concludes that, unlike the rest of DH, which went

[84] Peterson, *Locating a Tradition*.

[85] Ibid., 3.

[86] Ibid., 69–73.

[87] Ibid., 67–68. For the linguistic issues, Peterson draws heavily on Merrill, "Deuteronomy and de Wette," 25–42.

[88] Peterson, *Locating a Tradition*, 76–112.

[89] Peterson provides a helpful chart for the instances of "until this day" (ibid., 81–85).

[90] Ibid., 89–90.

[91] Ibid., 121–32.

[92] Peterson (ibid., 130–31) suggests that Deut 29:24–28[ET 25–29] could have been added by the prophet Jeremiah, since it refers to exile-like conditions.

through more significant editorial shaping, "the book of Deuteronomy . . . is one [*sic*] book within this corpus that appears to have had the least amount of shaping by any author/editor prior to Dtr's adoption of its theological principles as he/they fashioned the history of Israel."[93] According to Peterson, neither Josiah nor his reform played any role in the composition of Deuteronomy.

J. Gordon McConville: at least part of Deuteronomy is from the premonarchic period

In explaining the setting of Deuteronomy, McConville lays out his basic hypothesis: "Deuteronomy, or at least a form of it, is the document of a real political and religious constitution of Israel from the premonarchical period."[94] McConville supports his hypothesis in part by pointing out the significant differences between parts of the message of Deuteronomy and the Josianic setting envisioned by many scholars (seventh century BCE).[95] Even though King Josiah was a "bright light" in the history of Israel and Judah, even he did not measure up to the kingship envisioned in Deut 17. The king envisioned by Deuteronomy would not appoint judges (16:18) but would be appointed by the people (17:14–15). Furthermore, he should not view himself primarily as a warrior, possess a harem, or collect massive wealth (17:16–17). And Israel was to fulfill its political obligations by loyalty to YHWH rather than fealty to its human king. With strong support from other examples, McConville concludes that equating the original setting of Deuteronomy with the setting of Josiah's reforms ignores the theology of the book of Deuteronomy.[96]

In contrast to many scholars, McConville insists that there "was no time at which Deuteronomy was not a book."[97] He rejects attempts to describe the history of its composition as involving a transition from oral to written form. From its inception, the book of Deuteronomy served as the "document of the constitution" of Israel. Although Deuteronomy was intended for oral delivery, a hard copy always existed. However, McConville also affirms that there "is no reason to suppose that the content of the book may not have changed over time."[98] For example, McConville questions

---

[93] Ibid., 123.

[94] McConville, *Deuteronomy*, 34.

[95] Ibid., 34–36; McConville, "King and Messiah in Deuteronomy and the Deuteronomistic History," in *King and Messiah in Israel and the Ancient Near East: Proceedings of the Oxford Old Testament Seminar*, ed. J. Day, JSOTSup 270 (Sheffield: Sheffield Academic, 1998), 276–81.

[96] McConville, *Deuteronomy*, 34–36.

[97] Ibid., 38.

[98] Ibid., 39.

whether the premonarchic version of Deuteronomy contained passages that envisioned Israel's distant future beyond exile (e.g., 4:29–31; 30:1–10). He also rejects the efforts of critical scholars to contrast the law codes (Book of the Covenant, Holiness Code, Deuteronomy). He assumes that "no biblical law code was thought to be exclusive, but rather that the codes all operated in the public and intellectual world of Israel."[99]

Although McConville does not defend the Mosaic authorship of Deuteronomy, he acknowledges several lines of evidence that support a second-millennium BCE date for the book. Nevertheless, rather than attempting to date the book precisely, he prefers to identify its place within the life of Israel.[100]

Bill Arnold: Deuteronomy is the *ipsissima vox* of Moses from the time of Hezekiah

Bill Arnold addresses the question of the composition of Deuteronomy by using two phrases commonly employed in New Testament studies: *ipsissima verba* ("the very word," or exact words) and *ipsissima vox* ("the very voice," or basic message).[101] In Arnold's view, the book of Deuteronomy represents the basic message of Moses; in his words, Deuteronomy's "use of the speech of Moses, presented as his valedictory address, gives 'voice' to the *revising and updating of previous legal tradition*."[102] It is essential to distinguish this "Mosaic voice" from the idea of divine, prophetic, or narrative voice, because the "Mosaic voice" juxtaposes the continuities and discontinuities between what may have been said originally and the ongoing voice of *ipsissima vox*.[103] Drawing on the work of Bernard Levinson and Michael Fishbane,[104] Arnold posits that the tool of *ipsissima vox* demonstrates "the way the deuteronomic reformers respected and valued the Covenant Code, while at the same time moving past it with a new agenda."[105] Arnold characterizes this "innovation" as supplementing and updating what existed before (rather than refuting and replacing earlier

---

[99] Ibid.

[100] Ibid., 39–40.

[101] Arnold, "*Ipsissima Vox*," 53–55, 68–74. Arnold (68) also draws on two terms used in innerbiblical exegesis: *traditum* represents authoritative teachings, while *traditio* identifies those traditions that were reinterpreted for new historical contexts in the course of the transmission process.

[102] Ibid., 68–69, emphasis mine.

[103] Ibid., 69.

[104] Michael Fishbane, *Biblical Interpretation in Ancient Israel* (Oxford: Clarendon, 1985), 6–8, 163–277, 435–40; Bernard M. Levinson, *Deuteronomy and the Hermeneutics of Legal Innovation* (New York: Oxford University Press, 1997), 3–22.

[105] Arnold, "*Ipsissima Vox*," 70.

traditions[106]). According to Arnold, the way certain scholars have studied innerbiblical exegesis for the last two decades and the emerging emphasis on literary imitation "provide a new appreciation for the way Israel's legal traditions evolved over time."[107] In his view, the narrator explained what Moses was doing—he "began to elucidate the law" (Deut 1:5)—as an early example of adjusting inherited legal traditions.[108] In keeping with his view of the origin of Scripture in general, Arnold writes: "We simply cannot move beyond [or before] the 8th century as the beginning of biblical literature and the 7th century as a time of text revolution. We may theorize about pentateuchal sources as early as the 10th century but certainly no earlier."[109] Arnold concludes that it is "more likely that proto-Deuteronomy originated in the period of Hezekiah and was brought to the south after the fall of Samaria (722/721 B.C.E.), where it was discovered and used in the Josianic reforms in the late 7th century B.C.E."[110]

This brief overview demonstrates that scholars who question the link between Josiah's reforms and the composition of the book of Deuteronomy as commonly represented in critical scholarship are not unanimous in their views of its origins. Some of these scholars attribute most of the book to the time of Moses and date its actual composition at the latest to the time of David. However, none of them regards Josiah and his reforms as playing a significant role in bringing Deuteronomy into existence. All agree that a divinely authorized Mosaic message constitutes the heart of the book of Deuteronomy.[111] The most significant differences exist between the views of the first four presented above and Bill Arnold. The first three scholars affirm that Deuteronomy was first produced in written form and that a complete Deuteronomy scroll existed by the time of David. They also acknowledge that specific statements or phrases were added after the time of Moses. Although McConville is less willing to commit himself to a date of composition, he regards Deuteronomy as possessing a "book" status already during the second millennium BCE. Arnold contends to the contrary that Deuteronomy (along with other biblical books) could not have reached book status until the eighth or seventh

---

[106] Ibid., 71.

[107] Ibid., 72.

[108] Ibid., 73.

[109] Ibid., 65–66.

[110] Ibid., 67. Arnold does not reject the idea that some traditions in this proto-Deuteronomy may have derived from a time prior to the eighth century (Hezekiah's time), but he acknowledges that such connections are impossible to reconstruct and are of little heuristic value (67–68).

[111] Scores of issues that extend beyond the parameters of this essay would demand consideration in order to present fully the distinctions between these views at a methodological level.

centuries BCE and that only the Mosaic "message" (rather than its concrete statements) was divinely inspired.

Conclusion

At the outset, this essay provided a summary of the scholarly consensus concerning the potential role of the reformation commissioned by the godly king Josiah in the composition of the book of Deuteronomy or the development of DH. The common basis for this conclusion involves the terminological resonance between the legal and theological statements of Deuteronomy and Josiah's reform. A better handling of those intertextual examples demonstrates that the expressions shared by 2 Kgs 22–23 (and 2 Chr 34) and the book of Deuteronomy occur repeatedly in the intervening biblical passages (Joshua–2 Kgs 21), which describe the years between Moses and Josiah.

Although the intertextual evidence presented above will be cavalierly dismissed by DH proponents in light of their interpretive paradigm, noting the terminological resonance from Deuteronomy through 2 Kings provides clear evidence of what we already knew. YHWH gave Israel the Mosaic Law to serve as the theological engine meant to drive and direct its covenant loyalty.

In reality, this essay offers little new information. However, it reminds us that accepting biblical statements at face value provides evidence that a great God revealed his intentions for his chosen people. He accomplished this in the Pentateuch, and in Deuteronomy in particular, both of which had been primarily composed by the end of Moses' life. The impressive reform conducted by King Josiah was the result of a godly king who through his reading of the "book of the law" was motivated to seek to bring his nation back into conformity with those long-established divine intentions.

CHAPTER 5

The Book of Deuteronomy: Pseudepigraphy, Pseudonymity, or Something Else Altogether?

Bill T. Arnold

The book of Deuteronomy has been called the Archimedean point of pentateuchal research.[1] The metaphor is derived from Archimedes' alleged saying that, if he had a fulcrum and a lever long enough, he could move the earth. Thus, an Archimedean point is an objective point of reference from which a truer picture of something is obtainable.[2] Most scholars who use the metaphor are affirming the critical assessment of Deuteronomy as a book generally fixed to 622 BCE, which provides the reference point for a relative chronology for other sources of the Pentateuch. And yet it seems that the metaphor is relevant to our discussions more broadly. Our interpretation of this book has implications far beyond a simple chronological arrangement of pentateuchal sources. This book, like no other in the Old Testament's Primary History, presents us with a convergence of issues demanding our attention, requiring us to answer questions of composition, date, and methodology. Once we have done the hard work of

---

[1] Eissfeldt appears to have been the first to use the metaphor. He accepted de Wette's theory that the book was written not long before its discovery in 622 BCE, which establishes the precise time of origin of Deuteronomy and therefore a fixed point by which the age of the other component parts of the Pentateuch could be determined. "De Wette's thesis thus provided Pentateuchal criticism with 'a point of Archimedes' to which it could attach itself in order to deliver it from the bonds of church and synagogue tradition, and put in its place an alternative dating of the Pentateuch and its parts" (Otto Eissfeldt, *The Old Testament: An Introduction*, trans. Peter R. Ackroyd [New York: Harper & Row, 1965], 171). Others have followed; e.g., Eckart Otto, "Das Deuteronomium als archimedischer Punkt der Pentateuchkritik: Auf dem Wege zu einer Neubegründung der de Wette'schen Hypothese," in *Deuteronomy and Deuteronomic Literature: Festschrift C. H. W. Brekelmans*, ed. M. Vervenne and J. Lust, BETL 133 (Leuven: Peeters, 1997), 321–40; and Moshe Weinfeld, "Deuteronomy, Book of," *ABD* 2:168–83, esp. 174–75.

[2] Simon Blackburn, *The Oxford Dictionary of Philosophy* (Oxford: Oxford University Press, 2008), 21–22.

answering these questions, Deuteronomy provides a point of reference for discerning a truer picture of the Pentateuch, the Deuteronomistic History, and, indeed, biblical theology more generally. Our answers to the many questions on Deuteronomy bring into clearer focus almost all other questions related to the Torah and its interpretation, truly serving as an Archimedean point for biblical studies.

The following anecdote is unexceptional, but it illustrates the role of Deuteronomy in our field, and interestingly has significance for the history of Old Testament interpretation itself.

Some years ago, a young student walked into a classroom where the topic was Old Testament Introduction. The instructor was a well-known and respected scholar. One day in the course, the student heard that Deuteronomy was not entirely authored by Moses, even though the book seems to present itself as authored by him. Instead, the student learned that Deuteronomy was first composed centuries after Moses, perhaps six or seven centuries later, and that it addressed circumstances well defined for that much later historical context. Having come from an orthodox Lutheran family, the student was unsettled by the lecture precisely because, as he would say later, he found it compelling and persuasive. And so the student went to the professor's office later that day during his regular office hours. In their conversation about the class, the subject of Deuteronomy's origins came up naturally.

> "So then, is Deuteronomy what we might call a forgery?" the student asked.
>
> "For heaven's sake!" the professor replied. "That might be true, but one would never say such a thing!"

That brief conversation left an impact on the student. He remarked many years later that it seemed disingenuous for the professor to hesitate to say something he believed to be true. In fact, his teacher's words, "For heaven's sake," stayed with the man throughout his life. And, as he would say in his declining years, this conversation became something of a defining moment for him. It took place sometime in the early 1870s, and the young student became the renowned Friedrich Delitzsch, for whom his teacher's words "Um Gottes willen" would become an epigraph for his final work, *Die grosse Täuschung*.[3] Of course, Delitzsch went on to achieve

[3] This version of the encounter with his professor follows closely Delitzsch's own recounting of the conversation and its significance for him personally (Friedrich Delitzsch, *Die grosse Täuschung* [Stuttgart: Deutsche Verlags-Anstalt, 1921], 5–6). Delitzsch does not give the name of the celebrated professor, but it seems likely to have been Eberhard Schrader in Berlin. On the other hand, he may have taken Old Testament Introduction even earlier, in Leipzig, with his own father, Franz Delitzsch.

international fame as one of the fathers of modern Assyriology and the author of the "Babel und Bibel" lectures.[4] Sadly, in his last publication Delitzsch came to reject the Old Testament altogether, calling it completely unnecessary for Christian faith.[5]

With this crucial role of Deuteronomy in mind, I return in this study to my previous proposal to take Deuteronomy as the *ipsissima vox* of Moses rather than as his *ipsissima verba*. I will first explore the opening paragraph of the book (1:1–5) and its significance for the *vox* approach, especially in order to address the question of inspiration as a relevant factor. The paper will then briefly clarify the way in which Michael Fishbane's method informs such a *vox* approach. This is followed by a discussion of the bankrupt terminology used in biblical studies to describe Deuteronomy, and, finally, by a few concluding remarks.

The *Vox* Approach and the Nature of Divine Inspiration

Deuteronomy's first line throws us into the deep end of the pool: "These are the words Moses spoke to all Israel" (Deut 1:1). In Exodus–Numbers, Moses' role is defined as the lawgiver, summoned by YHWH to serve as a mouthpiece for divine proclamation (Exod 19:3, 7, 25; 25:1–2a; Lev 1:1; passim). In such cases, God speaks *through* Moses (Exod 20:1).[6] By contrast, Deuteronomy's opening line signals that the book presents the words *of* Moses rather than the "words of YHWH" *through* Moses. To a degree, Moses' function remains the same, since he is speaking to the Israelites "according to all that YHWH commanded him" (1:3). The narrator of Deut 1:1–5 explains that what follows is a confirmation and implementation of the Torah, since Moses undertook "to put this Torah into effect"

[4] And an advocate of so-called "Pan-Babylonianism"—see Bill T. Arnold and David B. Weisberg, "A Centennial Review of Friedrich Delitzsch's 'Babel und Bibel' Lectures," *JBL* 121 (2002): 441–57.

[5] "Das sogenannte 'Alte Testament' ist für die christliche Kirche und damit auch für die christliche Familie vollkommen entbehrlich" (Delitzsch, *Die grosse Täuschung*, 97).

[6] At times, God speaks to Moses and tells him what to say to the Israelites, although we are not shown Moses speaking (Lev 1:1–2a; 4:1–2a; 11:1–2a; 12:1–2a; etc.). So 'mosaicity' involves a set of nuancing ideas in the Pentateuch: Moses as author, Moses as auditor, Moses as actor, Moses as speaker, etc. (Lawson G. Stone, personal communication). Additionally, we might note that Moses' role of speaking the word of YHWH to Pharaoh foreshadows his role of speaking before all Israel (Exod 3:10; 5:1; 7:1, 2; passim).

(באר I, D-stem, Deut 1:5).[7] Moses the lawgiver has become Moses the first enforcer of the law; he functions here as the first Torah promulgator by formally putting the law into effect.[8] And related to the nuance of the verb is the debate that continues to confound scholars on the deictic referent of הַתּוֹרָה הַזֹּאת, "this Torah," which seems to have a disproportionate significance in the scholarship, considering the otherwise simple grammatical issues involved. On the one hand, "this Torah" may be anaphoric, referring *back* to Num 36:13 (and thus also to Lev 26:46 and 27:34), and therefore having in view the law revealed at Mount Sinai. In this case, the verb באר means simply to expound or interpret that law. At Sinai the law was introduced and proclaimed; here it is interpreted and explained.[9] On the other hand, "this Torah" may be cataphoric or anticipatory, referring *forward* to what follows in Deut 4:44 (and thus to Deut 5–26), and therefore having in view the law to be confirmed at Moab and put into full legal force at Mount Ebal (Deut 27:1–8). This yields the meaning of Deut 27:8 as "write upon the stones all the words of this Torah, thus correctly putting them in force."[10] Thus Deuteronomy relates to the Torah either as

---

[7] On the specific nuance of באר I in Deut 1:5 (and cf. 27:8) as either "to expound" or "to give legal force to [this Torah]," and the implications of the debate discussed in this paragraph, see Joachim Schaper, "The 'Publication' of Legal Texts in Ancient Judah," in *The Pentateuch as Torah: New Models for Understanding Its Promulgation and Acceptance*, ed. Gary N. Knoppers and Bernard M. Levinson (Winona Lake, IN: Eisenbrauns, 2007), 225–36, esp. 225–31. See now also Benjamin Kilchör, who rejects the "give legal force" interpretation (Benjamin Kilchör, *Mosetora und Jahwetora: Das Verhältnis von Deuteronomium 12–26 zu Exodus, Levitikus und Numeri*, BZABR 21 [Wiesbaden: Harrassowitz, 2015], 4).

[8] Some would say that Moses was the first law interpreter or exegete, as Israel's "first scribe"; see Eckart Otto, "Mose, der erste Schriftgelehrte: Deuteronomium 1,5 in der Fabel des Pentateuch," in *L'Écrit et L'Esprit: Études d'histoire du texte et de théologie biblique en hommage à Adrian Schenker*, ed. Dieter Böhler, Innocent Himbaza, and Philippe Hugo, OBO 214 (Fribourg and Göttingen: Academic Press and Vandenhoeck & Ruprecht, 2005), 273–84. For a different interpretation, see Georg Braulik and Norbert Lohfink, "Deuteronomium 1,5 באר את־התורה הזאת: 'er verlieh dieser Tora Rechtskraft,' " in *Textarbeit: Studien zu Texten und ihrer Rezeption aus dem Alten Testament und der Umwelt Israels: Festschrift für Peter Weimar zur Vollendung seines 60. Lebensjahres mit Beiträgen von Freunden, Schülern und Kollegen*, ed. Klaus Kiesow and Thomas Meurer, AOAT 294 (Münster: Ugarit-Verlag, 2003), 34–51; repr. in Norbert Lohfink, *Studien zum Deuteronomium und zur deuteronomistischen Literatur, 5*, SBAB 38 (Stuttgart: Katholisches Bibelwerk, 2005), 233–41.

[9] So Jean Louis Ska, "La structure du Pentateuque dans sa forme canonique," *ZAW* 113 (2001): 331–52, esp. 351, where Ska compares Deuteronomy to commentary on a text. See also Otto, "Mose, der erste Schriftgelehrte."

[10] Braulik and Lohfink, "Deuteronomium 1,5," esp. 240. Perhaps it is also suggestive that הַתּוֹרָה הַזֹּאת, "this Torah," occurs only once in the Tetrateuch in a completely non-paradigmatic way (Num 5:30), but 18 times in Deuteronomy (1:5; 4:8; 17:18, 19; 27:3, 8, 26; 28:58, 61; 29:20, 28[ET 21, 29]; 30:10; 31:9, 11, 12, 24, 26; 32:46).

exposition or implementation or some combination of these, depending on one's interpretation of 1:5. In any case, Deuteronomy is a presentation of "the words Moses spoke" instead of the word YHWH commanded "through" Moses (בְּיַד־מֹשֶׁה, Lev 26:46 and Num 36:13).

At 1:1–5 the narrator has placed Moses' voice in the foreground in a way that suppresses narration for the rest of the book.[11] Thus Deuteronomy has minimal narration because it is composed almost entirely of speeches of Moses, giving structure to the book as three or four main speeches of unequal length.[12] Drawing on an older discussion in New Testament scholarship, I proposed in 2010 that we approach the speeches of Deuteronomy as the *ipsissima vox* of Moses rather than the *ipsissima verba* of Moses.[13] The latter is the position most often favored by evangelical scholars, who take the book at large as the actual speech of Moses, allowing for post-Mosaica here and there, and in some cases allowing for considerable late editorial activity. In this case, questions of date and authorship are resolved easily enough, since *ex hypothesi*, Moses would have spoken these words in the late thirteenth century BCE (some arguing, of course, for a fifteenth-century date). The speeches of Moses would presumably have been preserved with limited redaction by scribes in Iron I, handed down through the monarchic period, and given something like their present form in the late preexilic period. Some advocates of this position have argued that Moses is responsible for the legal core of the

---

[11] Jean-Pierre Sonnet, *The Book within the Book: Writing in Deuteronomy*, BibInt 14 (Leiden: Brill, 1997), 237. So the four headings of the book (Deut 1:1–5; 4:44–5:1; 28:69–29:1a[ET 2a]; 33:1) function to "launch or re-launch Moses' represented speech acts" (ibid.). Paul Kleinert first discerned the *Vierüberschriftensystem* for Deuteronomy (Paul Kleinert, *Das Deuteronomium und der Deuteronomiker: Untersuchungen zur alttestamentlichen Rechts- und Literaturgeschichte* [Bielefeld and Leipzig: Velhagen & Klasing, 1872], 166–68). Thus the book's opening line, "These are the words Moses spoke" (1:1), signals a distinction from "The words of Jeremiah" (Jer 1:1), which is followed by a collection of other materials besides speeches, indicating a wider sense of discourse in that case.

[12] The speeches, minus the narrative frames, may be counted as follows: first address, 1:6–4:40; second address, 5:1b–26:19 plus 28:1–69[ET 29:1]; and third address, 29:1[ET 2]–30:20. To these are appended two poems, "The Song of Moses" (32:1–43) and "The Blessing of Moses" (33:2–29), and various shorter speeches. Cf. Daniel I. Block, "Recovering the Voice of Moses: The Genesis of Deuteronomy," *JETS* 44 (2001): 385–408, esp. 391 (repr. in Block, *The Gospel according to Moses: Theological and Ethical Reflections on the Book of Deuteronomy* [Eugene, OR: Cascade, 2012], 21–51). It is possible to count as many as fourteen separate Mosaic addresses in the book, which some suggest would lend support to literary structures built on the number seven and its multipliers, the septuples. See Udo Rüterswörden, "Moses' Last Day," in *Moses in Biblical and Extra-Biblical Traditions*, ed. Axel Graupner and Michael Wolter, BZAW 372 (Berlin: de Gruyter, 2007), 51–59, esp. 52.

[13] Bill T. Arnold, "Deuteronomy as the *Ipsissima Vox* of Moses," *JTI* 4 (2010): 53–74.

book (chs. 12–26) and perhaps even all of Deut 1–30.[14] Most would also allow for considerable updating of the actual words of Moses, especially since our present canonical book largely employs a late preexilic Hebrew dialect in grammar and orthography. Nevertheless, the *verba* approach takes these speeches of Moses as originating in the physical act of speaking by the historical Moses on the plains of Moab. Some of these attempts to read the book as the actual words of Moses do so directly and literally, although others have developed more subtle theories, that is, theories that make it plausible that Moses spoke these words on the plains of Moab.[15] In my 2010 study, I suggested that the *verba* approach, in all its iterations, is inadequate because it fails to give full consideration to the process of literary composition in antiquity, the nature and role of literacy in the Levant, along with the role of orality in ancient cultures, the process of text production, and the nature of scribal culture as it pertains to the practices and perceptions of authorship in antiquity.[16] At the end of the day, the *verba* approach is possible as a theory of Deuteronomy's Mosaic origins but, in my view, unlikely, and, in any event, it holds little heuristic value.

The conclusion of mainline historical-critical scholarship is usually perceived as the only alternative to the *verba* approach. Following a nearly hegemonic consensus around the theories of Wilhelm M. L. de Wette, this reconstruction takes the book of Deuteronomy as coming from a different author than the other books of the Pentateuch. This approach assumes further that Deuteronomy was a relatively recent composition connected in some way to the "book of the law" discovered in the Jerusalem temple in 622 BCE, and that it served as the impetus for Josiah's reforms (2 Kgs 22–23). The details of this critical consensus are, of course, well documented and need not detain us here.[17]

---

[14] For further discussion of the *verba* approach, see ibid., esp. 61–64.

[15] I have in mind here theories of northern origins (a variation of which I hold likely to be true, although not as a way of tracing Deuteronomy back to the eleventh or twelfth centuries BCE), denials of cult centralization as part of the book's reforming agenda, or a combination of these created by theorizing about a sequence of central locations over a long period of Israelite history (i.e., Shechem, Bethel, Gilgal, Shiloh, and finally Jerusalem). Of course, absolute certainty in these matters is not an attainable goal. But adequate certainty and reasonable certainty are legitimate objectives in our work, and so we might helpfully distinguish between theories that are possible, plausible, probable, or proven; for discussion, see Bill T. Arnold, "The Genesis Narratives," in *Ancient Israel's History: An Introduction to Issues and Sources*, ed. Bill T. Arnold and Richard S. Hess (Grand Rapids: Baker Academic, 2014), 23–45, esp. 25.

[16] Arnold, "*Ipsissima Vox*," 64–65.

[17] For a recent summary of the *status quaestionis*, see Ernest W. Nicholson, "Deuteronomy in Old Testament Research: A Brief Overview," in *Deuteronomy and the Judaean Diaspora* (Oxford: Oxford University Press, 2014), 3–15.

Suffice it to say that I considered my proposal to take Deuteronomy as the actual voice of Moses to be a *tertium quid*, or third option, avoiding the extremes of fideism and skepticism.[18] Instead of impaling the book of Deuteronomy on the horns of a dilemma—assuming that the substance of the book is either from the thirteenth century BCE or entirely new in the seventh century BCE—I believe we have space for affirming the book as the *ipsissima vox Moysi*, the very voice of the historical Moses.[19] This approach takes the speeches of the book as capturing the concepts of Moses, and maximizes the scripturalization of the figure of Moses in Deuteronomy's closing words (Deut 34:10–12), subordinating the historical man Moses to the book of Moses as the primal voice of prophetic authority.[20] He becomes the fountainhead of prophecy and the inspiration for Mosaic scribes who followed him, who saw themselves as heirs of the Mosaic message and who perpetuated his voice in the canonical shape of Deuteronomy. The *vox* approach also fully exploits the process of transmission history at work in the production of Israelite legal material on its way to becoming torah, which was meant to replace Moses. In my view then, the *vox* approach finally comes to grips with Deuteronomy's "communicational pattern" that led Jean-Pierre Sonnet to conclude that neither the traditional nor the critical interpretation of the book adequately probes the way Deuteronomy serves as the surrogate to another "book," which is out of the reader's range, safely tucked away beside (מִצַּד, *DCH* 7:73) the ark of the covenant (31:9–13, 24–26).[21] This approach acknowledges the self-understanding of the scribes responsible for Deuteronomy, who "projected their working silhouette in the book" in the numerous references to the scribal acts of writing down and copying, especially in Deut 31–32.[22]

I understand that one's view of inspiration may be a hindrance to accepting this *vox* approach to Deuteronomy. It might be helpful at this point to take up the question of how we understand the Scriptures

---

[18] Arnold, "*Ipsissima Vox*," 54.

[19] Thus I believe the dilemma itself is false, and that we can indeed escape from between its horns by means of this *vox* approach.

[20] And anticipating the movement from the Law to the Prophets canonically; see Stephen B. Chapman, *The Law and the Prophets: A Study in Old Testament Canon Formation*, FAT 27 (Tübingen: Mohr Siebeck, 2000), 113–31.

[21] Sonnet, *Book within the Book*, 259–62.

[22] Ibid., 262–67, esp. 265. The formulae of Deut 31:24 echo scribal activity that signals the completion of writing, and, as Sonnet observes, the leading characters of the book—God, the people, Joshua, and Moses—appear in the role of scribes. Additionally, as many have observed, Jer 8:8 relates to this question, and may suggest the role of scribes in the composition of Deuteronomy. See Moshe Weinfeld, *Deuteronomy and the Deuteronomic School* (Oxford: Clarendon, 1972), 158–60; William L. Holladay, *Jeremiah 1: A Commentary on the Book of the Prophet Jeremiah, chapters 1–25*, Hermeneia (Philadelphia: Fortress, 1986), 281–83.

and the role of inspiration in our critical research. In my own tradition, we speak of Scripture as containing "all things necessary to salvation," to be received "through the Holy Spirit as the true rule and guide for faith and practice," and as "the primary source and criterion for Christian doctrine."[23] Our understanding of inspiration and special revelation has, of course, come down to us from Scripture itself (e.g., Ps 19; 2 Tim 3:16–17; 2 Pet 1:20–21), and is rooted in God's work in the whole people of Israel, culminating in the person and ministry of the Messiah. Unlike the claims of other religions about divine revelation and inspiration, our Judeo-Christian traditions bear testimony to multiple hands active in the reception and transmission of our sacred texts.[24] This is in distinct contrast to most other religions, where claims about divine revelation rest largely on trust in the private revelations of their respective and very individual founders and prophets. Both Muhammad and Joseph Smith, for example, had private revelations, which they recorded without other human witnesses. Most other sacred writings of the world, the Vedas and Buddhist

[23] *The Book of Discipline of the United Methodist Church, 2016* (Nashville: United Methodist Publishing House, 2016), 66, 73, 83. Most traditionalists in the Wesleyan movement would be content with a definition of evangelicalism as conversionism, activism, biblicism, and crucicentrism—à la David Bebbington, *Evangelicalism in Modern Britain: A History from the 1730s to the 1980s* (London: Unwin Hyman, 1989), 3. Wesleyan-Arminianism has generally lived in an uneasy tension with the evangelical movement at large, especially at the interstice between human freedom and various forms of determinism, and most also acknowledge that inerrancy is an extrinsic admixture in our theology. In general, we would argue that inerrancy is a twentieth-century North American and largely Reformed teaching, owing more to Calvinistic determinism than to the early church; see Laurence W. Wood, *Theology as History and Hermeneutics: A Post-Critical Conversation with Contemporary Theology* (Lexington, KY: Emeth, 2004), 29–30, 36; Kenneth J. Collins, *The Evangelical Moment: The Promise of an American Religion* (Grand Rapids: Baker Academic, 2005), 70–78. Kenton Sparks puts entirely too fine a point on the subject by attempting to distinguish between the classical inerrancy of the church fathers, on the one hand, which admits that the Bible accommodates human error in its pages, and the concept of inerrancy as held by today's evangelicals in the Cartesian tradition, on the other hand. He argues that the latter is driven by a Cartesian thirst for incorrigible truth, which leads inevitably into an epistemological cul-de-sac (Kenton L. Sparks, *God's Word in Human Words: An Evangelical Appropriation of Critical Biblical Scholarship* [Grand Rapids: Baker Academic, 2008], 54–55, 357–58).

[24] The *vox* approach I am advocating could be seen as exploring the πολυμερῶς καὶ πολυτρόπως ("many and various ways") God spoke through the prophets of old (Heb 1:1). Perhaps also there is significance in the plurals of "long ago God spoke to our *ancestors* (τοῖς πατράσιν)" (Heb 1:1) and "*men and women* (ἄνθρωποι) moved by the Holy Spirit spoke from God" (2 Pet 1:21 NRSV). Since most of the Old Testament books are written anonymously, our doctrine of inspiration includes all these unknown authors, and I am suggesting, as well, the Mosaic scribes who gave us Deuteronomy.

scriptures included, are similarly subjective and unverifiable in their origins. By contrast, the authority of Christian Scripture is preserved first in Israel's Scriptures, rooted in God's salvific work in the world, recorded by the prophets, and subsequently by the witness of countless tradents and copyists who carefully transmitted the written record.[25]

So far, my comments on inspiration are uncontroversial and widely held by ecumenical Christianity. Why raise them here? Because my approach to Deuteronomy as the *vox* of Moses simply acknowledges the larger number of hands involved, testifying to the validity, the truth, and the dependability of this book. The countless contributors and scholars that I refer to here as the "scribes of Moses" served collectively and corporately as witnesses to the tradition, testifying that the words of Deuteronomy are good and true and "useful for teaching, for reproof, for correction, and for training in righteousness" (2 Tim 3:16). And a corporate understanding of authorship accords well with our knowledge of the composition of lengthy literary texts from antiquity. *In nuce*, the role of the individual as author was much less central, for we know that such compositions were the result of a scribal culture in which many hands contributed to the final product, resulting in a "stream of tradition" over time that was the collective property of the scribal community.[26]

The composition of numerous texts illustrates for us that some ancient texts were indeed composite, being a collection of originally unconnected writings, transformed and integrated into a continuous series (as in the case of the *Gilgamesh Epic*), while others were conflations, being composed of two or more variant versions of the same topic and woven together by a redactor (as in the case of the so-called *All Souls Deuteronomy* [4QDeut^{n}], which conflates the two motive clauses for the Sabbath command, Exod 20:11 and Deut 5:15).[27] These comparisons suggest that

[25] "Whatever the origins and history of our biblical materials . . . they became manuscripts in the hands of scribes, and it is as such that we have received them" (Michael A. Fishbane, *Biblical Interpretation in Ancient Israel* [Oxford: Clarendon, 1985], 23–43, esp. 23).

[26] For the concept "stream of tradition" as applied to cuneiform literature transmitted by scribal schools, see A. Leo Oppenheim, *Ancient Mesopotamia: Portrait of a Dead Civilization* (Chicago: University of Chicago Press, 1977), 13, 235–75.

[27] Jeffrey H. Tigay, *Empirical Models for Biblical Criticism* (Philadelphia: University of Pennsylvania Press, 1985), 21–52 for *Gilgamesh* as a composite, and 53–95 for *All Souls Deuteronomy* and many others as examples of conflations. This volume gives many examples, such as how a composite text can be produced by supplementation, resulting in inconsistencies, and how sometimes a composite text includes stylistic inconsistencies, like vocabulary or formulaic phraseology, which constitute traces of the redactional process. On 4QDeut^{n}, see Eugene Ulrich et al., *Qumran Cave 4.IX: Deuteronomy, Joshua, Judges, Kings*, DJD 14 (Oxford:

in antiquity lengthy texts of literary quality were written in the same manner as that reconstructed by redaction critics of the Pentateuch, at times leaving older and later versions of a text interwoven side by side and incorporated into a new composition. What we know of the role of ancient scribes in the production of literary masterpieces in the ancient Near East confirms that such works typically developed through several stages, sometimes spanning many centuries, while scribal authors incorporated diverse ancient sources in their work.[28]

When we combine this evidence with the information we have at our disposal regarding literacy and scribal activity in the Levant, we have a compelling picture of the general time period when text production began to occur in ancient Israel.[29] All indications point to the eighth century BCE

Clarendon, 1995), 117–28. For the ideal specimen, in which the history of composition can be traced empirically from different periods, illuminating the compositional process itself, see the *Gilgamesh Epic* (Jeffrey H. Tigay, *The Evolution of the Gilgamesh Epic* [Philadelphia: University of Pennsylvania Press, 1982], 1–3, 241–50). The end result of the process was a literary masterpiece in mature form. To deny these data would be to argue that *Gilgamesh* was composed all at once by a single author without literary strata or stages of development. But in light of the abundant documentary evidence, we simply must admit that the ancient scribes and redactor-authors were responsible for the continued expansion and development of the text. For a theoretical discussion of the diverse redactional strategies involved in the composition of the Pentateuch, see Stephen A. Kaufman, "The Temple Scroll and Higher Criticism," *HUCA* 53 (1982): 29–43.

[28] For an understanding of scribes and redactors as far more than automaton-like transcribers or anthologists, whose work was limited to copying and pasting, see Lawson G. Stone, "Redaction Criticism: Whence, Whither, and Why? Or, Going beyond Source and Form Criticism without Leaving them Behind," in *A Biblical Itinerary: In Search of Method, Form, and Content: Essays in Honor of George W. Coats*, ed. Eugene E. Carpenter, JSOTSup 240 (Sheffield: Sheffield Academic, 1997), 77–90, esp. 80–85; Stone, "Redaction Criticism, OT," *NIDB* 4:752–53. Unlike earlier source- and form-critical scholars, we understand the Israelite redactors as scribal authors—interpreters of the *traditum* with a seriousness and sophistication of literary activity that also evinces a serious theological intention. Stone ("Redaction Criticism," 85) summarizes their role by citing the insight of Franz Rosenzweig, who suggested that the siglum "R," far from signifying "Redactor," should be taken to signify *rabbenu*, "our teacher"!

[29] See recently Christopher A. Rollston, "Scribal Curriculum during the First Temple Period: Epigraphic Hebrew and Biblical Evidence," in *Contextualizing Israel's Sacred Writings: Ancient Literacy, Orality, and Literary Production*, ed. Brian B. Schmidt, SBLAIL 22 (Atlanta: SBL Press, 2015), 71–101, and Rollston's several other contributions on this point. Other studies have confirmed that writing itself played a limited role until the eighth century BCE (William M. Schniedewind, *How the Bible Became a Book: The Textualization of Ancient Israel* [New York: Cambridge University Press, 2004], 48–90). Education, beginning with alphabetic training, was available to the ruling classes as early as the united monarchy; see David M. Carr, *Writing on the Tablet of the Heart: Origins of Scripture and Literature*

as the beginning of biblical literature and the seventh century as a time of text revolution.[30] We may theorize about the origins of Deuteronomy earlier—for example, among northern priests in the ninth or even tenth centuries BCE—but such early sources (other than perhaps legal collections) were likely oral literature, which puts them beyond our ability to investigate. Thus a *vox* approach that acknowledges the work of "Mosaic scribes" in the eighth and seventh centuries BCE accords well with these data. On a spectrum of human participation—with the historical Moses as single author on one extreme and a host of Mosaic scribes on the other extreme—the *vox* approach that I proposed in 2010 is likely to be perceived as defending the latter, and perhaps rightly so. Such a position does not necessarily minimize the role of the historical Moses as authorizer of Israel's Torah. Rather, this approach simply acknowledges that we have a clearer picture of the later stage of composition and that earlier stages are unrecoverable.

Michael Fishbane Again: The Significance of the *Traditum* for the *Traditio*

In my previous work, I have traced how research on ancient Israel's legal corpora illumines the process by which the Mosaic scribes became the voice of Moses, exploring especially the way Deuteronomy's original core (Deut 12–26) relates to the older Tetrateuchal legal material diachronically.[31] In what follows, I expand the discussion to include also the

(New York: Oxford University Press, 2005), 112–24; Nili Sacher Fox, *In the Service of the King: Officialdom in Ancient Israel and Judah*, HUCM 23 (Cincinnati: Hebrew Union College Press, 2000), 96–110, 195–96.

[30] Schniedewind, *How the Bible Became a Book*, 64–117. For the seventh century BCE as the "starting point for the Deuteronomistic literary production" generally, see Thomas Römer, *The So-Called Deuteronomistic History: A Sociological, Historical, and Literary Introduction* (London: T&T Clark, 2005), esp. 41–43. We certainly have epigraphic evidence for Hebrew prior to this time, but these data are not determinative when theorizing about the production of belles lettres in ancient Israel. For the alternative view that the epigraphic evidence from Syria-Palestine does, in fact, suggest that written literature was being produced from at least the tenth century BCE onward, see A. R. Millard, "The Knowledge of Writing in Iron Age Palestine," *TynBul* 46 (1995): 207–17; Richard S. Hess, "Literacy in Iron Age Israel," in *Windows into Old Testament History: Evidence, Argument, and the Crisis of "Biblical Israel,"* ed. V. Philips Long, Gordon J. Wenham, and David W. Baker (Grand Rapids: Eerdmans, 2002), 82–102; and Hess, "Questions of Reading and Writing in Ancient Israel," *BBR* 19 (2009): 1–9.

[31] Arnold, "*Ipsissima Vox.*" In this work I drew in particular upon the work of Bernard M. Levinson, *Deuteronomy and the Hermeneutics of Legal Innovation* (New York: Oxford University Press, 1997).

book's inner and outer framing units—the later, outer frame (Deut 1–3[4] and 31–34) and the older, inner frame (Deut 5–11 and 27–30)—both of which also reflect the voice of Moses. Once again, my approach is greatly influenced by Michael Fishbane's distinction between *traditum* and *traditio*, or between the content of tradition and the long and varied process of transmission, respectively.[32] The "voice" of Moses is pertinent in both the legal core of Deuteronomy and the development of Israel's Torah, including the book's frameworks. The *traditum* of Israel's old legal material (especially the Covenant Code, Exod 20:22–23:33) has been updated and recast in Deut 12–26, and portions of Genesis, Exodus, and Numbers have also been updated and recast in the book's narrative and paraenetic frameworks.[33] The process of how the *traditio* works in developing the book's framing units differs from that used for the legal materials, although the result is the same. The voice of Moses is clear in the work of the Mosaic scribes, through their updating, revising, preaching, and teaching.[34]

Another important distinction in Fishbane's approach is pertinent to this discussion. When exploring the idea of scribal development of the *traditum*, he raises the question of a continuum between purely scribal-redactional procedures, on the one hand, and authorial-compositional

---

[32] A distinction first proposed by Douglas A. Knight, *Rediscovering the Traditions of Israel: The Development of the Traditio-Historical Research of the Old Testament, with Special Consideration of Scandinavian Contributions*, SBLDS 9 (Missoula, MT: Scholars Press, 1975), 5–20. For further discussion of the definitions, see Arnold, "*Ipsissima Vox*," 68–69.

[33] We have no real consensus about the extent or date of these frameworks. Wellhausen proposed three stages of diachronic development: first, the original Deuteronomy, chs. 12–26; second, two accretions independent of each other, (a) chs. 1–4, 12–26, and 27, and (b) chs. 5–11, 12–26, and 28–30; and finally, the conflation of these two editions (Julius Wellhausen, *Die Composition des Hexateuchs und der historischen Bücher des Alten Testaments* [Berlin: G. Reimer, 1899], 193). Van der Toorn believes he has discerned four editions of the book, in chronological order: the Covenant Edition, the Torah Edition, the History Edition, and the Wisdom Edition (Karel van der Toorn, *Scribal Culture and the Making of the Hebrew Bible* [Cambridge: Harvard University Press, 2007], 150–66). In any case, one can discern two types of Mosaic *traditum* in Deuteronomy, reflecting Fishbane's legal and aggadic exegesis (the legal core of Deut 12–26 was likely primary, with the framing units added subsequently). While we cannot agree on specific dates for these additions, the diachronic development seems certain. Synchronically oriented approaches are also helpful, but they are limited in their ability to explain the current canonical shape of Deuteronomy.

[34] The book itself is, after all, an interpretation and implementation of the old Mosaic law of Sinai, a re-presentation of the revelation at Sinai as "this Torah," which is also why it came to be referred to in rabbinic literature as משנה תורה; cf. *Sipre Deb.* 160; *ʿAbod. Zar.* 25a; *Ḥul.* 63b. See Hindy Najman, *Seconding Sinai: The Development of Mosaic Discourse in Second Temple Judaism*, JSJSup 77 (Leiden: Brill, 2003), 39.

ones, on the other.[35] The fact is, such a distinction between scribes and authors is difficult to discern in biblical literature.

> Many scribes undoubtedly saw themselves as the cultural allies of the composers—teachers of their meanings and reporters of their teachings—and so composers in a derivative sense. And if, in fact, the scribes also belonged to the institutional groups which composed and taught these texts, and therefore regarded their addenda as part and parcel of the larger guild composition, there would be additional reason to consider the demarcation between scribe and author somewhat artificial.[36]

If, on the one hand, we think of scribes as distinct from authors—assuming that authors only compose texts and scribes only copy them—then emendations and scribal activity would produce a *traditum* with multiple levels of authority. As we have seen, our views of inspiration are all too often tied to this view of authorship, so that authority is located in a single individual author who gave us his autographs. Scribes then would be merely preservers of that *traditum*; they would make no substantive contribution to its content.

On the other hand, if scribes and authors cannot be distinguished, or if the scribal craft is considered formally and functionally allied to that of authors, "sharing with them a diversity of knowledge, concern, and technique,"[37] then the emending work of scribes presents no interruption of the *traditum*, and their work is no less authoritative as it supplements, changes, and updates the *traditum*. Again, Fishbane:

> Viewed in this way, the *traditum* dominates the *traditio* and conditions its operations. And to the extent that the scribal *traditio* makes the *traditum* lexically more accessible, theologically more palatable, or materially more comprehensive, its operations are intended to reinforce the authority of the *traditum* and to serve it. . . . Thus, scribal exegesis derives from the *traditum*, articulates and underscores its content, and ultimately shares in its composition. From this perspective, the *traditio* of scribal exegesis simply brings obscure or problematic dimensions of the *traditum* to the level of textuality. It neither alters nor rivals the centrality and authority of the textual artefact.[38]

---

[35] See Fishbane, *Biblical Interpretation*, 84–88, for discussion. See also numerous other publications by Fishbane: "Revelation and Tradition: Aspects of Inner-Biblical Exegesis," *JBL* 99 (1980): 343–61; "Inner Biblical Exegesis: Types and Strategies of Interpretation in Ancient Israel," in *Midrash and Literature* (New Haven: Yale University Press, 1986), 19–37; "The Hebrew Bible and Exegetical Tradition," in *Intertextuality in Ugarit and Israel*, ed. Johannes Cornelis de Moor, *OtSt* 40 (Leiden: Brill, 1998), 15–30; "Types of Biblical Intertextuality," in *Congress Volume, Oslo 1998*, ed. André Lemaire and Magne Sæbø, VTSup 80 (Leiden: Brill, 2000), 39–44.

[36] Fishbane, *Biblical Interpretation*, 85.

[37] Ibid., 86.

[38] Ibid., 87.

This vision of innerbiblical exegesis[39] comes near the end of Fishbane's general discussion of scribal comments and corrections as part of the exegetical dynamics of the *traditum-traditio* relationship. And so his comments are apropos with regard to both legal and aggadic exegesis, which are the categories of his approach immediately pertinent for the interpretation of Deuteronomy (both its legal core and its narrative and paraenetic frameworks). The idea that the message of the tradition drove scribal interpreters forward in their work of reformulation and transmission is suggestive for Deuteronomy precisely because the book is by definition an exegetical enterprise. While the name "Deuteronomy" may be an unfortunate translation of "copy of this law" (17:18) in the LXX, it is oddly enough somewhat appropriate because of the way the book exegetes and interprets the Torah for a new audience.[40] The message the scribes had before them as a *Vorlage* (the *traditum*) drove a process of reformulation and continuation in a method of composition (*traditio*) that we can trace by careful exegesis of our own. In a sense, today's interpreters of Deuteronomy have much in common with the Mosaic scribes who gave us the book. Whenever scribes chose to explain a difficult text rather than simply to remove it, they "insured that future readers would be forced to a realization not far removed from their own: that they are latecomers to the text, who must read it with the guidance of an oral—now written—exegetical tradition."[41] Their authoritative work is in our Bible because, in my view, they were scribal authors working under divine inspiration to illustrate how the people of God appropriate and reapply the revelation of the Mosaic covenant for a new generation. These Mosaic scribes did not present their work in some sort of disingenuous attempt to deceive their seventh-century readers, nor did they intentionally archaize their writing in order to add authenticity to what they feared would otherwise be unaccepted. They presented Deuteronomy as an updating and recasting of the Mosaic tradition they

[39] I avoid the less carefully defined term "intertextuality" for this discussion.

[40] This is not to diminish the difficulties in the way Deut 1–3, for example, relates to Exodus and Numbers, for which see the recent work of Angela Roskop Erisman, "Transjordan in Deuteronomy: The Promised Land and the Formation of the Pentateuch," *JBL* 132 (2013): 769–89.

[41] Fishbane, "Types and Strategies," 22. This is close to the concept of "Mosaic Discourse," which is said to have originated with the gradual production of a collection that became Deuteronomy and to have become increasingly important in Second Temple Judaism. This Mosaic Discourse extrapolates authoritative teachings from Moses' presentation of divine instructions as recorded in older documents (Najman, *Seconding Sinai*, 1–40; cf. also John H. Choi, *Traditions at Odds: The Reception of the Pentateuch in Biblical and Second Temple Period Literature*, LHBOTS 518 [London: T&T Clark, 2010], 15–46).

had received, in order to perpetuate that Mosaic *traditum* faithfully for a new generation.[42]

Pseudepigraphy, Pseudonymity, Fictionality, Fraud, and Other False Leads

My proposal is that Deuteronomy is the result of a long process in which scribal transmitters received, reworked, contributed to, and handed on authoritative Mosaic teachings, although they were not "authors" in a way that suggests "intellectual property" to our minds today. Indeed, Moses himself, the founder of the tradition, may be thought of as the "author" of these teachings, although again, that designation is an anachronism if we impose modern conceptions of authorship upon it.[43] The concept of "attributed authorship" might be helpful. But here again, the approach I am advocating relies on the intentional development of *traditum* in a communally accepted process of *traditio*, which is categorically different from attributing one's work to a fictive author from the remote past in order to lend legitimacy to the composition. And so this raises a question: Does this mean Deuteronomy is "pseudepigraphic"? Taking us back to the conversation Friedrich Delitzsch had with his professor those many years ago—are designations like "pseudonymous," "fictive," "forgery," and "pious fraud" appropriate for the book of Deuteronomy? In other words, does it make a difference whether we think the scribes who gave us Deuteronomy wrote in the *name* of Moses, or in the *voice* of Moses?

Perhaps the most common designation for Deuteronomy in the secondary literature is *pseudepigraphy*.[44] This literary phenomenon has been

---

[42] Ziony Zevit draws a similar conclusion when he states that Deuteronomy does not present itself as "an archaic, authentic teaching" pretending to be something it is not, but presents itself as "a post-Mosaic revelation about Moses' authentic teaching" (Ziony Zevit, "Deuteronomy in the Temple: An Exercise in Historical Imagining," in *Mishneh Todah: Studies in Deuteronomy and Its Cultural Environment in Honor of Jeffrey H. Tigay*, ed. Nili Sacher Fox, David A. Glatt-Gilad, and Michael J. Williams [Winona Lake, IN: Eisenbrauns, 2009], 201–18, esp. 212).

[43] Hartmut Gese, "The Biblical View of Scripture," in *Essays on Biblical Theology* (Minneapolis: Augsburg, 1981), 9–33, esp. 21.

[44] E.g., Morton Smith says that Israelite literature was "originally and customarily anonymous. When interest in history became acute in the 7th century and later centuries B.C. a considerable number of anonymous works were falsely attributed to famous historical figures. . . . The first great representative of this genre is probably, but not certainly, the Deuteronomic Code (*Dt.* 12–26 and 28), written shortly before 621 B.C." (Morton Smith, "Pseudepigraphy in the Israelite Literary Tradition," in *Pseudepigrapha I*, ed. Kurt von Fritz, Entretiens sur l'Antiquité

defined recently as denoting "a process in which literary documents are attributed to someone other than the actual author and so possess false authorial ascriptions."[45] Of course, we know of pseudepigraphic literature from the Second Temple period, and I am not addressing the question of whether pseudepigraphy is an appropriate category for portions of Isaiah, the Gospel of John, or various Pauline epistles.[46] Rather, I am more narrowly asking whether such a term is profitable for Deuteronomy, in light of my proposal that the authoritative revelatory *traditum* of Moses was expanded, reworked, and rewritten by Mosaic scribes and eventually textualized in the book of Deuteronomy. Indeed, in at least one case, the *vox* approach I proposed in 2010 has been categorized as taking Moses as a "legendary figure" and the speeches of the book as "pseudepigraphic."[47]

Classique 18 [Vandoeuvres-Geneva: Fondation Hardt, 1972], 214–15); cf. also van der Toorn, *Scribal Culture*, 33–34, who uses "pseudonymity" and "pseudepigraphy" interchangeably; and Joseph Blenkinsopp, who states that the early attribution of Deuteronomy to Moses makes it one of "the earliest examples of Jewish pseudepigraphy" (Joseph Blenkinsopp, *The Pentateuch: An Introduction to the First Five Books of the Bible*, ABRL [New York: Doubleday, 1992], 2). Fishbane also refers to the pseudepigraphic Mosaic voice in Deuteronomy (Fishbane, *Biblical Interpretation*, 436, 530–33), which I think needs to be stated differently.

[45] Christopher B. Ansberry, Casey A. Strine, Edward W. Klink III, and David Lincicum, "Pseudepigraphy and the Canon," in *Evangelical Faith and the Challenge of Historical Criticism*, ed. Christopher M. Hays and Christopher B. Ansberry (Grand Rapids: Baker Academic, 2013) , esp. 125. Thus, a literary pseudepigraphon bears "a false attribution of authorship" (David A. deSilva, *Introducing the Apocrypha: Message, Context, and Significance* [Grand Rapids: Baker, 2002], 15).

[46] For discussion of the possibility of pseudepigraphic literature in these other canonical cases, see Ansberry et al., "Pseudepigraphy and the Canon," esp. 133–56. Many years ago, Moisés Silva dealt with the question of authorship for conservative scholars (Moisés Silva, "Old Princeton, Westminster, and Inerrancy," *WTJ* 50 [1988]: 65–80, drawing upon the example of E. J. Young [p. 75]; repr. in *Inerrancy and Hermeneutic*, ed. Harvie M. Conn [Grand Rapids: Baker, 1988], 67–80). Silva's discussion implies that pseudepigraphy might be considered part of an inerrant New Testament, which is to suggest that evangelicals should accept the idea that the biblical canon has pseudepigraphical portions. On pseudepigrapha in Second Temple literature, such as the Wisdom of Solomon, Book of Baruch, and Second Esdras, see deSilva, *Introducing the Apocrypha*, 127–52, 198–213, and 323–51, respectively; and James C. VanderKam, *An Introduction to Early Judaism* (Grand Rapids: Eerdmans, 2001), 56–58. Annette Yoshiko Reed has rightly challenged not only the heurism of the term, but its appropriateness for the so-called Old Testament Pseudepigrapha (Annette Yoshiko Reed, "The Modern Invention of 'Old Testament Pseudepigrapha,' " *JTS* 60 [2009]: 403–36).

[47] Daniel I. Block, *Deuteronomy*, NIVAC (Grand Rapids: Zondervan, 2012), 28–29 and n13 there. To be sure, Professor Block nuances my position in the footnote, but he nonetheless appears to categorize my view with that of Moshe Weinfeld as one that puts "programmatic speeches into the mouth" of Moses, a position that is "diametrically opposed to the internal evidence of the book." Others have

The definition given above includes a "false authorial ascription," which I believe is not accurate to describe the work of the scribes behind Deuteronomy. They and the community of which they were a part perceived their task as perpetuating and contributing to the venerated Mosaic tradition, and their anonymity was only natural since they did not think of themselves as initiating and authorizing that tradition. Their task was one of developing, expanding, and recontextualizing the Mosaic *traditum*, and it involved no prevarication, deception, falsehood, or perfidy. My objection to the use of "pseudepigraphy" is not simply derived from evangelical theology, which a priori might conclude that the book cannot be "false" because it is divinely inspired.[48] The point is that such a denotation for Deuteronomy is inadequate and misrepresentative because it does not reflect the way the Mosaic scribes who produced the book perceived themselves or the text they wrote. The use of "pseudo" is a cultural imposition on the book of Deuteronomy and the faithful theologians and scholars who produced it.

Another term that is closely related, but which for my purposes is defined distinctly and narrowly, is *pseudonymity*. Borrowing again from a recent definition, this is "a literary convention in which an author deliberately writes under a name other than his/her own."[49] The nuances of these two—pseudepigraphy and pseudonymity—reflect different perspectives on essentially the same literary phenomenon. The definition given above for "pseudepigraphy" highlights the process in which an anonymous document is attributed falsely. Although the author may be complicit, the focus is on someone else who attributes the document to a different person. The definition provided for "pseudonymity" highlights the process in which

---

used my proposal approvingly; see Christopher B. Ansberry and Jerry Hwang, "No Covenant before the Exile? The Deuteronomic Torah and Israel's Covenant Theology," in *Evangelical Faith and the Challenge of Historical Criticism*, ed. Christopher M. Hays and Christopher B. Ansberry (Grand Rapids: Baker Academic, 2013), 74–94, esp. 82–89; Stephen L. Cook, *Reading Deuteronomy: A Literary and Theological Commentary*, Reading the Old Testament, ed. Mark E. Biddle (Macon, GA: Smyth & Helwys, 2015), 27, 56.

[48] In my view, the authors of the aforementioned article on "Pseudepigraphy and the Canon" (Ansberry et al.) are correct that pseudepigraphy itself is not a problem for canonical texts. However, I differ from them in that, for the Pentateuch, and more particularly for Deuteronomy, I believe the term "pseudepigraphy" itself is misleading and unhelpful.

[49] Ansberry et al., "Pseudepigraphy and the Canon," 125. See also Richard N. Soulen and R. Kendall Soulen, *Handbook of Biblical Criticism*, 4th ed. (Louisville: Westminster John Knox, 2011), 168; Arthur G. Patzia and Anthony J. Petrotta, *Pocket Dictionary of Biblical Studies* (Downers Grove, IL: InterVarsity Press, 2002), 97, although both of these popular handbooks fail to distinguish between pseudepigraphy and pseudonymity, as I am doing here.

authors themselves intentionally falsify a document.[50] This designation is as inappropriate for Deuteronomy as pseudepigraphy. I have attempted to construct a new (or, in my view, to (re)construct an "old") way of understanding the composition of Deuteronomy. I believe the *vox* approach is a different way of thinking about Mosaic authorship, one that avoids characterizing the book as either pseudepigraphic or pseudonymous, or anything else that is rightly described by the prefix "pseudo."

Another designation one often finds in the secondary literature on Deuteronomy is of the book's *fictive* or *fictitious* nature.[51] An exacting problem arises here from the use of the English word "fiction," because in literary studies the term is notoriously difficult to define, no less so than the word "history."[52] Robert Alter complicated the issues by referring to "historicized fiction" and "fictionalized history," at times interchangeably and with little distinction.[53] The former connotes an account that is essentially nonfactual, irrespective of bits of factual information included in the telling. By contrast, "fictionalized history" connotes an account representing real events in the past, however much (or little) fictionalizing may be involved in the telling of those events.[54] In any case, care must be used to clarify and define our terms, as always. Yet even the scholarly discussions of "fiction" and "history" are more complicated because those discussions focus largely on narrative historiography, and we have precious little of that genre in Deuteronomy. Cast as a framed collection of speeches of Moses delivered to the Israelites on the plains of Moab, and defining itself essentially as a book pointing to another book or, more pre-

[50] On pseudonymous attribution to Moses, see Najman, *Seconding Sinai*, 36–39; and Patrick D. Miller, " 'Moses My Servant': The Deuteronomic Portrait of Moses," in *A Song of Power and the Power of Song: Essays on the Book of Deuteronomy*, ed. Duane L. Christensen, SBTS 3 (Winona Lake, IN: Eisenbrauns, 1993), 301–12, esp. 306; repr. of *Int* 41 (1987): 245–55.

[51] For example, Römer refers in passing to the idea that Deuteronomy makes no attempt at all "to conceal its fictive character" (Thomas Römer, "Deuteronomy in Search of Origins," in *Reconsidering Israel and Judah: Recent Studies on the Deuteronomistic History*, ed. Gary N. Knoppers and J. G. McConville [Winona Lake, IN: Eisenbrauns, 2000], 119–20).

[52] V. Philips Long, *The Art of Biblical History*, Foundations of Contemporary Interpretation 5 (Grand Rapids: Zondervan, 1994), 58–86; repr. as "History and Fiction: What Is History?" in *Israel's Past in Present Research: Essays on Ancient Israelite Historiography*, ed. V. Philips Long, SBTS 7 (Winona Lake, IN: Eisenbrauns, 1999), 232–54.

[53] Robert Alter, *The Art of Biblical Narrative*, 2nd ed. (New York: Basic Books, 2011), 25–54.

[54] Thus Long, *Art of Biblical History*, 61–62. He also draws upon the views of Baruch Halpern, according to whom "history. . . is all fictionalized, and yet history" (Baruch Halpern, *The First Historians: The Hebrew Bible and History* [San Francisco: Harper & Row, 1988], 68).

cisely, pointing to a "scroll of this Torah" (29:20[ET 21]; 30:10; 31:26), Deuteronomy has a distinctive quality from the outset that complicates this question still further. It seems that similarly to fictionalized history, we might think of the Cisjordan author as imagining an early version of ancient Israel encamped on the plains of Moab (1:1–5) as a general context, and the rest of the book as placed in that imagined context.[55] In fictional writing an author's imagination from the outset creates a text that is entirely or mostly nonfactual. But this is certainly not the idea behind a *vox* approach to the composition of the book of Deuteronomy. Sonnet refers to Deuteronomy's "represented world" as a narrative stage, established by the book's opening.[56] So the terms "fictive," "fictional," and "fictitious" are hardly required by this approach to Deuteronomy's represented world. I would add that an imagined stage for the speeches of Moses is not the same as "imaginary" literature. In other words, we have in Deuteronomy a mental viewpoint or attitude but not a fantasy. The *vox* approach I am advocating does not mean the book is ahistorical or antihistorical; "fictive" is, strictly speaking, inappropriate for Deuteronomy.

In my opening anecdote, Friedrich Delitzsch asked his professor if, in light of what he learned in the lecture earlier that day, Deuteronomy might be considered a *Fälschung*, or *forgery*. Although not as common as "fictive" or other labels discussed here, the idea that Deuteronomy is a forgery has been considered occasionally and has at times been distinguished from the idea of pseudepigraphy.[57] Hindy Najman has observed

---

[55] The concept of "point-of-view," which has been influential in narratival studies as applied to the Old Testament, is helpful in this regard; cf. Boris Uspensky, *A Poetics of Composition: The Structure of the Artistic Text and Typology of a Compositional Form*, trans. Valentina Zavarin and Susan Wittig (Berkeley: University of California Press, 1973); and for Uspensky's significance in biblical studies, see, e.g., Meir Sternberg, *The Poetics of Biblical Narrative: Ideological Literature and the Drama of Reading*, ISBL (Bloomington: Indiana University Press, 1985), 129–52.

[56] Sonnet, *Book within the Book*, 4–6, 11–12, 259–62. See also Jean-Pierre Sonnet, "De Moïse et du narrateur: Pour une pensée narrative de l'inspiration," *RSR* 93 (2005): 517–31, esp. 528–31, where he suggests that Moses' voice hypostatizes all anonymous voices of Israel's legal tradition and that the dramatization of the book establishes the objective moment of inspiration, as well as its teleology, building faith by means of language. None of this would require that the narrative stage is fictional, although admittedly this is not Sonnet's point.

[57] Bruce Metzger was careful to distinguish between pseudepigraphy and forgery by emphasizing the intention to deceive. In his view, forgeries were created in a calculated attempt to deceive, which is not true of pseudepigraphical writing (Metzger, "Literary Forgeries and Canonical Pseudepigrapha," *JBL* 91 [1972]: 3–24, esp. 4). On the error of "intentional fallacy" committed by both conservative and liberal scholars, see the interesting discussion in Ansberry and Hwang, "No Covenant before the Exile?" 86–87.

that scholars have suggested, either explicitly or implicitly, that the scribes who produced Deuteronomy and other Old Testament books "committed what we would call *forgery*, an activity that is not only unhistorical, but also morally tainted."[58] As she goes on to demonstrate, by "unhistorical" she means that books in antiquity were not written intentionally as forgeries, and that associated concepts of plagiarism and tampering are historical anachronisms. Rather than a fraudulent or even criminal-sounding activity, the work of the Mosaic scribes who produced Deuteronomy is like that of other Israelite scribes who worked so hard over centuries to draw attention away from their labor, while pointing always to Moses' originary voice. It is anachronistic to call their work forgeries, for they themselves saw their work as expository, expansive, and, in the case of Deuteronomy, paraenetic.

Finally, it hardly needs to be said at this point that Wilhelm M. L. de Wette's often (mis)quoted "pious fraud" designation for Deuteronomy is off the mark.[59] In fact, while de Wette considered the possibility that Deuteronomy could have been planted by the priest Hilkiah, perhaps assisted by Shaphan and Huldah the prophetess, he refused to give this much consideration, asserting that such detail is beyond our ability to reconstruct.[60] As with other false leads, this one is anachronistic because its concept of "authorship" imposes modern connotations on the work of Israel's tradents, conjuring up illicit claims of literary origins, whereas in Deuteronomy the voice of Moses represents "a declaration of authoritative tradition."[61] In sum, all approaches to the composition of the book of Deuteronomy that characterize it as "pseudo" or fraudulent are themselves false leads. The legal core of the book may be identified under

[58] Najman, *Seconding Sinai*, 5. She also speculates that this scholarly impulse to characterize the scribal "practices and intentions" of ancient Israel's scribes as forgeries stems from the "hostile attitude toward religious authorities characteristic of many key figures of the Enlightenment, the period in which modern biblical criticism was crystallized" (6).

[59] Wilhelm M. L. de Wette, *Beiträge zur Einleitung in das Alte Testament*, (Hildesheim: Olms, 1971 [1806]), 1:179. And for a twist on this concept, see Levinson's comment that Deuteronomy is, in fact, an "impious fraud" (*Legal Innovation*, 150; and cf. Najman, *Seconding Sinai*, 5).

[60] De Wette, *Beiträge* 1:179. A. J. Droge claims that no scholar of the nineteenth century actually used language of fraud to describe Deuteronomy (A. J. Droge, " 'The Lying Pen of the Scribes': Of Holy Books and Pious Frauds," *Method and Theory in the Study of Religion* 15 [2003]: 117–47, esp. 121). Biblical scholars have essentially propagated the concept by quoting each other and giving de Wette credit for something he never seriously proposed.

[61] Ansberry and Hwang, "No Covenant before the Exile?" 84. Ansberry and Hwang agree that, when Deuteronomy is properly understood as preserving the Mosaic *traditum*, referring to it as pseudepigraphical or fraudulent is going too far (85).

the category of attributed authorship due to its so-called promulgation formula, which uses the first-person personal pronoun to assume the identity of Moses, in the expression "that I command you/have commanded you."[62] The *vox* approach I am advocating relies on the intentional development of the Mosaic *traditum* in a communally accepted process of *traditio*, and envisions more than the attribution of one's work to a venerated figure from the remote past in order to gain legitimacy and authority. Ultimately, this *vox* approach requires new categories for understanding "authorship," since none of the ones discussed here are accurate or adequate.

Conclusion

In this general way, then, we may think of "Mosaic authorship" for the legal portions of the Pentateuch, including Deuteronomy. Indeed, Mosaic authorship is an important concept for canonization, parallel to apostolic authority in the development of New Testament books.[63] On the one hand, we might envision Mosaic authority as follows—although again, these are mere speculations beyond the scope of critical investigation. The historical Moses promulgated the law in germinal form at Horeb, perhaps some early version of the Covenant Code (Exod 20:22–23:33; cf. 24:3–4). Moses issued this Torah as *res judicata*, declaring the law officially in effect (Deut 1:5) and putting it into the hands of a new generation of Israelites on the plains of Moab for the sake of all Israelites in perpetuity. We can only speculate further about the preservation of this Torah: perhaps it was pretextualized until preserved first in the hands of royal scribes or wisdom priests in the tenth century BCE, and ultimately in the late eighth century BCE, when tradents from the north became refugees in Jerusalem, most likely settling in the new western section of the city, the מִשְׁנֶה (cf. 2 Kgs

[62] Moses is the antecedent of 15 occurrences of the nominative first-person-singular pronoun (12:11, 14, 21, 28; 13:1[ET 12:32], 19[ET 18]; 15:5, 11, 15; 17:3; 19:7, 9; 24:8, 18, 22) and of two occurrences of the objective first-person-singular pronoun (18:15, 17).

[63] "The claim of Mosaic authorship . . . functioned theologically within the community to establish the continuity of the faith of successive generations with that which had once been delivered to Moses at Sinai. Unfortunately, in the nineteenth-century debate over authorship the canonical role of Moses in relation to the Pentateuch was misunderstood by both parties. When correctly interpreted, the Mosaic authorship of the Pentateuch is an important theological affirmation which is part of the canonical witness" (Brevard S. Childs, *Introduction to the Old Testament as Scripture* [Philadelphia: Fortress, 1979], 135).

22:14), and integrating themselves gradually in their new surroundings.[64] By 622 BCE, while pondering what could have gone wrong in the north and hoping to avoid the same disastrous results in Judah, they embraced and (re)promulgated the old Mosaic way articulated in their texts—which had already been esteemed, copied, and proclaimed for a century. This reconstruction is a maximalizing historical speculation. On the other hand, reconstructing any part of Deuteronomy as the *ipsissima verba* of Moses strains our credulity beyond that which is necessary. Perhaps the *verba* approaches ought to be abandoned for the *vox* approach, which I believe makes the best sense of Deuteronomy's data and honors the Mosaic scribes who gave us this book.[65]

In Jeremiah's day, a circle of tradents and scribes in the ancient Israelite wisdom traditions were engaged in the composition of Torah literature (Jer 8:8). It is not without reason that many scholars have linked the Torah written by the pen of these scribes to our current book of Deuteronomy.[66] Perhaps this verse even gives us a glimpse of the original "Mosaic scribes," who developed the Mosaic *traditum* handed down through the centuries in what became typical Jewish fashion, while they themselves were becoming the "voice" of Moses.

---

[64] On the archaeological evidence for the expansion of Jerusalem, see Magen Broshi, "The Expansion of Jerusalem in the Reigns of Hezekiah and Manasseh," *IEJ* 24 (1974): 21–26; and Nadav Na'aman, "The Growth and Development of Judah and Jerusalem in the Eighth Century BCE: A Rejoinder," *RB* 116 (2009): 321–35.

[65] I have used the term *vox* by way of comparison with the older notion of *ipsissima vox Jesu* in New Testament studies, although perhaps for our purposes *ipsissima spiritus Moysi* or *ipsissima notio Moysi* would be better.

[66] If this is correct, it is important to remember that Jeremiah was not condemning the composition itself as false, but rather insincere scribes who claimed some inalienable privilege while not observing the teaching they themselves had committed to writing. See Fishbane, *Biblical Interpretation*, 33–36; Weinfeld, *Deuteronomic School*, 158–71; Holladay, *Jeremiah 1*, 282; Peter C. Craigie, Page H. Kelley, and Joel F. Drinkard, *Jeremiah 1–25*, WBC 26 (Dallas: Word, 1991), 134.

CHAPTER 6

SLAVES AND REBELS: INSCRIPTION, IDENTITY, AND TIME IN THE RHETORIC OF DEUTERONOMY[1]

Brent A. Strawn

> Those who composed [Deuteronomy] in this form did not consider themselves to be guilty of some pious fraud and were not using a literary artifice either. Moses' voice, as it was heard in their imaginations in the late royal era, went forth to this declining period, taking account of its specific troubles and grappling with the disorder of its religious and social life. Over a distance of many centuries past it was possible once again to stand at the foot of Mount Sinai and hear God's will. Thus Israel introduced her divine history into the present! Perhaps we may express it better by saying that history itself intruded again and again into Israel. (Gerhard von Rad)[2]

> Moses shifts back and forth between that day at Horeb and this day in Moab; so too the Deuteronomist, by breaking frame throughout the book, subtly—almost subliminally—forces us to shuttle back and forth between the narrated past and the narrator's present. Both Moses and the narrator shift temporal gears in the process of teaching. (Robert Polzin)[3]

Two Key Texts

The inspiration for the present essay (as well as its title) is taken from two passages in the book of Deuteronomy that situate the Israelites in

[1] I thank the editors and conveners of the Wheaton conference at which this paper was originally presented for their kind invitation and assistance, and am grateful to the other participants for a very collegial and enjoyable exchange. I am indebted to Bill T. Arnold for his feedback, encouragement, and bibliographical suggestions, and am particularly grateful to Aubrey E. Buster for her close reading of an earlier draft, which helped me reformulate several important aspects of the argument.

[2] Gerhard von Rad, "How to Read the Old Testament," in *God at Work in Israel*, trans. John H. Marks (Nashville: Abingdon, 1980 [German orig.: 1974]), 14.

[3] Robert Polzin, "Deuteronomy," in *The Literary Guide to the Bible*, ed. Robert Alter and Frank Kermode (Cambridge: Belknap, 1987), 94. Cf. Polzin, *Moses and the Deuteronomist*, part 1, *Deuteronomy, Joshua, Judges* (New York: Seabury, 1980), 32.

two modes. The first text is Deut 6:21, which discusses *Israel's Egyptian servitude*:

> Tell your children: "We were Pharaoh's slaves in Egypt, but YHWH brought us out from Egypt with a strong hand."[4]

The second text is Deut 9:7, which mentions *Israel's seemingly incessant rebellion*:

> From the day that you left the land of Egypt, until you arrived at this place, you've been rebels against YHWH.

These two verses have more than a few things in common, including some repeated words and several syntactical details, but perhaps the most striking commonality is the use of a masculine plural substantive fronted before a Qal suffix-conjugation verb form of היה in order to describe the Israelites in two very different states and within two distinct temporal frames: "Slaves *we were*" (עֲבָדִים הָיִינוּ) vs. "Rebels *you've been*" (מַמְרִים הֱיִתֶם).

The present essay argues that Deuteronomic rhetoric can be aptly summarized by this twinned presentation of the audience as "slaves" and "rebels," insofar as this presentation functions to constantly (re)situate its readers (or hearers)[5] into these two roles and their correlate temporal frames. This (re)situation has great significance for the construction of the audience's identity, as signaled already in the two verbal subjects employed in 6:21 and 9:7 ("we" and "you," respectively), even as it also affords insight into the *telos* of this rhetoric. To put matters in words borrowed from Gerhard von Rad, used as the first epigraph above, while the rhetoric of Deuteronomy is no "pious fraud," it is nevertheless nothing if not high artistry and thus an *artifact*—that is, a rhetorical construction[6]—

---

[4] Translations are my own, and have been made as fluid as possible, with an eye on the CEB.

[5] For present purposes, no significant difference obtains between these two forms of reception, though they are obviously distinct. Hereafter, I prefer to speak more generally of "audience."

[6] So, if nothing else, Deuteronomy's rhetoric is marked by what is known in the classical study of rhetoric as "arrangement" (*dispositio*, *taxis*). See Richard A. Lanham, *A Handlist of Rhetorical Terms*, 2nd ed. (Berkeley: University of California Press, 1991), 165–66, 171–74. For rhetoric in Deuteronomy proper, see, inter alia, Moshe Weinfeld, *Deuteronomy and the Deuteronomic School* (Oxford: Clarendon, 1972; repr. Winona Lake, IN: Eisenbrauns, 1992), 320–65; Timothy A. Lenchak, *"Choose Life!" A Rhetorical-Critical Investigation of Deuteronomy 28,69–30,20*, AnBib 129 (Rome: Pontifical Biblical Institute, 1993), 63–66; Brent A. Strawn, "Keep/Observe/Do—Carefully—Today! The Rhetoric of Repetition in Deuteronomy," in *A God So Near: Essays on Old Testament Theology in Honor of Patrick D. Miller*, ed. Brent A. Strawn and Nancy R. Bowen (Winona Lake, IN: Eisenbrauns, 2003), 215–40; Jerry Hwang, *The Rhetoric of Remembrance: An Investigation of the "Fathers" in Deuteronomy*, Siphrut 8 (Winona Lake, IN: Eisenbrauns, 2012); and Shin Wook Hur,

and thus an *artifice* in the best sense of the term.[7] Similarly, Deuteronomy's rhetoric definitely makes it "possible once again to stand at the foot of Mount Sinai and hear God's will," and to do so "[o]ver a distance of many centuries," but that distance should not be restricted only to "the late royal era." Instead, it is better to cite Robert Polzin's opinion, used as the second epigraph above, that Deuteronomy "forces us to shuttle back and forth between the narrated past and the narrator's present." Of course, von Rad, too, speaks of Deuteronomy consistently intersecting with the present; even so, that intersection is not solely nor primarily a matter of "divine *history*" being introduced or somehow intruding (so von Rad), as much as it is a case of "divine *presence*" doing that work in Israel—a divine presence that is facilitated, in the end, not by history per se or as such, but *by rhetoric*,[8] which means that this intersection is ever mobile, always (re) applicable, and ultimately *trans*historical. In what follows, these points are argued more fully through attention to inscription, identity, and time in Deuteronomy's rhetoric, though all three of these elements are interrelated, even inextricably so. The essay concludes with a consideration of the several functions and effects of this rhetoric.

Inscription: "We" and "You"

Perhaps the easiest way to describe what transpires in Deut 6:21 and 9:7 is to term both verses instances of (literary) "inscription."[9] By this term I

"The Rhetoric of the Deuteronomic Code: Its Structures and Devices" (PhD diss., Emory University, 2013). See also Jack R. Lundbom, *Deuteronomy: A Commentary* (Grand Rapids: Eerdmans, 2013), and the earlier work by the same author: *Jeremiah: A Study in Ancient Hebrew Rhetoric*, 2nd ed. (Winona Lake, IN: Eisenbrauns, 1997), esp. xix–xliii; and his volume of collected essays: *Biblical Rhetoric and Rhetorical Criticism*, HBM 45 (Sheffield: Sheffield Phoenix, 2013), esp. chs. 1, 11–13.

[7] Both "artifice" and "artifact" trace back to Latin and have to do with making with skill. See *OED Online*, 2nd ed., s.v. "artifice" and "artefact," accessed September 11, 2015. Cf. Polzin, "Deuteronomy," 93: "We are dealing with an unusually sophisticated and artfully constructed work of the first millennium B.C.E."

[8] This should not be taken as a suggestion that history and rhetoric are completely discrete, which of course is not the case. See, inter alia, V. Philips Long, *The Art of Biblical History*, FCI 5 (Grand Rapids: Zondervan), 58–87; and Hayden White, *The Content of the Form: Narrative Discourse and Historical Representation* (Baltimore: Johns Hopkins University Press, 1987).

[9] Not entirely unrelated is the notion of interpellation, though critics use that term in slightly different ways, often with strong connections to ideology and its manifestation. If interpellation applies in this case, it would be in a somewhat "weaker" form: "the constitutive process where individuals acknowledge and respond to ideologies [or, in this case theologies], thereby recognizing themselves as subjects" (Cindy Nguyen, "Interpellation," online at https://lucian.uchicago.edu/blogs/mediatheory/keywords/interpellation/; accessed September 9, 2015). See

simply mean that, via the rhetorical presentation, the audience is *written into* the story, made to be (and feel) a part of it. That is to say that the members of the audience are inscribed directly as "Pharaoh's slaves in Egypt" (6:21) and "rebels against YHWH" (9:7), and this is true whether or not they agree to the inscription and whether or not such an identification is accurate or otherwise feasible. Both of these points deserve further discussion.

First, the audience is not given space—at least within the rhetoric as we now have it—to respond to this literary inscription, whether affirmatively or negatively. There are instances elsewhere in the Bible where the literary audience responds positively (see, e.g., Exod 19:8; cf. also Josh 24:21–22, 24; Neh 8), but that does not take place in these two specific passages—nor, indeed, almost anywhere else in Deuteronomy proper.[10] The audience is simply identified as "slaves" and "rebels"; that is who they are, whether they like it or not.

Second, the literary *fabula*[11] of both Deuteronomy and the Torah writ large (see esp. Num 14:26–35 and 26:63–65)[12] suggests that this inscrip-

---

also Carol A. Newsom, "Woman and the Discourse of Patriarchal Wisdom: A Study of Proverbs 1–9," in *Gender and Difference in Ancient Israel*, ed. Peggy L. Day (Minneapolis: Fortress, 1989), 142–60. Richard B. Hays has shown how Pauline rhetoric, too, often relies heavily on literary inscription. See, e.g., his *The Conversion of the Imagination: Paul as Interpreter of Israel's Scripture* (Grand Rapids: Eerdmans, 2005).

[10] Deuteronomy 26:17; 27:15–26 might be considered here. See also below for the important case of 32:31. Whatever the case, another way to put the matter at hand is to say that, if the audience of Deuteronomy does have a choice, it is not unlike the choice offered the youth in Proverbs or the individual in Ps 1: yes, there may be two ways, but no one in their right mind (after succumbing to the rhetoric) would pick the foolish or wicked way. In this light, Deuteronomy's rhetoric begins to approach that of wisdom canons. See, in this regard, Weinfeld, *Deuteronomic School*; Stephen A. Geller, "Fiery Wisdom: The Deuteronomic Tradition," in *Sacred Enigmas: Literary Religion in the Hebrew Bible* (London: Routledge, 1996), 30–61; and Georg Braulik, "Wisdom, Divine Presence and Law," in *The Theology of Deuteronomy: Collected Essays of Georg Braulik*, trans. Ulrika Lindblad (North Richland Hills: BIBAL Press, 1994), 1–25.

[11] I mean by this term simply "the narrated world," following Norbert Lohfink, "Reading Deuteronomy 5 as Narrative," in *A God So Near*, 261–81. Cf. the distinction drawn in Russian Formalism between plot and story: plot (*syuzhet*) refers "to the order and manner in which events are actually presented in the narrative," and story (*fabula*) refers "to the chronological sequence of events" (J. A. Cuddon and C. E. Preston, *The Penguin Dictionary of Literary Terms and Literary Theory*, 4th ed. [London: Penguin, 1998], 328). In this article, my use of *fabula* is closer to "plot," not "story," following Lohfink as well as Meike Bal, *Narratology: Introduction to the Theory of Narrative*, 3rd ed. (Toronto: University of Toronto Press, 2009), who defines *fabula* as "the sequence of events as they 'occur' in the imaginative world." See ibid., 5–12 and passim for Bal's differentiation between narrative, text, story, and *fabula*.

[12] See Dennis T. Olson, *The Death of the Old and the Birth of the New: The Framework of the Book of Numbers and the Pentateuch*, BJS 71 (Chico, CA: Scholars Press, 1985).

tion is simply not accurate in terms of historical/temporal sequence.[13] In Deuteronomy, the literary audience that hears Moses' address is comprised extensively, if not exclusively, of those who were neither actual slaves in Egypt nor rebels in the wilderness—at least not as major participants in the foundational redemptive act, nor as agents in the paradigmatic moments of rebellion (the golden calf and spy incidents). Rather, it is precisely those who were *not* disobedient (either because they were not yet born or were minors) who have survived the wilderness wanderings and who now stand poised to take possession of Canaan.[14] This generational change is specified early in Deuteronomy in its recapitulation of the spy debacle in Deut 1:34–40, and signaled again slightly later with the chronological reference (thirty-eight years) and the notification of the death of "every one of the previous generation, those of fighting age, from the camp . . . just as YHWH had sworn about them" in Deut 2:14 (cf. 2:15–16).[15] Assuming something like a forty-year generation,[16] this means that many if not most (or even all) of those listening at Moab were not born in Egypt but represent the second generation from there—the notable exceptions, which in this instance proverbially prove the rule, being Caleb and Joshua (see 1:36 and 1:38; 3:28; 31:3, 7, respectively).

These considerations indicate that Deuteronomic inscription is somewhat "out of order." Perhaps the clearest example of the issue at hand is Deut 5:3, especially given its over-the-top syntactical emphasis:

---

[13] So similarly Hwang, *Rhetoric of Remembrance*, 6.

[14] For more on Deuteronomy's *Generationswechsel* (generational changing), see Hwang, *Rhetoric of Remembrance*, passim; and Bill T. Arnold, "Reexamining the 'Fathers' in Deuteronomy's Framework" in *Torah and Tradition: Papers Read at the Sixteenth Joint Meeting of the Society for Old Testament Study and the Oudtestamentisch Werkgezelschap, Edinburgh 2015*, ed. Klaas Spronk and Hans Barstad, *OtSt* 70 (Leiden: Brill, 2017), 10–41, both of whom argue that the rhetorical blending of generations is an intentional rhetorical device. Arnold believes "this intentional ambiguity" functions to create "deliberate solidarity . . . among Israel's generations. . . . This intentional indeterminateness draws Israelite readers into solidarity with each generation of ancestors" (19). Arnold speaks of "trans-generational Israel" (18–19), "transgenerational solidarity" (39–40), "rhetorical generation-blending" (39), and the "rhetorical conflation of Israel's generations" (28). Bernd Biberger, *Unsere Väter und Wir: Unterteilung von Geschichtsdarstellungen in Generationen und das Verhältnis der Generationen im Alten Testament*, BBB 145 (Berlin: Philo, 2003), 332–61, has catalogued no fewer than five generational groups: (1) the patriarchal generation; (2) the exodus generation; (3) the wilderness generation; (4) the generation in the plains of Moab; and (5) future generations.

[15] Note also the mention of "forty years" in the wilderness in Deut 2:7; 8:2, 4; 29:4.

[16] See, inter alia, the data on average life expectancy in Hans Walter Wolff, *Anthropology of the Old Testament*, trans. Margaret Kohl (Philadelphia: Fortress, 1974), 119–20; and Philip J. King and Lawrence E. Stager, *Life in Biblical Israel*, LAI (Louisville: Westminster John Knox, 2001), 37, 58.

> YHWH did not make this covenant with our ancestors, *but with us, those of us here now, all of us who are alive* (כִּי אִתָּנוּ אֲנַחְנוּ אֵלֶּה פֹה הַיּוֹם כֻּלָּנוּ חַיִּים).

Once again, according to the literary *fabula* of Deuteronomy and the sweep of the pentateuchal narrative from Exodus until this point, this is simply not true—at least not entirely. Even if this statement is true with respect to the "ancestors" Abraham, Isaac, and Jacob,[17] it would not hold true for all who are alive in the plains of Moab. Their more immediate ancestors *were* present at the covenant-making on Horeb; conversely, many of the "us here now, all of us who are alive" *were not*.

Rather than considering Deut 5:3 some sort of slip—whether one that was somehow accidental, related to composition/redaction, or downright duplicitous ("pious fraud")—it is better to recognize it as another instance of literary inscription, a device that characterizes Deuteronomy's rhetoric and that is robustly employed throughout the book. Indeed, the very first unit of Deuteronomy after the opening superscription manifests this very same kind of inscription. Immediately after we learn that Moses was willing (or began) to explain this Torah (הוֹאִיל מֹשֶׁה בֵּאֵר אֶת־הַתּוֹרָה הַזֹּאת, 1:5), a statement that is followed by a recitative לֵאמֹר ("saying" or "as follows"), Moses speaks:

> YHWH our God spoke *to us* (אֵלֵינוּ) at Horeb: "You've stayed at this mountain long enough (רַב־לָכֶם שֶׁבֶת)."

The very same problems of the addressed audience vis-à-vis the literary *fabula* obtain here, just as they did in the other texts cited thus far (along with the many others that might be added). That is, many if not most of the members of the audience addressed in the plains of Moab were *not* present at Horeb because, according to the *fabula*, they were not yet alive. But no matter: they are inscribed as if they were.

The presence of this type of literary inscription at the very outset of Deuteronomy signals its importance in the book's rhetoric. Therefore it is not surprising to find inscription used throughout much of what follows, whether that be in 5:3 or 6:21 or 9:7, and whether that inscription is ac-

---

[17] Much depends on the definition of "ancestors" here: does it refer only to the great patriarchs and matriarchs of old? If so, Deut 5:3 would be correct: Horeb represents a new thing not experienced by them. But if it refers more generally to the previous generation(s), then it is patently *in*accurate (see below). The precise referent of the "fathers" in Deuteronomy has occasioned much discussion, esp. after Thomas Römer, *Israels Väter: Untersuchungen zur Väterthematik im Deuteronomium und in der deuteronomistischen Tradition*, OBO 99 (Göttingen: Vandenhoeck & Ruprecht, 1990). Here is not the place to engage Römer's "insertion theory," for which see Norbert Lohfink, *Die Väter Israels im Deuteronomium*, OBO 111 (Göttingen: Vandenhoeck & Ruprecht, 1991); Hwang, *Rhetoric of Remembrance*; and esp. Arnold, "Reexamining."

complished by means of the first-person common plural or second-person (singular and/or plural) forms.[18] Stated most simply, inscription is a hallmark of Deuteronomic rhetoric, perhaps even *the* hallmark of that rhetoric. The pervasiveness of this technique and its presence from the very start of the book in the transition from Deut 1:5 to 1:6ff. suggests that one of the primary ways Torah is expounded (בֵּאֵר) in Deuteronomy is not only by means of storytelling (as opposed to some sort of formal legal explication) but by *storytelling that inscribes the audience into the very story being told*—once again, whether they like it or not, and whether or not the inscription "fits" the temporal sequence of events. The main point, regardless of agreement or accuracy, is, once again, to inscribe the audience directly into the story that Moses tells. That story revolves around two primary nodes: redemption from slavery and rebellion against the Lord.

"*We* Were Slaves" (Deut 6:21)

The first of the two key texts mentioned above exemplifies the workings of Deuteronomic inscription even as it showcases how central this rhetorical move is for the way the book of Deuteronomy works. In Deut 6:20–25, a hypothetical (or inevitable) scenario[19] is raised in which children inquire about the "laws, regulations, and case laws" (הָעֵדֹת וְהַחֻקִּים וְהַמִּשְׁפָּטִים). In a move that is entirely familiar from the shift from 1:5 to 1:6, the parental answer that is commended has virtually nothing to do with legal explication proper but, instead, with inscription into the story of the exodus:

> Tell your children: "We were Pharaoh's slaves in Egypt, but YHWH brought us out from Egypt with a strong hand. Before our own eyes, YHWH performed great and terrible signs and wonders against Egypt, against Pharaoh and his dynasty. But he brought us out from there in order to bring us in—to give us the land that he promised our ancestors. YHWH commanded us to perform all these regulations by fearing YHWH our God, for our good always, to preserve

[18] For the alteration in second person forms (plural and singular)—the famous *Numeruswechsel*—see further below.

[19] Note 6:20a: כִּֽי־יִשְׁאָלְךָ בִנְךָ מָחָר, "If [or: when] your child asks you, in the future . . . ." Bill T. Arnold and John H. Choi, *A Guide to Biblical Hebrew Syntax* (Cambridge: Cambridge University Press, 2003), 151, note that "the distinction between temporal and conditional [instances of כִּי] is somewhat vague, especially when dealing with future temporal statements," and illustrate the conundrum with reference to Deut 6:20. See further Anneli Aejmelaeus, "Function and Interpretation of כי in Biblical Hebrew," *JBL* 105 (1986): 193–209, esp. 197, who writes, again with reference to Deut 6:20: "In several cases, the interpreter may freely choose either interpretation [temporal or conditional] according to one's own consideration of the wider context."

> us alive, just as we are right now. Furthermore, we will be righteous if we carefully perform all this commandment before YHWH our God, exactly as he commanded us." (6:21–25)

The parent's answer precisely imitates the rhetorical movement found in Deut 1:5–6 (and elsewhere). Hence, inscribing future generations into the story is not simply a rhetorical device that can be *identified* in a particular passage and *subsequently described*; in Deuteronomy, this type of inscription is also—and far more importantly—*applied prescriptively, even mandated.*

Deuteronomy 6:20–25 is an important passage in still other ways, insofar as verse 20 casts light on *why* rhetorical inscription is necessary in the first place, or, put differently, how such inscription addresses a specific rhetorical situation.[20] The clue is found in how the children who will ask this question about the legislation carefully differentiate themselves from their parents:

> "What is the meaning of the laws, regulations, and case laws that YHWH our God commanded *you*?" (6:20b)

The exact meaning of this question, which is verbless in Hebrew, is somewhat uncertain. Perhaps the child is simply asking about the *content*: *what are* the laws, regulations, and case laws? However, it seems more likely—precisely because of the pronominal distinction that, though it acknowledges YHWH as *our* God, nevertheless makes clear that the legislation itself and the command to obey it applies only to the parents (אֶתְכֶם: "you," second masculine plural)—that the child is asking not simply about the content of this legislation but about its *meaning for* and/or *pertinence to* the child. This latter option is confirmed by both the details and rhetoric of the parental answer.

Before addressing those details and that rhetoric, it should be noted that the versions reflect variants in the pronouns used in 6:20b, with some having the child say "commanded *us*" (אֹתָנוּ: first common plural).[21] If the

---

[20] For more on the rhetorical situation, see below, and, more generally, Chaïm Perelman and L. Olbrechts-Tyteca, *The New Rhetoric: A Treatise on Argumentation*, trans. John Wilkinson and Purcell Weaver (Notre Dame: University of Notre Dame Press, 1969 [French orig.: 1958]), esp. 17–26, 35–40, 59–62, 495–502.

[21] אֶתְכֶם ("you," pl.) is found in SamPent, LXX^{mss}, Syr, and Targ; אתָנו ("us") is reflected in LXX and Vulg. Carmel McCarthy, *Biblia Hebraica Quinta: Deuteronomy* (Stuttgart: Deutsche Bibelgesellschaft, 2007), 24 (hereafter *BHQ*) thinks the latter is a case of harmonization of syntax, though she seems to posit the same for the reading in MT^{L}. This confusion is clarified in McCarthy's textual commentary where she notes that John Wevers, who edited the Göttingen Septuagint of Deuteronomy, has changed his mind on the original reading of LXX, which he now deems was ημων υμιν, "*our* [God commanded] *you*," because the distinction in pronouns seems intentional and because he deems the temptation to level the

latter reading is correct, there would be no difference between the child's and the parent's reception of the laws after all. However, the difference in the pronouns as reflected in MT seems most likely to be original ("*our* God," "commanded *you*"), the versional evidence constituting what is the easier reading and therefore the likely result of harmonization. "Commanded *you*" is not only the more difficult reading; it is also the most interesting one, since it draws a clear distinction between what God commanded the previous generation ("you," plural) and everything thereafter, since the prior generation does not include the child, apparently (if only) because the child was not there.[22] The generational, temporal, and historical differential evoked by the child's shrewd use of pronouns is quite legitimate and accurate—as far as such things go—but in this specific case none of that goes very far at all since the distinction is granted neither legitimacy nor accuracy because the parental answer to what seems to be an entirely sensible question functions to collapse all distance—generational, temporal, and historical—by means of literary inscription. The child says "you," but the parent responds with an onslaught of "we" language. The child says "you" once, but the parent uses some form of "we" or "us" no fewer than fifteen times in a tour de force of literary inscription. This "we" language is not restricted to the parents themselves (the speaking subjects in vv. 21–25) but necessarily includes the child for several reasons, one of which is the first-person common plural subject[23] and another of

---

pronouns to have been too powerful to resist (*BHQ*, 72*). A similar but reversed case of such leveling is found in the case of אֱלֹהֵינוּ, "our God," since, according to J. Hempel in *BHS*, אֱלֹהֶיךָ ("your [sg.] God") is reflected in Cairo and LXX[Lmin], with אֱלֹהֵיכֶם ("your [pl.] God") reflected in LXX[min] OL.

[22] I.e., at Sinai; but, as per the preceding discussion, the very same situation likely obtained for the child's parents! This is to consider only generations 2.0 and 3.0 (or generations 1.5 and 2.0). It is even truer for future generations further down the line. This is the force of von Rad's remarks used as the first epigraph in this essay, and, further, von Rad's comment in *Studies in Deuteronomy*, trans. David Stalker, SBT (London: SCM, 1953 [German orig.: 1948²]), 70: "this Israel which is addressed by Moses is, of course, *completely different* from the one that stood at the foot of Mount Horeb. It knows Palestine with all its religious temptations, it has a king and a graded civil service; economically its life is no longer the patriarchal, but it has entered upon the stage of an economy based on currency, with all its perilous consequences; it knows the prophets, and has indeed already had unpleasant experiences with these men; and so on . . . . [T]his Israel *has in actual fact no longer any points of comparison* with the Israel that in the past stood at Horeb; [it is] separated from the events at Horeb by a very long and extremely incriminating history . . . . six centuries wasted in sin and constant apostasy" (my emphasis). See further ibid., 71–73.

[23] Note that the pronouns in 6:20a are second masculine singular (בִנְךָ, יִשְׁאָלְךָ), as is the verbal form in 6:21a (וְאָמַרְתָּ), suggesting, as it were, a *singular* parent interacting with a *singular* child. Given this, the instructed response of "we" does

which is the climax of the parental response in verses 24b–25 (especially לְחַיֹּתֵנוּ כְּהַיּוֹם הַזֶּה). The child has asked a question—perhaps innocently, but perhaps frustrated by the imposition of so many חֻקִּים וּמִשְׁפָּטִים—and, in reply, gets overwhelmingly and inescapably narrated into the story of Israel. In the process, the parents play the part of "little Moseses," rhetorically inscribing their children into the story, with the children becoming the "little Israelites" so inscribed.[24]

It bears repeating that 6:20–25 not only exemplifies the Deuteronomic rhetoric of inscription, it *legislates* the same. What Moses provides throughout the book is not simply a model, then, it is a *mandate*—one that can be and will need to be enacted for all generations: "*whenever* your child asks you in the future." Still further, as noted above, the child's question reflects a likely rhetorical situation that calls for (or calls forth) this particular rhetorical move—namely, the problem younger generations face when they encounter (often with some measure of dissatisfaction) religious systems for themselves. It is at exactly this significant and tenuous moment in the transgenerational communication of religious values that Deuteronomy commends and commands inscription: narrating the next generation into the story of Israel with its God—a story that begins, fundamentally and paradigmatically, with "we were slaves."

---

not imagine a mother-father pairing talking to a child but a singular parent addressing a child, with the two of them together subsequently comprising the "we" of the discourse in vv. 21–25.

[24] For Moses as the model teacher, see Dennis T. Olson, *Deuteronomy and the Death of Moses: A Theological Reading*, OBT (Minneapolis: Fortress, 1994), 11; David G. Firth, "Passing on the Faith in Deuteronomy," in *Interpreting Deuteronomy: Issues and Approaches*, ed. David G. Firth and Philip S. Johnston (Downers Grove, IL: IVP Academic, 2012), 164. For more on Deuteronomy, children, and instruction in the faith, see Firth, "Passing on the Faith," passim; Mark A. Awabdy, "Teaching Children in the Instruction of Amenemope and Deuteronomy," *VT* 65 (2015): 1–8, who speaks of how Deuteronomy uses "the common human desire for formative parental teaching and filial obedience in order to contextualize Israel's exodus experience in quotidian life" (8); and esp. Patrick D. Miller, "That the Children May Know: Children in Deuteronomy," in *The Child in the Bible*, ed. Marcia J. Bunge, Terence E. Fretheim, and Beverly Roberts Gaventa (Grand Rapids: Eerdmans, 2008), 45–62. For research supporting the importance of parents and parental instruction in children's faith in contemporary North America, see Kenda Creasy Dean, *Almost Christian: What the Faith of Our Teenagers is Telling the American Church* (Oxford: Oxford University Press, 2010), 109–30; and Christian Smith with Melinda Lundquist Denton, *Soul Searching: The Religious and Spiritual Lives of American Teenagers* (Oxford: Oxford University Press, 2005), 54–61.

"*You've* Been Rebels" (Deut 9:7)

While the story begins with slavery and the exodus from Egypt, it certainly does not end there, because there is the second key text to consider, Deut 9:7, which also evidences literary inscription but to very different effect. To allude to a much later legal discussion (see Matt 22:34–40), if this second inscription is not quite equal to the first and greatest one (Deut 6:21), it is at least "like it," such that one might say that "on these two hang" all instances of Deuteronomic inscription. This is to say that the second inscription—the one concerning Israel's rebelliousness—is also basic to and pervasive in Deuteronomy's rhetoric, even if it remains somewhat secondary to the first inscription, which concerns Israel's deliverance from Egyptian servitude.[25]

Deuteronomy 9:7 appears as the introduction to the golden calf incident, which belongs, in turn, to the third in a series of "do not say/think" passages in Deut 7–9. These passages are united by the thrice-repeated use of the phrase "speaking" (אמר) + "in your heart" (בִּלְבָבְךָ) in 7:17; 8:17; and 9:4. In each case, what Israel says in its heart concerns possible estimations of its life-situation or life-status that are expressly forbidden.[26] Coming hard upon the heels of the positive reformulation of the first commandment in the Shema, as these three passages do, and taking their place amid the larger oration on the Great Commandment in chapters 6–11,[27] these three passages comprise vignettes—sermon illustrations, as it were—that deal with possible rivals to Israel's sole allegiance to YHWH, each of which must be vigorously resisted. But if these rivals are false gods, as suggested by the larger literary context, they are very subtle ones: the kind that haunt the human heart (hence בִּלְבָבְךָ + אמר!), not necessarily an Iron Age cult site.

In the first vignette, Israel is tempted to trust in *military might*, or, perhaps more precisely, to despair in its absence (7:17–24); in the second, the temptation is *wealth or self-sufficiency* (8:17–20); in the third, *morality or false piety* (9:4–10:11).[28] In each case the struggle is with estimations of Israel's "self," especially vis-à-vis the facts "on the ground," at least from YHWH's perspective. So it is that these three rivals to Israel's sole

[25] If nothing else, the secondary nature of this second inscription is due to the pentateuchal *fabula*: Israel was in slavery first and rebelled thereafter.

[26] See Olson, *Deuteronomy and the Death of Moses*, 52–58.

[27] On which, see Norbert Lohfink, *Das Hauptgebot: Eine Untersuchung literarischer Einleitungsfragen zu Dtn 5–11*, AnBib 20 (Rome: Pontifical Biblical Institute, 1963).

[28] Olson, *Deuteronomy and the Death of Moses*, 52, names these "gods of death" as militarism, materialism, and moralism.

allegiance could be termed the struggle with the *untrusting, overconfident,* and *immodest* self.[29]

Once again, Deut 9:7 appears in the third and final vignette, which forbids Israel from overestimating its own righteousness vis-à-vis the disinherited nations. Here Deuteronomy finally mentions the golden calf debacle. Norbert Lohfink has made a compelling case that it is precisely for rhetorical effect that Deuteronomy does not mention this incident earlier.[30] Deuteronomy 1:6 begins with the departure from Horeb, and the *fabula* moves forward in time from that point, through the spy incident and the victories in the Transjordan (1:19–3:29) until Moses' flashback to the fireworks at Horeb (4:1–24), which is replete with an accompanying sermon that focuses on the second commandment (4:25–40). After a short interlude (4:41–49), Moses returns to Horeb with a recapitulation of the Decalogue (5:1–22) and remarks about his intercessory role thereafter (5:23–33). All of this is in concert with the *fabula* as known from Exod 19:1–20:21. Perhaps the legislation of Exod 20:22–31:18 could be located "between the lines" of Deut 5:23–33; what is certain, regardless, is that the events of Exod 32–34 are held in reserve. It is altogether possible, that is, that the golden calf story could have been mentioned earlier, at some point in chapter 6, with its focus on the first commandment, or even in chapter 4, with its attention to the second commandment.[31] Instead, it is saved until chapter 9. It fits perfectly well there, to be sure, within the extended sermon on the first commandment found in chapters 6–11, but it seems to have been held back until this moment for rhetorical reasons: in brief, it comprises definitive proof countering Israel's final temptation to immodesty and overestimation of its own self-righteousness. The most pertinent verses follow:

> Once YHWH your God drives them [i.e., the nations] out before you, do not say in your heart: "It's because of my righteousness that YHWH has brought me to possess this land." Rather, it's because of the wickedness of these nations that YHWH is removing them before you! It is not because of your righteousness or the uprightness of your heart that you are entering to take possession of their land, but because of the wickedness of these nations that YHWH your God is removing them before you in order that YHWH might

---

[29] See Brent A. Strawn, "Deuteronomy," in *Theological Bible Commentary*, ed. Gail R. O'Day and David L. Petersen (Louisville: Westminster John Knox, 2009), 70; also Strawn, "Deuteronomy," in *The Wesley Study Bible: NRSV* (Nashville: Abingdon, 2009), 226–29.

[30] See Lohfink, "Reading Deuteronomy 5," esp. 263–65, 277–78.

[31] I leave aside here the issue of the combination or division of what the Reformed Christian tradition numbers as the first (no other gods) and second (no idols) commandments. In my judgment, even if they are numbered separately, these prohibitions are closely related and best interpreted together. This may be reflected in the way they overlap in Deut 4, 6, and 9.

> prove what he promised to your ancestors: to Abraham, Isaac, and Jacob. So, know that it is not because of your righteousness that YHWH your God is giving you this good land to possess—because you are a stubborn people! Remember—do not forget!—how you made YHWH your God furious in the wilderness. From the day that you left the land of Egypt, until you arrived at this place, you've been rebels against YHWH. (Deut 9:4–7)

The passage continues with specifics about the golden calf incident as proof par excellence that Israel is not more righteous than the nations but is, in fact, just as wicked as they are. For present purposes, however, the point is simply that the dynamics of literary inscription are clearly at work in 9:7 and function in the very same way(s) that the inscription of 6:21 does. Once again, the audience is not granted space to dispute the inscription. They are simply identified as rebels—and persistent and intractable ones at that. This point is underscored still further in what might be seen as the negative climax of this second paradigmatic inscription, at least as found in chapter 9:

> Also at Taberah, and at Massah, and at Kibroth-hattaavah you've been the kind of people who make YHWH furious (מַקְצִפִים הֱיִיתֶם אֶת־יְהוָה). And, when YHWH sent you from Kadesh-barnea, saying, "Go up and take possession of the land that I have given to you," you rebelled (מרה) against YHWH your God's command. You did not trust in him and you did not listen to his voice. You've been rebels against YHWH (מַמְרִים הֱיִיתֶם עִם־יְהוָה) from the day <he>[32] knew you. (Deut 9:22–24)

This second inscription, which might be termed the rebel- or מַמְרִים-type, is similar to the first inscription (the slave- or עֶבֶד-type of inscription) in several ways: (1) not only is the audience not given permission to respond (approvingly or disapprovingly), as already noted, but (2) this second type of inscription is also *contra-fabula*. This is to say that the same problems that obtained for the literary audience's identification as Pharaoh's slaves in Egypt also obtain for that selfsame audience being identified as those who rebelled at Horeb or at Kadesh-barnea. The guilt of most, if not all, of those hearing Moses in Moab is at best by association only, since they are generation 2.0 (or 1.5, at the very least). If this Moab audience were *truly* guilty, they would be dead in the wilderness. The precious few—make that two—people who are not dead from generation 1.0 are precisely those who were *not*

[32] Here there is another text-critical issue with MT (דַּעְתִּי), Syr, and Targ reading "I (Moses) knew you," but SamPent, σ', and θ' reflecting דַּעְתּוֹ: "he (i.e., YHWH) knew you." The latter is to be preferred, with LXX and Vulg offering something of a middle position (see *BHQ*, 32) and MT probably reflecting a theological smoothing. For discussion, see *BHQ*, 78*; *HOTTP* 1:279. Covenantal connotations of עדי are likely operative here (for which, see *TLOT* 2:515–18; *NIDOTTE* 2:411–13).

rebels, namely, Caleb and Joshua.[33] Finally, (3) the מַמְרִים-inscription, like the עֶבֶד-inscription found in Deut 6:20–25, affords insight into the rhetorical situation lying behind or perhaps before it—that is, why such rhetoric is required in the first place. In the case of Deut 9:4–10:11, it is not a frustrated question from the next generation in the middle of a confirmation class; it is, instead, the settled self-righteous estimation of the elect lording it over those who are *not*—not elect and thus (presumably) not righteous. In the עֶבֶד-inscription, the child's question imposed distance between the next generation and the faith community—at least to some degree—and so the inscription narrated the child into the story of the faith community that undergirds its religious system and motivates adherence to the same. In the מַמְרִים-inscription, the immodest and inaccurate estimation of the faith community imposes distance between it and all others, simultaneously aligning it unrealistically close(r) to the deity. It is thus the burden of this second type of inscription to disabuse the faith community of all such false (self-righteous) estimations. While the wickedness of the nations cannot be denied, the gap between Israel and them is not large; conversely, the distance between Israel and YHWH remains significant because who Israel is and what Israel does, at least according to the מַמְרִים-inscription, is to be (היה) rebels/rebellious (מרה) and to make YHWH furious (קצף)—incessantly. The palpable difference in rhetorical situations explains the very different content of this second type of literary inscription: in this case, Israel is no longer comprised of "slaves" who receive the benefits of YHWH's redeeming activity; they are now nothing more than "rebels" entirely deserving of YHWH's judgment.

The Song of Moses

These, then, are the two types of literary inscription in Deuteronomy's rhetoric: the עֶבֶד-type and the מַמְרִים-type. The preceding discussion has already touched on how these two relate to matters of *identity* (slaves vs. rebels) and *time* ("in Egypt"; "from then until now"), but these call for additional discussion. Before turning to these topics, one particularly im-

[33] To be sure, one should not ignore issues of corporate responsibility, identity, or punishment at this point. See, e.g., H. Wheeler Robinson, *Corporate Personality in Ancient Israel* (Philadelphia: Fortress, 1964); Joel S. Kaminsky, *Corporate Responsibility in the Hebrew Bible*, JSOTSup 196 (Sheffield: Sheffield Academic, 1995); and Jurrien Mol, *Collective and Individual Responsibility: A Description of Corporate Personality in Ezekiel 18 and 20*, SSN 53 (Leiden: Brill, 2009). Even so, Deut 7:10 and 24:16 loom large here in promising individual retribution (contrast 5:9!); even more important is the larger literary *fabula*.

portant instance of the מַמְרִים-inscription deserves mention.[34] It is found in Deut 32:15. There, in the middle of a section describing Israel's rebellion in the third person, the Song of Moses (*Haʾăzînû*) suddenly inscribes the audience directly into the story by means of second-person address before it returns to third-person discourse:

(a) Jacob ate until he was stuffed;

(b) Jeshurun got fat, then rebellious.

(c) *It was you who got fat, thick, stubborn!* (שָׁמַנְתָּ עָבִיתָ כָּשִׂיתָ)

(d) He gave up on the God who made him,

(e) thought the Rock of his salvation was worthless. (Deut 32:15)[35]

The lineation offered here shows how verse 15c intrudes upon the poetry and syntax of the verse. Without it, the discourse remains in the third person, recounting the failures of Jacob/Jeshurun in two nicely balanced bicola.[36] Verse 15c manifests similar colometry,[37] but its second-person forms are completely unexpected and out of place within the third-person context,[38] rendering verse 15d understandable only if it is taken as a direct resumption of verse 15b. Such factors make it tempting to excise verse 15c altogether as a secondary addition,[39] if it were not for the text-critical data supporting it[40] and, even more to the point at hand, the fact

---

[34] For another instance of inscription in ch. 32, this one akin to the עֶבֶד-type, see below.

[35] See *BHS* and *BHQ* for the many text-critical issues that plague this verse. In addition to CEB, see also NRSV; contrast NJPS.

[36] Bicola a–b: 3 + 3 words and stresses, 8 + 9 syllables; bicola d–e: 3 + 3 words and stresses, 8 + 9 syllables. All such counts are of mixed utility, of course, and should not be depended upon overmuch. For the approach more generally, see Oswald Loretz and Ingo Kottsieper, *Colometry in Ugaritic and Biblical Poetry: Introduction, Illustrations, and Topical Bibliography* (Altenberge: CIS-Verlag, 1987).

[37] 3 + 3 words and stresses, 9 syllables.

[38] Cf., e.g., LXX, S, T^{O} (singular), as well as T^{JNF} (plural), which read third-person forms in v. 15c, in a clear case of harmonizing with the surrounding context (see *BHQ*, 94, 144*). The singular forms are supported by SamPent and, in the first instance, by 4QPhyl^{n}, σ', and θ'.

[39] À la *Wiederaufnahme* (repetitive resumption) or *Ringkomposition*, for which, see, e.g., Shemaryahu Talmon, "The Textual Study of the Bible—A New Outlook," in *Qumran and the History of the Biblical Text*, ed. Frank Moore Cross and Shemaryahu Talmon (Cambridge: Harvard University Press, 1975), 321–400, esp. 363–64 and 395n174; and Bernard M. Levinson, *Deuteronomy and the Hermeneutics of Legal Innovation* (Oxford: Oxford University Press, 1997), 17–20.

[40] That is, v. 15c is not missing from the versions, though note MT, which lost the first three words of v. 15 (colon a), apparently through haplography (see *BHQ*, 94, 144*).

that literary inscription is a hallmark of Deuteronomic rhetoric and thus not unexpected, even here. So, whether or not verse 15c was originally part of some *Urform* of the Song of Moses is of little significance. Even if it is somehow a Deuteronomic plus—an addition to some early/earlier form of the poem as received into Deut 32—it would be a plus that is completely at home in Deuteronomy's rhetoric of inscription.

Identity: "Slaves" and "Rebels"

Much of what has been said in the preceding section demonstrates how Deuteronomy's rhetoric of inscription bears directly on the construction of the audience's identity. In a word—or, better, in two words—this rhetoric figures Israel as either "slaves" or "rebels," or rather *both*. As noted above, the audience is given no space to accept or reject this identification: the inscription simply makes them either one of these two subjects alternatively, if not both simultaneously. Of course, we might presume that the audience's reception of this inscription matters in crucial ways. If the audience accepts the inscription, that would make the rhetoric somehow more active or effective; alternatively, if the audience rejects the inscription, all bets are off. But, again, in terms of rhetorical effect (see further below), the inscription figures the audience as, or in, one (or both) of these categories quite apart from their say in the matter. Inscription and identity are therefore indelibly linked. The former leads directly to the latter; the latter is entirely contingent on the former.

As observed above, these two "existential categories"—that of redeemed slave and/or obstinate rebel—are found throughout Deuteronomy, not just in the two key texts 6:21 and 9:7. The book repeatedly circles back, in one way or another, to these two possibilities and, in doing so, underscores how each is in some way *fundamental* and/or *paradigmatic* for Israel. The following delineation of these two identities is brief but representative.

Israel's Identification as (Former) Slaves Rescued from Egypt: The עֶבֶד-Inscription

In the warp and woof of the *fabula*—in both Deuteronomy and in Exodus–Deuteronomy—Egyptian slavery stands at the head of all other elements of Israel's relationship with God, the only possible exception being the (still earlier) promises to the ancestors (see Deut 1:8, 11, 21, 35; 4:1, 31, 37; 6:3, 10, 18, 23; 7:8, 12, 13; 8:1, 18; 9:5; 10:11, 15; 11:9, 21; 12:1; 13:18[ET 17]; 19:8; 26:3, 15; 27:3; 28:11; 29:13[ET 14]; 30:20; 31:7, 20;

cf. 26:7; 29:24[ET 25]).[41] In this way, Egyptian servitude and the release therefrom are *fundamental*. It is *paradigmatic* insofar as it is constantly and consistently referenced throughout Deuteronomy, often at crucial junctures, including its deployment as motivation for obedience to key legislation. A few examples suffice:[42]

(a) I am YHWH your God who brought you out of the land of Egypt, out of the house of slavery (בֵּית עֲבָדִים). (5:6)

(b) Remember that you were a slave (עֶבֶד הָיִיתָ) in the land of Egypt, but YHWH your God brought you out of there with a strong hand and an outstretched arm. That's why YHWH your God commanded you to keep the Sabbath day. (5:15)

(c) Tell your children: "We were Pharaoh's slaves (עֲבָדִים הָיִינוּ) in Egypt, but YHWH brought us out from Egypt with a strong hand." (6:21)

(d) Remember that you were a slave (עֶבֶד הָיִיתָ) in the land of Egypt, but YHWH your God rescued you. That's why I am commanding you to do this thing right now. (15:15)

(e) Remember that you were a slave (עֶבֶד הָיִיתָ) in Egypt, so be careful to perform these regulations. (16:12)

(f) Remember that you were a slave (עֶבֶד הָיִיתָ) in Egypt, but YHWH your God rescued you from there. That's why I am commanding you to do this thing. (24:18)

---

[41] The importance of the ancestors makes Deut 5:3 that much more unexpected. Similarly striking in this perspective are 8:1, 16; 30:5, 9 (texts that have the audience somehow surpassing the ancestors), as well as 13:7[ET 6]; 28:36, 64; 32:17 (the invocation of the ancestors in judgment passages). Of course, the precise valence of these passages depends in no small measure on the specific referent of "ancestors" (for which see note 17 above). For those who hold to a redactional theory like Römer's and its relationship to a certain understanding of the composition and formation of the Pentateuch, Deuteronomy's origin story began with Egyptian slavery and thus the exodus and did not include the ancestors as known from Genesis.

[42] In addition to the texts that follow, see also, inter alia, 1:30; 4:20, 34, 37; 6:12, 22; 7:8, 18; 8:14; 9:12; 11:3; 13:6, 11[ET 5, 10]; 16:1, 3, 6; 20:1; 23:5[ET 4]; 24:9; 25:17; 26:8; 29:2, 16; 34:11; cf. 4:45–46; 29:24[ET 25]. This is but a partial listing compiled by tracing the presence of מִצְרַיִם in Deuteronomy. In any event, the pervasive import of the servitude in and deliverance from Egypt is no doubt what makes the sentiment expressed in 1:27 appear so shocking and unfaithful. It is also what lends power to the different expressions in 9:12 and 9:26, even as it underscores the severity of 28:27, 60, 68 (cf. 7:15).

(g) Remember that you were a slave (עֶבֶד הָיִיתָ) in the land of Egypt. That's why I am commanding you to do this thing. (24:22)

Outside of example (a), the passages conjoin היה with עֶבֶד, always in the singular, save for the one plural instance found in the parent's reply in 6:21 (example [c]; see above). However, example (a) deserves to be mentioned, since the reference to Egyptian slavery at the very start of the Decalogue more than suffices to indicate the importance of that experience and its place within YHWH's relationship to Israel as well as its role in motivating Israel's obedient response to YHWH's covenant. The function of the עֶבֶד-inscription in the prologue to the Decalogue is quite similar in this regard to the way the mention of Egyptian slavery functions in the fourth commandment. It should also be recalled that Deuteronomy uniquely formulates its version thereof (example [b]) by mentioning the oppression under Pharaoh and not God's rest on the seventh day of creation (contrast Exod 20:11).

Although they do not employ the language of slavery proper (עבד), two additional verses should also be included here since they evoke the same situation (life in Egypt) and with the same verbal construction, only this time with גֵּר-language:[43]

(h) Love the immigrant because you were immigrants (גֵּרִים הֱיִיתֶם) in the land of Egypt. (10:19)

(i) Do not detest any Edomite because they are your kin. Do not detest any Egyptian because you were an immigrant (גֵּר הָיִיתָ) in their land. (23:8[ET 7])

More texts could be cited, but examples (a)–(i) demonstrate that the story of Egyptian servitude (and sojourn) pervades Deuteronomy, crisscrossing the various parts of the book and comprising a consistent and repeated element in its rhetorical program.[44] This is to say that, once inscribed into this story, the audience is never allowed to forget it. Or, perhaps it would be better or more accurate to put the matter in reverse: given the importance of this story, the audience is not allowed to escape it, but is thoroughly and repeatedly inscribed into it.

[43] For more on the גֵּר in Deuteronomy, see Mark A. Awabdy, *Immigrants and Innovative Law: Deuteronomy's Theological and Social Vision for the* גר, FAT 2/67 (Tübingen: Mohr Siebeck, 2014), who draws a careful distinction between גֵּר-Egypt and עֶבֶד-Egypt traditions (see ibid., 127–64).

[44] On the rhetorical function of repetition in Deuteronomy, see Strawn, "Keep/Observe/Do." For an extended recent study of (poetic) repetition, see Knut Martin Heim, *Poetic Imagination in Proverbs: Variant Repetitions and the Nature of Poetry*, BBRSup 4 (Winona Lake, IN: Eisenbrauns, 2013).

Israel's Identification as (Constant) Rebels: The מַמְרִים-Inscription

While this second inscription is not as pervasive as the עֶבֶד-inscription, it is important nevertheless. Three of the key passages from chapter 9 have already been discussed above:

(a) From the day that you left the land of Egypt, until you arrived at this place, you've been rebels (מַמְרִים הֱיִתֶם) against YHWH. (9:7)

(b) Also at Taberah, and at Massah, and at Kibroth-hattaavah you've been the kind of people who make YHWH furious (מַקְצִפִים הֱיִיתֶם). (9:22)

(c) You've been rebels (מַמְרִים הֱיִיתֶם) against YHWH from the day <he> knew you. (9:24)

To these three, a fourth should be added:

(d) Because I know your rebelliousness and stubbornness. If you've been rebels (מַמְרִים הֱיִתֶם) against YHWH while I'm still alive and with you here and now, then how much more after my death! (31:27)

The syntax of these four verses is remarkably similar—a *hiphil* masculine plural participle conjoined with the *qal* suffix-conjugation of היה. This construction is also quite similar to that found in the גֵּר/עֶבֶד + היה passages outlined above. However, a signal difference between the two types of inscription is that, when the עֶבֶד-inscription is constructed with a second-person form of היה, the verbal form is singular, whereas the מַמְרִים-inscription is consistently plural. This difference is related to the famous problem of *Numeruswechsel* in Deuteronomy and may simply be another example of the same. Either way, like the *Numeruswechsel*, it is best treated as a stylistic device: the singular emphasizing the responsibility of each individual Israelite, the plural emphasizing the collective responsibility of the people as a whole.[45] If so, then the עֶבֶד-inscription would be primarily a point of attention for an *individual* Israelite, each one of whom is specifically and personally inscribed into the story of Israel's

[45] See, e.g., Lundbom, *Deuteronomy*, 9–10; cf. Jeffrey H. Tigay, *Deuteronomy*, דברים (Philadelphia: Jewish Publication Society of America, 1996), 62; and further, Moshe Weinfeld, *Deuteronomy 1–11: A New Translation with Introduction and Commentary*, AB 5 (New York: Doubleday, 1991), 15–16. The most extensive work is Christopher T. Begg, "Contributions to the Elucidation of the Composition of Deuteronomy with Special Attention to the Significance of the *Numeruswechsel*" (PhD diss., Louvain, 1987).

rescue from Egypt.[46] The מַמְרִים-inscription would be different, however, and would focus the audience's attention on their *collective* guilt as rebels, since this is how they are so inscribed: as a people group, as a whole.

Although it may not be coextensive with the עֶבֶד-inscription, there is sufficient mention of rebellion and disobedience outside of the three instances in chapter 9 and the fourth mention in 31:27 to demonstrate that the מַמְרִים-inscription, too, is *fundamental* and *paradigmatic*. The early positioning and significance of the spy disaster (1:19–46) has already been mentioned. The specific language of disobedience is varied here (e.g., אבה + לֹא, שמע + לֹא, אמן + אַיִן), but it is significant that מרה is found in 1:26 and 1:43. As noted earlier, the foundational failure in the golden calf episode is held in reserve until chapter 9, but the persistent rhetoric of obedience, remembering, not forgetting, and being on constant guard implies the very real potential of future failure—and in these specific ways.[47] This possibility is also suggested by the syntactically similar construction found in 7:26a,[48] but it comes to its fullest fruition (or deepest nadir) in chapter 28, especially in the transition evident from the hypothetical "*if* you will not obey" (אִם־לֹא תִשְׁמַע) of verse 15 to the certain "*because* you did not obey" (כִּי־לֹא שָׁמַעְתָּ) in verses 45 and 62 and the firm "*because* you did not serve" (תַּחַת אֲשֶׁר לֹא־עָבַדְתָּ) in verse 47. Here, in Deut 28, one finds a dense concatenation of second-person waw-consecutive suffix-conjugation forms of היה—seven of the nine such forms that appear in the book (78 percent).[49] The first is a *positive* instance in the event of *obedience*:

> YHWH will make you the head of things, not the tail. You will always be at the top of things (וְהָיִיתָ רַק לְמַעְלָה); you will not be at the bottom because you will obey the commandments of YHWH your God that I am commanding you right now by carefully doing them. (28:13)

But this bright potential future quickly fades from view after the sea change wrought in the curse section of Deut 28 (vv. 15–68). The rest of the instances are *negative* and concern the dread results of *disobedience*:

---

[46] Despite the plural "we"-constructions in 6:21–25, this receives further support from the introductory frame of 6:20–25, since it is the singular child (בִּנְךָ) that is so inscribed (see above).

[47] See, among many others, J. G. Millar, "Living at the Place of Decision: Time and Place in the Framework of Deuteronomy," in J. G. McConville and J. G. Millar, *Time and Place in Deuteronomy*, JSOTSup 179 (Sheffield: Sheffield Academic, 1994), 15.

[48] "Do not bring any detestable thing into your house or you will be *ḥērem* (וְהָיִיתָ חֵרֶם) like it!"

[49] The other two instances are 7:26 (see preceding note) and 16:15: וְהָיִיתָ אַךְ שָׂמֵחַ, "then you will surely rejoice." Note that all nine instances are singular.

> YHWH will hand you over to your enemies, defeated. You will go out against them by one direction, but you will run for your life away from them in seven different directions! You will be a terrifying example (וְהָיִיתָ לְזַעֲוָה) to every kingdom on earth. (28:25)

> You will grope around (וְהָיִיתָ מְמַשֵּׁשׁ) at high noon just like blind people grope around in darkness. Your plans will not succeed. Instead, you will be constantly oppressed and taken advantage of (וְהָיִיתָ אַךְ עָשׁוּק וְגָזוּל) without any one to help. (28:29 [2x])

> The produce of your land and all your hard work will be consumed by people you do not know. You will be nothing but oppressed and mistreated (וְהָיִיתָ רַק עָשׁוּק וְרָצוּץ) constantly. (28:33)

> You will go insane (וְהָיִיתָ מְשֻׁגָּע) by what your eyes see. (28:34)

> You will become something horrible (וְהָיִיתָ לְשַׁמָּה), fit only for use in proverbs and in insults by all the peoples where YHWH drives you. (28:37)

In this expansive curse section, every blessing in the blessing section is systematically refuted, leaving no doubt that *Israel's undoing* is *YHWH's direct doing,* precisely because of Israel's inevitable disobedience (vv. 45, 47, 62).[50] The coup de grâce is the final verse of this unit (and of the central section of the book):[51]

> Finally, YHWH will take you back to Egypt in ships, by the route I promised you would never see again. There you will try to sell yourselves to your enemies as slaves—male and female (לַעֲבָדִים וְלִשְׁפָחוֹת)—but no one will buy you. (28:68)

There is no specific use of היה here, but this, too, is an instance of מַמְרִים-inscription, and a vision of its most horrific future.[52] It is stunning though not surprising (rhetorically ironic, at the very least) that the end result of being מַמְרִים is a precise reversal of the עֶבֶד-inscription; the audience is no longer a people *freed from Egypt* but a people *returned to Egypt*, with their slavery now self-imposed in order to eke out some sort of existence (וְהִתְמַכַּרְתֶּם). However, despite this worst-case scenario, even these measures are completely ineffectual (וְאֵין קֹנֶה). This change of status—from עֲבָדִים to מַמְרִים back to עֲבָדִים—is figured in terms of the past versus the

---

[50] See Strawn, "Deuteronomy," 73.

[51] I understand 28:69 as a superscription for what follows, not a subscription to what precedes. The debate here is a lively one. See recently Lundbom, *Biblical Rhetoric and Rhetorical Criticism*, 102–20.

[52] Deuteronomy 28:62 deserves mention here. This verse employs הֱיִיתֶם in a contrast between the multitude of Israelites prior to the devastation wrought by destruction: "Instead of being as many as the stars of the sky (תַּחַת אֲשֶׁר הֱיִיתֶם כְּכוֹכְבֵי הַשָּׁמַיִם לָרֹב), only a few of you will survive because you did not obey YHWH your God's voice."

future and the future versus the past, and so leads directly into the next topic to be discussed: time. But before turning to that matter, it should be noted that the מַמְרִים-inscription is found in Deuteronomy even after the brutal ending promised in chapter 28. The striking instance in Deut 32:15c, for example, has already been mentioned above, as has 31:27, but other texts, too, might be included (see, e.g., 29:21[ET 22]–30:5; 31:16–22), all of which offer further proof that this second type of inscription is also well attested across the book of Deuteronomy and is a generative rhetorical device.

Time: "Were," "Are/Have Been," and "Will Be"

The two main types of Deuteronomy's rhetoric of inscription map not only onto two primary identities but also onto two different temporal frames:

- The עֶבֶד-inscription is almost exclusively a *past-tense phenomenon*: you (or we) *were* slaves to Pharaoh, but are no longer because of God's act of הוֹצִא (i.e., deliverance). YHWH's exodus-activity marks the decisive point that restricts the time of being עֲבָדִים to the past. Israel was a slave once, but *is* such *no longer*, though Israel must never forget that former state of being.

- The מַמְרִים-inscription is *a past-tense phenomenon with continuing effects up to the current moment*. The addition of a temporal complement in texts like 9:7 (לְמִן־הַיּוֹם אֲשֶׁר־יָצָאתָ . . . עַד־בֹּאֲכֶם עַד־הַמָּקוֹם הַזֶּה, "from the day that you left . . . until you arrived at this place") or 9:24 (מִיּוֹם דַּעְתּוֹ אֶתְכֶם, "from the day <he> knew you")[53] signals that the action of being מַמְרִים is something that happened in the *past but continues* into the contemporary moment of rhetorical exchange. In this way, Israel *has been* rebellious *and still is*.

Thus far the inscription corresponds to simple past (*were*) and present perfect (*have been and still are*), but the *future* is also at play in this rhetoric:

- There is only one instance of עֶבֶד-language that threatens a *future* existence as slaves, though that is unique and rather distinctive (28:68; see discussion above); in terms of its semantic content and rhetorical force (future judgment), it actually belongs with the next category.[54]

[53] For the emendation, reading דַּעְתּוֹ for דַּעְתִּי, see note 32 above.

[54] Cf. 17:16 for a somewhat similar syntactical construction, though the statement there is negated and the action it describes is expressly forbidden.

- Since Israel's past rebelliousness continues up to the present, it has a *possible if not likely future afterlife*. This is the burden of Moses' constant exhortation *not* to disobey, *not* to forget, *not* to go astray. However, chapters 28 and 31 (among others) indicate that such a disobedient future is both imminent and (or so it would seem) inevitable. In chapter 28, the use of the waw-consecutive on the suffix-conjugation of היה signals the *futurity* of the disobedience (28:25, 29 [2x], 33, 34, 37; see above), while the negated suffix-conjugations constructed with כִּי in verses 45 and 62 or with תַּחַת אֲשֶׁר in verse 47 indicate the *certainty* of the same.[55] The syntax and semantic content of 31:16–21, 27 follow suit.

However, the future is not a time solely for failure or for an inescapable recapitulation of life as מַמְרִים. Indeed, the force of so much Deuteronomic rhetoric to *avoid* disobedience, amnesia, and sin envisions a possible future that is *not* marked by the same; otherwise the rhetoric would be unnecessary and altogether futile. But this is to anticipate the next section of the present study, which attends to the several functions and effects of the book's literary inscription. Here too a final temporal frame in Deuteronomic rhetoric must be considered that has not yet been sufficiently treated: namely, the place of the *present tense*.

The Functions/Effects of Deuteronomy's Rhetoric of Inscription

In this final section, I wish to highlight three primary functions or effects of Deuteronomy's rhetoric of inscription. Each can be captured by a single word: involvement, transhistoricism, and "bothness."

Involvement

The first major function or effect of Deuteronomy's rhetoric of inscription is to *involve its audience*. By means of literary inscription, the audience is written directly into the story in both positive and negative ways: as slaves who have been rescued and as rebels who are recalcitrant and heading for doom. The rhetoric grants no pause, no stay in its onslaught consistently and constantly to involve the audience in this way and in these modes. The only way to escape would be to shut down the stimulus altogether and walk away from Deuteronomy completely.

[55] Note that תַּחַת אֲשֶׁר also occurs in v. 62. Elsewhere in Deuteronomy this construction appears only in 21:14; 22:29.

But according to the logic of Deuteronomy, to do that would be to no longer be Israel.[56]

Inasmuch as the rhetoric of the entire book consistently situates the audience between these two poles—as slaves and as rebels—the audience is incessantly pressed with the existential moment of decision.[57] This is indeed the whole point of the rhetoric: Which pole will dominate and be the way forward? Will Israel remember its prior servitude and be motivated by its redemption to unswerving fealty to its redeeming Lord? Or will the predilection toward rebellion triumph, with all ending in ruin? Deuteronomic inscription presses this dilemma relentlessly and intensely upon the audience. Like it or not, "accurate" or otherwise, these are the two identities the audience manifests. For this reason, the present moment of existential decision, the pervasive Deuteronomic "now/today," is the ultimate temporal frame manifested in the book, created, sustained, and maintained by its rhetorical art.[58]

Transhistoricism

This existential quality of "always being in the moment of decision" creates a *transhistorical effect*, constantly taking the members of the audience out of their own historical situation (whatever, wherever, or whenever that might be) and *re*situating them in the plains of Moab, *re*configuring them as slaves and rebels, and *repeatedly* calling them to choose life rather than death.[59] Insofar as this *resituation*, *reconfiguration*,

---

[56] Cf. Strawn, "Keep/Observe/Do."

[57] See Millar, "Living at the Place of Decision," 15–88.

[58] יוֹם occurs 167 times in Deuteronomy, and while not all instances of the word are directly related to the book's hortatory rhetoric, the majority are. See Strawn, "Keep/Observe/Do," 217, 229 and n. 76; Weinfeld, *Deuteronomic School*, 356–57; and cf. von Rad, *Studies*, 70: " 'This day' appears throughout the Deuteronomic utterances, highlighting the existential quality of this divine *praedicatio impii*." Note also Hwang, *Rhetoric of Remembrance*, 6–7.

[59] See Strawn, "Keep/Observe/Do," 222–24, for other non-time-constrained aspects of repetition within Deuteronomy's rhetoric. See also Millar, "Living at the Place of Decision," 15: "The effect is to gather up *every significant moment in Israel's past experience in the present dilemma at Moab*" (my emphasis), and 88: "Yesterday, Today, and Tomorrow, wherever the nation finds itself—in the land or outside it—a simple decision faces Israel: to live for Yahweh or not—to move further into the land with Yahweh or to go back to Egypt. There can be no standing still." Cf. von Rad, *Studies*, 70–71: "six centuries . . . *are cancelled out and Israel is set once more* at Horeb to hear Jahweh's word of salvation. . . . It is the tremendous 'here and now' in the divine election that lies at the back of Deuteronomy's attempt to *re-comprehend* the Israel that was now in the grip of an inner disintegration as the holy people of God" (my emphases). Hwang, *Rhetoric of Remembrance*, 8, speaks of

and *repetition* is temporal—"we were slaves," "you've been rebels," etc. (see above)—the proper adjective to describe Deuteronomy's rhetoric is not "timeless,"[60] as if the rhetoric were somehow or fundamentally *unrelated* to matters of time and history, but rather "transhistorical"; it is thoroughly related to the audience's life within time and history and yet, simultaneously, is somehow and nevertheless *above* the same.

It is instructive to compare the transhistorical quality of Deuteronomic rhetoric to the eighth principle of Judaism and what Jon Levenson has called "the literary simultaneity of Scripture."[61] The eighth principle, as known in "Ani Ma'amin," states, "I believe with perfect faith that the entire Torah presently in our possession is the one given to Moses our master (may he rest in peace)."[62] This is a paraphrase of one of the thirteen principles of Maimonides (1138–1204 CE), which reads, in part:

> That the Torah is from heaven . . . that is: that we believe that the entire Torah presently in our possession is the one given to Moses our master (may he rest in peace), [and] that it is all from the mouth of God, that is, that it was all given to him from the Lord (may he be blessed) in the manner that is metaphorically called "speaking."[63]

According to Levenson, this principle has to do with the ultimate "unity and divinity of the Torah."[64] Moving in reverse order, this means that the *divine* origin of the Torah must not be expunged, and that all parts of the Torah—its most exalted verses and its most mundane—come from the mouth of God.[65] Levenson defines the *unity* of the Torah as "the simultaneity, self-referentiality, and mutual implication of *all* its parts."[66]

Levenson notes that such a disposition toward the Torah's divine and unified nature is at variance with (at least some) modern critical approaches to the Bible as practiced widely for the past few centuries. This is especially true for the second point, regarding whether the Bible can

---

how Deuteronomy "recreate[s] imaginatively the experiences of Moab for future generations."

[60] Contra Hwang, *Rhetoric of Remembrance*, 233, who speaks of the "fathers" as a "timeless symbol" in Deuteronomy. However, Hwang is quite right in his understanding of the rhetorical flexibility of Deuteronomic rhetoric on this subject (and others).

[61] Jon D. Levenson, "The Eighth Principle of Judaism and the Literary Simultaneity of Scripture," in *The Hebrew Bible, the Old Testament, and Historical Criticism: Jews and Christians in Biblical Studies* (Louisville: Westminster John Knox, 1993), 62–81 (the essay was originally published in 1988).

[62] Ibid., 63.

[63] Ibid.

[64] Ibid., 65.

[65] Ibid., 64.

[66] Ibid., 75 (his emphasis).

be treated (even if only in some final, ultimate fashion) as a unity rather than as an agglutinative pastiche that must be surgically filleted so as to arrive at the right literary-compositional-historical stratification and, correlatively, the right interpretation (presumably). Levenson cites Menahem Haran's apt summary:

> The postulate of [premodern or pre-critical] exegesis is that Scripture, being the word of God and not subject to change, is not bound to time and place, whereas the [modern] critical method regards Scripture as a human manifestation (to be sure, a most brilliant one) of a culture confined to its own bounds of time and space—the culture of the ancient Near East.[67]

According to Levenson, the price to be paid for many of modern historicizing approaches "is the dismemberment—the decomposition—of the synchronic literary reality that was the Bible and the displacement of authority from the text as a whole onto those aspects of it *with which the interpreter is already in sympathy*."[68]

This is not the place to discuss all the aspects of Levenson's argument, specifically, or the idea of literary simultaneity, more generally,[69]

---

[67] Menahem Haran, "Midrashic and Literal Exegesis and the Critical Method in Biblical Research," in *Studies in Bible*, ed. Sara Japhet, ScrHier 31 (Jerusalem: Magnes, 1986), 36–37; also cited in Levenson, "Eighth Principle," 69–70. The additions of "premodern or pre-critical" and "modern" to Haran's citation are my own, not Levenson's, due to the larger argument Levenson is making. Perhaps "traditional or confessional" versus "non-confessional" would work just as well. Haran himself goes on to speak of "classical exegesis" versus the "secular essence" of modern criticism ("Midrashic," 37). In my judgment, the dichotomy—however construed—is a false one, and the poles need not be construed antithetically or as completely discrete sets. Cf., among others, David C. Steinmetz, "The Superiority of Pre-Critical Exegesis," in *The Theological Interpretation of Scripture: Classic and Contemporary Readings*, ed. Stephen E. Fowl (Malden: Blackwell, 1997), 26–38; and Michael C. Legaspi, *The Death of Scripture and the Rise of Biblical Studies* (Oxford: Oxford University Press, 2010). See also further below.

[68] Levenson, "Eighth Principle," 72–73 (my emphasis).

[69] For example, when, exactly, "was" the Bible "the synchronic literary reality" of which Levenson speaks (see previous note)? As Levenson notes elsewhere, "the juxtaposition of these various sorts of literature [now found in the Old Testament] in the same book [i.e., within the covers of one Bible] is a matter of *literary* context; it becomes a fact of *history* per se only very late in the period of the Second Temple—long after the original historical contexts of the Pentateuchal literature and perhaps also the proverb collections [for example] had vanished" ("Why Jews Are Not Interested in Biblical Theology," in *The Hebrew Bible, the Old Testament, and Historical Criticism*, 37; his emphasis [orig. 1987]). But Levenson's formulation in "Eighth Principle" suggests a point (or points) in time in which this literary juxtaposition was also (or became) something real: a reality from which modern biblical scholarship subsequently prescinded. When did that happen and how? And how do we know about that, and how can we access it, assuming that we can and should?

but at least two points of comparison with Deuteronomic rhetoric deserve mention.

The first is that, on the one hand, Deuteronomy's rhetoric of inscription may be seen as an instance or manifestation of Levenson's notion of literary simultaneity. If so, in the case of Deuteronomy one is not simply fideistically believing (אֲנִי מַאֲמִין) the Torah (or סֵפֶר הַתּוֹרָה!) to be literarily simultaneous; the Torah *is* in fact literarily simultaneous *precisely by means* of Deuteronomy's own rhetoric. That Deuteronomy manifests such simultaneity, inscribing the same on its audience, suggests that simultaneity might be found elsewhere in Scripture and that it may even (and as a result) be a reasonable understanding of Scripture's rhetoric writ large, and thus a matter worthy of belief (or disposition) regarding how Scripture as a whole functions—exactly as per the eighth principle.

Even so—and this is the proverbial "on the other hand"—Deuteronomy's literary simultaneity, regardless of its pre- or post-critical nature, is (to reverse Haran's language) *not* above alteration (contra Haran's "not subject to change") and also *not* unmoored from circumstance and location (contra Haran's "not bound to time and place"). To the contrary, Deuteronomy's rhetoric—and its rhetorical situation(s)—live, move, and have their being in *changed times* and in *altered circumstances*—in repetition that always comes replete with its two aspects of sameness and difference.[70] Deuteronomy's rhetoric is thus *thoroughly* bound to time and space; the audience receiving Deuteronomy is inscribed into the twin poles of slavery and rebellion, into the existential locations of Egypt, Horeb/Sinai, and Kadesh—not to mention other points along the way. This is not timelessness, like some proverb that could be applied anywhere at any time. Take Prov 6:6, for example:

> Go to the ant, you lazy person;
> observe its ways and grow wise. (CEB)

This is a far cry indeed from "we were slaves *to Pharaoh in Egypt*" (Deut 6:21) and "you've been rebels until you arrived *at this place* [i.e., the plains of Moab]" (9:7). In contrast to wisdom literature, which can instruct an audience from twenty-first-century Georgia as directly as one from Iron Age Judah, Deuteronomy re-places and re-situates its audience by inscribing them into the past, but always so as to force the existential decision today (*trans*historicism).[71] Thus, while Deuteronomy can be seen as an instance

---

[70] See above and, further, Strawn, "Keep/Observe/Do."

[71] Cf. Polzin, "Deuteronomy," 92: "The *temporal perspectives* of both audiences *merge in the book* through the phrases 'that day' and 'this day.' Moses' 'that (future) day' becomes 'this (present) day' of the narrator"; 92–93: an important "temporal aspect of the book's composition is Moses' and the narrator's practice of shuttling back and forth *between 'that day' of the speaker's past and 'this day' of his here-and-*

of literary simultaneity, it is a rather particular and peculiar sort thereof. And while not entirely "confined to its own bounds of time and space—the culture of the ancient Near East" (Haran), it is equally at home there, even as it is always equally at home *beyond* there; and so, ultimately, it is not "confined" there at all or in the least. Here, again, Deuteronomy may offer an instructive model for how Scripture as a whole functions.

This leads directly to the second point, which is to note, as Levenson himself has, that an appropriate method of interpretation that takes seriously the literary simultaneity of the text—or, in the present case, that takes seriously Deuteronomy's transhistoricism—need not *deny* historical investigation even though it would almost certainly *relativize* it.[72] Speaking concretely about biblical scholarship—specifically pentateuchal criticism—Levenson writes:

> The efforts to take the text apart would not cease; they are informative and . . . not without precedent in the premodern tradition of biblical interpretation. They would, however, be dialectically checked by a continual awareness of the need to put the text back together in a way that makes it available in the present and in its entirety—not merely in the past and [not merely] in the form of historically contextualized fragments.[73]

Once again, Deuteronomy serves as a parade example of the kind of constructive move Levenson advocates, offering this example *from within the pages of Scripture itself*. So despite, or perhaps better, in spite of the seemingly endless attempts to analyze compositional strata within Deuteronomy, find its earliest form, and so on, the rhetoric of the book consistently resists such attempts to fix its primary semantic value in this or that location, period, or century.[74] Deuteronomy's rhetoric traffics in the "back then," to be sure, but primarily and ultimately so as to address the audience in the eternal "now,"[75] which is an eternal now-*cum*-then. Among other things, this explains why scholars have successfully located multiple

---

now"; and 93: "Both Moses and the narrator use *'that day' to help them put into context this day's recitation* of the law" (emphases added).

[72] See Levenson, "Eighth Principle," 79.

[73] Ibid.

[74] Cf., somewhat similarly, J. G. McConville's understanding that "the silence of Deuteronomy on the identity of the place [where God will set the divine name] . . . encapsulates (not to say enshrines) the *non-significance of individual places*" ("Time, Place and the Deuteronomic Altar-Law," in *Time and Place in Deuteronomy*, 139; my emphasis).

[75] I am conscious of the echo here of Paul Tillich's *The Eternal Now* (New York: Scribner's, 1963), esp. 122–32, though I am thinking more of Bruce F. Kawin's sense of the transcendent aspects of repetition (the continuous present) in his *Telling It Again and Again: Repetition in Literature and Film* (Boulder: University Press of Colorado, 1989). For application to Deuteronomy, see Strawn, "Keep/Observe/Do," esp. 220–24. See also notes 57–60 and 71 above.

audiences within Deuteronomy and have appropriately placed the book (or some of its parts) in different eras. Within the rhetoric of inscription, *all* such audiences and eras are correct! This is an impossible scenario for a thin historicism to conceive, but, per Luke 1:37 (similarly Matt 19:26 // Mark 10:27 // Luke 18:27), nothing is impossible for God, and, in Deuteronomy, Moses says much the same thing (e.g., Deut 30:11–14).[76] Put differently, Deuteronomy's rhetoric summons all people and times to itself (cf. John 12:32), inscribing them yet again—always again!—into the roles of slaves and rebels, pressing on them to decide, here and now, today.

This rhetoric is not *non*historical, and certainly not *a*historical, for the reasons expressed above, but it is definitely *trans*- or *supra*historical. And yet, if this is correct, then it may not be going too far to say that, in some important ways, Deuteronomy's rhetoric *does* approach the nonhistorical, for the reasons expressed above. It is not constrained or confined by the limits of history, and certainly not ultimately. Deuteronomy is not (only) about *then*, it is (equally if not more so) about *now*. Once again, Deuteronomy is about *both then and now*, along with *what yet will be*, but the clear accent in terms of literary effect is on *now*. Whatever the case, the transhistorical nature of Deuteronomy's rhetoric—its point and purpose—need not pose a threat to those who care deeply about matters of history and historicity, facticity or verity,[77] though it puts all those commitments in considerable and relativized perspective, indicating, among other things, that Scripture's truthfulness is not reducible (solely) to matters of "history" or "fact," however those are defined. So, while one might still care deeply about such matters, whether in Deuteronomy or elsewhere in Scripture, one must not care about them too much, and certainly not ultimately. This is the lesson that the transhistoricism of Deuteronomy's powerful theological rhetoric (or its powerful rhetorical theology) teaches and manifests. That theological rhetoric/rhetorical theology can be encapsulated rather pithily by another, much later text:

> I tell you, now is the time of God's favor, now is the day of salvation. (2 Cor 6:2 NIV)[78]

And, Deuteronomy would be quick to add, now is also "the time of God's judgment, now is the day of decision."

---

[76] The whole Moab covenant might be considered at this point, on which see Olson, *Deuteronomy and the Death of Moses*, 126–58; and Olson, "How Does Deuteronomy Do Theology? Literary Juxtaposition and Paradox in the New Moab Covenant in Deuteronomy 29–32," in *A God So Near*, 201–13.

[77] It is worth observing that such people are found on both poles of the confessional/non-confessional spectrum.

[78] Note that this text from 2 Corinthians cites Isa 49:8, which is, in turn, replete with exodus motifs.

"Bothness"

Finally, "bothness" indicates that Deuteronomy's rhetoric of inscription will not permit the audience to identify with *only one* of the two poles: either that of slaves or that of rebels. Instead, the audience is *both* of these and so must hear what it means to be both—both in the past and for the possible future, but above all and especially in and for the present. If given the choice, most modern readers are probably wont to identify with only the "positive" pole—in Deuteronomy's case, that of rescued and redeemed slaves—letting the "negative" part about being rebels go. This applies whether it is due to supersessionist tendencies[79] or simply to old-fashioned Freudian projection, or both.[80] The reverse is also possible, though I suspect that overidentification with the pole representing judgment is far less common, at least in many Christian circles in affluent North America.

Regardless, in Deuteronomy the point is that you cannot pick just one pole: you must read (and be!) *both*—both "good" parts and "bad" parts are part and parcel of the rhetoric. Furthermore, the "bad" parts prove to be as good for the soul as the "good" parts. That is how Deuteronomy's inscription works: *writing the audience into the story's most noble and most ignoble moments for salutary ends*.

The benefits of accepting such inscription, of learning how to read in Deuteronomy's way, are exemplified in chapter 32, in the second of the two striking instances of inscription that are found in that famous poem. The first instance, found in verse 15c, was discussed at some length above. In that verse, the poem writes the members of the audience directly into the storyline, if by chance they somehow did not realize this song of torah was really about them: "*It was you* who got fat, thick, stubborn!" The audience is *acted upon* in verse 15c, as is always the case with Deuteronomic inscription; their permission is not sought, they are not asked if they agree with, let alone appreciate, the identification. By means of this rhetoric they are simply told, "This is a story about you."

The second instance of inscription is found in verse 31, where, just when it seems that all is lost after the apostasy that has led to divine judgment and total devastation (vv. 5–6, 15–30), suddenly and unexpectedly Israel *writes itself* into the poem:[81]

---

[79] See the trenchant insights of Levenson, "Eighth Principle," and passim in *The Hebrew Bible, the Old Testament, and Historical Criticism*.

[80] Cf. Levenson's remark ("Eighth Principle," 72–73; cited above at note 68) on how such "dismemberment" and "decomposition" of Scripture "as a whole" results in a "displacement of authority from the text . . . onto those aspects of it *with which the interpreter is already in sympathy*" (my emphasis).

[81] What follows is indebted to Brent A. Strawn, *The Old Testament Is Dying: A Diagnosis and Recommended Treatment* (Grand Rapids: Baker Academic, 2017), 205–11.

But no! Their rock is not like our Rock!
Our enemies are completely foolish.[82]

This proves to be the turning point in the poem. Hereafter, all is most assuredly *not* lost, and things change decisively with YHWH doing an about-face vis-à-vis the enemies who were previously the divine instrument of punishment. Hereafter, YHWH chooses instead to "acquit" (דין) and "have compassion" (נחם) on helpless Israel.

In this second case of inscription in chapter 32, Israel is not inscribed into the song *passively* as an *object acted upon*, but *reinscribes itself as an active subject, reinserting* itself into the stanza, and to stunning effect. The first inscription, in verse 15, was for *judgment*: "You grew fat!" This is a case of מַמְרִים-inscription. This second self-inscription, in verse 31, is for *hope*, if not for *doxology*: "Our God is incomparable!" And this second inscription works: the hope pays off and God attends to Israel, saving it once again.[83]

It is essential that the hope undergirding this second instance of (re-) inscription, in verse 31, is entirely predicated on the עֶבֶד-type inscription—it depends on knowing that God is a saving and redeeming God who has cared for Israel in the past and still does so (cf. the dynamics in Deut 6:20–25: "for our good always, to preserve us alive, just as we are right now"). The self-inscription of the audience in verse 31 is only possible because the audience has learned what inscription is about and how it works, and because—in this crucial moment at least, if not also at last—the audience accepts all of that, applying the tools of Deuteronomy's rhetorical trade just in time, exactly when it is needed most.

What Deuteronomy shows in this verse and throughout its rhetoric of inscription, therefore, is how the "good" and "bad" parts of Scripture go together; both are equally important, and both are equally precious. No less than in the case of existential involvement or transhistoricism, in this way Deuteronomy offers us a model for reading Scripture—*all* of Scripture—every nook and cranny, whether we like it or not, whether we want to or not, and reading ourselves therein. We must read all of Scripture this way, deeming each part important, holding each part precious, because, in the end, it is we, all of us here alive today, who are both slaves and rebels.

---

[82] The last colon is in some doubt. J. Hempel (in *BHS*, 347) suggests inserting כֻּלָּם ("all of them") after וְאֹיְבֵינוּ, *metri causa*, which is always a dubious reason, especially in the absence of text-critical support. Perhaps something is simply gapped from the first colon. However, the real question concerns פְּלִילִים. The translation above follows LXX's ἀνόητοι (so also NRSV), which may actually be ignorant of the Hebrew lexeme (see *BHQ*, 96, *149–50). Other solutions are possible, of course, for which see the commentaries.

[83] For other examples of how Deut 32 worked, as attested in texts like 2 Macc 7; 4 Macc 18; and Rev 15, see Strawn, *The Old Testament Is Dying*, 209–11.

CHAPTER 7

Literary and Other Observations on Passages Dealing with Foreigners in the Book of Deuteronomy: The Command to Love the *Gēr* Read in Context

Markus Zehnder

Introduction

The aim of this study is to explain the command to love the גֵּר in Deut 10:19, in connection with the related command found in Lev 19:34. The thematic and literary connections of these two verses will be explored with respect to the larger contexts in which they are embedded. This leads to observations concerning the relationship between the "Book of the Covenant," priestly laws, including what is often called the "Holiness Code," and the Deuteronomic law collection. The study will focus mainly on texts that relate to the גֵּר, though in some instances I will also consider others that concern a second type of "foreigner," the נָכְרִי. It is not possible to treat all passages dealing with the גֵּר (or the נָכְרִי) in the biblical law collections in this essay; I will rather consider only those that can in some ways be related to the love-command in Deut 10:19 (and its counterpart in Lev 19:34).[1]

Broadly speaking, the word גֵּר designates a person of foreign origin who has settled permanently among the Israelites, or perhaps an internally displaced person or migrant from within the territories covered by Israel and Judah.[2] This differs from the second category of individuals

[1] This essay expands on observations made in my *Habilitationsschrift*, *Umgang mit Fremden in Israel und Assyrien: Ein Beitrag zur Anthropologie des "Fremden" im Licht antiker Quellen*, BWANT 168 (Stuttgart: Kohlhammer, 2005). I presented the preliminary results of my earlier investigation at the SBL International Meeting in Singapore in 2005 and at the University of Nottingham in 2011.

[2] Scholars continue to discuss whether the term גֵּר in Deuteronomy or the Covenant Code refers ethnically to a non-Israelite. Among recent voices who are

with a foreign background mentioned in the biblical law collections, the נָכְרִי or בֶּן־נֵכָר.[3]

Concerning my method in assessing the literary relationship between laws dealing with the גֵּר found in the various biblical law collections, the following general remarks are crucial. First, we must distinguish between thematic—including possible ideational—overlap, on the one hand, and direct literary influence, on the other. Second, in cases of literary influence, we must distinguish among citation, quotation, allusion, echo, and trace.[4] Third, concerning the direction of literary influence, no comprehensive, agreed-upon catalog can be taken as a starting point. However, some general points of orientation help in addressing such issues:[5]

- Some kind of textual "disturbance," such as the use of otherwise unattested language, or "friction" with regard to the embedding in the literary context, points to a text being dependent on an external source text.
- Receiving texts may be recognizable by the clarification they offer of the source text or by modifications they make to the source document based on their overall ideological outlook.
- If an obscure text gains clarity when one reads a related text, the latter probably predates the former.
- In accordance with a principle used in textual criticism (*lectio brevior/lectio difficilior*), a shorter and/or more difficult text is probably the source text, which provides a base for the received text.

We need to handle such general indicators circumspectly and with a degree of flexibility that takes into account distinctive features of individual cases. To assess questions of literary or ideational influence, we must also make a counterexamination, checking whether the reverse

---

critical of the "non-Israelite" interpretation, see Thomas Römer, "Fremde," in *Wörterbuch alttestamentlicher Motive*, ed. Michael Fieger, Jutta Krispenz, and Jörg Lanckau (Darmstadt: Wissenschaftliche Buchgesellschaft, 2013), 162–66.

[3] For details see Zehnder, *Umgang mit Fremden*, esp. 279–87, 323–84. In this monograph I occasionally note observations on the relative sequence of laws pertaining to foreigners. These generally suggest that P/H antedate the Deuteronomic laws (see 358–59n5, 362n3, 366n2, 371n3).

[4] See the classification in Michael R. Stead, *The Intertextuality of Zechariah 1–8*, LHBOTS 508 (New York: T&T Clark, 2009), 21–23.

[5] For such a list see, e.g., Mark A. Awabdy, *Immigrants and Innovative Law: Deuteronomy's Theological and Social Vision for the* גֵּר, FAT 2/67 (Tübingen: Mohr Siebeck, 2014), 178.

direction of dependence could provide a satisfactory or better explanation of the data under scrutiny. We also need to be open to the possibility that we are dealing with parallel, yet literarily independent, traditions, especially if the thematic overlap is limited and the linguistic discrepancies are large.

The specific contribution of this study lies in its combination of observations concerning thematic, linguistic, and broader literary and compositional factors, along with indicators of literary or conceptual lines of development. At the same time, the observations adduced below do not aim to shed light on all possible aspects of the discussion of the sequence of the biblical law collections. However, the approach offered here may bring to the fore evidence that is often overlooked.

In the cases under investigation here, it seems more plausible to conclude that the Deuteronomic laws postdate the comparative material in both the Covenant Collection (= CC) and in their priestly analogs, specifically in the Holiness Collection (= HC).[6]

Deut 10:18–19 and Lev 19:34: The Command to Love the גֵּר

The command that will get primary attention in this study is the ordinance to love the גֵּר. The Deuteronomic version of this ordinance, which

[6] My use of the term HC (= Holiness Collection; in many scholarly discussions labelled H) does not entail any commitment regarding whether or to what degree this collection (generally delimited to Lev 17–26) should be separated from (other) priestly legal material. Critical continental European scholarship generally assumes that H (= Heiligkeitsgesetz/Holiness Code) presupposes both CC and the Deuteronomic laws (and sometimes P as well). See, e.g., Christophe Nihan, "The Holiness Code between D and P: Some Comments on the Function and Significance of Leviticus 17–26 in the Composition of the Torah," in *Das Deuteronomium zwischen Pentateuch und Deuteronomistischem Geschichtswerk*, ed. Eckart Otto and Reinhard Achenbach, FRLANT 206 (Göttingen: Vandenhoeck & Ruprecht, 2004), 81–83; Eckart Otto, "Innerbiblische Exegese im Heiligkeitsgesetz Levitikus 17–26," in *Levitikus als Buch*, ed. Heinz-Josef Fabry and Hans-Winfried Jüngling, BBB 119 (Berlin/Bodenheim: Philo, 1999), 141, 151, and passim; see also Jeffrey Stackert, *Rewriting the Torah: Literary Revision in Deuteronomy and the Holiness Legislation*, FAT 2/52 (Tübingen: Mohr Siebeck, 2007). Some also maintain that H and D developed independently and more or less contemporaneously. See, e.g., Moshe Weinfeld, *Deuteronomy and the Deuteronomic School* (Oxford: Clarendon, 1972), 179–244. For the most comprehensive recent study arguing for the sequence CC–HC–D, see Benjamin Kilchör, *Mosetora und Jahwetora: Das Verhältnis von Deuteronomium 12–26 zu Exodus, Levitikus und Numeri*, BZABR 21 (Wiesbaden: Harrassowitz, 2015).

occurs outside the Deuteronomic laws in the strict sense (Deut 12–26), is found in Deut 10:18–19. The command reads as follows:[7]

עֹשֶׂה מִשְׁפַּט יָתוֹם וְאַלְמָנָה	He executes justice for the orphan and the widow,
וְאֹהֵב גֵּר לָתֶת לוֹ לֶחֶם וְשִׂמְלָה׃	and shows His love for the alien by giving him food and clothing.
וַאֲהַבְתֶּם אֶת־הַגֵּר	So show your love for the alien,
כִּי־גֵרִים הֱיִיתֶם בְּאֶרֶץ מִצְרָיִם׃	for you were aliens in the land of Egypt.

This law has its closest analog in the command to love the גֵּר in Lev 19:34:

כְּאֶזְרָח מִכֶּם יִהְיֶה לָכֶם הַגֵּר הַגָּר אִתְּכֶם	The stranger who resides with you shall be to you as the native among you,
וְאָהַבְתָּ לוֹ כָּמוֹךָ	and you shall love him as yourself;
כִּי־גֵרִים הֱיִיתֶם בְּאֶרֶץ מִצְרָיִם	for you were aliens in the land of Egypt:
אֲנִי יְהוָה אֱלֹהֵיכֶם׃	I am the LORD your God.

If it is possible to identify some kind of dependence between these two laws, does one represent an earlier stage in the development of the concept of "loving" the גֵּר?[8]

As opposed to what one finds in Deut 10:19, in Lev 19:34 the command is addressed to a singular "you" and supplemented by the phrase כָּמוֹךָ. Furthermore, in Lev 19 the command to love the גֵּר is preceded by the command to love the רֵעַ (v. 18),[9] whereas in Deut 10 the command to love YHWH is first (v. 12).

---

[7] All the translations in this study are taken from the New American Standard Bible 1977. The verses are numbered according to the BHS, not the English translation. Many see Deut 10:18–19 as a late addition, chronologically later than the laws concerning the גֵּר found in Deut 12–26/28. See, e.g., Alfred Cholewiński, *Heiligkeitsgesetz und Deuteronomium: Eine vergleichende Studie*, AnBib 66 (Rome: Biblical Institute Press, 1976), 275. This precludes using Deut 10:18–19 to make any judgments concerning the sequence of HC and the Deuteronomic laws. As I will show below, Deut 10:18–19 is so tightly connected to various passages in the Deuteronomic law collection proper that such a division is problematic.

[8] Awabdy leaves open the question whether the two texts are "genetically related" (*Immigrants*, 205–6).

[9] Christophe Nihan (*From Priestly Torah to Pentateuch: A Study in the Composition of the Book of Leviticus*, FAT 2/25 [Tübingen: Mohr Siebeck, 2007], 464), following Otto, rightly identifies Lev 19:34 as structurally parallel to Lev 19:17–18.

Based on the context, Deut 10 seems to have in mind a "love" of the גֵּר that is characterized by the community's practical help for the גֵּר, whereas Lev 19 envisions a "love" that can better be described in terms of a general sense of equality and respect. Whereas in Deut 10 the command is preceded in verse 18 by עֹשֶׂה מִשְׁפַּט יָתוֹם וְאַלְמָנָה ("He executes justice for the orphan and the widow") and its sequel לָתֶת לוֹ לֶחֶם וְשִׂמְלָה ("by giving him food and clothing"), in Lev 19 the preceding theme of honoring elderly people and the subsequent phrase כָּמוֹךָ set the tone. Thus one could argue that the love-command in Lev 19:34 exhibits a more developed state by placing the גֵּר on the same level as the אֶזְרָח and the addressee, which goes beyond the injunction in Deut 10:19, where the love spoken of seems to be restricted to the socioeconomic area.[10]

However, the issues are more complex than this. The ordinance in Deut 10:19 is dependent on the description of YHWH's action in the preceding verse, while Deut 10:18 expands on the description of who YHWH is in verse 17. Introduced by the particle כִּי, this verse provides the motivation for Israelites to circumcise their hearts, as verse 16 commands them to do.[11] There is, then, a dimension that transcends the socioeconomic sphere: to "love" the גֵּר is ultimately a matter of the heart.[12] Another observation points in the same direction: the foundation for the love-command in Deut 10:19 is the claim in verse 18 that YHWH himself "loves" the גֵּר. However, in all other instances in the book of Deuteronomy where YHWH is the subject of אָהַב, the object is Israel, and in these instances "love" obviously has a broader meaning and cannot be reduced to the socioeconomic sphere. Conversely, Lev 19:35, which directly follows the command to love the גֵּר, also mentions the specific realm of מִשְׁפָּט ("justice"), measurements, and weights. These observations caution against exaggerating the difference between a narrow social understanding of the love of the גֵּר in Deut 10 and a lofty philosophical understanding of this love in Lev 19.

The two versions of the command differ in another respect. Whereas Deut 10:19 involves the free landowning Israelite, who, as head of an extended family, is the implied addressee of the ordinance, Lev 19:34 is addressed to each Israelite without reference to his social position. This suggests a more socially oriented concept of "love" in Deut 10 than in Lev 19.

---

[10] This type of reasoning can also be found in Nihan's treatment of the passage (see *From Priestly Torah*, 476). He claims that the גֵּר is "identified" with the native and is "like a (full) citizen." However, this goes beyond the precise meaning of Lev 19:33–34, which concerns not a matter of identification but the just treatment of the גֵּר.

[11] Thus also Awabdy, *Immigrants*, 50.

[12] For a similar remark see J. Gordon McConville, *Deuteronomy*, ApOTC 5 (Downers Grove, IL: InterVarsity Press, 2002), 201.

The phrase לָתֶת לוֹ לֶחֶם וְשִׂמְלָה in Deut 10:18 shows that here (as in most texts in the Deuteronomic law collection) the גֵּר is considered to be part of the socially weak classes of society, as not belonging directly to the extended family of a landowning Israelite. This low social position is further stressed by the mention of YHWH's care for the יָתוֹם and the אַלְמָנָה at the beginning of verse 18.

Deuteronomy's lack of a command to love one's neighbor, whether the רֵעַ or the אָח, is striking. The following consideration may explain this: On the level of interpersonal relationships, love of the גֵּר is understood as the apex of what can be aspired to. If the Israelites are called to love the גֵּר, it is a matter of course that also their Israelite neighbor must be loved, and therefore the רֵעַ or אָח need not be mentioned explicitly as the recipients of the divinely ordained love.

Both Deut 10:18–19 and Lev 19:34 refer to the Israelites' experience as גֵּרִים in Egypt in an added motive clause. Since the formula כִּי־גֵרִים הֱיִיתֶם בְּאֶרֶץ מִצְרָיִם appears only here in Deuteronomy—elsewhere the Israelites in Egypt are referred to as עֲבָדִים—Deut 10:19 was probably influenced by Lev 19:34, which suggests that the priestly regulation preceded the Deuteronomic law. On the other hand, whenever Leviticus refers to the Israelites' stay in Egypt, rather than using a form of the verb הָיָה, as here, H uses יָצָא, with YHWH as the subject. Presumably, by referring to גֵּרִים instead of עֲבָדִים in Deut 10:19 the author intends to remind the addressees of the early positive phase of the Israelites' stay in Egypt, as opposed to the later phase, when they were oppressed. The Israelites are to remember the kindness the Egyptians showed them in the days of Joseph and follow this model in their own treatment of the גֵּר living among them.[13]

One additional observation also points to the chronological priority of the Leviticus law over the Deuteronomic law. Deuteronomy 10 not only commands the Israelites to love the גֵּר, but also speaks of YHWH's love for the גֵּר. Since this represents the theological climax of the lawgiver's comments about the גֵּר, it seems more likely that this passage postdates its counterpart, in which the divine paradigm is missing.

The location of the reference to YHWH's love for the גֵּר immediately following a hymnlike praise for God in Deut 10:17 highlights its significance. In the context of the chapter, especially in light of verse 17, this love is best understood as a demonstration of God's impartiality.[14]

[13] Thus also Awabdy, *Immigrants*, 54. This would square nicely with Deut 23:8.

[14] Cf. Christopher Wright's comment: "In some ancient Near Eastern royal texts the exaltation of national gods is commonly followed by the derivative exaltation of the royal household. It was human kings who basked in the reflected glory of the ruling gods. But who . . . are the beneficiaries of Yahweh's supreme lordship? The fatherless and the widow and . . . the alien! Nothing could be more characteristic of Israel's 'counter-cultural' faith. The majestic monotheistic superlatives of verses 14 and 17 are harnessed, not to the glory

YHWH's love for the גֵּר provides the Israelites with further motivation to love the גֵּר, in addition to their own experience as גֵּרִים in Egypt; whomever God loves, the Israelites also should love. Accordingly, obedience to the command represents a case of *imitatio Dei*, one that is intimately bound up with empathy. *Imitatio* and empathy are two sides of the same coin: as גֵּרִים in Egypt and during the exodus the Israelites experienced God's love, demonstrated in practical help. Accordingly, if the Israelites love the גֵּר, they will pass on the love that they themselves received from God[15]—and from the Egyptians during the first phase of their sojourn in Egypt. Deuteronomy is clear about *how* this *imitatio* should be lived out practically. YHWH demonstrated love for the גֵּר by giving him food and clothing (לָתֶת לוֹ לֶחֶם וְשִׂמְלָה), but it is also clear that the love-command can never be exhausted by such specifications.

The reference to YHWH's love for the גֵּר also provides motivation for the Israelites' love for the גֵּר in a negative way by serving as a warning: the Israelites' special relationship to God does not release them from the duty to act justly and compassionately toward גֵּרִים, because God also acts as an impartial advocate for them.[16]

The fact that all other commands to "love" in Deuteronomy have YHWH as their object highlights the theological significance of the command to love the גֵּר. This goes beyond the parallelism between the love of the גֵּר and love of the neighbor in Lev 19.[17] This is not to suggest that the concept of *imitatio Dei* is lacking in Lev 19; it is present but formulated differently and somewhat less explicitly. Leviticus 19:2 summons the Israelites to be holy as YHWH himself is holy. The imitation does not involve an imitation of God's love, as in Deut 10, but of God's holiness. By following the ethical and social commands in Lev 19, which include those relating to the love and protection of the גֵּר, the Israelites implement God's own justice and righteousness in the everyday life of this world.[18]

---

and power of the wealthy and strong, but to the needs of the poor, the weak and the vulnerable" (*Deuteronomy*, NIBCOT [Peabody, MA: Hendrickson, 1996], 149).

[15] See Friedrich Vinzenz Reiterer, "Du sollst den Fremden lieben wie Dich selbst (Lev 19,34)," in *Die Fremden*, ed. Gottfried Bachl (Regensburg: Transfer, 1993), 86.

[16] Cf. Jeffrey H. Tigay's comment on Deut 10:18: "the point of this verse is to demonstrate that God is beyond influence and favoritism and that Israel cannot expect to sin and escape punishment because of its special relationship with Him" (*Deuteronomy*, דברים [Philadelphia: Jewish Publication Society of America, 1996], 108).

[17] Significantly, in the context of Deuteronomy love of YHWH is not restricted to the political loyalty of a vassal to his suzerain, even if this dimension is important. See the remarks by Awabdy, *Immigrants*, 55 (referring to Lapsley's and Arnold's correction of Moran's too one-sided approach).

[18] See Thomas Hieke, *Levitikus 16–27*, HThKAT (Freiburg im Breisgau: Herder, 2014), 762.

Several additional observations argue for the chronological priority of the Lev 19 version of the love-command. Jacob Milgrom notes that, in contradistinction to Deut 10:19, Lev 19:34 does not use the plural verb form in the phrase "you shall love him" (i.e., "the גֵּר"), even though the immediate context in Lev 19:33–34 uses plural verb forms.[19] This suggests that the command to love the גֵּר in Lev 19:34 is modeled after the singular command to love the רֵעַ in Lev 19:18 and not after the command in Deut 10:19. The plural in Deut 10:19 can be explained simply by the consistent use of plural verb forms from verse 15 onward, and the command to love the גֵּר in Lev 19:34a can easily be explained as an extrapolation of Lev 19:18, the command to love the neighbor. The subsequent motive clause כִּי־גֵרִים הֱיִיתֶם בְּאֶרֶץ מִצְרָיִם can be explained as derived from Exod 22:20[ET 21].[20]

We should also note that the command to love the גֵּר in Deut 10:19 is placed before the law corpus proper that begins in Deut 12. This literary position puts it in a category similar to the Shema and the V'ahavta (6:4–5), which is linked to Deut 10:12 through the repetition of the command to love YHWH. This command in 10:12 confirms that the ordinance to love the גֵּר in Deut 10:19 is not out of place in its present literary context. By being placed before the law collection proper beginning in Deut 12, rather than, for example, in the paragraph on the protection and economic support of the גֵּר in Deut 24:10–22, the ordinance to love the גֵּר is given extra weight. The injunction was probably introduced in its present context because *imitatio Dei* is such an important point for Deuteronomy. Leviticus has no parallel to the Deuteronomic command to love YHWH, and in this respect it does not reach the same theological level. It is gratuitous to assume that it simply presupposed the Deuteronomic command and felt no need to repeat it.

The specific placement of the injunction to love the גֵּר in Lev 19:34 bears no sign of an alleged influence of Deuteronomy; it seems to be merely a natural expansion of the theme of not oppressing the גֵּר mentioned in verse 33 and to be connected to the injunction to treat the גֵּר like an אֶזְרָח, a common topic in Leviticus. The specific formulation of the law in Lev 19:34 can easily be explained as an analogy—and structural complement—to the preceding command to love one's neighbor in Lev 19:18.[21]

Further complicating the question of dependence is that it is difficult to understand why Deuteronomy would take over the command to love the גֵּר and not add to it the more general command to love one's neighbor, which is so closely related to the former command in Lev 19, all the more so since the love-theme is important in Deuteronomy.

---

[19] See Jacob Milgrom, *Leviticus 17–22*, AB 3A (New York: Doubleday, 2000), 1704.

[20] Cf. Kilchör, *Mosetora*, 290–91, with a refutation of conflicting views presented by Van Seters and Nihan.

[21] Not only with respect to the use of the singular for the addressee, as mentioned above. Thus also Hieke, *Levitikus*, 755.

Exploring the possible direction of dependence from a different angle, one could argue that the first part of Lev 19:34 goes further than Deut 10:19 in prescribing an equality of sorts between the גֵּר and the native Israelite, an equality that is underlined by the parallelism between Lev 19:18 (love of neighbor) and Lev 19:34 (love of the גֵּר).[22] As was demonstrated above, however, this argument does not consider the full dynamics and scope of the love-commands in Deuteronomy. Furthermore, the formulation found at the beginning of Lev 19:34 does not imply a general equality of the גֵּר and the native Israelite.[23]

The Inclusion of Lev 19:33 and Its Ramifications

Leviticus 19:34 is preceded by and intimately connected to the prohibition not to wrong or oppress a גֵּר (v. 33).[24] This prohibition points to a network of interconnected texts:

Exod 22:20[ET 21]:

וְגֵר לֹא־תוֹנֶה וְלֹא תִלְחָצֶנּוּ כִּי־גֵרִים הֱיִיתֶם בְּאֶרֶץ מִצְרָיִם׃

And you shall not wrong a stranger or oppress him, for you were strangers in the land of Egypt.

Similarly, Exod 23:9:

וְגֵר לֹא תִלְחָץ וְאַתֶּם יְדַעְתֶּם אֶת־נֶפֶשׁ הַגֵּר כִּי־גֵרִים הֱיִיתֶם בְּאֶרֶץ מִצְרָיִם׃

---

[22] Thus Cholewiński, *Heiligkeitsgesetz*, 276. If Lev 19:34 is understood as the structural complement to Lev 19:17–18 (see Nihan, *From Priestly Torah*, 464), a far-reaching prohibition not to hate the גֵּר—which would have no analogue in Deuteronomy—may also be in view. However, one could also argue that, since there is no explicit prohibition against hating the גֵּר, the גֵּר is intentionally not put on the same level as the אָח/עָמִית.

[23] For more details see Zehnder, *Umgang*, 340. Awabdy, *Immigrants*, 206, takes a contrasting position, calling the Deuteronomic position toward the גֵּר "accommodation" to meet the immigrants' needs that is not found in HC (see ibid., 207, 214, 219). However, Awabdy's view that Deuteronomy intentionally relaxes the rules—especially cultic regulations—for the social benefit of the גֵּר (see ibid., 219, 224, 226) disregards the possibility that Deuteronomy presupposes many of the cultic rules in Leviticus and Numbers and senses no need to repeat (and possibly modify) them.

[24] This verse is structurally related to Lev 19:13–14; see Nihan, *From Priestly Torah*, 464. For a short discussion of the possible redactional-critical relationship of Lev 19:33–34 (as well as vv. 35–36) to their literary context see, e.g., Cholewiński, *Heiligkeitsgesetz*, 50–51. His and other commentators' similar reconstructions remain speculative and are prone to circular reasoning.

And you shall not oppress a stranger, since you yourselves know the feelings of a stranger, for you also were strangers in the land of Egypt.

Lev 19:33–34:

וְכִי־יָגוּר אִתְּךָ גֵּר בְּאַרְצְכֶם לֹא תוֹנוּ אֹתוֹ׃

When a stranger resides with you in your land, you shall not do him wrong.

כְּאֶזְרָח מִכֶּם יִהְיֶה לָכֶם הַגֵּר הַגָּר אִתְּכֶם וְאָהַבְתָּ לוֹ כָּמוֹךָ כִּי־גֵרִים הֱיִיתֶם בְּאֶרֶץ מִצְרָיִם אֲנִי יְהוָה אֱלֹהֵיכֶם׃

The stranger who resides with you shall be to you as the native among you, and you shall love him as yourself; for you were aliens in the land of Egypt: I am the LORD your God.

Deut 10:19:

וַאֲהַבְתֶּם אֶת־הַגֵּר כִּי־גֵרִים הֱיִיתֶם בְּאֶרֶץ מִצְרָיִם׃

So show your love for the alien, for you were aliens in the land of Egypt.

Omitting for the moment Exod 23:9, which does not add substantially to Exod 22:20[ET 21], the relationships among the three texts can be represented as in Table 1:[25]

Table 1

	Oppression	**Love**
CC	And you shall not wrong a stranger or oppress him, for you were strangers in the land of Egypt. (Exod 22:20)	
Deut		So show your love for the alien, for you were aliens in the land of Egypt. (Deut 10:19)
HC	When a stranger resides with you in your land, you shall not do him wrong. (Lev 19:33)	The stranger who resides with you shall be to you as the native among you, and you shall love him as yourself; for you were aliens in the land of Egypt: I am the LORD your God. (Lev 19:34)

[25] For a short explanation of the relationship between Lev 19:33–34 and Exod 22:20[ET 21] see David L. Baker, *Tight Fists or Open Hands? Wealth and Poverty in Old Testament Law* (Grand Rapids: Eerdmans, 2009), 184–85. He also mentions Deut 10:17–19 (187).

The picture emerging from this presentation looks straightforward: CC only has a command not to oppress the גֵּר, while Deuteronomy only has a command to love the גֵּר; HC has both elements. Taken in isolation, this might suggest that HC combines CC and Deuteronomy and therefore is dependent on both CC and Deuteronomy. Thus Lev 19:33–34 would seem to combine the phrase לֹא־תוֹנֶה ("do not wrong") in Exod 22:20[ET 21] (cf. 23:9) and the command to love the גֵּר in Deut 10:19, while retaining the element כִּי־גֵרִים הֱיִיתֶם בְּאֶרֶץ מִצְרָיִם ("for you were aliens in the land of Egypt"), which is found in both Exod 22:20[ET 21] (cf. 23:9) and Deut 10:19, and adding a formula at the end that is typical of HC, "I am the LORD your God."[26]

This explanation of the relationships among the three law collections accords with the dominant view in continental Europe, which sees Deuteronomy as dependent on CC only, and HC, the latest work, as dependent on both CC and Deuteronomy. However, it conflicts with the observations adduced above that focus on the two specific commands to love the גֵּר. Moreover, the verses in question should not be interpreted in isolation but rather investigated within their broader literary contexts.

While arguments concerning the precedence of HC or Deuteronomy conflict at this point, there seems little doubt that the prohibitions in CC mark the earliest step in the development; the prohibition against the oppression of the גֵּר lacks an admonition to love him.

However, when we consider the literary context of some of the verses quoted above and other texts that are topically or lexically related to those considered thus far, the issues turn out to be more complex. We first have to note that Deuteronomy does in fact lack a command not to oppress the alien that uses the verbs found in Exod 22:20[ET 21] and 23:9 or in Lev 19:33. This could mean that Deuteronomy *presupposes* the prohibition not to oppress the alien. Alternatively, this prohibition may be included in the injunction to love the גֵּר, that is, as the minimal first step toward heeding it. If these assumptions are correct, there is no longer a clear line of dependence between HC and Deuteronomy, as suggested by an exclusive consideration of the synopsis presented above.

Taking the issue further, while it is true that Deuteronomy contains no prohibition against oppressing the גֵּר that closely matches Exod 22:20[ET 21] (cf. Exod 23:9) and Lev 19:33, the book contains a prohibition concerning the oppression of other persons expressed with the same verb יָנָה that is found in Exod 22:20[ET 21] and Lev 19:33. This prohibition is related to the treatment of the runaway slave in Deut 23:16–17[ET 15–16]:

[26] Cf., e.g., Cholewiński, *Heiligkeitsgesetz*, 275, who claims that the only direct correspondence to Lev 19:33 is found in Deut 24:17–18. Because this passage has a narrower focus than the one in HC, he concludes that HC must represent a later stage of development. However, as I will demonstrate below, Deut 24:17–18 is not the only passage in Deuteronomy to which Lev 19:33 is lexically and topically related.

לֹא־תַסְגִּיר עֶבֶד אֶל־אֲדֹנָיו	You shall not hand over to his master a slave
אֲשֶׁר־יִנָּצֵל אֵלֶיךָ מֵעִם אֲדֹנָיו׃	who has escaped from his master to you.
עִמְּךָ יֵשֵׁב בְּקִרְבְּךָ	He shall live with you in your midst,
בַּמָּקוֹם אֲשֶׁר־יִבְחַר בְּאַחַד שְׁעָרֶיךָ	in the place which he shall choose in one of your towns
בַּטּוֹב לוֹ	where it pleases him;
לֹא תּוֹנֶנּוּ׃	you shall not mistreat (יָנָה) him.

In addition, there is a text prohibiting the oppression of the גֵּר using the verb עָשַׁק, Deut 24:14–15:

לֹא־תַעֲשֹׁק שָׂכִיר עָנִי וְאֶבְיוֹן	You shall not oppress a hired servant who is poor and needy,
מֵאַחֶיךָ אוֹ מִגֵּרְךָ	whether he is one of your countrymen or one of your aliens
אֲשֶׁר בְּאַרְצְךָ בִּשְׁעָרֶיךָ׃	who is in your land in your towns.
בְּיוֹמוֹ תִתֵּן שְׂכָרוֹ	You shall give him his wages on his day
וְלֹא־תָבוֹא עָלָיו הַשֶּׁמֶשׁ	before the sun sets,
כִּי עָנִי הוּא	for he is poor
וְאֵלָיו הוּא נֹשֵׂא אֶת־נַפְשׁוֹ	and sets his heart on it;
וְלֹא־יִקְרָא עָלֶיךָ אֶל־יְהוָה	so that he may not cry against you to the LORD
וְהָיָה בְךָ חֵטְא׃	and it become sin in you.

It is possible that the fugitive slave mentioned in Deut 23:16[ET 15] represents a subcategory of the גֵּר, especially since he is likely of foreign extraction. As far as Deut 24:14–15 is concerned, taking its use of a different Hebrew verb for "oppress" as not implying a fundamental conceptual difference, it can be said that Deuteronomy also contains a prohibition against the oppression of the גֵּר, although it is formulated more narrowly by pointing to the hired laborer or the poor as subcategories of the גֵּר rather than to the גֵּר in general.[27]

We may therefore interpret Deut 23:17[ET 16] and 24:14 as *specifying* the general command of Exod 22:20[ET 21], identifying two subgroups of

[27] For a discussion of the various ways in which שָׂכִיר עָנִי וְאֶבְיוֹן מֵאַחֶיךָ אוֹ מִגֵּרְךָ in Deut 24:14a can be understood and of the variant readings in the ancient versions, see Awabdy, *Immigrants*, 84–85.

the category גֵּר that must not be oppressed, namely, the עֶבֶד who has fled his foreign master and the day laborers and poor among the גֵּרִים. This fits well with Deuteronomy's interest in the specification of social categories. The relationships among the relevant texts are illustrated in Table 2:

Table 2

	Oppression		**Love**
CC	And you shall not wrong a stranger or oppress him, for you were strangers in the land of Egypt. (Exod 22:20[ET 21])		
Deut	You shall not hand over to his master a slave who has escaped from his master to you. He shall live with you in your midst, in the place which he shall choose in one of your towns where it pleases him; you shall not mistreat him. (Deut 23:16–17[ET 15–16])	You shall not oppress a hired servant who is poor and needy, whether he is one of your countrymen or one of your aliens who is in your land in your towns. (Deut 24:14)	So show your love for the alien, for you were aliens in the land of Egypt. (Deut 10:19)
HC	When a stranger resides with you in your land, you shall not do him wrong. (Lev 19:33)		The stranger who resides with you shall be to you as the native among you, and you shall love him as yourself; for you were aliens in the land of Egypt: I am the LORD your God. (Lev 19:34)

With respect to the sequence of texts, it is more likely that an original general command has prompted specific thoughts on the broad topic at different places in a later law collection than that different texts from unrelated contexts have been combined under a general heading in such a way that, at least in one case (Deut 23:17[ET 16]), the source text is almost unrecognizable.

Considering the wider picture as presented above, one can assume that the Deuteronomic version of the laws postdates not only CC but also HC, reflecting both linguistic innovation and a more developed differentiation of the social stratigraphy. The latter trait characterizes a number of other cases as well. However, we must consider two problems before accepting this explanation too quickly. On the Deuteronomic side, the "love" element only appears outside the generally accepted limits of the Deuteronomic law collection (chs. 12–26), and the motive clause pointing to the Israelites' own status as גֵּרִים in Egypt is missing from both Deut 23:16–17[ET 15–16] and Deut 24:14–15. However, the placement of the love-command outside the law corpus proper is not conclusive in itself. Furthermore, only a few verses after Deut 24:14–15, and still belonging to the same extended paragraph, the formula וְזָכַרְתָּ כִּי עֶבֶד הָיִיתָ בְּמִצְרַיִם ("and you shall remember that you were a slave in Egypt") appears twice (in v. 18 and v. 22, the latter adding אֶרֶץ before מִצְרַיִם).

The Inclusion of the Literary Contexts of Exod 22:20 [ET 21] and Deut 24:14–15

As observed above, Deut 24:14 prohibits the oppression of certain groups that we may understand as belonging to the גֵּרִים. This statement is part of a literary composition that exhibits many links with Exod 22 (see Table 3 below). The pertinent parallel passages are Exod 22:20–26[ET 21–27] and Deut 24:10–22,[28] excluding Deut 24:16, which addresses another topic.

> Exod 22:20 And you shall not wrong a stranger or oppress him, for you were strangers in the land of Egypt. [21] You shall not afflict any widow or orphan. [22] If you afflict him at all, and if he does cry out to Me, I will surely hear his cry; [23] and My anger will be kindled, and I will kill you with the sword; and your wives shall become widows and your children fatherless. [24] If you lend money to My people, to the poor among you, you are not to act as a creditor to him; you shall not charge him interest. [25] If you ever take your neighbor's cloak as a pledge, you are to return it to him before the sun sets, [26] for that is his only covering; it is his cloak for his body. What else shall he sleep in? And it shall come about that when he cries out to Me, I will hear him, for I am gracious.

> Deut 24:10 When you make your neighbor a loan of any sort, you shall not enter his house to take his pledge. [11] You shall remain outside, and the man to whom you make the loan shall bring the pledge out to you. [12] And if he is a

[28] There are additional thematic and lexical connections between each of the two texts and their respective literary contexts. For example, the theme of the pledges mentioned in Deut 24:10–13 and 17 also appears in Deut 24:6. If the break between Deut 24 and 25 is interpreted as a soft break and Deut 25:1–3 is included as the natural literary extension of Deut 24:10–22, we also need to consider Exod 23:6–9 in the CC parallel (see Kilchör, *Mosetora*, 279–81). Because Exod 23:9 closely parallels Exod 22:20[ET 21]—and may be interpreted as a structural element framing the whole passage that begins in Exod 22:20[ET 21]—these expansions reinforce the case. However, Exod 22:27[ET 28]–23:5 lacks any parallel in Deut 24. In any event, my delimitation of the passages is not absolute. However, the selection of these specific verses helps the focus on regulations related to resident aliens/foreigners.

poor man, you shall not sleep with his pledge. [13] When the sun goes down you shall surely return the pledge to him, that he may sleep in his cloak and bless you; and it will be righteousness for you before the LORD your God. [14] You shall not oppress a hired servant who is poor and needy, whether he is one of your countrymen or one of your aliens who is in your land in your towns. [15] You shall give him his wages on his day before the sun sets, for he is poor and sets his heart on it; so that he may not cry against you to the LORD and it become sin in you. . . . [17] You shall not pervert the justice due an alien or an orphan, nor take a widow's garment in pledge. [18] But you shall remember that you were a slave in Egypt, and that the LORD your God redeemed you from there; therefore, I am commanding you to do this thing.

Deut 24:19 When you reap your harvest in your field and have forgotten a sheaf in the field, you shall not go back to get it; it shall be for the alien, for the orphan, and for the widow, in order that the Lord your God may bless you in all the work of your hands. [20] When you beat your olive tree, you shall not go over the boughs again; it shall be for the alien, for the orphan, and for the widow. [21] When you gather the grapes of your vineyard, you shall not go over it again; it shall be for the alien, for the orphan, and for the widow. [22] And you shall remember that you were a slave in the land of Egypt; therefore I am commanding you to do this thing.

Themes found in Exod 22:20–23[ET 21–24] are also addressed in Deut 24:14–22, while themes in Exod 22:24–26[ET 25–27] are addressed in Deut 24:10–18. That several of these elements in CC exhibit more than one correspondence in Deuteronomy suggests that CC antedates Deuteronomy. The three most salient examples are the pledge theme, which is mentioned in Exod 22:25[ET 26] and in Deut 24:10–13 and 17; the oppression theme, mentioned in Exod 22:20–22[ET 21–23] and in Deut 24:14 and 17; and the sojourn in Egypt theme, mentioned in Exod 22:20 and in Deut 24:18 and 22.[29] Table 3 demonstrates further how elements of CC are developed and expanded in Deuteronomy.

[29] The theme of crying to the Lord recurs in Exod 22:22 and 26, but it appears only once in Deuteronomy (Deut 24:15). The repetition in Exod 22 can easily be explained as a structural marker found at the end of two thematically related passages.

Table 3

CC (Exod 22:20–26)		DC (Deut 24:10–22)		
[20] And you shall not wrong a stranger or oppress him, for you were strangers in the land of Egypt. [21] You shall not afflict any widow or orphan. [22] If you afflict him at all, and if he does cry out to Me, I will surely hear his cry; [23] and My anger will be kindled, and I will kill you with the sword; and your wives shall become widows and your children fatherless.		[17] You shall not pervert the justice due an alien or an orphan, nor take a widow's garment in pledge. [18] But you shall remember that you were a slave in Egypt, and that the LORD your God redeemed you from there; therefore I am commanding you to do this thing.	[19] When you reap your harvest in your field and have forgotten a sheaf in the field, you shall not go back to get it; it shall be for the alien, for the orphan, and for the widow, in order that the LORD your God may bless you in all the work of your hands. [20] When you beat your olive tree, you shall not go over the boughs again; it shall be for the alien, for the orphan, and for the widow. [21] When you gather the grapes of your vineyard, you shall not go over it again; it shall be for the alien, for the orphan, and for the widow. [22] And you shall remember that you were a slave in the land of Egypt; therefore I am commanding you to do this thing.	[14] You shall not oppress a hired servant who is poor and needy, whether he is one of your countrymen or one of your aliens who is in your land in your towns. [15] You shall give him his wages on his day before the sun sets, for he is poor and sets his heart on it; so that he may not cry against you to the LORD and it become sin in you.

24 If you lend money to My people, to the poor among you, you are not to act as a creditor to him; you shall not charge him interest. 25 If you ever take your neighbor's cloak as a pledge, you are to return it to him before the sun sets, 26 for that is his only covering; it is his cloak for his body. What else shall he sleep in? And it shall come about that when he cries out to Me, I will hear him, for I am gracious.		10 When you make your neighbor a loan of any sort, you shall not enter his house to take his pledge. 11 You shall remain outside, and the man to whom you make the loan shall bring the pledge out to you. 12 And if he is a poor man, you shall not sleep with his pledge. 13 When the sun goes down you shall surely return the pledge to him, that he may sleep in his cloak and bless you; and it will be righteousness for you before the LORD your God.	14 You shall not oppress a hired servant who is poor and needy, whether he is one of your countrymen or one of your aliens who is in your land in your towns. 15 You shall give him his wages on his day before the sun sets, for he is poor and sets his heart on it; so that he may not cry against you to the LORD and it become sin in you.	17 You shall not pervert the justice due an alien or an orphan, nor take a widow's garment in pledge. 18 But you shall remember that you were a slave in Egypt, and that the LORD your God redeemed you from there; therefore I am commanding you to do this thing.

These are the most important parallels between Exod 22:20–23[ET 21–24] and Deuteronomy: The prohibition against perverting justice in Deut 24:17 takes up the oppression theme, which is described in Exod 22:20–22[ET 21–23] with three different verbs. Deuteronomy 24:17 also mentions the orphan and the widow in addition to the alien, corresponding to Exod 22:20–21[ET 21–22]. Deuteronomy 24:18 is linked to Exod 22:20 through the reference to the sojourn in Egypt.

Deuteronomy 24:19–22 is loosely related to Exod 22:20–23[ET 21–24] through the transformation of CC's prohibition of affliction into a positive command mandating economic support for the alien, as well as by the addition of references to the orphan and the widow. The reference to the sojourn in Egypt in Deut 24:22 also links this passage to Exod 22:20[ET 21]. Deuteronomy 24:14–15 is related to Exod 22:20–23[ET 21–24] through the prohibition against oppressing the alien (Exod 22:20[ET 21]; Deut 24:14) and by the motif of oppressed persons crying to YHWH (Exod 22:22[ET 23]; Deut 24:15).

The most important parallels between Exod 22:24–26[ET 25–27] and Deut 24:10–26 are the following: (1) Deuteronomy 24:10–13 takes up the loan theme, with Deut 24:10 expanding Exod 22:24[ET 25] to include loans of all sorts. (2) Although they use different expressions, the "pledge" motif found in all four verses in Deut 24:10–13 (עֲבוֹט) relates to the "pledge" in Exod 22:25[ET 26] (חָבַל). (3) Both Deut 24:13 and Exod 22:25–26[ET 26–27] mention the debtor's sleep and his cloak. (4) Both Deut 24:14–15 and Exod 22:24–25 refer to the "poor." (5) The temporal modifier "before the sun sets" links Exod 22:25[ET 26] with Deut 24:15. (6) Like Exod 22:25[ET 26], Deut 24:17 speaks of taking a garment in pledge.

As Table 4 indicates, the closest parallels occur between Exod 22:24–26[ET 25–27] and Deut 24:10–13.[30] Although these passages exhibit considerable lexical overlap, neither the main technical terms nor the structure of the passages are parallel. This rules out a simple process of copying.

Table 4

Exod 22:24–26[ET 25–27]	Deut 24:10–13
24 If you lend money to My people, to the poor among you, you are not to act as a creditor to him; you shall not charge him interest. 25 If you ever take your neighbor's cloak as a pledge, you are to return it to him before the sun sets, 26 for that is his only covering; it is his cloak for his body. What else shall he sleep in? And it shall come about that when he cries out to Me, I will hear him, for I am gracious.	10 When you make your neighbor a loan of any sort, you shall not enter his house to take his pledge. 11 You shall remain outside, and the man to whom you make the loan shall bring the pledge out to you. 12 And if he is a poor man, you shall not sleep with his pledge. 13 When the sun goes down you shall surely return the pledge to him, that he may sleep in his cloak and bless you; and it will be righteousness for you before the LORD your God.

If one only looks at these two passages, it is clear that Deuteronomy is the later text. Whereas Exod 22:24–26[ET 25–27] addresses only the poor and money loans, Deut 24:10–13 covers a wider range of loans and offers a more developed description of the debtor. Initially it uses the broader term "neighbor," but later speaks of the "poor" as a subcategory of this group.

Following the order of Exod 22:20–26[ET 21–27], Table 5 identifies the common elements:

---

[30] For a recent treatment of "security, pledge" in the Hebrew Bible and its ancient Near Eastern context, see Baker, *Tight Fists*, 266–75.

Table 5

Theme	Exod 22:20–26[ET 21–27]	Deut 24:10–22
Oppression of the גֵּר	22:20[ET 21] (יָנָה/לָחַץ)	24:14 (עָשַׁק) [24:19–21 (economic support)]
Israel's experience in Egypt	22:20[ET 21] (גֵּר)	24:18 (עֶבֶד) 24:22 (עֶבֶד)
Affliction of widows and orphans	22:21[ET 22] (עָנָה)	24:17 (חָבַל ;נָטָה מִשְׁפָּט) [24:19–21 (economic support)]
Crying out to YHWH	22:22[ET 23] 22:26[ET 27]	24:15
Lending	22:24[ET 25] (לָוָה), to poor	24:10 (נָשָׁה), to neighbor 24:12, to poor
Charging interest	22:24[ET 25]	(Deut 23:20–21)
Taking a pledge	22:25[ET 26]	24:10–13 24:17
A cloak as pledge	22:25[ET 26]	24:13 24:17
Returning the pledge before sunset	22:25[ET 26]	24:12–13 24:15
Sleep of the debtor	22:26[ET 27]	24:13

As this list indicates, most elements in CC have two analogues in Deut 24, the main exceptions being the theme of the crying out to YHWH and the prohibition of taking interest. Significantly, Deuteronomy goes beyond the negative, prohibitive orientation of CC by adding positive measures for the benefit of (potentially) disadvantaged persons. Taken together, these factors suggest strongly that Deuteronomy reflects a later stage in the development of the laws. As observed earlier, it is more likely that an original general command has informed more specific and variegated treatments of the same themes at various places in a later law collection than that different texts from unrelated contexts have been combined under a general heading in such a way that the source text is unrecognizable. And if the sequence of the two passages that contain the closest network of parallels (Exod 22:24–26[ET 25–27] and Deut 24:10–13) can be determined with relative certainty, we may reckon with the same sequence with regard to the rest of the material found in Exod 22:20–26[ET 21–27] and Deut 24:10–22.

Nevertheless, we must be cautious when making claims about direct literary dependence. The variations in terminology are considerable, and both CC and the Deuteronomic passages exhibit a clear structure, particularly with the respective repetition of the cry motif in Exod 22:22–23[ET 23–24] and 26[ET 27] and the Egypt motif in Deut 24:18 and 22.

The Inclusion of Deut 23:20–21 [ET 19–20] and Its Ramifications

As seen in Table 5, one significant element in Exod 22:20–26[ET 21–27] is missing in Deut 24:10–22, namely, the "prohibition of interest" mentioned in Exod 22:24[ET 25]. However, it is found in Deut 23:20–21 [ET 19–20]. We must also note that while the tripartite command in Deut 24:19–21 involving economic support of the גֵּר (and other groups in need of special protection) has no direct parallel in CC, it finds a close analogue in Lev 19:9–10.[31] Therefore, we also need to consider this passage.

With respect to the topic of interest, Exod 22:24[ET 25] contains the following statement:

אִם־כֶּסֶף תַּלְוֶה אֶת־עַמִּי אֶת־הֶעָנִי עִמָּךְ לֹא־תִהְיֶה לוֹ כְּנֹשֶׁה לֹא־תְשִׂימוּן עָלָיו נֶשֶׁךְ׃

If you lend money to My people, to the poor among you, you are not to act as a creditor to him; you shall not charge him interest.

In this case, it is clear that the loans in question involve loans for Israelites who suffer economic hardship, rather than loans requested for mercantile reasons.[32] Deuteronomy 23:20–21[ET 19–20] contains the following related regulations:

לֹא־תַשִּׁיךְ לְאָחִיךָ	You shall not charge interest to your countrymen:
נֶשֶׁךְ כֶּסֶף נֶשֶׁךְ אֹכֶל	interest on money, food,
נֶשֶׁךְ כָּל־דָּבָר אֲשֶׁר יִשָּׁךְ׃	or anything that may be loaned at interest.

[31] For a short discussion of the possible redaction-critical relationship of these verses to their literary context see Cholewiński, *Heiligkeitsgesetz*, 49. However, such reconstructions are speculative and prone to circular reasoning, as noted above with respect to Lev 19:33–34 and Lev 19:35–36.

[32] Cf. Baker, *Tight Fists*, 257–58. He points out that, in spite of this restriction, it is unlikely that taking interest was accepted in other cases (see 262; however, a different assessment is found on p. 265).

לַנָּכְרִי תַשִּׁיךְ	You may charge interest to a foreigner,
וּלְאָחִיךָ לֹא תַשִּׁיךְ	but to your countryman you shall not charge interest,
לְמַעַן יְבָרֶכְךָ יְהוָה אֱלֹהֶיךָ	so that the LORD your God may bless you
בְּכֹל מִשְׁלַח יָדֶךָ עַל־הָאָרֶץ	in all that you undertake in the land
אֲשֶׁר־אַתָּה בָא־שָׁמָּה לְרִשְׁתָּהּ׃	which you are about to enter to possess.

The law stipulates that an Israelite is not allowed to take interest from an Israelite "brother" (אָח), but he is explicitly entitled to take interest from a foreigner (נָכְרִי). As in Deut 15:3, here the נָכְרִי is excluded from a regulation that protects the אָח. Presumably because the נָכְרִי is only distantly related to the people of Israel and Yahwism, the special measures intended to protect the אָח do not apply to him; he remains under international rules governing economic life. Because the נָכְרִי is permitted to charge his Israelite business partners interest and probably stays in close contact with partners outside of Israel, he is not as dependent on Israel's internal economic climate, as Israelite citizens would be. Thus, he would be unduly privileged if he did not have to pay interest for loans from Israelite business partners.[33]

We may understand the Deuteronomic command as an extension of the ordinance found in Exod 22. It expands the prohibition of interest in three respects: (1) by extending loans of money to loans of all kinds, (2) by extending loans to an עָנִי to all members of the Israelite community, and (3) by explicitly excluding the נָכְרִי. There is no explicit analogue to this third element in CC, though it may be implied by the reference to "my people" in Exod 22:24[ET 25]. These Deuteronomic extensions are best understood as reflecting a later stage in the development of the law.

As is often the case when Deuteronomy uses earlier law collections, Deut 23 and 24 appear to split up legal topics that occur together in CC and treat them at different places. To propose the opposite process—namely, that the author(s) of CC combined material from widely separated places in Deuteronomy and relegated one of the borrowed elements to a subor-

[33] See Zehnder, *Umgang*, 371; see also Baker, *Tight Fists*, 263; Michael Guttmann, "The Term Foreigner (נָכְרִי) Historically Considered," *HUCA* 3 (1926): 7; Tigay, *Deuteronomy*, 218. Nihan refers to Deut 15:3 and 23:20–21[ET 19–20] in his explanation of Lev 25:44–46, claiming that this passage "seems clearly to be based upon one of the principles of the D legislation on debt, where it is systematically stipulated that brotherly compassion does not apply to the foreigner (cf. Dtn 15,3 and 23,20–21 . . .)" ("Holiness Code," 88). The situation, however, is more complex than Nihan suggests, because the passage in Leviticus speaks of the גֵּר, while the Deuteronomic verses refer to the נָכְרִי.

dinate clause or an afterthought—is unconvincing, especially because the application in Exodus is narrower in focus than in the assumed source text in Deuteronomy (loans just of “money” and just for the “poor”).

A prohibition against taking interest from the אָח is also found in Lev 25:35–38:[34]

וְכִי־יָמוּךְ אָחִיךָ	Now in case a countryman of yours becomes poor
וּמָטָה יָדוֹ עִמָּךְ	and his means with regard to you falter,
וְהֶחֱזַקְתָּ בּוֹ גֵּר וְתוֹשָׁב	then you are to sustain him, like a stranger or a sojourner,
וָחַי עִמָּךְ׃	that he may live with you.
אַל־תִּקַּח מֵאִתּוֹ נֶשֶׁךְ וְתַרְבִּית	Do not take usurious interest from him,
וְיָרֵאתָ מֵאֱלֹהֶיךָ	but revere your God,
וְחֵי אָחִיךָ עִמָּךְ׃	that your countryman may live with you.
אֶת־כַּסְפְּךָ לֹא־תִתֵּן לוֹ בְּנֶשֶׁךְ	You shall not give him your silver at interest,
וּבְמַרְבִּית לֹא־תִתֵּן אָכְלֶךָ׃	nor your food for gain.
אֲנִי יְהוָה אֱלֹהֵיכֶם	I am the Lord your God,
אֲשֶׁר־הוֹצֵאתִי אֶתְכֶם מֵאֶרֶץ מִצְרָיִם	who brought you out of the land of Egypt
לָתֵת לָכֶם אֶת־אֶרֶץ כְּנַעַן	to give you the land of Canaan
לִהְיוֹת לָכֶם לֵאלֹהִים׃	*and* to be your God.

We may describe this law best in terms of its logical development, as standing between the versions in CC and Deuteronomy:[35] On the one hand, the priestly law is closer to the Deuteronomic law in not restricting the prohibition of interest to loans of money, but it is not as broad as the Deuteronomic version. Leviticus mentions only money and food, while

---

[34] For a considerably different translation (and corresponding interpretation) see Jacob Milgrom, *Leviticus 23–27*, AB 3B (New York: Doubleday, 2001), 2147, 2204–12; see also Bruce Wells, “The Quasi-Alien in Leviticus 25,” in *The Foreigner and the Law: Perspectives from the Hebrew Bible and the Ancient Near East*, ed. Reinhard Achenbach, Rainer Albertz, and Jakob Wöhrle, BZABR 16 (Wiesbaden: Harrassowitz, 2011), 135–55.

[35] That only Lev 25 describes the socioeconomic circumstances in which loans would be requested and granted poses a significant problem for comparing the three laws prohibiting the taking of interest. Scholars differ widely in their interpretation of these circumstances.

Deuteronomy adds "anything" as an object of the loan.[36] If Lev 23:35–38 were dependent on Deuteronomy, it is difficult to explain why "anything" was omitted. On the other hand, the regulation in Leviticus is closer to the Exodus law in naming only the poor Israelite as the person protected by the stipulation and in not explicitly excluding the נָכְרִי. Deuteronomy represents a more advanced and therefore likely later version of the law, because only Deuteronomy mentions the נָכְרִי, and only Deuteronomy extends the prohibition against charging interest to cases where the borrower is not necessarily poor.[37]

The relationship between Lev 25:35–38 and the law in CC, however, is more complex. While Exod 22:24[ET 25] involves a general prohibition against taking interest from any Israelite experiencing economic hardship, Lev 25:35 seems to narrow this prohibition to more specific cases.[38] This means that HC is not simply repeating—and in some respects broadening—the prohibition found in CC, but rather applying it to specific situations that are more precisely defined than in CC. This "middle" position of the HC law may suggest that it preceded the Deuteronomic law.[39] However, apart from אָח, כֶּסֶף, אֹכֶל, and נֶשֶׁךְ, the linguistic overlap is too limited to argue for direct literary dependence of the Deuteronomic version on HC. The fact that Deuteronomy deviates from CC, which reads אֶת־עַמִּי אֶת־הֶעָנִי, but is in accordance with Leviticus by using אָח, may indicate that the Deuteronomic lawgiver was familiar with both Exod 22:24 [ET 25] and the HC regulation concerning interest.

The independence of Lev 25:35–38 from Deuteronomy is evident in the tight structural embedding of this passage in its literary context and in its stylistic coherence.[40] The fact that the root מוך occurs only in HC and nowhere else in the Hebrew Bible reinforces the view that Lev 25:35–38 was an original text not dependent on Deuteronomy.[41] On the other side of the equation, the formulation of Deut 23:20–21[ET 19–20] appears somewhat detached from its literary context,[42] and it is only here within the

---

[36] Thus also Baker, *Tight Fists*, 262–63, with references to earlier authors holding the same view.

[37] Thus also Georg Braulik, "Weitere Beobachtungen zur Beziehung zwischen dem Heiligkeitsgesetz und Deuteronomium 19–25," in *Das Deuteronomium und seine Querbeziehungen*, ed. Timo Veijola, Schriften der Finnischen Exegetischen Gesellschaft 62 (Helsinki: Finnische Exegetische Gesellschaft, 1996), 48.

[38] See Kilchör, *Mosetora*, 270–71. Scholars debate how we should understand the specific character of the case envisioned in Lev 25:35.

[39] Thus also Hillel Gamoran, "The Biblical Law against Loans and Interest," *JNES* 30 (1971): 132–33.

[40] As is demonstrated at length by Braulik, "Weitere Beobachtungen," 35–39.

[41] All the more so, since no unique linguistic traits are found in Deut 23:20–21.

[42] See Braulik, "Weitere Beobachtungen," 41–42.

context of verses 16–26 that the legal prohibition is supplemented with a reference to the blessing that those who follow the regulation will receive.

The issues become more complicated when we observe that in Lev 25:36 the technical term standing in the center of all three versions of the regulation, נֶשֶׁךְ, is augmented by מַרְבִּית/תַּרְבִּית. We could explain this phenomenon as follows: because Lev 25 has a narrow understanding of the term נֶשֶׁךְ as related to the means of exchange ("money"), it requires another term for loans of food, namely, מַרְבִּית/תַּרְבִּית. On the other side, Deuteronomy broadens the meaning of נֶשֶׁךְ to cover loans of any kind.[43] This again indicates that Deuteronomy contains the latest version of legal regulations concerning interest.

By contrast, one could argue that Lev 25:35–38 goes a step further than Deut 23:20–21[ET 19–20] by stressing the importance of the support of one's "brother" with a free loan. This could mean that HC represents a later development. However, this topic finds its counterpart in Deut 15:7–11, which treats it more thoroughly than HC does. Therefore, this argument that Lev 25:35–38 is later is invalid. Instead, we encounter another case of Deuteronomy splitting up a topic and treating it at different places in a more thorough manner than the other law collections.[44] Deuteronomy 23:20–21[ET 19–20] also goes beyond Lev 25:35–38 by not limiting the prohibition against taking interest from an Israelite "brother" to a specific point in time.

One could also argue that Lev 25:35–38 combines Deut 15:7–11 and Deut 23:20–21,[45] but this is unlikely. Leviticus 25:35–38 makes perfect sense in its current location within the sequence of progressively greater economic hardships that an Israelite male could face, beginning in verse 25

---

[43] See Gamoran, "Biblical Law," 131; see also the discussion in Baker, *Tight Fists*, 260; Kilchör, *Mosetora*, 266; Milgrom, *Leviticus 23–27*, 2209–10. Cf. also the short discussion in Cholewiński, *Heiligkeitsgesetz*, 301. Cholewiński distinguishes between "Zins" and "Zuschlag," the former applying to loans of money, the latter to loans of food. Although he offers no further reasons for this interpretation, Cholewiński understands the new level of differentiation as indicating a later stage. He also understands v. 35 as an addition to Deut 23:20–21[ET 19–20] (see *Heiligkeitsgesetz*, 301–2). However, if one also takes Deut 15:7–11 into account, an addition is precluded.

[44] Otto ("Innerbiblische Exegese," 170–71) claims a dependence of Lev 25:35–38 on both Exod 22:24 and Deut 23:20[ET 19], without, however, giving any specific reasons.

[45] As is done by Nihan, *From Priestly Torah*, 532; "Holiness Code," 87. In the latter work, he sees the author of H involved in an act of "inner-biblical exegesis" "inasmuch as the instruction of Dtn 15,7–11 is now harmonized with Dtn 23,20 and Ex 22,24." It is not clear, however, where this harmonization occurred. Elsewhere Nihan points to the parallelism between Lev 25:35–38 and Deut 15:7–11 (see "Holiness Code," 85). However, if Deut 23:20–21[ET 19–20] is disregarded, the picture remains incomplete and such deductions are therefore unsubstantiated.

and continuing after verse 38. Accordingly, this passage can be explained completely on the basis of internal reasons relating to Lev 25, independent of external sources.[46] The texts exhibit no lexical overlap that suggests any connection between Lev 25:35–38 and Deut 15:7–11. Furthermore, Deut 15:7–11 and Lev 25:35–38 appear to have two different cases in view. Whereas the first case concerns impoverished "brothers" in general, the latter addresses a more specific situation involving a brother who is midway between a lighter degree of economic distress in which he is forced to sell part of his property (v. 25) and a more serious degree requiring him to sell himself (v. 39). In addition to its connection to the sequence beginning in Lev 25:25 that was just discussed, Lev 25:35–38 appears to have been influenced by Lev 19:17–18, rather than Deuteronomy.[47]

Deuteronomy 23:20–21[ET 19–20] and 15:3 exhibit a clear relationship in that both deny the נָכְרִי special economic protection. This focus, which is absent in Leviticus, likely points to a later stage in the development of these topics. Significantly, the prohibition against taking interest from the אָח in Deut 23:20–21[ET 19–20] follows closely on the prohibition not to oppress the עֶבֶד, being separated by only two verses that forbid cultic prostitution and the use of money derived therefrom for the cult of YHWH (Deut 23:18–19[ET 19–20]). This sequence (i.e., prohibition of interest—unacceptable cult—prohibition of oppression) in Deut 23:16–21[ET 15–20] resembles the sequence (i.e., unacceptable cult—prohibition of oppression—prohibition of interest) in Exod 22:19–24[ET 20–25]. However, because neither an A-B-C—A′-B′-C′ nor an A-B-C—C-B-A pattern exists, again claims of direct literary dependence are weak, all the more so given the minimal lexical overlap. But the increased specificity of the cultic prohibition in Deut 23:18–19 [ET 17–18] and the reflection in that passage of a more complex society than the one presented in Exod 22:19[ET 20] suggest again the chronological priority of CC over Deuteronomy.

Deut 24:19–22 and Parallel Regulations in HC

As noted above, the commands to love the גֵּר intensify the prohibition against the oppression of the גֵּר (see Table 1). This prohibition occurs for the first time in a canonical law collection in Exod 22:20[ET 21], which introduces Exod 22:20–26[ET 21–27], which in turn finds its closest parallel in Deut 24:10–22 (see pp. 205–6). The last four verses of the latter (vv. 19–22) exhibit ties to other laws in the biblical law collections out-

[46] See Braulik, "Weitere Beobachtungen," 35–36.
[47] For details see ibid., 46–48.

side of Exod 22. We need to explore these connections further, because the passage explicitly addresses the treatment of the גֵּר.

Deut 24:19–22 reads as follows:[48]

כִּי תִקְצֹר קְצִירְךָ בְשָׂדֶךָ	19 When you reap your harvest in your field
וְשָׁכַחְתָּ עֹמֶר בַּשָּׂדֶה	and have forgotten a sheaf in the field,
לֹא תָשׁוּב לְקַחְתּוֹ	you shall not go back to get it;
לַגֵּר לַיָּתוֹם וְלָאַלְמָנָה יִהְיֶה	it shall be for the alien, for the orphan, and for the widow,
לְמַעַן יְבָרֶכְךָ יְהוָה אֱלֹהֶיךָ	in order that the LORD your God may bless you
בְּכֹל מַעֲשֵׂה יָדֶיךָ׃	in all the work of your hands.
כִּי תַחְבֹּט זֵיתְךָ	20 When you beat your olive tree,
לֹא תְפָאֵר אַחֲרֶיךָ	you shall not go over the boughs again;
לַגֵּר לַיָּתוֹם וְלָאַלְמָנָה יִהְיֶה׃	it shall be for the alien, for the orphan, and for the widow.
כִּי תִבְצֹר כַּרְמְךָ	21 When you gather the grapes of your vineyard,
לֹא תְעוֹלֵל אַחֲרֶיךָ	you shall not go over it again;
לַגֵּר לַיָּתוֹם וְלָאַלְמָנָה יִהְיֶה׃	it shall be for the alien, for the orphan, and for the widow.
וְזָכַרְתָּ	22 And you shall remember
כִּי־עֶבֶד הָיִיתָ בְּאֶרֶץ מִצְרָיִם	that you were a slave in the land of Egypt;
עַל־כֵּן אָנֹכִי מְצַוְּךָ	therefore I am commanding you
לַעֲשׂוֹת אֶת־הַדָּבָר הַזֶּה׃	to do this thing.

This passage states that the owner of a field (שָׂדֶה), an olive grove, or a vineyard may not collect the gleanings, but must leave them for the גֵּר,

[48] For a recent, if brief, discussion of this passage, see Baker, *Tight Fists*, 236–37.

the orphan, and the widow. The combination of גֵּר with יָתוֹם and אַלְמָנָה demonstrates that the גֵּר is included in the group of the *personae miserae*. The lawgiver assumes that none of these three owns land or belongs to the family of an Israelite landowner.

Verse 19 provides motivation for the command by pointing to the blessing that would result from obedience.[49] Instead of suffering negative economic consequences for leaving the gleanings, the landowner would experience positive results. Verse 22 adds further motivation by referring to the Israelites' own experience in Egypt. Since this points implicitly to YHWH's care for his people, to obey the command represents a practical act of *imitatio Dei* (cf. Deut 10:18–19). The placement of the injunction after the general command not to deprive the גֵּר of justice shows that this concerns a basic right of the socially weak, rather than an act of mercy granted by the landowner.[50]

The tripartite law of Deut 24:19–22 finds its closest parallels in Lev 19:9–10 and Lev 23:22, which may be read as on the facing page:[51]

In contradistinction to Deut 24, Lev 19 omits any mention of gleaning in an olive grove, while Lev 23 speaks only about the שָׂדֶה. The Deuteronomic law appears to combine the respective priestly laws, suggesting that the priestly laws preceded the Deuteronomic law. To argue that a Deuteronomic *Vorlage* has been taken over partially at two different points in Leviticus seems less likely. Why would Leviticus draw on a *Vorlage* twice, without elaborating on it, and in two contexts where the reason for the insertion is not transparent?

---

[49] The same motivation is found in Deut 14:29.

[50] Just how far such a stipulation could effectively further the livelihood of the *personae miserae* is a matter of dispute. Based on information provided by the Mishnaic tractate Pe'ah, Joseph D. Amusin, on the one hand, thinks that the combined yield of both gleaning and tithing was rather low; see "Die Gerim in der sozialen Legislatur des Alten Testaments," *Klio* 63 (1981): 17–18. Christoph Bultmann, on the other hand, claims that גֵּרִים and other socially deprived persons were actually able to live on the basis of gleaning and tithing; see *Der Fremde im antiken Juda: Eine Untersuchung zum sozialen Typenbegriff "ger" und seinem Bedeutungswandel in der alttestamentlichen Gesetzgebung*, FRLANT 153 (Göttingen: Vandenhoeck & Ruprecht, 1992), 37–38, 53.

[51] We may assume that Lev 23:22 was taken over directly from Lev 19:9–10 (see Hieke, *Levitikus*, 719; Milgrom, *Leviticus 17–22*, 1624). Baker (*Tight Fists*, 235) suggests that the law is repeated in Lev 23:22 "to teach the people that fulfilling religious obligations by giving to God does not excuse them from fulfilling social obligations to give to the poor." Michael Fishbane surmises that v. 22b may be a demythologizing reinterpration of v. 22a, with the latter being understood as referring to offerings to chthonic spirits. See *Biblical Interpretation in Ancient Israel* (Oxford: Clarendon, 1985), 299n21. However, this interpretation is speculative. According to Otto ("Innerbiblische Exegese," 160, 167), Lev 23:22 involves a quotation from Lev 19:9–10.

Lev 19:9–10

וּבְקֻצְרְכֶם אֶת־קְצִיר אַרְצְכֶם	9 Now when you reap the harvest of your land,
לֹא תְכַלֶּה פְּאַת שָׂדְךָ לִקְצֹר	you shall not reap to the very corners of your field,
וְלֶקֶט קְצִירְךָ לֹא תְלַקֵּט׃	neither shall you gather the gleanings of your harvest.
וְכַרְמְךָ לֹא תְעוֹלֵל	10 Nor shall you glean your vineyard,
וּפֶרֶט כַּרְמְךָ לֹא תְלַקֵּט	nor shall you gather the fallen fruit of your vineyard;
לֶעָנִי וְלַגֵּר תַּעֲזֹב אֹתָם	you shall leave them for the needy and for the stranger.
אֲנִי יְהוָה אֱלֹהֵיכֶם׃	I am the LORD your God.

Lev 23:22

וּבְקֻצְרְכֶם אֶת־קְצִיר אַרְצְכֶם	When you reap the harvest of your land,
לֹא־תְכַלֶּה פְּאַת שָׂדְךָ בְּקֻצְרֶךָ	moreover, you shall not reap to the very corners of your field,
וְלֶקֶט קְצִירְךָ לֹא תְלַקֵּט	nor gather the gleaning of your harvest;
לֶעָנִי וְלַגֵּר תַּעֲזֹב אֹתָם	you are to leave them for the needy and the alien.
אֲנִי יְהוָה אֱלֹהֵיכֶם׃	I am the LORD your God.

Whereas Deuteronomy uses the triad גֵּר, יָתוֹם, and אַלְמָנָה, both Lev 19 and 23 use the pair גֵּר and עָנִי. Furthermore, Deuteronomy also uses the term עָנִי elsewhere. Therefore, the replacement of this term likely reflects a conscious shift in meaning. While Leviticus has in mind a measure aimed at helping the poor, Deuteronomy comes closer to establishing rights for groups of persons who should be protected from poverty.[52] This

[52] See Georg Braulik, "Die dekalogische Redaktion der deuteronomischen Gesetze: Ihre Abhängigkeit von Levitikus 19 am Beispiel von Deuteronomium 22,1–12; 24,10–22 und 25,13–16," in *Bundesdokument und Gesetz: Studien zum Deuteronomium*, ed. Georg Braulik, HBS 4 (Freiburg im Breisgau: Herder, 1995), 18. He also explains Deut 24:19–22 as "eine Reduzierung eines älteren, in Levitikus noch bezeugten Brauches . . . , den man zwar nicht völlig aufgeben wollte, der aber z.B. durch den Drittjahreszehnten (14,28–29) seine wirtschaftliche Bedeutung verloren hatte" (17). Awabdy follows Braulik in proposing that Deut 24:19–22 is part of a

interpretation makes sense especially if one takes into account Deut 15:4–11, which prescribes measures to prevent Israelites from becoming poor.[53] This shift from charity to rights is more easily understood if Deuteronomy represents the later stage in the development of the respective regulations.[54]

Nihan reverses the argument, claiming that Lev 19:9–10 goes further than Deut 24:19–22 in specifying that "the abandonment of the harvest's gleanings and of the vineyard's leftover grapes to the poor and the alien is mandatory, whereas the parallel law of Deut 24:19–22 merely forbade coming back to collect them in case they had been omitted initially."[55] However, nothing in the formulation of the two passages warrants such a contrast. Deuteronomy 24:20–21 envisions occasions when part of the harvest was not unintentionally forgotten.[56] Nihan also claims that the failure of HC to include the גֵּר among the *personae miserae* outside of Lev 19:10 indicates that this verse is dependent on D.[57] However, this is incorrect, since the גֵּר is clearly reckoned among the *personae miserae* in Lev 19:33. Moreover, HC and the priestly laws in general that involve the גֵּר are less interested in issues of social justice than in cultic matters.[58]

Only Deuteronomy attaches reasons to the commands related to God's future blessings, on the one hand, and the addressees' experience in Egypt, on the other. Proposals that assume the priority of Deuteronomy must explain why Leviticus deleted all specific reasons. The lesser degree of specification in Lev 19 (and 23) suggests it is farther removed from a situation in which Israelites are actually dwelling in the land. In addition, specific linguistic features argue for the dependence of Deut 24:19–22 on Lev 19:9–10. Since the combination of the verb קָצַר with the noun קָצִיר is attested elsewhere in HC but nowhere else in Deuteronomy, it is unlikely

program that aims to create a society in which socially vulnerable persons do not become poor (see *Immigrants*, 89)—a program not found in HC.

[53] For more details see Kilchör, *Mosetora*, 294.

[54] Against this background, Cholewiński's claim (*Heiligkeitsgesetz*, 270) that Lev 19:9–10 is later than Deut 24:19–22 because the term עָנִי in Leviticus is broader in meaning than יָתוֹם and אַלְמָנָה in Deuteronomy is weakened. Cholewiński also notes the higher degree of precision in Leviticus with regard to the gleaning process. However, this is not decisive, because Deuteronomy did not view this as particularly important. His final argument, that the concluding formula "I am YHWH" in Leviticus opens a wider horizon than Deuteronomy's motivation based on salvation history, is groundless. In his conclusion, Cholewiński concedes that, while the law in Lev 19:9–10 is much older (i.e., pre-Deuteronomic), only its introduction by the HC redaction is more recent (see *Heiligkeitsgesetz*, 270–71).

[55] Nihan, *From Priestly Torah*, 471; similarly McConville, *Deuteronomy*, 364.

[56] If we treat וְשָׁכַחְתָּ in Deut 24:19 as the first element of the apodosis, then the owner of the field is expected to intentionally "forget," that is, to knowingly leave part of the harvest behind.

[57] See Nihan, *From Priestly Torah*, 471.

[58] See the overview in Zehnder, *Umgang*, 326.

that it is original in Deut 24:19. Furthermore, Lev 19:10 uses the *hapax legomenon* פֶּרֶט, which likewise points to the originality of this text.[59]

As noted previously, Deut 24:19–22 belongs to a larger unit that begins in verse 10. The entire passage concerns the protection of the weak, primarily the economically weak, though verse 17a deals with the judicially weak. Deuteronomy 24:10–22 appears to offer an explanation and extension of Exod 22:20–26[ET 21–27]. The combination of גֵּר with יָתוֹם and אַלְמָנָה in Deut 24:19–21 finds its precedent in Exod 22:20–21[ET 21–22], though the sequence of יָתוֹם and אַלְמָנָה is reversed in Deuteronomy, in line with its normal usage.

Unlike the intertextual connections of Deut 24:19–21 with both CC and Lev 19:9–10/23:22, direct connections between Lev 19:9–10 and 23:22, on the one hand, and between these Leviticus texts and CC, on the other, are lacking. Against this background, Deut 24:19–22 appears to combine Exod 22:20–21[ET 21–22] and Lev 19:9–10/23:22. Furthermore, Lev 19:9–10 makes good sense in its present context, as a bridge between religious (vv. 4–9) and ethical (vv. 12–18) duties.[60] There is no hint that Lev 19:9–10 is compositionally dependent on Deuteronomy.

However, subsequent verses in Lev 19 raise other issues. Leviticus 19:13 parallels Exod 22:21–22[ET 22–23] and 22:25[ET 26] (the prohibition of oppression; the requirement to pay a day laborer on the same day),[61] and Lev 19:15 parallels Exod 22:20–21[ET 21–22] (the prohibition of judicial oppression) in content. Thus, while parallels to one specific passage in CC occur in Lev 19:9–10, 13, and 15, the same contents are found in a more compact form in Deut 24:10–22. If HC were dependent on Deuteronomy, the question arises as to why Leviticus would split up what was concentrated in Deuteronomy and include only select elements found there without clear motivation for omitting others. It is more plausible that Deuteronomy took what was extant in Exodus and Leviticus and formed it into a compact, comprehensive whole.

Leviticus 19:13 is related not only to Exod 22:21–22[ET 22–23] and 22:25[ET 26] but also to Deut 24:14–15 (see Table 6).

---

[59] For similar observations see Braulik, "Die dekalogische Redaktion," 17.

[60] Thus also Milgrom, *Leviticus 17–22*, 1624.

[61] The connection is particularly close between Lev 19:13b and Deut 24:14. In an additional argument, Nihan states that, by including Lev 19:9–10 here and its structural counterpart in Lev 19:23–25, the lawgiver refers to the creation order, which goes beyond Deuteronomy's limited focus on economic measures (see *From Priestly Torah*, 471). However, why one should see hints of a "creational order," as Nihan puts it, remains unclear. The only specific indication Nihan gives is the use of the root ערל, which occurs in both Lev 19:23 and Gen 17:14 (see *From Priestly Torah*, 471n292). Even if one agrees that the creational order is in view here, this difference in perspective indicates neither a chronological sequence nor a direction of dependence.

Table 6

Exod 22:21–22	Lev 19:13	Deut 24:14–15
No oppression (עַנֵּה) of אַלְמָנָה and יָתוֹם	No oppression (עָשַׁק) of neighbor	No oppression (עָשַׁק) of שָׂכִיר, עָנִי, and אֶבְיוֹן, whether a brother or a גֵּר
	payment of the wages of the שָׂכִיר on the same day	payment of the שָׂכָר on the same day, because he is עָנִי
so that they do not cry out to the LORD		so that he does not cry to the LORD

As in the previous cases, the Deuteronomic version of this command is best explained as a combination of earlier versions in CC and HC. Regarding the relationship between Lev 19:13 and Deut 24:14–15, the line of development most likely runs from HC to the Deuteronomic law. The latter clearly expands and clarifies the former by adding a reason (the person to be protected is poor) and a consequence (crying out to YHWH). It also explicitly protects both fellow Israelites and the גֵּרִים.[62] If Lev 19:13 were dependent on Deut 24:14–15, it would be difficult to explain why the noun שָׂכָר was replaced by פְּעֻלָּה, which occurs only here in the Pentateuch, and why the verb לִין was introduced, since it is not found elsewhere in Leviticus. Leviticus 19:13 exhibits clear traits of an original text.[63]

This leads to the following reconstruction: In Deut 24:10–15, the Deuteronomic author first draws on Exod 22:25–26[ET 26–27], reworking these regulations in Deut 24:10–13, and then draws on Lev 19:13, reworking this verse in Deut 24:14–15. Borrowing from Lev 19:13 was not necessarily instigated by the relationship between Lev 19:13 and Exod 22:25[ET 26], but this relationship made the subsequent step easier.[64] The catchword מִשְׁפָּט in Lev 19:15 then led to Deut 24:17a taking up the topic of the just treatment of the גֵּר in the judicial realm.

Exod 22:20 [ET 21] /23:9 and the Protection of the גֵּר in the Judicial Realm

A similar prohibition against oppressing the גֵּר is attested twice in CC, namely, in Exod 22:20 and 23:9. This calls for some explanation. A widespread view attributes the distinctions between these two verses to

[62] For a similar evaluation see Baker, *Tight Fists*, 298; cf. also McConville, *Deuteronomy*, 362. The גֵּר may be *implicitly* in view in Lev 19:13, as well, because the שָׂכִיר may be from the גֵּרִים. This is then made *explicit* in Deuteronomy. Cf. also Milgrom, *Leviticus 17–22*, 1637.

[63] Thus also Braulik, "Die dekalogische Redaktion," 15.

[64] Cf. Kilchör, *Mosetora*, 281.

the different literary contexts in which they are embedded: Whereas Exod 22:20 relates to the general social and especially the economic maltreatment of the גֵּר, Exod 23:9 focuses on the maltreatment of the גֵּר in judicial procedures.[65] However, not only does the use of the verb לָחַץ argue against this view, but also there is no reason to exclude judicial aspects from the oppression mentioned in both Exod 22:20 and 23:9. Although not all the commands in Exod 23:1–9 deal with judicial issues, the literary context points to the problem of justice in court as a major focus of Exod 23:9.[66]

Because of this, this study also needs to take into account passages that speak specifically of the treatment of the גֵּר in the judicial realm. Whether or not such texts occur in the priestly law collections/HC is difficult to determine. A case can be made for Lev 19:33–36, where the injunction to "love" the גֵּר is followed immediately by the prohibition not to do wrong in judgment (בַּמִּשְׁפָּט), in measurement, weight, or capacity:

וְכִי־יָגוּר אִתְּךָ גֵּר בְּאַרְצְכֶם	33 When a stranger resides with you in your land,
לֹא תוֹנוּ אֹתוֹ׃	you shall not do him wrong.
כְּאֶזְרָח מִכֶּם יִהְיֶה לָכֶם הַגֵּר הַגָּר אִתְּכֶם	34 The stranger who resides with you shall be to you as the native among you,
וְאָהַבְתָּ לוֹ כָּמוֹךָ	and you shall love him as yourself;
כִּי־גֵרִים הֱיִיתֶם בְּאֶרֶץ מִצְרָיִם	for you were aliens in the land of Egypt:
אֲנִי יְהוָה אֱלֹהֵיכֶם׃	I am the LORD your God.
לֹא־תַעֲשׂוּ עָוֶל בַּמִּשְׁפָּט	35 You shall do no wrong in judgment,
בַּמִּדָּה בַּמִּשְׁקָל וּבַמְּשׂוּרָה׃	in measurement of weight, or capacity.
מֹאזְנֵי צֶדֶק אַבְנֵי־צֶדֶק אֵיפַת צֶדֶק וְהִין צֶדֶק יִהְיֶה לָכֶם	36 You shall have just balances, just weights, a just ephah, and a just hin:
אֲנִי יְהוָה אֱלֹהֵיכֶם	I am the LORD your God,
אֲשֶׁר־הוֹצֵאתִי אֶתְכֶם מֵאֶרֶץ מִצְרָיִם׃	who brought you out from the land of Egypt.

[65] Thus, e.g., Winfried Thiel, *Die soziale Entwicklung Israels in vorstaatlicher Zeit* (Neukirchen-Vluyn: Neukirchener Verlag, 1980), 155.

[66] For an overview discussion of the problem, see Zehnder, *Umgang*, 316–18.

Since the גֵּר is not explicitly mentioned in verses 35–36, the relationship of these instructions to him is only indirect.[67] Leviticus 19:35 is obviously closely connected with Lev 19:15, repeating the initial words in exactly the same order (לֹא־תַעֲשׂוּ עָוֶל בַּמִּשְׁפָּט).

Deuteronomy also commands just treatment of the גֵּר in the judicial realm in several instances:

Deut 1:16

וָאֲצַוֶּה אֶת־שֹׁפְטֵיכֶם בָּעֵת הַהִוא לֵאמֹר	Then I charged your judges at that time, saying,
שָׁמֹעַ בֵּין־אֲחֵיכֶם	"Hear the cases between your fellow countrymen,
וּשְׁפַטְתֶּם צֶדֶק בֵּין־אִישׁ וּבֵין־אָחִיו	and judge righteously between a man and his fellow countryman,
וּבֵין גֵּרוֹ׃	or the alien who is with him."

Deut 24:17–18

לֹא תַטֶּה מִשְׁפַּט גֵּר יָתוֹם	You shall not pervert the justice due an alien or an orphan,
וְלֹא תַחֲבֹל בֶּגֶד אַלְמָנָה׃	nor take a widow's garment in pledge.
וְזָכַרְתָּ כִּי עֶבֶד הָיִיתָ בְּמִצְרַיִם	But you shall remember that you were a slave in Egypt,
וַיִּפְדְּךָ יְהוָה אֱלֹהֶיךָ מִשָּׁם	and that the LORD your God redeemed you from there;
עַל־כֵּן אָנֹכִי מְצַוְּךָ לַעֲשׂוֹת אֶת־הַדָּבָר הַזֶּה׃	therefore, I am commanding you to do this thing.

Deut 27:19

אָרוּר מַטֶּה מִשְׁפַּט גֵּר־יָתוֹם וְאַלְמָנָה	"Cursed is he who distorts the justice due an alien, orphan, and widow."
וְאָמַר כָּל־הָעָם אָמֵן׃	And all the people shall say, Amen.

[67] Cf. Eckart Otto, who maintains: "Wie in Ex 23,1–9 wird das Verbot, den Fremden zu unterdrücken, mit dem Verbot, Unrecht vor Gericht zu begehen, konkretisiert" ("Das Heiligkeitsgesetz Leviticus 17–26 in der Pentateuchredaktion," in *Altes Testament—Forschung und Wirkung: Festschrift für Henning Graf Reventlow*, ed. Peter Mommer and Winfried Thiel [Frankfurt am Main: Lang, 1994], 70). For him, then, there is no doubt about the גֵּר being the main beneficiary of the prohibition of Lev 19:35–36.

How do these passages in three law collections dealing with the protection of the גֵּר in the judicial realm relate to each other?[68] To begin with, Deut 1:16 is not comparable to Exod 22:20[ET 21]/23:9, because it lacks overlapping terminology and stands outside the Deuteronomic law collection proper, which highlights that it is different in character from the other texts dealing with the same topic listed above. This leaves us with Deut 24:17–18 and Deut 27:19, as far as Deuteronomy is concerned. Since the latter seems to be directly depe ndent on the former, we may restrict our investigation to Deut 24:17–18.

As indicated above, this passage forms part of a larger literary context that parallels Exod 22:20–26[ET 21–27]. We may understand Deut 24:17–18 as an explanation of Exod 22:20–21[ET 21–22], interpreting the prohibition not to oppress גֵּר, widow, and orphan first with respect to justice in court and then with respect to the social question of pledged clothing, which also links with Exod 22:25[ET 26].[69] At the same time, a close connection also exists with Exod 23:6:

לֹא תַטֶּה מִשְׁפַּט אֶבְיֹנְךָ בְּרִיבוֹ׃	You shall not pervert the justice due to your needy brother in his dispute.

Regarding the specific connection between Exod 23:6 and Deut 24:17, the Deuteronomic lawgiver seeks not only to protect the poor, but also more generally to prevent persons from falling into poverty in the first place.[70]

In theory, the direction of influence may run from Deuteronomy to Exodus. However, this is improbable, because it is difficult to explain why the author(s) of CC in Exod 22:20–21[ET 21–22] changed the sequence גֵּר–orphan–widow to גֵּר–widow–orphan. In contrast, if a Deuteronomic author used CC as a source, we may easily explain this change as an assimilation to the sequence that is always used elsewhere in Deuteronomy.[71]

The issues become more complex if Lev 19:35–36 also involves the גֵּר. As seen above, Lev 19:35–36 relates judicial wrongdoing to false measurements, which direct us again to the socioeconomic realm. Exodus

---

[68] The phrase לֹא־תַטֶּה מִשְׁפָּט is also found in Deut 16:19 but without reference to the גֵּר.

[69] In this case, there is a direct lexical correspondance with the use of the verb חָבַל ("to take a pledge") followed by שַׂלְמָה in Exod 22:25 and בֶּגֶד in Deut 24:17.

[70] Cf. Kilchör, *Mosetora*, 291–92. We can detect the same principle in relation to Lev 9:9–10, where only the גֵּר and the עָנִי are protected, and Deut 23:20[ET 19], where the prohibition against taking interest seeks to protect all Israelites—not only the עָנִי, as in Exod 22:24[ET 25].

[71] See Deut 14:29; 16:11, 14; 24:19–21; 26:12–13; 27:19. Deuteronomy 10:18 preserves the sequence orphan–widow as well, but mentions the גֵּר last rather than first.

22:20[ET 21]/23:9 and Lev 19:33–36 also share content; both texts address both judicial and socioeconomic questions. The main difference is that Lev 19 makes the judicial aspect explicit and complements its prohibition not to oppress the גֵּר with a positive command to love him, suggesting a sequence CC–Lev 19.

Deuteronomy 25:13–16 also involves false measurement, though it is disconnected from court justice and fails to mention the גֵּר. This likely indicates a splitting of topics dealt with in other law collections, which often happens in Deuteronomy. While this can be explained more easily if Deuteronomy follows Leviticus rather than the other way around, three additional more specific reasons point in the same direction. First, Deuteronomy (in 24:17) makes clear that the protection of the גֵּר also relates to the judicial realm, a point left ambiguous in Lev 19. Second, the combination of the verb עָשָׂה with the noun עָוֶל is more at home in Lev 19:15, 35 than in Deut 25:16.[72] Whereas in Lev 19 the phrase לֹא־תַעֲשׂוּ עָוֶל בַּמִּשְׁפָּט is fundamental to the respective commands, the phrase כֹּל עֹשֵׂה עָוֶל at the end of Deut 25:16 is expendable, since it adds nothing new to the combination of תּוֹעֵבָה and כֹּל עֹשֵׂה עָוֶל. This may indicate that the Deuteronomic author is familiar with the literary formulation now found in Lev 19:15, 35 (or some similar version). Third, Lev 19 does not differentiate between protected persons like Deut 24:17 and Exod 22:20–21[ET 21–22] do; Lev 19:34 mentions only the גֵּר, and Lev 19:15 only refers to the עָמִית.[73] It is unlikely that the less specific version represents the last step in the development of these regulations.[74]

---

[72] Leviticus 19:35 is structurally parallel to Lev 19:15 (thus also Nihan, *From Priestly Torah*, 464; cf. Braulik, "Die dekalogische Redaktion," 20).

[73] A differentiation is also made between דָּל and גָּדוֹל, but this is not on the same level as גֵּר, יָתוֹם, and אַלְמָנָה.

[74] Nihan (*From Priestly Torah*, 476) claims that the addition of the measure "hin" in Lev 19:36 indicates that Lev 19 presupposes and postdates Deut 25. This argument is already found in Cholewiński (*Heiligkeitsgesetz*, 278), who also observes that מאזְנֵים (balances) in Lev 19:36 has no parallel in Deut 25. However, an additional element does not automatically prove a later date. The "hin" (as well as the "balances") could easily be viewed as devoid of any independent information by a later editor and therefore dispensable. Cholewiński (*Heiligkeitsgesetz*, 278) rightly also claims that Lev 19:35–36 has a broader, more general outlook than Deut 25:13–16. However, this does not argue for the dependence of HC on Deuteronomy, because it ignores the fact that Deuteronomy contains other passages that are related to Lev 19:35–36.

According to Otto ("Innerbiblische Exegese," 147–48), Lev 19:15 takes up Exod 23:3, 6 and corrects the "Fortschreibung" of Exod 23:6, 8 found in Deut 16:18–19. While the Deuteronomic law focuses on the protection of the weak, HC widens the perspective by prohibiting an unjustified special treatment of both the strong and the weak. This argumentation, however, overlooks the fact that Deuteronomy takes up the question of proper justice elsewhere, where the focus

Two additional observations concerning the relationship between Lev 19:35–36 and Deut 25:13–16 reinforce the view that Lev 19 antedates Deuteronomy.[75] In contrast to Lev 19, where verse 15 prepares for verse 35a and the final colon of verse 34 prepares for the first part of the second colon of verse 36, there are no thematic or literary connections between Deut 25:13–16 and its context. Although common in priestly language, the noun עָוֶל is not characteristic of Deuteronomy.[76] Moreover, Lev 19:35–36a is closely connected to the two preceding verses: the topics of abusive court proceedings (relating to business dealings) and false weights and measures offer concrete examples of how a גֵּר could be mistreated.[77]

Nothing in the specific linguistic shape of Exod 22:20[ET 21] (//23:9), Lev 19:35–36, and Deut 24:17 points to a direct literary dependence in any direction. A close lexical relationship exists only between Lev 19:33b and Exod 22:20[ET 21]. The relationship of these three legal texts to the judicial realm is schematically summarized below:

Table 7

Exod 22:20[ET 21] (//23:9)	Lev 19:35–36	Deut 24:17 and 27:19
general protection of the גֵּר in court	specific protection of the גֵּר in court	general protection of the גֵּר in court
	related to right measurements	(right measurement in Deut 25:13–16)

is not merely on the protection of the weak. It also ignores the possibility that the author(s) of Deuteronomy in certain cases deemed it unnecessary to repeat a preexistent regulation. Otto (pp. 148–49) also claims that the sequence in Lev 19:33–36 reflects the redactor of H first taking up Exod 23:1–9 (in vv. 33–34; v. 33 relates directly to Exod 23:9, and v. 34 links with Exod 23:4–5) and then Deut 25:13–16 (in vv. 35–36). This reasoning is questionable. Why would the redactor of H change the wording of his sources this way? And how do the Deuteronomic texts that also deal with the prohibition against oppressing the גֵּר (and other weak persons), as well as the command in Deut 10:19 to love the גֵּר, fit into this picture?

[75] For further arguments see Braulik, "Die dekalogische Redaktion," 19–22.

[76] The term "priestly" here includes the book of Ezekiel, which contains the highest density of the use of this noun in the Hebrew Bible. In Deuteronomy the term is attested only in 32:4, where it occurs in the context of describing YHWH as a God without iniquity.

[77] Thus also Milgrom, *Leviticus 17–22*, 1708.

The Overall Network of Relationships among the Texts Referring to the Love and Protection of the גֵּר

We may summarize as follows the connections discussed above between Exod 22:20[ET 21] (// 23:9) and its literary context, on the one hand, and related texts in other law collections in the Hebrew Bible, on the other, as well as between the love-command in Deut 10:19 and the passages to which it is related:[78]

Table 8

Topic	CC	HC	DC	Deut
General prohibition of oppression of the גֵּר	Exod 22:20 [ET 21] (Exod 23:9)	Lev 19:33		
General prohibition of oppression of a subgroup of the גֵּר		(Lev 19:13)	Deut 24:14 Deut 23:17 [ET 16]	Deut 1:16
Specific protection of a subgroup of the גֵּר related to extradition			Deut 23:16 [ET 15]	
Prompt payment of wages to the גֵּר or subgroup of the גֵּר		(Lev 19:13)	Deut 24:14	
Economic support of the גֵּר		Lev 19:9–10 Lev 23:22	Deut 24:19–21	
Crying out to YHWH by the גֵּר or by a subgroup of the גֵּר	Exod 22:21–22 [ET 22–23]		Deut 24:15	

[78] Whether one begins with Exod 22:20[ET 21] or Deut 10:19 is inconsequential. Texts explicitly *or* implicitly relating to the גֵּר are considered. I include in the last row a case regulating the treatment of the נָכְרִי instead of the גֵּר because of the close literary relationship of the regulation in Exod 22:24[ET 25] to Exod 22:20.

General protection of the גֵּר in court	(Exod 22:20) [ET 21] Exod 23:9		Deut 24:17 Deut 27:19	
Specific protection of the גֵּר in court related to honest measures		Lev 19:35–36	(Deut 25:13–16)	
Love of the גֵּר		Lev 19:34		Deut 10:19
Prohibition of charging a fellow Israelite interest ——— ——— Allowance of charging נָכְרִי interest	Exod 22:24 [ET 25] (prohibition only)	Lev 25:35–37 (prohibition only)	Deut 23:20–21 [ET 19–20] (prohibition) ——— ——— Deut 23:21 [ET 20] (allowance)	

We may now summarize the overall picture. The closest linguistic parallels exist between Exod 22:20[ET 21] and Lev 19:33b and between Lev 19:34 and Deut 10:19. In principle, Lev 19:33–34 could serve either as an intermediate "bridge" between Exod 22:20[ET 21] and Deut 10:19 and Deut 23:17/24:14, or as an "heir" to both Exod 22:20[ET 21] and the Deuteronomic texts. The analysis presented above demonstrates that the first option is preferable. Generally, HC is more restrained than Deuteronomy in elaborating topics found in CC. Whereas Deuteronomy often seems to depend on CC and sometimes also on HC, the direction of dependence between Deuteronomy and HC is never clearly in the inverse order. In many cases, CC evidently functions as a kind of "root" that is complemented by more comprehensive passages in other law collections.

These limited observations preclude broader conclusions about the relationship between CC, HC, and Deuteronomy. Because of the special nature of the position of Lev 19 (and Lev 25) within the broader literary context of HC and the priestly laws,[79] a logical or chronological priority

[79] Leviticus 19 stands out as a legal summary formally set apart from its context by the constant repetition of the formula "I am YHWH your God." This raises questions regarding the chapter's literary-critical position within HC. Cf., e.g., David T. Stewart, "Leviticus 19 as Mini-Torah," in *Current Issues in Priestly and Related Literature: The Legacy of Jacob Milgrom and Beyond*, ed. Roy E. Gane and Ada Taggar-Cohen, RBS 82 (Atlanta: SBL Press, 2015), 299–323. On the special literary position of Lev 25, see, e.g., Baruch A. Levine, "Late Language in the

of Lev 19 (and 25) over Deuteronomy need not apply to HC as a whole.[80] That a segment of Deut 10 is part of the web of connections binding Exod 22, Lev 19, and Deut 24 cautions against an overly strict separation between the law collection proper in Deuteronomy (chapters 12–26/28) and the rest of the book, or at least chapters 5–11.[81]

Conclusion

Attested twice in the Pentateuch, literarily the command to love the גֵּר is tightly connected to other commands related to the גֵּר. We may view it as a "crown" or climax in biblical legal instructions on the relationship between Israelites and aliens, both structurally and in terms of content. In both HC and Deuteronomy this kind of love represents perhaps the loftiest command in the realm of interpersonal relationships. The fact that it is embedded in contexts that assert YHWH's love for both Israel and the גֵּר and is complemented by the command to love YHWH only in Deuteronomy, in contradistinction to HC, likely supports the temporal sequence HC–Deuteronomy. However, because only HC explicitly formulates a command to love one's neighbor before it issues a similar command to love the גֵּר, we may conclude that Deuteronomy does not intend to replace HC, but rather to complement it.

This last observation deserves an additional comment. Based on the relationships of the laws examined in this study, arguments for the replacement theory are not compelling; rather, the composers of the laws intended them to be read alongside each other. This applies especially to the relationship between HC and CC. Although the issues are somewhat more complex with Deuteronomy, in most cases Deuteronomy appears to update and complement rather than replace preexistent laws. Further-

Priestly Source: Some Literary and Historical Observations," in *Proceedings of the Eighth World Congress of Jewish Studies* (Jerusalem: World Union of Jewish Studies, 1983), 69–82. Focusing on the גֵּר, it is striking that the noun is consistently combined with תּוֹשָׁב in Lev 25, a phenomenon that occurs elsewhere within the biblical law collections only in Num 35:15.

[80] In each instance in the law collections we should also check whether the texts in question (or parts of them) are integral to and an original part of their immediate literary contexts. However, in the absence of unequivocal signs (that were not detected in our treatment of the passages under investigation in this study), we must be wary of circular or subjective arguments for literary-critical dissection.

[81] For a similar caution against reading chapters 12–26/28 in isolation from chapters 5–11, see Daniel I. Block, "Deuteronomic Law," in *The Oxford Encyclopedia of the Bible and Law,* ed. Brent Strawn (Oxford: Oxford University Press, 2015), 182–84.

more, in general the relationship between later and earlier regulations cannot be described in terms of simple copying, even in cases where there is strong continuity between the respective laws.

Some Additional Observations

First, it is clear that both in the law collection proper found in chapters 12–26/28 and outside of it, Deuteronomy presents a more differentiated classification of aliens and foreigners than HC. Besides the גֵּר, Deuteronomy mentions the נָכְרִי and a series of specific ethnic groups: the various peoples of Canaan, the Amalekites, Egyptians, Edomites, Moabites, and Ammonites. This differs from HC, where only the נָכְרִי has its analogue in the בֶּן־נֵכָר. This may indicate that Deuteronomy represents a later, more advanced stage in the development of the regulations concerning aliens and foreigners.

Second, the fact that aliens/foreigners play a larger role and even appear within the boundaries of Israel in the curses contained in Deut 28, in contrast to Lev 26, may also suggest that Deuteronomy represents a later stage than HC.

Third, a final observation regarding the relative sequence of the law collections concerns the thematic overlap or lack thereof between CC, HC, and the Deuteronomic laws or Deuteronomy in general, both with respect to aliens or foreigners, and where this focus is lacking. Here are the findings:[82]

Relatively few laws in CC find no echo in HC and Deuteronomy. The amount of overlap between CC and Deuteronomy surpasses the overlap between CC and HC by a ratio of three to two.

The Deuteronomic laws contain a relatively large quantity of *Sondergut* (i.e., "unique material"), involving roughly one-third of the regulations. Parallels with both CC and HC are found in about one-third of all cases respectively. However, only 10 of 90 cases exhibit overlap with both CC and HC.

Roughly one-fourth of the laws in HC overlap with CC, while the overlap with regulations in Deuteronomy exceeds one-half of the laws. If we exclude Lev 19, the amount of overlap with CC drops to slightly less than one-fifth.

It seems best to account for these statistical figures by viewing Deuteronomy as the final, most elaborate law collection; it apparently makes use of the other two.

---

[82] The statistics are based on a comprehensive unpublished classification that I have created of the biblical laws contained in the various law collections.

CHAPTER 8

The Cult in Deuteronomy and Its Relationship to the Book of the Covenant and the Holiness Code

Richard E. Averbeck

As is well known, there are three major parallel units of law in the Torah. They are commonly referred to as: (1) the Covenant Code, or Book of the Covenant (Exod 21–23), (2) the Holiness Code (Lev 18–26, or 17–27; see the discussion below), and (3) the Deuteronomic Code (Deut 12–26).[1] The focus of this essay is on the relationships between these three parallel units of law and, in particular, the cultic regulations in Deuteronomy as compared to those in Exodus and Leviticus. There are cultic regulations in all three units, but none of them focuses on the cult to the same degree and in the same way as the tabernacle, sacrificial, and purity regulations of Exod 25–Lev 16, the so-called Priestly Code. Although there are a few exceptions, most of the shorter units of cultic regulations embedded in the Numbers narrative are similar and supplementary to those in the Priestly Code (e.g., the festival offering regulations in Num 28–29, cf. Lev 23; the vow regulations in Num 30, cf. Lev 27).

Strictly speaking, "Torah" means "instruction," and instruction is done in the Torah in a variety of ways and from diverse perspectives. In general terms, for example, the narrative genre instructs, but it does so in a very different way from genealogy, itinerary, poetry, or law. Similarly, the various law collections mentioned above are also of different types and look at things from different perspectives. The Covenant Code views Moses as the legislative and judicial mediator of YHWH's covenant law to Israel (see the narrative context of Exod 19–24; cf. also Exod 18).[2] Moses'

[1] Some scholars object to the use of "Code" in these expressions because to them it suggests a kind of comprehensive system of law. They would prefer something like "Collection," which has no such implications. I use the term "Code" in this essay only as a convention.

[2] On the compositional features of the Exod 19–24 covenant-making narrative see now Richard E. Averbeck, "Pentateuchal Criticism and the Priestly Torah," in *Do Historical Matters Matter for Faith: A Critical Appraisal of Modern and Postmodern*

priestly role begins to emerge in Exod 24:1–11 at the ratification of the covenant, and in the Priestly Code of Exod 25–Lev 16 he is the one who directs the construction of the tabernacle and actually serves as the priest who ordains Aaron and his sons to function as the priestly family (see Exod 40 and Lev 8). The regulations in the Priestly Code are written from the perspective of the priests standing inside the tabernacle looking out toward the community. By way of contrast, in the Holiness Code the perspective is generally priestly, but in this case the standpoint is out in the community looking in at the tabernacle rather than the other way around. The focus is on community holiness and purity rather than tabernacle holiness and purity, as in the Priestly Code.

General Approaches to Deuteronomy

Deuteronomy is another matter altogether. There are diachronic considerations, of course, even without the support of any historical-critical reconstructions. According to the narrative of the Pentateuch as it stands, a great deal had taken place since Israel's time at Sinai about forty years earlier, including the long years of wandering in the wilderness and the passing away of the first generation of men of war (Num 1:45–46; 14:29; Deut 2:14–15). The new day called for Moses to expound the law (Deut 1:5), but now to a new second generation facing essentially the same challenges of faith, obedience, and perseverance as the first. Moses' posture also changed with the new time and the shift in historical situation. Here he stood outside the priestly system and perspective, looking at the people as a whole from a prophetic rather than a priestly point of view, exhorting them to live according to the covenant, in obedience to the law (see, e.g., Deut 18:15, "a prophet like me," i.e., Moses; Deut 34:10, "Since then, no prophet has risen in Israel like Moses, whom the LORD knew face to face").[3] Thus, Deuteronomy shows little interest in how the priests and people should practice their faith inside the tabernacle. That was the main concern of the earlier Priestly Code. In Deuteronomy, therefore, there are no instructions for how one should present various kinds of offerings (cf. Lev 1–5), for example, but there is a great deal of concern over the presenting of them to YHWH alone, and only at the place where YHWH has placed his name, after Israel had entered, conquered, occu-

---

Approaches to the Bible, ed. James K. Hoffmeier and Dennis R. Magary (Wheaton, IL: Crossway, 2012), 159–79, and the literature cited there.

[3] Unless otherwise noted, translations are from the New International Version (2011 edition).

pied, and found rest in the land.[4] We will return to this point below as an essential part of this essay.

This way of reading Deuteronomy is dependent, of course, on the validity of the biblical storyline. Those who take this storyline seriously generally explain the differences between Deuteronomy and the other "codes" according to the new historical circumstances of the people, as outlined above, along with Moses' prophetic rather than priestly standpoint. Already at the beginning of the nineteenth century, however, Wilhelm Martin Leberecht de Wette argued for linking the composition of Deuteronomy to the reforms of Josiah in the middle of the first millennium BCE rather than to the second millennium, and three-quarters of a century later Julius Wellhausen followed him without question or hesitation.[5] Since then, many others have followed this long-standing higher-critical consensus and have expanded the scope of time for its compositional stages to anywhere from between the eighth century (before the exile) to the exilic or postexilic periods, depending on literary-critical analysis and the rationale proposed for Deuteronomy's supposedly diverse theological emphases.

On the one hand, from a religious point of view, most have understood Deuteronomy to contain the theological rationale for the purifying and centralizing reforms of Hezekiah (late eighth century; 2 Kgs 18:1–6; 2 Chr 29–31) and/or Josiah (late seventh century; 2 Kgs 22–23; 2 Chr 34–35). On the other hand, from a political point of view, many have also argued that Deuteronomy was composed as a polemic against Assyrian imperial dominance in order to promote submission to YHWH, Israel's God, as its sovereign king. Others have argued that Deuteronomy was

[4] In his monograph, Benjamin Kilchör works through the details and shows how Deut 12 and other chapters in Deuteronomy resonate with various passages in Exodus through Numbers, even some of the laws in the Priestly Code (Benjamin Kilchör, *Masetora und Jahwetora: Das Verhältnis von Deuteronomium 12–26 zu Exodus, Levitikus und Numeri*, BZABR 21 [Wiesbaden: Harrassowitz, 2015], esp. 71–95, 309–32 for Deut 12). I will not review all that material here but will focus instead on how the altar and slaughter laws at the beginning of the Deuteronomic Code in Deut 12 relate to the parallel passages at the beginning of the Covenant Code in Exod 20:24–26 and the Holiness Code in Lev 17:1–8.

[5] See the review of the history of scholarship in Julius Wellhausen, *Prolegomena to the History of Israel* (Edinburgh: A. & C. Black, 1885; repr., Atlanta: Scholars Press, 1994), 4–9. For a relatively recent complete review and critique of this position, see Eugene H. Merrill, "Deuteronomy and de Wette: A Fresh Look at a Fallacious Premise," *JESOT* 1 (2012): 25–42. A careful look at the history of scholarship will show that de Wette was not the first to suggest this general approach to the date and composition of Deuteronomy, but he did indeed establish it as the basic starting point for the proposed relative chronology of the sources of the Pentateuch.

composed during or even after the Babylonian exile in response to the loss of the land, setting the agenda for the postexilic restoration.[6]

Regardless, according to this overall approach to the date and composition of Deuteronomy, the centralization of worship "in the place the LORD your God will choose" (Deut 12:5, 11) is a masked reference to Jerusalem, and Moses had nothing to do with writing Deuteronomy. Some date P and H before Deuteronomy, in which case the cultic centralization in Deut 12 is nothing new, in light of the regulation in Lev 17.[7] Others take the standard critical position, in which P and H are later than Deuteronomy, making the centralization of worship in Deut 12 an innovation that was either assumed or confirmed later by H in Lev 17.

Cultic Worship and Profane Slaughter in Deut 12

The issue of the centralization of altar worship as called for in Deut 12 is a key feature of the cult in Deuteronomic law. In calling for exclusively Yahwistic altar worship, of course, Deuteronomy agrees with the Sinai regulations (compare Deut 12:1–14, 17–18, 26–27 with Exod 20:22–26 and Lev 17:1–9, in particular). Deuteronomy 12:5–14, 17–19, 26–27, however, demands that when they occupy the promised land the Israelites must carry out their exclusive Yahwistic altar worship only at the one place that YHWH will choose among all their tribes. Most agree that this regulation differs from Exod 20:24–25, which instructs them to construct sacrificial altars of packed earth or uncut stones "in every place where I cause my name to be remembered" (v. 24). Therefore Exod 20 allows for multiple solitary sacrificial altars, while Deut 12 does not. Furthermore, on the one hand, Deut 12:15–16, 20–25 allows for the nonsacrificial slaughter of domestic animals anywhere in the land, as long as the Israelites pour the blood out on the ground like water, as they would do with the blood of wild game. On the other hand, Lev 17:1–9 allows the

---

[6] For a very helpful review of the historical-critical debate over the date and composition, with references to specific internal evidence, see Jeffrey H. Tigay, *Deuteronomy*, דברים (Philadelphia: Jewish Publication Society of America, 1996), xix–xxiv. See also Jack R. Lundbom, *Deuteronomy: A Commentary* (Grand Rapids: Eerdmans, 2013), 6–21; and J. G. McConville, *Deuteronomy*, ApOTC (Downers Grove, IL: InterVarsity Press, 2002), 21–33. Most recently, see the helpful review of some of these major issues in Bill T. Arnold, "Israelite Worship as Envisioned and Prescribed in Deuteronomy 12," *ZABR* 22 (2016): 161–75, in which he critiques Moshe Weinfeld's treatment of Deuteronomy as a text driven by a demythologizing and secularizing agenda.

[7] See, e.g., Jacob Milgrom, *Leviticus 1–16*, AB 3 (New York: Doubleday, 1991), 28–29, 713–18.

Israelites to slaughter their domestic animals for meat only at the central sanctuary, so that they would not offer them to the "goat demons" in the wilderness (Lev 17:7).

So there are at least two major issues at hand. First, with regard to the relationship between the Book of the Covenant and the law in Deuteronomy, Exod 20 allows for multiple Yahwistic solitary sacrificial altars, while Deut 12 calls for only one sacrificial altar at a single central place of worship. Second, with regard to the relationship between the Holiness Code and Deuteronomy, Lev 17 calls for the slaughter of domestic animals for eating meat only at the central tabernacle altar, while Deut 12 allows for such slaughter anywhere in the land, as long as it is non-sacrificial slaughter and the blood is handled properly.[8] Deuteronomy 12:20–25 clarifies the rationale for the non-sacrificial slaughter. When God had enlarged their territory (v. 20) so that some of the people lived too far away from the central place to slaughter their meat there for regular meals, they could slaughter domestic animals non-sacrificially. It was still a solemn occasion marked by pouring the blood out on the ground like water (vv. 23–24), but it did not rise to the level of sacrificial slaughter, which would require that the blood be poured out on the altar at the central place (v. 27). Both of these issues require further examination below. Before that, however, there is the question of the unity of Deut 12.

Structure and Compositional Unity

Although there are variations, many scholars divide Deut 12 into four major units (vv. 2–7, 8–12, 13–19, and 20–28).[9] Some argue that the repetitions of similar expressions in the chapter (see, e.g., the place YHWH chooses or puts his name in vv. 5, 11, 14, 18, 21, 26) and the shift from second-person plural to second-person singular pronouns at verse 13 reflect different strata of tradition and stages of redaction.[10] Bernard Levinson, for example, divides the main substance of the chapter into five units with a chiastic structure:

---

[8] For the rationale of including Lev 17 in the Holiness Code, see Richard E. Averbeck, "The Egyptian Sojourn and Deliverance from Slavery in the Framing and Shaping of the Mosaic Law," in *"Did I Not Bring Israel Out of Egypt?": Biblical, Archaeological, and Egyptological Perspectives on the Exodus Narratives*, ed. James Hoffmeier, Alan Millard, and Gary Rendsburg, *BBRSup* 13 (Winona Lake, IN: Eisenbrauns, 2016), 150–51n15.

[9] For an earlier treatment of some of the details of Deut 12, see Richard E. Averbeck, "מזבח altar," in *NIDOTTE* 2:895–97.

[10] See the extensive discussion and the literature cited in Bernard M. Levinson, *Deuteronomy and the Hermeneutics of Legal Innovation* (New York: Oxford University Press, 1997), 23–28.

A 12:2–7 Cultic purification and centralization (plural)

B 12:8–12 *Temporal* condition for centralization (plural)

C 12:13–19 Centralization and secular slaughter (singular)

B′ 12:20–28 *Geographical* condition for slaughter (singular)

A′ 12:29–31 Conclusion: Cultic purification (singular)[11]

Levinson follows the common view in supposing that Deut 12:13–19 (the center of the chiasm) is the oldest stratum since it is in the singular, although he doubts that the diachronic development of the chapter can be fully discerned.[12] Others deny the adequacy of these criteria and argue for a relatively synchronic reading of the chapter.[13] Gordon McConville, for example, is fully aware of the repetitions, but he regards them as synchronic rhetorical elaborations rather than marks of compositional strata that were redacted together at a later time.[14]

The battle continues to rage over the (dis)unity of this chapter. For instance, Levinson argues that those who read the chapter synchronically "fail to do justice to the degree of philological difficulty in the chapter."[15] According to him, they cannot take full account of the redundant nature of the chapter along with the shift from plural to singular at Deut 12:13. Furthermore, they ignore the fact that the recognized structural coherence of the chapter may just as well have been imposed on it by the processes of redaction as it could have been an original compositional unity. McConville, in turn, follows Norbert Lohfink when he points out that verses 13–19 cannot be deemed a coherent altar law because they refer only to "your burnt offerings" (עֹלֹתֶיךָ; v. 13). There is no reference to "your sacrifices" (זְבָחֶיךָ) in the entire unit. How could such a tradition be anything but confusing? Are "sacrifices" abolished as part of altar worship?[16]

In light of the fact that the Deuteronomic law is by nature expository (see Deut 1:5, "Moses undertook to explain the law," and the sermonic character and structure of the book as a whole), the repetitions do not

---

[11] Adapted from Levinson, *Legal Innovation*, 25. He also includes v. 1 in his analysis as a superscription, as does McConville, *Deuteronomy*, 213.

[12] Levinson, *Legal Innovation*, 26, 28. See also, e.g., Gerhard von Rad, *Deuteronomy: A Commentary*, OTL (Philadelphia: Westminster, 1966), 92.

[13] See, e.g., the remarks and literature cited in Tigay, *Deuteronomy*, 364n3; and Levinson, *Legal Innovation*, 27n12.

[14] McConville, *Deuteronomy*, 214–16. See also his earlier, more detailed discussion in J. G. McConville, *Law and Theology in Deuteronomy*, JSOTSup 33 (Sheffield: JSOT Press, 1984), 58–67.

[15] Levinson, *Legal Innovation*, 27.

[16] McConville, *Deuteronomy*, 215.

seem problematic. Levinson himself admits this. However, he sees the combination of the redundancy and the shift from plural to singular at verse 13 as being lethal for any synchronic reading of this chapter. In my view, such a claim is unjustified. It is not as if such shifts occur erratically back and forth throughout the chapter. The main substance of the chapter actually falls into two large sections according to this shift in number. Moreover, the rhetorical effect of the shift to the singular would or could have served to highlight the move away from national, corporate, centralized altar worship to local, non-centralized, non-sacrificial eating of meat and the individual, familial, and communal responsibility for pouring out the blood on the ground.

According to Levinson's own analysis, the singular stretches across the boundaries of the three final units and the plural across the first two (see his chiastic structure cited above). This makes the shift from plural to singular appear to be intentional and, therefore, original to the composition of the chapter. The first two (plural) units of Levinson's chiasm make good sense as a larger section. The commands in Deuteronomy 12:2–7 belong together. Verses 2–3 command the Israelites to eliminate everything that belongs to the Canaanite worship system when they come to live in the land. Verse 4 (לֹא־תַעֲשׂוּן כֵּן לַיהוָה אֱלֹהֵיכֶם, "you must not do thus for the LORD your God") refers back to verses 2–3 and binds them forward to the commands in verses 5–7 (beginning with כִּי אִם, "but") to worship YHWH exclusively and only in the one place that YHWH himself would choose amid all their tribes.

Similarly, the commands in Deut 12:8–12 belong together, and these verses expand on verses 5–7 much like verses 5–7 expand on verses 2–3. Like verse 4, this section begins with "You must not (לֹא־תַעֲשׂוּן) . . ." (v. 8a). Thus, verses 4–7 tell the Israelites that they must not worship the way the Canaanites do, while verses 8–12 command them not to worship the way they were worshipping when they were on the plains of Moab, "every man [doing] all that is right in his own eyes" (אִישׁ כָּל־הַיָּשָׁר בְּעֵינָיו, v. 8b; see more on this below). Instead, when they enter and occupy and, most importantly, when YHWH "gives you rest from all your enemies all around and you dwell securely" (וְהֵנִיחַ לָכֶם מִכָּל־אֹיְבֵיכֶם מִסָּבִיב וִישַׁבְתֶּם־בֶּטַח), then they are to do what was commanded in verses 5–7—namely, worship YHWH exclusively and only in the one place that YHWH himself would choose amid all their tribes (vv. 11–12). Thus, one step leads to the next and, similarly, all the way through the chapter (see presently).

Deuteronomy 12:13–19 is the center of the chiasm and the first unit in the chapter to use second-person singular forms. It is often considered the oldest stratum of the chapter by those who read it diachronically (recall the discussion above). This is where non-sacrificial slaughter is first introduced in the chapter, which is likely the reason for the shift from plural to singular pronouns as well. It is addressed to family heads and community leaders in their "gates" (v. 15). Non-sacrificial slaughter is a matter of individual prerogative in their homes and communities, not religious unity of the nation through exclusively Yahwistic worship. Verses 13–14 reiterate the call for centralized corporate worship found in the previous units (see vv. 5–7 and, similarly, vv. 11–12). But here it is in abbreviated form, mentioning only burnt offerings, without peace offering sacrifices or any other features of the worship system (v. 13, הִשָּׁמֶר לְךָ פֶּן־תַּעֲלֶה עֹלֹתֶיךָ בְּכָל־מָקוֹם אֲשֶׁר תִּרְאֶה, "Be careful lest you offer up your burnt offerings in any place you see"). Verses 17–19 come back again to centralized worship and list many of the other kinds of tithes and offerings, but again without peace offering sacrifices (זְבָחִים).

The middle of the unit (vv. 15–16) begins with the limiting (restrictive) particle "only" (רַק, v. 15a), which binds verse 15 back to verses 13–14 as a restriction on the call for centralized worship, allowing for the local non-sacrificial slaughter of domestic animals.[17] The same limiting particle at the beginning of verse 16, in turn, binds it back to verse 15 as a restriction on how the Israelites should eat such meat. They must not eat the blood of the animal but should pour it out on the ground like water. It is of special interest that the verb used for "slaughter" in verse 15 is זָבַח (cf. also v. 21, discussed below), which is almost always used for making "sacrifice(s)" at an altar and is cognate to the noun זְבָחִים/זֶבַח, "sacrifice(s)," used elsewhere in the chapter. The latter term is paired with עֹלוֹת/עֹלָה, "burnt offering(s)," in verses 6, 11, and 27, but, as noted above, it is not paired with "burnt offerings" in the current unit (v. 13).

This use of זָבַח has been noted and discussed by scholars and will be treated in more detail below. What is important at this point in the discussion is to note that the root זבח is reserved here for the slaughter of domestic animals to be eaten at a local family or community gathering, not in the worship of YHWH at the central sanctuary. In the latter case, the blood must be poured out on the altar rather than on the ground (cf. v. 27). This would include, for example, the three annual festivals mentioned in Deut 16 as well as the occasions when individuals or families would visit the central sanctuary for the purpose of sacrificial worship (see, e.g., Elkanah with his family in 1 Sam 1). But these were not the only occasions on which they could eat meat, and that is the main point of the regulations in verses 15–16. Since it was non-sacrificial meat, both the unclean and clean could eat it (v. 15).

Deuteronomy 12:20–28 makes the reason for non-sacrificial slaughter explicit. It is a matter of simple logistics. When YHWH gives the Israelites

---

[17] See also the remarks to this same effect in Michael Fishbane, *Biblical Interpretation in Ancient Israel* (Oxford: Clarendon, 1985), 533.

full possession of the land, many of them will live too far away from the central sanctuary to slaughter meat there and then eat it at home. Here the rationale for non-sacrificial slaughter is stated clearly (i.e., the distance from the central sanctuary), as is the rationale for pouring out the blood on the ground: "Only be sure not to eat the blood, for the blood is the soul-life and you must not eat the soul-life with the meat" (v. 23, רַק חֲזַק לְבִלְתִּי אֲכֹל הַדָּם כִּי הַדָּם הוּא הַנָּפֶשׁ וְלֹא־תֹאכַל הַנֶּפֶשׁ עִם־הַבָּשָׂר). Note the same restrictive particle here again as in verses 15 and 16 in the previous section (רַק). Perhaps one might have surmised both points in verses 13–19 (i.e., the rationale for non-sacrificial slaughter and for pouring out the blood on the ground), but here they are made explicit.

Further exposition of the blood restriction follows immediately in verses 24–25. Both verses begin with לֹא תֹּאכְלֶנּוּ, "you must not eat it." The first simply adds that the Israelites should pour it out on the ground rather than eat it—something that was clear in the previous unit. The second verse, however, expands on that point with the rationale: "you must not eat it so that it may go well for you and your children after you because you do what is right in the eyes of the LORD" (v. 25). The phraseology of the last clause (כִּי־תַעֲשֶׂה הַיָּשָׁר בְּעֵינֵי יְהוָה, "because you do what is right in the eyes of the LORD") echoes the beginning of the explanation in the plural section, by way of contrast (v. 8b, אִישׁ כָּל־הַיָּשָׁר בְּעֵינָיו, "a man [doing] all that is right in his own eyes"). There is an *inclusio* here, especially with the reiteration of the same terminology at the very end of the unit (v. 28b, כִּי תַעֲשֶׂה הַטּוֹב וְהַיָּשָׁר בְּעֵינֵי יְהוָה אֱלֹהֶיךָ, "because you do that which is good and right in the eyes of the LORD your God"). This framing emphasizes the importance of both the centralization of sacrificial worship and the localized non-sacrificial slaughter, especially the proper handling of the blood in both cases (vv. 25 and 27b–28).

Levinson places verses 29–31 in chiastic parallel to verses 2–7, but the former actually matches only verses 2–3. There are other details that we are unable to discuss here. For example, our analysis deals with neither the mixed number in the pronouns of Deut 12:1 in the MT nor with the question of the relationship of Deut 13:1[ET 12:32] to Deut 12 and 13, nor with the mixed number also there in the MT and the related text-critical data.[18] Nevertheless, the main substance of chapter 12 moves naturally step by step through the topics it treats. There are no disjunctions here that betray any kind of long-term redactional process. Just as the plural section of the chapter (12:2–12) sets forth the basic call to centralized sacrificial worship (12:2–7) and then expounds on it with further explanation of the details (12:8–12), so the singular section (12:13–28) gives

[18] For the connection of Deut 13:1[ET 12:32] back to Deut 12 see, e.g., Tigay, *Deuteronomy*, 128, and for the meaning of the verse see his remarks on Deut 4:2 (43–44).

the basic regulation for non-sacrificial local slaughter first (12:13–19) and then expounds on it with further explanatory details (12:20–28). The shift from plural to singular at verse 13 can easily be explained without resorting to diachronic rationale. Moreover, the supposedly oldest unit that some think forms the basis for the buildup of the traditions (verses 13–19) does not constitute a workable altar law in the first place (see above).

Arguments for diachronic redactional strata in the main substance of Deut 12 (leaving aside Deut 12:1 and the relationship of Deut 13:1[ET 12:32] to Deut 12; see the remarks above) are not as cogent as they are often made out to be. To argue that the current coherence of the chapter only demonstrates that the redaction has been done so well that the redactor himself has disappeared is to assume one's conclusion counter to the available evidence,[19] betraying the bias of the method itself. A sounder method that is more respectful of the text as it stands would be to read it as a unified compositional whole and assess how that contributes to the development of Israelite religion according to Deuteronomy. The text is "expository" and, therefore, resumptive in a step-by-step manner, not made up of fragments redacted together over time. There is, nevertheless, a non-redactional diachronic element called for and supplied by the text itself. That is, Deuteronomy presents itself as originating forty years after the Israelites arrived at Sinai and thirty-eight years after their rebellion at Kadesh-barnea (Deut 2:7, 14). In the meantime, they had arrived at Moab and were about to enter the land to take possession of and settle in it. The situation was changing, and the law needed to change with it. The "diachrony" in the text reflects the actual historical situation assumed by Deuteronomy rather than any redactional process.

Centralization and the Historical-Critical Consensus

Jeffrey Tigay provides a helpful summary of the possible reasons for restricting sacrifices to a central sanctuary in Deut 12.[20] The major proposals include: (1) to curtail cultic sacrifice in favor of prayer as the primary mode of worship in Israel; (2) to unify the people in their devotion to Jerusalem against the Assyrians, like Jeroboam had earlier sought to unify northern Israel against southern Judah (1 Kgs 12:26–33); (3) to gain control of economic resources for Josiah's government; (4) to clarify the fact that there is only one God by having only one central sanctuary (monotheism); (5) to clarify that the Israelites should worship only one God, not the demons in the wilderness (cf. Lev 17:1–10) or any other gods

---

[19] Levinson, *Legal Innovation*, 27 and n. 11, where he refers to John Barton's "disappearing redactor."

[20] Tigay, *Deuteronomy*, 459–64, Excursus 14 on Deut 12.

(Deut 12:2–4, monolatry); (6) to clarify that there is only one YHWH, not multiple YHWHs with shrines in various locations (mono-Yahwism); and (7) to eliminate multiple sites of worship, which is an "inherently pagan" practice. The latter view, proposed by Moshe Greenberg, is the one Tigay takes most seriously, although he admits that there is not a great deal of difference between this view and the monotheistic view (#4 above).[21] The fact of the matter is that the last four options are closely related, but Tigay thinks the primary point is that "sacrificing at multiple sites . . . smacks of paganism."[22] It seems difficult, however, to stop short of the fact that the reason it "smacks" of paganism is that the multiple places of worship in paganism are associated with multiple deities, as Deut 12:3 and verses 30–31 indicate.

None of the last four views reviewed above requires any particular date for the prohibition of multiple altars—or for the composition of Deuteronomy. As noted above, however, one of the main reasons historical-critical scholarship has assigned (much of) Deuteronomy to the time of Josiah (or from Hezekiah to Josiah, with later redactions as well), is that the centralization regulation in Deut 12 seems to have motivated Josiah's reforms in 2 Kgs 23, after the scroll was "discovered" in the temple (2 Kgs 22). Many scholars would argue that Moses had nothing to do with the writing of Deuteronomy and that his name was given to it merely to provide the backing of ancient tradition for its religious and political agenda (i.e., the book is pseudepigraphic). Others are less committed to this view and allow for a much longer process of composition, perhaps even beginning with Moses.[23]

The standard historical-critical position concerning the relationship of Deut 12 to Exod 20:24–26 was articulated long ago, for example, by S. R. Driver. He argued that from earlier pre-Mosaic times down to the time of Solomon multiple altars were sanctioned, as legislated in Exod 20. This practice continued until the time of Josiah's reforms, as reflected in 1–2 Kings. However, by then it had become clear that "the old law (Ex. 20:24), which sanctioned an indefinite number of local sanctuaries, had been proved to be incompatible with purity of worship." Deuteronomy 12, therefore, "marks the final, and most systematic, effort made by the prophets to free the public worship of Jehovah from heathen accretions."[24]

Over half a century later Gerhard von Rad argued similarly to Driver in some regards, but he added the observation that there is probably

---

[21] Ibid., 463–64.

[22] Ibid., 463.

[23] See, e.g., the review of the history of this discussion in ibid., xix–xxvi.

[24] S. R. Driver, *A Critical and Exegetical Commentary on Deuteronomy*, ICC (Edinburgh: T&T Clark, 1895), 139–40.

> much that is traditional in this Deuteronomic rule which appears to be so revolutionary. This is evident in the resemblance of the form of the basic Deuteronomic law to the law of the altar in the Book of the Covenant. When compared with the latter, the formulation in Deuteronomy appears rather to be only a fresh wording. . . . Yahweh's will was indeed announced in the old commandments, but how it was to be obeyed in the constantly changing circumstances of practical life was a matter which Israel had to work out afresh for itself in its own conscience again and again.[25]

Therefore, von Rad saw the shift from the altar law in Exod 20 to the centralization in Deut 12 as a reflection of the changing circumstances of Israel's life as a people. To the ancient Israelites it would have been a natural part of their ongoing adjustments along the way. Similarly, according to Michael Fishbane, Deut 12:20–28 was added to verses 13–19 as a new exegetical solution to the readily apparent contradiction between the private slaughter admitted (or permitted?) in Deut 12:13–19 and restricted in Lev 17 (see more on this below). The new exegetical solution was to prohibit private slaughter within the original boundaries of the land while permitting it in the new territories.[26]

Over the last twenty years or so there have been some significant developments in the scholarly treatment of the relationship between the altar laws in Deut 12 and Exod 20. Bernard Levinson, for example, has proposed that "Deuteronomy represents a radical revision of the Covenant Code."[27] On the one hand, this is neither a completely new nor extreme suggestion, but rather one that is consonant with the reading of Deuteronomy as a late preexilic or exilic revision of the law under the influence of one set of religious or political reforms or another, or some combination of them. On the other hand, Levinson takes this way of reading Deuteronomy to a whole new level. In some ways his approach is reminiscent of the work of his dissertation mentor, Michael Fishbane, who has done much to put the study of innerbiblical exegesis on solid ground.[28] However, Levinson proposes to the contrary:

---

[25] Von Rad, *Deuteronomy*, 91.

[26] Fishbane, *Biblical Interpretation*, 534.

[27] Levinson, *Legal Innovation*, 3.

[28] Fishbane, *Biblical Interpretation*. See Bernard M. Levinson, *Legal Revision and Religious Renewal in Ancient Israel* (New York: Cambridge University Press, 2008), 95–181, for his thorough review of the history and development of scholarship on innerbiblical exegesis and rewriting, beginning with Wellhausen. Some of the other scholars included in the review are Moshe Greenberg, Samuel Sandmel, Nahum Sarna, James Sanders, Geza Vermes, Moshe Weinfeld, Jacob Weingreen, Shemaryahu Talmon, Joseph Blenkinsopp, Jacob Finkelstein, André Lemaire, Jeffrey Tigay, James Kugel, Norbert Lohfink, Yair Zakovitch, Eckart Otto, Konrad Schmid, Emanuel Tov, David Carr, Jeffrey Stackert, Christophe Nihan, and William Schniedewind. Levinson has obviously cast his net very wide here, and he sees himself

> In the end, however, inner biblical exegesis does not provide a satisfactory model to describe the achievements of the authors of Deuteronomy. The concern of the authors of Deuteronomy was not to explicate older texts but to transform them. Neither "interpretation" nor "exegesis" adequately suggests the extent to which Deuteronomy radically transforms literary and legal history in order to forge a new vision of religion and the state.[29]

According to Levinson, the writers of Deuteronomy were not only interpreters of the previous legal traditions, but also revisionists who camouflaged their abrogation and subversion of what their forerunners had written in order "to propound and justify" their own "program of cultic and legal reform."[30] Moreover, they "borrowed pseudepigraphically from the very textual authority that they subverted" in order to lend the authority of Moses to their own innovations.[31]

Levinson follows the standard higher-critical sequence of the Covenant Code (pre-exilic), then Deuteronomy (late pre-exilic), and finally the Holiness Code (exilic and postexilic), and assumes that the Covenant Code was largely known to the authors of Deuteronomy as an authoritative traditional text. In turn, the Holiness Code revises both the Covenant Code and the Deuteronomic Code that came before it. He accepts the higher-critical consensus that Deuteronomy was the law code that stood behind Josiah's reforms, which were viewed by the authors as critically important to the survival of the nation during the Neo-Assyrian crisis. So, for example, the centralization of worship called for in Deut 12 subverts the solitary altar regulations in Exod 20:24–26, which would have stood in the way of religious and political unity and stability in Judah. These legal revisions and innovations left markers in the present text, and these markers, in turn, betray the fact that the regulations as promulgated in Deuteronomy are just that—revisions, innovations, and, in fact, subversions of the previous cultic legal traditions.[32] So the question becomes: How does Levinson actually argue from the text to his theory of the hermeneutics of legal innovation?

---

and his approach as being within this scholarly tradition and contributing to it in substantial ways, especially as it relates to the book of Deuteronomy.

[29] Levinson, *Legal Innovation*, 15.

[30] Ibid., 4.

[31] Ibid., 6.

[32] Ibid., 9–10. Levinson, *Legal Revision*, 149–50, briefly summarizes his own work, largely as found in his *Deuteronomy and the Hermeneutics of Legal Innovation*. Many of his related articles are republished in revised form in Bernard M. Levinson, *"The Right Chorale": Studies in Biblical Law and Interpretation*, FAT 54 (Tübingen: Mohr Siebeck, 2008).

Like Wellhausen in his famous *Prolegomena to the History of Israel*, Levinson begins his discussion with places of worship.[33] In Levinson's view, the altar centralization and profane slaughter regulations in Deut 12:2–28 use the diction of the solitary altar regulations found in Exod 20:24–26.[34] But Levinson argues that the reason this was done was to subvert the teaching of the latter passage while, at the same time, recognizing it as an authoritative text in the antecedent legal tradition; Levinson calls this "lemmatic transformation."[35] He starts with the combined regulations for centralized worship and profane slaughter in Deut 12:13–19, especially the relationship between the lemma "in every place" in Exod 20:24 as compared to related lemmas in Deut 12:13–15 (the translations and highlighting are mine):

מִזְבַּח אֲדָמָה תַּעֲשֶׂה־לִּי וְזָבַחְתָּ עָלָיו אֶת־עֹלֹתֶיךָ וְאֶת־שְׁלָמֶיךָ אֶת־צֹאנְךָ וְאֶת־
בְּקָרֶךָ בְּכָל־הַמָּקוֹם אֲשֶׁר אַזְכִּיר אֶת־שְׁמִי אָבוֹא אֵלֶיךָ וּבֵרַכְתִּיךָ׃

You shall make for me an altar of earth and you shall sacrifice upon it your burnt offerings and your peace offerings, your sheep and your cattle; **in every place** where I make my name remembered I will come unto you and I will bless you. (Exod 24:24)

13 הִשָּׁמֶר לְךָ פֶּן־תַּעֲלֶה עֹלֹתֶיךָ בְּכָל־מָקוֹם אֲשֶׁר תִּרְאֶה׃ 14 כִּי אִם־בַּמָּקוֹם
אֲשֶׁר־יִבְחַר יְהוָה בְּאַחַד שְׁבָטֶיךָ שָׁם תַּעֲלֶה עֹלֹתֶיךָ וְשָׁם תַּעֲשֶׂה כֹּל אֲשֶׁר אָנֹכִי
מְצַוֶּךָּ׃ 15 רַק בְּכָל־אַוַּת נַפְשְׁךָ תִּזְבַּח וְאָכַלְתָּ בָשָׂר כְּבִרְכַּת יְהוָה אֱלֹהֶיךָ אֲשֶׁר
נָתַן־לְךָ בְּכָל־שְׁעָרֶיךָ הַטָּמֵא וְהַטָּהוֹר יֹאכְלֶנּוּ כַּצְּבִי וְכָאַיָּל׃

(13) Watch yourself lest you offer up your burnt offerings ***in* every place** that you see. (14) Instead, **in the place** that the Lord chooses in one of your tribes, there you shall offer up your burnt offerings, and there you shall do all that I am commanding you. (15) Nevertheless, whenever you desire you may slaughter and eat meat according to the blessing of the Lord your God that he has given you **in all your gates**; the unclean and the clean may eat it like the gazelle and like the deer. (Deut 12:13–15)

From these comparisons Levinson offers two main points. First, "in every place" in Deut 12:13 actually sets up a "straw man" in relation to the altar law in Exod 20:24, which limits the places to those where YHWH has made his name remembered (v. 24b). In fact, this "rhetorical *straw man* erected by the authors of Deuteronomy thus *camouflages* the real point of the exercise: functionally to abrogate that law with its affirmation of multiple altar sites as legitimate for sacrifice."[36]

---

[33] See the relatively complete summary of Wellhausen's view and subsequent discussions of the altar law in Averbeck, "מזבח altar," 893–94.

[34] Note the similar remarks in this regard by von Rad cited above.

[35] Levinson, *Legal Innovation*, 28–52.

[36] Ibid., 31 (italics mine).

Second, he argues from his comparison of the combined lemmas in the two passages that,

> the Deuteronomic authors skillfully break up and recast the syntax of the older Exodus altar law. . . . By means of this reworking, the Deuteronomic authors turn the older Exodus altar law against itself. . . . This literary recycling allows the Deuteronomic authors to *retain the ostensible validity of the older Exodus altar law* or, at least, to cast their innovations in light of the older sacrificial norm and *to minimize their departure from it.* Nonetheless, in substantive terms, they abrogate it. Indeed, they doubly disenfranchise it. . . . The authors of Deuteronomy have *atomistically restricted the older law's authority to individual, recycled lexemes* shorn from their original semantic context.[37]

Thus, Levinson actually takes the highlighted lemmas in the two passages and reads them as lending validity to the older altar law while at the same time undermining and abrogating it. It seems that the "straw man" essentially distracts the reader from seeing what is happening as the passage continues.

Unfortunately, the most likely way of reading the comparisons is clearly the opposite of what Levinson is proposing. It is hard to imagine anyone reading Deut 12:13–15 with previous knowledge of Exod 20:24 and not immediately recognizing that it abrogates what is taught in the earlier law. There is no "camouflage" here. In fact, the use of the same lemmas with variants would only highlight the innovations and make the reader fully aware that the author of Deut 12:13–15 was repealing the law of Exod 20:24. The questions that might actually have occured to an Israelite would be: Why is this happening? Why would Moses, of all people, reverse the altar law in Exod 20 that God had given through him at Sinai forty years earlier?[38]

The many problems with the historical-critical consensus have been recognized by some who handle the centralization of altar worship very differently. One approach is to minimize the distinctions between Exod 20 and Deut 12.[39] Since in Exod 20:24 the word "altar" is singular, as is

---

[37] Ibid., 32–33 (italics mine).

[38] For a more comprehensive and recent review and negative critique of Levinson's "subversive" approach to legal revision in the Pentateuch as a whole, see Joshua Berman, "Supersessionist or Complementary? Reassessing the Nature of Legal Revision in the Pentateuchal Law Collections," *JBL* 135 (2016): 201–22. Berman also criticizes Jeffrey Stackert's version of the "subversion" theory, as set forth in *Rewriting the Torah: Literary Revision in Deuteronomy and the Holiness Legislation* (Tübingen: Mohr Siebeck, 2007). Berman finds the "complementary" theory, in which the parallel laws in the various collections of law in the Pentateuch complement rather than subvert each other, to be much more convincing.

[39] See Peter T. Vogt, "Centralization and Decentralization in Deuteronomy," in *Interpreting Deuteronomy: Issues and Approaches*, ed. David G. Firth and Philip S. Johnston (Downers Grove, IL: InterVarsity Press, 2012), 122–31; and Vogt,

"place" in the expression בְּכָל־הַמָּקוֹם, "in every place" (not "places"), it is proposed that this verse may refer to one particular place, or at least one particular place at a time. The point, therefore, would not be that there can be multiple altars, but that YHWH will be with the Israelites wherever they go, so they need not worry about leaving YHWH behind when they leave Sinai. And, in any case, the passage is focused on worship devoted solely to YHWH and to no other god(s). Thus, Exod 20 and Deut 12 share the same primary concern.[40]

The problem for this view of Exod 20 is the distributive כָּל־ in the expression rendered "in every place" (Exod 20:24, cited above), which explicitly allows for and implies that there were multiple altars simultaneously. Moreover, according to Exod 20:24–25, the Israelites were to construct these altars out of packed earth (אֲדָמָה) or uncut stones (אֲבָנִים). This eliminates the supposition that the passage refers to the Israelites moving the tabernacle from place to place as they traveled through the wilderness or even after they entered the land. The bronze burnt offering altar in the tabernacle (Exod 27:1–8) does not meet the requirements of Exod 20:24–25. Rather, Exod 20 refers to the kind of altars in view in such passages as Exod 24:4; Deut 27:5–7 (cf. Josh 8:30–31); Judg 6:24; 1 Kgs 18:30–32; 19:10, etc.[41] Elijah, for example, repaired such an altar on Mount Carmel (1 Kgs 18:30–32) and bemoaned the fact that the Israelites had torn down

---

Deuteronomic Theology and the Significance of Torah: A Reappraisal (Winona Lake, IN: Eisenbrauns, 2006); also Daniel I. Block, *Deuteronomy*, NIVAC (Grand Rapids: Zondervan, 2012), 306n13, and the literature cited there.

[40] Vogt, "Centralization," 122–23.

[41] We agree, however, that the "most likely explanation" for the regulation in Deut 12 is that it "envisions a single sanctuary," *not* solitary altars, "chosen by YHWH, but that this requirement could be and was met in a series of places in succession"; see Vogt, "Centralization," 126n23, and my discussion below.

With regard to the tabernacle altar, some have proposed that, aside from the bronze burnt offering altar (Exod 27:1–8; 30:28; 40:6; etc.), there also would have been altars like the ones commanded in Exod 20:24–25 constructed within the tabernacle court whenever it was set up. This is by no means certain, however; see the summary discussion in Averbeck, "מזבח altar," 889–90, 897–900. More recently, Paul Heger, *The Three Biblical Altar Laws: Developments in the Sacrificial Cult in Practice and Theology: Political and Economic Background*, BZAW 279 (Berlin: de Gruyter, 1999), has argued that there never was a bronze burnt offering altar in the tabernacle in the first place. Instead, this so-called altar was actually a display table for offerings that were not immolated. His historical-critical analysis, as well as his archaeological and exegetical investigations, have been severely critiqued by Baruch Schwartz and Dennis Pardee; see their reviews in *CBQ* 63 (2001): 112–14 and *JNES* 65 (2006): 296–303, respectively. The latter provides substantial archaeological and textual evidence favoring the viability of a bronze burnt offering altar as described in Exod 27:1–8 (cf. also Averbeck, "מזבח altar," 890, 898–900).

the altars of YHWH (1 Kgs 19:10), along with their rejecting YHWH's covenant and killing his prophets, all of which are referred to in the same sentence. Clearly, in the experience and understanding of Elijah, YHWH approved of such altars and the offerings presented there.

Another alternative to the historical-critical consensus is the argument that Deut 12 does not call for only one centralized "place" that YHWH would choose for the Israelites to worship him with their offerings and tithes.[42] This explanation takes the singular "place" in verse 5 to be generic, referring to any particular location where YHWH might place his name. Deuteronomy 12:3b uses such a generic singular to refer to the many Canaanite worship places that needed to be destroyed. This is taken as a justification for the same interpretation in verse 5 and following.[43] The problem, of course, is the binding of the singular noun in verse 3 with the plural at the beginning of verse 2 in parallel expressions to form an *inclusio* (my translation):

אַבֵּד תְּאַבְּדוּן אֶת־כָּל־הַמְּקֹמוֹת אֲשֶׁר עָבְדוּ־שָׁם . . . אֶת־אֱלֹהֵיהֶם

> (2a) You must certainly eradicate all the places where they serve . . . their gods . . .

וּפְסִילֵי אֱלֹהֵיהֶם תְּגַדֵּעוּן וְאִבַּדְתֶּם אֶת־שְׁמָם מִן־הַמָּקוֹם הַהוּא׃

> (3b) . . . and the images of their gods you shall cut down, so you **shall eradicate their name from that place**.

The point here is that this kind of worship and everything associated with it must be completely eliminated in order to expunge the names of these gods from any and every place in the land. There is no such plural used for "**the place** the LORD your God will choose to put his name" anywhere in Deuteronomy.

One could perhaps understand Deut 12:14 (כִּי אִם־בַּמָּקוֹם אֲשֶׁר־יִבְחַר יְהוָה בְּאַחַד שְׁבָטֶיךָ) as more flexible in this regard, rendering it either "but in the place that the LORD shall choose in one of your tribes . . . ," or, in a more distributive sense, "but at whatever place the LORD will choose in any of your tribes . . ." The latter case allows for multiple places distributed throughout the tribal regions.[44] Deuteronomy 12:5, however, would not allow such a distributive rendering: כִּי אִם־אֶל־הַמָּקוֹם אֲשֶׁר־יִבְחַר יְהוָה אֱלֹהֵיכֶם מִכָּל־שִׁבְטֵיכֶם לָשׂוּם אֶת־שְׁמוֹ שָׁם לְשִׁכְנוֹ תִדְרְשׁוּ וּבָאתָ שָּׁמָּה, "But you shall seek the place where the LORD your God shall choose from all your tribes to put his name there as its (i.e., the name's) dwelling, and you

---

[42] See, e.g., Christopher J. H. Wright, *Deuteronomy*, NIBCOT 4 (Peabody, MA: Hendrickson Publishers, 1996), 169–70.

[43] Ibid., 170.

[44] Ibid., 169.

shall come there."[45] Some have argued that the flexibility in verse 14—in the section of Deut 12 that employs singular pronouns—indicates that this is an earlier tradition around which later and stricter traditions have accumulated through an extended process of composition, but this places more weight on the latter rendering of the verse than it can bear.

This does not necessarily mean, however, that there could not have been a series of places where the central sanctuary could have been located. In fact, there was. Jeremiah 7:12a and 14 are especially important here: "Indeed, go now to my place that is in Shiloh where I first made a dwelling for my name" (v. 12a); "and just as I did to Shiloh I will do to the house upon which my name is called, in which you are trusting, and to the place that I gave to you and to your fathers" (v. 14). Thus, the first place YHWH chose to put his name was Shiloh; the last was the temple in Jerusalem, up until the time of the Babylonian exile. In between there was at least one other place (Gibeon; see, e.g., 1 Kgs 3:4; 1 Chr 16:39–40; 21:29). The central place could move around while it was in the form of a tabernacle—a movable tent—but the Jerusalem temple became the permanent location from the time of Solomon at least until its destruction in 586 BCE (see the removal of YHWH's name and glory presence in Ezek 8–11).[46]

"Rest" in the Land and Centralization of Altar Worship

The most likely explanation for the shift from multiple solitary earthen altars in Exod 20:24–26 to the centralized worship in only one place at a time, with that place to be chosen by YHWH, according to Deut 12, turns on the issue of "rest" in the land (vv. 9–10).[47] After the initial call for worship at this sole centralized place in Deut 12:4–7, the text supplies an immediate rationale:

---

[45] For this rendering, which follows the MT, see the remarks in McConville, *Deuteronomy*, 211. Lundbom, *Deuteronomy*, 428 repoints לְשִׁכְנוֹ as a *piel* verb (as in v. 11) and renders v. 5, "But to the place that YHWH your God will choose out of all your tribes to put his name there, to make it (i.e., the name) reside, you shall seek and each of you shall go there." This rendering is more awkward, but both renderings are possible and, in either case, the "place" is clearly one place, not multiple places, which is the point we are concerned with here.

[46] See also the same conclusion reached by Vogt, "Centralization," 126n23; and Vogt, *Deuteronomic Theology*, 177–79.

[47] The discussion here is an abbreviation and update of my earlier treatment of this subject in Averbeck, "מזבח altar," 892–97, where more detail can be found. A former student of mine, Sean McNulty, first drew my attention to the significance of this textual detail.

8 לֹא תַעֲשׂוּן כְּכֹל אֲשֶׁר אֲנַחְנוּ עֹשִׂים פֹּה הַיּוֹם אִישׁ כָּל־הַיָּשָׁר בְּעֵינָיו׃
9 כִּי לֹא־בָאתֶם עַד־עָתָּה אֶל־הַמְּנוּחָה וְאֶל־הַנַּחֲלָה אֲשֶׁר־יְהוָה אֱלֹהֶיךָ נֹתֵן לָךְ׃
10 וַעֲבַרְתֶּם אֶת־הַיַּרְדֵּן וִישַׁבְתֶּם בָּאָרֶץ אֲשֶׁר־יְהוָה אֱלֹהֵיכֶם מַנְחִיל אֶתְכֶם וְהֵנִיחַ לָכֶם מִכָּל־אֹיְבֵיכֶם מִסָּבִיב וִישַׁבְתֶּם־בֶּטַח׃

(8) You must not do according to all that we are doing here today, each man (doing) whatever is right in his own eyes.

(9) For until now you have not entered into the **resting place** and inheritance that the LORD your God is about to give you.

(10) But you will cross over the Jordan and dwell in the land that the LORD your God is causing you to inherit, **and he will give you rest** from all your enemies round about, and you dwell there securely. (Deut 12:8–10, my translation)

As noted above, Deut 12:4 tells the Israelites they must not worship the way the Canaanites do, while verse 8 commands them not to worship the way they themselves were worshipping when they were on the plains of Moab. They had been there for some time now, during the conquest of the territories of Sihon the Amorite and Og, King of Bashan (Num 21:21–25:18; Deut 2:24–3:17), and the initial occupation of the region by the two and a half tribes that would occupy it after the conquest of Canaan (Num 32; cf. Josh 12:1–6; 22:1–6, etc.).

Deuteronomy 12:8 does not clarify what is meant by the expression "each man (doing) whatever is right in his own eyes" (cf. Judg 17:6; 21:25). But since they were no longer all dwelling in a camp around the tabernacle while they were settling the Transjordan region (contrast Lev 17:1–8 and see the discussion below), it seems that at least some of them would have been worshipping at solitary altars in their local regions. In fact, they may have been doing this in ways that Deut 12:3–4 prohibits, for example, with Asherahs and sacred pillars. This is precisely what Deut 16:21–22 forbids:

21 לֹא־תִטַּע לְךָ אֲשֵׁרָה כָּל־עֵץ אֵצֶל מִזְבַּח יְהוָה אֱלֹהֶיךָ אֲשֶׁר תַּעֲשֶׂה־לָּךְ׃
22 וְלֹא־תָקִים לְךָ מַצֵּבָה אֲשֶׁר שָׂנֵא יְהוָה אֱלֹהֶיךָ׃

(21) You must not plant for yourself an Asherah, any tree, beside the altar of the LORD your God that you shall make for yourself. (22) And you must not set up for yourself a (sacred) pillar, which the LORD your God hates. (my translation)

A regulation against offering blemished or defective animals on YHWH's altar follows in the next verse (Deut 17:1).[48]

Such regulations would have had ongoing importance, since centralized altar worship was intended to take place only when Israel rested securely in the promised land, without unconquered internal enemies disrupting their rest within the land. Then, and only then, were they to be careful to bring their burnt offerings, sacrifices, tithes, special gifts, and votive offerings to YHWH only at the one central place he would choose "to make his name dwell there" (לְשַׁכֵּן שְׁמוֹ שָׁם, v. 11).[49] They must not worship at the places where the gods of Canaan had been worshipped; in

---

[48] See the related higher-critical remarks in Levinson, *Legal Innovation*, 102, 148. In my view, these verses are rather loosely linked with their context, probably because they were inserted as regulations to be taken seriously whether in Transjordan or Cisjordan.

[49] There has been considerable scholarly discussion about the so-called "name theology" expressed in Deut 12:5, 11, 21 (cf. also, e.g., Deut 14:23; 16:2, 6, 11; 26:2; Jer 7:12; Ezra 6:12; Neh 1:9; Pss 20:1; 33:21; 44:5). The standard historical-critical understanding of this expression is that it stands between the conception of the earlier JE altar law in Exod 20:24–26 and the later P description of presence and guidance (see, e.g., Exod 33:7–16; 40:34–38; Lev 9:22–10:2; 16:2; Num 9:15–23). According to Exod 20:24–26, the Lord would not dwell at the solitary altar, but the altar was to be built in the "place where I [YHWH] cause my name to be remembered" (v. 24, אֲשֶׁר אַזְכִּיר אֶת־שְׁמִי). In the Deuteronomic name theology, "The name dwells on the earth in the sanctuary; YHWH himself is in heaven (Deut 26:15)" (von Rad, *Deuteronomy*, 90). Basically, this is "a theologically very striking conception of the name, which is present at the shrine in almost material form, is regarded almost as a person, and acts as a mediator between YHWH and his people" (ibid.). The priestly (P) conception moves "toward the more abstract, demythologized, and transcendent image of the deity," that is, "the present, yet ephemeral, presence of the deity" (Sandra L. Richter, *The Deuteronomistic History and the Name Theology:* l^{e}šakkēn š^{e}mô šām *in the Bible and the Ancient Near East*, BZAW 318 (Berlin: de Gruyter, 2002), 7–8, 12. See also her helpful review of the related literature (7–14, 26–36).

In her extensive study, Richter proposes that לְשַׁכֵּן שְׁמוֹ שָׁם is a Hebrew expression borrowed from Akkadian *šuma šakānu*, which means "to place the name." She reviews the use of the Akkadian expression in various kinds of dedicatory and victory inscriptions where it refers to ownership and sovereignty obtained through conquest. Similarly, the Deuteronomistic expression has nothing to do with divine presence, but was all about "the sovereignty and fame of YHWH by right of conquest." She concludes that, by means of this expression, "YHWH states that he has 'placed his name' in the Promised Land. The king has captured this new territory; he has claimed it as his own. Let the people be subject, let them bring tribute, and let them always remember that it is he who has defeated their foes and it is he to whom allegiance is due" (217). There is no "name theology" here alluding to any kind of personal, ephemeral, or other kind of "presence," according to Richter.

Despite Richter's helpful discussion of the Akkadian parallel, not all scholars agree with her that there is no conception of divine presence attached to the

fact, they "must wipe out their name" (i.e., the names of the gods) from any such place (v. 3b, וְאִבַּדְתֶּם אֶת־שְׁמָם מִן־הַמָּקוֹם הַהוּא). Note the direct contrast between the names of those gods (v. 3) and the name of YHWH (v. 5). The Israelites must worship only at the particular place where YHWH himself has put his own name. Moreover, they would "eat there in the presence (לִפְנֵי) of the LORD" (v. 7; cf., e.g., the parallel in Exod 33:14), so that "making his name dwell there" is somehow related to YHWH's actual presence in the place he would choose.

Historically, two points are especially important here. First, the "rest" in the land referred to in Deut 12:9–10 did not become a reality until the time of David (2 Sam 7:1, "After the king was settled in his palace and the LORD had given him rest from all his enemies around him"). Only then would such centralization have made sense. It is true that Josh 21:43–45 tells us that "the LORD gave Israel all the land he had sworn to give their ancestors . . . The LORD gave them rest on every side, just as he had sworn to their ancestors. Not one of their enemies withstood them . . . Not one of all the LORD's good promises to Israel failed; every one was fulfilled." Yet in Josh 23 the elderly Joshua warned the people to neither associate with the people of the nations still living in their midst nor worship their gods. If they failed in this, "the LORD your God will no longer drive out these nations before you" (v. 13). Judges 1 expands on this ongoing reality (see also Judg 2:20–3:6), which continued through the judges period and up until the time of David.

We do not actually know when and by whom the book of Joshua was originally written or redacted into the unit we now know as part of the Former Prophets (Joshua–2 Kings), since the text offers us no explicit information regarding this. Certain internal considerations indicate that it was not put into its current form until at least late in the judges period (compare, e.g., Judg 18:27–29 with Josh 19:47–48). This suggests that the remark in Josh 21:43–45 (cited above) concerning total rest in the land comes from a later time, perhaps during or after the time of David. In other words, this passage may have been written from a viewpoint later than that of Joshua, sometime after the ultimate goal of the conquest of the land had been reached, namely, full control and rest in the land. In any case, Joshua reflects the tension between the fulfillment of God's promise to give the Israelites rest in the land and the rather lengthy process through which that would be accomplished, that is, from the time of Joshua all the way through the judges period until David's reign.

The second key historical point is that both the Former Prophets and Chronicles make it clear that the legitimate Yahwistic use of solitary

---

expression in this context; see below, as well as Block, *Deuteronomy*, 307–8, and especially McConville, *Deuteronomy*, 223.

rock and earthen altars as called for in Exod 20:24–26 did not stop with Joshua's conquest and the apportioning of the promised land to the tribes of Israel (see, e.g., Judg 6:26; 1 Sam 7:17). It apparently continued even beyond the period of the united monarchy (see, e.g., Elijah on Mount Carmel, 1 Kgs 18:30–38; 19:10). The kind of "rest" referred to in Deut 12:9–10 was not attained until the time of David and did not endure beyond Solomon's reign, since the division of the kingdom between north and south occurred shortly after Solomon's death (1 Kgs 12). This was part of Jeroboam's rationale for setting up golden calves in Bethel and Dan, as well as for instituting houses of worship on high places (1 Kgs 12:26–30). As he put it, "The kingdom will now likely revert to the house of David. If these people go up to offer sacrifices at the temple of the LORD in Jerusalem, they will again give their allegiance to their lord, Rehoboam king of Judah" (1 Kgs 12:26–27). The divided kingdom period by definition was not a time of rest in the land. This is why tearing down the Yahwistic solitary altars was such an abomination, at least in the Northern Kingdom, according to Elijah (1 Kgs 19:10).

Nevertheless, there was a semblance of rest in the land that came with Joshua's initial conquest. The narrator noted this in Josh 23:1, and Joshua himself included the non-Israelites who still remained in the land along with those whom they had already defeated as peoples they would disinherit (vv. 4–5). Because of the Israelites' initial military success there was also an impetus toward centralization even from the start, although they did not connect this to the elimination of solitary altars at other locations (see, e.g., 1 Sam 16:1–5; 20:6, 24–26, 28–29). Accordingly, this underlying tendency toward centralization of altar worship rises to the surface of the text in numerous places.

For example, occasionally individuals, families, or the nation as a whole would go to the tabernacle, wherever located, in order to sacrifice on the altar located there (see, e.g., 1 Sam 1:3, 9; 2:22; 3:3; 9:12; 1 Kgs 3:4; 2 Chr 1:3–6).[50] Even as early as Josh 22:10–34 it is clear that the Israelites were thinking of only one central sanctuary altar. Before crossing over the Jordan to their homeland, the two and a half Transjordanian tribes built an imposing altar as a "copy of the altar of the LORD" (v. 28, אֶת־תַּבְנִית מִזְבַּח יְהוָה) that was in front of the tabernacle at Shiloh. They built it on the Canaan side of the Jordan as a witness that they had rights to the central sanctuary altar on that side of the Jordan. It was not an altar for sacrifice. At first, however, the other tribes misunderstood their

---

[50] See the helpful discussion in Menahem Haran, *Temples and Temple Service in Ancient Israel: An Inquiry into Biblical Cult Phenomena and the Historical Setting of the Priestly School* (Oxford: Clarendon, 1978; repr., Winona Lake, IN: Eisenbrauns, 1985), 304–16.

intentions and saw this as a violation of the one central sanctuary law and an act of idolatrous rebellion against YHWH. They even prepared to go to war against the two and a half tribes over it.

First Kings 3:1–4 is especially instructive regarding the transition from multiple solitary altars to the sole central sanctuary as the only place of sacrifice to YHWH. Solomon had not yet built the temple, so the people were still sacrificing on the high places (1 Kgs 3:2). Also, Solomon loved YHWH and followed his father David's instructions, "except that he was sacrificing and offering incense on the high places" (v. 3, רַק בַּבָּמוֹת הוּא מְזַבֵּחַ וּמַקְטִיר). It appears that these places were already under suspicion then, even if they were devoted to YHWH. The next verse is especially interesting: "The king went to Gibeon to sacrifice there, for that was the great high place" (v. 4a). The tabernacle was there, and David had already considered it to be the central sanctuary even though the ark of the covenant was not there (1 Chr 16:39–42; cf. 2 Chr 1:3–6 for special clarity). Sacrificing at Gibeon was especially pleasing to YHWH, so when Solomon "offered a thousand burnt offerings on that altar" (1 Kgs 3:4b) YHWH appeared to him that night in a dream and granted him the special wisdom he asked for as well as abundant prosperity.

Throughout the remainder of the preexilic period, high places became increasingly associated with idolatrous practices. (Compare 1 Kgs 3:2–3 and 15:13–14 with 2 Kgs 17:9–13 and the reforms of Hezekiah [2 Kgs 18:4, 22; 2 Chr 31:1] and Josiah [2 Kgs 23:5, 12–20; 2 Chr 34:1–7].) However, as noted above, during the divided kingdom period the practice of building Yahwistic altars was highly approved in the Northern Kingdom since access to the temple in Jerusalem was cut off for faithful Yahwists living in the Northern Kingdom. After all, there was no longer rest in the land, but instead ongoing or at least intermittent conflict between the north and the south. This building of solitary Yahwistic altars naturally continued with approval in the north until the exile of the Northern Kingdom. The same practice, however, also extended illegitimately into the Southern Kingdom, as we can see from the religious reforms of Hezekiah immediately afterward and through the time of Josiah until the Babylonian exile. Centralization of altar worship was designed and instituted for times of rest in the land, as we can see from Deut 12:8–9 as well as from the historical developments displayed in Joshua through Kings and Chronicles, as noted above.

Localization of Non-Sacrificial Slaughter

The second half of Deut 12 (vv. 13–28) focuses on practices for eating meat in local regions after the Israelites entered, occupied, and had rest in the land. According to the narrative storyline and Sinai theology, Lev 17:1–9 made perfectly good sense while they were traveling through the wilderness as a camp that followed the glory cloud of God's presence, and when they were camping around the tabernacle occupied by his manifest presence. They were all near to the tabernacle, and the tabernacle was essentially a movable Sinai by means of which YHWH walked and dwelt among them as they traveled and camped (Lev 26:11–12). Across the Jordan on the plains of Moab forty years later, however, Moses was anticipating their conquest and occupation of the land when their travels through the wilderness would end. At that time they would no longer camp around the tabernacle but would instead spread throughout the land, with most of them residing too far away from the central place to slaughter their meat at the tabernacle altar for regular meals or other local events.[51]

However, as noted above, many scholars do not accept this narrative storyline. Instead, according to their view, Deuteronomy was originally written not by Moses, but five or six centuries later, when it was composed as the law book for the religious reforms of Hezekiah (eighth century BCE) and/or, more importantly, of Josiah (seventh century BCE). Assigning it to Moses was a pseudepigraphic effort to give authoritative and traditional force to its regulations. These scholars commonly regard the profane slaughter in Deut 12:15–16, 20–25 as part of a larger secularizing tendency by the Deuteronomist.[52] But there are also scholars who argue that this is actually a non-cultic but still fundamentally religious rather than secular turn.

Levinson, for example, emphasizes that there is still a special promise attached to the non-sacrificial slaughter: "according to the blessing of the LORD your God" (v. 15, כְּבִרְכַּת יְהוָה אֱלֹהֶיךָ; cf. Exod 20:24b, "I will come to you and bless you," אָבוֹא אֵלֶיךָ וּבֵרַכְתִּיךָ).[53] As he puts it,

> In face of the dismantling of the countryside cultus begun by Hezekiah and intensified by Josiah, it was crucial for the Deuteronomic authors to establish for the citizens of Judah that the loss of the local altars did not entail complete loss of local access to God or, more seriously, that God had abandoned the local sphere. They went out of their way to provide the local sphere with its own integrity. Yahweh continues to be active and to grant his blessing there.[54]

Peter Vogt makes the same point, but bases it on the use of the term זבח, "to sacrifice" (Deut 12:15, 21): "you may slaughter and eat meat" (v. 15, תִּזְבַּח וְאָכַלְתָּ בָשָׂר) and "and you may slaughter from your herd and your flock" (v. 21, וְזָבַחְתָּ מִבְּקָרְךָ וּמִצֹּאנְךָ). He also points to the pouring out

[51] See, e.g., the explanation in Tigay, *Deuteronomy*, 124–26.

[52] See n. 6 above.

[53] Levinson, *Legal Innovation*, 49–52.

[54] Ibid., 49–50.

of blood on the ground as a solemn act, especially since the same verb is used in verses 16 and 24 as in verse 27, where it describes pouring out the blood on the altar in sacrificial slaughter.[55] Vogt acknowledges that local slaughter was not a sacrifice but insists that it still had religious significance.[56] Accordingly, "Deuteronomy 12 centralizes *sacrifice* to the central sanctuary, but *worship* is decentralized."[57]

Scholars agree that this passage refers to non-sacrificial (sometimes termed "secular" or "profane") slaughter even though the verb זבח "to sacrifice" (Deut 12:15, 21) almost always refers to sacred sacrificial slaughter. There are a few exceptions where the non-sacrificial nature of the slaughter is explicit, as it is here in Deut 12:15, 21, but this usage is truly exceptional.[58] As noted earlier in our discussion of structure, in Deut 12:13–19 this verb is used only in verse 15 for non-sacrificial slaughter, and there is no mention of "sacrifices" (noun or verb) anywhere else in the unit. It appears many times elsewhere in the chapter, however, often paired with "burnt offerings." The point of this usage in Deut 12:13–19 seems to be that non-sacrificial slaughter was, nevertheless, slaughter that was to be managed according to religious concerns.

The Outside Cultic Frame of the Law Collections

All three of the parallel law collections under consideration here (the Covenant Code, the Holiness Code, and the Deuteronomic Code) are

---

[55] Vogt, "Centralization," 130, notes that Lev 4:7, 18, 25, 30, 34 refer to pouring out "all [the rest of] the blood at the base of the altar (אֶל־יְסוֹד מִזְבַּח) of burnt offering." This was the way they disposed of the leftover blood after some of it had already been used for the sprinkling ritual to make atonement (see vv. 5–7a). This blood was not "poured out upon the altar (עַל־מִזְבַּח)," as Deut 12:27 states. Moreover, when the priestly material refers to offering the blood of burnt or peace offerings on the burnt offering altar it describes it in this way: "and they (the priests) shall splash (זרק) the blood all around upon the altar (וְזָרְקוּ אֶת־הַדָּם עַל־הַמִּזְבֵּחַ סָבִיב)" (Lev 1:5, 11; 3:2, 13; etc.). The verb שפך is never used this way in the Levitical material. The reason it is used this way in (non-Levitical) Deut 12:27 for pouring the blood out on the altar is in order to express the corresponding opposite of pouring out the blood on the ground like water in Deut 12:16, 24. There is no mimicking of sacrifice here—quite the opposite. It is like hunting and killing wild game (vv. 15, 22). This does not mean, however, that there is nothing solemn or worshipful about the act of pouring out the blood like water. In my view, Vogt is correct here. See also Block, *Deuteronomy*, 318, 320–22, who makes the same point.

[56] Vogt, "Centralization," 129–31.

[57] Ibid., 131.

[58] See *HALOT*, 262, meaning 1; note esp. 1 Sam 28:24 with vv. 22–23. See also, e.g., Block, *Deuteronomy*, 317; Lundbom, *Deuteronomy*, 435; Tigay, *Deuteronomy*, 125; and Vogt, "Centralization," 129n28.

framed by cultic regulations even though, as noted above, they are not dominated by the cult, at least not to the extent that the Priestly Code is. Therefore the present essay has focused on the beginning of each of these three law collections, since the altar laws occur at the beginning of each of them. The laws of the Book of the Covenant in Exod 21–23 actually begin with the solitary altar regulations at the end of the previous chapter, Exod 20:22–26. This law collection concludes with the command to participate in the three major annual pilgrimage festivals—Unleavened Bread, Harvest, and Ingathering (Exod 23:14–17). This is followed by the related regulations against offering leavened bread at Passover and Unleavened Bread (v. 18a), the requirement to consume the Passover lamb completely in one night (v. 18b), and finally the obligation to offer the firstfruits of the soil to YHWH, along with the rather enigmatic concluding prohibition, "You must not boil a kid in its mother's milk" (v. 19; cf. Deut 14:21).

The major unit of cultic regulations in Deuteronomy likewise begins with an altar law in Deut 12 and concludes with an explanation of the same three annual festivals in Deut 16, much like the cultic frame of the Book of the Covenant. But there is a major difference: there is no reference in Deut 16 to the offering of firstfruits (cf. Exod 23:19). Instead, the Deuteronomic Code places its treatment of the celebration of firstfruits at the end of its regulations in Deut 26. Thus, the last chapter of the Deuteronomic Code highlights the firstfruits offering from the soil after the Israelites have entered the promised land (Deut 26:1–11), just as the final section of the Book of the Covenant does in Exod 23:19, but in Deuteronomy a liturgy accompanies it: "My father was a wandering Aramean . . ." (Deut 26:5b–10a). The third-year tithe festival regulations in Deut 26:12–15 also contribute to this cultic conclusion to the laws in the book of Deuteronomy.[59]

The discussion of the Holiness Code is more complicated. Scholars sometimes limit the Holiness Code to Lev 18–26, since the standard holiness terminology does not appear in Lev 17 or 27.[60] The full holiness

[59] The concluding verses of Deut 26 seem to reflect some kind of cultic ceremony for the ratification or renewal of the covenant on the plains of Moab (vv. 16–17), thereby echoing the introduction to the covenant-making narrative in Exod 19 (cf. Deut 26:18–19 with Exod 19:5–6). Thus, the end of the law echoes its beginning in the Torah. This subject is treated in Averbeck, "Egyptian Sojourn," 143–75. See also Thomas H. McClendon Jr., "The Book of the Torah as a Gospel of Grace: A Synthesis of Daniel I. Block's Biblical Theology of Deuteronomy," in *For Our Good Always: Studies on the Message and Influence of Deuteronomy in Honor of Daniel I. Block*, ed. Jason S. DeRouchie, Jason Gile, and Kenneth J. Turner (Winona Lake, IN: Eisenbrauns, 2013), 528–29, and the literature cited there.

[60] See, e.g., Gordon J. Wenham, *The Book of Leviticus*, NICOT (Grand Rapids: Eerdmans, 1979), 7, and the literature cited there. For a helpful summary of the

formula appears first in Lev 19:2, קְדֹשִׁים תִּהְיוּ כִּי קָדוֹשׁ אֲנִי יְהוָה אֱלֹהֵיכֶם, "You shall be holy because I, the LORD your God, am holy" (cf. 20:7, 26; 21:6–8), but the related formula אֲנִי יְהוָה אֱלֹהֵיכֶם, "I am the LORD (your God)," appears regularly throughout Lev 18–26 (see 18:2, 4, 5, 6, 21, 30; 19:3, 4, 10, 12, 14, 16, 18, 25, 28, 30, 31, 32, 34, 36, 37; 20:7, 8, 24; 21:8, 12, 15, 23; 22:2, 3, 8, 9, 16, 30, 31, 32, 33; 23:22, 43; 24:22; 25:17, 38, 55; 26:1, 2, 13, 44, 45).

Most scholars today extend the Holiness Code back into Lev 17, viewing this chapter as part of a priestly redaction.[61] On the one hand, Lev 17 looks back to chapters 1–16 in that it emphasizes making offerings in the tabernacle (Lev 17:1–9), along with blood "atonement" and, therefore, the prohibition against eating blood (vv. 10–16). On the other hand, the primary goal of the regulations in Lev 17 is to reinforce the absolute exclusivity of YHWH worship, one of the major concerns of chapters 18–26. Thus, cultic altar regulations are found at the beginning of the Holiness Code, the Book of the Covenant (Exod 20:22–26), and the core legislation in the book of Deuteronomy (Deut 12).

Leviticus 27, which concludes the book, is normally treated as an appendix because of the colophon at the end of Lev 26 (v. 46, "These are the statutes, the judgments, and the laws that the LORD established between himself and the Israelites at Mount Sinai by the hand of Moses").[62] A similar colophon, however, also appears at the end of Lev 27 (v. 34, "These are the commandments which the LORD commanded Moses for the Israelites at Mount Sinai"). Although, like Lev 17, chapter 27 does not use the standard formulas of Lev 18–26, some note that its general content is nevertheless appropriate and, again, suggest that its location here is due to a late H redaction.[63] In my view, however, there are good reasons to believe that this was the way the law was put together in the first place, not a late redaction.

Just as the festival regulations in Exod 23:14–19 conclude the laws in the Book of the Covenant and the firstfruits and third-year tithe festival

---

larger discussion, see John E. Hartley, *Leviticus*, WBC 4 (Dallas: Word, 1992), 250–60, and the references cited there.

[61] See, e.g., Jacob Milgrom, *Leviticus 17–22*, AB 3A (New York: Doubleday, 2000), 1332.

[62] There are no curses and blessings at the end of the Book of the Covenant (Exod 21–23), for two reasons. First, the Book of the Covenant is embedded in a covenant-making narrative (Exod 19–24), not a covenant document. It concludes, therefore, with a covenant-making ceremony in which there is a covenant-making oath procedure (Exod 24:6–8; cf. also, e.g., the covenants/treaties in Gen 21:24, 31; 26:31; 31:53). Second, the Sinai covenant material actually extends beyond Exod 24 all the way through Lev 26, as the colophon in Lev 26:46 indicates. The blessings and curses of the covenant, therefore, are given in Lev 26.

[63] See, e.g., Milgrom, *Leviticus 17–22*, 1333–34.

regulations in Deut 26 conclude the core law section of Deuteronomy, so Lev 27 contains a series of diverse cultic regulations. The presentation of firstborn animals in Lev 27:26–27 parallels the firstfruits offerings in Exod 23:19 and Deut 26:1–11, while Lev 27:30–33 and Deut 26:12–15 both discuss tithes. If, as it appears, Exod 20:22–26 corresponds to 23:14–19, Deut 12 to 26, and Lev 17 to 27, we have a regular pattern of the cultic framing of the three parallel non-cultic law collections in the Pentateuch. In my view, this offers a better explanation for why Lev 27 is placed after Lev 26, despite the colophon in Lev 26:46.

The main point here is that all three parallel units of law in the Pentateuch both open and close with cultic regulations. The law is framed by cultic law. This is the place to start when considering the cult in Deuteronomy and its relationship to that of the Book of the Covenant and the Holiness Code. Everything begins and ends with the Israelites' relationship and devotion to their God, which is the purpose of the cult in the first place. The rest of the law makes no sense without its cultic context.

In turn, the cultic context and framework on which the law is suspended find their underlying rationale in the historical narrative within which they are embedded. The defining feature of ancient Israel was to be their worship and service of YHWH, the one and only Most High God, who had brought them out of Egypt, from the house of slavery, to give them rest in the land that he had promised to their patriarchal fathers, Abraham, Isaac, and Jacob. This historical anchor provides another closely associated inside frame around the law; that is, within the cultic frame.

Conclusion

As is well known, the Ten Commandments given at Sinai begin with the historical point of departure: "I am the LORD your God, who brought you out of Egypt, out of the land of slavery" (Exod 20:2). Moreover, directly following the cultic introduction to the Book of the Covenant (Exod 20:22–26), the laws begin with the Israelite debt slave laws (Exod 21:2–11; v. 2, "If you buy a Hebrew servant . . ."). No other ancient Near Eastern law collection begins with slave law; in Israel the law begins here precisely because the whole premise of the law is the Israelites' deliverance from slavery. Immediately prior to the cultic conclusion to the law as it was given at Sinai (Lev 27; see the remarks above), following the curses and blessings of the covenant (see Lev 26 and especially the colophon in v. 46; cf. Lev 27:34), Lev 25:39–55 returns once again to the laws of Hebrew debt slavery. The concluding verses emphatically call attention to the basic historical premise of the law: "Even if someone is not redeemed in any of these ways, they and their children are to be released in the Year of Jubilee, for the Israelites belong to *me* as servants. They are *my* servants, whom *I* brought out of Egypt. *I* am the LORD your God" (vv. 54–55; note the emphasis on YHWH through first-person expressions).

Finally, at the conclusion of the law as given on the plains of Moab forty years later, the historical credo for the offering of the firstfruits of the land back to YHWH in Deut 26:5–10 emphasizes the importance of the Egyptian sojourn and YHWH's deliverance from slavery. And the following verses emphasize the ethos of the law embodied in bringing the firstfruits and third-year tithe to YHWH as a way of providing for the foreigners, Levites, and poor in Israel (vv. 11–15).[64] So although the cult provides the *outside* frame on which the three main parallel units of law in the Torah are suspended, there is also an *inside* frame. YHWH's deliverance of Israel from slavery in Egypt and its implications for the treatment of the poor, resident aliens, and other disadvantaged people in Israel play a significant role in the literary, sociological, and theological framing and shaping of the law as it is presented in the canonical form of the Pentateuch.

Cultic law is by nature *worship* law. The exodus from Egypt provides the basic rationale for the Israelites' worship of YHWH, as is clear from the very beginning of the Ten Words. The faithful are, first of all and above all, worshippers of the God who delivered them from their slavery in Egypt to give them rest in the land he had promised them.

---

[64] For a more detailed discussion of this framing of the law collections in the Pentateuch, see Averbeck, "Egyptian Sojourn."

CHAPTER 9

Wisdom and Torah in Deuteronomy

J. Gordon McConville

Introduction

While the supreme importance of torah in Deuteronomy is well known, the profile of "wisdom" in the book is less so, and indeed the relationship between torah and wisdom remains a matter of ongoing scholarly debate. In what follows, I aim to make a contribution to that debate by paying attention to key passages in Deuteronomy and relating them to the phenomenon of wisdom in other parts of the Old Testament.

The idea of wisdom occurs at key points in the book: at the beginning, when Moses is advised to appoint wise leaders tribe by tribe (1:9–18); on the threshold of the book's long section of Mosaic teaching (4:5–8); at the beginning of the uniquely Deuteronomic extended provisions for administration (16:19); and at two points in the closing chapters, following the long section of detailed instruction. The first is in the Song of Moses, in which the people's characteristic unfaithfulness to YHWH, as portrayed in the book, is conveyed in a cluster of recognizably "wisdom" vocabulary (Deut 32:15, 28–29).[1] The second is in the last few verses of the book, in the narrative of the transition of leadership from Moses to Joshua, where Joshua is said to have been "full of the spirit of wisdom (מָלֵא רוּחַ חָכְמָה) because Moses laid his hands upon him" (34:9).[2] Wisdom texts, therefore, take prominent positions at the beginning and the end of the book; they may also be said to bracket the long legal section of the book (chs. 4 and 32),[3] and they feature in two of the book's key passages concerning leadership (1:9–18; 16:18–20). Overt wisdom language is relatively infrequent, yet significant because of its placement.

---

[1] The terms are עֵצוֹת, תְּבוּנָה, חָכְמוּ, יַשְׂכִּילוּ, and יָבִינוּ. In the context these are cast either as a lack or as a desideratum. Wisdom also has its obverse in 32:15, where the verb נבל ("to be foolish") occurs in the *piel* in the sense of "scoff at" or "scorn" (YHWH).

[2] All Bible translations in this essay are the author's unless otherwise noted.

[3] See Gerald T. Sheppard, *Wisdom as a Hermeneutical Construct: A Study in the Sapientializing of the Old Testament*, BZAW 151 (Berlin: de Gruyter, 1980), 65.

The question regarding wisdom's relation to torah gains a particular stimulus from Deut 4:5–8. This passage forms part of Moses' long speech in Deut 4, which is the book's most extensive treatise on the "statutes and ordinances" (חֻקִּים וּמִשְׁפָּטִים) or the "commandments" (מִצְוֹת) of YHWH. These are in effect the substance of Deuteronomic torah (4:8, כֹּל הַתּוֹרָה הַזֹּאת, "this whole torah"; cf. 5:31), given to Israel at Mt. Horeb (4:10–14), to which the long central portion of the book (Deut 12–26) corresponds. Deuteronomy 4 also highlights the role of Moses himself as mediator of the Horeb covenant, and above all as the teacher of torah (4:14). The chapter is therefore crucial to the self-understanding of Deuteronomy as "the book of this law" (סֵפֶר הַתּוֹרָה הַזֹּאת, Deut 28:61; cf. 31:9).

What is distinctive about the verses in question is their correlation of torah with wisdom. In Deut 4:6 Moses exhorts Israel: "Keep them and do them [that is, the "statutes and ordinances"], for that will be your wisdom and your understanding in the sight of the peoples" (ESV; כִּי הִוא חָכְמַתְכֶם וּבִינַתְכֶם לְעֵינֵי הָעַמִּים).[4] This statement may seem to posit an equation of wisdom and torah, but in fact three possibilities are permitted by the syntax: the pronoun "that" might mean the "statutes and ordinances" themselves (v. 5), Israel's action of keeping them, or even, as Thomas Krüger expresses it, the condition implied in verse 6b, namely, "if they will hear . . . they will say."[5] It may be unnecessary to select one of these as the only correct meaning.[6] But it is important to note at this stage that the text does not determine the outcome of our inquiry in advance.

Our question about wisdom and torah in Deuteronomy will consider the place of wisdom broadly in the book and also the nature of the relationship between the interpretation of Deuteronomy and wisdom literature. In the context of the religious history of Israel, do the wisdom texts in Deuteronomy attest to a convergence between the originally disparate phenomena of torah and wisdom?

---

[4] Deuteronomy's consonantal text regularly lacks the feminine form הִיא, and always has the form הִוא even where we would expect a feminine. MT sometimes, as here, points it to be read as הִיא.

[5] Thomas Krüger, "Law and Wisdom according to Deut 4:5–8," in *Wisdom and Torah: The Reception of 'Torah' in the Wisdom Literature of the Second Temple Period*, ed. Bernd U. Schipper and D. Andrew Teeter, JSJSup 163 (Leiden: Brill, 2013), 38–39. Richard D. Nelson also sees this final option as a possibility in *Deuteronomy*, OTL (Louisville: Westminster John Knox, 2002), 64–65.

[6] Krüger, "Law and Wisdom," 39–40. It is best to follow translations, such as ESV, that retain the verb "to be" in the latter clause of this sentence, in order to illustrate the interpretive possibilities, rather than NIV and NRSV, which have "this will show your wisdom . . . ." This leaves open certain interpretive possibilities which the latter make impossible.

Deuteronomy and Wisdom Literature

The Old Testament wisdom literature consists primarily of the books of Proverbs, Job, and Ecclesiastes, but wisdom also more broadly refers to a kind of thinking that may be identified in other books of the Old Testament, especially the Psalms and Prophets (e.g., Ps 37:16; Isa 28:23–29; Amos 3:3–8). The literature is classed as wisdom both because it deploys a vocabulary recognizable as belonging to the semantic field of wisdom and because it has affinities with the literary legacy of an intellectual tradition that was widespread in the ancient Near East. The religious content of wisdom literature has long been felt to be in tension with the broadly "covenantal" line in Old Testament theology, constituted by the election of Israel, exodus from Egypt, Sinai/Horeb covenant, and possession of a given land.[7] The question of wisdom and torah, therefore, has important implications for Old Testament theology and interpretation on a broad level. Our question is whether Deuteronomy indeed attests to a convergence between disparate types of religion in the Old Testament period, or whether wisdom and torah maintain separate identities within Yahwism.[8]

In order to approach this question, we turn now to consider the seminal work of Moshe Weinfeld, together with the counterproposal of Georg Braulik. The scholarly discussion has moved beyond their conversation, as we shall see, yet their exchange still identifies the essential issues.

Weinfeld believes that Deuteronomy was strongly influenced by wisdom thought. He points out affinities of both phraseology and content between Deuteronomy and Proverbs. The related topics of leadership and legal judgment are common to both books. Thus in Deuteronomy, the first occurrence of wisdom concepts (as one reads the book) is in Deut 1:9–18, in connection with Moses' appointment of "wise, discerning, and experienced (or reputable) men" (1:13, אֲנָשִׁים חֲכָמִים וּנְבֹנִים וִידֻעִים; cf. 1:15) for purposes of both military leadership (1:15) and judging cases (1:17). The text has parallels in Exod 18:23–27 and Num 11:11–30, in comparison

[7] Gerhard von Rad famously found little place for wisdom in his magisterial *Old Testament Theology I, II* (London: Oliver & Boyd, 1962), and subsequently devoted a separate volume to the topic, *Wisdom in Israel* (London: SCM, 1972). The roots of Old Testament wisdom in the ancient Near East have led some to see its relationship with Yahwism as problematic. For James L. Crenshaw, wisdom could evince a "skepticism [which] was a means of coping for those who proposed a viable alternative to traditional Yahwism" (James L. Crenshaw, *Old Testament Wisdom: An Introduction* [London: SCM, 1982], 238).

[8] The question implies a further question, namely, the journey of wisdom into Yahwism. The reception of wisdom into Yahwism is an accomplished fact in the Old Testament, at least by the time of the completion of Prov 1–9. The way in which this happened cannot be investigated here.

with which Deuteronomy is distinguished by its use of wisdom vocabulary. In Exod 18:21 Moses is advised by Jethro to select "able men who fear God" (אַנְשֵׁי־חַיִל יִרְאֵי אֱלֹהִים) and who have moral integrity. The Numbers text foregrounds the concept of "spirit." Deuteronomy differs in these ways from its parallels in the Pentateuch, not only in Deut 1:9–18 but also in 16:18–20. The latter text, in the context of the book's detailed provisions for life in the land, again provides for the appointment of "judges and officers." Its dominant criterion is the pursuit of justice (צֶדֶק); but tellingly, whereas Exod 23:8 has "a bribe blinds the officials/those who see (פִּקְחִים)," Deut 16:19 has "a bribe blinds the eyes of *the wise*" (עֵינֵי חֲכָמִים).[9] Deuteronomy 16:18–20 varies from Deut 1:9–18 in that it focuses on the decisions of judges in court and omits military leadership. Nevertheless, in both texts Deuteronomy postulates wisdom as an indispensable quality of leadership.[10]

In this assignment of wisdom as a quality of leadership, Deuteronomy has close affinities with Proverbs. In the great speech of personified Wisdom in Prov 8, the rule of kings and princes is said to be owed to it (Prov 8:15–16). Proverbs also expressly associates wisdom with right judgment (Prov 24:23, cf. 28:21).[11] These texts also show an affinity with Deuteronomy in linguistic expression, as forms of the phrase הַכֵּר־פָּנִים בְּמִשְׁפָּט occur in the Old Testament only in Prov 24:23 and Deut 1:17 (cf. Deut 16:19).[12] Weinfeld notes further a parallel for this expression in Egyptian literature.[13]

Weinfeld extends his study of Deuteronomy into the Deuteronomic History, paying special attention to the Solomon narratives. Solomon prays for "an understanding heart/mind" (לֵב שֹׁמֵעַ, 1 Kgs 3:9),[14] and YHWH responds by granting him "a wise and discerning heart/mind"

---

[9] Moshe Weinfeld, *Deuteronomy and the Deuteronomic School* (Oxford: Clarendon, 1972), 244–45.

[10] For the distribution of wisdom vocabulary in Deuteronomy, see also Sheppard, *Wisdom as a Hermeneutical Construct*, 63–64.

[11] Weinfeld, *Deuteronomic School*, 245. He also describes the Deuteronomist's view of "true wisdom" as "the intellectual faculty which enables man to distinguish between good and evil in the judicial sphere" (ibid., 246–47).

[12] Deuteronomy 16:19 also has מִשְׁפָּט in the close context of תַכִּיר פָּנִים, though not in the same phrase.

[13] Weinfeld, *Deuteronomic School*, 245. He also notes the widespread occurrence of the verb "to hear" in connection with court judgments in Egypt and Mesopotamia.

[14] שֹׁמֵעַ is probably to be taken here in the sense of "understanding" (*HALAT* s.v. שמע 5). Cf. 2 Sam 14:17, where "hearing" implies the capacity to distinguish between good and evil; see also Num 24:4; Ezek 3:12; Job 4:6, 8. The phrase "a listening heart" derives, according to *HALAT*, from Egyptian wisdom literature (*HALAT* 4:1454).

(לֵב חָכָם וְנָבוֹן, v. 12). The purpose of both prayer and response is that Solomon might be able to judge, or govern, his people rightly. Weinfeld further argues that Solomon's vision at Gibeon is distinct from sanctuary-founding dream-visions in Ugarit and Mesopotamia in making the dream the vehicle for imparting wisdom.[15] On the strength of his study of both Deuteronomy and Kings, and the perceived affinities of these with ancient Near Eastern wisdom literature, Weinfeld argues for wisdom influence on the Deuteronomic literature broadly conceived. And he explains this by postulating a Deuteronomic school of scribes working in Jerusalem at the time of Josiah, who were influenced by wisdom language and concepts. These scribes subjected received traditions to their own overarching viewpoint in such a way that it is possible to detect pre-Deuteronomic and Deuteronomic layers in the literature. Solomon's dream-vision is a case in point, the vision-report itself belonging to pre-Deuteronomic tradition concerning a type of vision widely known in the ancient world, while the Deuteronomists re-presented it in accordance with their own program.

That program, as Weinfeld sees it, was broadly characterized by "secularizing" and "demythologizing" interests, which he takes to account for many of the features of Deuteronomy, such as the tendency that he calls "humanism," namely, its heightened concern for marginalized groups compared with earlier Old Testament legal material. This Deuteronomic program is also conceived as somewhat rational. Thus, for Weinfeld, the "wisdom and understanding" that Solomon prays for are "intellectual qualities" needed to judge well.[16] His analysis depends, therefore, on a sharp disjunction between what are perceived to be pre-Deuteronomic and Deuteronomic concepts of wisdom. The former include practical capabilities, such as the technical skills of artisans, like Bezalel, who was "filled with the spirit of God" to excel in all manner of craftsmanship (Exod 31:3–5), "native shrewdness," persuasive speech, and "general knowledge."[17] The latter is the result of nothing less than a revolution of thought, begun in the time of Hezekiah, marked by "a resurgence of intellectual literary activity," in which wisdom becomes "synonymous with the knowledge and understanding of proper behaviour and with morality."[18]

Weinfeld's analysis, therefore, has four essential components: first, the observation of conceptual and linguistic parallels between Deuteronomy and wisdom literature; second, the belief that wisdom in Israel evolved from an earlier form, characterized by practical skills, to a later

[15] Weinfeld, *Deuteronomic School*, 250.

[16] Ibid., 253.

[17] Ibid., 249–50, 254. He lists as cases of pre-Deuteronomic wisdom: 2 Sam 13:3; 1 Kgs 2:9; 2 Sam 14:2; 20:16; Gen 41:8, 33, 39; Exod 7:11; 28:3; 31:6; 35:25–26; 36:1; etc.; 2 Sam 14:20.

[18] Ibid., 255.

more intellectual or morally enlightened type; third, the view that this development could be observed within the Deuteronomic corpus; and fourth, the postulate of a Deuteronomic school of scribes in Jerusalem that was influenced by this developed form of wisdom, and that was responsible for the essential characteristics of Deuteronomy as we know it.

Weinfeld's powerful account of the wisdom tendency in Deuteronomy was challenged by Georg Braulik, among others. Braulik shows that there are differences as well as similarities between Deuteronomy and wisdom, such as the near absence in Old Testament wisdom literature of the verb למד (*qal* and *piel*), meaning respectively "learn" and "teach," whereas these are the most important terms in Deuteronomy for its learning and teaching program.[19] He finds no evidence for a distinct school of wisdom tradents in Jerusalem, arguing that the Jerusalem literary elite would have been educated in the full range of ancient Near Eastern ideas, and would have been familiar with treaty forms such as those of Esarhaddon (VTE). Instead of Weinfeld's concept of an intellectual revolution inspired by international wisdom, Braulik proposes that Deuteronomic wisdom was influenced by other external forms, notably the Assyrian treaty form, and that it developed a radical view of Israel as a society in response to the events before and after the Babylonian exile.[20] Thus, Deuteronomy's accentuated sympathy for the marginalized groups derives, not from a generalized moral-intellectual enlightenment, but from a very specific Deuteronomic vision, based on absolute loyalty to YHWH. It is a vision for a society characterized not only by justice but also by a distinctive kind of egalitarianism in which Israel is seen as a brother-/sisterhood. The enhanced position of women in Deuteronomy may be a consequence of its rejection of the Asherah cult, but with a concession to the degree of acceptance that that cult had given women.[21] Braulik explains the Deuteronomic interest in leaders' wisdom in Deut 1:9–18 as being in keeping with Isaiah's ironic ascription of "wisdom and understanding":

> Woe to those who are wise in their own eyes (הוֹי חֲכָמִים בְּעֵינֵיהֶם),
> And shrewd in their own sight (וְנֶגֶד פְּנֵיהֶם נְבֹנִים)! (Isa 5:21 RSV)

---

[19] Georg Braulik, " 'Weisheit' im Buch Deuteronomium," in *Studien zum Buch Deuteronomium*, SBAB 24 (Stuttgart: Verlag Katholisches Bibelwerk, 1997), 228–29; repr. from *Weisheit ausserhalb der kanonischen Weisheitsschriften*, ed. B. Janowski, VWGT 8 (Gütersloh: Gütersloher Verlagshaus, 1996), 39–69. The only exceptions are in Prov 5:13 and 30:3.

[20] Braulik actually inverts Weinfeld's chronological relationship between the concept of wisdom in Deut 4:5–8 and that found in Prov 1–9, which he thinks was not in its present form until the Persian period ("Weisheit," 255).

[21] Ibid., 229.

The wisdom and understanding demanded of leaders, therefore, are simply the requisite attributes of true leaders, conceived according to Deuteronomy's "democratic" theology of the nation.[22]

Braulik's response to Weinfeld challenges him on two fundamental points, namely, on the nature of wisdom as found in Deuteronomy, and on the provenance of the book from Jerusalem scribal schools. In his own analysis of wisdom in the book, he considers it in terms of concerns and features of Deuteronomy itself, and in doing so he offers a different proposal regarding the interrelationship of the various wisdom texts.

Braulik traces a narrative of wisdom in Deuteronomy against the backdrop of the Deuteronomic account of events before and after the exile. Deuteronomy 1:9–18 is integral to Deut 1–3 and belongs to the period of Josianic expansionism. The Josianic program ultimately failed with the fall of the state to Babylon. Deuteronomy 1:9–18 therefore belongs to a pattern of failure that is also predicated in DH's account of Solomon and his successors. In this context, Deut 4:5–8, set near the end of the exile, is a promulgation of torah, in which wisdom now belongs to the people through torah.[23] It presupposes Deut 1:13 and 15, both synchronically and diachronically, and imparts to the whole Deuteronomic law its character as torah.[24] The ideological context of this development is the Babylonian self-understanding as wise and learned. Israel's wisdom and learning cannot compete with Babylon's cultural and intellectual sophistication. After the fall of monarchy and temple, however, Israel still possesses one perceived advantage, namely, a superior concept of social order. "Wisdom," therefore, is henceforth understood, not as individual education, but as being exhibited in the Deuteronomic vision of society. When Israel properly manifested this, it would be seen to be the equal of its neighbors and a "great nation."[25] Central to this vision would be the elimination of poverty, through the full assimilation of the marginal groups as "brothers/sisters" in Israel. In this vision, YHWH would hear his people when they called to him in distress, apart from the need for any special place for meeting with him.[26] Deuteronomy was in this regard engaged in a critical dialogue with the revered tradition of justice deriving from Hammurabi.[27]

In favor of Braulik's account is his view of wisdom in Deuteronomy as having a background, not in the wisdom tradition exclusively, but more generally in the traditions of both the Old Testament and the ancient

[22] Ibid., 239–40.
[23] Ibid., 248.
[24] Ibid., 249.
[25] Ibid., 249–50.
[26] Ibid., 253.
[27] Ibid., 254.

Near East. Braulik's Deuteronomists are in touch with the Old Testament prophets as well as with broad currents of ancient Near Eastern thought. His explanation of Deut 4:5–8 as a commendation of torah to the nations also identifies the key point of that text. And he attempts to understand wisdom in Deuteronomy within the logic of that book, as he sees it. In common with Weinfeld, however, he bases his account on a theory about the positioning of Deuteronomy within a certain religio-historical scenario, entailing views about the dating of the book and the stages of its growth and development.

The key difference between Weinfeld and Braulik is in the extent to which they find convergence between the postulated identifiable strands of religious thought, namely, torah and wisdom. On this point Braulik is rightly more cautious than Weinfeld.

Evolving Wisdom?

In the foregoing we have seen how attempts to understand wisdom in Deuteronomy are attended by reconstructions both of the story of wisdom in Old Testament Israel and of the redactional history of Deuteronomy in relation to this. A recent study illustrates this point, and shows how the questions addressed by both Weinfeld and Braulik continue to dominate the field.

Reinhard Müller explores the "sapiential tradition" in relation to Deut 16:19–20.[28] Broadly accepting that Deuteronomy shows evidence of influence by the sapiential (wisdom) tradition, he notes the parallel (observed by Weinfeld) between Deut 16:19 and Exod 23:8,[29] in which Deuteronomy substitutes "the wise" for the Exodus text's more general "open-eyed." Whereas Weinfeld saw this simply as evidence of a sapiential tendency in Deuteronomy, Müller finds a more complicated state of affairs. For him, Deut 16:19 implies a criticism of "the wise": "being wise does not protect from the influences of bribery."[30] In his view, the author of Deut 16:19 has in mind a particular group, designated "the wise," namely, those elected as Israel's "heads" and "judges" in Deut 1:15–16. Regarding this relationship between Deut 16 and Deut 1:9–18, he sees an important difference between 16:18 and 16:19. Deuteronomy 16:18 finds a corresponding echo in 1:15–16, in that both texts provide for the appointment of judges throughout the tribes who were to judge justly. Deuteronomy 1:13 and

[28] Reinhard Müller, "The Blinded Eyes of the Wise: Sapiential Tradition and Mosaic Commandment in Deut 16:19–20," in *Wisdom and Torah*, 9–33.

[29] See above, note 8.

[30] Müller, "Blinded Eyes of the Wise," 15.

15 supply a gap left in 16:18 by spelling out the qualities needed for the exercise of such judgment, namely, that they should be "wise, discerning, and experienced." Deuteronomy 16:19, however, takes a critical stance toward Deut 1:9–18. In this text, "the peculiar change of the proverbial saying from Exod 23:8b was likely motivated by the way in which Israel's judges were chosen according to Deuteronomy 1."[31] Müller develops this point by arguing that the wisdom exemplified by the qualities required of these leaders lacks any "spiritual dimension," when compared with other texts on leadership qualities, such as Num 11:24–30, or the portrayal of Joseph in Gen 41.[32] The wisdom of these judges "seems to have been completely acquired by themselves."[33] Deuteronomy 16:19, therefore, is a critique of the view expressed in Deut 1:9–18 and Deut 16:18. However, all this occurs within the scribal tradition that is attested in Deuteronomy. Deuteronomy 16:19, indeed, together with verse 20, is a kind of "self-critique" on the part of the scribes themselves.[34] Müller considers this to be a remarkable critique of wisdom, comparable to a prophetic text such as Jer 8:8–9.[35]

This convoluted argument has in common with Weinfeld a belief that Deuteronomy is broadly indebted to the wisdom tradition, and it shares with Braulik an attempt to reconstruct a history of wisdom in Deuteronomy with a theory about the growth of the text. The weakness of the argument lies in its uncritical assumption that texts must be read as if referring to some phenomenon lying behind them that can only be deciphered by scholarly art. In reality, Deut 16:19 requires for its understanding no reference to some specific body of "the wise," but only the premise that even wise people need to be forearmed against the blandishments of the powerful. Nor is his recourse to an elaborate self-critique convincing; Deut 16:18–20 is an entirely coherent overture to the book's extended section on administration (Deut 16:18–18:20), providing for the appointment of judges tribe by tribe, recalling their obligation not to be corrupt, and building its exhortation into a general plea to seek justice uncompromisingly (16:20). It has elements in common with the wisdom tradition (Prov 24:23), but this merely shows that law and wisdom in Israel had points in common, rather than demonstrating dependence or assimilation. And its hortatory style, with its sharp awareness of the chosen people's corruptibility, is entirely Deuteronomic.

---

[31] Ibid., 22.

[32] Ibid., 24–25.

[33] Ibid., 25. He cites Braulik ("Weisheit," 246) in support of this view.

[34] Müller, "Blinded Eyes of the Wise," 27.

[35] Ibid., 29.

This example illustrates some of the problems involved in any attempt to match the study of Deuteronomy to an account of the development of wisdom. Such attempts almost inevitably have an air of circularity about them. This is true, for example, when distinctions perceived between forms of wisdom are plotted on a timeline. Weinfeld, as we have seen, makes a sharp division between an older, pre-Deuteronomic concept of wisdom, consisting of practical or technical forms of human capability, as exemplified by Bezalel (Exod 31), and the kinds of accomplishment nurtured in the more advanced moral-intellectual hothouse of wisdom circles in which he finds the origins and genius of Deuteronomy.[36] But this is unsustainable. One can respond to it in part with a semantic point, namely, that the term חָכָם ("wise") has a range of possible meanings in the Old Testament. For example, there is the "wisdom" of Jonadab, who offers his friend Amnon advice regarding his consuming desire for his half-sister Tamar. Jonadab's advice to Amnon is disastrous, leading to the murder of Amnon by Tamar's full brother Absalom and arguably to the devastating civil war between Absalom and David and Absalom's own wretched death. Yet Jonadab is אִישׁ חָכָם מְאֹד (lit., "a very wise man," 2 Sam 13:3)! The adjective here clearly has the pejorative sense of "crafty" or "wily." It would be wrong to assign this to a "pre-Deuteronomic" meaning of the word; it is simply one of the things the word can mean. The point may be extended by observing that the Jonadab passage occurs within the extended narrative of David's reign (2 Sam 7–1 Kgs 2) that embeds a nuanced reflection on the meaning of wisdom. Joab co-opts a "wise woman" to his purpose of containing the threat of Absalom; she in turn attributes wisdom to David, who has spoken (wisely) against himself in interpreting her case: he "has wisdom like the wisdom of the angel of God to know all things that are on the earth" (2 Sam 14:20). In verse 17, the king is (again) "like the angel of God to discern good and evil" (cf. Deut 30:15). (Weinfeld calls this "general knowledge," but that is far too bland.[37]) Finally, 1 Kgs 2:9 portrays David advocating to Solomon a kind of "wisdom" that ruthlessly achieves a political purpose. The whole story may be seen as a reflection on and exploration of what is entailed in acquiring, and possibly losing, wisdom. This reflection may or may not be "Deuteronomic." But when we consider the actual usage of "wisdom" language we find that it resists being slotted neatly into preconceived categories.

One can respond further to Weinfeld's polarization with the substantial point that Old Testament wisdom simply embraces all kinds of human

---

[36] See above, note 16.

[37] Weinfeld, *Deuteronomic School*, 254.

capability. Taking issue with R. N. Whybray,[38] Raymond van Leeuwen makes the point effectively in an essay on temple-building in the ancient Near East and the Old Testament. Drawing on extrabiblical models, he shows that the building and provisioning of temples was long regarded as being accomplished through divine wisdom. In the Old Testament, there are close analogies between the wisdom language used for the building of the tabernacle (Exod 31:3; 35:31) and temple (1 Kgs 7:13–14) and the language found in Proverbs for YHWH's creation of the world (Prov 3:19–20; 24:3–4).[39] For van Leeuwen, wisdom embraces the wide range of activities attributed to it in the Old Testament because YHWH created, or "built," the world with wisdom. The technical forms of it are not inferior: "Rather it is Wisdom per se, from which all other forms are derived."[40] Humans, in exercising wisdom across a range of endeavors, are imitating the mind of the creator.

Wisdom therefore includes the applied skills and knowledge of artisans as well as the personal, moral, and intellectual capacities that are in accord with the way things are in the world. And conversely in Deuteronomy, the individual laws include provisions that look very much like practical common sense (e.g., Deut 22:1–4, 6–8). So while it is true that Deuteronomy and wisdom draw predominantly on different streams of ancient Near Eastern thought, there are features of both that testify to a greater range of perception and reception on the part of the biblical writers.

Taken together, Weinfeld and Braulik highlight the complexity of the Old Testament's interrelationships. Deuteronomy and Old Testament wisdom literature evidently have much in common, yet they are distinctive. It is difficult to express the relationship of the two corpora neatly in terms

---

[38] R. N. Whybray, *The Intellectual Tradition in the Old Testament*, BZAW 135 (Berlin: de Gruyter, 1974). Whybray's thesis (ibid., 83) is similar to Weinfeld's. As van Leeuwen points out, Whybray regards all instances of the root חכם that refer to manual skill as "non-significant," and includes among his examples of this all its occurrences in Exodus pertaining to the constructing of the tabernacle, ark, and priestly garments (Raymond van Leeuwen, "Cosmos, Temple, House: Building and Wisdom in Mesopotamia and Israel," in *From the Foundations to the Crenellations: Essays on Temple-Building in the Ancient Near East and Hebrew Bible*, ed. Mark J. Boda and Jamie Novotny [Münster: Ugarit Verlag, 2010], 418 and note).

[39] Van Leeuwen, "Cosmos, Temple, House," 418; cf. 412–15. He cites also Prov 8:22–31; 9:1; 14:1. See also Angelika Berlejung, "Der Handwerker als Theologe: Zur Mentalitäts- und Traditionsgeschichte eines altorientalischen und alttestamentlichen Berufstands," *VT* 46 (1996): 154. Berlejung shows that in the ancient Near East and in Israel the artisans of temple and tabernacle had especially close relationships with and understanding of their God, and because of this they could rightly be called "theologians."

[40] Van Leeuwen, "Cosmos, Temple, House," 418.

of either similarity or difference: neither is one the child of the other, nor are they reducible to some kind of commonality. There are several clear differences between the two. While Deuteronomy may be said to be politically radical, Proverbs is rather conservative—there is no critical analysis of kingship here. Proverbs lacks an account of Israel's history, or any evident concern with it, and it includes foreigners as well as Israelites within its reach of potential learners and, indeed, teachers (Prov 30–31).[41] The "exotic" setting of Job in the land of Uz also seems to imply an international orientation. Finally, Proverbs lacks a systematic teaching and learning program, in contrast to Deuteronomy's extensive record of Moses' teaching, and the book's intention to create a "community of learning" in Israel based on it.[42]

Nor (conversely) are they conceptually opposed. Both Deuteronomy and wisdom are set within ancient Near Eastern currents of thought, and in distinctive ways. Deuteronomy, I think, owes more to the streams of treaty and law, while Proverbs and related Old Testament literature partake rather of the ancient Near East's wisdom heritage. Yet it is a mistake to force either into a Procrustean bed formed of either of these. The topic is beset by a temptation to polarize.

Wisdom in Deuteronomy

How then does Deuteronomy understand wisdom? Braulik rightly attempts to answer this by attending to the developing logic of the relevant texts within the book. He is correct, I believe, to find in it a close relationship between wisdom and the vision for Israel as a society that is enshrined in the laws. As we saw at the outset, wisdom language occurs at key points in the book. It is also true that wisdom is in a sense "democratized" here. This does not imply some advance of 4:5–8 over 1:9–18, however, as Braulik thought. Rather, it belongs within the spirit of Deuteronomy as a whole, with its pervasive address to the whole people, and their obligation, individually and corporately, to learn all that is involved in obedience to the torah.[43] Braulik's argument that Deuteronomy embod-

[41] For a full account of the similarities and differences between Deuteronomy and Proverbs in relation to teaching and learning see Karin Finsterbusch, *Weisung für Israel: Studien zu religiösem Lehren und Lernen im Deuteronomium und in seinem Umfeld*, FRLANT 44 (Tübingen: Mohr Siebeck, 2005), e.g., 111–14, for her summary of Proverbs.

[42] This is one of the major differences between the two identified by Finsterbusch (ibid., 316).

[43] Braulik seems to hesitate on this point. Having read 1:9–18 as a provision that failed, he nevertheless concedes that Deuteronomy regards it as continuing

ies a conception of peoplehood that constitutes not merely a utopian vision but a direct ideological challenge to forms of society in the ancient Near East is also correct. In my view, however, one does not need to locate this in the late exilic period; it could equally well be preexilic.

As we have seen, it is by no means clear that the key text in Deut 4:5–8 aims to express an equivalence between wisdom and the "statutes and ordinances." It is even less clear that it equates torah with a particular concept of wisdom, namely, as a specific movement or ideological tendency, at least not without other evidence to support this. As Braulik saw, it is likely that the passage means that the torah, and Israel's observance of it, will be taken by other nations to demonstrate the wisdom of Israel, in the same way that other nations saw their own laws as just. For Krüger, "Deut 4:5–8 is not a discussion of the relationship between Wisdom and Torah in principle. Rather, the verses express the desire that Israel's obedience to the Mosaic Law will lead to its recognition by the nations."[44] And for this to be true, it is not necessary to adopt any theory of the relationship between Deuteronomy and wisdom groups.

The passage suggests, therefore, that when the nations "hear" the statutes, they will attribute wisdom to the people (v. 6). Content and enactment can hardly be separated in this wisdom. The torah as a whole, as the totality of Moses' instruction, is wise in its conception, and its wisdom becomes manifest in its implementation. This interpretation fits, I think, with the character of Deuteronomic torah as instruction to be learned and digested by all Israelites (6:4–9) and to be applied to all areas of their life. One can take the point further and suppose that Israel could be said to *become* wise through the learning and doing of torah. If there is wisdom in the torah and the keeping of it, this might be expected to have good outcomes. The wisdom of the torah's measures to eliminate chronic poverty, for example, could only be learned through the actions that Israelites were required to take in order to effect this. Such actions might indeed have been counterintuitive, especially where—as frequently in the laws—they entailed the voluntary giving up of goods that might

---

to have validity, and that it is no mere historical reminiscence of the wilderness period ("Weisheit," 249n82). He also finds a democratic spirit generally in Deuteronomy, and specifically in 1:9–18 (ibid., 239–40).

[44] Krüger, "Law and Wisdom," 51–52. He thought a setting of the text in the time of the Achaemenids fits well with their known positive interest in the laws of other nations, citing Ezra 7:25–26, as well as texts in Herodotus (48–51). Compare on this Joseph Blenkinsopp, *Wisdom and Law in the Old Testament* (Oxford: Oxford University Press, 1983), 76: "*torah* is said to constitute for Israel what wisdom is to those nations which host an ancient and well established scribal tradition"; see also Jack R. Lundbom, *Deuteronomy: A Commentary* (Grand Rapids: Eerdmans, 2013), 238.

have been considered one's own due. Examples are the release of debt-slaves in the sixth year, together with sufficient provision for them to become economically viable again (Deut 15:12–18), and the pilgrimage feasts of Weeks and Tabernacles, in which family wealth was to be shared with "the Levite, the stranger, the orphan, and the widow" (Deut 16:11, 14, cf. 14:29). The dynamic of sacrificial action leading to blessing is a feature of the persuasive rhetoric of Deuteronomy (Deut 14:29b; 15:6, 10; 16:15). It is misunderstood when regarded as a crude ethic of reward and punishment, because such a view reckons without, chiefly, the principled acceptance of a strong ethic of solidarity, not to mention the enormous act of faith involved in adopting the self-sacrificial measures. The laws, therefore, and the rhetoric of motivation that accompanies them, may be said to have a didactic—or better, a formative—function. Those who keep torah learn by doing it that the torah is good and true, or put differently, that it is wise.[45]

Related to this is the nature of the Mosaic instruction. One of the unavoidable features of torah in Deuteronomy is its differences from parallel texts in the Pentateuch. The laws of slave-release in Exodus and Deuteronomy may be cited as an example. One way of accounting for such differences is that, far from being accidental, or merely evidence of the historical development of Israelite law over time, they are essential to the characterization of the Mosaic instruction. By this I mean that Moses is portrayed, not as one who simply subjects Israel to a kind of learning drill, but as one who acts as an interpreter of torah, and who thus models the same for Israel. Therefore, as a learning community, Israel is invited into a life-practice that yields a deepening knowledge of the meaning of torah. Finsterbusch rightly sees Moses' *freedom* in his expression of the statutes as a corollary of his great authority as a teacher, and it is this concept of teaching torah that operates in the constitution of Israel as a learning community. In this way, torah is not frozen in any particular form (despite the declaration of its immutability in the formula that warns against adding to or taking away from the Deuteronomic instruction). Rather, it points beyond itself to an understanding of YHWH's work in history, and to an undergirding attitude, namely, the *fear of YHWH*.[46]

To say that the torah is wise, therefore, is not the same as postulating an absolute congruity between torah and "wisdom."[47] With this in mind

[45] Finsterbusch argues that Moses in Deuteronomy does not simply pass on the statutes; his *teaching* them constitutes Israel as a *learning community*; moreover, Moses as teacher motivates Israel to *do* the commandments (Finsterbusch, *Weisung für Israel,* 307–8).

[46] Ibid., 307–11.

[47] Probably not even Sirach does this, in spite of Sir 24:23. Gerhard von Rad thought that Sirach was not centrally interested in the Torah, but was much more

it is important to take into account the full picture of wisdom in Deuteronomy. Curiously, having identified Deut 32:29 and 34:9 as wisdom texts, Braulik entirely omits the former from consideration (despite his interest elsewhere in his argument in synchronic considerations), and the latter he assigns not strictly to Deuteronomy but more broadly to the Pentateuch.[48] These are important texts, not least because they invoke wisdom quite apart from the torah. The Song of Moses (Deut 32:1–43) lacks any reference to torah. This is no doubt one reason why it has been regarded as deriving from a separate source and as having an ambivalent relationship with the rest of the book. The Song has in common with the rest of the book, however, its concern that Israel should learn and understand its true identity in the context of YHWH's history with them and the other nations. The aspect of historical understanding is clear throughout Deut 1–11, with its reminiscences of Egypt and the wilderness (e.g., 4:34–40; 8), and also in the laws, in which the same memory becomes a spur to compassionate behavior toward the marginal groups (15:15) and also serves as an antithesis to the ideal of living in the land according to torah (17:16). The Song locates wisdom in the understanding of YHWH's purposes throughout all this history. Israel's position on the borders of the promised land is inexplicable apart from the astoundingly unexpected events that have brought them there:

> How can one man chase a thousand
> Or two see off a host,
> Unless their Rock had sold them,
> Unless the Lord had given them up? (Deut 32:30)

Only by being "wise" can Israel hope to understand this mystery in the way things are. Wisdom here means nothing less than the spiritual readiness and capacity to know the ways of YHWH. And the thought is evidently capable of being expressed without appeal to the role of torah in it.

---

at home with wisdom language and concepts (von Rad, *Wisdom in Israel*, 244). For him, Sirach endeavors "to legitimize and to interpret Torah from the realm of understanding characteristic of wisdom" (245); the Torah is (merely) "the primeval order inherent in the whole world appearing in a new guise" (246). Sirach belongs to a conceptual world in which Mosaic torah is coming to take a dominant place; he probably meant by torah, not Deuteronomy alone, but the canonical Pentateuch (Braulik, "Weisheit," 255). Yet wisdom in Sirach both remains indebted to traditional Israelite wisdom and engages in contemporary debate about it. For example, Sirach contends that wisdom is available to all, in the manner of Lady Wisdom's invitation (Sir 24:19), in contrast with 1 Enoch, which presents it as esoteric and remote. See on this Randal A. Argall, *1 Enoch and Sirach: A Comparative, Literary and Conceptual Analysis of the Themes of Revelation, Creation and Judgment*, SBLEJL 8 (Atlanta: Scholars Press, 1995), 92–94.

[48] Braulik, "Weisheit," 263.

In Deut 34:9, Joshua is "filled with the spirit of wisdom, for Moses had laid hands on him." There is an allusion to the torah in the following clause, which tells that the people listened to him, "and they did all that the LORD had commanded Moses." However, it is significant that stress is laid on the wisdom that Moses imparts to Joshua, and indeed on "the spirit of wisdom," rather than on a body of teaching. There is evidently more to wisdom than torah. It is something that can be transmitted from person to person and can be qualified by a phrase with "spirit" (רוּחַ). Here is something that cannot be exhausted by an objective body of teaching.

Conclusion

I have argued that Deuteronomy and wisdom literature have their own irreducible individuality, deriving from the distinctive engagement of each with ancient Near Eastern traditions. Deuteronomy is oriented toward the ancient Near East's heritage of treaty and law, while Old Testament wisdom faces primarily toward ancient Near Eastern wisdom. Neither of these is exclusive, and the biblical writers are aware of other intellectual currents both within the Old Testament and in the ancient Near East. Each has subjected streams of thought to a fundamental Yahwistic vision, so that both Deuteronomy and Old Testament wisdom can properly be said to be fully in the service of YHWH. Yet their individuality remains intact.

A corollary of this is that the wisdom of YHWH, and indeed the wisdom commended to Israel in both Deuteronomy and the Old Testament wisdom literature, cannot be equated without remainder with any given body of teaching. Wisdom may indeed be seen, with van Leeuwen, as an overarching category, capable of enfolding within it the wisdom that is manifested in the Deuteronomic law and the ability to discern the meaning of YHWH's acts in history on behalf of Israel, as well as that which consists in the experimental discovery of YHWH's world that may be said to characterize Old Testament wisdom. Both corpora appeal in their own ways to YHWH's creative ordering of history and nature. Deuteronomy asserts the wisdom of holding to covenant faithfulness, the knowledge of YHWH and the governing of life under torah; Proverbs adapts all of wisdom's thinking about human capacity and possibility, the snakes and ladders lying along the "two ways," equally to a view of the world ordered by YHWH. The wisdom of both encourages us to think that we can hope to live well in YHWH's world. But there is wisdom too, I think, in a readiness to allow both these parts of Scripture to have their individual integrity, without letting the reading of the one overly influence the reading of the other.

CHAPTER 10

When a Prophet Quotes Moses: On the Relationship between the Book of Hosea and Deuteronomy

Carsten Vang

Introduction

One of the distinctive features of the book of Hosea is the prophet's frequent use of diverse traditions from the early history of Israel.[1] This includes the claim that God chose Israel in its early days and gave it binding obligations. In Hos 10:11–12, the prophet describes in vivid figurative language how YHWH placed a yoke on a young, eager heifer (Ephraim/Israel) to harness the plow, a metaphor for serving YHWH and following his precepts.[2] References such as these are often so concise and lapidary that the prophet must assume a rather extensive knowledge on the part of his listeners in order for them to grasp the meaning of his message.

In addition to diverse references to Israel's early history, there are striking connections between Hosea and Deuteronomy. This relationship appears in shared words, phrases, and sentences, e.g., the sequence of expressions שָׂבַע—רָם לֵב—שָׁכַח אֶת יהוה ("be satisfied—be proud—forget YHWH"), in Hos 13:6 and Deut 8:12–14. Many parallels also turn up in shared theological ideas, e.g., a strong opposition to non-Yahwistic worship and cultic sites on the hills, or the notion that Israel's history from its beginning is inextricably linked with God's love for his people (Hos

[1] Cf. Dwight R. Daniels, *Hosea and Salvation History: The Early Traditions of Israel in the Prophecy of Hosea*, BZAW 191 (Berlin: de Gruyter, 1990); Else K. Holt, *Prophesying the Past: The Use of Israel's History in the Book of Hosea*, JSOTSup 194 (Sheffield: Sheffield Academic, 1995); Jerry Hwang, " 'I Am Yahweh Your God from the Land of Egypt': Hosea's Use of the Exodus Traditions," in *"Did I Not Bring Israel Out of Egypt?": Biblical, Archaeological, and Egyptological Perspectives on the Exodus Narratives*, ed. James K. Hoffmeier, Alan R. Millard, and Gary A. Rendsburg, BBRSup 13 (Winona Lake, IN: Eisenbrauns, 2016), 243–53; Heinz-Dieter Neef, *Die Heilstraditionen Israels in der Verkündigung des Propheten Hosea*, BZAW 169 (Berlin: de Gruyter, 1987).

[2] See Göran Eidevall, *Grapes in the Desert: Metaphors, Models, and Themes in Hosea 4–14*, ConBOT 43 (Stockholm: Almqvist & Wiksell, 1996), 159–61.

11:1; Deut 7:7–8).[3] Both works share a prominent covenantal dimension. They also share several metaphors and similes, e.g., a father and son (Hos 11:1; Deut 8:5; 14:1) or a swooping eagle (Hos 8:1; Deut 28:49). Moses is called a נָבִיא ("prophet") only in Deuteronomy (18:15, 18; 34:10) and in Hos 12:14[ET 13]. Israelite prophecy has Mosaic roots according to both Deuteronomy and Hosea. On several levels, therefore, strong intertextual links between Hosea and Deuteronomy can be observed.[4]

The Question of Dependence

How are these links to be understood? Are they just accidental, a witness to the fact that Hosea and Deuteronomy in their present forms address the same problems and share a similar theological understanding, and for these reasons draw from the same stock of stereotype formulas? Some of the verbal parallels may be explained in that manner, but not all. Most scholars are convinced that a majority of the verbal and thematic parallels in Hosea and Deuteronomy are not chance occurrences but bear witness to some sort of literary dependence. This article will address the question of dependence: Who influenced whom? Who—the author/editors of Deuteronomy or of Hosea—reused verbal elements from the other tradition and transformed them to fit into their own rhetoric and arguments? Was it Hosea who in multifarious ways influenced the later Deuteronomic covenantal exposition? Or was it the reverse, with Hosea reusing elements from an already existing Deuteronomic exposition that he and his circle considered authoritative?

This question is extremely important, and not only for a correct historical evaluation of the relationship between the two books in question. It also makes a crucial difference in the interpretation of texts like Deut 8:12–14 and Hos 13:4–6—which one should be considered the depen-

[3] The root אהב is very common in Hosea and Deuteronomy but is nearly absent from other prophetic books or the Covenant Code. The root is found seventeen times in Hosea and eighteen times in Deuteronomy, referring either to God's love for Israel or Israel's relationship to God/other gods.

[4] In addition, see the surveys in H. Louis Ginsberg, *The Israelian Heritage of Judaism* (New York: The Stroock Publication Fund, 1982), 19–24; Jack R. Lundbom, *Deuteronomy: A Commentary* (Grand Rapids: Eerdmans, 2013), 33–35; James Robson, "The Literary Composition of Deuteronomy," in *Interpreting Deuteronomy: Issues and Approaches*, ed. David G. Firth and Philip S. Johnston (Downers Grove, IL: InterVarsity Press, 2012), 19–59, at 47–48; Moshe Weinfeld, *Deuteronomy and the Deuteronomic School* (Oxford: Clarendon, 1972), 366–70; Weinfeld, *Deuteronomy 1–11*, AB 5 (New York: Doubleday, 1991), 44–49; Hans W. Wolff, *Hosea: A Commentary on the Book of the Prophet Hosea*, trans. Gary Stansell, Hermeneia (Philadelphia: Fortress, 1974), xxxi.

dent text? Either Deut 8:12–14 quotes Hos 13:4–6—i.e., Deuteronomy has rephrased Hosea's accusation against Israel for having forgotten YHWH into a general admonition not to forget him—or Hos 13:4–6 prophetically actualizes the injunction in Deut 8 for Israel not to forget YHWH when it enters the promised land and enjoys its blessings.

In order to address this question, we will first describe the literary phenomenon of quotation and review recent discussions about possible literary criteria for determining the direction of dependence in cases of quotation. Next, we will study three examples of verbal parallels between Hosea and Deuteronomy and examine the contexts of each for indications of who has reused and adapted phrases and ideas from whom. Thematic parallels fall outside the scope of this essay.[5] In the first place, however, we will sketch the problem by reviewing the most common scholarly positions today.

Outline of the Major Positions

Scholars have given very different answers about the direction of influence and impact involving Deuteronomy and Hosea. The dominant position within historical-critical scholarship has been to view Hosea as one of the forerunners of the later Deuteronomic movement. Accordingly, the Deuteronomists took up certain Hosean phrases and theological concepts and transformed them into general covenantally embedded legislation. In other words, the intertextuality of Hosea and Deuteronomy suggests that *Ur-Deuteronomium* has roots in the Northern Kingdom of Israel. This understanding dominates Hans Walter Wolff's magisterial commentary on Hosea. He claims, "Entire complexes of thought characteristic of Deuteronomic paraenesis occur first in Hosea"; and further, "Here [Hos 13:6] we again recognize in Hosea one of the fathers of the early Deuteronomic movement."[6] In this interpretation Wolff is followed by most recent

[5] See Carsten Vang, "God's Love according to Hosea and Deuteronomy: A Prophetic Reworking of a Deuteronomic Concept?" *TynBul* 62 (2011): 173–94.

[6] Wolff, *Hosea*, xxxi and 226. In German: "Ganze Dankbewegungen, die für die deuteronomische Paränese kennzeichnend sind, finden wir erstmals bei Hosea" and "Wieder ist Hosea als einer der Väter der frühdeuteronomischen Bewegung zu erkennen." The quotations in German are taken from the 4th German ed. (1990, xxvi and 294), an imprint of the reworked 3rd ed. (1975). In his understanding that Deuteronomy is rooted in Hosea's preaching, Wolff builds upon, among others, Albrecht Alt, "Die Heimat des Deuteronomiums," in *Kleine Schriften zur Geschichte des Volkes Israel* (Munich: C. H. Beck, 1953), 2:250–75, at 271–73.

scholars,[7] and in particular by Konstantin Zobel, who has written the only specialized monograph on the subject.[8] These works frequently lack literary arguments for the claimed direction of influence. Hosean priority is simply assumed on the premise that *Ur-Deuteronomium* was composed during the latter days of the Judahite kingdom. The literary relationship is assumed in advance without seeking literary indications of the direction of influence in the texts.

Other scholars have stressed the individuality of the books of Hosea and Deuteronomy. They find that the differences in outlook between them are so extensive that the intertextuality should be explained rather in terms of dependence on a shared Ephraimite tradition. Both Hosea and Deuteronomy appear to be heirs to a shared tradition.[9] Accordingly, the many verbal and thematic parallels between these two books are not intentional.

Scholars with a more conservative orientation have tended to understand the direction of influence the other way around. In their magisterial commentary on Hosea, Andersen and Freedman maintain that "Hosea's discourses . . . are threaded with Deuteronomic ideas in a way that shows that they already were authoritative in Israel. Whether already written in an early form or still largely oral, Deuteronomic material served as background for much of Hosea's thought."[10] The fact that many Deuteronomy-

---

[7] E.g., G. I. Davies, *Hosea*, NCB (Grand Rapids: Eerdmans, 1992), 36; Jörg Jeremias, *Der Prophet Hosea*, ATD 24/1 (Göttingen: Vandenhoeck & Ruprecht, 1983), 44, 70, 141, 164; Jeremias, "Hosea/Hoseabuch," *TRE* 15 (1986): 586–98, at 594; Robert A. Kugler, "The Deuteronomists and the Latter Prophets," in *Those Elusive Deuteronomists: The Phenomenon of Pan-Deuteronomism*, ed. Linda S. Schearing and Steven L. McKenzie, JSOTSup 268 (Sheffield: Sheffield Academic, 1999), 127–44, at 138–39; Lundbom, *Deuteronomy*, 33–34; Eduard Nielsen, *Deuteronomium*, HAT 1/6 (Tübingen: Mohr Siebeck, 1995), 6–7; Alexander Rofé, "The Book of Deuteronomy: A Summary," in *Deuteronomy: Issues and Interpretation*, OTS (London: T&T Clark, 2002), 7–8; Jeffrey H. Tigay, *Deuteronomy*, דברים (Philadelphia: Jewish Publication Society of America, 1996), xxiii; Weinfeld, *Deuteronomic School*, 366–70; Hans-Jürgen Zobel, "Hosea und das Deuteronomium: Erwägungen eines Alttestamentlers zum Thema 'Sprache und Theologie,'" *TLZ* 110 (1985): 13–24.

[8] Konstantin Zobel, *Prophetie und Deuteronomium: Die Rezeption prophetischer Theologie durch das Deuteronomium*, BZAW 199 (Berlin: de Gruyter, 1992).

[9] Thus, e.g., Daniels, *Hosea and Salvation History*, 120–22; Cees Houtman, *Der Pentateuch: Die Geschichte seiner Erforschung neben einer Auswertung*, CBET 9 (Kampen: Kok Pharos, 1994), 306. J. Andrew Dearman, *The Book of Hosea*, NICOT (Grand Rapids: Eerdmans, 2010), voices sympathy for this model (36–39).

[10] Francis I. Andersen and David N. Freedman, *Hosea: A New Translation with Introduction and Commentary*, AB 24 (New York: Doubleday, 1980), 75. To a great extent, they build upon Walter Brueggemann's study of the traditions in Hosea, *Tradition for Crisis: A Study in Hosea* (Richmond, VA: John Knox, 1968). It should be noted, however, that Brueggemann has modified his earlier strong affirmation

like phrases are embedded in Hosea's preaching suggests that Hosea is indebted to a prevalent Deuteronomic tradition.[11] Literary arguments for this interpretation are not offered, however.

In his commentary Douglas Stuart claims that Hosea's oracles of doom and salvation are directly dependent on the blessing and curse sections in Lev 26 and Deut 28, which is seen either through direct references or through allusions.[12] Unfortunately, Stuart offers no support for this claim, which is based on a literary analysis of the shared themes. Mark Rooker similarly offers a list of many diverse connections between Hosea and Deuteronomy and states: "Hosea appears to be aware of the book of Deuteronomy in its entirety. This awareness may be demonstrated not only through the common themes prevalent in each work but also by the borrowing of technical legal phraseology on the part of Hosea."[13] Rooker, however, offers no literary analysis of these parallels that might substantiate his understanding of the diachronic relationship.

In a recent dissertation on the hermeneutical aspects of Hosea's use of literary traditions, Derek D. Bass argues that Hosea extensively quotes and alludes to the Pentateuch, particularly Deuteronomy.[14] He finds that Hosea must be dependent on Deuteronomy from two considerations: (1) The sheer extent and scope of Hosea's allusions to prior material make it probable that he is dependent on the Pentateuch. (2) "Numerous scholars have demonstrated the plausibility of early dates for separate portions of the Pentateuch by comparison of the biblical data to ANE analogues."[15]

Some critical scholars would agree that the extant book of Hosea is dependent on Deuteronomy. However, they explain the diverse affinities between these two books as a result of extensive Deuteronomistic

---

of Hosea's dependence on Deuteronomic traditions; cf. his commentary *Deuteronomy*, AOTC (Nashville: Abingdon, 2001), 21.

[11] Other scholars envisage the Hosea-Deuteronomy relationship in a similar manner, e.g., J. G. McConville, *Deuteronomy*, ApOTC 5 (Leicester: Apollos, 2002), 20; Chaim Rabin, "Discourse Analysis and the Dating of Deuteronomy," in *Interpreting the Hebrew Bible: Essays in Honour of E. I. J. Rosenthal*, ed. J. A. Emerton and Stefan C. Reif, UCOP 32 (Cambridge: Cambridge University Press, 1982), 171–77; Edward J. Woods, *Deuteronomy*, TOTC 5 (Downers Grove, IL: InterVarsity Press, 2011), 31.

[12] Douglas Stuart, *Hosea–Jonah*, WBC 31 (Waco, TX: Word, 1987), xxxii–xlii, 17–18. See also Daniel I. Block, *Deuteronomy*, NIVAC (Grand Rapids: Zondervan, 2012), 34.

[13] Mark F. Rooker, "The Use of the Old Testament in the Book of Hosea," *CTR* 7 (1993): 51–66, at 62.

[14] Derek D. Bass, "Hosea's Use of Scripture: An Analysis of His Hermeneutics" (PhD diss., The Southern Baptist Theological Seminary, 2008). Used by kind permission from the author. I am indebted to Jason S. DeRouchie for directing my attention to this dissertation.

[15] Ibid., 92–93.

redactions or "Fortschreibungen" in the book of Hosea.[16] The direction of influence thus goes from a postexilic Deuteronomy to an even later Deuteronomistic expansion of Hosea's prophecies.

The disturbing fact is that both historical-critical and conservative scholars appeal to the same pool of intertextual links and shared phrases but come to opposite conclusions. In their evaluation of the shared ideas and phraseology, they seem to be governed by an a priori understanding of the relationship between Deuteronomy and the book of Hosea. However, none of the sources cited above offer the kind of literary study of the shared locutions that would demonstrate either that Hosea is influenced by Deuteronomy or that the putative Deuteronomic movement took over and reused textual elements from Hosea. It is precisely this type of study of the *literary* relationship between the books of Hosea and Deuteronomy that is the subject of this article.

Quotation and the Direction of Dependence

In a study of the diachronic relations between two biblical books, clear definitions of literary terms like "quotation" and "allusion" are crucial. A quotation or allusion is created when an author adopts textual elements from a source text or tradition and makes them part of his own rhetoric. Here Richard Schultz's definition of "quotation" will be followed. According to Schultz, a quotation is a conscious textual repetition of interconnected words from another text "in which an exegetical purpose in reusing earlier material can be demonstrated or where an understanding of the earlier text and context is helpful, if not essential, for a proper interpretation of the new text."[17] This definition stresses the *functional* aspects of quotation more than its degree of formal agreement with its source. The quotation comes to life again when the audience recognizes the reference to the earlier text/tradition and is able to draw this earlier tradition into their understanding. The quotation has the power

[16] Martti Nissinen, *Prophetie, Redaktion und Fortschreibung im Hoseabuch: Studien zum Werdegang eines Prophetenbuches im Lichte von Hos 4 und 11*, AOAT 231 (Kevelaer: Butzon & Bercker, 1991). Similarly, with different accentuations, Gale A. Yee, *Composition and Tradition in the Book of Hosea: A Redaction-Critical Investigation*, SBLDS 102 (Atlanta: SBL Press, 1987); Henrik Pfeiffer, *Das Heiligtum von Bethel im Spiegel des Hoseabuches*, FRLANT 183 (Göttingen: Vandenhoeck & Ruprecht, 1999).

[17] Richard L. Schultz, *The Search for Quotation: Verbal Parallels in the Prophets*, JSOTSup 180 (Sheffield: Sheffield Academic, 1999), 221; cf. 227. Michael A. Lyons, *From Law to Prophecy: Ezekiel's Use of the Holiness Code*, LHBOTS 507 (London: T&T Clark, 2009), is sympathetic to Schultz's definition; however, he prefers to speak of "shared locutions" instead of "quotation" (56–59).

to refer the listener or the reader not only to the borrowed text itself but also to its context. When the quotation has been recognized, the context of the source rings in the background and enriches the interpretation of the quoting text. Often it turns out that several words from the source text recur in the borrowing text.

What Schultz terms "quotation," many other scholars call "allusion."[18] While an allusion may consist of a verbal parallel of two or more words in a similar syntactical construction, this is not necessarily the case. Allusion may also be effective where there are no verbal elements in common, e.g., when Hosea refers to יְמֵי הַגִּבְעָה ("the days of Gibeah") in Hos 10:9. Here the allusion functions even though the specific phrase יְמֵי הַגִּבְעָה is absent from the account in Judg 19–20.[19] For that reason, the term "quotation" is preferred in this study for designating *verbal* parallels that show signs of purposeful reuse and interpretation.

The observation that certain words in a given text recur in another text does not in itself qualify them as involving the phenomenon of quotation. Words in a verbal parallel should occur in the same or a similar syntactical relation to one another in order to be considered a quotation.[20]

In the study of verbal parallels in Hosea and Deuteronomy, it is crucial to differentiate between verbal parallels that were intended by the author (quotation) and random parallels, e.g., proverbial expressions, stock phrases, or shared vocabulary due to convergent topics (e.g., cultic language). Shared vocabulary in itself indicates nothing about literary priority. If the locution in common is found in other parts of the Old Testament as well, the probability that Hosea is alluding to Deuteronomy or vice versa is not very high. As an example, there is no basis for the assumption that Hos 5:10b is quoting Deut 27:17, because the shared locution הִסִּיג גְּבוּל ("move boundary marks") is also found verbatim in Prov 22:28 and 23:10.[21] However, if the shared phrase appears only in two books, the probability of a conscious literary reference is much higher.[22]

---

[18] E.g., Jeffery M. Leonard, "Identifying Inner-Biblical Allusions: Psalm 78 as a Test Case," *JBL* 127 (2008): 241–65; Russell L. Meek, "Intertextuality, Inner-Biblical Exegesis, and Inner-Biblical Allusion: The Ethics of a Methodology," *Bib* 95 (2014): 280–91.

[19] The specific reference of the allusions in Hos 9:10 and 10:9 need not concern us here.

[20] Schultz, *Search for Quotation*, 222–23.

[21] Against, e.g., Andersen and Freedman, *Hosea*, 408; Bass, "Hosea's Use of Scripture," 176; Thomas E. McComiskey, "Hosea," in *Hosea, Joel, and Amos*, ed. Thomas E. McComiskey, vol. 1 of *The Minor Prophets* (Grand Rapids: Baker, 1992), 82; Stuart, *Hosea–Jonah*. Rooker, "Use of the Old Testament," 64, terms it an example of "Hosea's borrowing of language from Deuteronomy."

[22] Schultz, *Search for Quotation*, 214, 224, 273–74. See also Leonard, "Identifying Inner-Biblical Allusions," 251; Lyons, *From Law to Prophecy*, 68–69.

Schultz adds the observation that if one of the texts in a verbal parallel shows signs of reinterpretation, this adds weight to the claim that this text is alluding to the other through quotation.[23] In Hos 11:8 it is fairly evident that Hosea not only refers his audience to the horrifying episode of the destruction of the cities on the plain (Gen 19) but also reinterprets this episode and takes up several phrases from the tradition in Gen 19 in order to proclaim that, instead of overturning (הפך; Gen 19:21, 25, 29) Israel in his judgment, God's own heart has "turned over" (הפך). Thus, reinterpretation of the original text or tradition is an essential trait of quotations.

If our analysis of a verbal parallel leads us to conclude that the parallel is not random but rather due to a purposeful quotation, this leads to the next question: How can one determine *the direction of dependence* in quotations? Can any reliable literary criteria be established for deciding which text in a verbal parallel that involves a quotation is reusing the other? This question is most complex. Until Schultz published his monograph *The Search for Quotation* in 1999, few scholars had attempted to formulate the question. It was easier simply to make a decision concerning literary priority in advance. Some suggested that the shorter text in a verbal parallel is the parent text; for that reason, Deut 8:12–14 was interpreted as an elaboration of Hos 13:6.[24] Other scholars argued, to the contrary, that the concise shorter text in Hos 13:6 is an abbreviation of the longer text in Deut 8:7–14.[25] Thus, in two publications appearing in the same year (1999), the same criterion (i.e., conciseness versus verbosity) was used to draw opposite conclusions.

During the last fifteen years, however, the discussion has moved forward considerably, because the methodology for establishing criteria for dependence has been addressed in a more rigorous manner.[26] Schultz stresses, on the one hand, the tentative nature of any effort to determine the direction of borrowing in quotation.[27] On the other hand, he proposes

[23] Schultz, *Search for Quotation*, 224.

[24] Reginaldo Gomes de Araújo, *Theologie der Wüste im Deuteronomium*, ÖBS 17 (Frankfurt am Main: Lang, 1999), 262–63.

[25] Pfeiffer, *Heiligtum von Bethel*, 172–73: "Vor allem die prägnante Kürze des Hoseatextes gegenüber Dtn 8,7–14 spricht für die Ursprünglichkeit der Dtn-Stellen."

[26] David Carr, "Method in Determination of Direction of Dependence: An Empirical Test of Criteria Applied to Exodus 34,11–26 and Its Parallels," in *Gottes Volk am Sinai: Untersuchungen zu Ex 32–34 und Dtn 9–10*, ed. Matthias Köckert and Erhard Blum, VWGT 18 (Gütersloh: Gütersloher Verlagshaus, 2001), 107–40; Leonard, "Identifying Inner-Biblical Allusions," 261–64; Lyons, *From Law to Prophecy*, 61–67; Schultz, *Search for Quotation*, 230–31.

[27] Schultz recently has stressed the inadequacy of most suggested criteria for determining the direction of quotation; see Richard L. Schultz, "Isaianic Intertex-

that any indications of reinterpretation in one text of the verbal parallel suggest that the interpretive text is the dependent one: "By making a discriminating use of word statistics and examining evidence of interpretive reworking, one can suggest, at least in terms of degrees of probability, the direction and nature of the quotation."[28]

Lyons puts forward four helpful guidelines for determining the direction of quotation:[29] concrete indications (1) that one of the texts has *modified* the transmitted material; (2) that the shared material is incompletely integrated into the dependent text and therefore contains elements that fit only to some degree into the borrowing text; (3) that the later text is dependent on information in the source text in order to be fully comprehensible;[30] and (4) that the dependent text introduces expansions that evidence interpretation of the appropriated text.

It must be stressed here, on the one hand, that criteria like these are not objective. They only indicate possible solutions to the challenging question of which text in a quotation-like verbal parallel has influenced which. On the other hand, a meticulous study of the literary parallels between Hosea and Deuteronomy has the intriguing potential of yielding an independent confirmation of scholarly theories about the diachronic relationship between Hosea and Deuteronomy.

Is Quotation Possible?

Before addressing specific examples of verbal parallels, we must ask: Would it be conceivable either for Hosea to refer to Deuteronomy (or to a relatively fixed Deuteronomic[31] tradition) or for Deuteronomy to allude to Hosea (and other prophetic collections)?

---

tuality and Intratextuality as Composition-Historical Indicators: Methodological Challenges in Determining Literary Influence," in *Bind Up the Testimony: Explorations in the Genesis of the Book of Isaiah*, ed. Daniel I. Block and Richard L. Schultz (Peabody, MA: Hendrickson, 2015), 37–39.

[28] Schultz, *Search for Quotation*, 231.

[29] Lyons, *From Law to Prophecy*, 61–67.

[30] Leonard has a similar criterion ("Identifying Inner-Biblical Allusions," 261).

[31] The use of terms like "Deuteronomic" and "Deuteronomistic" is somewhat confusing in the scholarly debate; see, e.g., Norbert F. Lohfink, "Was There a Deuteronomistic Movement?" in *Those Elusive Deuteronomists: The Phenomenon of Pan-Deuteronomism*, ed. Linda S. Schearing and Steven L. McKenzie, JSOTSup 268 (Sheffield: Sheffield Academic, 1999), 37–40. In this essay, I use the term "Deuteronomic" for texts found in the book of Deuteronomy and "Deuteronomistic" for the so-called "school" that is supposed to have edited many texts in the Old Testament and for texts resembling Deuteronomy.

The issue of the redaction history of the book of Hosea complicates the question further. In recent decades, several studies have argued that the book of Hosea went through an extensive redaction in Persian Yehud.[32] The Deuteronomy-like phrases and themes in Hosea could be the result of a later Deuteronomistic redaction of the book. Macintosh, however, argues convincingly that the book of Hosea may be dated confidently to Hosea's time, apart from a few Judean additions and exilic and postexilic glosses.[33] This position forms the basis for this study.

Most scholars today would instinctively deny the possibility that Hosea could have quoted an existing Deuteronomic tradition because they consider *Ur-Deuteronomium* to be a literary product of late seventh-century Judah. On the basis of the contents of the book of Hosea, however, it is a possibility to be considered seriously. As mentioned above, Hosea often evokes traditions about the exodus, the wilderness wandering, and the settlement in the land. He also makes explicit references to wide-ranging divine instruction being available as an authoritative repository of knowledge that Israel rejected as irrelevant. According to 8:12, God complains about Ephraim: אֶכְתּוֹב־לוֹ רִבּוֹ[34] תּוֹרָתִי כְּמוֹ־זָר נֶחְשָׁבוּ ("I wrote him the multitude of my instructions,[35] but they are regarded as something strange").[36] Hosea stresses that God *wrote* (אֶכְתּוֹב)[37] these instructions, implying a divinely sanctioned document. This suggests that the law collection is ancient and has an authoritative status, since its divine source is stated so clearly. Furthermore, this law collection must be extensive, since God describes it as רִבּוֹ תּוֹרָתִי ("the multitude of my instructions"). Hosea 8:1 and 4:6 contain additional references to an existing תּוֹרָה ("law") that has been neglected.[38] Therefore, it certainly is possible that Hosea could have quoted or alluded to a covenant renewal tradition similar to the one in Deuteronomy.

---

[32] Cf., e.g., Nissinen, *Prophetie, Redaktion und Fortschreibung*; Roman Vielhauer, *Das Werden des Buches Hosea: Eine redaktionsgeschichtliche Untersuchung*, BZAW 349 (Berlin: de Gruyter, 2007).

[33] A. A. Macintosh, *Hosea*, ICC (Edinburgh: T&T Clark, 1997), lxv–lxxiv; see also Dearman, *Hosea*, 6. Wolfgang Schütte has recently argued that most of the book was redacted by exilic Israelites in Hezekiah's time (see "Die Entstehung der juda-exilischen Hoseaschrift," *Bib* 95 [2014]: 198–223).

[34] *Qere* is followed. Cf. *BHQ*; G. Jeshurun, "A Note on Hosea VIII, 12," *JSOR* 11 (1927): 222–24; and Wolff, *Hosea*.

[35] All the versions, apart from Tg. Neb., have plural.

[36] All translations from the Hebrew Bible in this essay are by the author.

[37] אכתוב here should be understood as a *yiqtol* with a simple preterite sense, which is sometimes the case in poetic texts (Joüon §113h).

[38] With most exegetes, I take 8:1b to be Hosean and not Deuteronomistic (cf. Kugler, "Deuteronomists and the Latter Prophets," 139; Macintosh, *Hosea*, 293).

Is the reverse option also possible—that Deuteronomy could refer to Hosea through quotation?[39] Deuteronomy frequently directs its audience to earlier traditions, such as God's promises to the fathers,[40] and in its law exposition Deut 12–26 reinterprets older law collections (e.g., the Covenant Code).[41] If Deuteronomy underwent several redactions in sixth- and fifth-century Judah, it is a realistic possibility that Deuteronomistic redactions of Deuteronomy might have taken over verbal and thematic elements from the prophetic writings (e.g., from Hosea). It is reasonable to assume that Hosea in many aspects has influenced the book of Jeremiah,[42] and similarly Hosea might also have had an impact on a Deuteronomistic "school."

However, the option that Deuteronomy might contain literary references to Hosea runs into the problem that quotations like this would disturb the presumed fiction of a law-focused exhortation delivered by Moses. The reason is that quotations (and allusions) only function when recognized by the audience or readers. But quotations in Deuteronomy to the prophets would undercut the Deuteronomic authors' intention of presenting Deuteronomy as an exposition of the law given by Moses, the model and forerunner of all true YHWH prophets. In this case, we should talk about a Deuteronomistic reuse of prophetic phraseology rather than quotations. That Deuteronomy could take over Hosean phrases and themes is certainly possible from a literary point of view, but it runs into some difficulties when viewed from Deuteronomy's own clear-cut rhetorical perspective.

We will now examine three specific examples of verbal parallels in Hosea and Deuteronomy that bear the characteristics of quotation/reuse and ask which literary corpus appears to interpret the other.

---

[39] To his surprise, K. Zobel observed that Deuteronomy never directly quotes a prophetic word (*Prophetie und Deuteronomium*, 216–17).

[40] Cf. Jerry Hwang, *The Rhetoric of Remembrance: An Investigation of the "Fathers" in Deuteronomy*, Siphrut 8 (Winona Lake, IN: Eisenbrauns, 2012).

[41] Benjamin Kilchör, *Mosetora und Jahwetora: Das Verhältnis von Deuteronomium 12–26 zu Exodus, Levitikus und Numeri*, BZABR 21 (Wiesbaden: Harrassowitz, 2015).

[42] Jörg Jeremias, "The Hosea Tradition and the Book of Jeremiah," *OTE* (1994): 21–38; Martin Schulz-Rauch, *Hosea und Jeremia: Zur Wirkungsgeschichte des Hoseabuches*, Calwer Theologische Monographien, Reihe A: Bibelwissenschaft 16 (Stuttgart: Calwer, 1996).

Hos 13:4–6 ~ Deut 8:12–14

Hos 13:4–6*	Deut 8:12–14
4וְאָנֹכִי יְהוָה אֱלֹהֶיךָ מֵאֶרֶץ מִצְרָיִם וֵאלֹהִים זוּלָתִי לֹא תֵדָע וּמוֹשִׁיעַ אַיִן בִּלְתִּי׃ 5אֲנִי יְדַעְתִּיךָ בַּמִּדְבָּר בְּאֶרֶץ תַּלְאֻבוֹת׃ 6כְּמַרְעִיתָם **וַיִּשְׂבָּעוּ** **שָׂבְעוּ** **וַיָּרָם לִבָּם** עַל־כֵּן **שְׁכֵחוּנִי**׃	12פֶּן־תֹּאכַל . . . **וְשָׂבָעְתָּ** וּבָתִּים טוֹבִים תִּבְנֶה וְיָשָׁבְתָּ׃ 13וּבְקָרְךָ וְצֹאנְךָ יִרְבְּיֻן וְכֶסֶף וְזָהָב יִרְבֶּה־לָּךְ וְכֹל אֲשֶׁר־לְךָ יִרְבֶּה׃ 14**וְרָם לְבָבֶךָ** **וְשָׁכַחְתָּ אֶת־יְהוָה** אֱלֹהֶיךָ הַמּוֹצִיאֲךָ מֵאֶרֶץ מִצְרַיִם מִבֵּית עֲבָדִים׃
4 But I am YHWH your God from the land of Egypt; a God apart from me you do not know, and no savior besides me. 5 It was I who knew you in the wilderness, in the parched land; 6 according to their grazing, **they were satisfied;** **they were satisfied,** **and their heart was lifted up**; therefore, **they forgot me**.	. . . 12 lest, when you eat and **become satisfied** and build good houses and live in them, 13 and when your cattle and flocks multiply and you achieve much silver and gold and all that you have is multiplied, 14 **your heart will be lifted up,** **and you will forget YHWH** your God, who led you out from the land of Egypt, from the house of slavery.

*Bold and highlighted type indicate shared locutions.

The verbal parallels here are probably the clearest example of quotation involving Hosea and Deuteronomy. In Hos 13:5–6 Hosea recapitulates how YHWH chose Israel and took care of it in the wilderness. He fed the Israelites like a shepherd feeding his flock, but in their satiety they became proud and forgot their benefactor. In Deut 8:11–16 Moses admonishes the Israelites not to forget YHWH when they enter the good land and enjoy its gifts. Three verbal constructions recur in both texts and in the same order: שׂבע ("be satisfied"), רָם לֵב/לֵבָב ("be proud"), and שׁכח ("forget") YHWH. This peculiar sequence of locutions appears only in these two places in the entire Old Testament. Accordingly, the concept of divinely provided satiety resulting in arrogance and self-reliance leading to a fatal ignorance of YHWH is found only in Hos 13 and Deut 8.[43]

In Deut 8:12, as well as generally in Deuteronomy, the verb שׂבע ("be satisfied") never stands alone, appearing rather in the hendiadys stock phrase אָכַל וְשָׂבַע ("eat and be satisfied").[44] In Hos 13:6a, however, this notion appears in a metaphor of a flock grazing on a rich and abundant pasture: כְּמַרְעִיתָם[45] וַיִּשְׂבָּעוּ ("according to their grazing they were satisfied"). Thus, Hos 13:6a contains a poetic, metaphorical synonym to Deuteronomy's locution אָכַל וְשָׂבַע ("eat and be satisfied"). Accordingly, the verbal parallel consists not of three locutions, but actually four (counting אָכַל וְשָׂבַע / מַרְעִית וְשָׂבַע ["eat and be satisfied" / "according to their grazing they were satisfied"] as two locutions).

Further intertextual connections can be recognized. In Hos 13:5 Hosea refers to God's provision for Israel בַּמִּדְבָּר ("in the desert"); ידע ("know") expresses both God's election and his care;[46] and the wilderness is described as אֶרֶץ תַּלְאֻבוֹת ("a parched land").[47] Corresponding to these, Deut 8:15–16 describes God's miraculous guidance of Israel in the terrible מִדְבָּר ("desert"), which is described as צִמָּאוֹן אֲשֶׁר אֵין־מָיִם ("a thirsty area where there is no water"), where God provided his people with food and water. In addition, the concept of having a personal experience (ידע, "know")

[43] The same idea and similar verbal elements also occur in Deut 6:10–13 and 32:15, 18. However, 6:10–13 lacks רָם לֵבָב ("lift up a heart"), while 32:15, 18 employs other terms to express the notion of becoming satisfied and forgetting the divine benefactor. Thus, the closest verbal parallel (i.e., the one that shares the most elements) is Hos 13:5–6 // Deut 8:12–14.

[44] 6:11; 8:10, 12; 11:15; 14:29; 26:12; 31:20. See also 23:25[ET 24], where the verb אכל ("eat") is followed by the noun שֹׂבַע ("satiation"), similar to the Old Testament stock phrase אָכַל לָשֹׂבַע ("eat to the full").

[45] The tendency in older commentaries to emend כְּמַרְעִיתָם ("according to their grazing") on the basis of some of the versions (cf. Andersen and Freedman, *Hosea*, 634–35; *BHS*) is unnecessary (*BHQ*; Dominique Barthélemy, *Critique textuelle de l'Ancien Testament*, vol. 3, *Ézékiel, Daniel et les 12 Prophètes*, OBO 50/3 [Fribourg: Éditions Universitaires, 1992], 610–11). Because of the plural suffix in מַרְעִיתָם, the noun מַרְעִית here signifies the flock's grazing actions rather than its pasturage (cf. *DCH* 5:491).

[46] ידע here expresses "Yahweh's establishment and maintenance of a relationship of love with Israel" (Macintosh, *Hosea*, 528).

[47] For the translation options for the *hapax legomenon* תַּלְאֻבוֹת ("parched"), see *HALOT*, 1737.

with the salvific deeds of YHWH referred to in Hos 13:4b is akin to Israel's knowing (ידע, "know") YHWH during the wilderness experience in Deut 8:5. Finally, almost the entire sentence in Hos 13:4a—a remarkable self-proclamation without any verbal element[48]—occurs in Deut 8:14b (i.e., "YHWH your God . . . from the land of Egypt").

Thus there are also several remarkable links between the immediate contexts of Hos 13:6 and Deut 8:12–14, which appear to be intentional; that is, one text in the parallel is quoting the other.

Can we discover anything about the direction of dependence? The dominant understanding today is that the verbal parallel in Deuteronomy is a Deuteronomistic reuse of phrases from Hos 13:5–6.[49] Often Deuteronomy's dependence is taken for granted.

Several literary considerations, however, call for a different assessment. The concept of having enough to eat to be satisfied (אָכַל וְשָׂבַע) is a prevalent Deuteronomic concept, since it is a direct expression of God blessing his people in response to their covenant loyalty. In Hosea, this idea occurs only in 13:6, where it is characteristically an element in a historical retrospect. It does not belong to Hosea's typical vocabulary.

In Deuteronomy, the opposite of שָׁכַח אֶת יהוה ("forget YHWH") is זָכַר אֶת יהוה ("remember YHWH," 8:2, 18; cf. 9:7). The verb זכר ("remember") is often used in the Old Testament, especially in Deuteronomy, as an antonym to שׁכח ("forget"). Hosea 13:4, however, uniquely employs יָדַע אֶת יהוה ("know YHWH") as a contrast to שָׁכַח אֶת יהוה ("forget YHWH").[50] It is difficult to conceive of Deuteronomy adopting the Hosean idea of "forgetting YHWH because of arrogance" without also taking over Hosea's peculiar contrast of knowing YHWH in his salvation and in his right ordi-

[48] This self-proclamation recalls the introductory word of the Decalogue. Hosea 13:4a (and 12:10a[ET 9a]) probably is a deliberate quotation from the Decalogue, since (1) the wording with the "long" (אנכי, "I") self-proclamation clause is found verbatim in Exod 20:2 and Deut 5:6; (2) self-proclamation statements like Hos 13:4a are not typically prophetic and do not appear elsewhere in the prophetic corpus; and (3) read literally, the proclamation וְאָנֹכִי יְהוָה אֱלֹהֶיךָ מֵאֶרֶץ מִצְרָיִם ("but I am YHWH your God from the land of Egypt") is ambiguous (i.e., is YHWH an Egyptian god?). However, read with the self-proclamation formula of the Decalogue in mind, this quotation is filled with meaning and allusive force.

[49] E.g., Davies, *Hosea*, 285, 290; Gomes de Araújo, *Theologie der Wüste*, 262–65; Holt, *Prophesying the Past*, 77n88; Lundbom, *Deuteronomy*, 33; Macintosh, *Hosea*, 531; Richard D. Nelson, *Deuteronomy: A Commentary*, OTL (Louisville: Westminster John Knox, 2002), 7; Tigay, *Deuteronomy*, xxiii; Wolff, *Hosea*, 226; Zobel, *Prophetie und Deuteronomium*, 149.

[50] The same opposition between ידע ("know") and שׁכח ("forget") also occurs in הִיא לֹא יָדְעָה ("she does not know") in Hos 2:10[ET 8], contrasted with אֹתִי שָׁכְחָה ("me she forgot") in 2:15[ET 13] (cf. also וְיָדַעַתְּ אֶת־יְהוָה ["and you shall know YHWH"] in 2:22[ET 20]).

nances, especially since Deut 8 uses ידע ("know") to describe the proper recognition of YHWH's works (8:5). In fact, it is for this reason that Martti Nissinen asserts that Deut 8 could not have been modeled on Hos 13:4–6; instead, he claims that 13:4–6 results from a later Deuteronomistic redaction of Hosea![51]

Another aspect to consider is that אָכַל וְשָׂבַע ("eat and be satisfied") is used in a straightforward sense in Deut 8:10–14. It refers to Israel receiving and enjoying the abundance of agricultural products and water that it severely lacked during the preceding wilderness period, and it appears in conjunction with building houses, raising cattle, and increasing in wealth. In Hos 13:6, the corresponding term for "eat"—מַרְעִית ("grazing")—is used metaphorically with regard to a grazing flock. Here, as well, it is easier to conclude that Hosea modified the straightforward hendiadys אָכַל וְשָׂבַע ("eat and be satisfied") into a multidimensional metaphor (i.e., Israel as God's herd being abundantly provided for by its shepherd) than to suggest that Deut 8 picked up the locution from Hosea but stripped it of any metaphorical connotation.[52]

In addition, Hos 13:5–6 seems to presuppose information from Deut 8.[53] Read in isolation, the Hosean description of the wilderness as אֶרֶץ תַּלְאֻבוֹת ("a parched land") where God once "knew" Israel is ambiguous. Deuteronomy 8:3–4 and 15–16, however, describe this terrible and uninhabitable desert as one without food or water. God's miraculous provision for his "flock" in the "parched land" can be understood from Deut 8. And while God previously delivered Israel from poisonous desert creatures (Deut 8:15), he now will act like carnivorous predators in the land (Hos 13:7–8).

Thus, the evidence indicates that Hos 13:4–6 is dependent on Deut 8 and can appropriately be labelled a quotation. Hosea 13 reinterprets the locution of eating and being satisfied by incorporating it into a metaphor, contains "Deuteronomic" language atypical of Hosea, and evokes Deut 8 as supplying essential background information for the message

---

[51] Nissinen, *Prophetie, Redaktion und Fortschreibung*, 162–64. Nissinen is followed by, e.g., Timo Veijola, *Das fünfte Buch Mose: Deuteronomium: Kapitel 1,1–16,17*, ATD 8.1 (Göttingen: Vandenhoeck & Ruprecht, 2004), 186. Contra Nissinen, a conceptual affinity between Hos 13:4 and Isa 43:10–11 and 45:5 does not inherently indicate the work of a redactor in Hos 13:4.

[52] Cf. Eidevall, *Grapes in the Desert*, 196. The shepherd-flock metaphor, although often used in the prophets and in the Asaphite psalms (cf. Regine Hunziker-Rodewald, *Hirt und Herde: Ein Beitrag zum alttestamentlichen Gottesverständnis*, BWANT 155 [Stuttgart: Kohlhammer, 2001]), never occurs in Deuteronomy, nor does the root רעה ("graze; herd"), used in Hos 13:6.

[53] Cf. Leonard's criterion of dependence on information in the source text (Leonard, "Identifying Inner-Biblical Allusions," 261) and Lyons' third criterion (discussed above; *From Law to Prophecy*, 64–65).

in 13:5–8.[54] In Deut 6 and 8, Moses warned the Israelites not to forget YHWH and his commandments, telling them rather to remember all his gracious acts. Israel, however, not only displayed ingratitude and forgot YHWH, but also ignored his warnings, not due to disappointments and difficulties but because of disobedience. The intertextual device of quotation in Hos 13:6 suggests that the succinct metaphor of the grazing flock is rich in meaning: God gave them a good land full of possibilities for eating their fill, constructing safe and stable dwellings, and increasing their wealth, but they abandoned their shepherd.

Although several critical scholars agree that Hos 13:4–6 is heavily influenced by Deuteronomy, they explain the relationship in terms of an exilic or postexilic Deuteronomistic reworking of Hosea's preaching. Some scholars take the very fact that Hos 13:5–6 betrays a close affinity to Deuteronomic phrases and motifs as indicating a priori that this passage belongs to a later redactional stratum.[55]

However, there are no signs of later redactional activity in Hos 13:4–6. The change in person from second-person singular in verse 5 to third-person plural in verses 6–7 is a common Hosean device. It therefore provides no basis for suspecting a literary-critical insertion after verse 5 (against Pfeiffer). In addition, the atypical phrase וַיִּשְׂבְּעוּ שָׂבֵעוּ ("they were satisfied; they were satisfied") in 13:6, with a *wayyiqtol* immediately followed by a *qatal* of the very same verb, is unprecedented in the entire Hebrew Bible.[56] It is certainly not a Deuteronomic trait, but goes well with Hosea's predilection for repetitious language.[57] There is therefore no reason for questioning the Hosean origin of 13:4–6.

This example of intertextuality suggests that here Hosea is quoting an existing Deuteronomic tradition that is very similar to what is found in Deut 8. Whether this tradition is oral or written is difficult to know. Another example of a close linguistic and conceptual correspondence with Deuteronomy is found in Hos 2:10[ET 8]. Like Hos 13:5–6, the verbal parallel is found in Deut 8; moreover, it is repeated in 17:17.

---

[54] Thus also Bass, "Hosea's Use of Scripture," 249–50; Walter Gisin, *Das Buch Hosea*, Edition C Bibelkommentar Altes Testament 37 (Witten: SCM R. Brockhaus, 2014), 529; McConville, *Deuteronomy*, 167–68.

[55] Thus, e.g., Reinhard Achenbach, *Israel zwischen Verheißung und Gebot: Literarkritische Untersuchungen zu Deuteronomium 5–11,* Europäische Hochschulschriften: Theologie 422 (Frankfurt am Main: Lang, 1991), 331–32; Pfeiffer, *Heiligtum von Bethel*, 172–74. See also Nissinen, *Prophetie, Redaktion und Fortschreibung*, 162–64; Vielhauer, *Das Werden des Buches Hosea*, 150.

[56] Second Kings 8:14b is not a true parallel because of a subject change.

[57] Cf. Macintosh, *Hosea*, lxiv.

Hos 2:10 [ET 8] ~ Deut 8:13 / 17:16–17

Hos 2:10[ET 8]	Deut 8:13
וְהִיא לֹא יָדְעָה כִּי אָנֹכִי נָתַתִּי לָהּ הַדָּגָן וְהַתִּירוֹשׁ וְהַיִּצְהָר וְכֶסֶף הִרְבֵּיתִי לָהּ וְזָהָב עָשׂוּ לַבָּעַל׃	וּבְקָרְךָ וְצֹאנְךָ יִרְבְּיֻן . . . וְכֶסֶף וְזָהָב יִרְבֶּה־לָּךְ וְכֹל אֲשֶׁר־לְךָ יִרְבֶּה׃ Deut 17:16–17 16 רַק לֹא־יַרְבֶּה־לּוֹ סוּסִים וְלֹא־יָשִׁיב אֶת־הָעָם מִצְרַיְמָה לְמַעַן הַרְבּוֹת סוּס וַיהוָה אָמַר לָכֶם לֹא תֹסִפוּן לָשׁוּב בַּדֶּרֶךְ הַזֶּה עוֹד׃ 17 וְלֹא יַרְבֶּה־לּוֹ נָשִׁים וְלֹא יָסוּר לְבָבוֹ וְכֶסֶף וְזָהָב לֹא יַרְבֶּה־לּוֹ מְאֹד׃
10 But she does not know that it was I who gave her the grain, the new wine, and the fresh oil, and **I multiplied for her silver and gold,** which they used for Baal.	8:13 13 and when your cattle and flocks multiply **and you multiply for yourself silver and gold** and all that you have is multiplied . . . 17:16–17 16 Only he [i.e., the king] must not multiply for himself many horses, and he must not return the people to Egypt in order to get many horses, since YHWH has told you: "You must never again return that way." 17 And he must not multiply for himself wives, lest his heart turn away, and **he must not multiply for himself** much **silver and gold**.

Hosea 2:10[ET 8] forms part of God's speech of indictment against his wife, Israel, for idolatry and whoredom (2:4–15[ET 2–13]). She did not realize who the actual provider of grain, new wine, olive oil, and precious metals was.[58] What she ascribed to the Baals were, in fact, YHWH's gifts. The parallel in Deut 8 is from the same passage as the preceding parallel: God intends to lead Israel into a land that will produce all fine agricultural products and where the societal surplus will allow acquisition of much silver and gold. The economic growth, however, may lead to arrogance and the neglect of God. The repetition of the verbal parallel in Deut 17:16–17 stems from the "law of the king" in Deut 17:14–20, where the king is cautioned against obtaining much silver and gold.

We can observe strong intertextual links between Hos 2:10[ET 8] and Deut 8:13; 17:17. The use of the locution כֶּסֶף וְזָהָב ("silver and gold"), followed by some form of the verb רבה ("multiply") and the preposition לְ of "interest," is common to all three texts. Furthermore, this particular sequence is unattested outside Deuteronomy and Hosea. The notion of acquiring much silver and gold is expressed in various ways in the Old Testament, but כֶּסֶף וְזָהָב + רבה + לְ appears only three times—in Deut 8:13; 17:17; and Hos 2:10b[ET 8b]. In all three occurrences, the object כֶּסֶף וְזָהָב ("silver and gold") precedes the verb.[59] Hosea states directly that these highly valued metals are gifts from YHWH ("I provided her . . ."), while Deuteronomy hints in a more veiled manner that economic growth is due to God blessing the efforts of the people.

In addition, the triad הַדָּגָן וְהַתִּירוֹשׁ וְהַיִּצְהָר ("the grain, the new wine, and the fresh oil") in Hos 2:10a[ET 8a] is very common in Deuteronomy, though it is found elsewhere in the Old Testament.[60] It sums up all the agricultural products of the land that Israel may harvest due to God's blessing.

Another verbal link occurs in the immediate context: In Hos 2:11[ET 9] God threatens to take (לקח) "my grain" (דְּגָנִי) "in its time" (בְּעִתּוֹ) and "my new wine" (תִּירוֹשִׁי) "in its season" (בְּמוֹעֲדוֹ). Deuteronomy 11:14 promises that God will give (נתן) the rain "in its time" (בְּעִתּוֹ) that Israel may harvest "your grain" (דְגָנֶךָ), "your new wine" (תִירֹשְׁךָ), and "your fresh oil" (יִצְהָרֶךָ). The verb לקח ("take") in Hos 2:11a[ET 9a] is the antonym of נתן ("give") in Deut 11:14a.

---

[58] The authenticity of 2:10b[ET 8b] is sometimes doubted, e.g., by Jeremias, *Der Prophet Hosea*, 44n10 (cf. text note in *BHS*). Some scholars consider the phrase עָשׂוּ לַבָּעַל ("used for Baal") a later gloss (e.g., Macintosh, *Hosea*, 54; Wolff, *Hosea*, 37). However, since 2:10bβ forms an *inclusio* with 2:15aβγ[ET 13aβγ], there is no reason to treat עָשׂוּ לַבָּעַל as an insertion.

[59] In Deut 8:13 the inverted object position is in keeping with the immediate context in verses 12–13. Hosea 2:10b[ET 8b] has the same order (object–verb), despite its context.

[60] Deut 7:13; 11:14; 12:17; 14:23; 18:4; 28:51. Moreover, cf. 2 Kgs 18:32; 2 Chr 31:5; Neh 10:40[ET 39]; Jer 31:12; Joel 1:10; 2:19.

All the words in this verbal parallel are rather common, so it might be sheer coincidence that Hosea expresses himself similarly to Deuteronomy. But the exact sequence combined with the לְ of "interest" is found only in these three texts. Hence the intertextual relationship may qualify as a quotation, though it is admittedly linguistically weaker than the Hos 13:4–6 parallel.

Accordingly, it seems impossible to determine the direction of influence based on literary considerations, since there are no clear indications in the parallel as to who is dependent on whom. However, Hosea states that Israel's guilt consists in the fact that לֹא יָדְעָה ("she does not know," i.e., "acknowledge") the one who actually gives her abundant crops and wealth (2:10[ET 8]). Expressing guilt in these terms suggests that she ought to know; her ignorance is inexcusable. This lack of knowledge warrants punishment despite her stated intention to return to her first husband (v. 9[ET 7]), for there is a particular knowledge concerning YHWH and his gifts that she has not considered. "Knowing" YHWH and his covenantal requirements is a Hosean key word.[61]

The charge . . . וְהִיא לֹא יָדְעָה כִּי אָנֹכִי ("but she does not know that it was I . . .") suggests that she has neglected some key traditions about YHWH as the giver of the land and its products. This repository of knowledge encompasses not only that YHWH will provide the agricultural products of the land and precious metals acquired through trade but in particular that he is the *sole* provider of all these goods. How should she have known this? From her earlier experiences of receiving gifts from her "spouse" and recognizing their true source she could have reflected on that tradition and realized that YHWH and no other deity was the giver.

This verbal parallel displays the phenomenon of "splitting." Deuteronomy 8:13 and 17:17 use the usual sequence כֶּסֶף וְזָהָב ("silver and gold"). Hosea 2:10b[ET 8b], however, has split off the second noun וְזָהָב ("and gold") from the stock phrase כֶּסֶף וְזָהָב ("silver and gold"), placed it after the verbal element הִרְבֵּיתִי לָהּ ("I multiplied for her"), and added an asyndetic relative clause עָשׂוּ לַבָּעַל ("which they used for Baal"),[62] thereby creating a two-line expression. According to Benjamin Sommer, the phenomenon of splitting indicates that the splitting text is alluding to the non-split text.[63]

---

[61] See M. Douglas Carew, "To Know or Not to Know: Hosea's Use of *ydʿ/dʿt*," in *The Old Testament in the Life of God's People: Essays in Honor of Elmer A. Martens*, ed. Jon Isaak (Winona Lake, IN: Eisenbrauns, 2009), 73–85.

[62] In all probability the relative clause has both כֶּסֶף ("silver") and זָהָב ("gold") as its antecedents.

[63] Benjamin D. Sommer, *A Prophet Reads Scripture: Allusion in Isaiah 40–66* (Stanford: Stanford University Press, 1998), 68–69. Lyons notes many examples of the split-up phenomenon in Ezekiel (*From Law to Prophecy*, 67).

A notable trait in Hos 2:10–11[ET 8–9] is that the indictment and judgment are expressed metaphorically in terms of an adulterous wife ascribing fertility and wealth to her imagined lovers and YHWH depriving his wife of the husband's gifts. This whoredom metaphor is not found in Deut 8 or 17,[64] which is peculiar if Deuteronomy is supposedly reusing phrases and ideas from Hosea.

A striking difference between Hosea and Deuteronomy can be noted precisely where they are addressing the same topic and sharing identical phraseology: Hosea accuses Israel of having misconstrued reality and misused the silver and gold for the idols ("the lovers"). In contrast, Deuteronomy does not associate Israel's acquisition of wealth with the danger of idolatry. Although Deuteronomy contains stern warnings against making idols, coveting the silver and gold of the Canaanites' idols, or taking an interest in Canaanite religion, it does not share Hosea's linkage of wealth with idolatry. According to Deuteronomy, the problem with acquiring silver and gold is that it might mislead Israel to think that its wealth resulted from its own effort and skill. This, in turn, would lead to pride and the failure to acknowledge YHWH. It is difficult to view Deuteronomy as the one that develops Hosea's thought when the great danger of ascribing agricultural products and economic progress to the Baals is totally absent in the former.[65]

It is difficult to claim with certainty that Hosea is alluding to Deuteronomy in this case, since the referential markers are rather ambiguous. However, the oft-stated assessment that Deuteronomy is building on Hosea's vocabulary and ideology here[66] cannot be maintained. The indictment that Israel has lost its knowledge of YHWH as the sole provider of its wealth, the splitting up phenomenon in Hos 2:10b[ET 8b], the lack of metaphorical language in Deut 8:12–14, and Deuteronomy's disinterest in the danger of misconceiving economic wealth as the gift of local gods all suggest that Hosea is referring to and developing a Deuteronomic tradition.[67] The dif-

[64] Even Hosea's prominent marriage and adultery metaphor is absent from Deuteronomy, despite the fact that Deuteronomy shares Hosea's emphasis on God's love for his people and God's warnings against religious infidelity. See Vang, "God's Love," 191–92.

[65] The fact that certain nouns in Deut 7:13, such as דָּגָן ("grain") and תִּירוֹשׁ ("new wine"), as well as שֶׁגֶר ("offspring") and עַשְׁתְּרֹת ("increase"), may be linguistically related to the names of Canaanite deities does not indicate that the Deuteronomic authors here are opposing rival gods (against, e.g., Nelson, *Deuteronomy*, 102–3; Block, *Deuteronomy*, 213). Agricultural products and cattle are consistently described in Deuteronomy as *Israel's* possession, not YHWH's.

[66] E.g., Ginsberg, *Israelian Heritage of Judaism*, 19; Lundbom, *Deuteronomy*, 33; Macintosh, *Hosea*, 56; Nelson, *Deuteronomy*, 7; Nielsen, *Deuteronomium*, 101; Wolff, *Hosea*, 37; Zobel, *Prophetie und Deuteronomium*, 62, 76, 142–43.

[67] Andersen and Freedman, *Hosea*, 243; Bass, "Hosea's Use of Scripture," 136; Gisin, *Hosea*, 124; Shmuel Sperber, "השפעת ספר דברים על הושע [The Influence of the Book of Deuteronomy on Hosea]," *Melilah* 1 (1944): 221.

ferences between Hosea and Deuteronomy are easier to explain if Hosea is alluding to a Deuteronomic tradition about YHWH as the sole giver of all of the land's products. The fact that Hos 2:10[ET 8] can function as a quotation of Deut 8:13, while nothing in Deut 8:13 or 17:17 indicates that Deuteronomy is evoking a prophetic tradition, suggests that Hosea is the quoter and Deuteronomy the source.

Through the device of quotation, Hosea indicates in 2:10[ET 8] the specific knowledge that Israel has failed to take into consideration. Hosea underlines the people's guilt by referring them to the covenant tradition that they have ignored. While Deut 8 warns its audience that an abundance of silver and gold might lead to self-complacency, Hosea reinterprets this warning as a statement that Israel misunderstood the precious metals as something the Baals had given, so that, metaphorically, the adulterous wife misused for her lovers her spouse's abundant gifts.

In another indictment against idolatry, Hosea again makes use of locutions that have a close verbal and conceptual parallel in Deuteronomy.

Hos 4:13 ~ Deut 12:2

Hos 4:13	Deut 12:2
עַל־רָאשֵׁי הֶהָרִים יְזַבֵּחוּ וְעַל־הַגְּבָעוֹת יְקַטֵּרוּ תַּחַת אַלּוֹן וְלִבְנֶה וְאֵלָה כִּי טוֹב צִלָּהּ עַל־כֵּן תִּזְנֶינָה בְּנוֹתֵיכֶם וְכַלּוֹתֵיכֶם תְּנָאַפְנָה׃	אַבֵּד תְּאַבְּדוּן אֶת־כָּל־הַמְּקֹמוֹת אֲשֶׁר עָבְדוּ־שָׁם הַגּוֹיִם . . . אֲשֶׁר אַתֶּם יֹרְשִׁים אֹתָם . . . אֶת־אֱלֹהֵיהֶם עַל־הֶהָרִים הָרָמִים וְעַל־הַגְּבָעוֹת וְתַחַת כָּל־עֵץ רַעֲנָן׃
13 **On** the tops of **the mountains** they sacrifice, **and on the hills** they burn offerings, **under oak and poplar and terebinth**, because their shadow is good. Therefore your daughters commit harlotry, and your daughters-in-law commit adultery.	2 You shall utterly destroy all the places where the nations . . . whom you shall dispossess . . . give worship to their gods, **on the** high **mountains** **and on the hills** and **under every leafy tree**.

In Hos 4:13 the prophet condemns the community for its widespread involvement in the fertility cult[68] on mountains and hills and under large trees—for offering sacrifices in every possible location. In Deut 12:2–3[69] Moses commands Israel to destroy all Canaanite cult places, whether on mountains or hills or under trees with wide crowns of shady leaves (תַּחַת כָּל־עֵץ רַעֲנָן).[70] The entire hemistich verse 2b expands on the expression כָּל־הַמְּקֹמוֹת ("all the places") in 12:2a.

There appear to be strong verbal links between Hos 4:13 and Deut 12:2. The word sequence עַל הֶהָרִים וְעַל־הַגְּבָעוֹת ("on the mountains and on the hills") followed by the preposition תַּחַת ("under") and some word for "tree" is common to both. This three-part expression occurs in only three places in the Old Testament—in these two texts and in Ezek 6:13. Ezekiel 6:13, however, has reversed the sequence of הַר ("mountain") and גִּבְעָה ("hill") and is dependent on Hos 4:13 and Deut 12:2.[71] The Old Testament often contains shorter versions of the expression, such as "hills and every richly leafed tree," or "mountains" followed by תַּחַת כָּל־עֵץ רַעֲנָן ("under every leafy tree"), especially in Kings and Jeremiah, and thus this is a rather common locution.[72] But the full sequence with the shared elements in this order—foreign worship on the mountains, on the hills, and under every leafy tree—appears only in Hos 4 and Deut 12. Both Hosea and Deuteronomy accentuate the height of the mountains—"on the *tops* of the mountains" (עַל־רָאשֵׁי הֶהָרִים, Hos 4:13) or "on the *high* mountains" (עַל הֶהָרִים הָרָמִים, Deut 12:2)—while the rest of the Old Testament more

[68] The intense debate over whether the cult denounced in 4:13–14 also involved sacred prostitution will not be discussed here. See the most recent studies on the topic by Christel M. Maier, "Myth and Truth in Socio-Historical Reconstruction of Ancient Societies: Hosea 4:11–14 as a Test Case," in *Thus Says the Lord: Essays on the Former and Latter Prophets in Honor of Robert R. Wilson*, ed. John J. Ahn and Stephen L. Cook, LHBOTS 502 (New York: T&T Clark, 2009), 256–72; Hermann-Josef Stipp, "Die Qedešen im Alten Testament," in *Die Erzväter in der biblischen Tradition: Festschrift für Matthias Köckert*, ed. Anselm C. Hagedorn and Henrik Pfeiffer, BZAW 400 (Berlin: de Gruyter, 2009), 209–40.

[69] Deuteronomy 12:1–12 is often held to include several exilic and postexilic Deuteronomistic redactional layers that were added to an original core demanding cult centralization. Cf. Nelson, *Deuteronomy*, 150–59; Udo Rüterswörden, *Deuteronomium 12,1–26,19*, BKAT 5/3 fasc. 1 (Neukirchen: Neukirchener Verlag, 2011), 7–9. McConville, however, has argued for the compositional unity of Deut 12; cf. his *Deuteronomy*, 214–16.

[70] The meaning of רַעֲנָן is "fresh, leafy" and not "green," as previously claimed. See, e.g., P. Mommer, "רַעֲנָן *ra*ᶜ*ᵃnān*," *ThWAT* 7:580–82.

[71] Daniel I. Block, *The Book of Ezekiel: Chapters 1–24*, NICOT (Grand Rapids: Eerdmans, 1997), 237–38.

[72] See the list in William L. Holladay, " 'On Every High Hill and under Every Green Tree,' " *VT* 11 (1961): 170–76.

often emphasizes the height of the *hills* (גְּבָעוֹת).[73] While most occurrences of the "hill formula" in the Old Testament have the particle of totality כָּל ("all") attached to either "mountain" or "hill," this word is absent from Hos 4:13 and Deut 12:2. In both Hosea and Deuteronomy worship on hills and under trees is condemned.

Interestingly, Hos 4:13 illustrates the meaning of the term כָּל־עֵץ רַעֲנָן ("every leafy tree"). Instead of this general Deuteronomic phrase, Hosea mentions three specific trees, אַלּוֹן וְלִבְנֶה וְאֵלָה ("oak, poplar,[74] and terebinth"), and comments on their ability to offer shade from the blazing sun.

The correspondence in vocabulary, syntactical arrangement, and religious outlook in the verbal parallel suggests that this is not simply a random variation of a widespread Old Testament phrase, but rather that one text draws on and reuses elements from the other text. The next question is: What is the probable direction of dependence here?

Neither text in this verbal parallel contains any "foreign" element that would indicate that it is an adaptation of phrases from the other.[75] We can, however, observe some differences in outlook between the two units. While Deuteronomy describes worship on the hills in general terms, Hos 4:13 is specific and definite. Not only does Hosea refer to three specific leafy trees—instead of using the phrase כָּל־עֵץ רַעֲנָן ("every leafy tree")—but Deuteronomy also uses the general term עבד to describe the nations' "worship" on the hills. In contrast, Hosea describes the condemnable worship with זבח ("sacrifice") and קטר ("burn offerings"). Deuteronomy only notes that the Canaanite cultic practices take place on high mountains (עַל־הֶהָרִים הָרָמִים); Hosea locates the Israelite idolatry on the mountaintops (עַל־רָאשֵׁי הֶהָרִים). In sum: whereas Deuteronomy is general and indefinite in its description of the condemnable worship, Hosea is concrete and specific.[76]

It is easy to conceive of the literary dependence as the work of a later Deuteronomistic redactor who turned Hosea's specific phraseology into a general description of foreign worship—that is, that the line of borrowing extends from Hosea to the Deuteronomistic redactor of the "Altar Law" in

---

[73] E.g., גִּבְעָה גְּבֹהָה, "high hill" (Jer 2:20; 1 Kgs 14:23; 2 Kgs 17:10; cf. Jer 17:2), and כָּל־גִּבְעָה רָמָה "any high hill" (Ezek 20:28; 34:6).

[74] The meaning of לִבְנֶה is often taken to be "storax-tree." This tree, however, is rather small and bushlike, and given the mention of the shade the לִבְנֶה provides, it is preferable to identify this as the "poplar."

[75] Cf. Lyons' second criterion, the "criterion of incongruity" (*From Law to Prophecy*, 62–63).

[76] Deuteronomy always describes the Canaanite cult and its idols in very general, non-specific terms, avoiding concrete expressions like Baal and בָּמָה ("high place").

Deut 12 and then further to Kings/Jeremiah.[77] It is also possible to view Hos 4:13a as the prophetic elaboration of a Deuteronomic phrase that aims to stigmatize the cult in Hosea's day.[78]

One feature suggests that Hos 4:13 is alluding to Deut 12:2 and not the other way around. Hosea 4:13 draws particular attention to the various places in nature where Israel's worship takes place. From the context in 4:12 it is clear that this worship was illegitimate and warranted prophetic critique. However, Hos 4:12–14 does not address the question of why offering sacrifices on these many sites constituted spiritual adultery. What is wrong with sacrificing on mountains and hills and under large trees, that Hosea should vehemently attack these practices as manifestations of רוּחַ זְנוּנִים ("a spirit of adultery," v. 12b) in the people? Moreover, why does the cultic activity on these sites lead to the literal promiscuity of their women (עַל־כֵּן, "therefore," v. 13b)? The significance of this "cultic geography" in Hos 4:13a remains unexplained, since the verbs describing the cult are neutral terms (זָבַח, "sacrifice," and קִטֵּר, "burn offerings") and no gods are mentioned. Deuteronomy 12:2, however, provides the reason why Hosea must even condemn the *sites* of their religious activity: they are slaughtering and burning their sacrifices in the same manner and on the same sites as the indigenous nations have done and where they served their gods. Because of the "Canaanite geography" of Israelite religion, widespread promiscuity took place within the context of its cult.

According to Lyons' criterion, if one parallel text supplies essential information for understanding the full implications of the message in the other text, a quotation is present and the text that receives elucidation from the other text is the borrower.[79] While the indictment in Hos 4:13a is clarified by Deut 12:2–3, the description of the Canaanite cultic sites in Deut 12:2 does not need any illumination from Hosea. The phrase עַל־הֶהָרִים הָרָמִים וְעַל־הַגְּבָעוֹת וְתַחַת כָּל־עֵץ רַעֲנָן ("on the high mountains and on the hills and under every leafy tree") simply expands on the phrase אֶת־כָּל־הַמְּקֹמוֹת ("all the places") in verse 2a.

It is attractive to see Hosea as the one who refers his audience to the Deuteronomic depiction through the device of quotation. By evoking the

[77] Thus Holladay, "On Every High Hill," 175–76. Most scholars follow Holladay in this diachronic assessment: e.g., Frédéric Gangloff, "A l'ombre des Déesses-arbres? (Os 4:12–14)," *BN* 106 (2001): 15–16; Macintosh, *Hosea*, 155; Maier, "Myth and Truth," 268; Mommer, *ThWAT* 7:581; Schulz-Rauch, *Hosea und Jeremia*, 45; Tigay, *Deuteronomy*, xxiii; Weinfeld, *Deuteronomic School*, 322; Steve A. Wiggins, *A Reassessment of 'Asherah': A Study according to the Textual Sources of the First Two Millennia B.C.E.*, AOAT 235 (Kevelaer: Butzon & Bercker, 1993), 97.

[78] Thus, e.g., Bass, "Hosea's Use of Scripture," 170; McConville, *Deuteronomy*, 218; Rooker, "Use of the Old Testament," 62.

[79] Lyons, *From Law to Prophecy*, 64–65.

description of the many foreign cultic sites in Deut 12, Hosea characterizes the faulty worship in his day. Israel is worshipping in the very places where the Canaanites previously served their gods. Simply by alluding to Deut 12:2, Hosea indicates the Canaanite character of the cult, the close verbal parallel functioning as a Hosean reference to a Deuteronomic tradition about the indigenous worship.

Furthermore, the Deuteronomy passage cannot function as a quotation or allusion to Hos 4:13, since Hos 4:13 does not enrich the interpretation of Deut 12:2. If Deut 12 turned a prophetic attack on the "geography" of the Israelite cult into a general description of the cult places of the גּוֹיִם ("nations"), that description might be interesting, but it would not be illuminating.[80] In fact, it is strange that the supposed Deuteronomistic reuse of Hosean phraseology omits the prominent adultery metaphor in Hos 4:12–15. Deuteronomy 12 contains no hint that the false worship it decries should be seen through the conceptual lens of marital infidelity. In the intertextual device of quotation, however, the source text always rings in the background and is crucial for the full understanding of the alluding text. A reuse of prophetic phrases from Hos 4 in Deut 12 without the powerful adultery imagery is therefore improbable.

Several scholars offer another understanding of the verbal parallel, according to which the shared locutions and concepts is rather the result of a late Deuteronomistic reworking of Hos 4. Nissinen argues that much of the phraseology in Hos 4:13 is formulaic and that the actual wording in which the concepts are presented is Deuteronomistic. For example, the word-pair זבח and קטר (*piel*) is often employed in late Old Testament texts describing illegitimate worship. Since Hos 4:13 is more elaborate than the other occurrences of the three-part phrase, Nissinen infers that Hos 4:13 is the latest Old Testament usage of the phrase.[81]

In my view, the proposal of a late Deuteronomistic redaction and "Fortschreibung" of Hos 4 is unconvincing. The alternation between poetic and prose elements in Hos 4:12–15 (Pfeiffer) is not a reliable criterion for suspecting redactional activity, since the distinction between poetry and prose is blurred in Biblical Hebrew in general and in the book of Hosea in particular.[82] In 1–2 Kings, the word-pair זבח and קטר (*piel*)

---

[80] Nothing in Deut 12:2–3 indicates that the referent for the worship on the hills is Israelite syncretism rather than the Canaanite cult.

[81] Nissinen, *Prophetie, Redaktion und Fortschreibung*, 110, 214–17. Nissinen is followed by, among others, Pfeiffer, *Heiligtum von Bethel*, 216–19; Christine Stark, *"Kultprostitution" im Alten Testament? Die Qedeschen der hebräischen Bibel und das Motiv der Hurerei*, OBO 221 (Fribourg: Academic Press, 2006), 135–36. Cf. also Yee, *Composition and Tradition*, 166.

[82] Cf. Andersen and Freedman, *Hosea*, 71: "We have found it impossible to draw a line between poetry and prose in Hosea."

appears as a stock phrase for worship on the high places (e.g., 1 Kgs 22:44[ET 43]—עוֹד הָעָם מְזַבְּחִים וּמְקַטְּרִים בַּבָּמוֹת ["the people still sacrificed and burned offerings on the high places"]). In Hos 4:13, however, we do not find a stock phrase but rather parallelism,[83] and the condemnable cultic activity is not related to the "high places" (בָּמוֹת). Since Hos 4:13 does not contain the standard Deuteronomistic phraseology,[84] ascribing Hos 4:13a to a later stratum is ill advised.

Conclusion and Outlook

This study has focused on three examples of claimed intertextuality between Hosea and Deuteronomy. These examples have demonstrated how complex the literary phenomenon of quotation is, and how difficult it can be to determine the direction of dependence. In the case of Hos 13:4–6, there seem to be good reasons for recognizing a dependence on a tradition similar to the one found in Deut 8. With regard to Hos 2:10–11[ET 8–9], Hosea is clearly suggesting that Israel ought to have known the Deuteronomic covenantal traditions concerning YHWH as the sole provider of the good land, its products, and its economic surplus. In the case of Hos 4:13, the verbal parallel does not allow us to draw a firm conclusion, but the likelihood that Hosea is quoting Deut 12:2 in order to stigmatize the non-Yahwistic nature of the cult is greater than that Deut 12:2b is a Deuteronomistic adaptation of an obscure prophetic critique. These conclusions may seem to be a meager outcome, but the texts do not allow us to be more certain when using literary criteria to evaluate the priority of the Deuteronomy tradition vis-à-vis the book of Hosea.

This study was undertaken without assuming any a priori understanding regarding the literary relationship between Hosea and Deuteronomy. In each case of apparent intertextuality, we looked for indications in the verbal parallels that signaled an interpretative reuse of phrases and ideas from the other source (i.e., either from Hosea or from a Deuteronomic source). In each case it turned out to be Hosea who alluded to an existing Deuteronomic tradition.

These three are not the only examples we could have examined. A similar in-depth literary study of additional parallels like Hos 3:1 and Deut 31:18, 20; Hos 5:11 and Deut 28:33; or Hos 11:5 and Deut 17:16 would probably yield the same result.[85] A study of the shared "love" theme in Hosea and Deuteronomy points in the same direction.[86]

---

[83] A similar parallelism is found in Hos 11:2.

[84] Maier, "Myth and Truth," 268.

[85] Cf. Andersen and Freedman, *Hosea*, 298, 409; Gisin, *Hosea*, 164, 265, 459.

[86] Cf. Vang, "God's Love."

Only if the interpreter assumes Hosean priority is it possible to "read" the verbal parallels as a Deuteronomistic reuse of Hosean phrases and concepts. Literary indications in the book of Hosea, however, suggest otherwise.

This result therefore confirms hints in the book of Deuteronomy that it reflects a fixed covenantal tradition that is older than the eighth century BCE.[87] Because Hos 8:12 alludes to a *written* collection of instructions bearing divine authority, Hosea's quotations of Deuteronomic traditions might imply that he was making use of written traditions. The evidence is inconclusive, however. From the literary character of the Hosean quotations, it is also a possibility that older authoritative Deuteronomic traditions were given the written form that we know today in the seventh century BCE.

In his references to the covenantal tradition of Deuteronomy, Hosea makes some decisive changes. Hosea turns the Deuteronomic concept of God's gracious provision for his people in an uninhabitable desert into a metaphor concerning a grazing flock. Moses' admonition against forgetting YHWH due to affluence is turned into an indictment. Whereas Deut 8 warns the Israelites of the danger that they might close their minds to the true giver of silver, gold, and agricultural abundance in the land, Hosea *changes* this admonition into an indictment that Israel falsely believed that its wealth was the result of its relationship to the Baals. Key Deuteronomic ideas are alluded to as a pool of knowledge that Israel has neglected. In addition, the prophet *modifies* the general Deuteronomic description of the indigenous cult system (Deut 12:2) into a characterization of Israelite worship in order to substantiate his indictment of whoredom.

A careful evaluation of quotational links between Hosea and Deuteronomy indicates the literary priority of an authoritative Deuteronomic tradition. The prophet Hosea appears to have read Moses in addition to other traditions, which he extensively utilizes. When Hosea describes Israel's early relationship with YHWH in terms of a heifer eager to serve its master (Hos 10:11), the Deuteronomic covenantal exposition may be part of that pool of divine instructions that Israel was once willing to follow.

---

[87] These hints include Deuteronomy's literary affinity with the forms and thought world of the political treaties from the late second millennium BCE (cf. K. Lawson Younger Jr. and Neal A. Huddleston, "Challenges to the Use of Ancient Near Eastern Treaty Forms for Dating and Interpreting Deuteronomy," in this volume); its portrait of an authority structure without any king or royal bureaucracy (cf. J. G. McConville, "Deuteronomy, Book of," in *Dictionary of the Old Testament: Pentateuch*, ed. T. Desmond Alexander and David W. Baker [Downers Grove, IL: InterVarsity Press, 2003], 188–91); the absence of a temple, capital city, professional soldiers, and business class in the book; the absence of references to the Mesopotamian superpowers of the eighth to fourth centuries BCE; and the nonmention of the Philistines in the description of Israel's enemies in the land.

CHAPTER 11

The Archaeology of Mount Ebal and Mount Gerizim and Why It Matters

Sandra L. Richter

Introduction

> And so it shall be when you cross the Jordan, you shall set up these stones which I am commanding you today on Mount Ebal (SamPent "Mount Gerizim") and you shall coat them with lime . . . and you shall write on the stones all the words of this law very clearly. (Deut 27:4–8)[1]

More than thirty years ago, Gordon Wenham stated: "Undoubtedly Deuteronomy 27 is the clearest clue to the provenance of Deuteronomy in the whole book."[2] Although it is unlikely that Wenham would have claimed to be a prophet, if scholarly attention is any indicator of prognostic data this particular statement has proven itself true. Identified in the past as an unfortunate intrusion between *Urdeuteronomium*'s chapters 5–26 and epilogue in chapter 28, Deut 27 is now demonstrating itself to be a pivot around which one of the most vexing questions of the book turns—*where* is the place that YHWH has chosen?[3] As this question has

---

[1] The combination of בַּאֵר הֵיטֵב is unique in the biblical text. Noting the Akkadian cognate *bāru* and the standard Piel translation "to explain, to elucidate," it is possible that this adverbial phrase has more to do with the *purpose* of the inscription than its method—"in order to clearly explain" to the people of Israel the commands of God (*HALOT*, s.v. "באר" [p. 106]). All biblical translations in this essay are the author's own.

[2] Gordon J. Wenham, "Deuteronomy and the Central Sanctuary," *Them* 11 (1985): 115.

[3] Deuteronomy 27 "is widely regarded as secondary. It is closely related to Joshua 8:30–35 and may therefore have been inserted into the book by the Deuteronomistic historian." Thus E. W. Nicholson, *Deuteronomy and Tradition* (Philadelphia: Fortress, 1967), 19, 36. Richard Nelson concurs: "It is widely agreed that this chapter intrudes between chapters 26 and 28" (*Deuteronomy*, OTL [Louisville: Westminster John Knox, 2002], 315). Cf. S. R. Driver, *A Critical and Exegetical Commentary on Deuteronomy*, ICC (Edinburgh: T&T Clark, 1895), 294–95.

been answered historically as Jerusalem, Deuteronomy has been repeatedly characterized as a book reflecting on events and issues relating to the Judean monarchy. However, more recent work has asked whether the site of corporate worship commanded in Deuteronomy might actually be *named* in Deuteronomy—specifically in the cultic celebration of Deut 27. If Deut 27 is indeed identifying "the place" of the centralizing formula, then either Mount Ebal (the MT) or Mount Gerizim (the SamPent) becomes the first "place of the name," and Deuteronomy becomes a book that casts light either on the early days of Israelite settlement or the postexilic perspectives of a returning (and recovering) refugee population.[4] As Wenham anticipated, Deut 27 is the fulcrum around which these questions turn.

Additional developments in the last decade have intensified the focus on Deut 27 and the mountains surrounding the ancient city of Shechem. The first of these is Adam Zertal's discovery of a small, exclusively Iron I cult site on the northeast shoulder of Mount Ebal.[5] The second is Yitzhak Magen's recent excavation of a Persian period Samarian sanctuary on Mount Gerizim.[6] The third is the discovery of a Dead Sea Scroll fragment of Deut 27:4b–6, which reinforces SamPent's reading: "[when yo]u [have crossed] the Jo[r]dan, you shall set up [these stones about which I charge you t]oday, on Mount *Gerizim*."[7] The last involves the growing interest throughout the discipline in the Persian period as the era of the composition of the Pentateuch. The thesis of this essay is that each of these questions and developments is intertwined with the provenance and message of the book of Deuteronomy. And to our great surprise, the archaeology of Mount Ebal and Mount Gerizim matters *very* much.

---

[4] See Sandra Richter, "The Place of the Name in Deuteronomy," *VT* 57 (2007): 242–366; Daniel Block, "What Do These Stones Mean? The Riddle of Deuteronomy 27," *JETS* 56 (2013): 17–41; and Andrew E. Hill, "The Ebal Ceremony as Hebrew Land Grant?" *JETS* 31 (1988): 399–406, for further discussion of this pericope.

[5] See Adam Zertal, "An Early Iron Age Cultic Site on Mount Ebal: Excavation Seasons 1982–1987: Preliminary Report," *TA* 13–14, no. 2 (1986–87): 105–65; "Has Joshua's Altar Been Found on Mt. Ebal?" *BAR* 11.1 (1985): 26–43; "Mount Ebal," *IEJ* 34 (1984): 55; "How Can Kempinski Be So Wrong!" *BAR* 12.1 (1986): 52; "A Cultic Center with a Burnt-Offering Altar from Early Iron Age I Period at Mt. Ebal," in *Wünschet Jerusalem Frieden*, ed. Matthias Augustin (Frankfurt: Lang, 1988), 137–47; "Ebal," *NEAEHL* 1:375–77; " 'To the Land of the Perizzites and the Giants': On the Israelite Settlement in the Hill Country of Manasseh," in *From Nomadism to Monarchy: Archaeological & Historical Aspects of Early Israel*, ed. Israel Finkelstein and Nadav Na'aman (Jerusalem: Israel Exploration Society, 1994), 47–69; Ralph K. Hawkins, *The Iron Age I Structure on Mt. Ebal: Excavation and Interpretation*, BBRSup 6 (Winona Lake, IN: Eisenbrauns, 2012).

[6] Yitzhak Magen, "Gerizim, Mount," *NEAEHL* 2:484–92; and "Gerizim, Mount," *NEAEHL* 5:1742–48.

[7] James H. Charlesworth, "What Is a Variant? Announcing a Dead Sea Scrolls Fragment of Deuteronomy," *Maarav* 16 (2009): 201–12.

Deut 27 and the "Place of the Name"

In 2002 I began a journey that plunged me into the long-lived debate regarding the location of Deuteronomy's sacred site by means of a comparative linguistic study of the name formulae in Deuteronomy's centralizing formula: "The place where YHWH your God will choose from all your tribes לְשַׁכֵּן שְׁמוֹ שָׁם" (Deut 12:5 [!], 11; 14:23; 16:2, 6, 11; 26:2); and "the place where YHWH your God will choose from all your tribes לָשׂוּם שְׁמוֹ שָׁם" (Deut 12:5, 21; 14:24).[8] Investigating these formulae via the semantics of their particular occurrences,[9] I demonstrated that Deuteronomy's לְשַׁכֵּן שְׁמוֹ שָׁם is actually a loan-adaptation of the common Akkadian idiom *šuma šakānu* and should be translated with that Akkadian idiom, "to place his name."[10] Moreover, I found that Akkadian *šuma šakānu* was well known throughout the ancient Near East from the third millennium BCE through the Neo-Babylonian period in an array of genres, with its most significant distribution occurring within the typology of the Mesopotamian royal monumental inscriptions. In other words, this Akkadian idiom, borrowed into the biblical text, was known throughout the ancient Near East for its use in a long-standing and consistent cultural context—the royal act of making inscriptions and installing monuments.[11]

The Levantine monumental corpus offered further insight by establishing that Deuteronomy's second name formula, לָשׂוּם שְׁמוֹ שָׁם, shares the same semantic range and cultural context as Akkadian *šuma šakānu*. The bilingual, ninth-century Tell Fakhariyeh inscription is particularly instructive, as it translates Akkadian *šumīma liškun* as Old Aramaic *wšmym lšm* and Akkadian *u šumšu išakkanu* as Old Aramaic *wyšym šmh*.[12] Hence, here

---

[8] Sandra Richter, *The Deuteronomistic History and the Name Theology:* lᵉšakkēn šᵉmô šām *in the Bible and the Ancient Near East*, BZAW 318 (Berlin: de Gruyter, 2002), esp. 43–48.

[9] James Barr, *The Semantics of Biblical Language* (London: Oxford University Press, 1961; repr. London: SCM, 1983), 274.

[10] "Loanwords are in no sense 'borrowed' from the donor language as intact entities but are new creations within the receptor language." These "new creations" that result from borrowing are the result of native speakers reproducing a linguistic form from a foreign language by "imitating it phonetically" (Paul Mankowski, *Akkadian Loanwords in Biblical Hebrew*, HSS 47 [Winona Lake, IN: Eisenbrauns, 2000], 4, 7; cf. S. Lieberman, *The Sumerian Loanwords in Old-Babylonian Akkadian,* vol. 1, *Prolegomena and Evidence,* HSS 22 [Missoula, MT: Scholars Press, 1977], 21).

[11] Richter, *Deuteronomistic History*, 45–49, 130–53, 199–205; cf. W. W. Hallo, "The Royal Inscriptions of Ur: A Typology," *HUCA* 33 (1962): 8.

[12] Richter, *Deuteronomistic History*, 199–205; cf. D. M. Gropp and T. J. Lewis, "Notes on Some Problems in the Aramaic Text of the Hadd-Yith'i Bilingual," *BASOR* 259 (1985): 46, lines 10–12, 16–17); Ali Abou-Assaf, Pierre Bordreuil, and Alan R. Millard, *La statue de Tell Fekherye et son inscription bilingue assyro-araméenne*, Éditions recherche sur les civilisations (Paris: Anatole de la Forge,

we find that Akkadian *šuma šakānu* is reiterated in the first-millennium Levantine corpus in a monumental context via the Northwest Semitic calque *šm šīm*, "to place (the) name."[13] These linguistic data establish that the once enigmatic Biblical Hebrew לְשַׁכֵּן שְׁמוֹ שָׁם is a synonym to לָשׂוּם שְׁמוֹ שָׁם—its reflex in the rest of Deuteronomy and the Deuteronomstic History. Most importantly, these data demonstrate that in utilizing לְשַׁכֵּן שְׁמוֹ שָׁם and לָשׂוּם שְׁמוֹ שָׁם to describe YHWH's "chosen place" the writers of Deuteronomy must have understood that these idioms somehow involved the kingly act of installing inscriptions.[14]

These conclusions led to a second question and a second study.[15] How does this new translation and interpretation of לְשַׁכֵּן שְׁמוֹ שָׁם and לָשׂוּם שְׁמוֹ שָׁם as idioms communicating the installation of an inscribed monument speak to the age-old question of the identity of Deuteronomy's chosen place? Three strategic pericopes were considered, each of which involves a cultic site in Deuteronomy identified in part by an inscribed monument: Deut 11:29–32; 12:1–4; and 27:1–8. In Deut 11 and 27, which serve as the bookends to the "old legal core," Israel is commanded, upon entering the land promised, to declare their allegiance to YHWH via a public ceremony on the mountains surrounding the ancient Canaanite city of Shechem. This public ceremony involves the installation of two stelae inscribed with "all the words of this law" (Deut 27:1–8). Moreover, as Deut 12:1–5 specifies, all other cultic monuments present in the land must be either destroyed or effaced. Specifically, the Israelites are commanded to "ut-

1982); Stephen A. Kaufman, "Reflections on the Assyrian-Aramaic Bilingual from Tell Fakhariyeh," *Maarav* 3 (1982): 137–75.

[13] In linguistics a calque, or "loan translation," is a word or phrase borrowed from another language by literal, word-for-word, or root-for-root translation.

[14] As Peter Machinist has summarized, Israel learned of Mesopotamian language and culture in a multifaceted fashion, often mediated through other languages and oral and visual communications ("Akkadian in the First Millennium BC: The View from Israel and Other Western Outposts" [paper presented at the Annual Meeting of the SBL, New Orleans, LA, 23 November 2009]). Multiple sources attest to exposure to the Akkadian idiom, including the victory stelae of the Amanus Mountains, the broad dispersion of the Gilgamesh Epic, the Amarna correspondence, and Neo-Assyrian political language. Of the growing bibliography on scribal culture in Israel, Susan Niditch's theories regarding the orality-literacy continuum are helpful for understanding the role of לְשַׁכֵּן שְׁמוֹ שָׁם in the ears of its audience. She describes a process by which certain formulae associated with particular settings develop in the "oral registry" of a people and are then transferred to the written word. These linguistic formulae functioned in part to establish a context or expectation through listener familiarity, and then moved into the written world by means of literary imitation to incite the same expectations in the reader (Susan Niditch, *Oral World and Written Word: Ancient Israelite Literature*, LAI [Louisville: Westminster John Knox, 1996], 130).

[15] Sandra Richter, "Place of the Name," 342–66.

terly destroy all the places where the nations whom you shall dispossess serve their gods" by "effacing" (אִבַּדְתֶּם)[16] their *name* from that place. In contrast, Israel is to worship only "at the place where YHWH 'places His *name*' " (Deut 12:5, 11, 21; 14:23, 24, 25; 16:2, 6, 11; 26:2). In the realm of human politics these actions of defacement and installation would be interpreted as the standard means of eradicating a past regime from public memory and announcing a new sovereign.[17] This is an apt message for the readers of Deuteronomy. Indeed, the gods of Canaan are about to be evicted and forgotten; YHWH will be the new lord of this promised land. Hence, from a theological, narrative, and literary perspective, the eradication of past monuments and the installation of YHWH's monuments frame the legal core and provide critical scaffolding to the whole—all of which culminates in Deut 27. And via this narrative and theological trajectory, the reader of every generation is ultimately directed to the mountains surrounding Shechem for the promulgation of the great *politeia* of ancient Israel.

Mount Ebal, Mount Gerizim, and Shechem

Why might the sister mountains of Ebal and Gerizim have been chosen for such a significant role in the book of Deuteronomy? The answer to this question is the ancient city-state of Shechem. Israel Finkelstein speaks of Shechem as "the most important city in the northern part of the central hill country from the Middle Bronze to Iron I periods."[18] The

---

[16] *Piel* 2mp of אבד; note *HALOT* אבד + מִן meaning 5: "to be carried off from" (s.v. "אבד" [*HALOT* 1.2]). Although *HALOT* lists no factitive equivalent to this meaning under the *piel*, to "cause to be carried off from" very effectively communicates the meaning of "to efface."

[17] In the ancient Near East the act of effacing a king's name from his monument in order to insert one's own was considered the ultimate sacrilege and was broadly recognized as the definitive mechanism for erasing a past ruler from public memory in order to announce his replacement. Hence, the Mesopotamian texts regularly rehearse that the act of finding and preserving the inscription of a former king was considered a sacred trust, and the curses protecting that trust were substantial. For example: "As for the one who removes the name of Narām-Sîn and places his own name (MU-*šu i-ša-kà-nu-ma*) on the statue of Narām-Sîn, the mighty, and says: 'My statue,' or shows (it) to a foreigner and says: 'Erase his name and place my name (on it),' may the god Sîn [. . .] curse him with a terrible curse" (RIME 2, E2.1.4.5, col. i′:4′–iii′:8; cf. Richter, *Deuteronomistic History*, 143–44, 153–56, 185–86).

[18] Israel Finkelstein, *The Archaeology of the Israelite Settlement* (Jerusalem: Israel Exploration Society, 1988), 80–91, with quotation at p. 81; cf. *The Forgotten Kingdom: The Archaeology and History of Northern Israel*, ANEM 5 (Atlanta: SBL Press, 2013), 13–36.

city's influence was both political and religious. The enormous LB/Iron I fortress-temple that occupied the heart of the city for generations demonstrates that Shechem was indeed "the premier religious center of the highlands."[19] The Amarna Letters portray Shechem as a leading political center with predominant military influence. Shechem's king Labayu is named on numerous occasions as an intimidating figure, feared and respected by his comrade kings in the hill country.[20] Most significant to the biblical narrative is that Shechem was situated in the heart of the hill country of Manasseh, seated upon the only east-west passage intersecting what would become Israel's National Highway. Two-thirds of the Iron I Israelite population in Canaan in the eleventh century BCE as well as one-third of the identified Iron I sites are located here.[21] As a result, Shechem is regularly featured in the biblical books that speak of the settlement and early monarchy.[22] The book of Joshua identifies Shechem as a city of refuge (20:7; 21:21) and the appropriate center of covenant renewal (24:1–28). The book of Judges recounts the story of Abimelech and the great Shechemite *migdal* temple in great detail (Judg 8:33–9:6, 22–57). And even though the religious center at Shechem was obliterated in 1100 BCE, the city apparently served as the capital of Solomon's first district (1 Kgs 4:8), the site of Rehoboam's inauguration (1 Kgs 12:1), and the first capital of the Northern Kingdom (1 Kgs 12:25). As Edward Campbell states, Shechem was so prominent that it was "the place to go to establish one's right to rule the region."[23] In light of Shechem's prominence in Israel's settlement period and early monarchy, it is entirely predictable that

---

[19] Lawrence Stager, "The Fortress-Temple at Shechem and the 'House of El, Lord of the Covenant,' " in *Realia Dei: Essays in Archaeology and Biblical Interpretation in Honor of Edward F. Campbell, Jr. at His Retirement*, ed. Prescott H. Williams Jr. and Theodore Hiebert (Atlanta: Scholars Press, 1999), 245. First discovered by Ernst Sellin in 1926, this enormous temple was multistoried, its footprint 70 x 86 ft. with stone foundations 17 ft. thick (ibid., 246).

[20] See EA 243–246, 248, 250, 252–254, 263, 280, 289. Labayu's Shechem was clearly a city to be reckoned with, the "uncrowned queen of Palestine" (G. Ernest Wright, *Shechem: The Biography of a Biblical City* [London: Gerald Duckworth, 1965], 9).

[21] See Zertal, "Hill Country of Manasseh," 47–69; and Finkelstein, *Israelite Settlement*, 80–91. Two hundred Iron Age I sites were registered in the Manasseh territory, fifty-six of these in the Shechem syncline, three times the number of LB sites. According to Ralph Hawkins, "thirty-eight of these sites were established on virgin soil or rebuilt after having been abandoned for some time," demonstrating "the incursion of an outside population" (*Iron Age I Structure on Mt. Ebal*, 207).

[22] The ongoing ambiguity in the biblical text regarding Israel's "friend or foe" relationship with Shechem, as well as the confusion as to whether the Shechemites were "in" or "out" of Israel, is reflected in Num 26:31 and Josh 17:2. The mixed population of the city is apparent in Judg 9:28.

[23] Campbell, "Shechem," *NEAEHL* 4:1346.

the Israelites would have been drawn to the environs of Shechem to announce their presence and establish their own sacred space, as is reported in Deut 11:29–32 and 27:1–8.

Geographically, the city of Shechem is also quite conspicuous. It is situated on the lowest flanks of Mount Ebal, which is the highest mountain in northern Samaria. Ebal rises 3,083 ft. (940 m.) above sea level, 1,200 ft. (366 m.) above the valley in which it stands. As famed geographer George Adam Smith stated: "The view from Ebal virtually covers the whole land. . . . No geography of Palestine can afford to dispense with the view from the top of Ebal."[24] Hence, as I have argued in the past, it should be no surprise that the biblical writers would find Mount Ebal an ideal location for the installation of YHWH's monument.[25] Like the victory stelae of Mesopotamia, this elevation—the highest peak in the most densely populated region of Israel's earliest settlement—would provide an optimal site for announcing the advent of a new sovereign.

With the divided monarchy Shechem's influence began to fade. As Lawrence Stager has demonstrated, by the time of Jeroboam I the sacred precinct at Shechem had been desacralized by its conversion into a grain storage area, and Jeroboam himself is credited with a large public building erected over the sacred site.[26] In Iron IIC Shechem garnered little attention, and its Persian period occupation was sparse. The city was eventually abandoned, from 475–325 BCE. It was only after Alexander's conquest of Samaria that Shechem was reoccupied, regaining its status as an "urban center" under the Ptolemies. With the advent of Antiochus III (ca. 200 BCE) until the city's subsequent destruction in 114 BCE, Shechem was closely associated with the Samarian sacred space on Mount Gerizim—a significant association indeed.

In sum, we are left with two time periods in which the sister mountains of Shechem might have been significant enough to the formation of the religion of Israel that they would have been deemed worthy of the installation of YHWH's monument inscribed with "all the words of this law." These are the LB/Iron I era of Shechem's golden age, associated with Shechem's famous *migdal* temple, and the Persian/Hellenistic era, associated with the Samarian sacred precinct on Mount Gerizim.

---

[24] George Adam Smith, *The Historical Geography of the Holy Land, Especially in Relation to the History of Israel and of the Early Church* (New York: George H. Doron, 1920), 94.

[25] Richter, "Place of the Name," 342–45.

[26] Stager, "Fortress-Temple at Shechem," 234, 246; cf. Amihai Mazar, "Temples of the Middle and Late Bronze Ages and the Iron Age," in *The Architecture of Ancient Israel: From the Prehistoric to the Persian Periods*, ed. Aharon Kempinski and Ronny Reich (Jerusalem: Israel Exploration Society, 1992), 169–73.

The Archaeology of Mount Ebal

For generations the association of Israelite worship with Mount Ebal in the book of Deuteronomy has been recognized as quite ancient—and quite odd. As several have voiced, if Deuteronomy is indeed a book whose *raison d'être* is an apologetic for religious centralization in Josiah's Jerusalem, it is nothing short of bizarre that the biblical author would portray *Moses* commanding sacrificial *worship* at Ebal.[27] Equally odd is Ebal's presence if the book emerged from the dissident Northern Kingdom; one would expect instead a focus on Dan, Bethel, or even Shiloh. An unexpected twist to this conundrum came in April 1980, when, in the midst of a routine archaeological survey of the territory of Manasseh, Israeli archaeologist Adam Zertal discovered an Iron I cult site on the northeast shoulder of Mount Ebal.

Known as el-Burnat Sitti Salaamiyya, the site sits in isolation 492 ft. (150 m.) below the peak of the mountain. Zertal began excavation in September 1982, completed four seasons, and published his finds in a popular article in January 1985, with a technical report following in 1987.[28] Perhaps more than any other datum connected to this site, Zertal's premature publication of it has resulted in ongoing controversy.

El-burnat is a simple, one-period site, consisting of a Late Bronze village/campsite (Stratum II) that was remodeled in the early Iron I (Stratum

---

[27] Adam C. Welch was one of the first to voice this incongruity in *The Code of Deuteronomy: A New Theory of Its Origin* (London: James Clarke & Co., 1924), 174–85. As William T. Koopmans states: "Why are these texts which focus on cultic activity in the area of Shechem permitted to play such a conspicuous place [*sic*] in the literary corpus which is alleged to have had as its *raison d'être* an apologetic for the centralization of the cultus in Jerusalem?" (*Joshua 24 as Poetic Narrative*, JSOTSup 93 [Sheffield: JSOT Press, 1990], 13). Cf. Richter, "Place of the Name," 349–50.

[28] Zertal, "Has Joshua's Altar Been Found on Mt. Ebal?" 26–43. Zertal's previous publications regarding the site included a note in the 1983 *Excavations and Surveys in Israel* (2:72) and a brief statement in the "Notes and News" section of the 1984 *Israel Exploration Journal*: "The unique character of the site and the importance of Mt. Ebal in the biblical tradition (e.g. Deut. 27; Josh. 8) made excavation desirable. . . . The structure was deliberately filled with stones, soil and ashes containing sheep bones, upon which was built a stone pavement. . . . The pottery at the site dates exclusively from the Iron Age I (twelfth century B.C.E.), and the complex was apparently deserted shortly after its construction. Part of a clay ox head, identical to examples found in 1982 at Shiloh, was found on the surface. The architecture of the site is, to our knowledge, unique in the Iron Age I" (Adam Zertal, "Mount Ebal: Notes and News," *IEJ* 34 [1984]: 55).

Zertal's technical report on the site emerged in 1987, "Preliminary Report," 105–65; cf. Zertal, "A Cultic Center with a Burnt-Offering Altar," 137–47. See Ralph Hawkins' exhaustive list of Zertal's publications touching on Ebal in *Iron Age I Structure on Mt. Ebal*, 274–75.

IB, ca. 1200–1140 BCE) and abandoned in approximately 1140 BCE (Stratum IA).[29] Founded on bedrock, the first stratum of occupation (Stratum II) boasts two areas, referred to as A and B. Area A consists of a bedrock surface, two fragmentary walls, a sizeable pit filled with hammer stones, potsherds, and a chalice, and Installation 94 (see Figure 1, p. 315). To the west is a courtyard, Area B. Both Areas A and B are enclosed within a "thin elliptical wall . . . [which] stands to a height of about one and a half feet,"[30] interpreted by the excavator as a *temenos* wall. Attached to this wall is what Ralph Hawkins names a "coarse domestic-type four-room house" also built on bedrock.[31] Surrounding the features of Area A were 70 to 80 stone-bordered circles, squares, and rectangles of irregular shape, ranging in diameter from 12 to 28 in. (ca. 30–70 cm.), intermingled and built atop each other. Their great number and location surrounding Area A—and the fact that half were filled with pithoi, jars, bowls, jugs, cooking pots, and votive vessels—led Zertal to interpret these installations as depositories designed for the offerings of pilgrims.[32] The overlapping placement of these installations suggests that these represented at least two stages of use (Strata II and IB).[33] Two Egyptian scarabs dating from ca. 1250–1200 BCE were among the finds in Areas A and B.[34] But most significant to Stratum II is Area A's Installation 94, a stone repository 6.6 ft. (2 m.) in diameter.

> In it, and over the entire floor, was a layer of ash mixed with a large amount of animal bones, most of them charred . . . a large amount of ash, potsherds, and animal bones was uncovered on bedrock. In the opinion of the excavators, feasts or ceremonies were held in this area.[35]

The pottery assemblage and abundance of burnt bones in Installation 94, which is located in the exact center of what would become the main building complex in Stratum IB, are such that Installation 94 has been broadly recognized as something *other* than domestic in character. Even Zertal's most vocal detractor, Aharon Kempinski, states: "I am ready to suppose there was cultic activity here."[36]

---

[29] Hawkins, *Iron Age I Structure on Mt. Ebal*, 8.

[30] Zertal, "Has Joshua's Altar Been Found on Mt. Ebal?" 33.

[31] Hawkins, *Iron Age I Structure on Mt. Ebal*, 37.

[32] See the seven similar deposits investigated at Tel Dan (Jonathan Greer, *Dinner at Dan: Biblical and Archaeological Evidence for Sacred Feasts at Iron Age II Tel Dan and Their Significance*, CHANE 66 [Boston: Brill, 2013], 49–74).

[33] Adam Zertal, "Preliminary Report," 118; cf. Hawkins, *Iron Age I Structure on Mt. Ebal*, 45–46.

[34] Hawkins, *Iron Age I Structure on Mt. Ebal*, 66–72; cf. Baruch Brandl, "Two Scarabs and a Trapezoidal Seal from Mount Ebal," *TA* 13–14 (1986–1987): 166–72.

[35] Zertal, "Ebal," *NEAEHL* 1:375.

[36] Aharon Kempinski, "Joshua's Altar—An Iron Age I Watchtower," *BAR* 12.1 (1986): 45; cf. Hawkins, *Iron Age I Structure on Mt. Ebal*, 34–36.

The controversy begins with Stratum IB. The structure in Area A was built of large, unhewn stones and its corners are oriented toward the four compass points. Excavation of the structure has produced no floor or entrance; the two interior walls do not meet. Moreover, the interior seems to have been deliberately filled with layers of bones, ash, and Iron I pottery.[37] Zertal interpreted this central structure of Area A as an altar—specifically Joshua's altar made after the design of Exod 20 and reflective of the events recorded in Deut 27 and Josh 8. What Zertal interpreted as a 3.9 ft. (1.2 m.) ramp descending 23 ft. (7 m.) from the altar is complemented on either side by two paved courtyards, each of which includes a number of stone installations filled with bones, ash, jars, jugs, juglets, and pyxides.[38] Area B (a low wall and four-room house in Stratum II) was rebuilt in Stratum IB. According to Zertal, the previous domestic area was filled and leveled for the construction of a large courtyard complemented by a broad staircase and entryway at its northern end (entrance 220). This courtyard served as "a kind of platform in front of the main complex."[39] Area C was added to the site to the north in this phase and encircled by fieldstone enclosure walls laid in shallow foundation trenches. In Stratum IA, the main structure in Area A as well as parts of Area B were covered over with stones and the site was apparently deserted. Zertal concludes that the site was abandoned and "buried" as a ritual act of religious respect, analogous to what transpired in Stratum VII at Arad.[40] Therefore, the site was in use for a very short period of time, ca. 1240–1140 BCE, the initial stages of Israelite settlement.[41]

Although Adam Zertal's interpretation of Area A in Stratum IB as an altar has received little scholarly acceptance up to this point, there is broad agreement that Zertal has identified Iron I cultic activity on Mount Ebal—even *Israelite* cultic activity.[42] The most compelling evidence for this

[37] Zertal, "Preliminary Report," 113; "Ebal," *NEAEHL* 1:376; cf. Hawkins, *Iron Age I Structure on Mt. Ebal*, 9, 39–42.

[38] Zertal, "To the Land of the Perizzites and the Giants," 61–63.

[39] Zertal, "Preliminary Report," 119–20; cf. Hawkins, *Iron Age I Structure on Mt. Ebal*, 48–49.

[40] Zertal, "Preliminary Report," 124; Zertal, "Ebal," *NEAEHL* 1:376; Hawkins, *Iron Age I Structure on Mt. Ebal*, 53.

[41] Zertal, "Ebal," *NEAEHL* 1:375. It is tempting to link the date of abandonment at Ebal to the founding of the cult center at Shiloh, which Finkelstein states occurred "not before the second half of the 12th century BCE" (*Israelite Settlement*, 231).

[42] See Hawkins' exhaustive roster of the scholarly response in *Iron Age I Structure on Mt. Ebal*, 198–99. Cf. Michael Coogan, "Of Cults and Cultures: Reflections on the Interpretation of Archaeological Evidence," *PEQ* 119 (1987): 2; Finkelstein, *Israelite Settlement*, 82–85; J. Alberto Soggin, "The Migdal Temple, Migdal Šᵉkem Judg. 9 and the Artifact on Mt. Ebal," in "*Wünschet Jerusalem Frieden": Collected Communications to XIIth Congress of the International Organization for the Study of the Old Testament, Jerusalem, 1986*, ed. M. Augustin and K. D. Schunk (Frankfurt

conclusion is the assemblage of burnt bones present. Of the 2,862 bones excavated, 96 percent are of domestic animals (cattle, sheep, and goats), with 10 percent of the total diagnostic bone sample coming from fallow deer (at least six animals).[43] No horse, ass, dog, pig, or carnivore remains were found—all of which were common at settlements of this time and region. Liora Kolska Horwitz of Hebrew University of Jerusalem states that

> only edible animals are present at Ebal, while at other sites animals possibly used for various purposes (such as equids) are present. The specific absence of gazelle and pig remains is of interest considering their presence in the immediate vicinity of the site, both in antiquity and today. . . . It is suggested that the Ebal faunal assemblage represents a narrow range of activities either in function or time. The absence of animals prohibited for consumption but frequent at other Iron Age sites, suggests conformity with Biblical tenets.[44]

In sum, el-Burnat Sitti Salaamiyya was a short-lived Iron I cult site characterized by what appears to be a uniquely Israelite bone assemblage and repeat visitation by worshippers. As such, it is a very rare find.[45] The

---

am Main: Lang, 1988), 115–19; Amihai Mazar, *Archaeology of the Land of the Bible*: vol. 1, *10,000–586 B.C.E.* (New York: Doubleday, 1990), 350; and Mazar, "Jerusalem and its Vicinity in Iron Age I," in *From Nomadism to Monarchy*, 85–86; Gösta W. Ahlström, *Ancient Palestine: An Historical Introduction* (Minneapolis: Fortress, 2002), 366. In his 2014 review of Ralph Hawkins' publication of the site, Larry Herr states: "Although I began reading the book with some doubt as to Zertal's interpretation, I finished the book being virtually certain that he was correct" (*BASOR* 371 [2014]: 219).

[43] Liora Kolska Horwitz, "Faunal Remains from the Early Iron Age Site on Mount Ebal," *TA* 13–14 (1986): 173–89. The slaughtering of deer (אַיָּל) is actually a significant focus in Deuteronomy (Deut 12:15, 22; 14:5; 15:22). The deer in the Ebal collection are *Dama dama mesopotamica* (a species included under the appellative אַיָּל). This is one of only three species of deer found in the region in the Iron Age, and it was the most prevalent. Sacrificial meals like those described in Deuteronomy would have included an array of foodstuffs besides the שְׁלָמִים portion—they were feasts with a full table that certainly included other clean meats, such as deer. These are reflected in Area T at Dan as well (Greer, *Dinner at Dan*, 43–53). Moreover, as deer are a "fringe" animal, a society concerned with the proper slaughter of this animal is typically non-urban (cf. Richter, "The Quest for a Core: Law and Social Location" [paper presented at the Annual Meeting of the SBL, San Diego, CA, 20 November 2014], 17n77, 20–21).

[44] Cited in Zertal, "How Can Kempinski Be So Wrong!" 51–52; cf. Horwitz, "Faunal Remains," 187.

[45] "Of some eleven other sites from the same time period in the region of Israel (mostly in the lowlands and plains), analysis revealed bones of dogs and donkeys elsewhere, but not here. Mount Ebal is the only site where only the bones of edible animals were found. Bones of gazelle and pigs were found elsewhere, but not here" (Richard Hess, *Israelite Religions: An Archaeological and Biblical Survey* [Grand Rapids: Baker Academic, 2007], 218). See Ziony Zevit's summary in *The Religions of Ancient Israel: A Synthesis of Parallactic Approaches* (New York: Continuum, 2001), 247–51. Although Zevit associates Ebal with "the short reign of Abimelech in the

site dates to the earliest stages of Israelite settlement, and was, according to the excavator, ritually retired in the same general time frame as the initiation of cultic activity at Shiloh. Can this site be associated with the tradition recounted in Deut 27:4? Although skeptics point out that the material remains of Stratum II are modest, and are troubled by the fact that the site neither is at the peak of Ebal nor faces Gerizim (and therefore may not be a strong candidate for the ceremony reported in Deut 11:29–32 or Josh 8:30–35[46]), the fact that el-Burnat is one of only a handful of Iron I cult sites, is unique in its assemblage of "clean" burnt bones, and is located on the obscure mountain named in Deut 27:4 remains extremely significant.

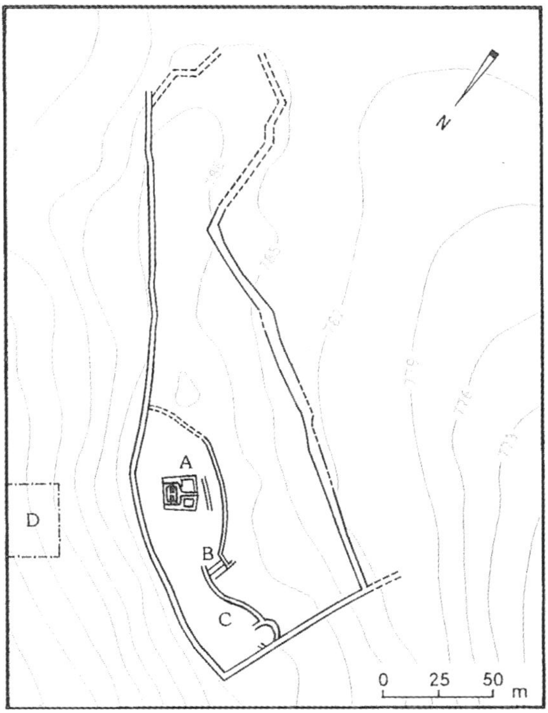

Figure 1. Excavations at Mount Ebal. (Used with permission of Dr. Shay Bar, Haifa University and the Manasseh Hill Country Survey.)

Shechem area"—a conclusion I believe goes beyond the evidence—his synthesis of Iron I sites emphasizes the uniqueness of Ebal (252).

[46] See Daniel I. Block, review of Hawkins, *Iron Age I Structure on Mt. Ebal*, in *BBR* 23 (2013): 94–96. Zevit argues, however, that the positioning of Iron Age temples on the north side of a site is found at Arad, Hazor, Dan, and Jerusalem, and may be a fully intentional expression of mythic and civic realities characterizing these eras (*Religions of Ancient Israel*, 250).

The Archaeology of Mount Gerizim

Like Mount Ebal, Mount Gerizim is strategically located on the perimeter of the ancient city-state of Shechem in the hill country of Manasseh. However, whereas Ebal lays claim to a holy place in the Iron I Age, Gerizim lays claim to a holy place in the Persian, Hellenistic, and modern periods.[47] In *Jewish Antiquities* 11:297–347 Josephus states that a Samaritan temple was built on Mount Gerizim "with the consent of King Darius" (11:311). This ancient testimony regarding a Persian-period temple on Gerizim and the long-standing identity of Mount Gerizim as sacred space among the ancient Samarians as well as the modern community of practicing Samaritans motivated Yitzhak Magen to tackle the site in 1982.[48] But after ten years of excavation Magen was forced to announce that "the excavations have so far produced no evidence of a temple or settlement from the time of the Ptolemies."[49] Rather, Magen found clear evidence of an impressive, but much later, Hellenistic city and sacred precinct on the southern ridge of Mount Gerizim. All the evidence indicated that both the city and precinct were established during the days of Antiochus III (ca. 200 BCE).[50] This same city and precinct were destroyed by

[47] Mount Gerizim lies southeast of the ancient city (now Nablus) and is slightly shorter than Ebal, rising 886 m. above sea level (Yitzhak Magen, *Mount Gerizim Excavations 2: A Temple City* [Jerusalem: Judea and Samaria Publications, 2008], 3). In Samaritan tradition Mount Gerizim (always written as a single word, הרגריזים) is sacred, being the intended "place" of Deuteronomy's centralizing formula. The command to build an altar on this site is present in the SamPent after Exod 20:14 and Deut 5:18 and constitutes what many call the Samaritans' "eleventh commandment." To this day more than half the world's Samaritan community lives in Qiryat Luza on Gerizim, and all practicing Samaritans celebrate their pilgrim feasts at the mountain (Reinhard Pummer, *The Samaritans* [Leiden: Brill, 1987], 289–301).

[48] The existence of a Roman temple and Byzantine church on the summit of Mount Gerizim confirms the mountain's established reputation as "sacred space." Magen believes that the Roman temple was built in the mid-second century CE, was rebuilt in the third century, and probably continued in use until the fourth century ("Gerizim," *NEAEHL* 2:490–92).

[49] Ibid., 487. Excavations at Mount Gerizim were carried out continuously from 1983 to 2003 under the direction of Yitzhak Magen. A four-quadrant, walled city with an area of about 100 acres was built on the upper ridge of the mount in the Hellenistic period, with a related sacred precinct on the summit of the hill (ca. 5 acres). Magen dates this city to the time of Antiochus III (ca. 200 BCE), destroyed by John Hyrcanus in 114–111 BCE ("Gerizim," *NEAEHL* 2:485–87, 492).

[50] Among the institutions that flourished under Antiochus III were local indigenous sanctuaries. Privileges similar to those given to Jerusalem (*Ant.* 12:138–144) were probably accorded by Antiochus III to Mount Gerizim as well (Jan Dušek, *Aramaic and Hebrew Inscriptions from Mt. Gerizim and Samaria between Antiochus III and Antiochus IV Epiphanes*, CHANE 54 [Leiden: Brill, 2012], 116).

John Hyrcanus in 114–111 BCE.[51] The site lay abandoned through the Roman period. Zeno completely absorbed this area when he erected a large church to Mary Mother of God directly over the ruins of the Samarian sacred precinct in 484 CE.[52] The excavator concluded that there was no evidence of either a temple or a settlement on Gerizim prior to the Hellenistic era.

But the 2008 supplemental volume to the *NEAEHL* has a different tale to tell. During the excavation seasons between 1993 and 2003 an accumulation of small finds (including an impressive bone assemblage of "clean" yearling animals and 68 Persian-period coins) along with the discovery of the footprint of a Persian-period square compound directly under the Hellenistic Samarian sacred precinct convinced Magen that he had at last located a Persian-period Samarian temple on Mount Gerizim.[53] The square compound measures 321 x 314 ft. (98 x 96 m.), is augmented by three six-chambered gates positioned north, east, and south, and is situated on the highest point of the mountain (see Figure 2, p. 321).[54] Magen dated the compound to the mid-fifth century BCE[55] and concluded that the sacred site was actually built one hundred years earlier than is indicated in Josephus' report. Moreover, he concluded that the catalyst for building the precinct was ongoing conflict between the Samarians

---

[51] This is contrary to Josephus' claim that the temple was destroyed in 128 BCE by John Hyrcanus (*Ant.* 13.254–257; *J.W.* 1.62). See Reinhard Pummer regarding the modern Samaritan cult ("The Samaritans: A Jewish Offshoot or a Pagan Cult?" *BR* 7.5 [1991]: 22–29, 40).

[52] Magen, "Gerizim," *NEAEHL* 2:485–87, 492.

[53] See Magen, *Mount Gerizim Excavations 2*, 97–137, for the full discussion. Based on the significant bone assemblage recovered from the large building just outside the northern six-chambered gate, Magen postulates that this area was utilized as a receptacle for ash from burnt sacrifices ("Gerizim," *NEAEHL* 5:1746). He further concludes that the assemblage demonstrates meticulous adherence to the requirements of "the Written Torah" (*Mount Gerizim Excavations 2*, 162). The Persian period coins come primarily from the sacred precinct. These include Sidonian and Samaritan exemplars, the oldest dating from 480 BCE ("Gerizim," *NEAEHL* 5:1746; *Mount Gerizim Excavations 2*, 168–69, 194–99). Jan Dušek states that 79 of the Antiochus III–era coins are dated to 223–187 BCE, and 1,419 remain undated. The quantity of coins minted by this ruler contrasts sharply with the meager number of Ptolemaic coins. Dušek hypothesizes that this may indicate some kind of Seleucid presence on Mount Gerizim, or the absence of Ptolemaic rule before 200 BCE (*Aramaic and Hebrew Inscriptions from Mt. Gerizim*, 3–4).

[54] The footprint of the western wall of the compound is preserved to a height of 2 m. along its entire 84 m. length. This western wall has no gate, probably due to the presence of a "holy of holies," which may be associated with the current holy site the Samaritans identify as "the twelve stones" (Magen, "Gerizim," *NEAEHL* 5:1746). According to the Samaritan tradition, this is the location of the altar commanded in Deut 27 and executed in Josh 8.

[55] Magen, "Gerizim," *NEAEHL* 5:1742.

and the people of Yehud (cf. Neh 13:28). And although Jan Dušek nudges the date to the last third of the fifth century BCE based on the epigraphic evidence (Darius II, 424–405 BCE), Magen's identification of the site as Persian is firm.[56]

> Today we can state with certainty that the first phase of the temple on Mount Gerizim was erected in the middle of the fifth century BCE by Sanballat the Horonite, a contemporary of Ezra and Nehemiah, who lived more than one hundred years before the Sanballat that is mentioned by Josephus.[57]

Magen further speculates that the erection of this temple was intended to sever all ties with Jerusalem and its temple and that, after building the sacred precinct, the Sanballat of Nehemiah's record gathered the unemployed Aaronic priests and Levites of Yehud to staff his new cultic center (cf. *Ant.* 11:312; Neh 13:10–11; Mal 1:6–10).

Of interest is the fact that the once great city-state of Shechem lay abandoned when Magen's Persian-period sanctuary was built on Mt. Gerizim.[58] The city would begin to recover in the late fourth century (Stratum IV, 325–250 BCE), when Alexander the Great's conquest of the city of Samaria forced the relocation of Samaria's population to Shechem.[59] With the rise of the Ptolemies Shechem once again became an urban cen-

---

[56] "The archaeologists distinguished two periods in the existence of the sanctuary with its sacred precinct. The first stage reflects Persian and Ptolemaic rule over Samaria. The sanctuary was founded in the first half of the 5th century BCE. The evidence for this dating is nevertheless scanty. . . . We have proposed dating the foundation of the sanctuary to the last third of the 5th century BCE, under Darius II (424–405 BCE). . . . only one published object seems plainly to predate the mid-5th century BCE: a drachma from Cyprus dated to 480 BCE. All other coins are of later date. Thus we maintain our earlier proposition" (Dušek, *Aramaic and Hebrew Inscriptions from Mt. Gerizim*, 3).

[57] Magen, "Gerizim," *NEAEHL* 5:1746–47. See Magen's recent article on the Israel Antiquities Authority website: "Sanballat from the time of Nehemiah was probably a resident of Hawara (Horon), located at the foot of Mount Gerizim, and was a descendant of the last Israelites who remained in Samaria after the destruction of the city by the Assyrians," http://www.antiquities.org.il/Article_eng.aspx? sec_id = 36&subj_id = 286&id = 472.

[58] Campbell identifies the era between Stratum V (Persian period, 600–475 BCE) and Stratum IVA-B (ca. 475–331 BCE) as an era in which Shechem was abandoned ("Shechem," *NEAEHL* 4:1347). Although Stern thinks these dates should be narrowed somewhat in light of newer evidence, Nancy Lapp reaffirms a period of abandonment from ca. 475–325 BCE (Ephraim Stern, *Archaeology of the Land of the Bible*, vol. 2, *The Assyrian, Babylonian, and Persian Periods (732–332 B.C.E.)* [New York: Doubleday, 2001], 427; Nancy L. Lapp, *Shechem IV: Persian-Hellenistic Pottery of Shechem/Tell Balâṭah*, ASORAR 11 [Boston: American Schools of Oriental Research, 2008], Table 1.1 [p. 4]).

[59] Campbell, "Shechem," *NEAEHL* 4:1353–54; cf. Stern, *Archaeology of the Land of the Bible*, 424–28.

ter (Stratum III, 250–190 BCE), as it would remain until its final destruction by John Hyrcanus in 107 BCE.[60] Alexander's conquest of Samaria also served as the catalyst for the founding of a small Hellenistic city on Mount Gerizim. With the victories of Antiochus III in the beginning of the second century BCE, and the ensuing period of stability under Antiochus IV, the city and sanctuary on Mt. Gerizim were largely rebuilt and significantly expanded, launching a second, "golden" phase for the sacred precinct that would also come to an end with the conquest of John Hyrcanus.

Mount Gerizim's "golden age" between 200–114 BCE is the period in which most ("perhaps all"[61]) of the 400 inscriptions excavated from the site originate. This assemblage of fragmentary inscriptions is written in Hebrew, Aramaic, and a "mixed script" of Aramaic and paleo-Hebrew.[62] These inscriptions are very important to the question of Samaritan origins and the nature of the sacred precinct on Mount Gerizim in that they exhibit a number of biblical names and phrases. An inscription of particular interest (no. 383) employs the Tetragrammaton in paleo-Hebrew script.[63] Based on this epigraphic evidence, Dušek concludes:

---

[60] "The most significant features of the Hellenistic reoccupation of Shechem are the extent and industry of the rebuilding and refortification. The whole tell was used . . . the Middle Bronze fortifications restored . . . so we must assume that Shechem was meant to be a powerful city in the Ptolemaic period, as strong as it had been when it had been the capital of a large city-state" (G. E. Wright, "The Samaritans at Shechem," *HTR* 55 [1962]: 358–89; cf. Stager, "Fortress-Temple at Shechem," 246; Campbell, "Shechem," *NEAEHL* 4:1354).

[61] Dušek, *Aramaic and Hebrew Inscriptions from Mt. Gerizim*, 116.

[62] Since 1985 excavations have yielded Aramaic, Hebrew, Samaritan, and Greek inscriptions. The *editio princeps* of the Aramaic, Hebrew, and Samaritan inscriptions was published by Naveh and Magen in 2004 and contains 381 inscriptions in Aramaic script, seven inscriptions in paleo-Hebrew script, several inscriptions in "mixed" script (Aramaic and paleo-Hebrew), an inscribed, square-shaped object (no. 390), an inscribed ring (no. 391), and four Samaritan inscriptions (Dušek, *Aramaic and Hebrew Inscriptions from Mt. Gerizim*, 5, 59–62, 116). Several taxonomies have been applied to these scripts. Magen himself speaks of "Neo-Hebrew," "lapidary Aramaic," and "Proto-Jewish" (Yitzhak Magen et al., *Mount Gerizim Excavations 1: The Aramaic, Hebrew and Samaritan Inscriptions* [Jerusalem: Judea and Samaria Publications, 2004], 41). Dušek prefers F. M. Cross's "paleo-Hebrew" to Magen's "Neo-Hebrew," and identifies Magen and Naveh's "mixed script" as "in reality the Aramaic cursive script with some letters taken from paleo-Hebrew" (Dušek, *Aramaic and Hebrew Inscriptions from Mt. Gerizim*, 41). The Gerizim inscriptions provide an important epigraphic link between the Persian and Hasmonean periods (Dušek, *Aramaic and Hebrew Inscriptions from Mt. Gerizim*, 54–59; Magen et al., *Mount Gerizim Excavations 1*, 31).

[63] Magen argues that inscription no. 383, which contains the Tetragrammaton, was written by priests since they "were the only ones to use the Tetragrammaton, a practice that had fallen into disuse among the other strata of society"

There is no doubt about the divinity worshipped in the sanctuary. One of the inscriptions in paleo-Hebrew script contains the name of God "YHWH." Two other finds indicate the divinity: a Greek inscription on a sundial discovered on the site contains ΘΕΩΙ ΥΨΙΣΤΩΙ "to the God Most High," and a Hebrew inscription on a silver ring contains יהוה אחד "the one Yahweh" in Aramaic letters.[64]

In sum, the first sacred precinct on Mount Gerizim dates to the last quarter of the fifth century BCE. The probable catalyst for that occupation was ongoing conflict with the Judeans returning to Yehud under the leadership of Ezra and Nehemiah. In 331 BCE Alexander the Great destroyed the city of Samaria, triggering the reoccupation of Shechem, which by this time had been long abandoned. A modest occupation near the sacred precinct on Mount Gerizim dates to this period as well.[65] This small settlement and sacred precinct on Mount Gerizim were significantly expanded at the beginning of the second century under Antiochus III. The epigraphic evidence indicates that this community understood their deity as the YHWH of the Pentateuch (albeit the *Samaritan* Pentateuch). Both the city and the sacred precinct were destroyed by John Hyrcanus in 114–111 BCE, marking the end of the Samarian Gerizim temple. *Hargerizim*, however, continues to this day as a site of utter holiness to the modern-day Samaritans. The SamPent identifies this site as the place of YHWH's dwelling, and the ruins continue to serve as the sacred destination of the three great pilgrim feasts of the Samaritan faith (Passover, Shavuot, and Sukkot). Here on *Hargerizim* we find the "Twelve Stones of Joshua," the "Altar of Isaac," and the Givat Olam (the "Eternal Hill"), among other sacred Samaritan relics.[66]

(Magen et al., *Mount Gerizim Excavations 1*, 255; cf. Dušek, *Aramaic and Hebrew Inscriptions from Mt. Gerizim*, 54). Dušek concurs that this inscription probably emerges from a priestly context. He states that dating the script is difficult, but, due to similarities with Qumran, it most likely emerges from the first half of the second century BCE (Dušek, *Aramaic and Hebrew Inscriptions from Mt. Gerizim*, 54).

[64] Dušek, *Aramaic and Hebrew Inscriptions from Mt. Gerizim*, 3.

[65] Campbell, "Shechem," *NEAEHL* 4:1347, 1353–54. It is likely that this residential area was occupied primarily by the priests connected to the temple. See Magen's diagram in "Bells, Pendants, Snakes & Stones: A Samaritan Temple to the Lord on Mt. Gerizim," *BAR* 36.6 [2010]: 24–36); cf. Figure 2, areas 3, 22, and 23.

[66] See Pummer, *Samaritans*, 289–301.

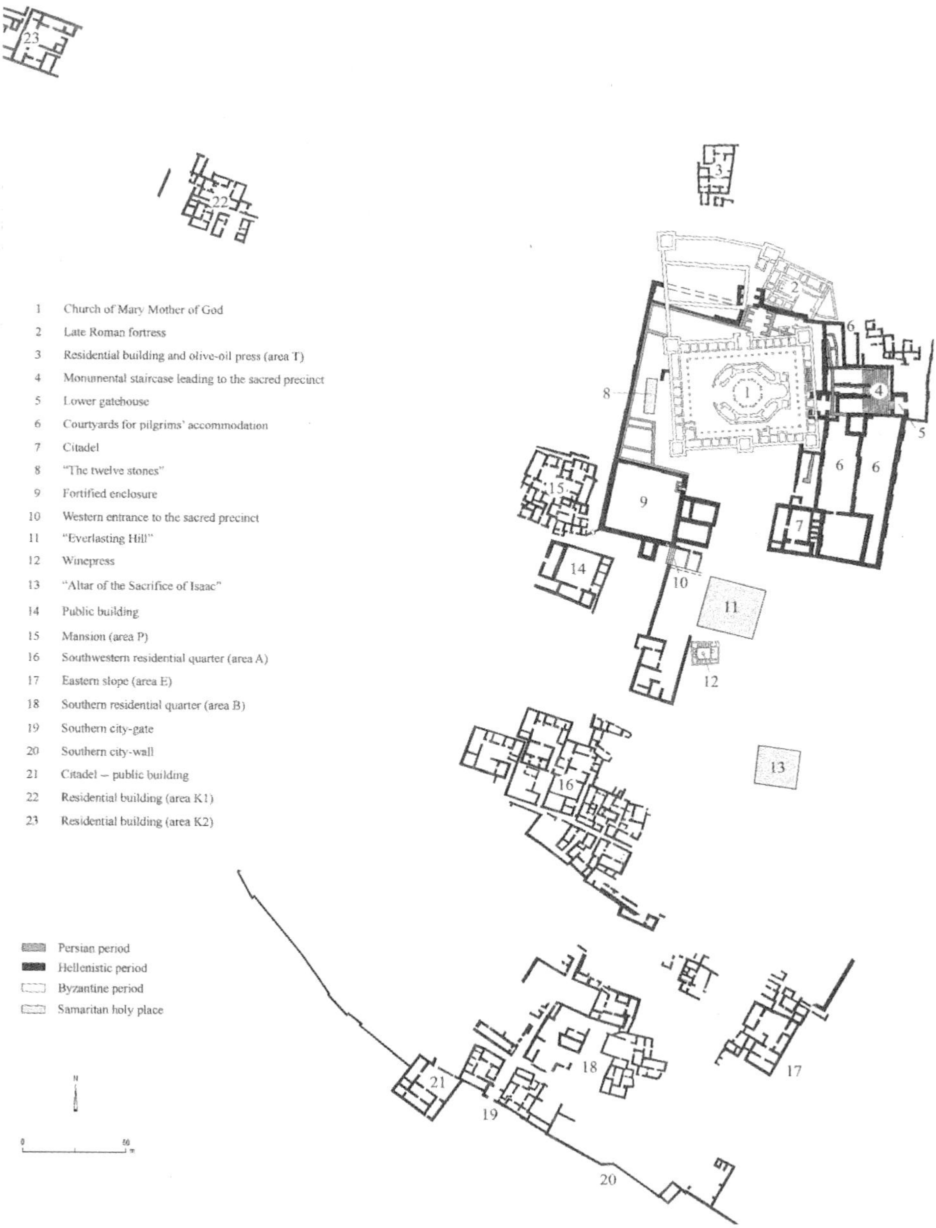

Figure 2. Excavations at Mount Gerizim. (Originally published in Yitzhak Magen, "Gerizim, Mount," in *NEAEHL* 5:1743. Used with permission of Dr. Ephraim Stern, The Institute of Archaeology, The Hebrew University of Jerusalem.)

A "Variant" Reading of Deut 27:4b

A third development ushering the mountains of ancient Shechem into prominence in recent years was the 2009 announcement of a new Dead Sea Scroll fragment of Deut 27:4b–6 (DSS F.154 [DSS F.Deut2]) (see Figure 3, pp. 326–27).[67] Unlike the only other existing Qumran witness to Deut 27:1–10 (4QDeut^{f} frgs. 32–35), the fragments of which are damaged at the critical point where the mountain should be named, the new fragment clearly names Israel's destination.[68] And the mountain named here is *not* the "Ebal" of the Masoretic Text and the Septuagint, but the "Gerizim" of the Samaritan Pentateuch. Although the new fragment is too small for AMS C14 analysis, Charlesworth assesses the script as "late Hasmonean Book Hand," and dates it to the second half of the first century BCE.[69] He concludes that the fragment should be identified as a proto-Samaritan text (Emanuel Tov prefers the term "pre-Samaritan"[70]), *not* a copy of the SamPent. Thus, the fragment should be dated to the late second or early first century BCE. As the reading of this new fragment is supported by Papyrus Giessen 19, the *Samareitikon*,[71] and, most compellingly, the Old

[67] James H. Charlesworth, "What is a Variant? Announcing a Dead Sea Scrolls Fragment of Deuteronomy," *Maarav* 16 (2009): 201–2. The full publication of this fragment is forthcoming in the Princeton Theological Seminary Dead Sea Scrolls Project series.

[68] See Eugene Ulrich, Frank Moore Cross, et al., *Qumran Cave 4, IX: Deuteronomy, Joshua, Judges, Kings* (Oxford: Clarendon Press, 1995), 53–54, plate xv.

[69] Charlesworth, "What is a Variant?" 202.

[70] Emanuel Tov, *Textual Criticism of the Hebrew Bible*, 3rd ed. (Minneapolis: Fortress, 2012), 74–92. The "pre-" or "proto-Samaritan" texts are defined as "ancient nonsectarian texts upon one of which the SamPent was based" (ibid., 81). The corpus is somewhat hypothetical as there is little material available on it, but the scribal tradition seems to share many similarities with texts of Qumran, from which the primary evidence for these texts comes. The important distinction between pre-Samaritan texts and the SamPent is that the former lack the distinctive ideological feature of the SamPent, namely, the regular reidentification of Israel's central cult site as Mount Gerizim (always offered as the single word *hrgryzym* [הרגריזים]) (ibid., 94). The pre-Samaritan texts and the SamPent share "the great freedom with which they approached the biblical text," resulting in many harmonizing alterations and a number of linguistic corrections (applied particularly to "correcting" archaic forms). Linguistic differences are evident as well, but less frequent (ibid., 84–94).

[71] The *Samareitikon* includes marginal readings in manuscripts of the Septuagint incorporated into Origen's Hexapla, marked as σαμ, το σαμ, or in one or two cases τὸ Σαμαρειτικόν, "the Samaritan." See Emanuel Tov, "Reflections on the Septuagint with Special Attention Paid to the Post-Pentateuchal Translations," in *Die Septuaginta—Texte, Theologien, Einflüsse*, ed. Wolfgang Kraus, Martin Karrer, and Martin Meiser, WUNT 252 (Tübingen: Mohr Siebeck, 2010), 3–22.

Latin Codex 100, Charlesworth concludes that the fragment represents the best original reading of Deut 27:4. In other words, it is the MT, not the SamPent, that preserves the "variant."[72] Since the SamPent's rendering of Deut 27:4 as "Gerizim" has been understood historically as one of many sectarian revisions of the MT (alterations that consistently identify any reference to Israel's central cult site as a reference to Mount Gerizim), Charlesworth's conclusions here are significant.[73]

Arguing against Charlesworth's position is the fact that DSS F.154 presents "Mount Gerizim" in the traditional and consistent SamPent fashion—as a single word, *hrgryzym* (הרגריזים). This indicates that this text has been influenced in the same fashion as the SamPent, which may identify it as a Samaritan, as opposed to a *pre*-Samaritan, text.[74] Moreover, as Carmel McCarthy clarifies, the MT reading of "Ebal" has the support of all the other textual witnesses, excluding the one Greek and one Latin manuscript named above.[75]

The weight Charlesworth places on the claim that Mount Ebal is the "Mountain of the Curse" is an additional problem.

> Most importantly, the text of Deuteronomy mentions two mountains: the Mountain of the Curse or Ebal and the Mountain of Blessing or Gerizim: "You shall pronounce the blessing at Mount Gerizim and the curse at Mount Ebal" (Deut 11:29 TANAKH). One would expect, therefore, that the author or compiler of Deuteronomy wrote that Moses conveyed the instruction to build God's altar on Mount Gerizim and not Mount Ebal as in the MT and LXX text of Deut 27:4.[76]

As it is quoted here, Deut 11:29 is one of three passages that report the covenant renewal ceremony at Shechem; the others are Deut 27:12–26

---

[72] Charlesworth, "What is a Variant?" 210. See Carmel McCarthy's helpful summary of the text critical situation in *BHQ: Deuteronomy*, 122*–23*.

[73] Space prohibits full discussion of opposing opinions here. See Emanuel Tov, *Textual Criticism*, 82–83, 94–100, 266n37; E. C. Ulrich, "4QJosh[a] [Pls. XXXII–XXXIV]," in *Qumran Cave 4*, vol. 9, *Deuteronomy, Joshua, Judges, Kings*, ed. E. C. Ulrich, F. M. Cross, et al., DJD 14 (Oxford: Clarendon, 1995), 146. Richard Nelson states: "it is unlikely that 'Ebal' is an anti-Samaritan reading as suggested by *BHS*" (*Deuteronomy*, OTL [Louisville: John Knox, 2002], 314 note "e").

[74] Central to the Samaritan faith is the "eleventh commandment" of the SamPent, offered in Exod 20:14, which identifies Mount Gerizim as the only legitimate site of Israelite worship. This inserted text is a composite of Deut 11:29a, Deut 27:2b–3a, Deut 27:4a, Deut 27:5–7, and Deut 11:30, and specifies "with clarity and geographical precision" that Mount Gerizim is the "place" that had been chosen as early as the patriarchs (Robert T. Anderson and Terry Giles, *The Samaritan Pentateuch: An Introduction to its Origin, History, and Significance for Biblical Studies* [Atlanta: SBL Press, 2012], 94–98).

[75] Carmel McCarthy, *BHQ: Deuteronomy*, 122*–23*.

[76] Charlesworth, "What is a Variant?" 210.

and Josh 8:33–34. When these passages are read together, it is fairly clear that the liturgical gathering envisioned directs the tribes to locate themselves in three spaces: half of the tribes are to gather on the slopes of Mount Gerizim, half are to gather on the slopes of Mount Ebal, and the Levites are to gather in a third area in between the two mountains (Deut 27:14; Josh 8:33). The objective of this ceremony is fairly straightforward: that all the people of Israel, native and alien, would hear and commit to the conditional blessings and curses of the Sinai covenant as spoken by YHWH's cultic mediators, the Levites. As Anne Marie Kitz states, the conditional curses itemized in the Dodecalogue of Deut 27:15–26 are well represented in the literature of the ancient Near East:

> They are proactive and protective. They are a tool in the arsenal of weapons that are designed to take preventative measures against future unwanted acts. It is for this reason that they [i.e., conditional curses] appear most frequently in treaties, dedicatory stela inscriptions such as the epilogue of the Code of Ḫammurabi and tomb inscriptions such as the sarcophagus of Aḫiram of Byblos.[77]

Charlesworth and others assume, however, that the command to "place (וְנָתַתָּה < נתן) the blessing on Mount Gerizim and the curse on Mount Ebal" (Deut 11:29), and for the tribes to "stand" (יַעַמְדוּ) in order "to bless" (לְבָרֵךְ) on Mount Gerizim (27:12), and "stand concerning the curse" (יַעַמְדוּ עַל־הַקְּלָלָה) on Mount Ebal (27:13) somehow identifies Mount Ebal as the mountain "of the curse." Based on this identification, Charlesworth concludes that Ebal could not have been the original choice for the installation of YHWH's altar. Rather, YHWH's chosen holy place should be upon the "mountain of the blessing," Gerizim. [78]

The logic of this broadly held belief regarding Mount Ebal as "the mountain of the curse" escapes me. Lexicography aside, one must ask if a curse is more potent to the one who *speaks* it or the one who *hears* it. Or better said in this particular case, does a conditional curse spoken by a second party, which entreats the deity to injure a target if certain provisions are not honored, impact the second party who is speaking, or the target of the curse? Obviously, the answer is the target of the curse.

---

[77] Anne Marie Kitz, *Cursed Are You! The Phenomenology of Cursing in Cuneiform and Hebrew Texts* (Winona Lake, IN: Eisenbrauns, 2015), 79–82.

[78] See n. 75 and S. R. Driver, *Deuteronomy*, 132–33, and Duane Christensen, *Deuteronomy 21:10–34:12*, WBC 6B (Nashville: Thomas Nelson, 2002), 227–28, for commentary and further bibliography. Cf. Gary Knoppers, "Mt. Gerizim and Mt. Zion: A Study in the Early History of the Samaritans and Jews," *SR* 34 (2005): 320; and Christophe Nihan, "The Torah Between Samaria and Judah," in *The Pentateuch as Torah: New Models for Understanding Its Promulgation and Acceptance*, ed. Gary N. Knoppers and Bernard M. Levinson (Winona Lake, IN: Eisenbrauns, 2007), 213.

In these passages the speaker is ultimately YHWH, who "announces and ordains human awareness of the inevitability of his activities should he be disobeyed."[79] YHWH's second party, his "professional curse practitioners," are the Levites.[80] As throughout the ancient Near East, it was those who would refuse to conform their behavior to the requirements of the pronounced maledictions who would be cursed—not the speakers or the place from which the curse was spoken.[81]

Returning to lexicography, Charlesworth's translation of the verb נתן as "pronounce" in Deut 11:29 is also problematic. Indeed, the text of Deut 11:29 is difficult. But as I have demonstrated elsewhere, a better translation of נתן in Deut 11:29 reflects the verb's use for the installation of a monument—a semantic field made explicit in Deut 27:1–8.[82] Hence, the text may indicate that one of the inscribed stelae described in Deut 27:2–4 is to be set up on Mount Gerizim to display the blessings of the Sinai covenant, and one on Mount Ebal to display the curses of the same. The utilization of a display monument to identify and protect barriers and boundaries or to provide a citizen of the ancient world with access to the written expectations of his superiors is widely represented in the ancient Near East.[83] But contrary to the interpretation espoused by Charlesworth and others, these monuments would not identify a locale as accursed. Rather, they were intentionally displayed in areas frequented by the community—primarily in areas of sacred space.

> Display maledictions are principally proactive. They are also public because their effectiveness depends on social awareness for their maintenance and ongoing respect. Therefore most of these imprecations are exhibited on monuments located in communal districts or in areas where the people might have occasional access such as temples and/or their courtyards.[84]

Thus, if נתן in Deut 11:29 refers to the installation of two stelae, one inscribed with the blessings on Mount Gerizim and one with the maledictions

---

[79] Kitz, *Cursed Are You!*, 81.

[80] Ibid., 394–99.

[81] Places considered "cursed" in the ancient world included destroyed cities, ruins, and wastelands. Kitz argues that these all shared a cultural association with "the final effect of maledictions, death" (*Cursed Are You!*, 247).

[82] Richter, "Place of the Name," 348; cf. Lev 26:1; *HALOT*, s.v. "נתן," meaning 12 (p. 734); and *DNWSI*, s.v. "נתן," meaning 2 (2:770).

[83] See Kitz, *Cursed Are You!*, 246–74. Even the illiterate utilized written display curses in this fashion. Kitz offers the lawcode of Ḫammurabi as an example. Here an *awīlum* who is illiterate is instructed to have a scribe orally recite the inscription on the *narû* such that he might obtain guidance in a lawsuit (ibid., 257–58; cf. Martha T. Roth, *Law Collections from Mesopotamia and Asia Minor* [Atlanta: Scholars Press, 1995], 134, col. 48, lines 3–19).

[84] Kitz, *Cursed Are You!*, 254.

on Mount Ebal, rather than consigning one location to a place of blessing and one to a place of curse, these stelae would mark both sites as public space, and likely as sacred space.

In sum, although the new Dead Sea Scroll fragment of Deut 27:4b–6 (DSS F.154 [DSS F.Deut2]) draws our attention back to the central role of the twin mountains in the book of Deuteronomy, and lends credence to the possibility that the original reading of Deut 27:4 was "Gerizim," not "Ebal," it does not exclude Ebal from the sacred space being delineated in this biblical text, nor does it resolve the question of *when* these twin mountains would be considered pivotal to Israelite religion.

Figure 3. DSS F.154 (DSS F.Deut2). (Images by Bruce and Kenneth Zuckerman and Marilyn Lundberg, West Semitic Research. Published with the permission of Azusa Pacific University.)

Pan-Persianism

A final development that affects our understanding of the role of Deut 27 in determining the provenance of the book of Deuteronomy is an emerging view within our discipline attributing the composition of Deuteronomy (and the Pentateuch) to the Persian period. As summarized by Christophe Nihan:

> The Torah is a sophisticated composition that, on the basis of earlier traditions, defines a new legend establishing the origins of "Israel," a legend capable of rivaling other prestigious national traditions inside the Achaemenid Empire, as is apparent for instance, in Deut 4:8: "And what great nation has statutes and ordinances as equitable as this whole law that I am setting before you today?"[85]

[85] Nihan, "Torah Between Samaria and Judah," 188.

In this new paradigm, the Pentateuch (and in particular Deuteronomy) becomes an "inner-Judean compromise" of the Persian period, its goal being to synthesize various scribal traditions in order to redefine the identity of "Israel" in the complex situation following the state's collapse.[86] Here Deut 27 (and Josh 8 and 24) become very late texts, revealing "concessions that were made to the Yahwistic community in the Persian province of Samaria so that the Torah would be just as acceptable to Samarians as to Judeans."[87]

Over the past ten years, Gary Knoppers has done a great deal to bring this discussion to American scholarship. In his book *Jews and Samaritans: The Origins and History of Their Early Relations* (2013),[88] Knoppers synthesizes these contributions and offers a new reading of the people group that remained in northern Israel after the Assyrian conquests. In contrast to traditional views, which emphasize cultural discontinuity following the collapse of the Northern Kingdom, Knoppers emphasizes cultural continuity.[89] Thus Knoppers argues that, although the communities of Samaria and Yehud suffered significant internal division, this division

[86] Ibid.," 188–89; cf. Jean-Louis Ska, *Introduction à la lecture du Pentateuque: Clés pour l'interprétation des cinq premiers livres de la Bible*, Le livre et le rouleau 5 (Brussels: Lessius, 2000), 310–21.

[87] Nihan, "Torah Between Samaria and Judah," 193. Yairah Amit in her "Shechem in Deuteronomy: A Seemingly Hidden Polemic" makes a similar argument regarding the era of these texts and the conflicts at hand serving as a catalyst: "To execute their anti-Shechem policy, the editors inserted two texts into the book of Deuteronomy regarding the ritual in Shechem's vicinity and a third into the book of Joshua . . . Such an ambivalent situation indicates a solution of compromise. . . . It seems to me that the original anti-Shechem polemic in Deuteronomy reflects an actual struggle at the beginning of the Second Temple period, before Nehemiah and Ezra. In this struggle, Jerusalem, with its miserable Temple, had to ensure its status versus Shechem" (*History, Memory, Hebrew Scriptures: A Festschrift for Ehud Ben Zvi*, ed. Ian D. Wilson and Diana Edelman [Winona Lake, IN: Eisenbrauns, 2015], 10–11).

[88] Gary Knoppers, *Jews and Samaritans: The Origins and History of Their Early Relations* (New York: Oxford University Press, 2013).

[89] Knoppers identifies Hezekiah's invitation to the northern tribes to celebrate the Passover in 2 Chr 30 as an important example of the Pentateuch as a document of compromise in the Persian period (*Jews and Samaritans*, 84–86; cf. Nihan's "tradition of administrative correspondence between the provinces of Yehud and Samaria," aimed at inviting unity between the communities ["The Torah Between Samaria and Judah," 191]). However, highlighting this particular exchange is problematic because the hope of restoration between the northern and Southern Kingdoms was not unique to the Chronicler's report of Hezekiah's Passover. Rather, the prophets all envision an *eschaton* in which the northern and southern tribes are reunited under "one (Davidic) shepherd" (e.g., Ezek 37:24). Therefore, if this message of reconciliation between north and south belongs only to the Samaria and Yehud provinces in the Persian period, the writing prophets would need to be relocated to this era as well.

was the result of gradual transformation, not "sudden breaks or sharp deviations."[90] Knoppers claims that these groups continued to recognize each other as kin and "coreligionists," who shared "substantial and persistent" contact until the great crisis of 114–111 BCE.[91] Knoppers envisions Samaria prior to this destruction as a wealthy and well-populated province of practicing Yahwists in regular contact with the people of Yehud.[92]

Noting the preponderance of Yahwistic names in the Hellenistic inscriptions emerging from the Gerizim excavations (as well as the mid-fourth-century Samaria papyri), Knoppers argues that the Samarians and Judeans were writing and speaking the same language. He concludes that both scribal communities were utilizing Aramaic script for diplomatic and commercial purposes, and paleo-Hebrew script for religious purposes."[93] Knoppers is particularly interested in the Hellenistic votive inscriptions, which regularly utilize biblical idiom (e.g., "house of sacrifice," כהן/כהנא for temple personnel, and Levitical names). From these inscriptions he argues for religious and cultural overlap between the temples at Gerizim and Jerusalem—both of which he identifies as "Yahwistic."[94] He concludes that "the majority of people in this province in the fourth cen-

---

[90] Knoppers, *Jews and Samaritans*, 108, 127, 133, 167; Knoppers, "Revisiting the Samarian Question in the Persian Period," in *Judah and the Judeans in the Persian Period*, ed. O. Lipshits and M. Oeming (Winona Lake, IN: Eisenbrauns, 2006), 272. Based on the Elephantine papyri, in which the colony at Elephantine requested assistance in rebuilding their temple in the late fifth century by appealing to the authorities in *both* Jerusalem and Samaria, Knoppers suggests that "normal diplomatic relations" between north and south were standard for the period. He finds this same diplomatic relationship echoed in Neh 6:10–14; 13:28; and Josephus, *Ant.* 11.306–312 ("Revisiting the Samarian Question," 278–79; cf. *Jews and Samaritans*, 9, 119–20).

[91] Knoppers, *Jews and Samaritans*, 133, 167.

[92] "My work concludes that of those who survived and remained in the land, the majority were Israelite. Significantly, then, portions of 'the ten lost tribes' were never lost" (Knoppers, *Jews and Samaritans*, 9). As evidence for his theory, Knoppers notes both the substantial growth in Samaria's population during the Persian period and the substantial resources necessary for the Hellenistic expansions to the Gerizim installations ("Revisiting the Samarian Question," 273; *Jews and Samaritans*, 171).

[93] Knoppers, "Revisiting the Samarian Question," 274. Quoting Naveh's 1998 publication of these inscriptions: "No differentiation whatsoever is discernible in the scripts used in Judah and Samaria in the Persian Period" (ibid.). One important distinction, however, is that from the fifth to the third centuries Yehud was utilizing paleo-Hebrew script for coins, but Samaria was not. In the third century, Yehud's use of the "Jewish Script" would further divide these two communities (ibid., 275).

[94] Knoppers, *Jews and Samaritans*, 184–88.

tury, or at least the majority of the elite, were Yahwistic."[95] Accordingly, Knoppers finds little evidence of a schism between the Yahwists of Gerizim and those of Jerusalem. Rather, he identifies the struggles reported in Ezra-Nehemiah as *internal* Judean debates.[96] In sum, Knoppers argues that the Pentateuch must be regarded as a "common patrimony" of the Judeans and the Samarians until the last two centuries BCE, and that prior to this time we should anticipate "considerable cooperation" between the elites of either community.[97] As a result, Knoppers concludes that the "imprecise language" of Deuteronomy's centralizing formula should be read as an intentional and strategic exercise in compromise between the two communities.[98]

> The textual and literary evidence from within the Pentateuch shared by Judeans and Samarians indicates that the Pentateuch was ultimately a compromise document, a work that could (and did, and does) function as scripture for both communities. It would not have been difficult for the framers of Deuteronomy (or the editors of the Pentateuch) to clarify YHWH's choice if they wanted to do so. The ambiguous phraseology in the centralization legislation in which the site of YHWH's own choosing goes unnamed was a critical component of the Judean-Samarian compromise.[99]

In this reconstruction, John Hyrcanus' destruction of the Hellenistic town and temple on Mount Gerizim marks the signal event precipitating hostile relations between these communities. This event was not the *result* of a

---

[95] Knoppers, "Revisiting the Samarian Question," 277. Among the 66 names with theophoric elements, the divine element *yhw* is by far the most common (57.57 percent). The other theophores are distributed among El (אל), 4.54 percent; Sin (סן), 4.54 percent; Baal (בעל), 3.03 percent; Shamash (שמש), 3.03 percent; and Qos (קוס), 3.03 percent (*Jews and Samaritans*, 115–16).

[96] Knoppers, *Jews and Samaritans*, 141–43.

[97] Ibid., 177, 188.

[98] Ibid., 195–97. "How long these two communities possessed the Pentateuch as a common literary corpus before the sectarian additions were added to what later became known as the SP is unclear. We do not know precisely how many centuries elapsed before the rise of a distinctive SP, because the date at which the Pentateuch was completed in the postmonarchic period is disputed. Also unclear is why the Samarians evidently chose one of the harmonistic texts of the Pentateuch, whereas one of the more common, less harmonistic, texts of the Pentateuch eventually prevailed in Jewish circles" (ibid., 189). Dušek states it this way: "The text that was used in their sanctuary during the first decades of the 2nd century was probably a harmonistic version of the Pentateuch, which was shared by other Yahwistic groups living in Palestine during the 2nd and 1st centuries BCE and perhaps even in later periods" (*Aramaic and Hebrew Inscriptions from Mt. Gerizim*, 117).

[99] Knoppers, *Jews and Samaritans*, 212. "From this vantage point, the very vagueness of the centralization formula—'the place YHWH will choose'—from within one of Israel's tribal territories (MT Deut 12:14) is a clue that the precise location of the central sanctuary is not to be found within Deuteronomy" (ibid., 211).

previously existing "downward spiral of bitter antagonism between the two groups," but instead triggered the schism between the two ancestral communities, thus serving as the genesis of the distinctive sectarian readings in SamPent.[100] According to Knoppers, the end result was the "addition of a thick layer of sectarian readings in the Pentateuch of the Samarians, and to a lesser extent, the addition of the occasional reading in the Pentateuch of the Judeans in the second-first centuries BCE [which] effectively transformed the Pentateuch in both communities."[101] Following Schenker, Knoppers further suggests that neither the *qal* perfect of בחר in the SamPent centralizing formula nor the naming of Gerizim in Deut 27:4 are late Samaritan sectarian readings. Rather, יבחר and the identification of Ebal in Deut 27:4 in the MT are late *Judean* sectarian alterations (as Charlesworth suggested; see above).[102] After the great divide of 114–111 BCE, "Judean scribes effectively eliminated a linchpin in the Samarian line of argumentation" regarding their election theology of Gerizim.[103] And having lost the place of the name of YHWH that they revered,

> Samaritan scribes sought to enshrine its unrivalled status in the very Pentateuch they shared with Judeans. The Samaritan sectarian additions ensured that their recently destroyed central shrine was indelibly and perpetually enshrined within the scriptures they held dear. [104]

Knoppers concludes that the LXX eventually embraced the politically motivated Judean emendation to "Ebal" (the timetable here is unclear). Thus, as Nihan details, the final form of the book of Deuteronomy (and

---

[100] Ibid., 179.

[101] Ibid., 13. Dušek dates this divide to the time of Antiochus IV Epiphanes in 168–167 BCE, when the Judean Yahwists became polarized between the Jerusalem orthodoxy (Judaism), on the one hand, and Hellenism and "foreignism," on the other. He concludes that at this juncture the Samarian Yahwists adopted Hellenism and openly declared their difference from the Judeans. From the Judean orthodox perspective, the Samarian Yahwists passed to the "wrong" side and were excluded from Israel as foreigners (*Aramaic and Hebrew Inscriptions from Mt. Gerizim*, 117).

[102] A. Schenker, "Textgeschichtliches zum Samaritanischen Pentateuch und Samareitikon: Zur Textgeschichte des Pentateuchs im 2. Jh. v.Chr.," in *Samaritans: Past and Present: Current Studies*, ed. Menachem Mor, Friedrich V. Reiterer, Studia Judaica: Forschungen zum Wissenschaft des Judentums 53; Studia Samaritana 5 (Berlin: de Gruyter, 2010), 105–21.

[103] Knoppers, *Jews and Samaritans*, 211.

[104] Dušek comes to similar conclusions, but places this after the events of 168–167 BCE. Here the legitimacy of the Yahwistic sanctuary on Mount Gerizim is formally denied by the Judean modification of Deut 27:4. For this reason John Hyrcanus destroyed Gerizim. Because the Samarian Yahwists did not share this perspective of orthodoxy, they continued to identify themselves as Israelites and modified their own Pentateuch. This modification emphasized the role of their sanctuary and excluded the temple of Jerusalem (*Aramaic and Hebrew Inscriptions from Mt. Gerizim*, 117).

of the Pentateuch as a whole) is to be located in the "late 5th or early 4th century B.C.E," and the ultimate issue at hand in Deut 27:4–8 is "to mediate between the competing claims of Zion and Gerizim" such that both sites might be legitimized despite Deuteronomy's centralization law.[105]

However, the testimony of the MT, LXX, and SamPent regarding the name formulae embedded in Deuteronomy's centralizing command evince a different timeline than the text-critical reconstruction offered above. As noted earlier, the Deuteronomic idiom לְשַׁכֵּן שְׁמוֹ שָׁם has a synonymous reflex in both Deuteronomy and the DH, לָשׂוּם שְׁמוֹ שָׁם (Deut 12:5, 21; 14:24; 1 Kgs 9:3; 11:36; 14:21; 21:4, 7).[106] In both corpora לָשׂוּם שְׁמוֹ שָׁם shares the same syntactical form and literary context as לְשַׁכֵּן שְׁמוֹ שָׁם. This is possible because לָשׂוּם שְׁמוֹ שָׁם is a Northwest Semitic calque of the original Akkadian formula *šuma šakānu*, which underlies Biblical Hebrew לְשַׁכֵּן שְׁמוֹ שָׁם, and the biblical authors recognized it as such. Hence, "the place where YHWH your God will choose to place his name" may be expressed with either formula.

The SamPent and the LXX affirm the correspondence between the two formulae by leveling the phrases. The SamPent renders both לָשׂוּם שְׁמוֹ שָׁם (Deut 12:21; 14:24) and לְשַׁכֵּן שְׁמוֹ שָׁם (Deut 12:11; 14:23; 16:2, 6, 11) as לְשַׁכֵּן אֶת־שְׁמוֹ שָׁם, indicating that the authors/editors of the SamPent understood these two formulae as interchangeable.[107] The LXX renders both formulae with ἐπικληθῆναι, "to be invoked," indicating that the LXX translators also understood the formulae as interchangeable, but apparently these translators were unaware of the idiomatic sense of the original Akkadian phrase.[108] It is significant that both the SamPent and the LXX have leveled these formulae but the MT has not.[109] It is also significant that the SamPent inserts the definite direct object marker אֶת־ before שְׁמוֹ in each

[105] Nihan, "Torah Between Samaria and Judah," 214–17.

[106] A third version of this formula exists, לִהְיוֹת שְׁמוֹ שָׁם, which I identify as a "periphrastic substitution" for the primary formulae. This form of the formula, outside of its debatable use in 1 Kgs 8, "may be unquestionably associated with the exilic and post-exilic eras" (Richter, *Deuteronomistic History*, 50; cf. fig. 2).

[107] The text-critical situation for Deut 12:5 is more complex. Note that unlike the Masoretes, the SamPent is not confused by the presence of both name formulae in Deut 12:5. Cf. Richter, *Deuteronomistic History*, 45–49. See Carmel McCarthy's helpful summary of the text-critical situation in *BHQ: Deuteronomy*, s.v. 12:5 (pp. 84*–86*).

[108] From ἐπικαλέω, "to summon a god to a sacrifice; to invoke" (*LSJ*, s.v. ἐπικαλέω [p. 635]).

[109] As McCarthy notes, those who hold the "Gerizim" reading as emerging from "an earlier, possibly non-sectarian text" argue that the MT's emendation to "Ebal" must have taken place prior to "G's translation of both books" (*BHQ: Deuteronomy,* 122*).

of its occurrences of the formulae, whereas the MT utilizes this particle only in Deut 12:5 (לָשׂוּם אֶת־שְׁמוֹ שָׁם), 2 Kgs 21:4, 7 (אָשִׂים אֶת־שְׁמוֹ עָם), and Neh 1:9 (לְשַׁכֵּן אֶת־שְׁמוֹ שָׁם). In the past I have demonstrated that these three MT occurrences with the ־אֶת particle involve the latest occurrences of these name formulae in the Hebrew Bible and in Deuteronomy.[110] The leveling evident in the LXX and the SamPent and the addition of the ־אֶת particle in the SamPent suggest that these are also later readings, and the best original reading of the name formulae in Deuteronomy's centralizing command is that of the MT, not that of the SamPent. Thus, although scenarios remain by which the "Ebal" reading of Deut 27:4 in the MT might be a late Judean variant, the formulae that first sent us looking for an installed monument on Ebal/Gerizim clearly are not.

Why It Matters

So why might the discovery of a small Iron I cult site on Mount Ebal, the excavation of a Persian-period sanctuary on Mount Gerizim, and the discovery of a Dead Sea Scroll fragment of Deut 27:4b–6 be of such consequence to the provenance of Deuteronomy? The answer is that, as envisioned by Wenham, the accumulating data surrounding Deut 27 are forcing us to ask and answer the following question: What sociohistorical setting might best suggest an imperative for Yahwistic worship on the mountains surrounding Shechem? The answer to this question provides the interpretive context for Deut 27:1–8. As I have demonstrated in this essay, there are only two candidates for that context: the LB/Iron I period of Israel's settlement and early monarchy, or the late Persian/Hellenistic eras of Samarian worship on Mount Gerizim. Nihan answers this question as follows:

> The various passages in Deuteronomy and Joshua describing a covenant ceremony in or near Shechem do not represent an ancient Northern tradition, as was usually assumed during the 20th century, but correspond to several attempts to acknowledge Samaria's religious and political role at the time of the Torah's composition.[111]

In Nihan's reconstruction Josh 24 is reinterpreted as the conclusion of a post-Priestly *Hexateuch* announcing a "new national unity between Judeans and Samarians after the fall of the two kingdoms and the end of

---

[110] Richter, *Deuteronomistic History*, 63n46. See Aaron D. Rubin, *Studies in Semitic Grammaticalization*, HSS 57 (Winona Lake, IN: Eisenbrauns, 2005), 91–109, for a full treatment of the development and grammaticalization of the direct object marker in Semitic.

[111] Nihan, "Torah Between Samaria and Judah," 223.

the monarchical state."[112] The supposed lack of specification regarding the "place" of Deuteronomy's centralization formula is construed as an intentional strategy to reconcile the conflicting traditions of the Yahwistic communities of Jerusalem and Gerizim. The Ebal "variant" of Deut 27:4 is identified as a polemical, anti-Samarian statement made by the post-Maccabean Judeans.[113] Thus, Nihan renders the text critical Ebal/Gerizim debate of Deut 27:4 as a Jerusalem/Gerizim debate. Moreover, the ancient city-state of Shechem known to the readers of both the MT and the SamPent becomes either the abandoned city of the Persian period or the Hellenistic reoccupation of the site known to Josephus under Alexander.[114] Most noteworthy, Deuteronomy, and the promulgation of the famed *politeia* of ancient Israel, become phenomena of the Persian and Hellenistic periods.

On the other hand, if the setting for Deut 27:1–4 (and the culmination of "placing" YHWH's name in the book of Deuteronomy) emerges from the settlement era, the point in question is where the newly arrived Israelites would establish their first place of corporate worship and announce their presence to Canaan. And whereas Shechem enjoyed the status of an "urban center" for less than a century during the Hellenistic period (ca. 200–114 BCE), Israel's settlement period corresponds to the "golden age" of the ancient city (1450–1150 BCE). As discussed above, Shechem was an enormously influential political and religious center throughout the Late Bronze and Iron I periods. Here covenants were made, oaths sworn, and stelae installed. Thirty-five references to the city in the books of Joshua and Judges illustrate and reiterate this profile. Moreover, the locus of earliest Israelite settlement in the territory of Manasseh confirms that Israel would have had regular contact with the city. With the dawn of Israel's monarchy, however, Shechem's influence began to fade. Shechem's *migdal* temple was destroyed in 1100 BCE. By the time of Jeroboam I the sacred precinct at Shechem had been converted into a storage area and repurposed.[115] Thus, the northern kings of Israel established their sanctuaries at Bethel and Dan, and Shechem's window of influence upon Israelite religion closed. This window would not reopen until ca. 325 BCE, when for a brief period Shechem served as the new center of Samarian faith. Therefore, the *only* two eras in which Shechem served as a religious center in Israel's experience are the settlement period of the LB/Iron I and the *re*settlement period of the Hellenistic era.

[112] Ibid.

[113] Ibid.

[114] Josephus refers to "the Samaritans, whose chief city at that time was Shechem, which lay beside Mount Garizein" (*Ant.* 11.340).

[115] Stager, "Fortress-Temple at Shechem," 234, 246; cf. Mazar, "Temples of the Middle and Late Bronze Ages and the Iron Age," 169–73.

As I have argued elsewhere, the nature of the religion described in Deut 27:1–8 requires consideration as well. Here Deuteronomy describes sacrificial Yahwistic religion characterized by a large, open-air altar and ink-on-plaster inscribed stelae. This description conforms precisely to what we know of religious practice in the Iron I.[116] The bone assemblage from the Mount Ebal excavations conforms to Israelite practice, clearly indicating that the people who repeatedly visited Mount Ebal for cultic feasting shared Israelite food taboos. The coating of prepared stelae with lime-based plaster in order to write upon the stelae with ink as described in the pericope is well attested in ancient Canaan. As Frank Moore Cross states: "I have long held that the lack of monumental inscriptions in early Israel is caused by the practice of making inscriptions with ink or paint on plastered stones."[117] Indeed, the LB/Iron I *migdal* temple at Shechem produced three such ink-on-plaster inscribed stelae. Lawrence Stager comments on these as follows:

> The quality of the size, shape, and preparation of this stela [i.e., one of the three] suggests that it once bore an elaborate inscription. The two stelae flanking the entrance to the temple must also have been inscribed. Obviously the inscriptions were not engraved; otherwise some traces of incised letters would have remained. It seems more likely that all of these stelae had once been plastered and inscribed with painted inscriptions.[118]

The Iron Age cult sites at Deir 'Alla (eighth–seventh century BCE) and Kuntillet 'Ajrud (eighth century BCE) have also yielded ink inscriptions on plaster.[119]

---

[116] Richter, "Place of the Name," 358–61. The LB/Iron I cultic sites at Shechem, the Bull Site, Tell el-Hayyat, Timna, and Bet Shean—to name only a few—as well as the critically important Iron II facility at Arad, have all produced large open-air sacrificial altars and stelae analogous to that described in Deut 27:1–8 (Coogan, "Of Cults and Cultures," 1–8; Mazar, "Temples of the Middle and Late Bronze Ages and the Iron Age," 165–86.

[117] Personal communication, September 23, 2003. Cf. Hershel Shanks, *Frank Moore Cross: Conversations with a Bible Scholar* (Washington, D.C.: BAS, 1994), 89, 91. Emmanuel Tov concurs (*Textual Criticism*, 201–2). Although no stelae have been found at Ebal, 20 pieces of white plaster have been recovered with traces existent from Stratum II and Stratum IA (Hawkins, *Iron Age I Structure on Mt. Ebal*, 42).

[118] Stager, "Fortress-Temple at Shechem," 233; cf. Wright, *Shechem*, 30–31, 80–85; cf. Mazar, "Temples of the Middle and Late Bronze Ages and the Iron Age," 165.

[119] Richter, "Place of the Name," 358–61; cf. H. G. Franken, "Archaeological Evidence," in *Aramaic Texts from Deir 'Alla*, ed. J. Hoftijzer and G. Van Der Kooij, Documenta et Monumenta Orientis Antiqui (Leiden: Brill, 1976); Jo Ann Hackett, *The Balaam Text from Deir 'Allā*, HSM 31 (Chico, CA: Scholars Press, 1984), 2–4; Zeev Meshel, "Kuntillet 'Ajrud," *ABD* 4:105, 107; Meshel, "Kuntilat 'Ajrud, 1975–1976," *IEJ* 27 (1976): 52–53; Tov, *Textual Criticism*, 201–2.

In comparison, Magen's reconstruction of the Persian and Hellenistic Samarian sanctuaries on Mount Gerizim predicts a large, open-air altar—but, due to the later construction of the Church of Mary Theotokos, such cannot be proven archaeologically. What does remain of the Hellenistic sacred precinct demonstrates the architecture had more in common with Greek forms than with the second temple in Jerusalem.[120] The bone assemblage and epigraphic evidence from Mount Gerizim clearly reflect Yahwistic worship. But unlike the dictates of Deut 27:1–8, as of now, no inscribed stelae have been recovered, only five "public" inscriptions have been identified, and no ink-on-plaster inscriptions have been found on Mount Gerizim.[121]

Conclusion

In conclusion, Gordon Wenham seems to have proven himself a prophet indeed. Whereas Deut 27 has long been marginalized within the larger book as an unfortunate interruption between chapters 5–26 and their epilogue in chapter 28, and the ceremony described in verses 1–8 has been obscured as an artificial conflation of two older and competing traditions, the question of the provenance of the book as reflected in this pericope has reemerged.[122] The core question is this: At what point in the experience of Israel might the twin mountains of Shechem be considered an appropriate arena for the culminating ceremony of the book of Deuteronomy? In what historical circumstance might "placing the name" of YHWH on one of these mountains be relevant? What occasion might serve as the catalyst for the promulgation of the *politeia* of ancient Israel from this northern arena?

---

[120] Magen, "Gerizim," *NEAEHL* 5:1746.

[121] "We can classify only five fragments as public inscriptions: no. 382, 383, 384, 385 and 387 with text ruled by horizontal lines separated by 6.3(–6.4) cm, written in Hebrew and in paleo-Hebrew script. All five fragments perhaps belonged to the same inscription" (Dušek, *Aramaic and Hebrew Inscriptions from Mt. Gerizim*, 62). These fragments are carved into prepared stone (not ink-on-plaster) and do not contain a biblical text (ibid.).

[122] Martin Noth and Gerhard von Rad have both proposed that Deut 27 presents us with an altar tradition based at Shechem commemorating Sinai, and a stelae tradition based at Gilgal commemorating the Settlement. See William T. Koopmans, *Joshua 24 as Poetic Narrative*, JSOTSup 93 (Sheffield: JSOT Press, 1990), 31–39; Otto Eissfeldt, "Gilgal or Shechem?" in *Proclamation and Presence: Old Testament Essays in Honour of Gwynne Henton Davies*, ed. John I. Durham and J. R. Porter (Richmond, VA: John Knox, 1970), 90–96; Nelson, *Deuteronomy*, 316–17.

This essay has demonstrated that there are only two possible answers to these questions: the LB/Iron I era of Israelite settlement, and the Persian/Hellenistic period of Samarian worship on Mount Gerizim prior to the Hasmonean destruction in 114 BCE. Concerning the evidence reviewed in this essay, Zertal's Iron I cult site on Mount Ebal unambiguously directs us to the first era. The site was in operation only during the Iron I period, which corresponds to the final phase of Shechem's tremendous religious influence via her *migdal* temple and the locus of early Israelite settlement. The DSS fragment of Deut 27:4 is less definitive. The fragment may be another expression of late Samarian sectarian views regarding *hargerizim*, or it may reflect the original reading of Deut 27:4. The evidence presented here inclines us toward the former. But as Gerizim and Ebal in their association with Shechem were well known in Israel's early history, either mountain, or both, could have served as Israel's first "place" of corporate worship in the settlement period. Thus, although at this point a final text-critical conclusion on Deut 27:4 is beyond our reach, the DSS fragment could support either historical scenario.

As we consider the sociohistorical setting most appropriate to the promulgation of the *politeia* of ancient Israel, however, the possibilities narrow. When the vast constellation of artifacts and memory attached to the great city-state of LB/Iron I Shechem and her *migdal* temple are compared to the remains and influence of Hellenistic Shechem, as well as the Persian-period Samarian temple and diminutive settlement on Mount Gerizim, the latter as the setting for the book of Deuteronomy is unlikely. Deuteronomy is focused upon the declaration of a new people of God standing on the cusp of a new identity in a new land. The possibility that the book remembers the location of the holiest precinct of the most influential city of the region at the time of Israel's earliest settlement and seeks to locate Israel's first place of corporate worship at that site is compelling. The fact that a humble expression of that sacred precinct has been found on one of Shechem's ancient mountains is constraining. Thus, at this point the evidence points us to an LB/Iron I setting for the historical memory captured in Deut 27:1–8. Here in Israel's first "place of the name" we find a people group committed to defining themselves against their social environment by the public declaration and installation of "all the words of this Torah" on the highest mountain of the most influential city of the most densely populated region of their new land. Deuteronomy 27 provides one of clearest clues to the provenance of the book of Deuteronomy, and the archaeology of Mount Ebal and Mount Gerizim do indeed matter very much.

CHAPTER 12

Hearing Galatians with Moses: An Examination of Paul as a Second and Seconding Moses[1]

Daniel I. Block

Introduction

In the last thirty years we have witnessed a revolution in scholarly perspectives on Paul's understanding of the relationship between the faith of Israel and Second Temple Judaism, on the one hand, and between the faith of Israel and the gospel of Jesus Christ, on the other. Especially in Protestant circles, it is widely accepted that the Hebrew Bible records the history of a failed system of life based on law in contrast to the effectual new covenant inaugurated by Jesus Christ and driven by the Spirit. Based on Rom 3–4 and Gal 3–4, some find an analogue to the New Testament way of faith in the Hebrew Bible by leapfrogging over almost a millennium of Israel's history as a nation back to Abraham, who modeled a righteousness based on faith, in opposition to a righteousness based on obedience to the law.[2]

Although the roots of this perspective date to the early centuries of Christianity, in the wake of the Reformation this approach has dominated Protestant scholarship. The forms of expression vary in different branches

---

[1] I am grateful to Nick Perrin, Seth Ehorn, Todd Wilson, and my brother George Block for reading an earlier draft of this paper and for offering many helpful suggestions, particularly with respect to New Testament issues and bibliography. I also thank my students Jordan Brown, Michelle Knight, Daniel Lanz, Franklin Wang, and Meredith Morris for their assistance along the way, and lastly my colleague Richard Schultz for his helpful suggestions as I prepared the final draft. Of course, any infelicities in style and content are my own responsibility.

[2] John Sailhamer, a Hebrew Bible scholar, interprets Exodus–Deuteronomy generically as a biography of Moses *sub lege* ("under the law") in contrast to the biography of Abraham, who lived *ante legem* ("before the law"). Abraham embodies the divinely approved pattern of a life of faith, while Moses demonstrates the inevitable failure of a life driven by law. See Sailhamer's *Introduction to Old Testament Theology: A Canonical Approach* (Grand Rapids: Zondervan, 1999), 272–89.

of Protestantism, but a generally negative view of Israel and of the Hebrew Bible itself has ruled the day for a long time—until the emergence three decades ago of what in Pauline scholarship is called the "new perspective." Scholars such as E. P. Sanders, James Dunn, and N. T. Wright do not agree on all points. However, based on a fresh look at Second Temple evidence, their work reflects a more positive disposition toward Judaism and a much more sympathetic reading of the Hebrew Bible.[3]

As an outsider to the debates between representatives of the "new" and "old" perspectives, I am struck by several features of the discussions. First, Hebrew Bible scholars are completely absent. Magnus Zetterholm's eight-page bibliography (135 entries) at the end of his volume on recent scholarship on Paul lacks the name of a single recognizable Hebrew Bible scholar.[4]

Second, and probably related to the previous observation, is that historically the course of the debate has been determined by the direction in which one reads the Scriptures. Proponents of the "old" perspective tend to read the Scriptures backward and interpret the Torah generally and the law particularly in the light of the New Testament. This approach often results in muffling the Hebrew Bible's own voice, forcing interpretations on earlier biblical texts that overlook internal evidence and marginalize natural readings of the texts. Representatives of the new perspective at least appear to listen more closely to the Hebrew Bible's own voice and to read later writings in the light of the earlier before they read the earlier in light of the later.

Third, proponents of the "old" perspective often appear uninterested in or unaware of the tensions their arguments create for an orthodox view of Scripture. Taking Paul's statements about the law at face value creates an intolerable opposition to the Torah. The Hebrew Bible perceives the law as an unprecedented gift (Deut 4:5–8) to be celebrated (Pss 19:7–14; 119). Obedience to it yields well-being and life (Deut 6:24), and results in the divine affirmation of law-observant Israelites: "You are righteous" (Deut 6:25; Ps 24:5; Ezek 18:9). But for Paul, the law brings (divine) wrath on people (Rom 4:13–15), animates sin (Rom 7:8–9), is associated with sin and death (Rom 8:2–4), is terminated in Christ (Rom 10:4–5), is/brings the curse (Gal 3:12–14), and imprisons and holds captive (Gal

[3] For a helpful introduction to the debates on Pauline views of gospel and law, see Magnus Zetterholm, *Approaches to Paul: A Student's Guide to Recent Scholarship* (Minneapolis: Fortress, 2009); John M. G. Barclay, *Paul and the Gift* (Grand Rapids: Eerdmans, 2015), 79–182.

[4] This impression is reinforced by recent collections of studies on Paul and the law, which rarely include Hebrew Bible scholars. See, for example, James D. G. Dunn, ed., *Paul and the Mosaic Law* (Grand Rapids: Eerdmans, 1994); Mark W. Elliott et al., eds., *Galatians and Christian Theology: Justification, the Gospel, and Ethics in Paul's Letter* (Grand Rapids: Baker, 2014).

3:21–24). In contrast to the Spirit, who animates (2 Cor 3:6), the letter (of the law) kills. If Moses and Paul were both inspired and their writings authoritative (as orthodox Christians believe), God appears minimally to speak out of both sides of his mouth and maximally to contradict himself.

I am admittedly a novice to the vast literature this discussion has spawned, and I present my response to these debates with considerable trepidation. However, having lived with Moses for three decades I have often found myself wondering what Moses, the statesman and theological trailblazer of ancient Israel, might have thought of Paul. And what would Moses have thought of our interpretations of the writings attributed to him and those attributed to the New Testament apostle? Breaking with my own past and popular practice, rather than reading Moses in the light of Paul in this paper I attempt to read Paul in the light of Moses. The challenge is huge, and this essay represents an initial foray into what must be a much larger project. John Barclay's recent work *Paul and the Gift* recognizes rightly that Paul's Epistles to the Romans and Galatians are at the heart of the debate. Although Romans represents a fuller theological statement and reflects Paul's thinking at a later stage, I begin my work in Galatians because this is where Paul began,[5] and frankly as a matter of expediency; this epistle is much shorter than Romans.

I sometimes imagine Moses and myself being present in one of the churches in Galatia as this epistle was read.[6] Occasionally I lean over to him and ask, "Did you say that?" or "How can Paul say that?" or "What do you think of that?" And I imagine looks on his face ranging from puzzlement to incredulity and surprise, perhaps even consternation.[7] However, at the same time I sense there is much in Galatians that Moses would have affirmed—much more than many modern readers will expect.

I begin this paper with summary observations from Gal 1–2 that present a portrait of Paul not merely as a prophet in the tradition of Jeremiah

---

[5] Scholars generally accept Galatians as Paul's earliest extant literary work, probably written prior to the Jerusalem Council (Acts 15), ca. 48 CE, though proponents of the North Galatian hypothesis suggest a date in the early 50s. See Richard N. Longenecker, *Galatians*, WBC 41 (Nashville: Thomas Nelson, 1990), lxxii–lxxxviii. The Epistle to the Romans was Paul's climactic literary work, produced in the mid-50s. See James D. G. Dunn, *Romans 1–8*, WBC 38 (Dallas: Word, 1988), xliii–xliv; Dunn, "Romans, Letter to the," *DPL*, 838.

[6] J. Louis Martyn rightly calls on modern readers to imagine themselves in the world of Paul's original addressees and invites us to "take a seat in one of the Galatian congregations, in order—as far as possible—to listen to the letter with Galatian ears" (*Galatians: A New Translation with Introduction and Commentary*, AB 33A [New York: Doubleday, 1997], 42).

[7] For an analogous rhetorical ploy, though from an unsympathetic perspective, see Jacob Neusner, *A Rabbi Talks with Jesus*, rev. ed. (Montreal: McGill-Queens University Press, 2000).

and Isaiah, as many have observed,[8] but as "a prophet like Moses," à la Deut 18:15–22.[9] If this is so, then Paul should have affirmed and built on Moses' work, rather than debunking or subverting him or his teaching.[10] Testing this hypothesis will be a complex task that will involve exploration of many of the key themes in Galatians. The second half of this paper concerns a single critical issue: What would Moses' disposition have been toward the debate between Paul and his detractors on whether or not gentile believers in Jesus needed to be circumcised?[11]

Paul's Status as a "Prophet Like Moses"

Despite the absence of any explicit claims by Paul to the title "prophet" (Hebrew נָבִיא, Greek προφήτης), many New Testament scholars have recognized the prophetic nature of his ministry.[12] In discussions of Paul as prophet, some refer to Moses in passing, but the apostle's relationship

---

[8] See further below.

[9] Cf. Jeffrey W. Aernie (*Is Paul Also among the Prophets? An Examination of the Relationship between Paul and the Old Testament Prophetic Tradition in 2 Corinthians*, LNTS 467 [New York: T&T Clark, 2012], 184), who concludes, "Although it is possible to argue at one level that Paul is either the expected prophet like Moses, the fulfillment of the servant tradition in Isaiah, or a type of second Jeremiah, the combination of all these parallels within 2 Corinthians seems to favour the understanding that Paul's emphasis is not on his connection with each prophet individually, but with the prophetic tradition corporately."

[10] For a fuller treatment of the use of Deuteronomy in Paul's letters, see David Lincicum, *Paul and the Early Jewish Encounter with Deuteronomy*, WUNT 2/284 (Tübingen: Mohr Siebeck, 2010), 117–68.

[11] In this essay I refer to Moses as speaker because everyone involved in the original conversation would have assumed that in Deuteronomy we hear Moses speaking, even as we assume we hear Paul's voice in Galatians.

[12] The vast literature on the subject is represented by Craig A. Evans, "Paul and the Prophets: Prophetic Criticism in the Epistle to the Romans (with Special Reference to Romans 9–11)," in *Romans and the People of God: Essays in Honor of Gordon D. Fee on the Occasion of His 65th Birthday*, ed. K. Soderlund and N. T. Wright (Grand Rapids: Eerdmans, 1999), 115–28; Tobias Nicklas, "Paulus—der Apostel als Prophet," in *Prophets and Prophecy in Jewish and Early Christian Literature*, ed. Joseph Verheyden, Korinna Zamfir, and Tobias Nicklas, WUNT 2/286 (Tübingen: Mohr Siebeck, 2010), 77–104; and fuller studies by Karl Olav Sandnes, *Paul—One of the Prophets?*, WUNT 2/43 (Tübingen: Mohr Siebeck, 1991); and Aernie, *Is Paul Also among the Prophets?* (n. 9 above). In an otherwise robust placement of Paul in the tradition of Israel's prophets (rooted in Isa 49:1 and Jer 1:5), Susan Eastman remarkably never mentions Moses or Deut 18:15–22, the foundational reference for a biblical understanding of the prophetic movement. See the chapter "Paul among the Prophets" in Eastman, *Recovering Paul's Mother Tongue: Language and Theology in Galatians* (Grand Rapids: Eerdmans, 2007), 63–88.

to Israel's paradigmatic prophet has not received the attention it deserves. Several features in Galatians appear to portray Paul as one in a long succession of "prophets like Moses" (promised by YHWH to Israel in Deut 18:9–22),[13] perhaps even as the new covenant Moses.[14] Moses had played a foundational role in establishing Israel as the covenant people of YHWH, interpreting YHWH's great acts of salvation associated with Israel's exodus and serving as an agent of divine revelation. In the wake of the "new exodus" that Jesus accomplished through his atoning work (cf. Matt 1:21), Paul functioned similarly to Moses. Indeed, we may perceive Paul as a "second" and "seconding Moses" who attempted to recover the heart of the faith of Israel's great leader.[15] Romans 7:12 declares Paul's default disposition: "So then, the Torah is holy, and the command is holy, righteous, and good" (cf. v. 16; 1 Tim 1:8).[16] While the subject demands an entire volume on its own, I offer a brief summary of features in Paul's *apologia* in Gal 1–2 that suggest he perceived himself as a Mosaic prophet.

[13] Against prevailing New Testament scholarship, I interpret Deut 18:9–22 as a promise of a succession of future prophets to carry on Moses' work, rather than a messianic prediction. See generally Daniel I. Block, *Deuteronomy*, NIVAC (Grand Rapids: Eerdmans, 2012), 433–47. For a more detailed argument, especially my interpretation of Acts 3:12–26 and 7:20–43, two critical New Testament texts often cited in the discussion, see my article " 'My Servant David': Ancient Israel's Vision of the Messiah," in *Israel's Messiah in the Bible and the Dead Sea Scrolls*, ed. R. S. Hess and M. D. Carroll R. (Grand Rapids: Baker, 2003), 26–32; and more recently, "A Prophet Like Moses: Another Look at Deuteronomy 18:9–22," in *The Triumph of Grace: Literary and Theological Studies on Deuteronomy and Deuteronomic Themes* (Eugene, OR: Cascade, 2017), 349–73.

[14] A notion suggested by Ernst Bammel ("Paulus, der Moses des Neuen Bundes," *Theologia* 54 [1983]: 399–408; repr. in Bammel, *Judaica et Paulina: Kleine Schriften II*, WUNT 91 [Tübingen: Mohr Siebeck, 1997], 205–14), though Bammel concludes that Paul cannot have viewed himself as the προφήτην . . . ὡς ἐμὲ, "the prophet . . . like me" (Deut 18:15 LXX). On Paul as the minister of the new covenant, see further Aernie, *Is Paul Also among the Prophets?*, 161–66; and more fully Scott J. Hafemann, *Paul, Moses, and the History of Israel: The Letter/Spirit Contrast and the Argument from Scripture in 2 Corinthians 3*, PBM (Milton Keynes: Paternoster, 2005).

[15] Secondary literature often suggests that in Galatians Paul has cast off his Jewish roots. See Zetterholm, *Approaches to Paul*, 69–94.

[16] Cf. N. T. Wright, "The Letter to the Galatians: Exegesis and Theology," in *Between Two Horizons: Spanning New Testament Studies and Systematic Theology*, ed. Joel B. Green and Max Turner (Grand Rapids: Eerdmans, 2000), 211–12; repr. in N. T. Wright, *Pauline Perspectives: Essays on Paul, 1978–2013* (Minneapolis: Fortress, 2013), 196–97. For a provocative discussion of what this might mean, see Pamela Eisenbaum, "On the Contrary, We Uphold the Law," in *Paul Was Not a Christian: The Original Message of a Misunderstood Apostle* (New York: HarperOne, 2009), 208–39. Unless otherwise noted, all translations of biblical texts in this essay are my own.

1. Paul's Self-Designation as "Apostle" (ἀπόστολος) of Jesus Christ (Gal 1:1)

In Gal 1:1 Paul introduces himself with his favorite title, an "apostle" called through Jesus Christ and God the Father.[17] Ἀπόστολος is a passive verbal adjective of the verb ἀποστέλλω, "to send, commission," used as a noun.[18] The word has long been understood as the Greek rendering of Hebrew שָׁלִיחַ, "envoy, commissioned officer," from שׁלח, "to send, commission."[19] By definition, apostles do not speak on their own initiative, but in response to a superior's commissioning. In Rom 1:1 Paul claims to have been "called" (κλητὸς) and "selected" (ἀφορίζω) to proclaim "the Gospel of God" (εὐαγγέλιον θεοῦ). Picking up on the former notion, in 1 Cor 1:1 he adds that he was called (κλητὸς) as an "apostle" of Christ Jesus by the will of God (διὰ θελήματος θεοῦ). Assuming the latter notion in Gal 1:15, Paul declares that he was "selected" (ἀφορίζω) before his birth and privileged to receive the revelation of God's Son that he might proclaim him among the gentiles (ἵνα εὐαγγελίζωμαι αὐτὸν ἐν τοῖς ἔθνεσιν).[20]

The Hebrew Bible offers little direct help in understanding Paul's preference for this professional epithet. The word ἀπόστολος appears only once in the LXX, translating the Hebrew participle שָׁלוּחַ, "sent," in an obscure variant reading of 1 Kgs 14:6.[21] While the absence of the lexeme

---

[17] Cf. the fuller expressions ἀπόστολος Χριστοῦ Ἰησου (1 Cor 1:1; 2 Cor 1:1; Eph 1:1; Col 1:1; 1 Tim 1:1; 2 Tim 1:1) and ἀπόστολος Ἰησοῦ Χριστοῦ (Titus 1:1; Peter prefers the latter in 1 Pet 1:1; 2 Pet 1:1). Paul also uses the word of other leaders in the early church in Gal 1:17, 19; cf. 1 Cor 9:5). Elsewhere it is used of Jesus' twelve disciples (Matt 10:2; Mark 3:14; 6:30; Luke 6:13; 9:10; 17:5; 22:14; 24:10; Acts 1:2, 26; 2:37, 43; 4:33, 36; 5:12, 18, 29, 40; etc.), and in Acts 14:14 it is applied to other leaders (Paul and Barnabas; cf. 1 Cor 9:5). In 1 Cor 15:5–11 Paul suggests that a key qualification for the title was the claim to having encountered the risen Christ.

[18] Thus Martinus C. de Boer, *Galatians: A Commentary*, NTL (Louisville: Westminster John Knox, 2011), 21. For lexical studies of the noun and the verb, see BDAG, 120–22; J. A. Bühner, "ἀποστέλλω *apostellō* send forth," *EDNT* 1:140–42; Bühner, "ἀπόστολος *apostolos* delegate, apostle," *EDNT* 1:142–46; M. Silva, "ἀποστέλλω (*apostellō*), to send . . . ," and "ἀπόστολος (*apostolos*), envoy, ambassador, apostle . . . ," *NIDNTTE* 1:365–76; K. H. Rengstorf, "ἀποστέλλω," *TDNT* 1:398–447.

[19] The *i*-class passive form is not attested in Biblical Hebrew (cf. *u*-class שְׁלוּחָה in Gen 32:19; Ezek 2:9). Aramaic-speaking Christians would probably have referred to the apostles as שְׁלִיחִין, a corresponding (plural) noun from the root שׁלח. On *i*-class passive forms common in Hebrew titular nouns, see J. Huehnergard, "On the Etymology and Meaning of Hebrew *nābîʾ*," *ErIsr* 26 (1999): 88*–93*.

[20] Cf. also Rom 1:5, and especially Paul's declaration in 11:13: "I am the apostle of the Gentiles" (εἰμι ἐγὼ ἐθνῶν ἀπόστολος).

[21] Hebrew וְאָנֹכִי שָׁלוּחַ אֵלַיִךְ קָשָׁה, "But I *have been sent* to you with bad news." The Greek text reads καὶ ἐγώ εἰμι ἀπόστολος πρός σὲ σκληρός, "and I am to you *an*

ἀπόστολος from the First Testament is striking, the notion of "envoy, messenger" is represented by Hebrew מַלְאָךְ, which the LXX translators regularly rendered as ἄγγελος, "angel."[22] The frequent linkage of this noun to the verb שׁלח, "to send, commission," reinforces the status of a מַלְאָךְ as a commissioned agent.[23] Moses is never identified as a מַלְאָךְ or a שָׁלוּחַ, but the frequent use of the verb שׁלח with YHWH as subject and Moses as object suggests that YHWH and the biblical writers perceived him as "the apostle" par excellence (cf. Deut 34:11). Although other human agents were also divinely commissioned,[24] with YHWH as subject the verb שׁלח overwhelmingly involves prophets,[25] and Moses appears as the object of this verb more frequently than all other prophets combined.[26] Paul's claim to the title ἀπόστολος locates him firmly in the prophetic train of Moses.[27]

2. Paul's Self-Designation as "Servant" (δοῦλος) of Jesus Christ (Gal 1:10)

Although ἀπόστολος was Paul's favorite titular epithet for himself, δοῦλος was a close second.[28] In the Greek world of Paul, this word and

---

apostle of bad news." See A. Rahlfs, ed., *Septuaginta* (Stuttgart: Württembergische Bibelanstalt, 1935), 1:668. For further discussion of this text, see Rengstorf, "ἀποστέλλω," 413–14. Since Ahijah is explicitly identified as a prophet (נָבִיא, 1 Kgs 14:2) and described as delivering a divine message to Jeroboam, here ἀπόστολος bears the technical sense of prophetic messenger of God.

22 Applied to agents of human authorities, see Gen 32:4, 7; Num 20:14; 21:21; 22:5; Judg 11:12–19; etc. Applied to envoys of God, see Gen 16:7–11; Exod 3:2; 32:34; Num 22:22–35; etc. For further references, see *DCH* 5:284–87. The New Testament uses ἄγγελος for human envoys (Matt 11:10; Mark 1:2; Luke 7:24, 27; 9:52; Jas 2:25), but Paul never claims this title.

23 More than seventy times. For references see *DCH* 5:285–86.

24 "Judge" deliverers: Judg 6:14; 1 Sam 12:11; King Saul: 1 Sam 15:18, 20; YHWH's servant: Isa 42:19; Aaron and Miriam, along with Moses: Josh 24:5; 1 Sam 12:8; Ps 105:26; Mic 6:4.

25 Prophets generally: Jer 25:4; 26:6; 35:15; 44:4 (cf. 29:19, where YHWH sends [שׁלח] his "word" [דָּבָר] by his servants the prophets). Individual prophets: Samuel (1 Sam 15:11), Nathan (2 Sam 12:1), Isaiah (Isa 6:8), Jeremiah (Jer 1:75; 8:17; 25:1; 26:12, 15), Ezekiel (Ezek 2:3, 4).

26 Exod 3:10, 12, 13, 14, 15; 4:28; 5:22; 7:16; Num 16:28, 29; Deut 34:11; Josh 24:5; 1 Sam 12:8; Mic 6:4; Ps 105:26.

27 Similarly Sandnes, *Paul—One of the Prophets?*, 68–69. On the tradition of Moses as apostle in Second Temple Judaism and in the book of Hebrews, see John Lierman, *The New Testament Moses: Christian Perceptions of Moses and Israel in the Setting of Jewish Religion*, WUNT 2/173 (Tübingen: Mohr Siebeck, 2004), 71–78.

28 Rom 1:1; Gal 1:10; Phil 1:1; Titus 1:1. The title was also claimed by James (Jas 1:1), Peter (2 Pet 1:1), and Jude, the brother of James (Jude 1:1), and applied to John (Rev 1:1) and Moses (Rev 15:3).

its cognate verbs were commonly used of slaves and their service, and Paul occasionally used it this way (Gal 3:28; 4:7, 22, 23, 30, 31).[29] However, given the conceptual and lexical legacy of the Hebrew Bible and the inscriptional use of the Semitic root עבד in the ancient Near East, it is misleading to render the word δοῦλος as "bond-slave" or "bond-servant" when Paul applies it to himself.[30] In royal circles, עֶבֶד הַמֶּלֶךְ, "servant of the king," was an honorific title designating persons equivalent to cabinet ministers in modern governments (2 Sam 18:29; 2 Kgs 22:12 [// 2 Chr 34:20]; 25:8). The expression occurs often in the Hebrew Bible,[31] but its courtly significance is confirmed by the plethora of ancient seals from Israel and its environs bearing epithets like עֶבֶד הַמֶּלֶךְ, "servant of the king,"[32] or more specifically, "servant of RN," where RN represents a royal name. Even more impressive is a recently discovered Anatolian monument erected by a "servant of the king."[33] No slave would have had the resources, authority, or chutzpah to erect a monument like this.

However, Paul's identification of himself as the δοῦλος of God and Christ involves a profoundly theological claim, probably rooted in Israelite tradition rather than in his Greek sociopolitical environment. The frequency of theophoric names involving עֶבֶד plus the name of a deity

---

[29] On the use of δοῦλος and cognates in the Greek world, see *LSJ*, 446–47; K. H. Rengstorf, "δοῦλος," *TDNT* 2:261–65; BDAG, 259–60, ("pert. to being under someone's total control, *slavish, servile, subject*" [259; italics original]); C. Spiqc, "δοῦλος," *TLNT* 1:380–86 ("The word *slave* refers above all to a legal status, that of an object or property [Latin *res mancipt*]. . . . A slave is an article of property that one buys, sells, leases, gives, or bequeaths, that one can possess jointly" [381]); A. Weiser, "δουλεύω," *EDNT* 1:349–50 ("In the Greek world and in Hellenism the word group has, because of the high valuation of personal freedom, almost exclusively a demeaning, scornful significance" [350]).

[30] NASB renders the word "bond-servant" in Luke 2:29; Rom 1:1; Gal 1:10; Phil 2:7; Col 1:7; 4:7; 2 Tim 2:24; Titus 1:1; Jas 1:1; 2 Pet 1:1; Jude 1:1; Rev 1:1; 15:3.

[31] The word עֶבֶד occurs frequently in construct with names of specific kings: e.g., Saul (1 Sam 29:3); Solomon (1 Kgs 11:26; 2 Chr 13:6); the king of Babylon (2 Kgs 25:8). Note also the personal name עֶבֶד־מֶלֶךְ in Jer 38:7–13; 39:15–18.

[32] For example, the Edomite seal inscribed "belonging to Qawsʿanal, servant of the king" (לקוסענל עבד המלך) from Tell el-Kheleifeh (John R. Bartlett, *Edom and the Edomites*, JSOTSup 77 [Sheffield: JSOT Press, 1989], 151–57); the seal "belonging to Shemaʿ, servant of Jeroboam" (לשמע עבד ירבעם) from Megiddo (see Mordechai Cogan and Hayim Tadmor, *II Kings: A New Translation with Introduction and Commentary*, AB 11 [New York: Doubleday, 1988], plate 12a); and the unprovenanced seal that reads "belonging to Obadiah, servant of the king" (לעבדיהו עבד המלך) (John C. L. Gibson, *Textbook of Syrian Semitic Inscriptions*, vol. 1, *Hebrew and Moabite Inscriptions* [Oxford: Clarendon, 1971], 62, 64).

[33] For translation and discussion of the text, see Dennis Pardee, "A New Aramaic Inscription from Zincirli," *BASOR* 356 (2009): 51–71.

in Israel[34] and in the world beyond demonstrates how widespread the notion of humans as "servants" of a deity was in the ancient Near East.[35] While biblical authors and characters in the narratives apply the epithet עֶבֶד יהוה/עֶבֶד אֱלֹהִים, "servant of YHWH/God," to many significant figures engaged in divine service,[36] for understanding Paul's status as δοῦλος of Christ/God, the treatment of prophets, often identified collectively as "my/his/your servants the prophets,"[37] is most important.[38] In these contexts עֶבֶד does not refer to a menial role, but designates one specially commissioned by YHWH and invited to stand in his council (סוֹד, Jer 23:16–22).

In contexts involving specific humans as servants of God, the LXX used five different expressions to translate עֶבֶד: in descending order of frequency, δοῦλος, παῖς, θεράπων,[39] ἄνθρωπος (2 Chr 24:6), and οἰκέτης (Deut 34:5). Δοῦλος occurs more than twice as often as all the others

---

[34] The name Obadiah (עֹבַדְיָה(וּ), "servant of YHWH") is ascribed to at least a dozen individuals in the Hebrew Bible and is frequently attested in Hebrew seals and inscriptions. See F. W. Dobbs-Allsopp et al., *Hebrew Inscriptions: Texts from the Biblical Period of the Monarchy with Concordance* (New Haven: Yale University Press, 2005), 611–12. On the name itself, see Jeaneane D. Fowler, *Theophoric Personal Names in Ancient Hebrew: A Comparative Study*, JSOTSup 49 (Sheffield: Sheffield Academic, 1988), 116, 353.

[35] For Ugaritic, see F. Gröndahl, *Die Personennamen der Texte aus Ugarit*, StPohl 1 (Rome: Biblical Institute, 1967), 104–6; for Punic and Phoenician, F. L. Benz, *Personal Names in Phoenician and Punic Inscriptions*, StPohl 8 (Rome: Pontifical Biblical Institute, 1972), 369–72; for Edomite, Bartlett, *Edom*, 203, 205–6, 211; for Ammonite, W. E. Aufrecht, *A Corpus of Ammonite Inscriptions*, ANETS 4 (Lewiston: Mellen, 1989), 371; for Aramaic and Canaanite, S. C. Layton, *Archaic Features of Canaanite Personal Names in the Hebrew Bible*, HSM 47 (Atlanta: Scholars Press, 1990), 122, 130–31. To these we should add Old Arabic, Akkadian, and Amorite names involving *[w]ardu*, their word for "servant." Cf. *CAD 1/II*, 250.

[36] Abraham (Gen 26:4; Ps 105:42); Jacob/Israel (1 Chr 16:23; Isa 41:8; etc.); Moses (Deut 34:5; Josh 1:1; etc.); Joshua (Josh 24:29; Judg 2:8); Caleb (Num 14:24); David (on which see Block, "My Servant David," 45–49); Hezekiah (2 Chr 32:16); Zerubbabel (Hag 2:23); and the Messianic Branch (Zech 3:8). Note also non-Israelites like Job (Job 1:8; 2:3; 42:7, 8) and Nebuchadnezzar (Jer 25:9; 27:6).

[37] For "my servants the prophets," see 2 Kgs 9:7; 17:13; Jer 7:25; 26:5; 29:19; 35:15; 44:4; Ezek 38:17; Zech 1:6; for "his servants the prophets," see 2 Kgs 17:23; 21:10; 24:2; Jer 25:4; Dan 9:10; Amos 3:7; Rev 10:7; 22:6; for "your servants the prophets," see Ezra 9:11; Dan 9:6; Rev 11:18.

[38] Note also the common identification of individual prophets as YHWH's servant: Ahijah (1 Kgs 14:18; 15:29), Elijah (2 Kgs 9:36; 10:10), Jonah (2 Kgs 14:25), Isaiah (Isa 20:3). This expression was especially useful for distinguishing true prophets from charlatans who claimed to speak for YHWH but whom he disowned (Ezek 12:21–13:23).

[39] Used primarily of Moses (Exod 14:31; Num 11:11; 12:7, 8; Josh 1:2; 9:2; 1 Chr 16:40, though עֶבֶד is lacking in Hebrew; cf. Heb 3:5), but also used of Job (Job 2:3; 42:7, 8), as an alternative to παῖς (1:8).

combined, and is preferred to παῖς by a 2:1 ratio.[40] Remarkably, outside the Gospels, in the New Testament παῖς occurs only in Acts, four times referring to Jesus (3:13, 26; 4:27, 30), once to David (4:25),[41] and once to a young lad (20:12). Why Paul avoided the word when identifying himself as "the servant" is unclear. Was it to avoid identification with the "servant" in the book of Isaiah whom the New Testament views as Jesus? By claiming the epithet δοῦλος, Paul identified himself with a long list of human beings whom YHWH had called into his service. But this was not menial service. Like Moses and the prophets of Israel, he served as a member of the heavenly council, received divine revelation, and spoke and wrote for God.

3. Paul's Call to Divine Service (Gal 1:15–16)

Paul's recollection of his call to divine service in Gal 1:15–16 is much sketchier than the classical "prophetical call narratives" of the Hebrew Bible, particularly the call of Moses (Exod 3–4)[42]—or than Luke's accounts of Paul's call in Acts (see Table 1).[43]

---

[40] While never used exclusively, the concentration of παῖς in Joshua, 1 and 2 Chronicles, and Isaiah suggests the choices reflected translators' preferences rather than deep-seated convictions regarding distinction between the two expressions. This conclusion is reinforced by the variation in readings of Dan 9:6 and 17; Vaticanus renders עֶבֶד as δοῦλος, while Theodotian prefers παῖς. The translator of Jeremiah generally preferred δοῦλος, but in references to prophets as "my servants" (26:5; 35:15; 44:4) he preferred παῖς (but see δοῦλος in 7:25 and 25:4).

[41] The use of παῖς here reflects the same impulse that led the editors to use this word in the superscription of Ps 18 (LXX Ps 17). The heading to Ps 36 uses δοῦλος. Nowhere else is David identified as the παῖς of God.

[42] Cf. the call narratives of Samuel (1 Sam 3:2–14), Isaiah (Isa 6:1–13), Jeremiah (Jer 1:3–16), and Ezekiel (1:1–3:27). For discussion of calls in the Hebrew Bible and the significance of the "Mosaic pattern" in establishing the authority of prophets, see Hafemann, *Paul, Moses, and the History of Israel*, 47–62. Although Paul's calling takes him in different directions, according to Hafemann, the apostle's allusion to Moses in 2 Cor 3:4–6 "is motivated by his conception of the parallels in function between his own ministry and the ministry of Moses" (p. 109).

[43] Though commonly interpreted as Paul's conversion experience, in all accounts this issue has been subordinated to the commission. On this event as a call to mission, see Krister Stendahl, *Paul among Jews and Gentiles* (Philadelphia: Fortress, 1976), 7–23; Richard M. Hays, "The Letter to the Galatians: Introduction, Commentary, and Reflections," in *NIB* 9:212–17.

Table 1. The Structure of Biblical Prophetic Appointment Accounts

Elements	Moses Exodus	Paul	Samuel (1 Samuel)	Isaiah (Isaiah)	Jeremiah (Jeremiah)	Ezekiel (Ezekiel)
(1) Divine Confrontation	3:1–4a	9:1–4a 22:3–7 26:9–14		6:1–4	1:4	1:1–28
(2) Introductory word (and response)	3:4b–9	9:4b–5a 22:8–9 26:15	3:2–10	6:5–7	1:5	2:1–2; 3:12–15, 22–24
(3) Divine Commission	3:10	9:5b–6a 22:10, 14–15 26:16, 18	3:11–14	6:8–13	1:10	2:3–5a; 3:4–6, 10–11 22–27
(4) Objections	3:11, 13 4:1, 10, 13				1:6	[2:6–8a] [3:16–21]*
(5) Divine Assurance	3:12, 14–22 4:2–9, 11–12 14–17	9:10–17 26:17			1:7–9, 17–19	3:7–9
(6) The Sign	4:2–9, 17	9:18–19 22:9, 11–13			1:11–16	2:8b–3:3

*The square brackets suggest that objections are implied, rather than explicitly declared.

Nevertheless, Werner Stenger has identified four elements of a prophetic call in Gal 1:15–16 (see Table 2):[44]

[44] The scheme is adopted by Sandnes, *Paul*, 59; and Roy E. Ciampa, *The Presence and Function of Scripture in Galatians 1 and 2*, WUNT 2/102 (Tübingen: Mohr Siebeck, 1998), 112–13.

Table 2. Elements of a Prophetic Call in Gal 1:15–16

15a,		Ὅτε δὲ εὐδόκησεν [ὁ θεὸς]	But when [God] . . . was pleased
	The Appointment (*Einsetzung*)		
16aα		ἀποκαλύψαι τὸν υἱὸν αὐτοῦ ἐν ἐμοί,	to reveal his Son in me,
15b	The Divine Calling (*Berufungswort*)	ὁ ἀφορίσας με ἐκ κοιλίας μητρός μου καὶ καλέσας διὰ τῆς χάριτος αὐτοῦ	. . . who had set me apart before I was born and called me through his grace . . .
16aβ	The Commission (*Dienstanweisung*)	ἵνα εὐαγγελίζωμαι αὐτὸν	so that I might proclaim him
16aβ	The Context of the Mission (*Zuständigkeitsbereich*)	ἐν τοῖς ἔθνεσιν.	among the gentiles.

Paul's being set apart "while in my mother's womb" alludes most obviously to Jeremiah's call (Jer 1:5).[45] However, the reference to God's revelation of his son in Paul recalls the revelatory purpose of the signs and wonders associated with the exodus (Deut 4:32–35), the theophany at Sinai (4:10–14, 36), and YHWH's revelation to Moses personally (Exod 33:11–34:7; cf. 34:29–35).[46]

4. Paul's Message (Gal 1:16)

Paul's Christocentric mission of proclaiming "the good news of him [Jesus]" is shorthand for the salvation from sin accomplished through Jesus' death and resurrection. While the word εὐαγγελίζω (Hebrew בִּשֵּׂר) is missing in Exod 3–4 LXX,[47] conceptually the notion corresponds to Moses' word of rescue for his people enslaved in Egypt (Exod 3:14–22).[48] Paul's

[45] But see also the Jewish tradition of a foreordained mission assigned to Moses in Assumption of Moses 1:14, according to which God "has devised and invented me [Moses], I who have been prepared from the beginning of the world to be the mediator of his covenant" (as translated by Johannes Tromp, *The Assumption of Moses: A Critical Edition with Commentary* [Leiden: Brill, 1992], 7; for commentary on this statement, see pp. 142–43).

[46] While an instrumental use of the preposition ἐν in ἐν ἐμοί (Gal 1:16aα) is not excluded (cf. 2 Cor 3:13), Paul later highlights the transforming effect of the revelation of the glory of the Lord (v. 18).

[47] The word is used in Isaiah with reference to the good news of Israel's return from exile, which was a new exodus (Isa 40:9; 52:7; cf. also 61:1).

[48] Cf. Isa 52:7, which identifies the proclamation of "peace" (שָׁלוֹם) and "salvation" (יְשׁוּעָה) as "gospel/good news" (εὐαγγελίζω).

focus on Jesus in the proclamation[49] answers to Moses' focus on YHWH as Israel's deliverer throughout Exod 3:6–22 and the specific event announced in Exod 14:13 and celebrated in the Song of the Sea (15:1–18). Many have found in Galatians a "cosmological apocalyptic theology," according to which the Christ-event signals God's intervention in the cosmos, liberating humankind from sin, which has enslaved it, and inaugurating a new age and resulting in a new creation.[50] While Moses' ministry could scarcely be characterized either as "eschatological" or "cosmological apocalyptic," as far as Israel was concerned he certainly announced the dawn of a new age and the birth of a new creation. Indeed, if the critical question for the Galatians was "What time is it?"[51] this was also the critical question for Moses and the Israelites. The narrative preamble to the call of Moses ends on a puzzling note:

> The Israelites groaned under their slavery, and they cried out. And their cry for help because of their slavery rose up to God. God heard their groaning, and God remembered his covenant with Abraham, Isaac, and Jacob. God saw the Israelites, and God knew (וַיֵּדַע אֱלֹהִים). (Exod 2:23b–25)

The last clause in the final sentence is incomplete. By omitting an object or a modifier, the narrator invites hearers to fill in the blank. Most translations assume the Israelites are the object, completing the sentence with something like "God took notice *of them*" (NRSV, NJPS; cf. NIV). However, the reference to the ancestral covenant in verse 24 suggests otherwise. The cry of the people signaled to God that the time had come to act in fulfillment of his promises in Gen 15: (1) the Israelites had become an innumerable host (Gen 15:5–6); (2) they had been aliens (גֵּר) in a foreign land for four hundred years (v. 13); (3) they had been enslaved (v. 13); and (4) the depravity of the Amorites (עֲוֹן הָאֱמֹרִי) had reached an intolerable level (v. 16). The time had come for YHWH to break into Israel's world, to defeat the forces of oppression in Egypt and of evil in Canaan, and to usher in a new era involving a new people in a new land.[52] The paradigmatic significance of this event for New Testament portrayals of the Christ-event is well documented.

---

[49] In Gal 1:7 he calls it τὸ εὐαγγέλιον τοῦ Χριστοῦ. Cf. Rom 1:16–17; 10:13–16; 15:16–20; 1 Cor 1:17–18; 15:1–8; but especially his summary of the gospel for gentiles in Eph 1–3.

[50] See especially M. C. de Boer, "Paul and Jewish Apocalyptic Theology," in *Apocalyptic and the New Testament: Essays in Honor of J. Louis Martyn*, ed. J. Marcus and M. L. Soards (Sheffield: Sheffield Academic, 1989), 169–90; J. Louis Martyn, "The Apocalyptic Gospel in Galatians," *Int* 54 (2000): 246–66.

[51] Thus Martyn, *Galatians*, 104–5.

[52] Note the announcement of the chronological significance of the timing of the exodus in Exod 12:2 and the subsequent emphasis on the timing of the event (Exod 13:4; 23:14; 34:18; Deut 16:1).

5. Paul's Inspiration (Gal 1:11–12)

The Torah presents Moses as having received his revelation of YHWH directly from God himself (Exod 3:1–4:17; 33:7–34:9), without a human mediator. Although Paul was aware of later tradition that had inserted angels into the process (Gal 3:19),[53] by emphasizing that he had received his message directly through a revelation of Jesus Christ (δι᾽ ἀποκαλύψεως Ἰησοῦ Χριστοῦ, 1:12c; cf. v. 16), he actually reinforced the linkage with Moses. In Gal 1:11–22 the apostle claimed that neither was he auto-inspired nor had he derived his gospel from any other human. Since it came directly from God himself, if his detractors rejected his message they would account to God and not to him. Paul makes this point repeatedly,[54] and in so doing he sounds particularly Mosaic. After the declaration of the Decalogue (Exod 19:16–20:21; Deut 4:9–15, 35; 5:1–27), all revelation at Sinai was given directly to Moses,[55] with whom YHWH spoke "face to face like someone speaks to a friend" (Exod 33:11; cf. Deut 34:10). In Deuteronomy both Moses and the narrator note that even his final speeches were delivered as YHWH had commanded him;[56] indeed, Moses occasionally equated his instructions/commands with the commands/voice of YHWH himself.[57] YHWH's defense of Moses in response to Aaron and Miriam's dispute over his monopoly of divine revelation (Num 12:1–9) is particularly pointed:

---

[53] Although the angel of YHWH (מַלְאַךְ יהוה) would figure as a guardian (Exod 14:9), guide (23:20–23; 32:34), and advance force for the Israelites in their battles for Canaan (33:2), in the remainder of the narratives of Exodus–Deuteronomy after Moses' original commission (Exod 3:2; cf. Acts 7:35) no angelic figure ever interacts with Moses. The tradition of the Torah being mediated through angels first appears in the Second Temple period: Deut 33:2 LXX; Josephus, *Ant.* 15.136; Philo, *Dreams* 1.140–44; Jubilees 1:27–2:1; Pseudo-Philo 11:5; cf. Gal 3:19; Acts 7:38, 53; Heb 2:2. Though without foundation in the Hebrew Bible, by New Testament times Jewish tradition claimed that prophecies generally were received through angelic mediators (cf. 3:16; Acts 7:53; Heb 2:2).

[54] (1) The gospel he preached was not a human message (1:11). In the phrase κατὰ ἄνθρωπον, the preposition marks a norm or standard, that is, "according to" human logic or imagination. Similarly, Barclay, *Paul and the Gift*, 355–56. (2) He did not receive his gospel from another human being (1:12a). (3) He was not taught this gospel (1:12b). (4) He received his gospel directly through a revelation of Jesus Christ (δι᾽ ἀποκαλύψεως Ἰησοῦ Χριστοῦ, 1:12c). (5) After his call to prophetic service, Paul cut himself off from the apostles for three years (1:16b–17).

[55] The formula וַיְדַבֵּר יְהוָה אֶל־מֹשֶׁה לֵּאמֹר occurs seventy times between Exod 20:22 and Num 35:9. The clause וַיֹּאמֶר יְהוָה אֶל־מֹשֶׁה לֵּאמֹר occurs an additional five times.

[56] The narrator: Deut 1:3; 28:69[ET 29:1]; Moses: 4:5, 14; 6:1, 25.

[57] Deut 4:2, 40; 6:2; 8:1, 11; 10:13; 11:27, 28; 12:28; 13:19[ET 18]; 15:5; 26:13–14; 28:1, 13, 15; 30:2, 8, 16; 31:29.

Listen to my words:
"When there are prophets among you,
I, YHWH, reveal myself to them in visions;
I speak to them in dreams.
Not so with my servant Moses:
In my whole household he is faithful.
With him I speak mouth to mouth,
clearly and not in riddles;
he gazes at the form of YHWH.
Then why were you not afraid
to speak against my servant Moses?" (vv. 6–8)

By declaring that he received his gospel directly from God, Paul claimed Moses-like privilege and reinforced the seriousness with which people needed to take his message. Cast in the roles of Aaron and Miriam, his detractors had set themselves up as the targets of divine fury.

6. Paul's Retreat to Arabia (Gal 1:17–18a)

Paul's enigmatic reference in Gal 1:17–18a to his three-year stay in Arabia raises all sorts of questions, especially since the narratives in Acts never allude to this journey. Against the prevailing view that Paul launched into his gospel mission immediately after his call and spent three years evangelizing the Nabateans,[58] N. T. Wright reads Ἀραβία as a cipher for Sinai/Horeb (cf. 4:25),[59] and argues that the purpose of his time spent there was to redirect his Phinehas- and Elijah-like zeal for Judaism to the mission of the crucified and risen Christ.[60] Wright is on the right track, but Paul returned from Arabia as more than an Elijah figure; he had been transformed into a second Moses, who had himself been transformed through his encounter with YHWH at this place.[61] If the

[58] On this view, see Eckhard J. Schnabel, *Early Christian Mission*, vol. 2, *Paul and the Early Church* (Downers Grove, IL: InterVarsity Press, 2004), 1032–45; Martin Hengel and Anna Maria Schwemer, *Paul between Damascus and Antioch: The Unknown Years,* trans. J. Bowden (Louisville: Westminster John Knox, 1977), 110–13; Jerome Murphy-O'Connor, "Paul in Arabia," *CBQ* 55 (1993): 732–37; Thomas R. Schreiner, *Galatians*, BECNT (Grand Rapids: Baker, 2013), 102–3; Douglas J. Moo, *Galatians*, BECNT (Grand Rapids: Baker, 2013), 106–7.

[59] N. T. Wright, "Paul, Arabia, and Elijah (Galatians 1:17)," *JBL* 115 (1996): 683–92.

[60] Ibid., 687–92.

[61] Suggesting that if the road to Damascus was the site of Paul's spiritual conversion, his theological conversion occurred at Sinai. For a Jewish perspective on conversion generally, and Paul's conversion specifically, see Alan F. Segal, *Paul the Convert: The Apostolate and Apostasy of Saul the Pharisee* (New Haven: Yale University Press, 1990), 72–149.

exodus from Egypt had signaled the dawn of a new era in *Heilsgeschichte*,[62] how much more had this been the case with the coming of Christ. Paul would declare Christ to be the redeemer of humankind, not in opposition to Moses, but as the climax and fulfillment of YHWH's grand covenantal plan. For Paul to understand this required reconsidering the "ancestral traditions" (αἱ πατρικαί μου παραδόσεις, Gal 1:14), abandoning his Judaizing agenda,[63] recovering the spirit of Moses and the heart of covenant theology, and grasping the cosmic significance of the new revelation. Like Moses (and Israel months later), Paul needed this divine appointment at Horeb (cf. Exod 3:12; 19:1–3) to experience personally the truth of Exod 19:4–5, to grasp anew YHWH's missionary vision for Israel, and to rediscover the spiritual foundations for his own mission, bringing people from every tribe and nation into the covenant community.[64]

7. Paul's Absolute Authority (Gal 1:6–9)

Although Paul's vocabulary differs from that of Moses (LXX), after the cordial opening to Galatians (1:1–5), conceptually Paul's denunciation of his detractors in 1:6–9 is thoroughly Mosaic. His reference to his detractors' divine election (τοῦ καλέσαντος ὑμᾶς ἐν χάριτι) recalls Moses' emphasis on YHWH's unmerited election of Israel, grounded in his love

[62] This is hinted at in the enigmatic ending to Exod 2:25, which fails to specify what God knew when he heard the groaning of the Israelites under the weight of the Egyptian bondage. The reference to the covenant with the ancestors in the previous verse suggests that God knew the time had come to rescue his people as promised in Gen 15:13–14 and to confirm (הָקִים) his covenant made with the ancestors as promised in Gen 17:7–8.

[63] With Matthew V. Novenson ("Paul's Former Occupation in *Ioudaismos*," in *Galatians and Christian Theology*, ed. Mark W. Elliott et al. [Grand Rapids: Baker, 2014], 24–39), and contra BDAG, 479, I understand Ἰουδαϊσμός in 1:13–14 not to refer to Judaism as a religion or set of beliefs but to a sectarian political program in defense of traditional Jewish practices. Neither in Galatians nor elsewhere does Paul give up the fundamentals of the Jewish/Israelite religion (summarized in Rom 9:4–5). While his former Ἰουδαϊσμός involved the defense of Jewish ancestral traditions within his own ethnic group (which the new "Christian" sect was undermining), in Galatians Judaizers insist on imposing traditional Jewish practices on gentile believers in Jesus. Novenson has rightly reined in Steven Mason's contention (Mason, "Jews, Judaeans, Judaizing, Judaism: Problems of Categorization in Ancient History," *JSJ* 38 [2007]: 457–512) that the word Ἰουδαϊσμός nominalizes the verb ἰουδαΐζω, "to behave like a Jew," and that it signifies actions only non-Jews can take.

[64] While Paul's involvement in the gentile mission undoubtedly shaped his rhetoric in Galatians (and Romans), contra Barclay (*Paul and the Gift*, 361, 481, 487, 541, 570), as noted above, he received his message (which includes his theology) directly from God.

for the ancestors (Deut 4:32–38) and their descendants (Deut 7:6–8).[65] His astonishment that they had deserted (μετατίθημι) their God for a different gospel (Gal 1:6) recalls Moses' references to Israel abandoning (עָזַב) YHWH in favor of alien gods (Deut 28:20; 31:16; cf. 29:24[ET 25]).[66] Most dramatically, in style and essence his denunciation of the Judaizers in Gal 1:8–9 appears to have been inspired by Deut 13,[67] where Moses imagines three scenarios involving false teachers who would invite YHWH's people to serve other gods.[68] Moses pronounced the death penalty over all who would lead the people astray, and in the third scenario (13:13–19[ET 12–18]) condemned to חֵרֶם towns that would abandon YHWH and go after other gods (13:16–19[ET 15–18]).[69] LXX renders Moses' command of "utter destruction" (הַחֲרֵם) emphatically as ἀναθέματι ἀναθεματιεῖτε, "you shall anathematize as an anathema" (13:16[ET 15]; cf. v. 19[ET 18]).[70] Paul employed the words of Moses to curse the Judaizers and highlight the exclusive nature of his gospel of Jesus Christ.[71]

Paul's invective against those who preach another gospel appears also to have been rooted in Deut 18:15–22. After sternly warning against refusing to listen to his authentic prophetic successors (vv. 18–19), Moses pronounced the death sentence on any prophet who falsely claimed to speak for YHWH or spoke by the authority of another deity (v. 20). The

---

[65] Except for Deut 7:6 (προαιρέω); 21:5 (ἐπιλέγω); and 23:17[ET 16] (missing), LXX renders בָּחַר with ἐκλέγομαι, "to choose," rather than καλέω, "to call." However, this word often means by extension "to choose for the receipt of a special benefit or experience" (BDAG, 503). Paul uses the word with this sense in Gal 1:15–16 and 5:13.

[66] This conceptual echo is reinforced by Paul's reference to "another" gospel (ἕτερον εὐαγγέλιον). Except for 31:18 and 20, which have θεοὺς ἀλλοτρίους, in Deuteronomy LXX always renders the adjective in the phrase אֱלֹהִים אֲחֵרִים with a form of ἕτερος (sixteen of eighteen times; 5:7; 6:14; etc.). In 1 Kgs 9:9 (// 2 Chr 7:22) Solomon linked the motifs of abandoning (עָזַב) YHWH, the "gospel" (אֲשֶׁר הוֹצִיא אֶת־אֲבֹתָם מֵאֶרֶץ מִצְרַיִם), and clinging to other gods (וַיַּחֲזִקוּ בֵּאלֹהִים אֲחֵרִים).

[67] Cf. the discussions in Sandnes, *Paul*, 70–73; Ciampa, *Presence and Function*, 83–90.

[68] Paul's reference to himself or "an angel from heaven" in Gal 1:8 answers to "a prophet or dreamer of dreams" in the first scenario who declares, " 'Let us go after other gods,' which you have not known, 'and let us serve them' " (13:2–3[ET 1–2]).

[69] Paul's pronouncement of ἀνάθεμα (vv. 8, 9) links his opponents' fate with that of the Canaanites (Deut 20:17), but more particularly with Israelites guilty of apostasy (הַתּוֹעֵבָה, Deut 13:14–15[ET 13–14]).

[70] LXX renders הַחֵרֶם consistently as ἀνάθεμα in Joshua, where the policy of Deut 20:17 is executed against the Canaanites (Josh 6:17, 18[3x]; 7:1[2x], 11, 12[2x], 13[2x]; 22:20).

[71] While Paul used the term ἀνάθεμα elsewhere in Rom 9:3 and 1 Cor 12:3 and 16:22, his invocation of a curse (ἀνάθεμα) on anyone who does not love the Lord in the last reference bears the strongest link to our text.

nature of Paul's condemnation of the Judaizers (Gal 1:8–9) suggests he perceived himself to be within this Mosaic prophetic train.

Moses and Paul on Circumcision

Having argued that in Galatians Paul functions as a second and seconding Moses,[72] I turn now to explore how this works out in the argument of the book. The issue is extremely complex, but because of space constraints I must limit my discussion to a single symbol of the gulf separating Paul and his opponents: whether or not gentile believers in Jesus needed to be circumcised. It seems that Paul never expected Jewish believers to give up circumcision as a cultural practice; indeed, Luke reports that apparently for the sake of the ministry to Jews in Lystra and Iconium he circumcised his protégé Timothy, whose father was Greek but whose mother was Jewish (Acts 16:1–3).[73] But in Galatia the issues were different. Whereas the Judaizers insisted that circumcision was required of gentile converts for their salvation and admission to the "inner circle" represented by Jewish Christians, Paul argued that the boundaries of the people of God transcend race (physical descent from Abraham) and that faith in Jesus Christ, rather than circumcision, is now the badge of membership in the covenant community.

The question for us is, if Moses had been an observer or participant in these debates, whose side would he have taken? Although the "circumcision party"[74] would have grounded their position in Gen 17,[75] as others of their persuasion did prior to the Jerusalem Council, they probably invoked the name of Moses to support their case:

---

[72] I do not hereby claim that he was the only "prophet like Moses," but that he viewed himself within this tradition, which suggests that by definition his message could not contradict Moses.

[73] Remarkably, this event shows Paul to have been more zealous about physical circumcision than Moses. On this event, see Thomas R. Schreiner, "Circumcision," *DPL*, 139.

[74] The phrase οἱ ἐκ περιτομῆς, "those of the circumcision," occurs in Acts 10:45; 11:2.

[75] Cf. Stephen's reference to "the covenant of circumcision" (διαθήκη περιτομῆς, Acts 7:8). If we must distinguish between the Abrahamic and Israelite covenants (which seems unwise to me), strictly speaking this refers to the Abrahamic covenant, rather than to the covenant established at Sinai. Presumably because the word בְּרִית occurs thirteen times in Gen 17, Maimonides concluded that God made thirteen covenants with Abraham. See Maimonides, "Laws of Circumcision," in *Mishneh Torah: The Book of Adoration,* trans. Moses Hyamson (Jerusalem: Feldheim, 1981), chapter 3.7–8 (165a).

> Unless you are circumcised according to *the custom of Moses* (τῷ ἔθει τῷ Μωϋσέως), you cannot be saved. (Acts 15:1)

> It is necessary to circumcise them [gentile believers in Jesus] and to order them to keep the law of Moses (τὸν νόμον Μωϋσέως). (Acts 15:5)

However, if we compare the biblical evidence for Moses' and Paul's treatments of the subject we discover the opposite: Moses would probably have sided with Paul.

The frequency with which the words περιτέμνω ("to circumcise"), περιτομή ("circumcision"), and ἀκροβυστία ("uncircumcision") appear in Paul's writings reflects the significance of circumcision in his thinking,[76] which contrasts with Moses' marginalization of the physical rite. Physical circumcision figures prominently in the Abraham narratives (Gen 17:10–27; 21:4; 34:14–25) but is rarely mentioned in Exodus–Deuteronomy. The verb מוּל, "to circumcise," never occurs in the Moses narratives,[77] and "foreskin" (עָרְלָה) appears only in Exod 4:25.[78] Since YHWH had declared that non-Israelite slaves (עֲבָדִים) and aliens (גֵּרִים) who wanted to participate in the original Passover event needed to be circumcised first (Exod 12:44–48), and that the same ordinance (תּוֹרָה) applied to native Israelites and aliens alike (v. 49), the descendants of Abraham who left Egypt were probably circumcised.

Given the foundational covenantal significance of circumcision in the patriarchal narratives, it is striking that in all of Israel's laws reference to the physical rite occurs only in Lev 12:3. In the context of regulations concerning female ritual cleanness, as a passing comment YHWH reiterated his command in Gen 17:3 that all male children be circumcised on the eighth day (Lev 12:3). Moses would undoubtedly have uttered the words relating to circumcision when he declared these divine ordinances to the people, but this would have been cast as divine speech, rather than his own. He never picked up the topic himself.

Apart from the absence of speech about physical circumcision, three striking facts reflect Moses' personal indifference to the practice. First, Exod 4:24–26 reports that YHWH would have killed him had not his Midi-

---

[76] περιτέμνω, "to circumcise": 1 Cor 7:18[2x]; Gal 2:3; 5:2, 3; 6:12, 13[2x]; Col 2:11; περιτομή, "circumcision": Rom 2:25–29[6x]; 3:1, 30; 4:9–12[6x]; 15:8; 1 Cor 7:19; Gal 2:7–9[3x], 12; 5:6, 11; 6:15; Eph 2:11; Phil 3:3, 5; Col 2:11; 3:11; 4:11; Titus 1:10; ἀκροβυστία, "foreskin, [state of] uncircumcision, uncircumcised person": Rom 2:25–27[4x]; 3:30; 4:9–12[6x]; 1 Cor 7:18, 19; Gal 2:7; 5:6; 6:15; Eph 2:11; Col 2:13; 3:11. For more detailed discussion of the relationship of circumcision and the covenant in Paul, see Lincicum, *Early Jewish Encounter*, 147–53.

[77] In Exod 4:25 the narrator uses the verb כָּרַת, "to cut off."

[78] עָרְלָה occurs in Gen 17:11, 14, 23, 24, 25; 34:14; עָרֵל, "having a foreskin," in Gen 17:14; מוּל in Gen 17:10–14[6x], 23–27[5x]; 21:4; 34:15, 17, 22[2x], 24. Cf. Lev 19:23, which metaphorically characterizes forbidden fruit as עָרְלָה.

anite wife instinctively circumcised their son. While this text is difficult at many levels, it raises questions regarding how God could have chosen Moses to be his agent of deliverance for his people when he had neglected the fundamental covenant rite applying to all Abraham's descendants.

Second, having noted that the Israelites had left Egypt as a circumcised multitude, in Josh 5:2–9 the narrator reports that the rite had been suspended during their four decades of wandering in the desert.[79] Either Moses intentionally neglected it because YHWH had rejected the exodus generation as the covenant people (cf. Deut 5:1–5),[80] or he simply did not deem it important. Ironically, the generation that had come out of Egypt and that bore the physical brand of the covenant would not enjoy the fulfillment of YHWH's covenant promises; they died in the desert (Deut 1:26–2:1). Meanwhile, despite the uncircumcised state of its males, the generation that stood before Moses was formally accepted as YHWH's covenant people (5:1–5; 26:16–19; 27:9–10; 29:9–12[ET 10–13]), and as such it would claim the land promised to the patriarchs.[81]

Third, in Deuteronomy Moses never speaks of physical circumcision, not even as a prerequisite to participation in Israel's annual festivals (cf. Exod 12:48).[82] In Deut 31:12 he charges the Levitical priests to read the

---

[79] YHWH's command to circumcise the Israelites "a second time" (שֵׁנִית, v. 2) is puzzling. LXX omits the word. Since this ritual (Josh 5:2–9) apparently preceded the first Passover celebration in the promised land (5:10–11), the natural impulse is to view the "first" circumcision as the rite that apparently preceded the original Passover event (Exod 12:44, 48). Thus Robert L. Hubbard, *Joshua,* NIVAC (Grand Rapids: Zondervan 2009), 181; David M. Howard, *Joshua,* NAC (Nashville: Broadman & Holman, 1998), 148. However, some suggest that the individuals were circumcised a second time because their previous circumcision had been according to the Egyptian practice, which did not involve the complete removal of the foreskin. Thus Jack Sasson, "Circumcision in the Ancient Near East," *JBL* 85 (1966): 473–76. For further discussion, see Richard S. Hess, *Joshua*, TOTC (Downers Grove, IL: InterVarsity Press, 1996), 118–19; Jason S. DeRouchie, "Circumcision in the Hebrew Bible and Targumim: Theology, Rhetoric, and the Handling of a Metaphor," *BBR* 14 (2004): 186–89. In light of Josh 5:7, the present argument is not affected by the interpretation one prefers.

[80] Note the narrator's reference to the people's resistance to the voice of YHWH in Josh 5:6.

[81] Both YHWH and Moses expressed pessimism about Israel's fidelity in the long run (Deut 4:25–28; 5:29; 29:17–27[ET 18–28]; 31:16–21, 27–29; 32:15–27), but on several occasions Moses commended this generation for its fidelity to YHWH (4:4; 5:1–6, 29).

[82] Deuteronomy 16 invites all sons and daughters, male and female servants, resident Levites, and the triad of alien, fatherless, and widow to participate in Shavuot and Sukkot. On aliens (הַגֵּר) participating in worship at the central sanctuary, see also 14:29; 26:11–13; 31:12. Moses' silence on physical circumcision might suggest that he simply assumed it. However, given its centrality in Gen 17, on the one hand, and Moses' personal neglect of the rite and his frequent identification

Torah publicly (before men, women, children, and "your alien" [גֵּרְךָ]) at the central sanctuary every seventh year, when they assembled for the covenant renewal ritual. This was the "assembly of YHWH" (קְהַל יְהוָה) from which Ammonites and Moabites were permanently barred, but to which Edomites and Egyptians would eventually be welcomed (23:4–9[ET 3–8]). Whatever the Israelites' physical state, the Torah they were to hear (presumably Moses' addresses in Deuteronomy) said nothing about the physical mark of the covenant.

Since Moses could use the metaphors "uncircumcised of lips" (עֲרַל שְׂפָתָיִם, Exod 6:12, 30) and "circumcision of the heart" (Deut 10:16; 30:6),[83] his neglect, both as a character in the narratives and as the speaker in Deuteronomy, of the physical rite obviously did not arise out of ignorance. Although Israel's covenant relationship with YHWH is front and center in the entire book, physical circumcision is never identified as *an* or *the* Israelite identity marker. Nevertheless, as the book of Judges suggests, it did not take long for the Israelites to treat this as *the* distinguishing mark of their ethnic identity and to disconnect the external rite from internal spiritual realities.[84] On the one hand, we may note the pejorative characterization of Philistines as "the uncircumcised" (הָעֲרֵלִים),[85] and on the other, we notice that Samson, who must have been circumcised, embodied all that was wrong with Israel and had himself become a virtual Philistine at heart (cf. 15:11; 16:30).[86]

---

of the fundamental covenant requirements in spiritual and ethical terms, on the other, this interpretation is unlikely.

[83] Note the graphic and physical nature of 10:16, וּמַלְתֶּם אֵת עָרְלַת לְבַבְכֶם, lit., "And you shall circumcise the foreskin of your heart" (similarly Jer 4:4). In 30:6 the reference to "foreskin" is dropped.

[84] At this point I have only one quarrel with Lincicum's observation that Paul essentially divorces the "physical observance from the demand of the law in order to claim that true circumcision is an eschatological state determined by the Spirit that enables one to fulfill the law—regardless of whether one is physically circumcised" (*Early Jewish Encounter*, 149). The problem here is the word "eschatological." It is true that Deut 30:1–10 and Ezek 36:26–36 envision the circumcision/transplant of Israel's collective heart as an eschatological reality, but nothing precludes this from having transpired in the hearts of individual Israelites in Moses' day or thereafter.

[85] Judg 14:3; 15:18. Cf. 1 Sam 14:6; 17:26, 36; 31:4; 2 Sam 1:20; 1 Chr 10:4. Cf. also Isa 52:1; Jer 9:25–26. On Israelite and Philistine dispositions toward circumcision, see most recently Avraham Faust, "The Bible, Archaeology, and the Practice of Circumcision in Israelite and Philistine Societies," *JBL* 134 (2015): 253–71. On the (un)circumcision of Philistines in the Hebrew Bible, see Matthew Thiessen, *Contesting Conversion: Genealogy, Circumcision, and Identity in Ancient Judaism and Christianity* (Oxford: Oxford University Press, 2011), 44–46.

[86] Cf. Daniel I. Block, *Judges, Ruth*, NAC 6 (Nashville: Broadman & Holman, 1999), 392. Jeremiah addresses the incongruity of physical circumcision apart from heart/spirit circumcision in Jer 9:23–25.

Moses' neglect of physical circumcision in speech and practice raises serious questions about the Judaizers' comment in Acts 15:1: "Unless you are circumcised according to the custom of Moses, you cannot be saved" (NRSV). The elevation of external identity markers above internal spiritual realities may have been traditional and customary (ἔθος) in Paul's day, but this development did not derive from Moses.[87] The association of Moses with circumcision was probably rooted in the fact that he (and Aaron) would have had to implement the rite as outlined in Exod 12:43–50, or in the notion that the entire Pentateuch came from him.[88]

If Not Circumcision, Then What?

In light of the foregoing discussion, a question arises inevitably: If physical circumcision was not *the* critical identity marker of the covenant people for Moses, then what was? Deuteronomy provides several potential answers.

1. True Israelites claimed the Shema as the fundamental declaration of Israelite identity: wholehearted and full-bodied covenant commitment to YHWH.

> Hear, O Israel: YHWH is our God, YHWH alone. You shall demonstrate love for YHWH your God with all your heart/mind (לֵב), and with all your being (נֶפֶשׁ), and with all your resources (מְאֹד). (Deut 6:4)[89]

Rather than functioning merely as a verbal badge of identity,[90] this declaration functions as a thesis statement for the segment of Moses' second address that is framed by two שְׁמַעs (6:4; 9:1) and highlights the importance of unreserved and unqualified commitment to YHWH. While

---

[87] A fact overlooked by Schreiner ("Circumcision," *DPL*, 138), who cites this text without comment under the heading "The Scriptures."

[88] Given Paul's focus on Abraham and God's covenant with him, it is ironic that *the sign* of the Abrahamic covenant should have become the premier symbol of the "cultural capital" (cf. Barclay, *Paul and the Gift,* 362–65) associated with Moses and the law that Paul rejected.

[89] On the interpretation presented here, see Daniel I. Block, "How Many Is God? An Investigation into the Meaning of Deuteronomy 6:4–5," *JETS* 47 (2004): 193–212; repr. in *How I Love Your Torah, O LORD: Studies in the Book of Deuteronomy* (Eugene, OR: Cascade, 2011), 73–97. On Hebrew אָהַב as "demonstrate love," see n. 115 below.

[90] For detailed instruction on the recitation/reading of the Shema, see Maimonides, "Laws of Reading the Shema," chs. 1–4 in *Mishneh Torah: The Book of Adoration,* trans. Moses Hyamson (Jerusalem: Feldheim, 1981), 94a–97b.

this commitment was obviously to be public (worn on the forehead and hands and inscribed on doors and gates, 6:8–9), in what follows the actual marks of identity include exclusive devotion to YHWH (6:10–15), doing what is right and good in his eyes (6:18, 24–25; 7:10–11; 8:1–5), repudiating all that is pagan (7:1–26), and blessing YHWH alone as the source of their well-being (8:7–20).

The commentary on the שְׁמַע offered by Deut 10:12–11:1 reinforces this interpretation. In catechetical style Moses poses a question, and then provides a three-part answer, with two literal appeals (vv. 12b–13, 20) sandwiching a metaphorical call for covenant loyalty (v. 16). All three are grounded doxologically in YHWH's transcendent sovereignty and his immanent grace (see Table 3).[91] The center of gravity in each answer involves deep internal spiritual and dispositional commitments. In the first answer Israel's identity is marked with five verbs: fearing YHWH, walking in his ways, loving him, serving him wholeheartedly, and obeying his commands (vv. 12b–13); the second calls for a circumcision of the heart, and the third for exclusive devotion to YHWH. The text is silent on the sorts of markers Judaizers were imposing on gentile believers in Galatians.

2. True Israelites received the story of Israel's redemption and the gift of the promised land as their story, and they responded to YHWH's grace demonstrated in these formative events with grateful obedience.

This disposition is reflected in two celebrative texts, which we may identify as the "Domestic Catechism" (6:20–25) and the "Little Creed" (26:1–11). While both statements prescribe a particular verbal response, the recitations themselves were not to be the identity marker, any more than merely reciting the שְׁמַע was to be. The point is receiving YHWH's salvation and the promised land as gracious gifts, rather than as entitlements (cf. 9:4–24), and responding to the privilege of being YHWH's people with overflowing gratitude and righteous living. Elsewhere the divine requirement is summarized as צֶדֶק צֶדֶק תִּרְדֹּף ("Righteousness, only righteousness, you shall pursue," 16:20). For Moses and Paul (and for Jesus, Matt 23:23), the primary badges of covenant relationship with God did not involve observance of rites and rituals but weightier matters of torah.

[91] For fuller discussions of this text, see Block, *Deuteronomy*, 268–79; Block, "In Spirit and in Truth: The Mosaic Vision of Worship," in *The Gospel according to Moses: Theological and Ethical Reflections on the Book of Deuteronomy* (Eugene, OR: Cascade, 2012), 290–93.

Table 3. The Structure of Deut 10:12–11:1

The Issue		So what does YHWH your God ask (דָּרַשׁ) of you? (10:12a)		
The Requirement		I (vv. 12b–15)	II (vv. 16–19)	III (vv. 20–22)
		You shall fear YHWH your God, walk in all his ways, demonstrate love for him, and serve YHWH your God with all your heart and with all your being, and keep the commands and statutes of YHWH, which I am commanding you today for your good. (10:12b–13)	Circumcise therefore the foreskin of your heart, and be no longer stubborn. (10:16)	You shall fear YHWH your God. You shall serve him and hold fast to him, and by his name you shall swear. (10:20)
The Basis of the Requirement	The Doxology	Look, to YHWH your God belong heaven and the heaven of heavens, the earth with all that is in it. (10:14)	For YHWH your God is God of gods and Lord of lords, the great, the mighty, and the awesome God, who is not partial and takes no bribe. (10:17)	He is your praise. He is your God, who has done for you these great and terrifying things that your eyes have seen. (10:21)
	The Application	Yet YHWH set his heart in love on your fathers and chose their offspring after them, you above all peoples, as you are this day. (10:15)	He executes justice for the fatherless and the widow, and demonstrates love for the sojourner, giving him food and clothing. So demonstrate love for the sojourner, for you were sojourners in the land of Egypt. (10:18–19)	Your fathers went down to Egypt seventy persons, and now YHWH your God has made you as numerous as the stars of heaven. (10:22)
The Summary Conclusion		You shall therefore demonstrate love for YHWH your God and keep his charge, his statutes, his rules, and his commands always. (11:1)		

3. True Israelites were marked by deep-seated and reverential trust in YHWH.

This discussion will be more complex than the preceding, but it is particularly necessary if we would understand Paul's identification of "faith working through love" (πίστις δι' ἀγάπης ἐνεργουμένη) as the true identity marker for the Christian community in Gal 5:6. Πίστις/πιστεύω words are scarce in LXX Deuteronomy, but conceptually the statement is thoroughly Deuteronomic. The verb πιστεύω (used for הֶאֱמִין in Gen 15:6) occurs twice in LXX Deuteronomy, but only 9:23 is relevant. Here Moses interprets Israel's refusal to listen to YHWH's voice and enter Canaan from Kadesh-barnea as rebellion and unbelief. When referring to this event in the first address, Moses had used the Hebrew word הֶאֱמִין: "But in spite of this, you would not trust (אֵינְכֶם מַאֲמִינִם) in YHWH your God" (1:32). However, instead of πιστεύω LXX renders הֶאֱמִין here with the rare but related word ἐμπιστεύω.

The noun πίστις occurs in Deuteronomy only in 32:20, where YHWH characterizes Israel as "a perverse generation, sons utterly lacking in faithfulness," which contrasts starkly with YHWH, whom 7:9 and 32:4 characterize as θεὸς πιστός (Hebrew הָאֵל הַנֶּאֱמָן and אֵל אֱמוּנָה, respectively).[92] If YHWH's faithfulness involved the divine Suzerain's actions in accord with his promises in the covenant, Israel's faithfulness would have involved the vassal's actions in keeping with the covenant to which they had committed themselves, first at Horeb and now on the plains of Moab.

Although this accounts for all the πίστις words in Deuteronomy, it does not mean that the notion of "faith"/"belief" is unimportant in the book. Indeed, יָרֵא, which normally means "to be afraid, to fear," often functions as a substitute for הֶאֱמִין.

This usage is evident already in the narratives that precede Deuteronomy. In Gen 15:6, the classic text for this conversation, Greek πιστεύω renders Hebrew הֶאֱמִין (cf. Gal 3:6; Rom 4:3), as expected. Although this is the last occurrence of the root אמן in a theological context in Genesis, it does not mean this was the last time Abraham's faith was tested. In 22:1 the narrator announces formally that what follows was designed as a divine test. Despite the absence of הֶאֱמִין in this context, YHWH's demand to sacrifice Isaac (22:2) obviously tested whether or not Abraham could trust YHWH to keep his promise to multiply his descendants *through Isaac* (21:8–12). However, the divine envoy used a different word in his assessment of Abraham's response: "Now I know that you are a God-fearer (כִּי־יְרֵא אֱלֹהִים אַתָּה; cf. LXX, ὅτι φοβῇ τὸν θεὸν σὺ), seeing you have not

[92] Deut 7:9: הָאֵל הַנֶּאֱמָן שֹׁמֵר הַבְּרִית וְהַחֶסֶד לְאֹהֲבָיו וּלְשֹׁמְרֵי מִצְוֹתָו לְאֶלֶף דּוֹר (θεὸς πιστός ὁ φυλάσσων διαθήκην καὶ ἔλεος τοῖς ἀγαπῶσιν αὐτὸν καὶ τοῖς φυλάσσουσιν τὰς ἐντολὰς αὐτοῦ εἰς χιλίας γενεὰς). Deut 32:4: אֵל אֱמוּנָה וְאֵין עָוֶל צַדִּיק וְיָשָׁר הוּא (θεὸς πιστός καὶ οὐκ ἔστιν ἀδικία δίκαιος καὶ ὅσιος κύριος).

withheld your son, your only son, from me" (v. 12). Although יָרֵא means fundamentally "to be afraid, to fear, to revere," here it connotes "trusting awe," or "awed trust," demonstrated by obedience.

The midwives' fear of God in Exod 1:17 and 21 may also be interpreted as trust in God to defend them against the fury of Pharaoh. However, the sense of "belief" for יָרֵא is nearer the surface in Exod 9:20, where the narrator notes that after Moses' announcement of impending hail, those Egyptian officials who "feared" (i.e., "believed") YHWH's word hastily removed their slaves and livestock to a secure place. Exodus 14:31 conjoins יָרֵא and הֶאֱמִין in a single statement: in the wake of YHWH's annihilation of Pharaoh's army "the people feared (יָרֵא) YHWH; they believed (הֶאֱמִין, LXX ἐπίστευσαν) in him and his servant Moses." This characterization reinforces Walter Moberly's proposal that in the Hebrew Bible "the fear of God" is the primary expression for the appropriate response to him:

> The First Testament use of "fear of God" is thus more or less equivalent *in function* to the New Testament's use of various forms of "believe/trust" and "have faith" (*pisteuō* and *pistis*) to depict appropriate human response to God; so in terms of function a Christian way of conveying the tenor of "one who fears God" might be "a believer," "a person of faith."[93]

The forty-plus occurrences of יָרֵא in Deuteronomy testify both to its breadth of meaning and significance in the book (Fig. 1). It often bears the common sense of fright or terror,[94] and the awesome/awe-inspiring character of YHWH's name and actions are represented by the cognate words הַנּוֹרָא (7:21; 10:17, 21; 28:58) and מוֹרָא (4:34; 26:8).[95] However, given the revelatory intention of these "signs and wonders,"[96] YHWH's awesome deeds should also have prompted the Israelites to trust him. The phenomena that precipitate this response offer clues to the nature of "fear": (1) the great fire and the sound of YHWH's voice at Horeb (4:10; 5:5, 29); (2) YHWH's signs and wonders in Egypt (4:34; 10:21; 26:8; cf. 34:12); (3) the judgment in criminal cases (13:12[ET 11]; 17:13; 19:20; 21:21); (4) eating in the presence of YHWH at the central sanctuary (14:23); (5) hearing the words of the Torah (17:19; 31:12–13; cf. 28:58). How the first four of these might prompt fear in the form of fright (1, 3) or awe (2, 4) is readily grasped, but how reading the Torah promotes either is not so clear—unless

---

[93] Walter Moberly, *Old Testament Theology: Reading the Hebrew Bible as Christian Scripture* (Grand Rapids: Baker, 2013), 245 (italics his).

[94] Without distinguishing the cause of the fright: 1:19, 21, 29; 2:4, 25; 11:25 (מוֹרָא); etc. In 1:19 and 8:15 the desert is characterized as "terrifying" (הַנּוֹרָא).

[95] In 34:12 the narrator exceptionally attributes these "awesome deeds" (הַמּוֹרָא הַגָּדוֹל) to Moses.

[96] Note the recurring recognition formula "They/you will know that I am YHWH" in Exodus: 6:7; 7:5, 17; 8:18[ET 22]; 10:2; 14:4, 18; 16:12; 29:46.

one follows LXX, which renders תּוֹרָה pervasively as νόμος, "law," in which case the word may refer to fear of punishment.

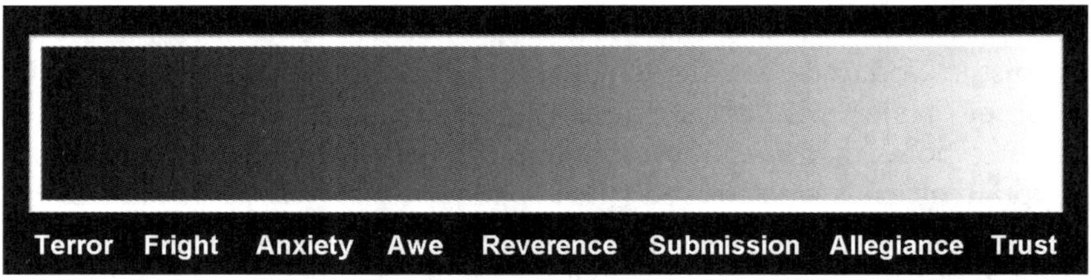

Figure 1. The Semantic Spectrum of ירא Words in Deuteronomy

Although Deuteronomy often links יָרֵא with obedience and righteous living,[97] important clues to its meaning are found particularly in the sequence of verbs scattered within the book: reading—hearing—learning—fearing—obeying—living well (Table 4).

Table 4. The Importance of Hearing the Torah

Reference	Reading	Hearing	Learning	Fearing	Obeying	Living well
1. 4:10		✓	✓	✓		
2. 5:23–29		✓		✓	✓	✓
3. 6:1–3			✓	✓	✓	✓
4. 17:13		✓		✓	✓	
5. 17:19–20	✓	[✓]	✓	✓	✓	✓
6. 19:20		✓		✓	✓	
7. 31:11–13	✓	✓	✓	✓	✓	

For our purposes, the fifth and seventh texts, which involve encounters with YHWH through the hearing of the Torah, are especially significant.[98] Whereas Israel's encounter with YHWH at Horeb had terrified the people (4:9–14, 36; 5:5, 23–33; 18:16), Deuteronomy portrays worship at the

[97] Deut 5:29; 6:2; 8:6; 10:12–13; 13:5[ET 4]; 17:19; 28:58; 31:12.

[98] In the first three the sound of YHWH's voice accompanied by awesome theophanic visual phenomena at Horeb evoked severe fright in the people. The fourth and sixth cases involve warnings against disregarding the divinely rendered decisions in criminal cases (17:13) or repeating the crime (19:20).

place where YHWH would establish his name as confident, intimate, and celebrative.[99]

The Torah itself answers how the verb יָרֵא fits this picture. If הַתּוֹרָה (i.e., Moses' addresses in Deuteronomy) is viewed primarily as "the law," as many assume, hearing "the law" could evoke fear of negative consequences analogous to the effect hearing verdicts in criminal cases had on the community (13:12[ET 11]; 17:13; 19:20; 21:21). However, if הַתּוֹרָה is understood as "instruction," whose goal is the promotion of יָרֵא in the sense of "faith, trust" (Paul's πίστις), then its significance for this discussion is readily apparent.

But how does hearing the Torah promote faith in YHWH? This preliminary essay cannot offer a full discussion of the issue, but we may begin by observing Deuteronomy's characterization of YHWH.

First, Deuteronomy portrays YHWH in gloriously transcendent terms, pointing to a trustworthy deity. By itself this image could evoke fright/awe, but in context it is intended to promote confidence (cf. Isa 40:12–31). The concluding "Song of YHWH" opens by ascribing greatness (גֹּדֶל) to him (32:3), a theme that had been declared in earlier doxological descriptions.

7:21	כִּי־יְהוָה אֱלֹהֶיךָ בְּקִרְבֶּךָ	YHWH your God is in your midst,
	אֵל גָּדוֹל וְנוֹרָא	a great and awesome God
10:17	יְהוָה אֱלֹהֵיכֶם הוּא אֱלֹהֵי הָאֱלֹהִים//וַאֲדֹנֵי הָאֲדֹנִים	YHWH your God is God of gods and Lord of lords,
	הָאֵל הַגָּדֹל הַגִּבֹּר וְהַנּוֹרָא	the great, the mighty, and the awesome God.
28:58	לְיִרְאָה אֶת־הַשֵּׁם הַנִּכְבָּד וְהַנּוֹרָא הַזֶּה	That you may fear this glorious and awesome name,
	אֵת יְהוָה אֱלֹהֶיךָ	YHWH your God.

YHWH's transcendent power and glory were demonstrated particularly through the "signs and wonders" performed against the Egyptians (4:34; 10:21; 26:8) and for Israel's benefit.[100]

---

[99] Signaled by the verb שָׂמַח, in 12:7, 12, 18; 14:26; 16:11, 14–15; 26:11 (cf. Lev 23:40). On the contrast between Israel's terrifying, one-time encounter with YHWH at Horeb and Israel's confident, regular meetings with him at the central sanctuary, see Daniel I. Block, "'A Place for My Name': Horeb and Zion in the Mosaic Vision of Israelite Worship," *JETS* 58 (2015): 221–47.

[100] Deuteronomy 11:2–7 includes YHWH's care for the Israelites in the desert and his punishment of Dathan and Abiram among "all the great acts of YHWH that he executed" (כָּל־מַעֲשֵׂה יְהוָה הַגָּדֹל אֲשֶׁר עָשָׂה). Cf. Exod 15:11.

Second, the Torah portrays YHWH in graciously personal terms. Although explicit verbal characterizations of YHWH as gracious are rare in Deuteronomy,[101] Israel's confidence in future restoration after judgment was based on his compassionate character (כִּי אֵל רַחוּם יְהוָה אֱלֹהֶיךָ, 4:31) and his change of heart toward his wayward people (וְעַל־עֲבָדָיו יִתְנֶחָם, 32:36). But Moses laced his recollections of past events with stories of divine grace: YHWH revealed his will to Israel (4:1–8; cf. 5:1–22; 6:20–25; 30:11–20); he invited Israel to assemble in his presence at Horeb and established his covenant with them there (4:9–31; cf. 5:2–3); he rescued his people from Egypt (4:32–40; cf. 5:6 et passim); he loved the ancestors and elected their descendants for his favor out of all the peoples on earth (4:37; cf. 7:6–7; 10:15; 14:2); he spared Israel and renewed the covenant at Horeb (9:19; 9:25–10:5); he cared for Israel in the desert (1:31; 8:1–5); he gave them a fruitful homeland (1:7–8; 6:10–11, 23; 8:7–10; 11:9–12; 26:9, 15; 27:3; 32:13–14); he provided leadership in the forms of king (17:14–20), prophets (like Moses; 18:9–20), and Levitical priests (10:8–9; 18:1–8; 21:5; 33:8–11); he confirmed the covenant with the present generation in Moab (26:16–19; 27:9; 28:69[ET 29:1]; 29:11[ET 12]; etc.); he invited Israel to worship and celebrate in his presence (12:1–14; 14:1–21, 26; 16:11–14; 26:1–11); and his ultimate goal was Israel's well-being (11:18–25; 12:7, 18; 15:10; 23:21[ET 20]; 28:1–14; 30:11–20). Even threats of punishment represent overtures of grace, reminding the people how passionately YHWH treasured his relationship with them and warning in advance of the consequences of apostasy. Hearing the Torah would remind the people of all these graces, hopefully evoking in them not fear in the sense of fright and awe, but especially in the sense of confidence in the one who had chosen them to be his treasured people.

Third, the Torah portrays YHWH as faithful to his word. The exordium to the "Song of YHWH" (ch. 32) begins by proclaiming YHWH's greatness (32:3), but the next strophe (v. 4) focuses on his faithfulness:

הַצּוּר תָּמִים פָּעֳלוֹ	The Rock, his work is perfect;
כִּי כָל־דְּרָכָיו מִשְׁפָּט	See, all his ways are justice.
אֵל אֱמוּנָה וְאֵין עָוֶל	A God of faithfulness and without iniquity,
צַדִּיק וְיָשָׁר הוּא	Righteous and upright is he.

While אֵל אֱמוּנָה conveys the notion of trustworthiness explicitly, this quality is also reflected in the last line: צַדִּיק וְיָשָׁר הוּא. In Deuteronomy

[101] The root חֵן occurs only in 24:1, which notes its absence in a man with a needy wife.

"righteousness" (צְדָקָה/צֶדֶק) means "conduct in accord with an objective standard," which is established by YHWH within the covenant that he made with his people. Moses celebrated YHWH's perfect embodiment of this trait doxologically in 7:9:[102]

יְהוָה אֱלֹהֶיךָ הוּא הָאֱלֹהִים	YHWH your God is God,
הָאֵל הַנֶּאֱמָן	the faithful God
שֹׁמֵר הַבְּרִית וְהַחֶסֶד	who maintains covenant loyalty
לְאֹהֲבָיו וּלְשֹׁמְרֵי מִצְוֹתָיו (Qere)	with those who love him and keep his command,
לְאֶלֶף דּוֹר	to a thousand generations.

While this summary declaration is covenantal from beginning to end, the Torah of Deuteronomy proclaims the faithfulness of YHWH with repeated reminders of how he has kept the promises associated with his covenant made with the ancestors, established with their descendants at Horeb,[103] and renewed with this generation:[104] (1) YHWH has multiplied the population like the stars of the sky;[105] (2) as predicted in Gen 15:13, after centuries in a foreign land, ending in slavery, YHWH rescued them from their oppressors;[106] (3) now, after the failure of the exodus generation (1:35; 4:25), YHWH is about to deliver the promised land of Canaan into their hands.[107] But YHWH's fidelity to his word is also reflected in his oath with which he guarantees the fulfillment of the imprecations for his people's infidelity built into the covenant (11:13–28; 28:1–69[ET 29:1]). However, building on Lev 26:40–45,[108] Moses declared that however horrendous

---

[102] Cf. Exod 34:6; Ps 86:15.

[103] Cf. Gen 17:6–8; Exod 6:2–8; 19:4–6; Deut 4:9–31.

[104] On "the covenant with the fathers," see Jerry Hwang, *The Rhetoric of Remembrance: An Investigation of the "Fathers" in Deuteronomy*, Siphrut 8 (Winona Lake, IN: Eisenbrauns, 2012), 178–232.

[105] Deut 1:10; 10:22; 26:5; cf. Gen 15:5; 22:17; 26:4.

[106] Deut 4:37; 5:6; 6:12, 21–23; 7:8; 8:14; 13:6, 11[ET 5, 10]; 26:6–8.

[107] References to the covenant oath involving the land occur a dozen times in the book: 1:8, 35; 4:21; etc.

[108] Assuming Lev 26 antedates Deut 4:25–31; 11:13–28; 28:1–69[ET 29:1]. See now Benjamin Kilchör, "The Direction of Dependence between the Laws of the Pentateuch: The Priority of a Literary Approach," *Ephemerides Theologicae Lovanienses* 89 (2013): 1–14; Kilchör, *Mosetora und Jahwetora: Das Verhältnis von Deuteronomium 12–26 zu Exodus, Levitikus und Numeri*, BZABR 21 (Wiesbaden: Harrassowitz, 2015); contra Jeffrey Stackert, who argues that while using the language of Deuteronomy the authors of the Holiness Code (which includes Lev 26) intentionally superseded, subverted, and supplanted the Deuteronomic Law. See his *Rewriting the Torah: Literary Revision in Deuteronomy and the Holiness Legislation*,

the punishment for rebellion might be (4:26–28; 28:15–68; 29:19–27[ET 20–28]), the judgment would not be the last word. With a compassionate heart and true to his commitments, YHWH would bring his people back from exile and reestablish them in the land promised to the ancestors (4:30–31; 30:1–10; 32:43). Both Moses and YHWH anticipated that the Israelites would soon forget their commitments by going after other gods (4:23; 6:12; 8:11, 14, 19; 31:16–18, 26–29), but YHWH would never forget his covenant (4:31). For this generation, YHWH guaranteed his people's future with his promise (32:36–43) and his oath.[109]

I return to the issue raised at the beginning of this lengthy excursus, namely, the importance of hearing the Torah in community. In addition to stimulating reverent awe (יָרֵא), hearing the reminders of YHWH's compassion toward his people in the past and his declarations of his faithfulness to his words, his covenant, and his people in the future should evoke in hearers the faith that Abraham exhibited in Gen 15:6 and 22:1–12. Since this confidence in YHWH represents part of the fuller meaning of יָרֵא in Deuteronomy, hearing the Torah would be critical for maintaining Israel's faith. At the festival of Sukkot, the priests were to "read" the Torah that the people might "hear," that they might "learn" to "fear" (i.e., trust) YHWH, that they might "obey," that they might "live" (Deut 31:9–13).[110] We now understand why the five markers of Israel's identity in Deut 10:12–13 begin with "fear/trusting awe" and then move successively through walking in the ways of YHWH, demonstrating love for him, wholehearted and full-bodied service, and finally to obedience to the commands. Borrowing from Deuteronomy, the wisdom writers had it right:

תְּחִלַּת חָכְמָה יִרְאַת יְהוָה	The fear of [trusting awe in] YHWH is the first principle of wisdom
וְדַעַת קְדֹשִׁים בִּינָה	And knowledge of the Holy One is understanding. (Prov 9:10)*

*Cf. Prov 1:7; 15:33; Job 28:28; Ps 111:10. On "fear" and its relation to wisdom, see Moberly, *Theology of the Old Testament*, 265–77.

FAT 52 (Tübingen: Mohr Siebeck, 2007); Stackert, "The Holiness Code," in *The Oxford Encyclopedia of the Bible and Law*, ed. Brent Strawn (Oxford: Oxford University Press, 2015), 1:389–96.

[109] Cf. the references to "a covenant . . . with an oath" in 29:11, 13, 20[ET 12, 14, 21].

[110] This sequence reinforces Nahum Sarna's contention (*Exodus*, JPS Torah Commentary [Philadelphia: Jewish Publication Society of America, 1991], 75) that "faith" in the Hebrew Bible "refers to trust and loyalty that find expression in obedience and commitment."

And now we also understand the conclusion to the book of Malachi, and indeed to the First Testament.[111] In a series of oracles from the Persian period responding to the absence of fear/trust in YHWH in the restored community in Jerusalem, Malachi prescribes the solution: "Remember the Torah of Moses my servant whom I charged at Horeb [to teach] ordinances and judgments for all Israel" (Mal 4:4).[112]

Based on the formulaic sequence reading—hearing—learning—fearing—obeying—living well, I imagine Moses standing beside me as the Epistle to the Galatians is being read and asking, "How shall they live, if they do not obey? How shall they obey if they do not have faith in YHWH? How shall they have faith if they have not learned of him? How shall they learn of him if they do not hear the Torah? How shall they hear the Torah if no one reads it for them?"[113]

With this conclusion we may have encountered another conceptual link between Paul in Galatians and Moses in Deuteronomy. In Gal 3:2, Paul asks, "Did you receive the Spirit by works of the law or by *hearing* with faith?" (ἐξ ἔργων νόμου τὸ πνεῦμα ἐλάβετε ἢ ἐξ ἀκοῆς πίστεως;). Just as Paul's proclamation of the gospel produced faith, so in an earlier time hearing the Torah of Moses should have produced faith. Although they refused to trust YHWH, the exodus generation did not need this Torah, for they had experienced firsthand YHWH's transcendent power, his gracious deliverance, and his confirmation of his word. Nevertheless, they failed YHWH and the covenant on this very count. Moses proclaimed the Torah for the present and future generations, to provide constant reminders of YHWH's grace and faithfulness (חֶסֶד וֶאֱמֶת) and to inspire awed trust in him, yielding righteous living (16:20) and securing his favor (6:25).

For Moses circumcision was not the primary badge of the Israel of God.[114] For him, as for Paul, "The only thing that counts is faith expressing itself through love" (NIV; Greek, ἀλλὰ πίστις δι᾽ ἀγάπης ἐνεργουμένη). Although the nuance of "faith/trust" is more explicit in Greek πίστις (Gal

---

[111] As arranged in LXX and all Christian translations. The Hebrew Bible concludes with 2 Chronicles.

[112] Malachi echoes Deut 4:1 and 4:14. Cf. also 6:1.

[113] My own adaptation of the words of Paul in Rom 10:14–15, which, of course, would not have been accessible to Moses, since the Epistle to the Romans would not be written for another millennium.

[114] The expression "Israel of God" (Ἰσραὴλ τοῦ θεοῦ) occurs only in Gal 6:16 and finds no equivalent in the Hebrew Bible. With Susan Grove Eastman ("Israel and the Mercy of God: A Re-reading of Galatians 6:16 and Romans 9–11," *NTS* 56 [2010]: 367–95), I interpret the phrase to refer, not to Christians as the new covenant community, but to the people of Israel (Paul's physical kin), for whom the apostle pleads for divine mercy. Similarly Barclay, *Paul and the Gift,* 420–21, 445. Cf. E. P. Sanders, *Paul, the Law, and the Jewish People* (Philadelphia: Fortress, 1983), 176.

5:6) than in Hebrew יָרֵא (Deut 17:18–19; 31:11–13), the apostle's statement reflects the Deuteronomic understanding of "love" (Hebrew אָהַב, Greek ἀγάπη)—"covenant commitment demonstrated in action in the interest of the other person."[115] While the supreme command recognized both vertical and horizontal dimensions of covenant love,[116] in Gal 5:13–15 Paul's primary concern was its horizontal expression (cf. Rom 13:8–9).

In Gal 5:16–26 Paul describes the reverse side of this badge of Christ followers—walking by the Spirit. The Hebrew Bible rarely uses such language to speak of faithful living, but we see it embodied by persons like Caleb, whom Moses characterized as "full after God" (1:36),[117] but whom YHWH identified as "my servant" and credited with "a different spirit" (הָיְתָה רוּחַ אַחֶרֶת עִמּוֹ; ἐγενήθη πνεῦμα ἕτερον ἐν αὐτῷ, Num 14:24). Whether or not this association is valid, the trajectory of Paul's ethic represented by "walking by the Spirit" (Gal 5:16) and "the fruit of the Spirit" (vv. 22–23) is certainly at home in Deuteronomy, and Paul's prioritizing of heart over physical circumcision is neither as innovative nor as radical as some suggest.[118] Correspondingly, Moses might have employed Paul's list of "deeds of the flesh" (vv. 19–21) to characterize the Canaanites. Paul's note that "those who practice such things will not inherit the kingdom of God" (v. 21b) is at home with the ubiquitous references in Deuteronomy to Israel possessing (יָרַשׁ, Greek κληρονομέω) the land, identified as their divine grant (נַחֲלָה, Greek κλῆρος).[119]

Returning to the issue of circumcision, when Moses spoke of circumcision, he—like Paul—was concerned with circumcision of the heart (Deut 10:16). Following YHWH's lead in Lev 26:41 (לְבָבָם הֶעָרֵל), for him this was the badge of the true Israel. Individuals like Caleb and Joshua and Josiah (cf. 2 Kgs 23:25) were circumcised of heart, but Deut 30:6–8 envisions the day when YHWH will circumcise the hearts of all Israel. Then they will collectively demonstrate covenant commitment to him (אָהַב, "love") with complete obedience.

---

[115] On אָהַב, "love," as active demonstration of commitment to the well-being of the next person, see Abraham Malamat, " 'You Shall Love Your Neighbor as Yourself': A Case of Misinterpretation?" in *Die Hebräische Bibel und ihre Nachgeschichte*, ed. E. Blum et al., Rendtorff Festschrift (Neukirchen-Vluyn: Neukirchener Verlag, 1990), 111–15.

[116] Matt 22:37–39; Mark 12:30–31; Luke 10:27.

[117] Hebrew מִלֵּא אַחֲרֵי יְהוָה, rendered periphrastically by LXX as προσκεῖσθαι αὐτὸν τὰ πρὸς κύριον, "attached to the LORD."

[118] Contra Lincicum (*Early Jewish Encounter*, 150): "Paul's innovation is to radically prioritize circumcision of the heart over physical circumcision, at the same time effectively accusing Christ-believing Jews of an 'ethical epispasm' that has rendered their physical circumcision null and void."

[119] Various forms of the verb κληρονομέω occur forty-nine times in LXX Deuteronomy.

Paul does not use the metaphor of heart circumcision in Galatians, but he develops it fully in Rom 2:25–29. His conviction that circumcision of the heart is the only kind that matters is entirely Mosaic and explains why the physical rite was a focal point in Paul's debate with the Judaizers over the nature of the new covenant community. In Gal 2:12 he identifies those who insisted that gentile believers in Jesus needed to submit to external Jewish identity markers as "the circumcision faction" (NRSV; Greek, περιτομή). For Paul, Peter's caving in to their pressure (2:11–14) nullified the grace of God (vv. 15–21). In 5:2–12 he declares that circumcising gentile believers neutralizes the work of Christ on their behalf (v. 2), obligates them to the fine print of the entire Law (νόμος, v. 3), cuts them off from Christ (v. 4a), and shows they have fallen away (ἐκπίπτω) from grace (v. 4b). At the end of this paragraph he declares physical circumcision to be irrelevant for gentiles and affirms the true identity marker for the Christian community: faith working through love (5:13–22; cf. v. 6).

Conclusion

Scholars debate whether Paul's apologia in Gal 1 was intended to defend himself and his gospel against the attacks of Judaizers,[120] or whether he was painting a self-portrait to contrast with the portrait of the agitators mentioned in the book.[121] However we answer the question, we should remember that Paul viewed the Galatian Christians as his pastoral charge. Rather than being self-interested, his defense of himself was driven by his passion for his people and the gospel. In both respects he resembles Moses.

The table of Christian fellowship, particularly the question of who is welcome there, symbolized the problem in Galatia (Gal 2:11–14). By focusing on external cultural identity markers that had eclipsed the badges of true Israelites as defined by Moses, the Judaizers promoted a two-tier Christianity. Apparently they did not deny Jesus the Messiah, but to faith in him they added "the works of the law" (2:16; 3:10), that is, the external

[120] Thus Schreiner, *Galatians*, 34; John M. G. Barclay, "Mirror-Reading a Polemical Letter: Galatians as a Test Case," *JSNT* 31 (1987): 73–93, esp. 87.

[121] Justin Hardin ("Galatians 1–2 without a Mirror: Reflections on Paul's Conflict with the Agitators," *TynBul* 65 [2014]: 302) concludes, "Paul's narrative aim was to provide himself as a foil to the agitators in an effort to persuade his dear children not to fall prey any longer to the Judaizing message of the agitators." Similarly Anton Fridrichsen ("Die Apologie des Paulus Gal. 1," in *Exegetical Writings: A Selection*, ed. Chrys C. Caragounis and Tord Fornberg [Tübingen: Mohr Siebeck, 1994; repr. of 1920 article], 173), who argues that Paul was not defending himself but campaigning against the threatening apostasy in Galatia.

markers of Judaism: circumcision, observing kosher dietary laws, and celebrating Jewish festivals.[122] By this standard, the new people of God consisted of Jews who believed in Jesus and gentile believers in Jesus who submitted to Jewish identity markers, which meant converting to Judaism and ceasing to be gentiles. In short, to gain access to the table gentiles needed to become Jews first.

These agitators could have learned from Moses the marks of the true Israel of God. Remarkably, Moses begins his own version of "table talk" in Deut 14:1–21 by describing those who are invited to YHWH's table (vv. 1–2, rearranged):

בָּנִים אַתֶּם לַיהוָה אֱלֹהֵיכֶם	You are children belonging to YHWH your God. . . .
כִּי עַם קָדוֹשׁ אַתָּה	Indeed you are a holy people
לַיהוָה אֱלֹהֶיךָ	belonging to YHWH your God,
וּבְךָ בָּחַר יְהוָה	and YHWH has chosen you
מִכֹּל הָעַמִּים אֲשֶׁר עַל־פְּנֵי הָאֲדָמָה	out of all the peoples who are on the face of the earth
לִהְיוֹת לוֹ לְעַם סְגֻלָּה	to belong to him as a treasured people.

Moses hereby summarizes the prerequisites to table fellowship in the presence of YHWH: (1) being adopted as God's sons and daughters; (2) being sanctified by God; (3) being engaged with God in covenant relationship; (4) being chosen by God from all the peoples on earth; and (5) being treasured by YHWH as his crown jewel (סְגֻלָּה). Fellowship with YHWH is a gift. This is precisely the ideal that Paul tried to establish in Galatia and all his churches. But the scope of invitees to the table had changed. Whereas in the past YHWH had called out for himself a people from among the nations (Israel) and set them high above the nations as lights of the world (Deut 4:5–8; 26:19), now Jesus Christ, the embodiment of divine χάριτος καὶ ἀληθείας (חֶסֶד וֶאֱמֶת, John 1:14), has called out for himself people from all the nations. This is the new covenant community, invited to fellowship and to celebrate in the presence of God. And this characterizes Paul's vision for the churches of Galatia.

* * * * *

[122] Cf. James D. G. Dunn, "Works of the Law and the Curse of the Law (Galatians 3:10–14)," *NTS* 31 (1985): 523–42; Segal, *Paul the Convert*, 124–25.

Postscript: While early Christian biblical scholarship and art tended to contrast Paul and Moses, the complementarity of the two figures is occasionally represented, as in a fifth-century Ravenna sarcophagus sculpture (Figure 2) and an early twelfth-century capital sculpture in the Church of St. Madeline, in Vezelay, France (Figure 3).

Figure 2. Twelve Apostles Sarcophagus with Sculpture of the *Traditio Legis*. Sant'Apollinare in Classe. Ravenna, Italy (fifth century CE). (Photo courtesy of Mary Ann Sullivan, Bluffton University. Used with permission.)

The figure on the right is the apostle Peter. He has received the cross from Jesus Christ, enthroned in the center. The figure on the left is the apostle Paul, who carefully receives a scroll from the hand of Jesus, presumably to treasure and use as the base of his own teaching. The object received may have been the entire Pentateuch, or more likely, the Torah scroll of Deuteronomy. Judging from the frequency of Jesus' citations from this book and allusions to it in the Gospels, Deuteronomy was most formative in his ministry. The size of the scroll favors identifying it as Deuteronomy.[123]

[123] According to Lincicum (*Paul and the Early Jewish Encounter with Deuteronomy*, 200–201), the scroll may be Deuteronomy, "given to the apostle to nourish the Gentile church and to make known the God of Israel's revelation in Jesus Christ: *Dominus Deuteronomium dat.*" For discussion of the sculpture, see Theodor Klausern, Frühchristliche Sarkophage in Bild und Wort, Beiheft zur Halbjahresschrift Antike Kunst 3 (Olten: Urs Grav-Verlag, 1966), 82–84. For discussion of the traditio legis ("transmission of the law") motif, see Reidar Hvalvik, "Christ Proclaiming the Law to the Apostles: The Traditio Legis-Motif in Early Christian Art and Literature," in *The New Testament and Early Christian Literature in Greco-Roman Context*, ed. John Fotopoulos; NovTSup 122 (Leiden: Brill, 2006), 405–37. Hvalvik interprets the scroll as "the new law of Christ," which replaces the Mosaic law.

Figure 3. Mystic Mill Capital. Benedictine Abbey, Church of Sainte-Marie-Madeleine, Vézelay, France (twelfth century CE). (Photo © Adrian Fletcher, www.paradoxplace.com. Used with permission.)

The figure on the left is Moses, who pours grain into a small mill. He stands in shadow since he belongs to the First Testament. The figure on the right is Paul, who carefully receives the flour. He stands in the light since he belongs to the New Testament. A wheel with cross-shaped spokes drives the mill, which implicitly stands for Christ, who extracts the life-giving essence of the Torah and transforms it into the renewed message of the New Testament.[124]

[124] For discussion, see Marian Moffatt, "The Mystic Mill from Vézelay," in *A World History of Architecture*, ed. Michael Fazio, Marian Moffat, and Lawrence Wodehouse, 2nd ed. (London: McGraw-Hill, 2008), 215–17; Kirk Ambrose, *The Nave Structure of Vézelay: The Art of Monastic Viewing* (Toronto: Pontifical Institute of Mediaeval Studies, 2006), 71–72.

CHAPTER 13

CONCLUDING REFLECTIONS

Richard L. Schultz

The Deuteronomy colloquium held on the campus of Wheaton College concluded without its participants necessarily drawing any substantive or dramatic "conclusions" regarding the composition or interpretation of the book of Deuteronomy. In organizing this colloquium, Daniel Block and I neither intended nor expected that, in the space of less than three days, we could achieve anything approaching a consensus regarding the disputed questions of the authorship, compositional date, structure, and purpose of the book of Deuteronomy, or of the relationship between its legal material and that of the other pentateuchal law codes. However, as noted below, some general patterns of agreement emerged. Our goal, rather, was to facilitate intense, open, and respectful dialogue among a group of scholars who share some core theological commitments, spiritual concerns, and academic interest in the book of Deuteronomy. We hoped that, in the process, the participants would give each other feedback that would help strengthen their respective papers prior to their publication in the present volume.

As an Isaiah scholar whose past academic engagement with Deuteronomy studies has been minimal, I was struck (but not surprised) while reading the essays by the features shared by contemporary critical studies of Isaiah and Deuteronomy, including the breakdown of what formerly was taken to be their "assured results," the assignment of an increasingly later date to much or most of each book (i.e., in the Persian period or beyond), and the denial that substantial shifts in the contents of each book could be accounted for by developments during the lengthy public ministry of each book's central figure (traditionally, its "author") rather than being the product of one or more later authorial or editorial hands. Especially intriguing to me are the similarities between what Bill Arnold understands as the role of the "Mosaic scribes" and the "disciples of Isaiah"—most prominently those designated by Bernhard Duhm as "Second" and "Third" Isaiah. Suddenly, I found myself in familiar territory!

I turn now to the colloquium and resultant essays on Deuteronomy to make a few observations. First, we began the colloquium with what, for me, was a somewhat surprising discussion of the label "evangelical" as applied to past and current Deuteronomy scholarship—surprising since such a discussion was completely absent from our Isaiah colloquium and since it made me wonder whether the participants in our "evangelical" dialogue that weekend also embraced the label as an acceptable self-description. That opening discussion prompted Daniel Block's helpful, hermeneutically focused characterization of "evangelical" biblical scholarship in the introduction to this volume. As his comments reflect, the tenor of our discussions indicated that our individual interests in Deuteronomy go beyond mere scholarly engagement to a commitment to this book as Scripture, which has practical implications, for example, for how we view the current immigration crisis. Even those essays that do not speak of Deuteronomy as the "words" of Moses are concerned with explaining how the present book is related to its purported source in Moses.

Second, most of the essays involve a *comparison* of some kind, and thus raise questions regarding the proper methodology for engaging in comparative studies, including between Deuteronomy and 2 Kings (Grisanti), the Gilgamesh Epic (Arnold), ancient Near Eastern treaty traditions (Huddleston and Younger), the Samaritan Pentateuch (Richter), legal material in Exodus and Leviticus (Averbeck and Zehnder), Hosea (Vang), Proverbs (McConville), and Galatians (Block). (Such a comparative perspective was foundational to only two of the essays in our Isaiah volume.)

This also raises the question of what constitutes a significant or adequate parallel—similar words or concepts, forms or structures, or emphases or concerns? Is the Deuteronomic "fear of God" the equivalent of Pauline "faith in God"? In my view, due caution was exercised in these matters and fair critiques were offered of the comparative analyses of other scholars. In this regard, we observed how an extensive knowledge of ancient Near Eastern texts and archaeological sites can offer a helpful corrective to the speculative tendencies of some biblical scholars, although the analysis of such texts and excavation data also involves considerable subjectivity.

Third, one issue that surfaces several times in the essays is the impact of prior conclusions, for example, regarding the dating of biblical texts, on the interpretive options that various scholars consider to be viable. This is illustrated by Carsten Vang's assessment that most scholars between the 1960s and 1990s concluded that Deuteronomy borrowed from Hosea rather than vice versa. However, this should remind us how prone we are to making similar hermeneutical moves in our biblical analyses and should banish from us any hint of critical smugness.

Considered positively, during the colloquium we also experienced both the specific research expertise and the particular interpretive lens of each participant enriching our deliberations. This was evident from one participant's repeated reminders to consider the anthropological, as well as the historical, theological, and ethical, dimensions of the texts, or to consider them from the perspective of the poor and disenfranchised migrants rather than simply from the perspective of the powerful. The presence of Professor Tigay in our midst was a special treat. During his public lecture, we learned how Jewish interpreters both ancient and modern wrestled with the ethical challenge posed by Deuteronomy's "annihilation" command, which, in turn, can help to illuminate the command in its biblical setting, as well.

In the case of our earlier Isaiah colloquium and the resulting volume of essays, we hoped to make a modest contribution not only to evangelical scholarship on Isaiah but also to academic Isaiah studies. As co-conveners of the Deuteronomy colloquium and coeditors of the essays, Daniel Block and I hope the same for the present volume. We are pleased to make these studies in the composition and interpretation of Deuteronomy available to a wider readership.

Bibliography

Achenbach, Reinhard. *Israel zwischen Verheißung und Gebot: Literarkritische Untersuchungen zu Deuteronomium 5–11*. Europäische Hochschulschriften. Theologie 422. Frankfurt am Main: Lang, 1991.

Aejmelaeus, Anneli. "Function and Interpretation of כי in Biblical Hebrew." *JBL* 105 (1986): 193–209.

Aernie, Jeffrey W. *Is Paul Also among the Prophets? An Examination of the Relationship between Paul and the Old Testament Prophetic Tradition in 2 Corinthians*. LNTS 467. New York: T&T Clark, 2012.

Ahlström, Gösta W. *Ancient Palestine: An Historical Introduction*. Minneapolis: Fortress, 2002.

Albertz, Rainer. *A History of Israelite Religion in the Old Testament Period*. OTL. 2 vols. Louisville: Westminster John Knox, 1994.

Allis, Oswald T. *The Five Books of Moses: A Reexamination of the Modern Theory That the Pentateuch Is a Late Compilation from Diverse and Conflicting Sources By Authors and Editors Whose Identity Is Completely Unknown*. 3rd ed. New York: Presbyterian & Reformed, 1969.

Allsopp, F. W., et al. *Hebrew Inscriptions: Texts from the Biblical Period of the Monarchy with Concordance*. New Haven: Yale University Press, 2005.

Alt, Albrecht. "Die Heimat des Deuteronomiums." In *Kleine Schriften zur Geschichte des Volkes Israel*, 2:250–75. Munich: C. H. Beck, 1953.

Alter, Robert. *The Art of Biblical Narrative*. 2nd ed. New York: Basic Books, 2011.

Altman, Amnon. *The Historical Prologue of the Hittite Vassal Treaties: An Inquiry into the Concepts of Hittite Interstate Law*. Bar-Ilan Studies in Near Eastern Languages and Culture. Ramat-Gan: Bar-Ilan University Press, 2004.

_____. "How Many Treaty Traditions Existed in the Ancient Near East?" In *Pax Hethitica: Studies on the Hittites and Their Neighbours in Honour of Itamar Singer*, edited by Yoram Cohen, Amir Gilan, and Jared L. Miller, 17–36. StBoT 51. Wiesbaden: Harrassowitz, 2010.

_____. "Reflections on the Alalaḫ Text AT 456." In *Looking at the Ancient Near East and the Bible through the Same Eyes: A Tribute to Aaron Skaist*, edited by Kathleen Abraham and Joseph Fleishman, 1–12. Bethesda, MD: CDL Press, 2012.

_____. *Tracing the Earliest Recorded Concepts of International Law: The Ancient Near East (2500–330 BCE)*. Edited by Randall Lesaffer. Legal History Library 8: Studies in the History of International Law. Leiden: Martinus Nijhoff, 2012.

_____. “What Kind of Treaty Tradition Do the Sefire Inscriptions Represent?” In *Treasures on Camels' Humps: Historical and Literary Studies from the Ancient Near East Presented to Israel Eph'al*, edited by Israel Eph'al, Mordechai Cogan, and Dan'el Kahn, 26–40. Jerusalem: Hebrew University Magnes Press, 2008.

Ambrose, Kirk. *The Nave Structure of Vézelay: The Art of Monastic Viewing*. Toronto: Pontifical Institute of Mediaeval Studies, 2006.

Amit, Yairah. “Shechem in Deuteronomy: A Seemingly Hidden Polemic.” In *History, Memory, Hebrew Scriptures: A Festschrift for Ehud Ben Zvi*, edited by Ian D. Wilson and Diana Edelman, 3–14. Winona Lake, IN: Eisenbrauns, 2015.

Amusin, Joseph D. “Die Gerim in der sozialen Legislatur des Alten Testaments.” *Klio* 63 (1981): 15–23.

Andersen, Francis I. *The Hebrew Verbless Clause in the Pentateuch*. SBLMS 14. Nashville: Abingdon, 1970.

Andersen, Francis I, and David N. Freedman. *Hosea: A New Translation with Introduction and Commentary*. AB 24. New York: Doubleday, 1980.

Anderson, Robert T., and Terry Giles. *The Samaritan Pentateuch: An Introduction to Its Origin, History, and Significance for Biblical Studies*. Atlanta: SBL Press, 2012.

Annus, Amar. *The God Ninurta in the Mythology and Royal Ideology of Ancient Mesopotamia*. SAAS 14. Helsinki: Neo-Assyrian Text Corpus Project, 2002.

Ansberry, Christopher B., and Jerry Hwang. “No Covenant before the Exile? The Deuteronomic Torah and Israel's Covenant Theology.” In *Evangelical Faith and the Challenge of Historical Criticism*, edited by Christopher M. Hays and Christopher B. Ansberry, 74–94. Grand Rapids: Baker Academic, 2013.

Ansberry, Christopher B., Casey A. Strine, Edward W. Klink III, and David Lincicum. “Pseudepigraphy and the Canon.” In *Evangelical Faith and the Challenge of Historical Criticism*, edited by Christopher M. Hays and Christopher B. Ansberry, 125–57. Grand Rapids: Baker Academic, 2013.

Argall, Randal A. *1 Enoch and Sirach: A Comparative, Literary and Conceptual Analysis of the Themes of Revelation, Creation and Judgment*. SBLEJL 8. Atlanta: Scholars Press, 1995.

Arnold, Bill T. “Deuteronomy as the *Ipsissima Vox* of Moses.” *JTI* 4 (2010): 53–74.

_____. “The Genesis Narratives.” In *Ancient Israel's History: An Introduction to Issues and Sources*, edited by Bill T. Arnold and Richard S. Hess, 23–45. Grand Rapids: Baker Academic, 2014.

_____. “Israelite Worship as Envisioned and Prescribed in Deuteronomy 12.” *ZABR* 22 (2016): 161–75.

_____. “Reexamining the ‘Fathers’ in Deuteronomy's Framework.” In *Torah and Tradition: Papers Read at the Sixteenth Joint Meeting of the*

Society for Old Testament Study and the Oudtestamentisch Werkgezelschap, Edinburgh 2015, edited by Klaas Spronk and Hans Barstad, 10–41. *OtSt* 70. Leiden: Brill, 2017.

Arnold, Bill T., and John H. Choi. *A Guide to Biblical Hebrew Syntax*. Cambridge: Cambridge University Press, 2003.

Arnold, Bill T., and David B. Weisberg. "A Centennial Review of Friedrich Delitzsch's 'Babel und Bibel' Lectures." *JBL* 121 (2002): 441–57.

Assaf, A. A., P. Bordreuil, and A. R. Millard. *La statue de Tell Fekherye et son inscription bilingue assyro-araméenne*. Éditions recherche sur les civilisations. Paris: Anatole de la Forge, 1982.

Aufrecht, W. E. *A Corpus of Ammonite Inscriptions*. ANETS 4. Lewiston, NY: Mellen, 1989.

Auld, A. Graeme. "The Deuteronomists and the Former Prophets, or What Makes the Former Prophets Deuteronomistic?" In *Those Elusive Deuteronomists: The Phenomenon of Pan-Deuteronomism*, edited by Linda S. Schearing and Steven L. McKenzie, 116–26. JSOTSup 268. Sheffield: Sheffield Academic, 1999.

Averbeck, Richard E. "מזבח altar." *NIDOTTE* 2:888–908.

______. "The Egyptian Sojourn and Deliverance from Slavery in the Framing and Shaping of the Mosaic Law." In *"Did I Not Bring Israel Out of Egypt?" Biblical, Archaeological, and Egyptological Perspectives on the Exodus Narratives*, edited by James K. Hoffmeier, Alan R. Millard, and Gary A. Rendsburg. BBRSup 13. Winona Lake, IN: Eisenbrauns, 2016.

______. "Pentateuchal Criticism and the Priestly Torah." In *Do Historical Matters Matter for Faith: A Critical Appraisal of Modern and Postmodern Approaches to the Bible*, edited by James K. Hoffmeier and Dennis R. Magary, 151–79. Wheaton, IL: Crossway, 2012.

Awabdy, Mark A. *Immigrants and Innovative Law: Deuteronomy's Theological and Social Vision for the* גר. FAT 2/67. Tübingen: Mohr Siebeck, 2014.

______. "Teaching Children in the Instruction of Amenemope and Deuteronomy." *VT* 65 (2015): 1–8.

Baer D. A., and R. P. Gordon. "חסד." *NIDOTTE* 2:211–18.

Baker, David L. *Tight Fists or Open Hands? Wealth and Poverty in Old Testament Law*. Grand Rapids: Eerdmans, 2009.

Bal, Meike. *Narratology: Introduction to the Theory of Narrative*. 3rd ed. Toronto: University of Toronto Press, 2009.

Bammel, Ernst. *Judaica et Paulina: Kleine Schriften II*. WUNT 91. Tübingen: Mohr Siebeck, 1997.

______. "Paulus, der Moses des Neuen Bundes." *Theologia* 54 (1983): 399–408.

Barclay, John M. G. "Mirror-Reading a Polemical Letter: Galatians as a Test Case." *JSNT* 31 (1987): 73–93.

______. *Paul and the Gift*. Grand Rapids: Eerdmans, 2015.

Barker, Paul A. "Contemporary Theological Interpretation of Deuteronomy." In *Interpreting Deuteronomy: Issues and Approaches*, edited by

David G. Firth and Philip S. Johnston, 60–90. Downers Grove, IL: InterVarsity Press, 2012.

_____. *Deuteronomy: The God Who Keeps Promises*. Melbourne: Acorn, 1998.

Barr, James. *Semantics of Biblical Language*. London: Oxford University Press, 1961. Repr., London: SCM Press, 1983.

Barrick, W. Boyd. *The Kings and the Cemeteries: Toward a New Understanding of Josiah's Reform*. VTSup 88. Boston: Brill, 2002.

Barthélemy, Dominique. *Critique textuelle de l'Ancien Testament*. Vol. 3, *Ézékiel, Daniel et les 12 Prophètes*. OBO 50/3. Fribourg: Éditions Universitaires, 1992.

Bartlett, John R. *Edom and the Edomites*, JSOTSup 77. Sheffield: JSOT Press, 1989.

Bass, Derek D. "Hosea's Use of Scripture: An Analysis of His Hermeneutics." PhD diss., The Southern Baptist Theological Seminary, 2008.

Beal, Richard Henry. *The Organisation of the Hittite Military*. THeth 20. Heidelberg: Winter, 1992.

Bebbington, David. *Evangelicalism in Modern Britain: A History from the 1730s to the 1980s*. London: Unwin Hyman, 1989.

Beckman, Gary M. *Hittite Diplomatic Texts*. Edited by Harry A. Hoffner. 2nd ed. SBLWAW 7. Atlanta: Scholars Press, 1999.

_____. "Hittite Treaties and the Development of the Cuneiform Treaty Tradition." In *Die deuteronomistischen Geschichtswerke: redaktions- und religionsgeschichtliche Perspektiven zur "Deuteronomismus"-Diskussion in Tora und Vorderen Propheten*, edited by Markus Witte, Konrad Schmid, Doris Prechel, and Jan Christian Gertz, 279–301. BZAW 365. Berlin: de Gruyter, 2006.

Begg, Christopher T. "Contributions to the Elucidation of the Composition of Deuteronomy with Special Attention to the Significance of the *Numeruswechsel*." Ph.D. diss., Louvain, 1987.

Benz, F. L. *Personal Names in Phoenician and Punic Inscriptions*. StPohl 8. Rome: Biblical Institute Press, 1972.

Berlejung, Angelika. "Der Handwerker als Theologe: Zur Mentalitäts- und Traditionsgeschichte eines altorientalischen und alttestamentlichen Berufstands." *VT* 46 (1996): 145–68.

Berman, Joshua. "Historicism and Its Limits: A Response to Bernard M. Levinson and Jeffrey Stackert." *JAJ* 4 (2013): 297–309.

_____. "Supersessionist or Complementary? Reassessing the Nature of Legal Revision in the Pentateuchal Law Collections." *JBL* 135 (2016): 201–22.

Biberger, Bernd. *Unsere Väter und Wir: Unterteilung von Geschichtsdarstellungen in Generationen und das Verhältnis der Generationen im Alten Testament*. BBB 145. Berlin: Philo, 2003.

Biggs, Robert D. šà.zi.ga*: Ancient Mesopotamian Potency Incantations*. Edited by Erich Ebeling. TCS 2. New York: J. J. Augustin, 1967.

Blackburn, Simon. *The Oxford Dictionary of Philosophy*. 2nd ed. Oxford: Oxford University Press, 2008.

Blenkinsopp, Joseph. *The Pentateuch: An Introduction to the First Five Books of the Bible*. ABRL. New York: Doubleday, 1992.

_____. *Wisdom and Law in the Old Testament: The Ordering of Life in Israel and Early Judaism*. Oxford: Oxford University Press, 1983.

Block, Daniel I. *The Book of Ezekiel: Chapters 1–24*. NICOT. Grand Rapids: Eerdmans, 1997.

_____. *Deuteronomy*. NIVAC. Grand Rapids: Zondervan, 2012.

_____. "How Many Is God? An Investigation into the Meaning of Deuteronomy 6:4–5." *JETS* 47 (2004): 193–212. Repr. in *How I Love Your Torah, O LORD: Studies in the Book of Deuteronomy*, 73–97. Eugene, OR: Cascade, 2011.

_____. "In Spirit and in Truth: The Mosaic Vision of Worship." In *Rediscovering Worship: Past, Present, and Future*, edited by Wendy Porter, 1–26. Eugene, OR: Pickwick, 2015. Previously published in *The Gospel according to Moses: Theological and Ethical Reflections on the Book of Deuteronomy*, 272–98. Eugene, OR: Cascade, 2012.

_____. *Judges, Ruth*. NAC 6. Nashville: Broadman & Holman, 1999.

_____. " 'My Servant David': Ancient Israel's Vision of the Messiah." In *Israel's Messiah in the Bible and the Dead Sea Scrolls*, edited by Richard S. Hess and M. Daniel Carroll R., 17–56. Grand Rapids: Baker Academic, 2003.

_____. " 'A Place for My Name': Horeb and Zion in the Mosaic Vision of Israelite Worship." *JETS* 58 (2015): 221–47.

_____. "Recovering the Voice of Moses: The Genesis of Deuteronomy." *JETS* 44 (2001): 385–408.

_____. Review of *The Iron Age I Structure on Mt. Ebal: Excavation and Interpretation*, by Ralph K. Hawkins. *BBR* 23 (2013): 94–96.

_____. "What Do These Stones Mean? The Riddle of Deuteronomy 27," *JETS* 56 (2013): 17–41.

Block, Daniel I., and Richard L. Schultz, eds. *Bind Up the Testimony: Explorations in the Genesis of the Book of Isaiah*. Peabody, MA: Hendrickson, 2015.

The Book of Discipline of the United Methodist Church, 2012. Nashville: United Methodist Publishing House, 2012.

Bordreuil, Pierre, and Dennis Pardee. *A Manual of Ugaritic*. LSAWS 3. Winona Lake, IN: Eisenbrauns, 2009.

Brandl, Baruch. "Two Scarabs and a Trapezoidal Seal from Mount Ebal." *TA* 14 (1987): 166–72.

Braulik, Georg. "Die dekalogische Redaktion der deuteronomischen Gesetze. Ihre Abhängigkeit von Levitikus 19 am Beispiel von Deuteronomium 22,1–12; 24,10–22 und 25,13–16." In *Bundesdokument und Gesetz. Studien zum Deuteronomium*, edited by G. Braulik, 1–25. Freiburg im Breisgau: Herder, 1995.

_____. " 'Weisheit' im Buch Deuteronomium." In *Weisheit ausserhalb der kanonischen Weisheitsschriften*, edited by B. Janowski, 39–69. VWGT 8. Gütersloh: Gütersloher Verlagshaus, 1996. Repr. in *Studien zum Buch Deuteronomium*, 225–71. SBAB 24. Stuttgart: Verlag Katholisches Bibelwerk, 1997.

_____. "Weitere Beobachtungen zur Beziehung zwischen dem Heiligkeitsgesetz und Deuteronomium 19–25." In *Das Deuteronomium und seine Querbeziehungen*, edited by T. Veijola, 23–55. Helsinki: Finnische Exegetische Gesellschaft, 1996.

_____. "Wisdom, Divine Presence and Law." In *The Theology of Deuteronomy: Collected Essays of Georg Braulik*, 1–25. Translated by Ulrika Lindblad. North Richland Hills: BIBAL Press, 1994.

Braulik, Georg, and Norbert Lohfink. "Deuteronomium 1,5 באר את־התורה הזאת: 'er verlieh dieser Tora Rechtskraft.' " In *Textarbeit: Studien zu Texten und ihrer Rezeption aus dem Alten Testament und der Umwelt Israels: Festschrift für Peter Weimar zur Vollendung seines 60. Lebensjahres mit Beiträgen von Freunden, Schülern und Kollegen*, edited by Klaus Kiesow and Thomas Meurer, 34–51. AOAT 294. Münster: Ugarit-Verlag, 2003.

Bray, Gerald. *Biblical Interpretation Past and Present*. Downers Grove, IL: InterVarsity Press, 1996.

Brinkman, John A. "Political Covenants, Treaties, and Loyalty Oaths in Babylonia and between Assyria and Babylonia." In *I trattati nel mondo antico: forma, ideologia, funzione*, edited by Luciano Canfora, Mario Liverani, and Carlo Zaccagnini, 81–111. Rome: L'Erma di Bretschneider, 1990.

Broshi, Magen. "The Expansion of Jerusalem in the Reigns of Hezekiah and Manasseh." *IEJ* 24 (1974): 21–26.

Bruce, F. F. *The Epistle to the Galatians: A Commentary on the Greek Text*. NIGTC. Grand Rapids: Eerdmans, 1982.

Brueggemann, Walter. *Deuteronomy*. AOTC. Nashville: Abingdon, 2001.

_____. *Tradition for Crisis: A Study in Hosea*. Richmond, VA: John Knox, 1968.

Bryce, Trevor R. *The Kingdom of the Hittites*. New ed. Oxford: Oxford University Press, 2005.

_____. *The World of the Neo-Hittite Kingdoms: A Political and Military History*. Oxford: Oxford University Press, 2012.

Bühner, J. A. "ἀποστέλλω *apostellō* send forth." *EDNT* 1:141–42.

_____. "ἀπόστολος *apostolos* delegate, apostle." *EDNT* 1:142–46.

Bultmann, Christoph. *Der Fremde im antiken Juda: Eine Untersuchung zum sozialen Typenbegriff "ger" und seinem Bedeutungswandel in der alttestamentlichen Gesetzgebung*. FRLANT 153. Göttingen: Vandenhoeck & Ruprecht, 1992.

Campbell, Antony F. "An Historical Prologue in a Seventh-Century Treaty." *Bib* 50 (1969): 534–35.

Campbell, Edward F. "Shechem." *NEAEHL* 4:1345–54.

Carew, M. Douglas. "To Know or Not to Know: Hosea's Use of *ydʿ/dʿt*." In *The Old Testament in the Life of God's People: Essays in Honor of Elmer A. Martens*, edited by Jon Isaak, 73–85. Winona Lake, IN: Eisenbrauns, 2009.

Carr, David. "Method in Determination of Direction of Dependence: An Empirical Test of Criteria Applied to Exodus 34,11–26 and Its Parallels." In *Gottes Volk am Sinai: Untersuchungen zu Ex 32–34 und Dtn 9–10*, edited by Matthias Köckert and Erhard Blum, 107–40. Veröffentlichungen der Wissenschaftlichen Gesellschaft für Theologie 18. Gütersloh: Gütersloher Verlagshaus, 2001.

______. *Writing on the Tablet of the Heart: Origins of Scripture and Literature.* New York: Oxford University Press, 2005.

Chapman, Stephen B. *The Law and the Prophets: A Study in Old Testament Canon Formation.* FAT 27. Tübingen: Mohr Siebeck, 2000.

Charlesworth, James H. "What Is a Variant? Announcing a Dead Sea Scrolls Fragment of Deuteronomy." *Maarav* 16 (2009): 201–12.

Charpin, Dominique. "Un traité entre Zimrî-Lim de Mari et Ibâl-pî-El II d'Ešnunna." In *Marchands, diplomates et empereurs: Études sur la civilisation mésopotamienne offertes à Paul Garelli*, edited by Dominique Charpin, Francis Joannès, and Paul Garelli, 139–66. Paris: Editions recherche sur les civilisations, 1991.

Cheyne, Thomas K. *Founders of Old Testament Criticism: Biographical, Descriptive and Critical Studies.* London: Methuen, 1893.

Childs, Brevard S. *Biblical Theology of the Old and New Testaments: Theological Reflection on the Christian Bible.* Minneapolis: Augsburg Fortress, 1993.

______. *Introduction to the Old Testament as Scripture.* Philadelphia: Fortress, 1979.

Choi, John H. *Traditions at Odds: The Reception of the Pentateuch in Biblical and Second Temple Period Literature.* LHBOTS 518. London: T&T Clark, 2010.

Cholewiński, Alfred. *Heiligkeitsgesetz und Deuteronomium: Eine vergleichende Studie.* AnBib 66. Rome: Biblical Institute Press, 1976.

Christensen, Duane L. *Deuteronomy 21:10–34:12.* WBC 6B. Nashville: Thomas Nelson, 2002.

______. "Deuteronomy in Modern Research: Approaches and Issues." In *A Song of Power and the Power of Song: Essays on the Book of Deuteronomy*, edited by Duane L. Christensen, 3–17. SBTS 3. Winona Lake, IN: Eisenbrauns, 1993.

Christensen, Duane L., and Marcel Narucki. "The Mosaic Authorship of the Pentateuch." *JETS* 32 (1989): 465–71.

Ciampa, Roy E. *The Presence and Function of Scripture in Galatians 1 and 2.* WUNT 2/102. Tübingen: Mohr Siebeck, 1998.

Clements, Ronald E. "The Deuteronomic Law of Centralisation and the Catastrophe of 587 BCE." In *After the Exile: Essays in Honour of Rex*

Mason, edited by John Barton and David J. Reimer, 5–25. Macon, GA: Mercer University Press, 1996.

_____. *Deuteronomy*. OTG. Sheffield: JSOT Press, 1989.

_____. "Deuteronomy and the Jerusalem Cult Tradition." *VT* 15 (1965): 300–312.

Cogan, Mordechai, and Hayim Tadmor. *II Kings: A New Translation with Introduction and Commentary*. AB 11. New York: Doubleday, 1988.

Cohen, Yoram, Amir Gilan, and Jared L. Miller, eds. *Pax Hethitica: Studies on the Hittites and Their Neighbours in Honour of Itamar Singer*. StBoT 51. Wiesbaden: Harrassowitz, 2010.

Collins, Billie Jean. *The Hittites and Their World*. SBLABS 7. Atlanta: Society of Biblical Literature, 2007.

Collins, Kenneth J. *The Evangelical Moment: The Promise of an American Religion*. Grand Rapids: Baker Academic, 2005.

Coogan, Michael. "Of Cults and Cultures: Reflections on the Interpretation of Archaeological Evidence." *PEQ* 119 (1987): 1–8.

Cook, Stephen L. *Reading Deuteronomy: A Literary and Theological Commentary*. Edited by Mark E. Biddle. Reading the Old Testament. Macon, GA: Smyth & Helwys, 2015.

Craigie, Peter C. *The Book of Deuteronomy*. NICOT. Grand Rapids: Eerdmans, 1976.

Craigie, Peter C., Page H. Kelley, and Joel F. Drinkard. *Jeremiah 1–25*. WBC 26. Dallas: Word, 1991.

Crenshaw, James L. *Old Testament Wisdom: An Introduction*. London: SCM, 1982.

Cross, Frank M. *Canaanite Myth and Hebrew Epic: Essays in the History of the Religion of Israel*. Cambridge: Harvard University Press, 1973.

Crouch, Carly L. *Israel and the Assyrians: Deuteronomy, the Succession Treaty of Esarhaddon, and the Nature of Subversion*. Edited by Ehud Ben Zvi. ANEM 8. Atlanta: Society of Biblical Literature, 2014.

Cuddon, J. A., and C. E. Preston. *The Penguin Dictionary of Literary Terms and Literary Theory*. 4th ed. London: Penguin, 1998.

d'Alfonso, Lorenzo. "Die hethitische Vertragstradition in Syrien (14.-12. Jh.v.Chr.)." In *Die deuteronomistischen Geschichtswerke: redaktions- und religionsgeschichtliche Perspektiven zur "Deuteronomismus"-Diskussion in Tora und Vorderen Propheten*, edited by Markus Witte, Konrad Schmid, Doris Prechel, and Jan Christian Gertz, 303–29. BZAW 365. Berlin: de Gruyter, 2006.

Daniels, Dwight R. *Hosea and Salvation History: The Early Traditions of Israel in the Prophecy of Hosea*. BZAW 191. Berlin: de Gruyter, 1990.

Davies, G. I. *Hosea*. NCB. Grand Rapids: Eerdmans, 1992.

Davies, Philip R. "Josiah and the Law Book." In *Good Kings and Bad Kings: The Kingdom of Judah in the Seventh Century BCE*, edited by Lester Grabbe, 65–77. LHBOTS 393. London: T&T Clark, 2005.

Dean, Kenda Creasy. *Almost Christian: What the Faith of Our Teenagers Is Telling the American Church.* Oxford: Oxford University Press, 2010.

Dearman, J. Andrew. *The Book of Hosea*. NICOT. Grand Rapids: Eerdmans, 2010.

de Boer, Martinus C. *Galatians: A Commentary*. NTL. Louisville: Westminster John Knox, 2011.

_____. "Paul and Jewish Apocalyptic Theology." In *Apocalyptic and the New Testament: Essays in Honor of J. Louis Martyn*, edited by J. Marcus and M. L. Soards, 169–90. Sheffield: Sheffield Academic, 1989.

Delitzsch, Friedrich. *Die grosse Täuschung.* Neuausgabe. Stuttgart: Deutsche Verlags-Anstalt, 1921.

del Monte, Giuseppe F. *Il trattato fra Muršili II di Ḫattuša e Niqmepaʿ di Ugarit.* OAC 18. Rome: Istituto per l'Oriente C. A. Nallino, 1986.

_____. "Note sui tratti fra Ḫattuša e Kizuwatna." *OrAnt* 20 (1981): 203–21.

DeRouchie, Jason S. *A Call to Covenant Love: Text–Grammar and Literary Structure in Deuteronomy 5–11.* Piscataway, NJ: Gorgias Press, 2007.

_____. "Circumcision in the Hebrew Bible and Targumim: Theology, Rhetoric, and the Handling of a Metaphor." *BBR* 14 (2004): 175–203.

_____. "Counting the Ten: An Investigation into the Numbering of the Decalogue." In *For Our Good Always: Studies on the Message and Influence of Deuteronomy in Honor of Daniel I. Block*, edited by Jason S. DeRouchie, Jason Gile, and Kenneth J. Turner, 93–125. Winona Lake, IN: Eisenbrauns, 2013.

deSilva, David A. *Introducing the Apocrypha: Message, Context, and Significance.* Grand Rapids: Baker, 2002.

Devecchi, Elena. "Treaties and Edicts in the Hittite World." In *Organization, Representation, and Symbols of Power in the Ancient Near East: Proceedings of the 54th Rencontre Assyriologique Internationale at Würzburg 20–25 July 2008*, edited by Gernot Wilhelm, 637–45. Winona Lake, IN: Eisenbrauns, 2012.

de Wette, Wilhelm Martin Leberecht. *Beiträge zur Einleitung in das Alte Testament.* 2 vols. Hildesheim: Olms, 1971 [1806].

_____. *A Critical and Historical Introduction to the Canonical Scriptures of the Old Testament.* Translated by Theodore Parker. Boston: Little, Brown, 1843.

_____. *Lehrbuch der historisch-kritischen Einleitung in die kanonischen und apokryphischen Bücher des Alten Testaments.* Berlin: G. Reimer, 1833.

_____. *Opuscula Theologica.* Berlin: G. Reimer, 1830.

Dietrich, Walter. *Prophetie und Geschichte: Eine redaktionsgeschichtliche Untersuchung zum deuteronomischen Geschichtswerk.* FRLANT 108. Göttingen: Vandenhoeck & Ruprecht, 1972.

Donbaz, Veysel. "An Old Assyrian Treaty from Kültepe." *JCS* 57 (2005): 63–68.

Draffkorn, Anne E. "Was King Abba-AN of Yamḫad a Vizier for the King of Ḫattuša?" *JCS* 13 (1959): 94–97.

Driver, Samuel R. *A Critical and Exegetical Commentary on Deuteronomy*. ICC. Edinburgh: T&T Clark, 1895.
Droge, A. J. " 'The Lying Pen of the Scribes': Of Holy Books and Pious Frauds." *Method and Theory in the Study of Religion* 15 (2003): 117–47.
Dunn, James D. G., ed. *Paul and the Mosaic* Law. Grand Rapids: Eerdmans, 1994.
_____. *Romans*. WBC 38. Dallas: Word, 1988.
_____. "Romans." *DPL* 838–50.
_____. "Works of the Law and the Curse of the Law (Galatians 3:10–14)." *NTS* 31 (1985): 523–42.
Durand, Jean-Marie. "Fragments rejoints pour une histoire élamite." In *Fragmenta Historiae Elamicae: Mélanges offerts à M.-J. Stève*, edited by M. J. Stève, Leon de Meyer, H. Gasche, and F. Vallat, 111–28. Paris: Editions recherche sur les civilisations, 1986.
_____. *Les Documents épistolaires du palais de Mari, I*. LAPO 16. Paris: Editions du Cerf, 1997.
Dušek, Jan. *Aramaic and Hebrew Inscriptions from Mt. Gerizim and Samaria between Antiochus III and Antiochus IV Epiphanes*. CHANE 54. Leiden: Brill, 2012.
Eastman, Susan Grove. "Israel and the Mercy of God: A Re-reading of Galatians 6:16 and Romans 9–11." *NTS* 56 (2010): 367–95.
_____. *Recovering Paul's Mother Tongue: Language and Theology in Galatians*. Grand Rapids: Eerdmans, 2007.
Edel, Elmar. *Der Vertrag zwischen Ramses II. von Ägypten und Ḫattušili III. von Ḫatti*. WVDOG 95. Berlin: Gebr. Mann, 1997.
Eidem, Jesper. "Apum: A Kingdom on the Old Assyrian Route." In *Mesopotamia: the Old Assyrian Period*, edited by K. R. Veenhof, Jesper Eidem, and Markus Wäfler, 265–352. OBO 160. Göttingen: Vandenhoeck & Ruprecht, 2008.
_____. "An Old Assyrian Treaty from Tell Leilan." In *Marchands, diplomates et empereurs: Études sur la civilisation mésopotamienne offertes à Paul Garelli*, edited by Dominique Charpin, Francis Joannès, and Paul Garelli, 185–207. Paris: Editions recherche sur les civilisations, 1991.
_____. *The Royal Archives from Tell Leilan: Old Babylonian Letters and Treaties from the Lower Town Palace East*. Archaeological introduction by Lauren Ristvet and Harvey Weiss. PIHANS 117. Leiden: Nederlands Instituut voor het Nabije Oosten, 2011.
Eidevall, Göran. *Grapes in the Desert: Metaphors, Models, and Themes in Hosea 4–14*. ConBOT 43. Stockholm: Almqvist & Wiksell, 1996.
Eisenbaum, Pamela. *Paul Was Not a Christian: The Original Message of a Misunderstood Apostle*. New York: HarperOne, 2009.
Eissfeldt, Otto. "Gilgal or Shechem?" In *Proclamation and Presence: Old Testament Essays in Honour of Gwynne Henton Davies*, edited by John I. Durham and J. R. Porter, 90–101. Richmond, VA: John Knox, 1970.

_____. *The Old Testament: An Introduction.* Translated by Peter R. Ackroyd. New York: Harper & Row, 1965.

Elliott, Mark W., et al., eds. *Galatians and Christian Theology: Justification, the Gospel, and Ethics in Paul's Letter*. Grand Rapids: Baker Academic, 2014.

Erisman, Angela Roskop. "Transjordan in Deuteronomy: The Promised Land and the Formation of the Pentateuch." *JBL* 132 (2013): 769–89.

Evans, Craig A. "Paul and the Prophets: Prophetic Criticism in the Epistle to the Romans (with special reference to Romans 9–11)." In *Romans and the People of God: Essays in Honor of Gordon D. Fee on the Occasion of His 65th Birthday*, edited by Sven K. Soderlund and N. T. Wright, 115–28. Grand Rapids: Eerdmans, 1999.

Fales, Frederick Mario. "After Taʿyinat: The New Status of Esarhaddon's *adê* for Assyrian Political History." *RA* 106 (2012): 133–58.

Faust, Avraham. "The Bible, Archaeology, and the Practice of Circumcision in Israelite and Philistine Societies." *JBL* 134 (2015): 253–71.

Finkelstein, Israel. *The Archaeology of the Israelite Settlement.* Jerusalem: Israel Exploration Society, 1988.

_____. *The Forgotten Kingdom: The Archaeology and History of Northern Israel.* Atlanta: SBL Press, 2013.

Finsterbusch, Karin. *Weisung für Israel: Studien zu religiösem Lehren und Lernen im Deuteronomium und in seinem Umfeld.* FRLANT 44. Tübingen: Mohr Siebeck, 2005.

Firth, David G. "Passing on the Faith in Deuteronomy." In *Interpreting Deuteronomy: Issues and Approaches*, edited by David G. Firth and Philip S. Johnston, 157–76. Downers Grove, IL: InterVarsity Press, 2012.

Fishbane, Michael. *Biblical Interpretation in Ancient Israel.* Oxford: Clarendon, 1988.

_____. "The Hebrew Bible and Exegetical Tradition." In *Intertextuality in Ugarit and Israel*, edited by Johannes Cornelis de Moor, 15–30. *OtSt* 40. Leiden: Brill, 1998.

_____. "Inner Biblical Exegesis: Types and Strategies of Interpretation in Ancient Israel." In *Midrash and Literature*, 19–37. New Haven: Yale University Press, 1986.

_____. "Revelation and Tradition: Aspects of Inner-Biblical Exegesis." *JBL* 99 (1980): 343–61.

_____. "Types of Biblical Intertextuality." In *Congress Volume, Oslo 1998*, edited by André Lemaire and Magne Sæbø, 39–44. VTSup 80. Leiden: Brill, 2000.

Fitzmyer, Joseph A. *The Aramaic Inscriptions of Sefire*. 2nd rev. ed. BibOr 19/A. Rome: Pontifical Biblical Institute, 1995.

Fohrer, Georg. *Introduction to the Old Testament.* Translated by David Green. Nashville: Abingdon, 1968.

Fowler, Jeaneane D. *Theophoric Personal Names in Ancient Hebrew: A Comparative Study*. JSOTSup 49. Sheffield: Sheffield Academic, 1988.

Fox, Nili Sacher. *In the Service of the King: Officialdom in Ancient Israel and Judah.* HUCM 23. Cincinnati: Hebrew Union College Press, 2000.

Franken, H. G. "Archaeological Evidence Relating to the Interpretation of the Text." In *Aramaic Texts from Deir 'Alla,* edited by J. Hoftijzer and G. Van Der Kooij, 3–16. Documenta et Monumenta Orientis Antiqui. Leiden: Brill, 1976.

Frankena, Rintje. "The Vassal-Treaties of Esarhaddon and the Dating of Deuteronomy." *OtSt* 14 (1965): 122–54.

Fridrichsen, Anton. "Die Apologie des Paulus Gal 1." In *Exegetical Writings: A Selection,* edited by Chrys C. Caragounis and Tord Fornberg, 168–85. WUNT 76. Tübingen: Mohr Siebeck, 1994. Repr. of 1920 article.

Friedrich, Johannes. "Ein Bruchstück des Vertrages Mattiwaza-Suppiluliuma in hethitischer Sprache?" *AfO* 2 (1924): 119–24.

_____. *Staatsverträge des Ḫatti-Reiches in hethitischer Sprache I.* MVAG 31/1. Leipzig: Hinrichs, 1926.

_____. *Staatsverträge des Hatti-Reiches in hethitischer Sprache II.* MVAG 34/1. Leipzig: Hinrichs, 1930.

Fronzaroli, Pelio. *Testi di cancelleria: i rapporti con le città (Archivio L. 2769).* With collaboration by Amalia Catagnoti. ARES 13. Rome: Missione Archeologica Italiana in Siria, 2003.

Fuhrmann, Justin M. "Deuteronomy 6–8 and the History of Interpretation: An Exposition on the First Two Commandments." *JETS* 53 (2010): 37–63.

Gamoran, Hillel. "The Biblical Law against Loans and Interest." *JNES* 30 (1971): 127–34.

Gangloff, Frédéric. "A l'ombre des Déesses-arbres? (Os 4:12–14)." *BN* 106 (2001): 13–20.

Geller, Stephen A. "Fiery Wisdom: The Deuteronomic Tradition." In *Sacred Enigmas: Literary Religion in the Hebrew Bible,* 30–61. London: Routledge, 1996.

Genz, Hermann. "Foreign Contacts of the Hittites." In *Insights into Hittite History and Archaeology,* edited by Hermann Genz and Dirk Paul Mielke, 301–31. ColAnt 2. Leuven: Peeters, 2011.

Gese, Hartmut. "The Biblical View of Scripture." In *Essays on Biblical Theology,* 9–33. Minneapolis: Augsburg, 1981.

Gibson, John C. L. *Textbook of Syrian Semitic Inscriptions.* Vol. 1 of *Hebrew and Moabite Inscriptions.* Oxford: Clarendon, 1971.

Gilan, Amir. "Hittites in Canaan? The Archaeological Evidence." *BN* 156 (2013): 39–52.

Ginsberg, H. Louis. *The Israelian Heritage of Judaism.* New York: Stroock Publication Fund, 1982.

Gisin, Walter. *Das Buch Hosea.* Edition C. Bibelkommentar Altes Testament 37. Witten: SCM R. Brockhaus, 2014.

Glatt-Gilad, David A. "Revealed and Concealed: The Status of the Law (Book) of Moses within the Deuteronomistic History." In *Mishneh*

Todah: Studies in Deuteronomy and Its Cultural Environment in Honor of Jeffrey H. Tigay, edited by Nili Sacher Fox, David A. Glatt-Gilad, and Michael J. Williams, 185–99. Winona Lake, IN: Eisenbrauns, 2009.

Gomes de Araújo, Reginaldo. *Theologie der Wüste im Deuteronomium*. ÖBS 17. Frankfurt am Main: Lang, 1999.

Grayson, A. Kirk. "Akkadian Treaties of the Seventh Century B.C." *JCS* 39 (1987): 127–60.

______. *Assyrian Rulers of the Early First Millennium BC I (1114–859)*. RIMA 2. Toronto: University of Toronto Press, 1991.

Graziani, Simonetta. "Note sui Sibitti." *AION* 39 (1979): 673–90.

Greenberg, Moshe. "What Are Valid Criteria for Determining Inauthentic Matter in Ezekiel?" In *Ezekiel and His Book*, edited by Johann Lust, 123–35. BETL 74. Leuven: Leuven University Press, 1986.

Greengus, Samuel. "Covenant and Treaty in the Hebrew Bible and in the Ancient Near East." In *Ancient Israel's History: An Introduction to Issues and Sources*, edited by Bill T. Arnold and Richard S. Hess, 91–126. Grand Rapids: Baker Academic, 2014.

______. *Old Babylonian Tablets from Ishchali and Vicinity*. PIHANS 44. Istanbul: Nederlands Historisch-Archaeologisch Instituut, 1979.

Greer, Jonathan. *Dinner at Dan: Biblical and Archaeological Evidence for Sacred Feasts at Iron Age II Tel Dan and Their Significance*. CHANE 66. Boston: Brill, 2013.

Grisanti, Michael A. "Deuteronomy." In *The Expositor's Bible Commentary*, rev. ed., edited by Tremper Longman III and David Garland, 2:457–814. Grand Rapids: Zondervan, 2012.

Gröndahl, F. *Die Personennamen der Texte aus Ugarit*. StPohl 1. Rome: Biblical Institute, 1967.

Gropp, D. M., and T. J. Lewis. "Notes on Some Problems in the Aramaic Text of the Hadd-Yith'i Bilingual." *BASOR* 259 (1985): 46.

Guichard, Michaël. "Political Space—Local Political Structures in Northern Syria: The Case of the Country of Ida-Maraṣ in the Eighteenth Century BC." In *Constituent, Confederate, and Conquered Space: The Emergence of the Mittani State*, edited by Eva Cancik-Kirschbaum, Nicole Brisch, and Jesper Eidem, 147–60. Topoi: Berlin Studies of the Ancient World 17. Berlin: de Gruyter, 2014.

_____. "Un traité d'alliance entre Larsa, Uruk et Ešnunna contre Sabium de Babylone." *Sem* 56 (2014): 9–34.

Günbatti, Cahit. "Two Treaty Texts Found at Kültepe." In *Assyria and Beyond: Studies Presented to Mogens Trolle Larsen*, edited by Mogens Trolle Larsen and Jan Gerrit Dercksen, 249–64. Leiden: Nederlands Instituut voor het Nabije Oosten, 2004.

Guttmann, Michael. "The Term Foreigner (נָכְרִי) Historically Considered," *HUCA* 3 (1926): 1–20.

Hackett, JoAnn. *The Balaam Text from Deir ʿAllā*. HSM 31. Chico, CA: Scholars Press, 1984.

Hafemann, Scott J. *Paul, Moses, and the History of Israel: The Letter/Spirit Contrast and the Argument from Scripture in 2 Corinthians 3*. Paternoster Biblical Monographs. Milton Keynes: Paternoster, 2005.

Hallo, William W. "The Royal Inscriptions of Ur: A Typology." *HUCA* 33 (1962): 8.

Hallo, William W., and K. Lawson Younger Jr., eds. *Archival Documents from the Biblical World*. Vol. 3 of *The Context of Scripture*. Leiden: Brill, 2002.

_____, eds. *Monumental Inscriptions from the Biblical World*. Vol. 2 of *The Context of Scripture*. Leiden: Brill, 2000.

Halpern, Baruch. *The First Historians: The Hebrew Bible and History*. San Francisco: Harper & Row, 1988.

Handy, Lowell K. "Historical Probability and the Narrative of Josiah's Reform in 2 Kings." In *The Pitcher Is Broken: Memorial Essays for Gösta Ahlström*, edited by Steven W. Holloway and Lowell K. Handy, 252–75. JSOTSup 190. Sheffield: Sheffield Academic, 1995.

Haran, Menahem. "Midrashic and Literal Exegesis and the Critical Method in Biblical Research." In *Studies in Bible*, edited by Sara Japhet, 19–48. ScrHier 31. Jerusalem: Magnes, 1986.

______. *Temples and Temple Service in Ancient Israel: An Inquiry into Biblical Cult Phenomena and the Historical Setting of the Priestly School*. Oxford: Clarendon, 1978. Repr. Winona Lake, IN: Eisenbrauns, 1985.

Hardin, Justin. "Galatians 1–2 without a Mirror: Reflections on Paul's Conflict with the Agitators." *TynBul* 65 (2014): 275–303.

Hardmeier, Christof. "King Josiah in the Climax of the Deuteronomic History (2 Kings 22–23) and the Pre-Deuteronomic Document of a Cult Reform at the Place of Residence (23.4–15): Criticism of Sources, Reconstruction of Literary Pre-Stages and the Theology of History in 2 Kings 22–23." In *Good Kings and Bad Kings: The Kingdom of Judah in the Seventh Century BCE*, edited by Lester Grabbe, 123–63. LHBOTS 393. London: T&T Clark, 2005.

Harrison, R. K. *Introduction to the Old Testament, with a Comprehensive Review of Old Testament Studies and a Special Supplement on the Apocrypha*. Grand Rapids: Eerdmans, 1969.

Harrison, Timothy P., and James F. Osborne. "Building XVI and the Neo-Assyrian Sacred Precinct at Tell Tayinat." *JCS* 64 (2012): 125–43.

Harvey, Paul B., Jr., and Baruch Halpern. "W. M. L. De Wette's *'Dissertatio Critica . . .'*: Context and Translation." *ZABR* 14 (2008): 47–85.

Hawkins, John David. "Karkamiš." In *Corpus of Hieroglyphic Luwian Inscriptions*. Vol. 1, *Inscriptions from the Iron Age, Part 1: Text: Introduction, Karatepe, Karkamiš, Tell Ahmar, Maraş, Malatya, Commagene*, edited by Roberto Gusmani, Anna Morpurgo Davies, Klaus Strunk, and Calvert Watkins, 72–223. UISK 8.1. Berlin: de Gruyter, 2000.

Hawkins, Ralph K. *The Iron Age I Structure on Mt. Ebal: Excavation and Interpretation*. BBRSup 6. Winona Lake, IN: Eisenbrauns, 2012.

Hays, Richard B. *The Conversion of the Imagination: Paul as Interpreter of Israel's Scripture*. Grand Rapids: Eerdmans, 2005.

_____. "The Letter to the Galatians: Introduction, Commentary, and Reflections." *NIB* 11:181–348.

Hecker, Karl. *Grammatik der Kültepe-Texte*. AnOr 44. Rome: Pontifical Biblical Institute, 1968.

Heger, Paul. *The Three Biblical Altar Laws: Developments in the Sacrificial Cult in Practice and Theology: Political and Economic Background*. BZAW 279. Berlin: de Gruyter, 1999.

Heim, Knut Martin. *Poetic Imagination in Proverbs: Variant Repetitions and the Nature of Poetry*. BBRSup 4. Winona Lake, IN: Eisenbrauns, 2013.

Hengel, Martin, and Anna Maria Schwemer. *Paul between Damascus and Antioch: The Unknown Years*. Translated by J. Bowden. Louisville: Westminster John Knox, 1977.

Herr, Larry. Review of *The Iron Age I Structure on Mt. Ebal: Excavation and Interpretation*, by Ralph K. Hawkins. *BASOR* 371 (2014): 218–19.

Hess, Richard. *Israelite Religions: An Archaeological and Biblical Survey*. Grand Rapids: Baker Academic, 2007.

_____. *Joshua*. TOTC. Downers Grove, IL: InterVarsity, Press, 1996.

Hieke, Thomas. *Levitikus 16–27*. HThKAT. Freiburg im Bresgau: Herder, 2014.

Hill, Andrew E. "The Ebal Ceremony as Hebrew Land Grant?" *JETS* 31/4 (1988): 399–406.

Hillers, Delbert R. *Covenant: The History of a Biblical Idea*. Baltimore: Johns Hopkins University Press, 1969.

Hinke, William John. *Selected Babylonian kudurru Inscriptions*. SSS 14. Leiden: Brill, 1911.

Hoffner, Harry A. "Ancient Israel's Literary Heritage Compared with Hittite Textual Data." In *The Future of Biblical Archaeology: Reassessing Methodologies and Assumptions: The Proceedings of a Symposium, August 12–14, 2001 at Trinity International University*, edited by Alan R. Millard and James K. Hoffmeier, 176–92. Grand Rapids: Eerdmans, 2004.

_____. "Hittite-Israelite Cultural Parallels." In *Archival Documents from the Biblical World*, vol. 3 of *The Context of Scripture*, edited by William W. Hallo and K. Lawson Younger Jr., xxix-xxxiv. Leiden: Brill, 2002.

_____. "The Hittites and Hurrians." In *Peoples of Old Testament Times*, edited by D. J. Wiseman, 197–228. London: Oxford University Press, 1973.

Hoffner, Harry A., Hans G. Güterbock, and Theo P. J. van den Hout, eds. *The Hittite Dictionary of the Oriental Institute of the University of Chicago*. Chicago: The Oriental Institute, 1980–.

Holladay, William L. *Jeremiah 1: A Commentary on the Book of the Prophet Jeremiah, chapters 1–25*. Hermeneia. Philadelphia: Fortress, 1986.

_____. " 'On Every High Hill and under Every Green Tree.' " *VT* 11 (1961): 170–76.

Holloway, Steven W. "Review of E. Otto, *Das Deuteronomium: Politische Theologie und Rechtsreform in Juda und Assyrien*, BZAW 284 (de Gruyter, 1999)." *JNES* 66 (2007): 204–8.

Hölscher, Gustav. "Komposition und Ursprung des Deuteronomiums." *ZAW* 40 (1923): 161–255.

Holt, Else K. *Prophesying the Past: The Use of Israel's History in the Book of Hosea*. JSOTSup 194. Sheffield: Sheffield Academic, 1995.

Horwitz, Liora. "Faunal Remains from the Early Iron Age Site on Mt. Ebal." *TA* 14 (1987): 173–89.

Houtman, Cees. *Der Pentateuch: Die Geschichte seiner Erforschung neben einer Auswertung*. CBET 9. Kampen: Kok Pharos, 1994.

Howard, David M. *Joshua*. NAC. Nashville: Broadman & Holman, 1998.

Hubbard, Robert L. *Joshua*. NIVAC. Grand Rapids: Zondervan, 2009.

Huddleston, Neal A. "Deuteronomy as *Mischgattung*: A Comparative and Contrastive Discourse Analysis of Deuteronomy and Ancient Near Eastern Treaty Traditions." PhD diss., Trinity International University, 2015.

Huehnergard, J. "On the Etymology and Meaning of Hebrew *nābîʾ*." *ErIsr* 26 (1999): 88*–93*.

Hunziker-Rodewald, Regine. *Hirt und Herde: Ein Beitrag zum alttestamentlichen Gottesverständnis*. BWANT 155. Stuttgart: Kohlhammer, 2001.

Hur, Shin Wook. "The Rhetoric of the Deuteronomic Code: Its Structures and Devices." Ph.D. diss., Emory University, 2013.

Hutton, Jeremy M. *The Transjordanian Palimpsest: The Overwritten Texts of Personal Exile and Transformation in the Deuteronomistic History*. BZAW 396. Berlin: de Gruyter, 2009.

Hvalvik, Reidar. "Christ Proclaiming the Law to the Apostles: The *Traditio Legis*-Motif in Early Christian Art and Literature." In *The New Testament and Early Christian Literature in Greco-Roman Context*, edited by John Fotopoulos, 404–37. NovTSup 122. Leiden: Brill, 2006.

Hwang, Jerry. " 'I Am Yahweh Your God from the Land of Egypt': Hosea's Use of the Exodus Traditions." In *"Did I Not Bring Israel Out of Egypt?": Biblical, Archaeological, and Egyptological Perspectives on the Exodus Narratives*, edited by James K. Hoffmeier, Alan R. Millard, and Gary A. Rendsburg, 243–53. BBRSup 13. Winona Lake, IN: Eisenbrauns, 2016.

_____. *The Rhetoric of Remembrance: An Investigation of the "Fathers" in Deuteronomy*. Siphrut 8. Winona Lake, IN: Eisenbrauns, 2012.

Ikeda, Yutaka. "Solomon's Trade in Horses and Chariots in Its International Setting." In *Studies in the Period of David and Solomon and Other Essays*, edited by T. Ishida, 215–38. Winona Lake, IN: Eisenbrauns, 1982.

Jeremias, Jörg. *Der Prophet Hosea*. ATD 24/1. Göttingen: Vandenhoeck & Ruprecht, 1983.

_____. "Hosea/Hoseabuch." *TRE* 15 (1986): 586–98.

_____. "The Hosea Tradition and the Book of Jeremiah." *OTE* (1994): 21–38.

Jeshurun, Geo. "A Note on Hosea VIII, 12." *JSOR* 11 (1927): 222–24.

Joannès, Francis "La traité de vassalité d'Atamrum d'Andarig envers Zimri-Lim de Mari." In *Marchands, diplomates et empereurs: Études sur la civilisation mésopotamienne offertes à Paul Garelli*, edited by Dominique Charpin, Francis Joannès, and Paul Garelli, 167–78. Paris: Editions recherche sur les civilisations, 1991.

Joosten, Jan. *People and Land in the Holiness Code: An Exegetical Study of the Ideational Framework of the Law in Leviticus 17–26*. VTSup 67. Leiden: Brill, 1996.

Josephus. Translated by Henry St. J. Thackeray et al. 10 vols. LCL. Cambridge: Harvard University Press, 1926–1965.

Kaminsky, Joel S. *Corporate Responsibility in the Hebrew Bible*. JSOTSup 196. Sheffield: Sheffield Academic, 1995.

Kaufman, Stephen A. "Reflections on the Assyrian-Aramaic Bilingual from Tell Fakhariyeh." *Maarav* 3 (1982): 137–75.

_____. "The Temple Scroll and Higher Criticism." *HUCA* 53 (1982): 29–43.

Kawin, Bruce F. *Telling It Again and Again: Repetition in Literature and Film.* Boulder: University Press of Colorado, 1989.

Kempinski, Aharon. "Joshua's Altar—An Iron Age I Watchtower." *BAR* 12.1 (1986): 45.

Kempinski, Aharon, and Silvin Košak. "Der Išmeriga-Vertrag." *WO* 5 (1970): 191–217.

Kilchör, Benjamin. "The Direction of Dependence between the Laws of the Pentateuch: The Priority of a Literary Approach." *Ephemerides Theologicae Lovanienses* 89 (2013): 1–14.

_____. *Mosetora und Jahwetora: Das Verhältnis von Deuteronomium 12–26 zu Exodus, Levitikus und Numeri*. BZABR 21. Wiesbaden: Harrasowitz, 2015.

King, Philip J., and Lawrence E. Stager. *Life in Biblical Israel*. LAI. Louisville: Westminster John Knox, 2001.

Kitchen, Kenneth A. *Ancient Orient and Old Testament*. London: Tyndale, 1966.

_____. *The Bible in Its World: The Bible and Archaeology Today*. Exeter: Paternoster, 1977.

_____. "Egypt, Ugarit, Qatna and Covenant." *UF* 11 (1979): 453–64.

_____. "The Fall and Rise of Covenant, Law and Treaty." *TynBul* 40 (1989): 118–35.

_____. *On the Reliability of the Old Testament*. Grand Rapids: Eerdmans, 2003.

_____. *Ramesside Inscriptions, Translated and Annotated: Notes and Comments*, vol. 2, *Ramesses II, Royal Inscriptions*. Cambridge: Blackwell, 1999.

Kitchen, Kenneth A., and Paul J. N. Lawrence. *Treaty, Law and Covenant in the Ancient Near East—Part 1: The Texts*. Wiesbaden: Harrassowitz, 2012.

_____. *Treaty, Law and Covenant in the Ancient Near East—Part 2: Text, Notes and Chromograms*. Wiesbaden: Harrassowitz, 2012.

_____. *Treaty, Law and Covenant in the Ancient Near East—Part 3: Overall Historical Survey*. Wiesbaden: Harrassowitz, 2012.

Kitz, Anne Marie. *Cursed Are You! The Phenomenology of Cursing in Cuneiform and Hebrew Texts*. Winona Lake, IN: Eisenbrauns, 2014.

Klausern, Theodor. *Frühchristliche Sarkophage in Bild und Wort*. Beiheft zur Halbjahresschrift Antike Kunst 3. Olten: Urs Grav-Verlag, 1966.

Kleinert, Paul. *Das Deuteronomium und der Deuteronomiker: Untersuchungen zur alttestamentlichen Rechts- und Literaturgeschichte*. Bielefeld: Velhagen & Klasing, 1872.

Kline, Meredith G. *Treaty of the Great King*. Grand Rapids: Eerdmans, 1963.

Knight, Douglas A. *Rediscovering the Traditions of Israel: The Development of the Traditio-Historical Research of the Old Testament, with Special Consideration of Scandinavian Contributions*. SBLDS 9. Missoula, MT: Scholars Press, 1975.

Knoppers, Gary N. "The Deuteronomist and the Deuteronomic Law of the King: A Reexamination of a Relationship." *ZAW* 108 (1996): 329–46.

_____. *Jews and Samaritans: The Origins and History of Their Early Relations*. New York: Oxford University Press, 2013.

_____. "Mt. Gerizim and Mt. Zion: A Study in the Early History of the Samaritans and Jews." *SR* 34 (2005): 320.

_____. "Revisiting the Samarian Question in the Persian Period." In *Judah and the Judeans in the Persian Period*, edited by O. Lipshits and M. Oeming, 265–89. Winona Lake, IN: Eisenbrauns, 2006.

_____. "Treaty, Tribute List, or Diplomatic Letter: KTU 3.1 Reexamined." *BASOR* 289 (1993): 81–94.

Koch, Christoph. *Vertrag, Treueid und Bund: Studien zur Rezeption des altorientalischen Vertragsrechts im Deuteronomium und zur Ausbildung der Bundestheologie im Alten Testament*. BZAW 383. Berlin: de Gruyter, 2008.

Koch, Heidemarie. "Elams Vertrag mit dem akkadischen König Narām-Sîn." In *TUAT, Neue Folge Band 2: Staatsverträge, Herrscherinschriften und andere Dokumente zur politischen Geschichte*, edited by Bernd Janowski and Gernot Wilhelm, 283–87. Gütersloh: Gütersloher Verlagshaus, 2005.

Koehler, Ludwig, and Walter Baumgartner. *The Hebrew and Aramaic Lexicon of the Old Testament*. Rev. by Walter Baumgartner and Johann Jakob Stamm. Translated and edited by by M. E. J. Richardson. 1st Eng. ed. Leiden: Brill, 2001.

Koopmans, William T. *Joshua 24 as Poetic Narrative*. JSOTSup 93. Sheffield: JSOT Press, 1990.

Kosyan, Aram. "Arnuwandas I in the East." *Aramazd* 1 (2006): 72–97.

Krüger, Thomas. "Law and Wisdom according to Deut 4:5–8." In *Wisdom and Torah: The Reception of 'Torah' in the Wisdom Literature of the Second Temple Period*, edited by Bernd U. Schipper and D. Andrew Teeter, 35–54. JSJSup 163. Leiden: Brill, 2013.

Kübel, Paul. "Zum Aufbau von Dtn 28." *BN* 122 (2004): 5–9.

Kugler, Robert A. "The Deuteronomists and the Latter Prophets." In *Those Elusive Deuteronomists: The Phenomenon of Pan-Deuteronomism*, edited by Linda S. Schearing and Steven L. McKenzie, 127–44. JSOTSup 268. Sheffield: Sheffield Academic, 1999.

Kühne, Cord, and Heinrich Otten. *Der Šaušgamuwa-Vertrag: Eine Untersuchung zu Sprache und Graphik*. StBoT 16. Wiesbaden: Harrassowitz, 1971.

Lambert, Wilfred G. "H. U. Steymans, Deuteronomium 28 und die *adê* zur Thronfolgeregelung Asarhaddons." *AfO* 44–45 (1997–1998): 397.

_____. "A Vizier of Ḫattuša? A Further Comment." *JCS* 13 (1959): 132.

Lanham, Richard A. *A Handlist of Rhetorical Terms*. 2nd ed. Berkeley: University of California Press, 1991.

Laroche, Emmanuel. *Catalogue des textes hittites*. Études et commentaires 75. Paris: Klincksieck, 1971.

_____. "Fragments hittites du traité mitannien de Šuppiluliuma Ier." *Ugaritica* 6 (1969): 369–73.

Larsen, Timothy. "Defining and Locating Evangelicalism." In *The Cambridge Companion to Evangelical Theology*, edited by Timothy Larsen and Daniel J. Treier, 1–14. Cambridge: Cambridge University Press, 2007.

Lauinger, Jacob. "Esarhaddon's Succession Treaty at Tell Tayinat: Text and Commentary." *JCS* 64 (2012): 87–123.

_____. "Some Preliminary Thoughts on the Tablet Collection in Building XVI from Tell Tayinat." *CSMSJ* 6 (2011): 5–14.

Layton, S. C. *Archaic Features of Canaanite Personal Names in the Hebrew Bible*. HSM 47. Atlanta: Scholars Press, 1990.

Legaspi, Michael C. *The Death of Scripture and the Rise of Biblical Studies*. Oxford: Oxford University Press, 2010.

Leichty, Erle. *The Royal Inscriptions of Esarhaddon, King of Assyria (680–669 BC)*. RINAP 4. Winona Lake, IN: Eisenbrauns, 2011.

Lemaire, André. "Une inscription araméenne du VIIe siècle avant J.-C. trouvée à Bukân." *StIr* 27 (1998): 15–30.

Lenchak, Timothy A. *"Choose Life!" A Rhetorical-Critical Investigation of Deuteronomy 28,69–30,20*. AnBib 129. Rome: Pontifical Biblical Institute, 1993.

Leonard, Jeffery M. "Identifying Inner-Biblical Allusions: Psalm 78 as a Test Case." *JBL* 127 (2008): 241–65.

Levenson, Jon D. "The Eighth Principle of Judaism and the Literary Simultaneity of Scripture." In *The Hebrew Bible, the Old Testament, and*

Historical Criticism: Jews and Christians in Biblical Studies, 62–81. Louisville: Westminster John Knox, 1993.

_____. “Why Jews Are Not Interested in Biblical Theology.” In *The Hebrew Bible, the Old Testament, and Historical Criticism: Jews and Christians in Biblical Studies,* 33–61. Louisville: Westminster John Knox, 1993.

Levine, Baruch A. “Late Language in the Priestly Source: Some Literary and Historical Observations.” In *Proceedings of the Eighth World Congress of Jewish Studies: Bible Studies and Hebrew Language,* edited by David Krone, 69–82. Jerusalem: World Union of Jewish Studies, 1983.

Levinson, Bernard M. *Deuteronomy and the Hermeneutics of Legal Innovation.* Oxford: Oxford University Press, 1997.

_____. *Legal Revision and Religious Renewal in Ancient Israel.* New York: Cambridge University Press, 2008.

_____. “The Reconceptualization of Kingship in Deuteronomy and the Deuteronomic History’s Transformation of the Torah.” *VT* 51 (2001): 511–34.

_____. *“The Right Chorale”: Studies in Biblical Law and Interpretation.* FAT 54. Tübingen: Mohr Siebeck, 2008. Repr. Winona Lake, IN: Eisenbrauns, 2011.

Lieberman, S. *Prolegomena and Evidence.* Vol. 1 of *The Sumerian Loanwords in Old-Babylonian Akkadian.* HSS 22. Missoula, MT: Scholars Press, 1977.

Lierman, John. *The New Testament Moses: Christian Perceptions of Moses and Israel in the Setting of Jewish Religion.* WUNT 2/173. Tübingen: Mohr Siebeck, 2004.

Lincicum, David. *Paul and the Early Jewish Encounter with Deuteronomy.* WUNT 2/284. Tübingen: Mohr Siebeck, 2010.

Lohfink, Norbert. “The Cult Reform of Josiah of Judah: 2 Kings 22–23 as a Source for the History of Israelite Religion.” In *Ancient Israelite Religion: Essays in Honor of Frank Moore Cross,* edited by Patrick D. Miller, Paul D. Hanson, and S. Dean McBride, 459–75. Philadelphia: Fortress, 1987.

_____. *Das Hauptgebot: Eine Untersuchung literarischer Einleitungsfragen zu Dtn 5–11.* AnBib 20. Rome: Pontifical Biblical Institute, 1963.

_____. *Die Väter Israels im Deuteronomium.* OBO 111. Göttingen: Vandenhoeck & Ruprecht, 1991.

_____. “Distribution of the Functions of Power: The Laws Concerning Public Offices in Deuteronomy 16:18–18:22.” In *A Song of Power and the Power of Song: Essays on the Book of Deuteronomy,* edited by Duane L. Christensen, 336–52. SBTS 3. Winona Lake, IN: Eisenbrauns, 1993.

_____. “The Laws of Deuteronomy: A Utopian Project for a World Without Any Poor?” *ScrB* 26 (1996): 2–19.

_____. “Reading Deuteronomy 5 as Narrative.” In *A God So Near: Essays on Old Testament Theology in Honor of Patrick D. Miller,* edited by Brent A. Strawn and Nancy R. Bowen, 261–81. Winona Lake, IN: Eisenbrauns, 2003.

_____. "Recent Discussion on 2 Kings 22–23: The State of the Question." In *A Song of Power and the Power of Song: Essays on the Book of Deuteronomy*, edited by Duane L. Christensen, 36–61. SBTS 3. Winona Lake, IN: Eisenbrauns, 1993.

_____. *Studien zum Deuteronomium und zur deuteronomistischen Literatur, 5.* SBAB 38. Stuttgart: Katholisches Bibelwerk, 2005.

_____. "Was There a Deuteronomistic Movement?" In *Those Elusive Deuteronomists: The Phenomenon of Pan-Deuteronomism*, edited by Linda S. Schearing and Steven L. McKenzie, 36–66. JSOTSup 268. Sheffield: Sheffield Academic, 1999.

_____. "Zur Fabel des Deuteronomiums." In *Bundesdokument und Gesetz: Studien zum Deuteronomium*, edited by G. Braulik, 65–78. HBS 4. Freiburg im Breisgau: Herder, 1995.

Long, V. Philips. *The Art of Biblical History*. FCI 5. Grand Rapids: Zondervan, 1994.

Longacre, Robert E. "Complementarity: Verb Types and Discourse Types in Biblical Hebrew." In *LACUS Forum XXIX: Linguistics and the Real World*, edited by Douglas W. Coleman, William J. Sullivan, and Arle Lommel, 123–33. Houston: LACUS, 2003.

_____. *The Grammar of Discourse*. 2nd ed. Topics in Language and Linguistics. New York: Plenum, 1996.

Longacre, Robert E., and Shin Ja J. Hwang. *Holistic Discourse Analysis*. 2nd ed. Dallas: SIL International, 2012.

Longenecker, Richard N. *Galatians*. WBC 41. Nashville: Thomas Nelson, 1990.

Longman, Tremper, III, and Raymond Dillard. *Introduction to the Old Testament*. 2nd ed. Grand Rapids: Zondervan, 2006.

Loretz, Oswald, and Ingo Kottsieper. *Colometry in Ugaritic and Biblical Poetry: Introduction, Illustrations, and Topical Bibliography*. Altenberge: CIS-Verlag, 1987.

Lundbom, Jack R. *Biblical Rhetoric and Rhetorical Criticism*. HBM 45. Sheffield: Sheffield Phoenix, 2013.

_____. *Deuteronomy: A Commentary*. Grand Rapids: Eerdmans, 2013.

_____. *Jeremiah: A Study in Ancient Hebrew Rhetoric*. 2nd ed. Winona Lake, IN: Eisenbrauns, 1997.

Lyons, Michael A. *From Law to Prophecy: Ezekiel's Use of the Holiness Code.* LHBOTS 507. London: T&T Clark, 2009.

Machinist, Peter. "Akkadian in the First Millennium BC: The View from Israel and Other Western Outposts." Paper presented at the Annual Meeting of the SBL. New Orleans, LA, 23 November 2009.

_____. "The Epic of Tukulti-Ninurta I: A Study in Middle Assyrian Literature." PhD diss., Yale University, 1978.

Macintosh, A. A. *Hosea.* ICC. Edinburgh: T&T Clark, 1997.

Magen, Yitzhak. "Bells, Pendants, Snakes & Stones: A Samaritan Temple to the Lord on Mt. Gerizim." *BAR* 36.6 (2010): 24–26.

_____. "Gerizim, Mount." *NEAEHL* 2:484–92.
_____. "Gerizim, Mount." *NEAEHL* 5:1742–48.
_____. *Mount Gerizim Excavations II: A Temple City*. Jerusalem: Judea and Samaria Publications, 2008.
Magen, Yitzhak, et al. *The Mount Gerizim Excavations 1: The Aramaic, Hebrew and Samaritan Inscriptions*. Jerusalem: Judea and Samaria Publications, 2004.
Maier, Christel M. "Myth and Truth in Socio-Historical Reconstruction of Ancient Societies: Hosea 4:11–14 as a Test Case." In *Thus Says the Lord: Essays on the Former and Latter Prophets in Honor of Robert R. Wilson*, edited by John J. Ahn and Stephen L. Cook, 256–72. LHBOTS 502. New York: T&T Clark, 2009.
Maimonides. *Mishneh Torah: The Book of Adoration*. Translated by Moses Hyamson. Jerusalem: Feldheim, 1981.
Malamat, Abraham. " 'You Shall Love Your Neighbor as Yourself': A Case of Misinterpretation?" In *Die Hebräische Bibel und ihre Nachgeschichte*, edited by Erhard Blum, Christian Macholz, and Ekkehard W. Stegemann, 111–15. Rolf Rendtorff Festschrift. Neukirchen-Vluyn: Neukirchener Verlag, 1990.
Mankowski, Paul. *Akkadian Loanwords in Biblical Hebrew*. HSS 47. Winona Lake, IN: Eisenbrauns, 2000.
Manley, George T. *The Book of the Law: Studies in the Date of Deuteronomy*. London: Tyndale, 1957.
Martyn, J. Louis. "The Apocalyptic Gospel in Galatians." *Int* 54 (2000): 246–66.
_____. *Galatians: A New Translation with Introduction and Commentary*. AB 33A. New York: Doubleday, 1997.
Mason, Steven. "Jews, Judaeans, Judaizing, Judaism: Problems of Categorization in Ancient History." *JSJ* 38 (2007): 457–512.
Mayes, A. D. H. *Deuteronomy*. NCB. Grand Rapids: Eerdmans, 1979.
Mazar, Amihai. *Archaeology of the Land of the Bible*. Vol. 1, *10,000–586 B.C.E.* ABRL. New York: Doubleday, 1990.
_____. "Jerusalem and Its Vicinity in Iron Age I." In *From Nomadism to Monarchy: Archaeological & Historical Aspects of Early Israel*, edited by Israel Finkelstein and Nadav Na'aman, 70–91. Jerusalem: Israel Exploration Society, 1994.
_____. "Temples of the Middle and Late Bronze Ages and the Iron Age." In *The Architecture of Ancient Israel: From the Prehistoric to the Persian Periods*, edited by Aharon Kempinski and Ronny Reich, 169–73. Jerusalem: Israel Exploration Society, 1992.
McCarthy, Carmel. *Biblia Hebraica Quinta: Deuteronomy*. Stuttgart: Deutsche Bibelgesellschaft, 2007.
McCarthy, Dennis J. *Treaty and Covenant: A Study in Form in the Ancient Oriental Documents and in the Old Testament*. Rev. ed. AnBib 21. Rome: Pontifical Biblical Institute, 1981 [1963].

McClendon, Thomas H., Jr. "The Book of the Torah as a Gospel of Grace: A Synthesis of Daniel I. Block's Biblical Theology of Deuteronomy." In *For Our Good Always: Studies on the Message and Influence of Deuteronomy in Honor of Daniel I. Block*, edited by Jason S. DeRouchie, Jason Gile, and Kenneth J. Turner, 511–33. Winona Lake, IN: Eisenbrauns, 2013.

McComiskey, Thomas E. "Hosea." In *Hosea, Joel, and Amos*, edited by Thomas E. McComiskey, 1–238. Vol. 1 of *The Minor Prophets*. Grand Rapids: Baker, 1992.

McConville, J. G. *Deuteronomy*. ApOTC 5. Downers Grove, IL: InterVarsity Press, 2002.

_____. "Deuteronomy, Book of." In *Dictionary of the Old Testament: Pentateuch*, edited by T. Desmond Alexander and David W. Baker, 182–93. Downers Grove, IL: InterVarsity Press, 2003.

_____. *Grace in the End: A Study in Deuteronomic Theology*. SOTBT. Grand Rapids: Zondervan, 1993.

_____. "King and Messiah in Deuteronomy and the Deuteronomistic History." In *King and Messiah in Israel and the Ancient Near East: Proceedings of the Oxford Old Testament Seminar*, edited by John Day, 271–95. JSOTSup 270. Sheffield: Sheffield Academic, 1998.

_____. *Law and Theology in Deuteronomy*. JSOTSup 33. Sheffield: JSOT Press, 1984.

_____. "Time, Place and the Deuteronomic Altar-Law." In *Time and Place in Deuteronomy*, edited by J.G. McConville and J. G. Millar, 89–139. JSOTSup 179. Sheffield: Sheffield Academic, 1994.

McKenzie, Steven L. "Deuteronomistic History." *ABD* 2:161.

Meek, Russell L. "Intertextuality, Inner-Biblical Exegesis, and Inner-Biblical Allusion: The Ethics of a Methodology." *Bib* 95 (2014): 280–91.

Melchert, H. Craig. *Cuneiform Luvian Lexicon*. Lexica Anatolica 2. Chapel Hill: University of North Carolina Press, 1993.

Mendenhall, George E. "Covenant Forms in Israelite Tradition." *BA* 17 (1954): 50–76.

Merrill, Eugene H. *Deuteronomy*. NAC. Nashville: Broadman & Holman, 1994.

_____. "Deuteronomy and De Wette: A Fresh Look at a Fallacious Premise." *JESOT* 1 (2012): 25–42.

_____. "Deuteronomy and History: Anticipation of Reflection?" *Faith & Mission* 18 (2000): 57–76.

Meshel, Zeev. "Kuntillet 'Ajrud." *ABD* 4:103–9.

_____. "Kuntilat 'Ajrud, 1975–1976," *IEJ* 27 (1977): 52–53.

Metzger, Bruce M. "Literary Forgeries and Canonical Pseudepigrapha." *JBL* 91 (1972): 3–24.

Meyer, Gerhard R. "Zwei neue Kizzuwatna-Verträge." *MIOF* 1 (1953): 108–23.

Milgrom, Jacob. *Leviticus 1–16*. AB 3. New York: Doubleday, 1991.

_____. *Leviticus 17–22*. AB 3A. New York, NY: Doubleday, 2000.

_____. *Leviticus 23–27*. AB 3B. New York, NY: Doubleday, 2001.

Millar, J. G. "Living at the Place of Decision: Time and Place in the Framework of Deuteronomy." In *Time and Place in Deuteronomy*, edited by J. G. McConville and J. G. Millar, 15–88. JSOTSup 179. Sheffield: Sheffield Academic, 1994.

_____. *Now Choose Life: Theology and Ethics in Deuteronomy*. NSBT 6. Leicester: Apollos, 1998.

Millard, Alan R. "Hadad-Yithʿi (2.34)." In *Monumental Inscriptions from the Biblical World*, vol. 2 of *The Context of Scripture*, edited by William W. Hallo and K. Lawson Younger Jr., 153–54. Leiden: Brill, 2000.

_____. "The Tell Fekheriyeh Inscriptions." In *Biblical Archaeology Today, 1990: Proceedings of the Second International Congress on Biblical Archaeology*, 518–24. Jerusalem: Israel Exploration Society, 1993.

Miller, Patrick D. " 'Moses My Servant': The Deuteronomic Portrait of Moses." In *A Song of Power and the Power of Song: Essays on the Book of Deuteronomy*, edited by Duane L. Christensen, 301–12. SBTS 3. Winona Lake, IN: Eisenbrauns, 1993.

_____. "That the Children May Know: Children in Deuteronomy." In *The Child in the Bible*, edited by Marcia J. Bunge, Terence E. Fretheim, and Beverly Roberts Gaventa, 45–62. Grand Rapids: Eerdmans, 2008.

Moberly, Walter. *The Old Testament of the Old Testament: Patriarchal Narratives and Mosaic Yahwism*. Minneapolis: Augsburg, 1992.

_____. *Old Testament Theology: Reading the Hebrew Bible as Christian Scripture*. Grand Rapids: Baker, 2013.

Moffatt, Marian. "The Mystic Mill from Vézelay." In *A World History of Architecture*, edited by Michael Fazio, Marian Moffat, and Lawrence Wodehouse, 215–17. 2nd rev. ed. London: McGraw-Hill, 2008.

Mol, Jurrien. *Collective and Individual Responsibility: A Description of Corporate Personality in Ezekiel 18 and 20*. SSN 53. Leiden: Brill, 2009.

Moo, Douglas J. *Galatians*. BECNT. Grand Rapids: Baker, 2013.

Morrow, William S. "Tribute from Judah and the Transmission of Assyrian Propaganda." In *"My Spirit at Rest in the North Country" (Zechariah 6.8): Collected Communications to the XXth Congress of the International Organization for the Study of the Old Testament, Helsinki 2010*, edited by Hermann Michael Niemann and Matthias Augustin, 183–92. BEATAJ 57. New York: Peter Lang, 2011.

Müller, Karl Friedrich. *Das Assyrische Ritual*. MVAG 41.3. Leipzig: Hinrichs, 1937.

Müller, Reinhard. "The Blinded Eyes of the Wise: Sapiential Tradition and Mosaic Commandment in Deut 16:19–20." In *Wisdom and Torah: The Reception of 'Torah' in the Wisdom Literature of the Second Temple Period*, edited by Bernd U. Schipper and D. Andrew Teeter, 9–33. JSJSup 163. Leiden: Brill, 2013.

Murphy-O'Connor, Jerome. "Paul in Arabia." *CBQ* 55 (1993): 732–37.

Na'aman, Nadav. "The Growth and Development of Judah and Jerusalem in the 8th Century BCE: A Rejoinder." *RB* 116 (2009): 321–35.

Najman, Hindy. *Seconding Sinai: The Development of Mosaic Discourse in Second Temple Judaism.* JSJSup 77. Leiden: Brill, 2003.

Neef, Heinz-Dieter. *Die Heilstraditionen Israels in der Verkündigung des Propheten Hosea.* BZAW 169. Berlin: de Gruyter, 1987.

Nelson, Richard D. *Deuteronomy*. OTL. Louisville: Westminster John Knox, 2002.

_____. *The Double Redaction of the Deuteronomistic History*. JSOTSup 18. Sheffield: JSOT Press, 1981.

Nestle, Eberhard. "Das Deuteronomium und 2 Könige 22." *ZAW* 22 (1902): 312–13.

Neusner, Jacob. *A Rabbi Talks with Jesus*. Rev ed. Montreal: McGill-Queens University Press, 2000.

Newsom, Carol A. "Woman and the Discourse of Patriarchal Wisdom: A Study of Proverbs 1–9." In *Gender and Difference in Ancient Israel*, edited by Peggy L. Day, 142–60. Minneapolis: Fortress, 1989.

Nicholson, Ernest. W. *Deuteronomy and Tradition*. Philadelphia: Fortress, 1967.

_____. "Deuteronomy in Old Testament Research: A Brief Overview." In *Deuteronomy and the Judaean Diaspora*, 3–15. Oxford: Oxford University Press, 2014.

_____. " 'Do Not Dare to Set a Foreigner Over You': The King in Deuteronomy and 'The Great King.' " *ZAW* 118 (2006): 46–61.

Nicklas, Tobias. "Paulus—der Apostel als Prophet." In *Prophets and Prophecy in Jewish and Early Christian Literature*, edited by Joseph Verheyden, Korinna Zamfir, and Tobias Nicklas, 77–104. WUNT 2/286. Tübingen: Mohr Siebeck, 2010.

Niditch, Susan. *Oral World and Written Word: Ancient Israelite Literature*. LAI. Louisville: Westminster John Knox, 1996.

Nielsen, Eduard. *Deuteronomium*. HAT 1/6. Tübingen: Mohr Siebeck, 1995.

Nihan, Christophe. *From Priestly Torah to Pentateuch: A Study in the Composition of the Book of Leviticus*. FAT 2/25. Tübingen: Mohr Siebeck, 2007.

_____. "The Holiness Code between D and P—Some Comments on the Function and Significance of Leviticus 17–26 in the Composition of the Torah." In *Das Deuteronomium zwischen Pentateuch und Deuteronomistischem Geschichtswerk*, edited by E. Otto and R. Achenbach, 81–122. Göttingen: Vandenhoeck & Ruprecht, 2004.

_____. "The Torah Between Samaria and Judah." In *The Pentateuch as Torah: New Models for Understanding Its Promulgation and Acceptance*, edited by Gary N. Knoppers and Bernard M. Levinson, 187–254. Winona Lake, IN: Eisenbrauns, 2007.

Nissinen, Martti. *Prophetie, Redaktion und Fortschreibung im Hoseabuch: Studien zum Werdegang eines Prophetenbuches im Lichte von Hos 4 und 11*. AOAT 231. Kevelaer: Butzon & Bercker, 1991.

Noth, Martin. *The Chronicler's History*. JSOTSup 50. Sheffield: JSOT Press, 1987.

_____. *Das System der zwölf Stämme Israels*. BWANT. Stuttgart: Kohlhammer, 1930.

_____. *The Deuteronomistic History*. JSOTSup 15. Sheffield: JSOT Press, 1981.

_____. *Überlieferungsgeschichtliche Studien*. 2nd ed. Tübingen: Niemeyer, 1957.

Nougayrol, Jean. *Le palais royal d'Ugarit IV: Textes accadiens des archives sud*. Edited by Claude F. A. Schaeffer. 2 vols. MRS IX. Paris: Imprimerie nationale and Librairie C. Klincksieck, 1956.

Novenson, Matthew V. "Paul's Former Occupation in *Ioudaismos*." In *Galatians and Christian Theology*, edited by Mark W. Elliott et al., 24–39. Grand Rapids: Baker, 2014.

O'Brien, Mark A. "The Book of Deuteronomy." *CurBS* 3 (1995): 95–128.

Olson, Dennis T. *The Death of the Old and the Birth of the New: The Framework of the Book of Numbers and the Pentateuch*. BJS 71. Chico, CA: Scholars Press, 1985.

_____. *Deuteronomy and the Death of Moses: A Theological Reading*. OBT. Minneapolis: Fortress, 1994.

_____. "How Does Deuteronomy Do Theology? Literary Juxtaposition and Paradox in the New Moab Covenant in Deuteronomy 29–32." In *A God So Near: Essays on Old Testament Theology in Honor of Patrick D. Miller*, edited by Brent A. Strawn and Nancy R. Bowen, 201–13. Winona Lake, IN: Eisenbrauns, 2003.

Oppenheim, A. Leo. *Ancient Mesopotamia: Portrait of a Dead Civilization*. Rev. ed. Chicago: University of Chicago Press, 1977.

Orr, James. *The Problem of the Old Testament Considered with Reference to Recent Criticism*. New York: Scribner's, 1906.

Otten, Heinrich. *Die Bronzetafel aus Boğazköy: Ein Staatsvertrag Tutḫalijas IV*. StBoTB 1. Wiesbaden: Harrassowitz, 1988.

_____. "Ein althethitischer Vertrag mit Kizzuvatna." *JCS* 5 (1951): 129–32.

_____. "Neue Quellen zum Ausklang des Hethitischen Reiches." *MDOG* 94 (1963): 1–23.

Otto, Eckart. "Das Deuteronomium als archimedischer Punkt der Pentateuchkritik: Auf dem Wege zu einer Neubegründung der de Wette'schen Hypothese." In *Deuteronomy and Deuteronomic Literature: Festschrift C. H. W. Brekelmans*, edited by M. Vervenne and J. Lust, 321–40. BETL 133. Leuven: Peeters, 1997.

_____. "Das Heiligkeitsgesetz Leviticus 17–26 in der Pentateuchredaktion." In *Altes Testament—Forschung und Wirkung: Festschrift für Henning Graf Reventlow*, edited by P. Mommer and W. Thiel, 65–80. Frankfurt am Main: Lang, 1994.

_____. *Deuteronomium 1–11: Erster Teilband: 1,1–4,43*. HThKAT. Freiburg im Breisgau: Herder, 2012.

_____. "Innerbiblische Exegese im Heiligkeitsgesetz Levitikus 17–26." In *Levitikus als Buch*, edited by H. J. Fabry and H. W. Jüngling, 125–96. Berlin: Philo, 1999.

_____. "Mose, der erste Schriftgelehrte: Deuteronomium 1,5 in der Fabel des Pentateuch." In *L'Écrit et L'Esprit: Études d'histoire du texte et de théologie biblique en hommage à Adrian Schenker*, edited by Dieter Böhler, Innocent Himbaza, and Philippe Hugo, 273–84. OBO 214. Fribourg: Academic Press, 2005.

Pardee, Dennis. "Le traité d'alliance RS 11.772+." *Sem* 51 (2003): 5–31.

_____. "A New Aramaic Inscription from Zincirli." *BASOR* 356 (2009): 51–71.

_____. Review of *The Three Biblical Altar Laws: Developments in the Sacrificial Cult in Practice and Theology, Political and Economic Background*, by Paul Heger. *JNES* 65 (2006): 296–303.

Parpola, Simo. "International Law in the First Millennium." In *A History of Ancient Near Eastern Law*, edited by Raymond Westbrook, 1047–66. HdO I/72. Leiden: Brill, 2003.

_____. "A Letter from Marduk-apla-uṣur of Anah to Rudamu/Urtamis, King of Hamath." In *Hama: Fouilles et recherches de la Fondation Carlsberg, II 2: Les objets de la période dite Syro-Hittite*, edited by P. J. Riis and Marie-Louise Buhl, 257–65. Copenhagen: Nationalmuseet, 1990.

Parpola, Simo, and Kazuko Watanabe. *Neo-Assyrian Treaties and Loyalty Oaths*. SAA 2. Helsinki: Helsinki University Press, 1988.

Patzia, Arthur G., and Anthony J. Petrotta. *Pocket Dictionary of Biblical Studies*. Downers Grove, IL: InterVarsity Press, 2002.

Perelman, Chaïm, and L. Olbrechts-Tyteca. *The New Rhetoric: A Treatise on Argumentation*. Translated by John Wilkinson and Purcell Weaver. Notre Dame: University of Notre Dame Press, 1969. Translation of *Traité de l'argumentation*. Paris: Presses universitaires de France, 1958.

Peterson, Brian N. *The Authors of the Deuteronomistic History: Locating a Tradition in Ancient Israel*. Minneapolis: Fortress, 2014.

Pfeiffer, Henrik. *Das Heiligtum von Bethel im Spiegel des Hoseabuches*. FRLANT 183. Göttingen: Vandenhoeck & Ruprecht, 1999.

Polzin, Robert. "Deuteronomy." In *The Literary Guide to the Bible*, edited by Robert Alter and Frank Kermode, 92–101. Cambridge: Belknap, 1987.

_____. *Moses and the Deuteronomist: A Literary Study of the Deuteronomistic History. Part 1: Deuteronomy, Joshua, Judges*. New York: Seabury, 1980.

Ponchia, Simonetta. "The Neo-Assyrian *adê* Protocol and the Administration of the Empire." In *From Source to History: Studies on Ancient Near Eastern Worlds and Beyond*, edited by Salvatore Gaspa, Alessandro Greco, Daniele Morandi Bonacossi, Simonetta Ponchia, and Robert Rollinger, 501–25. AOAT 412. Münster: Ugarit-Verlag, 2014.

Pummer, Reinhard. *The Samaritans*. Leiden: Brill, 1987.

_____. "The Samaritans: A Jewish Offshoot or a Pagan Cult?" *BRev* 7 (1991): 22–29, 40.

Rabin, Chaim. "Discourse Analysis and the Dating of Deuteronomy." In *Interpreting the Hebrew Bible: Essays in Honour of E. I. J. Rosenthal,* edited by J. A. Emerton and Stefan C. Reif, 171–77. UCOP 32. Cambridge: Cambridge University Press, 1982.

Radner, Karen. "Assyrische *ṭuppi adê* als Vorbild für Deuteronomium 28,20–44?" In *Die deuteronomistischen Geschichtswerke: Redaktions- und religionsgeschichtliche Perspektiven zur "Deuteronomismus"-Diskussion in Tora und Vorderen Propheten,* edited by Markus Witte, Konrad Schmid, Doris Prechel, and Jan Christian Gertz, 351–78. BZAW 365. Berlin: de Gruyter, 2006.

Rahlfs, A., ed. *Septuaginta.* Stuttgart: Württembergische Bibelanstalt, 1935.

Reed, Annette Yoshiko. "The Modern Invention of 'Old Testament Pseudepigrapha.' " *JTS* 60 (2009): 403–36.

Reichmuth, Silvio. "Mita von Pahhuwa (*CTH* 146)." In *Hethitologie in Dresden: Textbearbeitungen, Arbeiten zur Forschungs- und Schriftgeschichte,* edited by Robert Fischer, Detlev Groddek, and Henning Marquardt, 109–44. DBH 35. Wiesbaden: Harrassowitz, 2011.

Reiterer, Friedrich Vinzenz. "Du sollst den Fremden lieben wie Dich selbst (Lev 19,34)." In *Die Fremden,* edited by G. Bachl, 67–99. Regensburg: Transfer, 1993.

Rengstorf, K. H. "ἀποστέλλω." *TDNT* 1:398–447.

_____. "δοῦλος." *TDNT* 2:261–80.

Richter, Sandra L. "Deuteronomistic History." In *Dictionary of the Old Testament: Historical Books,* edited by Bill T. Arnold and H. G. M. Williamson, 219–30. Downers Grove, IL: InterVarsity Press, 2005.

_____. *The Deuteronomistic History and the Name Theology:* lᵉšakkēn šᵉmô šām *in the Bible and the Ancient Near East.* BZAW 318. Berlin: de Gruyter, 2002.

_____. "The Place of the Name in Deuteronomy." *VT* 57 (2007): 342–66.

_____. "The Quest for a Core: Law and Social Location." Paper presented at the Annual Meeting of the SBL. San Diego, CA, 20 November 2014.

Robinson, H. Wheeler. *Corporate Personality in Ancient Israel.* Philadelphia: Fortress, 1964.

Robson, James. "The Literary Composition of Deuteronomy." In *Interpreting Deuteronomy: Issues and Approaches,* edited by David G. Firth and Philip S. Johnston, 19–59. Downers Grove, IL: InterVarsity Press, 2012.

Rofé, Alexander. "The Book of Deuteronomy: A Summary." In *Deuteronomy: Issues and Interpretation,* 206–16. OTS. London: T&T Clark, 2002.

Rogerson, John W. *W. M. L. de Wette: Founder of Modern Biblical Criticism—An Intellectual Biography.* JSOTSup 126. Sheffield: Sheffield Academic, 1992.

Rollston, Christopher A. “Scribal Curriculum during the First Temple Period: Epigraphic Hebrew and Biblical Evidence.” In *Contextualizing Israel’s Sacred Writings: Ancient Literacy, Orality, and Literary Production*, edited by Brian B. Schmidt, 71–101. SBLAIL 22. Atlanta: SBL Press, 2015.

Römer, Thomas. “Deuteronomy in Search of Origins.” In *Reconsidering Israel and Judah: Recent Studies on the Deuteronomistic History*, edited by Gary N. Knoppers and J. G. McConville, 112–38. Winona Lake, IN: Eisenbrauns, 2000.

______. *Israels Väter: Untersuchungen zur Väterthematik im Deuteronomium und in der deuteronomistischen Tradition*. OBO 99. Göttingen: Vandenhoeck & Ruprecht, 1990.

______. *The So-Called Deuteronomistic History: A Sociological, Historical, and Literary Introduction*. London: T&T Clark, 2005.

Römer, Thomas, and Albert de Pury. “Deuteronomistic Historiography (DH): History of Research and Debated Issues.” In *Israel Constructs Its History: Deuteronomistic Historiography in Recent Research*, edited by A. de Pury, Thomas Römer, and Jean-Daniel Macchi, 24–141. JSOTSup 306. Sheffield: Sheffield Academic, 2000.

Rooker, Mark F. “The Use of the Old Testament in the Book of Hosea.” *CTR* 7 (1993): 51–66.

Roth, Martha T. *Law Collections from Mesopotamia and Asia Minor*. Atlanta: Scholars Press, 1995.

Rowley, H. H. *Men of God: Studies in Old Testament History and Prophecy*. London: Nelson, 1963.

Rubin, Aaron D. *Studies in Semitic Grammaticalization*. HSS 57. Winona Lake, IN: Eisenbrauns, 2005.

Rüterswörden, Udo. *Deuteronomium 12,1–26,19*. BKAT 5/3 fasc. 1. Neukirchen-Vluyn: Neukirchener Verlag, 2011.

______. “Moses’ Last Day.” In *Moses in Biblical and Extra-Biblical Traditions*, edited by Axel Graupner and Michael Wolter, 51–59. BZAW 372. Berlin: de Gruyter, 2007.

Sailhamer, John. *Introduction to Old Testament Theology: A Canonical Approach*. Grand Rapids: Zondervan, 1999.

Salazar, J. M. Gonzáles. “Tiliura, un ejemplo de la politica fronteriza durante el imperio hitita (*CTH* 89).” *AuOr* 12 (1994): 159–76.

Sanders, E. P. *Paul, the Law, and the Jewish People*. Philadelphia: Fortress, 1983.

Sandnes, Karl Olav. *Paul—One of the Prophets?* WUNT 2/43. Tübingen: Mohr Siebeck, 1991.

Sarna, Nahum M. *Exodus*. JPS Torah Commentary. Philadelphia: Jewish Publication Society of America, 1991.

Sasson, Jack. “Circumcision in the Ancient Near East.” *JBL* 85 (1966): 473–76.

Schaper, Joachim. “The ‘Publication’ of Legal Texts in Ancient Judah.” In *The Pentateuch as Torah: New Models for Understanding its Promulgation and Acceptance*, edited by Gary N. Knoppers and Bernard M. Levinson, 225–36. Winona Lake, IN: Eisenbrauns, 2007.

Schnabel, Eckhard J. *Early Christian Mission*. Vol. 2, *Paul and the Early Church*. Downers Grove, IL: InterVarsity Press, 2004.

Schniedewind, William M. *How the Bible Became a Book: The Textualization of Ancient Israel*. New York: Cambridge University Press, 2004.

Schreiner, Thomas R. "Circumcision." *DPL* 137–39.

_____. *Galatians*. BECNT. Grand Rapids: Zondervan, 2010.

Schultz, Richard L. "Isaianic Intertextuality and Intratextuality as Composition-Historical Indicators: Methodological Challenges in Determining Literary Influence." In *Bind Up the Testimony: Explorations in the Genesis of the Book of Isaiah*, edited by Daniel I. Block and Richard L. Schultz, 33–63. Peabody, MA: Hendrickson, 2015.

_____. *The Search for Quotation: Verbal Parallels in the Prophets*. JSOTSup 180. Sheffield: Sheffield Academic, 1999.

Schulz-Rauch, Martin. *Hosea und Jeremia: Zur Wirkungsgeschichte des Hoseabuches*. Calwer Theologische Monographien. Reihe A: Bibelwissenschaft 16. Stuttgart: Calwer, 1996.

Schütte, Wolfgang. "Die Entstehung der juda-exilischen Hoseaschrift." *Bib* 95 (2014): 198–223.

Schwartz, Baruch. Review of *The Three Biblical Altar Laws: Developments in the Sacrificial Cult in Practice and Theology, Political and Economic Background*, by Paul Heger. *CBQ* 63 (2001): 112–14.

Schwemer, Daniel. "The Storm-Gods of the Ancient Near East: Summary, Synthesis, Recent Studies (Part 1)." *JANER* 7 (2007): 121–68.

Scurlock, JoAnn, and Burton R. Andersen. *Diagnoses in Assyrian and Babylonian Medicine: Ancient Sources, Translations, and Modern Medical Analyses*. Urbana: University of Illinois Press, 2005.

Segal, Alan F. *Paul the Convert: The Apostolate and Apostasy of Saul the Pharisee*. New Haven: Yale University Press, 1990.

Sheppard, Gerald T. *Wisdom as a Hermeneutical Construct: The Sapientializing of the Old Testament*. BZAW 151. Berlin: de Gruyter, 1980.

Silva, Moisés. "Old Princeton, Westminster, and Inerrancy." *WTJ* 50 (1988): 65–80.

Silva, Moisés, ed. "ἀποστέλλω (*apostellō*), to send . . . "ἀπόστολος (*apostolos*), envoy, ambassador, apostle. . . ." *NIDNTTE* 1:365–76.

Singer, Itamar. "The Hittites and the Bible Revisited." In *"I Will Speak the Riddles of Ancient Times": Archaeological and Historical Studies in Honor of Amihai Mazar on the Occasion of His Sixtieth Birthday*, edited by Aren M. Maeir and Pierre de Miroschedji, 723–56. Winona Lake, IN: Eisenbrauns, 2006.

_____. "The Kuruštama Treaty Revisited." In Šarnikzel: *Hethitologische Studien zum Gedenkenan an Emil Orgetorix Forrer (19.02.1894—10.01.1986)*, edited by Detlev Groddek and Sylvester Rößle, 591–607. DBH 10. Dresden: Technische Universität, 2004.

Ska, Jean Louis. "La structure du Pentateuque dans sa forme canonique." *ZAW* 113 (2001): 331–52.

Smend, Rudolf. *Die Entstehung des Alten Testaments*. Theologische Wissenschaft 1. Stuttgart: Kohlhammer, 1978.

_____. "Ein Theologe zwischen den Fronten." In *Wilhelm Martin Leberecht de Wette. Ein Universaltheologe des 19. Jahrhunderts*, edited by H. P. Mathys and K. Seybold, 11–29. Studien zur Geschichte der Wissenschaften in Basel, Neue Folge 1. Basel: Schwabe, 2001.

_____. *From Astruc to Zimmerli: Old Testament Scholarship in Three Centuries*. Translated by Margaret Kohl. Tübingen: Mohr Siebeck, 2007.

_____. "The Law and the Nations: A Contribution to Deuteronomistic Tradition History." In *Reconsidering Israel and Judah: Recent Studies on the Deuteronomistic History*, edited by Gary N. Knoppers and J. Gordon McConville, 95–110. Winona Lake, IN: Eisenbrauns, 2000.

Smith, Christian, and Melinda Lundquist Denton. *Soul Searching: The Religious and Spiritual Lives of American Teenagers*. Oxford: Oxford University Press, 2005.

Smith, G. A. *The Historical Geography of the Holy Land, Especially in Relation to the History of Israel and of the Early Church*. New York: George H. Doron, 1920.

Smith, Gregory S. *The Testing of God's Sons: The Refining of Faith as a Biblical Theme*. Nashville: Broadman & Holman, 2014.

Smith, Mark S., ed. *The Ugaritic Baal Cycle*. Vol. 1, *Introduction, with Text, Translation and Commentary of KTU 1.1–1.2*. VTSup 55. Leiden: Brill, 1994.

Smith, Morton. "Pseudepigraphy in the Israelite Literary Tradition." In *Pseudepigrapha I*, edited by Kurt von Fritz, 191–227. Entretiens sur l'Antiquité classique 18. Vandoeuvres-Genève: Fondation Hardt, 1972.

Soggin, J. Alberto. "The Migdal Temple, Migdal Šᵉkem Judg 9 and the Artifact on Mount Ebal." In *Wünschet Jerusalem Frieden: Collected Communications of the XIIth Congress of the International Organization for the Study of the Old Testament, Jerusalem, 1986*, edited by Matthias Augustin and Klaus D. Schunk, 115–19. BEATAJ 13. Frankfurt am Main: Lang, 1988.

Sommer, Benjamin D. *A Prophet Reads Scripture: Allusion in Isaiah 40–66*. Stanford: Stanford University Press, 1998.

Sonnet, Jean-Pierre. *The Book within the Book: Writing in Deuteronomy*. BibInt 14. Leiden: Brill, 1997.

_____. "De Moïse et du narrateur: pour une pensée narrative de l'inspiration." *RSR* 93 (2005): 517–31.

Soulen, Richard N., and R. Kendall Soulen. *Handbook of Biblical Criticism*. 4th ed. Louisville: Westminster John Knox, 2011.

Spalinger, Anthony. "Considerations on the Hittite Treaty between Egypt and Hatti." *SAK* 9 (1981): 299–358.

Sparks, Kenton L. *God's Word in Human Words: An Evangelical Appropriation of Critical Biblical Scholarship.* Grand Rapids: Baker Academic, 2008.

Speiser, E. A. *Genesis: Introduction, Translation, and Notes.* AB 1. Garden City, NY: Doubleday, 1964.

Spencer, James. "Remembering Sabbath: An Application of Sociological Method in the Exposition of the Old Testament." PhD diss., Trinity Evangelical Divinity School, 2011.

Sperber, Shmuel. "השפעת ספר דברים על הושע [The Influence of the Book of Deuteronomy on Hosea]." *Melilah* 1 (1944): 205–31.

Spinoza, Benedict de. *Theological-Political Treatise,* edited by Jonathan Israel. Translated by Michael Silverthorne and Jonathan Israel. Cambridge Texts in the History of Philosophy. Cambridge: Cambridge University Press, 2007.

Spiqc, C. "δοῦλος." *TLNT* 1:380–86.

Stackert, Jeffrey. "The Holiness Code." In *The Oxford Encyclopedia of the Bible and Law,* edited by Brent Strawn, 1:389–96. Oxford: Oxford University Press, 2015.

______. *Rewriting the Torah: Literary Revision in Deuteronomy & the Holiness Legislation.* FAT 2/52. Tübingen: Mohr Siebeck, 2007.

Stager, Lawrence. "The Fortress-Temple at Shechem and the 'House of El, Lord of the Covenant.' " In *Realia Dei: Essays in Archaeology and Biblical Interpretation in Honor of Edward F. Campbell Jr. at His Retirement,* edited by Prescott H. Williams Jr. and Theodore Hiebert, 228–49. Atlanta: Scholars Press, 1999.

Stark, Christine.*"Kultprostitution" im Alten Testament? Die Qedeschen der hebräischen Bibel und das Motiv der Hurerei.* OBO 221. Fribourg: Academic Press, 2006.

Stead, Michael R. *The Intertextuality of Zechariah 1–8.* LHBOTS 508. New York: T&T Clark, 2009.

Steiner, Gerd. "Neue Alašija-Texte." *Kadmos* 1 (1962): 130–38.

Steinmetz, David C. "The Superiority of Pre-Critical Exegesis." In *The Theological Interpretation of Scripture: Classic and Contemporary Readings,* edited by Stephen E. Fowl, 26–38. Malden: Blackwell, 1997.

Stendahl, Krister. *Paul among Jews and Gentiles.* Philadelphia: Fortress, 1976.

Stern, Ephraim. *Archaeology of the Land of the Bible.* Vol. 2, *The Assyrian, Babylonian, and Persian Periods (732–332 B.C.E.).* New York: Doubleday, 2001.

Sternberg, Meir. *The Poetics of Biblical Narrative: Ideological Literature and the Drama of Reading.* ISBL. Bloomington: Indiana University Press, 1985.

Stewart, David T. "Leviticus 19 as Mini-Torah." In *Current Issues in Priestly and Related Literature: The Legacy of Jacob Milgrom and Beyond,* edited by Roy E. Gane and Ada Taggar-Cohen, 299–323. RBS 82. Atlanta: SBL Press, 2015.

Steymans, Hans Ulrich. *Deuteronomium 28 und die* adê *zur Thronfolgeregelung Asarhaddons: Segen und Fluch im Alten Orient und in Israel*. OBO 145. Göttingen: Vandenhoeck & Ruprecht, 1995.

_____. "Eine assyrische Vorlage für Deuteronomium 28,20–44." In *Bundesdokument und Gesetz: Studien zum Deuteronomium*, edited by Georg Braulik, 118–41. HBS 4. Freiburg im Breisgau: Herder, 1995.

Stipp, Hermann-Josef. "Die Qedešen im Alten Testament." In *Die Erzväter in der biblischen Tradition: Festschrift für Matthias Köckert*, edited by Anselm C. Hagedorn and Henrik Pfeiffer, 209–40. BZAW 400. Berlin: de Gruyter, 2009.

Stone, Lawson G. "Redaction Criticism, OT." *NIDB* 4:752–53.

_____. "Redaction Criticism: Whence, Whither, and Why? Or, Going beyond Source and Form Criticism without Leaving them Behind." In *A Biblical Itinerary: In Search of Method, Form, and Content, Essays in Honor of George W. Coats*, edited by Eugene E. Carpenter, 77–90. JSOTSup 240. Sheffield: Sheffield Academic, 1997.

Strawn, Brent A. "Deuteronomy." In *Theological Bible Commentary*, edited by Gail R. O'Day and David L. Petersen, 63–76. Louisville: Westminster John Knox, 2009.

_____. "Deuteronomy." In *The Wesley Study Bible: NRSV*, 213–62. Nashville: Abingdon, 2009.

_____ "Keep/Observe/Do—Carefully—Today! The Rhetoric of Repetition in Deuteronomy." In *A God So Near: Essays on Old Testament Theology in Honor of Patrick D. Miller*, edited by Brent A. Strawn and Nancy R. Bowen, 215–40. Winona Lake, IN: Eisenbrauns, 2003.

_____. *The Old Testament Is Dying: A Diagnosis and Recommended Treatment*. Grand Rapids: Baker Academic, 2017.

Streck, Michael P. "Die Flüche im Sukzessionsvertrag Asarhaddons." *ZABR* 4 (1998): 165–91.

Stuart, Douglas. *Hosea–Jonah*. WBC 31. Waco, TX: Word, 1987.

Sweeney, Marvin A. "The Critique of Solomon in the Josianic Edition of the Deuteronomistic History." *JBL* 114 (1995): 607–22.

_____. *King Josiah of Judah: The Lost Messiah of Israel*. Oxford: Oxford University Press, 2001.

Talmon, Shemaryahu. "The Textual Study of the Bible—A New Outlook." In *Qumran and the History of the Biblical Text*, edited by Frank Moore Cross and Shemaryahu Talmon, 321–400. Cambridge: Harvard University Press, 1975.

Thiel, Winfried. *Die soziale Entwicklung Israels in vorstaatlicher Zeit*. Neukirchen-Vluyn: Neukirchener Verlag, 1980.

Thiessen, Matthew. *Contesting Conversion: Genealogy, Circumcision, and Identity in Ancient Judaism and Christianity*. Oxford: Oxford University Press, 2011.

Thompson, John A. *The Ancient Near Eastern Treaties and the Old Testament*. London: Tyndale, 1964.

_____. *Deuteronomy: An Introduction and Commentary*. TOTC. London: Inter-Varsity Press, 1974.

Tigay, Jeffrey H. *Deuteronomy*, דברים. Philadelphia: Jewish Publication Society of America, 1996.

_____. *Empirical Models for Biblical Criticism*. Philadelphia: University of Pennsylvania Press, 1985.

_____. *The Evolution of the Gilgamesh Epic*. Philadelphia: University of Pennsylvania Press, 1982.

Tillich, Paul. *The Eternal Now*. New York: Scribner's, 1963.

Torri, Giulia. "Militärische Feldzüge nach Ostanatolien in der mittelhethitischen Zeit." *AoF* 32 (2005): 386–400.

Tov, Emmanuel. "Reflections on the Septuagint with Special Attention Paid to the Post-Pentateuchal Translations." In *Die Septuaginta: Texte, Theologien, Einflüsse*, edited by Wolfgang Kraus, Martin Karrer, and Martin Meiser, 3–22. WUNT 252. Tübingen: Mohr Siebeck, 2010.

_____. *Textual Criticism of the Hebrew Bible*. Minneapolis: Fortress, 1992.

Tromp, Johannes. *The Assumption of Moses: A Critical Edition with Commentary*. Leiden: Brill, 1992.

Ulrich, Eugene, Frank Moore Cross, Sidnie White Crawford, Julie Ann Duncan, Patrick W. Skehan, Emanuel Tov, and Julio Trebolle Barrera. *Qumran Cave 4:IX. Deuteronomy, Joshua, Judges, Kings*. DJD 14. Oxford: Clarendon, 1995.

Ünal, Ahmet. "A Hittite Treaty Tablet from Oylum Höyük in Southeastern Turkey and the Location of Ḫaššu(wa)." *AnSt* 65 (2015): 19–34.

Uspensky, Boris. *A Poetics of Composition: The Structure of the Artistic Text and Typology of a Compositional Form*. Translated by Valentina Zavarin and Susan Wittig. Berkeley: University of California Press, 1973.

van den Hout, Theo P. J. *Der Ulmitesub-Vertrag: Eine prosopographische Untersuchung*. StBoT 38. Wiesbaden: Harrassowitz, 1995.

VanderKam, James C. *An Introduction to Early Judaism*. Grand Rapids: Eerdmans, 2001.

van der Toorn, Karel. *Scribal Culture and the Making of the Hebrew Bible*. Cambridge: Harvard University Press, 2007.

Vang, Carsten. "God's Love according to Hosea and Deuteronomy: A Prophetic Reworking of a Deuteronomic Concept?" *TynBul* 62 (2011): 173–94.

_____. "The So-Called '*Ur-Deuteronomium*'—Some Reflections on Its Content, Size and Age." SEE-J Hiphil 6 (2009): http://www.see-j.net/hiphil.

van Leeuwen, Ray. "Cosmos, Temple, House: Building and Wisdom in Mesopotamia and Israel." In *From the Foundations to the Crenellations: Essays on Temple-Building in the Ancient Near East and Hebrew Bible*, edited by Mark J. Boda and Jamie Novotny, 399–421. Münster: Ugarit Verlag, 2010.

Veijola, Timo. *Das fünfte Buch Mose. Deuteronomium: Kapitel 1,1–16,17*. ATD 8/1. Göttingen: Vandenhoeck & Ruprecht, 2004.

Vielhauer, Roman. *Das Werden des Buches Hosea: Eine redaktionsgeschichtliche Untersuchung.* BZAW 349. Berlin: de Gruyter, 2007.

Vogt, Peter T. "Centralization and Decentralization in Deuteronomy." In *Interpreting Deuteronomy: Issues and Approaches*, edited by David G. Firth and Philip S. Johnston, 118–38. Downers Grove, IL: InterVarsity Press, 2012.

_____. *Deuteronomic Theology and the Significance of Torah: A Reappraisal.* Winona Lake, IN: Eisenbrauns, 2006.

_____. " 'These Are the Words Moses Spoke': Implied Audience and a Case for Pre-Monarchic Dating of Deuteronomy." In *For Our Good Always: Studies on the Message and Influence of Deuteronomy in Honor of Daniel I. Block*, edited by Jason S. DeRouchie, Jason Gile, and Kenneth J. Turner, 61–80. Winona Lake, IN: Eisenbrauns, 2013.

von Rad, Gerhard. *Deuteronomy: A Commentary*. Translated by Dorothea Barton. OTL. Philadelphia: Westminster, 1966.

_____. "How to Read the Old Testament." In *God at Work in Israel,* translated by John H. Marks, 9–18. Nashville: Abingdon, 1980. Translation of *Gottes Wirken in Israel.* Neukirchen-Vluyn: Neukirchener Verlag, 1974.

_____. *Old Testament Theology*. Vol. 1, *The Theology of Israel's Historical Traditions*. Translated by D. M. G. Stalker. New York: Harper & Row, 1962.

_____. *Old Testament Theology*. Vol. 2, *The Theology of Israel's Prophetic Traditions*. Translated by D. M. G. Stalker. New York: Harper & Row, 1965.

_____. *Studies in Deuteronomy*. Translated by D. M. G. Stalker. SBT. London: SCM, 1953. Translation of *Deuteronomium-Studien*. Rev. ed. Göttingen: Vandenhoeck & Ruprecht, 1948.

_____. *Wisdom in Israel.* London: SCM, 1972.

von Schuler, Einar. *Die Kaškäer: Ein Beitrag zur Ethnographie des alten Kleinasien*. Berlin: de Gruyter, 1965.

Watanabe, Kazuko. "Segenswünsche für den assyrischen König in der 2. Person Sg." *ASJ* 13 (1991): 347–87.

Weeks, Noel. *Admonition and Curse: The Ancient Near Eastern Treaty/Covenant Form as a Problem in Inter-Cultural Relationships*. London: T&T Clark, 2004.

Weidner, Ernst Friedrich. *Politische Dokumente aus Kleinasien: Die Staatsverträge in akkadischer Sprache aus dem Archiv von Boghazköi*. BoSt 8 and 9. Leipzig: Hinrichs, 1923.

Weinfeld, Moshe. "The Decalogue: Its Significance, Uniqueness, and Place in Israel's Tradition." In *Religion and Law: Biblical-Judaic and Islamic Perspectives*, edited by Edwin B. Firmage, Bernard G. Weiss, and John W. Welch, 3–47. Winona Lake, IN: Eisenbrauns, 1990.

_____. *Deuteronomy 1–11: A New Translation with Introduction and Commentary*. AB 5. New York: Doubleday, 1991. Repr. Winona Lake, IN: Eisenbrauns, 1992.

______. *Deuteronomy and the Deuteronomic School.* Oxford: Clarendon, 1972.

______. "Deuteronomy, Book of." *ABD* 2:168–83.

______. "Deuteronomy: The Present State of Inquiry." In *A Song of Power and the Power of Song: Essays on the Book of Deuteronomy*, edited by Duane L. Christensen, 21–35. SBTS 3. Winona Lake, IN: Eisenbrauns, 1993. Repr. from *JBL* 86 (1967): 249–62.

______. "Deuteronomy's Theological Revolution." *BRev* 12 (1996): 38–41, 44–45.

______. "The Emergence of the Deuteronomic Movement: The Historical Antecedents." In *Das Deuteronomium: Entstehung, Gestalt und Botschaft*, edited by Norbert Lohfink, 76–98. Leuven: Leuven University Press, 1985.

______. "On 'Demythologization and Secularization' in Deuteronomy." *IEJ* 23 (1973): 230–33.

______. "Traces of Assyrian Treaty Formulae in Deuteronomy." *Bib* 46 (1965): 417–27.

Weiser, Artur. "δουλεύω." *EDNT* 1:349–52.

______. *Old Testament: Its Formation and Development.* Translated by D. M. Barton. New York: Association, 1961.

Welch, Adam C. *The Code of Deuteronomy: A New Theory of Its Origin.* London: James Clarke, 1924.

Wellhausen, Julius. *Die Composition des Hexateuchs und der historischen Bücher des Alten Testaments.* 3d ed. Berlin: G. Reimer, 1899.

______. *Prolegomena to the History of Israel.* Edinburgh: A. & C. Black, 1885. Repr. with foreword by Douglas A. Knight. Atlanta: Scholars Press, 1994.

Wells, Bruce. "The Quasi-Alien in Leviticus 25." In *The Foreigner and the Law: Perspectives from the Hebrew Bible and the Ancient Near East*, edited by R. Achenbach, R. Albertz, and J. Wöhrle, 135–55. Wiesbaden: Harrassowitz, 2011.

Wenham, Gordon J. "The Date of Deuteronomy: Linch-pin of Old Testament Criticism (Part 1)." *Them* 10 (1985): 15–20.

______. "The Date of Deuteronomy: Linch-pin of Old Testament Criticism (Part 2)." *Them* 11 (1985): 15–18.

______. "Deuteronomy and the Central Sanctuary." *TynBul* 22 (1971): 103–18.

______. "Pondering the Pentateuch: The Search for a New Paradigm." In *The Face of Old Testament Studies: A Survey of Contemporary Approaches*, edited by David W. Baker and Bill T. Arnold, 116–44. Leicester: Apollos, 1999.

______. "The Structure and Date of Deuteronomy." Ph.D. diss., University of London, 1969.

White, Hayden. *The Content of the Form: Narrative Discourse and Historical Representation.* Baltimore: Johns Hopkins University Press, 1987.

Whybray, R. N. *The Intellectual Tradition in the Old Testament*. BZAW 135. Berlin: de Gruyter, 1974.

______. *The Making of the Pentateuch: A Methodological Study*. JSOTSup 53. Sheffield: JSOT Press, 1987.

Wiggins, Steve A. *A Reassessment of 'Asherah': A Study according to the Textual Sources of the First Two Millennia B.C.E.* AOAT 235. Kevelaer: Butzon & Bercker, 1993.

Wiseman, Donald J. "Abban and Alalaḫ." *JCS* 12 (1958): 124–29.

______. *The Alalakh Tablets*. OPSNKF 2. London: British Institute of Archaeology at Ankara, 1953.

______. "The Vassal-Treaties of Esarhaddon." *Iraq* 20 (1958): i–ii; 1–99; plates 1–53.

Wolff, Hans W. *Anthropology of the Old Testament*. Translated by Margaret Kohl. Philadelphia: Fortress, 1974.

______. *Hosea: A Commentary on the Book of the Prophet Hosea*. Translated by Gary Stansell. Hermeneia. Philadelphia: Fortress, 1974.

Wood, Laurence W. *Theology as History and Hermeneutics: A Post-Critical Conversation with Contemporary Theology*. Lexington, KY: Emeth Publisher, 2004.

Woods, Edward J. *Deuteronomy*. TOTC 5. Downers Grove, IL: InterVarsity Press, 2011.

Wright, Christopher J. H. *Deuteronomy*. NIBCOT 4. Peabody, MA: Hendrickson, 1996.

Wright, G. Ernest. "The Samaritans at Shechem." *HTR* 55 (1962): 357–66.

______. *Shechem: The Biography of a Biblical City*. London: Duckworth, 1965.

Wright, N. T. "The Letter to the Galatians: Exegesis and Theology." In *Between Two Horizons: Spanning New Testament Studies and Systematic Theology*, edited by Joel B. Green and Max Turner, 205–306. Grand Rapids: Eerdmans, 2000.

______. "Paul, Arabia, and Elijah (Galatians 1:17)." *JBL* 115 (1996): 683–92.

______. *Pauline Perspectives: Essays on Paul, 1978–2013*. Minneapolis: Fortress, 2013.

Yee, Gale A. *Composition and Tradition in the Book of Hosea: A Redaction-Critical Investigation*. SBLDS 102. Atlanta: SBL Press, 1987.

Younger, K. Lawson, Jr. "The 'Contextual Method': Some West Semitic Reflections." In *Archival Documents from the Biblical World*, vol. 3 of *The Context of Scripture*, edited by William W. Hallo and K. Lawson Younger Jr., xxxv–xlii. Leiden: Brill, 2002.

______. "The Scripts of North Syria in the Early First Millennium: The Inscription of Yariri (KARKAMIŠ A15b) Once Again." *Transeuphratène* 46 (2014): 169–83.

Yuhong, Wu. "The Treaty between Shadlash (Sumu-Numhim) and Neribtum (Hammi-dushur)." *JAC* 9 (1994): 124–36.

Zehnder, Markus. “Anstösse aus Dtn 23,2–9 zur Frage nach dem Umgang mit Fremden.” *FZPhTh* 52 (2005): 300–314.

_____. “Building on Stone? Deuteronomy and Esarhaddon’s Loyalty Oaths (Part 1): Some Preliminary Observations.” *BBR* 19 (2009): 341–74.

_____. “Building on Stone? Deuteronomy and Esarhaddon’s Loyalty Oaths (Part 2): Some Preliminary Observations.” *BBR* 19 (2009): 511–35.

_____. *Umgang mit Fremden in Israel und Assyrien: Ein Beitrag zur Anthropologie des “Fremden” im Licht antiker Quellen.* BWANT 168. Stuttgart: Kohlhammer, 2005.

Zertal, Adam. “A Cultic Center with a Burnt-Offering Altar from Early Iron Age I Period at Mt. Ebal.” In *Wünschet Jerusalem Frieden*, edited by Matthias Augustin, 137–47. Frankfurt am Main: Lang, 1988.

_____. “An Early Iron Age Cultic Site on Mount Ebal: Excavation Seasons 1982–1987: Preliminary Report.” *TA* 4 (1987): 105–65.

_____. “Ebal.” *NEAEHL* 1:375–77.

_____. “Has Joshua’s Altar Been Found on Mt. Ebal?” *BAR* 11.1 (1985): 26–43.

_____. “How Can Kempinski Be So Wrong!” *BAR* 12.1 (1986): 49–53.

_____. “Mount Ebal.” *IEJ* 34 (1984): 55.

_____. “ ‘To the Land of the Perizzites and the Giants’: On the Israelite Settlement in the Hill Country of Manasseh.” In *From Nomadism to Monarchy: Archaeological & Historical Aspects of Early Israel*, edited by Israel Finkelstein and Nadav Na’aman, 47–69. Jerusalem: Israel Exploration Society, 1994.

Zetterholm, Magnus. *Approaches to Paul: A Student’s Guide to Recent Scholarship.* Minneapolis: Fortress, 2009.

Zevit, Ziony. “Deuteronomy in the Temple: An Exercise in Historical Imagining.” In *Mishneh Todah: Studies in Deuteronomy and Its Cultural Environment in Honor of Jeffrey H. Tigay*, edited by Nili Sacher Fox, David A. Glatt-Gilad, and Michael J. Williams, 201–18. Winona Lake, IN: Eisenbrauns, 2009.

_____. *The Religions of Ancient Israel: A Synthesis of Parallactic Approaches.* New York: Continuum, 2001.

Zobel, Hans-Jürgen. “Hosea und das Deuteronomium: Erwägungen eines Alttestamentlers zum Thema ‘Sprache und Theologie.’ ” *TLZ* 110 (1985): 13–24.

Zobel, Konstantin. *Prophetie und Deuteronomium: Die Rezeption prophetischer Theologie durch das Deuteronomium.* BZAW 199. Berlin: de Gruyter, 1992.

Zsolnay, Ilona. “The Function of Ištar in the Assyrian Royal Inscriptions: A Contextual Analysis of the Actions Attributed to Ištar in the Inscriptions of Ititi through Šalmaneser III.” PhD diss., Brandeis University, 2009.

———. "Ištar, 'Goddess of War, Pacifier of Kings': An Analysis of Ištar's Martial Role in the Maledictory Sections of the Assyrian Royal Inscriptions." In *Proceedings of the 53e Rencontre Assyriologique Internationale*. Vol. 1, *Language in the Ancient Near East*, edited by Leonid Kogan, N. Koslova, S. Leosov, and S. Tishchenko, 389–402. Babel und Bibel 4: Annual of Ancient Near Eastern, Old Testament, and Semitic Studies. Winona Lake, IN: Eisenbrauns, 2010.

Index of Modern Authors

Index of Ancient Sources

Old Testament

NEW TESTAMENT

Septuagint and Apocrypha

Pseudepigrapha

Dead Sea Scrolls

Samaritan Scriptures

Old Latin

Philo

Josephus